A NEW DEAL FOR THE WORLD

ELIZABETH BORGWARDT

A
NEW DEAL
FOR THE WORLD

America's Vision for Human Rights

THE BELKNAP PRESS OF HARVARD UNIVERSITY PRESS

CAMBRIDGE, MASSACHUSETTS ■ LONDON, ENGLAND

2005

Library of Congress Cataloging-in-Publication Data

Borgwardt, Elizabeth
A new deal for the world : America's vision for human rights /
Elizabeth Borgwardt.
p.   cm.
Includes bibliographical references and index
ISBN 0-674-01874-5 (alk. paper)
1. United States—Foreign relations—20th century.   2. Atlantic Charter (1941).
3. International cooperation—History—20th century.
I. Title

JZ1480.B64 2005
327.1′7′097309044—dc22   2005048124

CONTENTS

CHARTING A NEW COURSE FOR HUMAN RIGHTS

The sunny Sunday morning of August 10, 1941, found President Franklin Roosevelt undertaking his longest public walk since contracting polio twenty years earlier. After crossing a narrow gangway, Roosevelt slowly made his way across the seemingly endless deck of the British battleship *Prince of Wales*. He advanced slowly, swinging his hips forward with each step and using a cane in one hand, while holding the arm of his son Elliott, a naval officer, with the other.

FDR's advisors had counseled against the president trying to walk—or to simulate walking—such a long distance on board ship. What if the deck pitched and the president fell? What if he lacked the strength to carry on to the end? But Roosevelt had insisted, completing his journey and taking his place at the right hand of British Prime Minister Winston Churchill. The two leaders, along with a few senior members of their diplomatic and military staffs, were moored in Placentia Bay, off the coast of Newfoundland, a place that Churchill described in a broadcast the following week as simply "somewhere in the Atlantic." The president was attending a joint Anglo-American Sunday service that had been meticulously stage-managed by Churchill. It was the second morning of a three-and-a-half-day conference that launched the closest wartime alliance in history. The meeting also marked the first personal encounter between Roosevelt and Churchill as leaders of the world's most powerful democracies.[1]

Roosevelt had personally devised what he called his "plan of escape" for sneaking away from sultry summertime Washington to meet with the British leader. "It was constantly emphasized, both in London and Washington, that the utmost secrecy before and during the trip was essential," he noted in a dictated memo. "The Summer of 1941 being extremely hot in June and July," the president continued, he would be spending the next week on a fishing trip off the coast of Maine, "in order to get some cool nights." First Lady Eleanor Roosevelt recalled that "my husband, after many mysterious consultations, told me that he was going to take a little trip up through the Cape Cod Canal and that he wished to do some fishing. Then he smiled and I knew he was not telling me all that he was going to do."[2]

After embarking from New London, Connecticut, on the presidential yacht *Potomac* "in full view of thousands, my Presidential flag sailing from the main top," Roosevelt and his entourage sailed to Martha's Vineyard in the middle of the night of August 3rd. There they met up with the heavy cruiser USS *Augusta,* and FDR transferred aboard. A substitute Navy crew then took over the *Potomac* and continued its scheduled fishing trip. The chief of the White House Secret Service detail lounged on the deck, flourishing a replica of the president's signature cigarette holder, while the *Potomac* issued periodic press releases ("President spent quiet day. His scotty Fala becoming restless for a little shore leave. All hands fishing")—a subterfuge that Roosevelt described in his notes as "delightful."[3]

Once aboard the *Augusta,* FDR was in fact headed for his secret shipboard rendezvous with Churchill. The historian Theodore Wilson has characterized this encounter as the first example in modern diplomatic history of what would now be called a superpower summit. The United States was not yet a combatant in the European war that had raged since the German invasion of Poland in September 1939. It only recently had begun to modify its restrictive Neutrality Acts of the 1930s. Roosevelt's innovative Lend-Lease program, conceived to offer material support to a beleaguered Britain, had been inching US public opinion toward more overt support for the embattled Allies, but the attack on Pearl Harbor was still four months away, and the United States had not yet joined Churchill's cause.[4]

On Saturday morning, August 9, 1941, HMS *Prince of Wales,* its flags flying and band playing "The Stars and Stripes Forever," pulled within sight of the *Augusta.* The cold, rainy day was brightened somewhat by the unexpected appearance of hundreds of small gift boxes for the British sailors. Each box held three pieces of fruit, a half-pound of cheese, two hundred cigarettes, and a signed note offering the compliments of the president of the United States, a gesture widely appreciated as "kindly and typically American."

Churchill was escorted aboard the American cruiser holding his right arm aloft to flash the new "V" for victory sign, while a Navy band played "God Save the King." Roosevelt held out his hand to Churchill, smiled, and said, "At last we've gotten together." Churchill then presented a surprisingly breezy letter of introduction from King George VI to Roosevelt, beginning "this is just a line to bring you my best wishes" and expressing "how glad I am that you have an opportunity at last of getting to know my Prime Minister. I am sure you will agree that he is a very remarkable man."[5]

The conference unfolded aboard the *Augusta* for most of Saturday and resumed with dinner in the evening. The next day, FDR paid a visit to the British battleship for the shipboard Sunday service. Along with the senior staff, some fifteen hundred British and American sailors looked on as Roosevelt's painful progress across the deck set the tone before a word was spoken. Churchill had directed an elaborate dress rehearsal of what he called the "Church parade," desiring that "every detail be perfect." "The PM had given much thought to the preparations for this Service," confirmed Churchill's personal secretary in a diary entry, "choosing the hymns . . . and vetting the prayers (which I had to read to him while he dried after his bath)."

Astutely emphasizing themes of duty, loyalty, and unstinting support to those in peril, the verse for the sermon was drawn from Joshua 1:5–6: "As I was with Moses, so will I be with thee: I will not fail thee, nor forsake thee. Be strong and of good courage." The assembled sailors and officials—sharing, as Churchill put it, "the same language, the same hymns, and, more or less, the same ideals"—prayed together: "Strengthen our resolve, that we fight . . . till all enmity and oppression be done away, and the people of the world be set free from fear to serve one another."[6]

Churchill recalled with satisfaction that "every word seemed to stir the heart, and none who took part in it will forget the spectacle presented that sunlit morning on the crowded quarterdeck—the symbolism of the Union Jack and the Stars and Stripes draped side by side on the pulpit . . . It was a great hour to live."

"You would have had to be pretty hard-boiled not to be moved by it all," agreed Churchill's secretary. "It seemed a sort of marriage service." Having Roosevelt walk down the aisle to consummate a symbolic diplomatic and strategic "marriage" was, of course, precisely the point, from Churchill's perspective. Roosevelt himself indicated that even "if nothing else had happened while we were here," this joint religious service "would have cemented us." Later that same evening Churchill ruminated, "I have an idea that something big may be happening—something really big."[7]

The Atlantic Conference with Churchill marked a bold attempt on the part of Roosevelt and his foreign policy planners to internationalize the New Deal. FDR hoped to apply the lessons of the Depression and interwar era to the world's burgeoning international crises and to sidestep the perceived mistakes of President Woodrow Wilson at the end of the First World War.

The most famous product of the Atlantic summit was a jointly authored eight-point statement of fewer than 400 words, released to the world via telegram on August 14, 1941. Quickly captioned the "Atlantic Charter" by an enterprising British journalist, this "simple, rough and ready wartime statement," as Churchill would soon characterize the brief message, was designed to shape the coming peace after what the charter referred to as the "final destruction of the Nazi tyranny." The Atlantic Charter called for self-determination of peoples, freer trade, and several New Deal–style social welfare provisions. It also mentioned establishing "a wider and permanent system of general security," arms control, and freedom of the seas. But this Anglo-American declaration was soon best known for a resonant phrase about establishing a particular kind of postwar order—a peace "which will afford assurance that all the men in all the lands may live out their lives in freedom from fear and want."[8]

To link anti-fascist politics and economic well-being was unusual in an international instrument. But to speak explicitly of individuals rather than state interests—to use the phrase "all the men in all the lands" in place of a more traditional reference to the prerogatives of nations—was positively revolutionary. The phrase hinted that an ordinary citizen might possibly have some kind of direct relationship with international law, unmediated by the intervening layer of a sovereign state. Though oblique, this hint that ideas about the dignity of the individual were an appropriate topic of international affairs was soon to catalyze groups around the world committed to fighting colonialism and racism as well as nazism. It marked a defining, inaugural moment for what we now know as the modern doctrine of human rights.

At the time of its drafting, however, the Atlantic Charter's radical implications were far from the minds of its negotiators, at least according to their later attempts to clarify their own intentions. Ironically, the specific phrase "all the men in all the lands" seems to have been a last-minute addition by the arch-imperialist Churchill. Earlier drafts had spoken of "peoples" and "nations"—terms redolent of interwar and even nineteenth-century diplomacy. Churchill's high-flown, abstract, and thin rhetoric would have unintended consequences when it collided with the changing "thick" realities of rough-and-tumble wartime politics, offering a rallying cry for postwar movements promoting self-determination in British colonies and civil rights reform in the United States.[9]

The Atlantic Charter also served as a focal point for movements promoting an expanded role for multilateral institutions. It prefigured the rule-of-law orientation of the Nuremberg Charter, the collective security articulated in the United Nations Charter, and even the free-trade ideology of the Bretton Woods charters that established the World Bank and the International Monetary Fund. Months before the Pearl Harbor attack would draw the United States into battle, the capacious Atlantic Charter was already sketching the outlines of a transformed postwar world, a world deliberately redesigned to transcend the economic and political conditions that had bred previous global conflicts. The charter's call for "all the men in all the lands" to be able to live out their lives in "freedom from fear and want" crystallized an ongoing transformation in the ideas and institutions underlying the modern human rights regime.[10]

This history explores this transformative moment in America's national identity as a global power. I begin with the story of the broader pedigree of the principles articulated in the Atlantic Charter and the political milieu from which these principles arose. The immediate purpose of the charter was to emphasize the moral contrasts between what Churchill and Roosevelt saw as Anglo-American values and those of their fascist enemies. To this end, the text echoed Roosevelt's famous "Four Freedoms" address of the previous January, which had highlighted freedom of speech and religion and freedom from fear and want as the distinctive characteristics of democracies. Contemporaries quickly began to cite the charter as the foundation stone for an internationalized set of "fundamental freedoms," using a particularly emblematic term for these universalist principles popularized during the war, "human rights." In several of his press conferences, FDR compared the aspirations articulated in the Atlantic Charter to those of the US Constitution, the British Magna Carta, and even the Ten Commandments.

But more than a statement of principles, policymakers saw the charter as a constitutive blueprint that would fill in the content of these thin and abstract freedoms and rights. If, as one prominent postwar sociologist has argued, "the greatness of free polities lies in their institutionalization of conflict," the Atlantic Charter and its more pragmatic progeny, such as the charters of the United Nations and the World Bank, represented an attempt to internationalize an Anglo-American vision of using institutions to entrench and extend order, prosperity, and legitimacy.[11]

Human rights may have represented a newly popular figure of speech in the early 1940s (though even this is a controversial point), but the concept was hardly a new idea. The elements of the underlying ideology shared a long pedigree, dating back to the first Hague and Geneva Conventions in the late nineteenth century and before. What was new about the modern human rights regime inaugurated by the Atlantic Charter was its synthesis of four essential qualities. First, it highlighted traditional political and civil rights as core values. Second, it broadened the conception of the Four Freedoms to incorporate vague references to economic justice. Third, it suggested that the subjects of this vision included individuals as well as sovereign nation-states. And finally, it emphasized that these principles applied within as well as across national borders. This was a fresh formulation of a much older principle, and all four of these elements continue to inform our conception of human rights today.[12]

But more than a new synthesis of old ideas, what we are called upon to explain is a new receptivity to these ideas. What were the sources of this receptivity, and how were they activated? We may find one answer in the way the Atlantic Charter reflected a new congruence between older ideas about international institutions and newer aspects of early 1940s society and political economy in the United States. This new capacity for an integrated vision of social and economic rights grew out of the mass experiences of the Depression era economy and its broad-gauge New Deal response. It was primarily the lived experience of the Depression that enabled Americans to see the world anew, and to lay the groundwork for the projection of New Deal–style multilateral institutions onto the wider world stage. Certainly, Roosevelt's many enemies identified multilateralism and international institutions with what they scornfully called a global New Deal, and they were correct to do so.

Roosevelt's advisors tended to use the term "New Deal" loosely, to refer to "the duty of government to use the combined resources of the nation to prevent distress and to promote the general welfare of all the people." Ideally, such governmental initiatives would be designed and implemented by cadres of professional planners—professional planners just like themselves. By the mid-1940s this ascendancy of professional bureaucrats combined with the devastation across the European landscape and the economic leverage offered by America's wartime boom to make the United States a willing leader in drawing up New Deal–style blueprints for multilateral institutions in the postwar period. A 1944 editorial in *The Nation* proclaimed that "only a New Deal for the world, more far-reaching and consistent than our own faltering New Deal, can prevent the coming of World War III."[13]

Standard accounts of the New Deal tend to limit themselves to domestic developments in the United States, positing a fading out of the New Deal even before the onslaught of the war, by 1938 or at the latest 1940. At a press conference in 1943, FDR himself rhetorically held the door for the departure of "Dr. New Deal," while heralding the housecall of the healer he called "Dr. Win-the-War." The return of prosperity triggered by the American entry into World War II presumably consolidated a sense of economic security—the very conditions that the New Deal had been struggling to generate.[14]

But just because the New Deal had expanded the idea of "security" to encompass economic and social security did not mean that the concept was now confined to these domestic dimensions. Such a perspective discounted the powerful and widespread anxieties glowering on the international horizon in the unsettled strategic landscape of the late 1930s. Whether Americans looked out across the Atlantic or across the Pacific, the idea of security was never exclusively economic or domestic. Rather, it was firmly engaged with ideas about national security—or insecurity. After the American entry into World War II, Americans continued to express anxieties about the shape of the postwar world, anticipating widespread unemployment and even chaos in the conflict's wake. It seemed only natural that the New Deal's sweeping institutional approaches to intractable problems would be translated to the international level by Roosevelt administration planners. This openness to large-scale institutional solutions was, arguably, the key difference between the World War I and World War II–era plans for a more stable and prosperous global order.[15]

America's receptivity to multilateral institutions such as the United Nations was enhanced by more cosmopolitan sensibilities growing out of widespread wartime service and vastly increased mobility on the home front. This new receptivity found expression in reduced opposition among key groups in Congress and in the business and financial communities, and helped the major multilateral institutions of the World War II era garner the legitimacy they needed to challenge traditional conceptions of state sovereignty. These wartime transformations in attitudes built upon the way the New Deal response to the Great Depression had led American policymakers of the World War II era to reconstrue the lessons of the First World War. After World War I, similar initiatives in international organization had failed to take root because they lacked this "cultural traction," or widespread grounding in popular experience.[16]

The ideology of the Atlantic Charter blueprint represented a new articulation of US national interests in the 1940s, expressed concretely through three sets of contentious international negotiations. The policy architecture of the United Nations, the IMF and World Bank, and the Nuremberg trials was designed both to manage the transition from war to peace and to shape the postwar world. These institutions set up mechanisms for promoting collective security, for stabilizing and coordinating international currency transactions and economic development, and for advancing ideas about international justice. The designers of the Bretton Woods, UN, and Nuremberg charters actively struggled to redefine the idea of "security" in the international sphere to include economic and political security, much as New Deal programs had redefined security domestically for individual American citizens.[17]

After Nuremberg, individuals would be held directly accountable to the international community, at least in theory. After the founding of the United Nations, the IMF, and the World Bank, the international community would in turn be able to reach back through the boundaries of state sovereignty to protect individuals or impose norms. The crushing impact of the war had reconfigured two of the most enduring constructions of the Enlightenment, the individual and the nation-state. Not only were traditional boundaries blurred, but new international entities would mean more players and a different playing field, as well as new rules and goals. And the efforts of American and British planners in particular would be not so much passively received as actively transformed.

Historians continue to speculate about Franklin Roosevelt's sincerity as an internationalist and an advocate of what we now call human rights. Very possibly, the universalistic language in the Atlantic Charter about human dignity, self-determination, and equal access to trade and raw materials was originally devised largely for its rhetorical effect. Roosevelt enthusiastically participated in a great American tradition of inspirational fiction linked to wartime mobilization. The unfolding of the Holocaust and the Allied failure to rescue its victims are the starkest examples of a dizzying gap between rhetoric and reality during the Roosevelt administration. The high-toned abstractions in the Atlantic Charter, intended to contrast Anglo-American principles with those of the Third Reich, inevitably served to highlight internal contradictions and hypocrisies within the democracies themselves.[18]

For example, in the summer of 1942, the Indian nationalist leader Mohandas Gandhi wrote to President Roosevelt that, even as the Western nations proclaim that "they are fighting to make the world safe for freedom of the individual and for democracy," their assertion "sounds hollow, so long as India, and for that matter, Africa are exploited by Great Britain, and America has the Negro problem in her own home." In discussing the worldwide impact of the Atlantic Charter, Roosevelt speechwriter Robert Sherwood wryly observed that sometimes, "when you state a moral principle, you are stuck with it, no matter how many fingers you have kept crossed at the moment."[19]

Such a dynamic relationship between proclamation and reception, between formal political content and actual social context, underlies how traditional antinomies such as "domestic" and "foreign" affairs have become increasingly obsolete in the study of the politics and ideas of the World War II era.[20] *A New Deal for the World* is an example of what is now sometimes called the "new international history," a field that combines traditional political, intellectual, or cultural history with cross-disciplinary approaches drawn from international relations, international law, and international economics.[21] The book contributes to an ongoing dialogue in a variety of disciplines about the transition from war to peace, particularly the changing role of the United States on the world stage as it took Britain's historic place at the strategic, financial, and even cultural center of the Western world. Some political scientists and international legal scholars have argued that there is something distinctive about the way societies, in the wake of mass atrocities or fallen authoritarian governments, deploy new ideologies, ideas, and institutions as instruments of recovery.[22] The Bretton Woods, United Nations, and Nuremberg charters are examples of such transitional regimes.[23] One question I address is how, during the postwar period, these multilateral institutions bridged the gap between facts and norms, that is, between the horrifying realities of wartime devastation and such aspirational abstractions as "justice" and "security."[24]

Not all such attempts at mediation were successful. A case in point was the prosecution of "crimes against humanity" at the main Nuremberg trial. Described by a recent commentator as "perhaps the boldest single effort to enshrine human rights as a universal value," the effort to bring legal norms to bear on the vast atrocities committed by the European Axis ultimately fell short. Such a wide-ranging category of crimes raised the specter of international jurisdiction over violations of the human rights of a domestic population—at Nuremberg, German Jews during the interwar era. Prosecuting internal human rights violations that were not even necessarily part of a transborder armed conflict presented an awkward prospect for the victorious allies, as it seemed likely to implicate what Gandhi had called America's "Negro problem." The executors of Nuremberg's legal mission accordingly developed the idea of crimes against universal human dignity in only a very limited way, choosing instead to emphasize responsibility for what they argued was the already-existing crime of waging aggressive war.[25]

Since the 1960s, it has become fashionable to observe that the Allies' ideological commitment to the rule of law was, in practice, staggeringly self-serving, particularly on the part of the United States. According to this view, "legitimacy" actually meant justifying American power; "prosperity" meant the imposition of free-market ideology; and "order" meant falling into line behind American hegemony. But setting up an opposition between motives that were and were not somehow self-serving is to pose a false duality. The political theorist Judith Shklar warns that it is an error to frame rule of law ideas as being the antithesis of "politics," as Americans seem peculiarly predisposed to do. A more nuanced approach would arrange transitional institutions on a spectrum of negotiation and compromise that is itself politically contested.

In this approach, "law"—as expressed through treaties, tribunals, and rule-following generally—becomes not an alternative to politics but a partner. In the Allies' negotiation of the postwar order, power always mattered, but it did not dictate outcomes in the linear way that an earlier generation of revisionist diplomatic historians has asserted. Granted, ideas may not be the engine of history. But ideas can often serve as a "switchman," to use Max Weber's image, determining along which sets of tracks the engine of power and interest advances.[26]

Why the United States chose to bind itself to multilateral institutions that would manifestly limit its historic obsession with unfettered freedom of action is a more interesting question than why it might try to dominate those institutions, once inside. At such a fluid historical moment, US policymakers chose to build institutions with enough legitimacy to induce other powers to join and, in so doing, endorse America's vision of order in the postwar world.[27] This legitimacy drew on earlier expressions of international aspirations, on Depression-era transformations in attitudes toward national and individual security, and on appeals to the self-interest of other nations. But ideas and institutions that may initially have been designed to safeguard or entrench American power eventually took on a life of their own.

In exploring the struggles of negotiators to design and explain their global plans for economic, political, and legal systems, I focus particularly on the transition to what is now sometimes called the modern human rights regime, using the 1941 Atlantic Charter as a point of departure. In the period from 1941 to 1945, policymakers saw economic security as supporting political stability, both at home and abroad, before this emerging synthesis was temporarily frozen by the bipolar imperatives of the Cold War.

When the strategic landscape thawed after the collapse of communism in 1989–1991, the multilateralist vision of international security encountered an altered strategic landscape of globalized finance, technology, trade, and communications, as well as narcotics trafficking, pollution, disease, and terror. Rather than framing the war on terror as an opportunity to build a robust, multilateral defense of civilization, however, the United States chose to look almost exclusively to its own devices, reasserting the unilateralist preferences of an earlier era. In the process, the United States pruned back its influence as a force promoting legitimacy, the rule of law, and, especially, international human rights.

Four years after making his dramatic walk across the deck of the *Prince of Wales*, President Roosevelt delivered his final inaugural address. This speech has taken on a fresh relevance in the unsettled early years of the twenty-first century. With characteristic simplicity, in a speech lasting less than five minutes, Roosevelt offered an activist, multilateralist vision of America's role in the world: "We have learned that we cannot live alone, at peace; that our own well-being is dependent on the well-being of other nations, far away." The European war was then entering its final stages, and the president explained that through terrible trials the American people "have learned to be citizens of the world, members of the human community. We have learned the simple truth, as Emerson said, that, 'The only way to have a friend is to be one.'"[28] Here was the promise not only of a new American foreign policy but of a new vision for the world.

PART I

SOMEWHERE IN THE ATLANTIC, AUGUST 1941

Somewhere in the Atlantic you did make some history, and like all truly historic events, it was not what was said or done that defined the scope of the achievement. It is the forces, the impalpable, the spiritual forces, the hopes, the expressions, and the dreams, and the endeavors that are released. That's what matters . . . We live by symbols, and we cannot too often recall them.

Supreme Court Justice Felix Frankfurter,
letter of August 18, 1941, congratulating President Roosevelt
on his meeting with Prime Minister Winston Churchill
at the Atlantic Conference

CHAPTER 1

THE GHOST
OF WOODROW WILSON

For many of its interpreters in the early 1940s, the Atlantic Charter was a unique opportunity to set the terms of American participation in world politics without repeating mistakes from the aftermath of the First World War. American policymakers drew different lessons from World War I at different times, but consistently seemed to extract four major guidelines from the previous conflagration and its post-conflict settlement.

Lesson number one was to bring putative opponents, as well as likely friends, into the postwar planning process at as early a stage as possible. This principle was based on the signal failure of Woodrow Wilson to fold Republican perspectives into the development of the postwar settlement a generation before.[1]

Lesson number two, from the perspective of Roosevelt administration planners, was to begin planning the peace while the war was still raging, counterintuitive as that allocation of resources seemed to some. While winning the war was of necessity the top priority—only victors are able to implement their peace plans, after all—the instructive failure of Wilsonian diplomacy taught that negotiating positions tended to harden quickly after an armistice, and nations soon turned inward once victory was assured, in a natural eagerness to focus on long-neglected domestic priorities. A corollary of these first two prescriptions was to work actively to bring public opinion along as well, ideally in ways that could be measured and heard by the Senate.

The third lesson drawn from the failed Versailles settlement was to seek a more integrated vision of collective security through combining political and military cooperation with economic security in the realm of trade, finance, and labor standards. This precept was based on the perceived successes of some of the League of Nations–affiliated agencies, such as the International Labor Organization, as well as the harsh experience of interwar economic diplomacy, where competitive currency depreciations and trade barriers had greatly magnified the global impact of the

Great Depression. A punitive reparations scheme for Germany, together with the deep indebtedness of the European Allies, had laid some of the groundwork for the Depression, which led to desperation and domestic instability, followed by an increased vulnerability to political extremism.

The final important lesson from the previous generation's mistakes was to avoid promising too much—to emphasize hardheaded realism, technical expertise, and practical progress for the "common man" rather than idealism or utopianism. As an anonymous editorial writer in *Life* magazine observed in 1942, "In the last war we used to talk of building 'a world fit for heroes to live in.' This time let us cut the talk and simply get on with building a world fit for everybody to live in."[2]

The sum of these four widely perceived lessons of the post–World War I settlement was that the United States had more to gain by participating in a new world order than by turning its back on international collaboration. The political scientist John Ikenberry elaborates that a hegemonic victor in possession of a preponderance of power is faced with three choices: "It can *dominate*—use its commanding material capabilities to prevail in the endless conflicts over the distribution of gains. It can *abandon*—wash its hands of postwar disputes and return home"; this was the choice of the United States following World War I. Or a victorious state "can try to *transform* its favorable postwar power position into a durable order that commands the allegiance of other states within the order."[3] The United States' choice during World War II to seek a postwar global transformation needs explaining, especially given its later decision to seek domination both during the Cold War era and in the wake of the terrorist attacks of September 11, 2001.

The negative example of the World War I settlement suggests why American planners were intent on avoiding "abandonment" after the global conflict ended. By the time of the Atlantic Charter, even before formally entering the war, they may have already concluded that the United States had the most to gain by actively working to parlay the fruits of a likely victory into a durable and stable institutional order. This was not so much an order created in America's own image—although, unsurprisingly, ideas about democracy, rights, and constitutionalism as promoted by US negotiators had a distinctly American flavor. Rather, it marked a new approach to using multilateral institutions to "lock in" wartime advantages.[4]

"No lover ever studied every whim of his mistress as I did those of President Roosevelt"

Isaiah Berlin once described Roosevelt as "a spontaneous, optimistic, pleasure-loving ruler who dismayed his assistants by the gay and apparently heedless abandon with which he seemed to delight in pursuing two or more totally incompatible policies." By contrast, wrote Berlin, the British prime minister "stands at almost the opposite pole." "Churchill's dominant category," Berlin explained, "the single, central, organising principle of his moral and intellectual universe, is a historical imagination so strong, so comprehensive, as to encase the whole of the present and the whole of the future in a framework of a rich and multicoloured past."[5]

In a famously evocative contrast, Berlin wrote in a later essay that "the fox knows many things, but the hedgehog knows one big thing." This image captures two incompatible intellectual and artistic temperaments. Berlin emphasized "the great chasm" between "those who pursue many ends, often unrelated and even contradictory, connected, if at all, only in some *de facto* way" (foxes) and those "who relate everything to a single, central vision" (hedgehogs). Early in 1941, presidential advisor Harry Hopkins had expressed concern that "the President is very like Winston in some ways—very temperamental" and that "if they were put together, in a ship for instance," the results might be more explosive than unifying.[6] How would an encounter between Roosevelt, the paradigmatic embodiment of Berlin's fox, and Churchill, the very avatar of his hedgehog, come off?

Hopkins had been sent ahead as FDR's personal envoy to get to know Churchill over the course of a twice-extended visit of five weeks. The ailing, rumpled former social worker got along famously with the patrician prime minister. In an informal after-dinner speech early in 1941, for example, Hopkins summarized his mission with the kind of world-historical idiom the prime minister loved best. "I suppose you wish to know what I am going to say to President Roosevelt on my return," began the presidential aide. "Well, I'm going to quote you one verse from that Book of Books in the truth of which . . . my own Scottish mother [was] brought up: 'Whither thou goest, I will go; and where thou lodgest, I will lodge: thy people shall be my people, and thy God my God . . . Even to the end.'"[7]

Recording this scene, Churchill's personal physician noted, "I was surprised to find the P.M. in tears. He knew what it meant . . . the words seemed like a rope thrown to a dying man." But Secretary of the Interior Harold Ickes noted dryly in his diary, "Probably a good deal of this is true and the attachment of Churchill to Harry Hopkins may be entirely genuine. However, I suspect that if, as his personal representative, the President should send to London a man with the bubonic plague, Churchill would, nevertheless, see a good deal of him."[8]

Hopkins had cut short a trip to the Soviet Union to accompany Churchill on the long and perilous journey to the coast of Newfoundland—six full days of travel, five of them over waters infested with U-boats. The American New Dealer passed the time by beating Churchill at backgammon for a shilling a game and responding to the prime minister's persistent queries about Roosevelt's personality and attitudes.[9]

The Atlantic Conference was to be Churchill's first meeting with Roosevelt, or, more precisely, his first encounter with FDR in the American politician's capacity as head of state. The two charismatic career politicians had been introduced in 1918 at a large ceremonial dinner in London, where the 44-year-old British cabinet member had given the 36-year-old assistant secretary of the Navy the brush-off, "an encounter Roosevelt remembered with distaste and Churchill had completely forgotten." Now, more than twenty years later, Churchill felt that the very survival of the British Empire might hinge on the American president's attitude. Given the precariousness of Britain's strategic situation in the summer of 1941, it seemed only fitting "that the Old World come, as it were, cap in hand to the New," writes the diplomatic historian Theodore Wilson.[10]

Shortly before his departure, Churchill ruminated about Roosevelt to the American diplomat and financier Averell Harriman. "I wonder if he will like me."[11] Churchill later remarked on this era in his relationship with FDR, "No lover ever studied every whim of his mistress as I did those of President Roosevelt."[12]

Churchill later recalled his modest expectation that "a conference between us would proclaim the ever closer association of Britain and the United States, would cause our enemies concern, make Japan ponder, and cheer our friends." Shy of attaining a formal, public American commitment to a military alliance with Britain, Churchill's overarching goal was to bring the United States to the threshold of such a step. Churchill's most specific objective, however, according to his official biographer, was a severe joint warning to Japan, ideally framed as an ultimatum, in response to Japan's recent occupation of French Indochina, the Dutch East Indies, and parts of the US-administered Philippines.[13]

Roosevelt's staff had also deliberately tamped down their expectations for this long-anticipated encounter. An American military aide later wrote that the main purpose of the clandestine meeting in the North Atlantic had been to reassure Roosevelt that the British prime minister was not a hopeless drunk, as some rumors had apparently suggested. With everyone seemingly satisfied on that point, one of FDR's speechwriters, striving mightily for an image of unity, finally observed that "the cigarette-in-holder and the long cigar were at last being lit from the same match."[14]

Undersecretary of State Sumner Welles later wrote that Roosevelt had two serious purposes in conferring with Churchill. First, the president had become interested in a face-to-face meeting after receiving an alarming 4,000-word letter from the prime minister on December 8, 1940. Described by Churchill as "the most important letter I ever wrote," it outlined Britain's desperate plight in the second year of a war Britain had entered after Germany invaded Poland in September 1939. During that autumn and through the following winter Germany abruptly ended its "phony war" with lightning strikes into Denmark, Norway, the Netherlands, Belgium, Luxembourg, and France. "Entrenched in their island citadel, the British alone stood between the Axis and complete domination of half the world," explained a 1942 Library of Congress publication discussing the context of the Atlantic Charter, written for American audiences. "May, June and July of 1940 represented the nadir of anti-Axis fortunes, with every prospect that Germany would attempt, and probably successfully complete, an outright invasion of England itself."[15]

The unexpectedly rapid capitulation of France in June 1940 left thousands of British troops and materiel stranded near the French port of Dunkirk. When over 300,000 soldiers (but not their equipment) were rescued and transported across the English Channel, Churchill famously intoned in the House of Commons: "We shall defend our island whatever the cost may be; we shall fight on the beaches, we shall fight on the landing grounds, in fields, in streets and on the hills. We shall never surrender . . . " The conclusion of this iconic assertion is quoted much less often: "even if, which I do not for the moment believe, this island or a large part of it were subjugated and starving, then our empire beyond the seas, armed and guarded by the British Fleet, will carry on the struggle until in God's good time the New World, with all its power and might, sets forth to the liberation and rescue of the Old." The historian Warren Kimball has argued that this famous exhortation, excerpted with its final sentence intact, was pleading as well as defiant, and was directed as much toward an American audience as toward the British home front.[16]

In the late summer of 1940, Germany initiated its air war over Britain, originally intended to soften up British defenses and civilian morale in preparation for a planned invasion. The Battle of Britain lasted from August 13 to October 31, 1940, and included fifty-seven consecutive nights of bombing civilian targets in London. At the peak of Britain's defensive effort, RAF fighter pilots were regularly flying two or three sorties per day, and six or seven daily scrambles were not unusual. Overstressed pilots sometimes instantly fell asleep upon landing, leaving ground crews to turn off the engines. In September 1940 Hitler postponed the invasion of Britain indefinitely. Although bombing continued into the winter, it was clear that Britain had survived the very worst that the Luftwaffe could deliver.[17]

But by autumn of 1940 Britain was suffering from a severe dollar shortage and was further squeezed by the denial of credit in the United States. During just one week in early 1940, Britain's dollar reserves dropped by close to four percent. Later that spring, the American journalists Joseph Alsop and Robert Kintner estimated that Britain would soon have no dollars or convertible assets left at all, and that Americans would have to choose between credits and donations or an outright German victory. But a myth of untapped British reserves being craftily withheld persisted through 1940, fueled by American assumptions about the British Empire's vast resources.

Kimball explained that "the exchange of sterling for dollars was the problem, not over-all British wealth" and that on the British side "the unspoken accusation was that the United States was using the wartime situation—as in World War I—to challenge Britain's overseas trade position." "Britain's broke, boys, it's your money we want," quipped a chipper Lord Lothian, Britain's ambassador to the United States, to a shocked American press corps in November 1940. These differences in perception would continue to cause problems in Anglo-American financial negotiations throughout the war.[18]

Churchill's "most important letter" of December 1940 accordingly emphasized to FDR that "the moment approaches when we shall no longer be able to pay cash for shipping and other supplies" and requested the "gift, loan or supply" of American warships. The prime minister's letter was "cleverly phrased to suggest that Britain was America's forward line of defence against the Axis," an argument that struck a chord with the American president. Roosevelt had an unusually quiet stretch of time to ponder the contents of this missive, as he sat on the deck of the cruiser *Tuscaloosa* on a post-election Caribbean cruise.[19]

At a press conference back in Washington the following week, Roosevelt articulated his rationale for a new program of aid to Britain, soon to be known as Lend-Lease. Comparing it to lending your neighbor a fire hose so that the fire does not spread to your own house, the president explained how the best security for the United States would result from resupplying Britain.[20] On December 29, 1940, during one of his famous fireside chats, FDR referred to the United States as the "arsenal of democracy," another gripping image broadcast around the world on the same night that large swaths of central London were being destroyed by the Luftwaffe. An important impetus for the Atlantic Conference was thus to buck up a beleaguered Britain.[21]

In addition to his interest in bolstering British morale, Roosevelt was on the lookout for opportunities to demonstrate to his domestic audience that American diplomacy could be both idealistic and hard-headed. A Roosevelt speechwriter described FDR at the Atlantic Conference as "haunted by the ghost of Woodrow Wilson." In the estimation of many of the president's foreign policy advisors, American foreign relations just after the First World War had suffered from an excess of naive idealism, followed by an excessively cold-eyed isolationist backlash. In an image typical of the New Dealers' approach, these advisors encouraged Roosevelt in his belief that American diplomacy could navigate between the Scylla of unfounded idealism and the Charybdis of economic isolationism.[22]

"Certain principles on which they base their hopes for a better world"

In his Annual Message to Congress in January 1941, FDR had proclaimed that he sought to establish what he called "four essential human freedoms" worldwide:

> The first is freedom of speech and expression—everywhere in the world.
>
> The second is freedom of every person to worship God in his own way—everywhere in the world.
>
> The third is freedom from want—which, translated into world terms, means economic understandings which will secure to every nation everywhere a healthy peacetime life for its inhabitants—everywhere in the world.

The fourth is freedom from fear—which, translated into international terms, means a world-wide reduction of armaments to such a point and in such a thorough fashion that no nation will be in a position to commit an act of physical aggression against any neighbor—anywhere in the world.

From the outset, these aspirations were expressed in explicitly international terms. "Freedom," the president continued, "means the supremacy of human rights everywhere. Our support goes to those who struggle to gain these rights or keep them." Roosevelt had added the Four Freedoms peroration himself, dictating it into the fourth draft of the speech in the presence of several speechwriters, including Hopkins. "That covers an awful lot of territory, Mr. President," Hopkins reportedly observed cautiously, commenting on the refrain "everywhere in the world." "I don't know how interested Americans are going to be in the people of Java." "I'm afraid they'll have to be some day, Harry," responded a ruminative Roosevelt. "The world is getting so small that even the people in Java are getting to be our neighbors now."[23]

Within months of delivering the Four Freedoms address, Roosevelt became interested in capitalizing on the favorable attention it had garnered by propounding "some kind of public statement of the objectives in international relations in which the Government of the United States believed." The president indicated he was seeking to use the internationalized conceptions in the Four Freedoms to advance the cause of "keeping alive some principles of international law, some principles of moral and human decency," in both US and world public opinion.[24]

In the spring of 1941 the public opinion expert Hadley Cantril advised the president to issue a statement of war aims as a way of educating the American public about "the personal effects of a Nazi victory or the whole Nazi ideology"; this vision should also include an elaboration on "what he means by the Four Freedoms." Such an inspirational and attention-grabbing statement would suggest that the best way to look out for the country's national interests would be for the United States to take the lead in creating a better world to come.[25]

FDR was interested in designing a statement that would articulate "our alternative to Hitler's new order," but his intent was specifically anti-Nazi, not broadly anti-totalitarian, as some commentators have recently suggested. It would be anachronistic to frame Roosevelt's purposes as anti-Soviet in August 1941. Hopkins had just returned from a fact-finding mission to the Soviet Union, where he had met with Premier Josef Stalin. Such unparalleled access to the Soviet leader astounded the American, British, and Soviet diplomatic staffs. At the Atlantic Conference,

Hopkins was determined to impart his increased confidence that American aid to the Soviet Union would not be wasted and that the Soviets should be supported, not antagonized. While absent in person, the Soviet leader attended the Atlantic Conference in spirit, as "a welcome guest at hungry table," in Churchill's words, and not as an ideological target.[26]

On the opening day of the conference, after presenting his credentials to Roosevelt, Churchill joined FDR for lunch on the *Augusta*. Their staffs shared a "cold plate" sniffily dismissed by Sir Alexander Cadogan, the British permanent undersecretary for foreign affairs, as "very unsatisfactory." Afterward, Cadogan and Sumner Welles had their first meeting, a marathon session which they spent discussing the merits of a diplomatic warning to Japan, the possibility of a German seizure of the Portuguese Azores, and the wisdom of continuing America's "Vichy gamble" by maintaining relations with the collaborationist regime in occupied France.[27]

It spoke volumes about Roosevelt's capricious, personality-driven management style that Welles was the senior diplomatic officer at the Atlantic Conference. Secretary of State Cordell Hull and the formidable secretary of war, Henry Stimson, had been left behind in favor of the aristocratic and sycophantic Welles. To Cadogan, Welles's opposite number in the British camp, the American diplomat was someone who "improves on acquaintance," even though it was "a pity that he swallowed a ramrod in his youth." Welles might have said the same of Sir Alexander. The fifth son of an earl, Cadogan was described by Churchill's bodyguard as "the coldest [person] I encountered—a real oyster."[28]

Turning to the final item on their agenda, the two career diplomats touched on the possibility of a joint declaration of war and peace aims. This discussion continued at a formal dinner that evening. Cadogan and Welles joined Hopkins, Averell Harriman, and the senior military staffs at a meal hosted by Roosevelt in Churchill's honor. It featured such "typical" American fare as candied sweet potatoes, chocolate ice cream, and cupcakes. This menu was considered so unusual by the British participants that Churchill's bodyguard reprinted it in an early draft of his memoirs, with exclamations over its exoticism.[29]

While Roosevelt had mentioned the desirability of a statement of war and peace aims some weeks before, he had not said anything specific about its being issued jointly. But the president seems to have realized that his two primary interests—bolstering British morale and educating the American public—might converge in a joint declaration. Welles had written a preliminary statement on his own in Washington but held it back when FDR suggested that the British should do the initial drafting. Before retiring, Churchill outlined both a joint warning to Japan and a joint declaration of objectives for Cadogan, who drafted both overnight.

The British version of the proposed joint declaration described "certain principles which [Roosevelt and Churchill] both accept for guidance in the framing of their policy and on which they base their hopes for a better world." Sensitive to American political constraints, this draft carefully avoided the language of a military alliance or the obligations of a formal treaty. The statement's opening provisions emphasized the Wilsonian ideal of seeking "no aggrandisement, territorial or other," and continued in this vein by enshrining the principle of self-determination, expressed as "no territorial changes that do not accord with the freely expressed wishes of the peoples concerned." An additional provision called for enhancing world security by means of "an effective international organization."[30]

The draft also featured references to what might be called Four Freedoms ideals—traditional civil rights leavened with vague economic aspirations. This British draft further declared that the United States and Britain would "respect the right of all peoples to choose the form of Government under which they will live: they are only concerned to defend the rights of freedom of Speech and Thought without which such choice must be illusory." The rather oblique anti-Soviet tenor of this provision was immediately softened by Welles and Roosevelt. An economic provision in the draft called for "a fair and equitable distribution of essential produce" and added the startling proviso "not only within their territorial boundaries but between the nations of the world."[31]

This unusual framing was intended to finesse the problem of imperial trade preferences, which the Americans could be counted on vehemently to oppose.[32] But the text itself, and the similar language that was inserted into the final version, was redolent of Keynesian internationalism, and over the course of the war smaller powers focused on these ideals to justify "compensation" for their wartime sacrifices. Similarly, the provision that later became the Atlantic Charter's sixth point, seeking to "afford to all nations the means of dwelling in safety within their own boundaries," reinforced the opening pronouncements on self-determination and soon created expectations in unexpected quarters (particularly with reference to expectations regarding racial equality). Finally, a catch-all proviso in this last article included a call for freedom of the seas and arms control.

FDR and Welles reviewed this draft in great detail late Sunday afternoon, the second day of the conference. To Welles's consternation, the president indicated that he did not favor an international organization along the lines of the defunct League of Nations. With an eye on the home front, the president was concerned about provoking an isolationist reaction that might overshadow any other war aims.

During his visit to Britain earlier in the summer, Harry Hopkins had noted that as the president's proxy he could not be too specific in expressing American support for Britain because "at home the isolationists were screaming bloody murder." "Isolationists" usually referred to influential congressional representatives such as Senator Robert A. Taft, Republican of Ohio, Senator Burton K. Wheeler, Democrat of Montana, and Senator Arthur Vandenberg, Republican of Michigan. But the term also encompassed shifting groups of New Dealers and labor leaders who were protective of fragile social programs; large numbers of working-class Catholics, especially women with draft-age sons (with notable exceptions in Polish communities); and assorted media figures, ranging from the peace activist and former socialist presidential candidate Norman Thomas and the historians Charles and Mary Beard to the celebrity aviator Charles Lindbergh and his wife, the writer Anne Morrow Lindbergh.[33]

To say that these constituencies were vocal would be something of an understatement. Midwestern business leaders had founded the isolationist America First Committee in 1940, for example, to sponsor speakers, rallies, congressional lobbying, and the distribution of literature. By the time the group disbanded thirteen months later, following the Pearl Harbor attack, it had roughly 800,000 members (future presidents Gerald Ford and John F. Kennedy were donors). Accordingly, FDR cautiously favored waiting until the war was under way to take up the question of how to organize the peace.

Welles spent Sunday evening editing the British draft to reflect the State Department's emphasis on free trade. Meanwhile, FDR was attending an informal dinner with Churchill and both of their personal staffs, where a lively exchange ensued on that very topic. According to an account by FDR's son Elliott, the debate was provoked by Roosevelt, who noted that "one of the preconditions of any lasting peace" would necessarily be "the greatest possible freedom of trade." When Churchill countered that Britain had no interest in losing its favored position among its dominions, Roosevelt drew what for the prime minister must have seemed a very uncomfortable connection. "Those Empire trade agreements," observed the president, "are a case in point. It's because of them that the peoples of India and Africa, of all the colonial Near East and Far East, are still as backward as they are." The younger Roosevelt noted that the prime minister's neck reddened as he retorted, "The trade that has made England great shall continue, and under conditions prescribed by England's ministers."[34]

Welles gave FDR his suggested changes the next morning, having softened the "joint" language of the preamble even more to suggest respective policies in harmony rather than a single common policy. Welles retained the provisions on territorial aggrandizement and self-determination, and—although he must have heard about the previous evening's colorful exchange of views—he also revised and significantly toughened the trade provision. It read: "[The parties] will strive to promote mutually advantageous economic relations between them through the elimination of any discrimination in either the United States of America or the United Kingdom against the importation of any product originating in the other country; and they will endeavor to further the enjoyment by all peoples of access on equal terms to the markets and to the raw materials which are needed for their economic prosperity." Despite its restrained and diplomatic tone, this language was in fact a frontal assault on Britain's imperial preference system.

Welles kept the substance of the final grab-bag provision as well, linking a future "effective international organization" to the idea of increased postwar security, along with a call for freedom of the seas and arms control, with only slight modifications. He revised the Four Freedoms provisions by removing the reference to specific civil rights and substituting a more general aspiration that "all human beings may live out their lives in freedom from fear." Welles now framed his own negotiation task as bringing the president around on the international organization provision and bringing the British around on the free trade provision.[35]

The two leaders met the next morning to review the American redraft, with Welles, Hopkins, and Cadogan participating. Churchill read Welles's draft aloud—which had been revised yet again, at the president's insistence, to remove any reference to an international organization. Predictably, the prime minister took strong exception to the revised trade provision. Churchill lectured the Americans about his lack of authority to repudiate a key policy of the British Commonwealth in the absence of approval from his cabinet and from the affected Commonwealth countries themselves. He claimed, rather cannily, that while he personally favored trade liberalization, "it would be at least a week before he could hope to obtain by telegraph the opinion of the Dominions with regard to this question."

This hard-hearted-partner strategy led to a capitulation by Roosevelt, who was hoping to have the declaration publicized immediately upon the conference's conclusion. Welles argued in vain that the trade provision was an important question of principle, and FDR seized upon Hopkins's placatory suggestion that the British take a crack at redrafting the offending passage.[36]

The remaining major point of difference was whether the declaration would include any reference to some international mechanism or multilateral institution designed to ensure collective security. When Churchill suggested reinserting the phrase "effective international organization," as framed in the original British draft, it was Roosevelt's turn to protest. While he agreed with the prime minister in principle, in practice he anticipated too much opposition on the home front to risk including the disputed provision. FDR explained that it was a matter of simple "realism" to postpone issues of collective security until after the war had been won and that, in addition, their two countries should anticipate a lengthy transition period where an Anglo-American alliance would be expected to police the world.[37]

Churchill agreed, but expressed concern about his own domestic public opinion, which he described as much more internationalist. The prime minister indicated that he attached so much importance to this provision that he was willing to stay an extra day and continue the negotiations. He also offered to cable his cabinet and dictate the contents of the draft for their discussion and approval. In consultation with the War Cabinet via cable a few hours later, Churchill expressed confidence to Deputy Prime Minister Clement Atlee that FDR would accede to the British version "for the sake of speedy agreement."[38]

The prime minister had read his future partner well. The final version of the Atlantic Charter contains a masterly elision by Churchill and Cadogan that significantly softened the arms control provision, combined it with the international organization provision, and pitched both at a high level of generality. Roosevelt concluded that this wording would not preclude his notion of a lengthy transition period. In the final version of the charter, the two leaders declared that "all the nations of the world, for realistic as well as spiritual reasons, must come to the abandonment of the use of force." The parties declared that, "since no future peace can be maintained if land, sea, or air armaments continue to be employed by nations which threaten, or may threaten, aggression outside of their

frontiers, they believe, pending the establishment of a wider and permanent system of general security, that the disarmament of such nations is
essential."[39]

Several historians have remarked on the extent to which a reluctant
Roosevelt needed to be dragooned into supporting even these rather
nebulous aspirations for international security. The president's unwillingness to take a principled stand in favor of what are generally assumed
to be his innate internationalist impulses might well have been due
entirely to the virulence of the isolationist reaction to his recently approved Lend-Lease bill. Just the previous January in a radio speech, Senator Wheeler had memorably asserted that active support for Britain
through the Lend-Lease program was "the New Deal's Triple-A foreign policy; it will plow under every fourth American boy." Roosevelt
later excoriated this statement "as the most untruthful, as the most das-
tardly, unpatriotic thing . . . that has been said in public life in my generation."[40]

Referring specifically to the president's attempts to strike out the clause
on an international organization, State Department economic advisor
Herbert Feis argued that FDR's "thoughts about a future international
organization were at this time cruising. He was sincerely convinced that a
collective organization akin to the League of Nations could not work,
and was restlessly searching for some other way to assure future political
and moral order." How Feis would have had such privileged access to the
president's state of mind is not clear, but the "cruising" image may well
have been apt, as was nautical imagery generally in describing Roosevelt's preferred approach to problem solving.[41]

Earlier language about economic prosperity from Welles's draft was
revived by a somewhat surprising contributor: the British War Cabinet.
Convening at 1 a.m. London time, the cabinet reviewed the draft version
and suggested inserting a more explicit reference to economic planning:
"[The United States and the United Kingdom] desire to bring about the
fullest collaboration between all nations in the economic field, with the
object of securing for all improved labor standards, economic advancement, and social security." Roosevelt readily agreed to this inclusion,
which was presented in flattering terms as folding in another of his Four
Freedoms. Still, the president's accession is somewhat surprising, given
that complaints about a labor standards provision were likely to emanate
from the same disgruntled domestic constituencies who opposed international entanglements.[42]

As Welles had gloomily predicted, the insertion of the British qualifier gutted the language of the trade provision. The final language read: "[The parties] will endeavor, *with due respect for their existing obligations,* to further the enjoyment of all states, great or small, victor or vanquished, of access, on equal terms, to the trade and to the raw materials of the world which are needed for their economic prosperity." This was a clear reference to the protectionist British program of trade preferences known as the Ottowa system. Feis observed dryly that with this provision, an early pattern was set in which "principle, in other words, proved vulnerable to circumstance."[43]

"When you state a moral principle, you are stuck with it"

The Atlantic Charter's more general Four Freedoms language asserted that the two countries hoped for a peace which would "afford assurance that all the men in all the lands may live out their lives in freedom from fear and want." The unusual phrasing of this provision explicitly mentioned individuals, supplementing the charter's earlier, more traditional references to "peoples," "countries," and "nations."

There was apparently no discussion of the inclusion of this reference to individuals ("all the men") at the time. The earlier draft of August 11, which Churchill described as having been "submitted to me by the President," refers to "a peace . . . which will afford assurance to *all peoples* that they may live out their lives in freedom from fear."[44] The substitution of "all the men in all the lands" for "all peoples" and the expansion of "freedom from fear" to "freedom from fear and want" were British modifications. The "all the men" locution likely originated with Churchill himself. The phrase appeared two months earlier in his June 1941 speech to a group of representatives of the European governments-in-exile in London: "Here we meet," Churchill began, "while from across the Atlantic Ocean the hammers and lathes of the United States signal in a rising hum their message of encouragement, and their promise of swift and ever-growing aid." He concluded in a typical Churchillian crescendo:

> This then is the message which we send forth today to all the states and nations bound or free,
>
> To all the men in all the lands who care for freedom's cause,
>
> To our allies and well-wishers in Europe, to our American

Friends and helpers drawing ever closer in their
might across the ocean—
Lift up your hearts. All will come right.[45]

(This excerpt preserves the original layout of the prime minister's speech. Many British politicians had their speeches typed out to resemble blank verse, to assist with a more fluid and dramatic reading. Churchill's consistently look the most like actual poems, however.)

The Atlantic Charter negotiators may have approved the new language about "all the men" merely for its inspirational or poetic effect. Yet this minor rhetorical modification went on to have a profound impact. It posited the individual as being in a relationship with a wider international order, and, by extension, implied that the individual was a legitimate object of international concern. This rather attenuated corollary was soon seized upon by a young black lawyer in South Africa. As Nelson Mandela later recounted: "The Atlantic Charter of 1941, signed by Roosevelt and Churchill, reaffirmed faith in the dignity of each human being and propagated a host of democratic principles." Mandela's reference to individual dignity is a precursor of what would soon become a standard human-rights reading of the Atlantic Charter.[46]

The idea that individual citizens could have a direct relationship to some kind of supranational legal order would hold an obvious appeal for an activist such as Mandela and for other subjects of oppressive regimes the world over. This enhanced role for the individual would later find a more explicit expression in the text of the 1945 United Nations Charter, where, as international lawyer Hersch Lauterpacht wrote in 1947, "the individual human being first appears in his full stature as endowed with fundamental rights and freedoms."[47]

Mandela directly addressed the question of the free translation of ideas from the international to the domestic level: "Some in the West saw the [Atlantic] Charter as empty promises, but not those of us in Africa. Inspired by the Atlantic Charter and the fight of the Allies against tyranny and oppression, the ANC created its own Charter . . . We hoped that the government and ordinary South Africans would see that the principles they were fighting for in Europe were the same ones we were advocating at home."[48] Roosevelt's speechwriter Robert Sherwood noted that "it was not long before the people of India, Burma, Malaya, and Indonesia were beginning to ask if the Atlantic Charter extended also to the Pacific and to Asia in general."[49]

Suffice it to say that Nelson Mandela's Atlantic Charter was not

Winston Churchill's. Such questions of universal application soon became "so acute and embarrassing" in the immediate aftermath of the charter's publication that Churchill was compelled to address them directly before the House of Commons the following month. The prime minister explained that "at the Atlantic meeting, we had in mind, primarily, the restoration of the sovereignty, self-government and national life of the States and nations of Europe now under the Nazi yoke." He then offered this firm elaboration: "So that is quite a separate problem from the progressive evolution of self-governing institutions in the regions whose peoples owe allegiance to the British Crown."[50]

Despite such narrow parsing, to many of its contemporary consumers the language of the Atlantic Charter spoke for itself. Point Three declared that the parties "respect the right of all peoples to choose the government under which they will live"—a phrase penned by Churchill himself that survived from the first draft—while Point Four referred to "all states, great or small." Point Five addressed itself to "all nations," as did Point Six, which also included the phrase "all the men in all the lands." Point Seven repeated "all men," and Point Eight spoke of "all the nations in the world." "Indeed," concluded Sherwood, "it may be said that one small word, 'all,' came to be regarded as the veritable cornerstone of the whole structure of the United Nations."[51]

The Atlantic Conference's immediate, substantive accomplishments were paltry on paper. The vaguely worded eight-point declaration was accompanied only by a commitment to extend US naval escort patrols as far as Iceland and a flaccid warning to Japan to cease its expansionist policies. This news was received—by a disappointed British press and public, in particular—as a "flop." Despite a few breathless headlines about a "New Deal for the World," it was clear that there was to be no hoped-for American declaration of war, no ultimatum to Japan, and no vastly increased share of American arms production. After hearing Deputy Prime Minister Clement Atlee read the text of the Atlantic Charter over the radio in an uninspiring monotone, an American military attaché in London "got the impression [British listeners] were all very much disappointed and had been hoping for some tangible movement toward war."[52]

The German press reviewed the Atlantic Charter with predictable disdain, as a fundamentally anti-Nazi manifesto, emphasizing the feeling of *katzenjammer*—a "hangover" implying disappointment—that the charter had elicited in Washington and London. Under the headline "Comedy at Sea," Goebbels's propaganda newspaper *Der Angriff* scoffed that "the lack of imagination and thought revealed by the two chieftains in Washington and London is amazing and incredible. The most antiquated phrases shot out of their theater cannons. They didn't even bother to brush them up or to try on a new costume." German editorials portrayed the eight points as a tired, hypocritical reprise of Wilsonianism—"A Super-Versailles with the Soviets as Watchdog," intoned a headline in *Der Völkische Beobachter*—while another article in the same edition observed dismissively that "this time the nations will not be taken in by these card sharks." The August 16, 1941, edition of the *Frankfurter Zeitung* concurred that "the German people have had experience with Wilson's 14 points and now know what to think about notions of autonomy when they are proclaimed by Anglo-Saxon nations." An editorial in the following day's edition concluded, "It is the same old salesman-jargon, only this time with a little more sugar."[53]

The German papers took advantage of their coverage of the Atlantic Charter to comment on America's burgeoning power and the shifting dynamics of the Anglo-American relationship. The *Frankfurter Zeitung* explained that "since England is losing its supremacy to America, and since the United States is indeed claiming leadership over the world for themselves, the only alternative to the autonomy of a wisely-ruled and newly-organized European continent is . . . indeed the Americanization of Europe." In something of a parallel with the American isolationist literature, another editorial in the same paper observed that the Atlantic Charter merely served "to drag the American people down the road towards war without asking them whether they want it or not," while a headline in *Der Angriff* mordantly concluded that "Uncle Sam wants to cash in, but not to bleed."[54]

Meanwhile, FDR's press secretary was annoyed that the news of the Atlantic Conference had broken with a London dateline. On the American side, as historian Robert Dallek observes, early reactions tended to "harden already existing battle lines." While some internationalists rejoiced and others complained that the charter did not go far enough, isolationists in Congress and the press muttered darkly about secret commitments. Churchill explained confidentially to his War Cabinet that "the President . . . made it clear that he would look for an 'incident' which would justify him in opening hostilities." As to more extensive or specific secret commitments, a British official present at the Atlantic Conference observed, "We wish to God there had been!"[55]

Yet actual "incidents" later that autumn did not prove all that provocative to American public opinion. German U-boat attacks on the

US destroyer *Greer* southeast of Greenland in September, which failed to sink the ship, prompted Roosevelt to announce an anti-submarine "shoot on sight" policy. In mid-October a German submarine torpedoed the US destroyer *Kearny,* killing eleven crew members, while the US destroyer *Reuben James* was torpedoed and sunk on October 30, with 115 lost.

The fact that there were as yet no conscripts in the Navy may have muted public outcry somewhat, but other more intangible elements of public memory may have been at work as well. As Sherwood noted bluntly, "The bereaved families mourned, but among the general public there seemed to be more interest in the Army–Notre Dame football game. There was a sort of tacit understanding among Americans that nobody was to get excited if ships were sunk by U-boats, because that's what got us into war the other time." American public opinion seemed fully prepared to avoid fighting the last war.[56]

A Gallup Poll taken immediately after the announcement of the Atlantic Charter reported that nearly three-quarters of interviewees favored the president's handling of foreign policy. And despite the wide reporting of the controversy between isolationists and interventionists, an American Institute of Public Opinion survey taken a few months after the charter's promulgation reported that, while the document enjoyed widespread name recognition, only one in ten Americans could name a charter provision. Despite this mixed reception, many contemporaneous commentators and subsequent analysts have held that the Atlantic Charter "marked the end of US isolationism." This "watershed" interpretation is especially astonishing for a statement issued before the Pearl Harbor attack.[57]

Immediately after the Atlantic Conference's closing luncheon, the president's secretary cabled the news of a hair's-breadth margin in the US House of Representatives (203 to 202) for extension of the Selective Service Act of 1940. The unexpected closeness of this vote on the limited military draft to rebuild the Army rattled the conference participants: "The news of it dropped like enemy bombs on the decks of the *Augusta* and the *Prince of Wales.*" The Selective Service Act had originally obligated draftees to twelve months' service, but as that deadline approached, Army Chief of Staff General George Marshall had warned that it would mean "the disintegration of the Army" to allow these newly trained draftees to disband. As far as the British were concerned, the combination of the Atlantic Charter agreement and the vote on the draft made for a puzzling message indeed. An American radio host in London quoted what he called a typical British reaction: "The Americans are curious people. I can't make them out. One day they're announcing they'll guarantee freedom and fair play for everybody everywhere in the world. The next day they're deciding by only one vote that they'll go on having an Army."[58]

Unsurprisingly, Army morale had been dampened by all this uncertainty, and the letters "OHIO"—"Over the Hill In October"—were appearing as graffiti on the walls of barracks and latrines. Political commentators argued that such resistance was "a symptom of a serious disease, a disease which shows itself more generally in the curious apathy of most American young men in the face of the most desperate crisis the country has ever known. The disease from which these young men suffer is this: they have not found a faith [to fight for]." In the words of an editorial in *The Nation*, "Relatively few of the recruits have any idea why they are in the army or what the army is for."[59]

The Atlantic Charter itself was intended as a partial answer to this very question. Cautious and confused as it was, the charter was nevertheless the first official statement—to the American and British people and to the world at large—outlining the war's aims and the shape of the postwar world to come. Yet it would be a mistake to evaluate the Atlantic Conference solely, or even primarily, on the basis of substantive criteria. The conference's concrete achievements were minimal. The discussions among military staffs at the Atlantic Conference were widely held to have been disorganized and inconclusive, producing "little of importance" besides the beginning of a close working relationship between American Army Chief of Staff George C. Marshall and British General Sir John Dill, chief of the Imperial General Staff. Besides the negotiation of the charter itself and the American commitment to extend its convoy routes in the Atlantic, other discussion topics failed to yield fruit. Either there was no agreement, as in Roosevelt's refusal to issue a firm joint warning to Japan, or the contingency under discussion failed to materialize, as in the discussion of plans relating to a possible German invasion of the Iberian peninsula.[60]

As Churchill himself summarized it, the biggest news of the conference was that he had established "warm and deep personal relations with our great friend." At the Atlantic Conference, Churchill and FDR were finally able to take the measure of each other, inaugurating what is widely held to be the closest wartime alliance in history. "The meeting with Winston Churchill at Argentia and the announcement of the Atlantic Charter came at a crucial point in the country's life," Eleanor Roosevelt concluded simply. "[It] lifted the morale of the people when that kind of inspiration was most needed."[61]

"Are we fighting for security of Europeans to enjoy the four freedoms?"

The document that immediately became known as the Atlantic Charter "quickly took on a life of its own," writes historian David Reynolds, hosting many divergent interpretations.[62] Some read it as a blueprint for expanding FDR's Four Freedoms into the rest of the world; it was the conceptual scaffolding for new thinking about human rights. Others read it as an anti-imperialist manifesto. But it could also be read as a mission statement that projected free trade and a New Deal–style economic order onto the wider world stage. Many contemporary commentators focused on the Atlantic Charter's similarities to Woodrow Wilson's Fourteen Points, seeing the 1941 document as a chance to enact revised versions of the failed diplomacy of the Wilsonian era.

Figuratively speaking, as we have seen, at least two visions of the Atlantic Charter circulated during the early war years—the charter of Winston Churchill's intentions and the charter of Nelson Mandela's aspirations. Churchill's charter was an ephemeral press release intended for European ears only, intended to shore up Britain's sagging morale and the hopes of the invaded countries of Europe. Mandela's charter was a global statement of principles with an anticolonial as well as an anti-Nazi message, promising freedom and equality to individuals worldwide, unconstrained by sovereign states or imperialist prerogatives.

Mandela was, of course, not the only person to read the charter in this way. Many other anticolonial writers—in Africa, India, Asia, and Latin America—advanced this "Mandela" interpretation with equal enthusiasm, as did the African-American press in the United States and prominent members of the British Labor Party on several notable occasions.[63] For example, Clement Atlee, in a controversial speech to a group of Nigerian students in London, offered this universalist interpretation: "Yesterday I was privileged to announce [the] declaration of principles by the President of the United States and the Prime Minister of this country. You will find their principles will apply, I believe, to all peoples of the world."[64] This specific speech was one of the factors prompting Churchill to offer his own careful retrenchment regarding the intended scope of the charter in the House of Commons several weeks later.

The seeming contradiction prompted a sharp telegram to the prime minister from the editor of a West African newspaper: "Must we assume that [Atlee's] statement to the West African Student's Union [in] London that the Atlantic Charter would benefit coloured races as well as white, misleading and unauthorized?" Yet more pointedly, linking the

Atlantic Charter with Four Freedoms ideas, the editor asked: "Are we fighting for security of Europeans to enjoy the four freedoms while West Africa continues on pre-war status? We naturally feel we are entitled to know what we are fighting for, and are anxious to know what our position is to be in the coming new world order."[65]

On the other side of the Atlantic, Roosevelt was not immune from such awkward questions, despite America's tradition of anti-imperialist rhetoric. "President Roosevelt, as a co-signatory of the Atlantic Charter, has assumed a real moral responsibility for enforcing a policy which will ensure freedom for all peoples, irrespective of their race, color and creed," argued an Indian nationalist pamphlet published during the war. Otherwise, the pamphleteer asserted, "the Atlantic Charter will become for hundreds of millions a symbol of hypocrisy."[66]

"The Atlantic Charter is not a law, it is a star"

"When Winston Churchill and Franklin Roosevelt met aboard a battleship off the coast of Newfoundland in August 1941," writes the political analyst Timothy Garton Ash, "singing 'Onward Christian Soldiers' with their massed British and American crews, they made one of the great symbolic bondings of the twentieth-century West." The Atlantic Charter quickly became "the classic statement of Allied principles, a set of criteria for subsequent wartime diplomacy," agrees the historian David Reynolds, while at the same time raising awkward questions about the incongruity of America's racial policies at home and Britain's imperial policies abroad.[67]

Whatever the interpretation of its specific principles, the Atlantic Charter and its underlying ideology crystallized a more expansive vision of the US national interest. The Atlantic Conference's main accomplishments were situated in this much more subjective realm of ideas, where participants' internal qualities met their external circumstances. The very breadth of the charter's principles meant that its symbolic value was contested and ambiguous. The document meant different things to different people, and deliberately so.[68]

The notoriously unreflective Roosevelt himself was soon describing the power of such symbols at a press conference shortly after his return to Washington in mid-August 1941. The president quoted at length from a letter he had just received from one of his many behind-the-scenes advisors, Supreme Court Justice Felix Frankfurter, including this statement:

"We live by symbols and we can't too often recall them. And you two in that ocean . . . in the setting of that Sunday service, gave meaning to the conflict between civilization and arrogant, brute challenge; and gave promise more powerful and binding than any formal treaty could, that civilization has brains and resources that tyranny will not be able to overcome."[69] As Frankfurter's letter suggests, the shipboard Sunday service symbolized the intangible achievements of the Atlantic Conference, while simultaneously magnifying and intensifying them. Echoing this iterative dynamic, the Atlantic Charter itself was both a symbol and a catalyst, crystallizing important shifts in the intellectual and policy milieu capping the interwar era.

The question of the scope and binding nature of the Atlantic Charter vexed contemporary commentators. First of all, to whom was the charter intended to apply? To European governments in exile? To the anti-Axis alliance? Or to all oppressed peoples, including enemy nationals? The mayor of New York City, Fiorello H. LaGuardia, offered this inflammatory assessment in 1944: to him, it was "so clear" that the charter "means that the colonies or islands that have been unhappy in the past and have had little or no say in their own destiny, in their own government, have been guaranteed the right of self-determination and of deciding whether or not they want to go back to the old status." From 1941, anticolonial activists had been demanding a "Pacific Charter," an "African Charter," or a "World Charter" as companions to the Atlantic one. The Australian diplomat Herbert Evatt offered his understanding that "the name 'Atlantic Charter' does not refer only to the Atlantic region or to Powers having interest in the Atlantic. The Charter derives its name from the place where it was signed. The 28 nations which have subscribed to it extend around the globe and the declaration is universal in its scope and application."[70]

A mildly exasperated Roosevelt clarified his own interpretation of the scope of the charter in a Washington's Birthday speech in 1942, just two months after the signing of the wartime anti-Axis alliance known as the Declaration by United Nations: "We of the United Nations are agreed on certain broad principles in the kind of peace we seek. The Atlantic Charter applies not only to the parts of the world that border the Atlantic but to the whole world."[71]

Equally vexed was a second question, concerning the charter's status as "law." Was it somehow binding on Britain and the United States? The original Atlantic Charter was an unsigned telegram sent out to the press. The piece of paper on which the telegram was printed was signed by Roosevelt, who then signed Churchill's name just below his own. This un-usual document was not the kind of material artifact that could comfort-ably be designated as "official," much less as a binding treaty or contract. Such a flimsy statement could presumably never rank among such vener-ated objects as the Declaration of Independence and the US Constitution, which the National Archives now calls "the Charters of Freedom."[72]

The term "charter" descends from the Latin term for paper and over time has come to denote "a legal document or deed written (usually) upon a single sheet of paper, parchment, or other material, by which grants, cessions, contracts and other transactions are confirmed and ratified." The term has long been entwined with ideas about rights and sovereignty or control; it denotes a document "delivered by the sovereign or legislature . . . granting privileges to, or recognizing rights of, the peo-ple." Shakespeare referred to charters as grants of right, while Hobbes wrote of them as "donations of the sovereign, and not laws, but exemp-tions from law." Historic English examples included the iconic Magna Carta obtained from King John in 1215, "guaranteeing the fundamental liberties of the English people" and "appealed to in all disputes between the sovereign and his subjects," as well as the so-called People's Charter of 1838, a document proposing a more democratic representation of the people in Parliament and promoted by democratic activists known as "Chartists."[73]

A copy of the Atlantic Charter, "beautifully framed and illuminated after the manner of an ancient document—like Magna Carta or the Dec-laration of Independence," according to one sarcastic contemporary ac-count, was displayed from 1942 to 1944 "on the wall of the National Museum in Washington."[74] Late in 1944, however, controversy erupted over the revelation that this display copy was not "the original." When questioned about the War Department's inability to produce "the origi-nal" Atlantic Charter, the president shocked his contemporaries by breez-ily noting at a press conference that really, there *was* no original. Only gradually did he come to realize that the absence of an official document was potentially a real problem, and not just an amusing quirk of history, as this exchange with reporters reveals:

Q: Mr. President, did Mr. Churchill ever sign the Atlantic Charter?
FDR: Nobody ever signed the Atlantic Charter. Now that's an amazing
    statement.
Q: Where is it, Mr. President?
FDR: Well, you're thinking in awfully—oh, what will I say?—banal

phrases and thought. There isn't any copy of the Atlantic Charter, so far as I know. I haven't got one. The British haven't got one. The nearest thing you will get is the radio operator on the *Augusta* and on the *Prince of Wales*. It's one of the things that was agreed to on board ship, and there was no formal document. And the aides were directed to have the scribbled thing, which was—great many corrections, some I suppose in Mr. Churchill's handwriting, and some in mine, and some in the—who was it?—Sir Alec Cadogan's handwriting, some in scraps of paper, some in Sumner Welles's handwriting—and the aides were directed to have it sent off to the British government, and to the United States government, and released to the press. That is the Atlantic Charter.

Q: Well, Mr. President, is it not true that all of the United Nations have signed the—

FDR: [interjecting] Oh, Yes.

Q: [continuing]—obligations of the Atlantic Charter—

FDR: [interjecting] There—Yes, that—

Q: [continuing]—through the Declaration of Washington [the January 1942 wartime statement of alliance, mentioning the Atlantic Charter]?

FDR: Yes . . .

Q: Mr. President, that Statement that was issued to the press said [the Atlantic Charter] was a Statement signed by yourself and by the British Prime Minister. Is that not literally true, sir, that it was merely presented through you—that it was not a document—

FDR: [interposing] What statement to the press?

Q: When the Atlantic Charter statement was issued? . . .

FDR: It isn't a formal document. [Churchill] has got a lot of his handwriting—some of mine—in it, and I don't know where it is now.

Q: I understand that, sir, but the caption on that Statement that we received said it was a Statement signed by yourself and the British Prime Minister. I was just trying to clarify whether that document actually had signatures on the bottom of it, or whether it did not? . . .

FDR: Well, we all agreed on it, that's all I know . . . It isn't considered signed by us both.

Q: My recollection is that the thing that came up to the Capitol said at the bottom, "Signed Roosevelt and Churchill."

FDR: It couldn't have. He went back to England . . .

Q: Mr. President, can you tell us—

FDR: It was signed in substance. Now whether—whether—There is no formal document—complete document—signed by us both. There are memoranda to the—to the people there and to the radio people.

MR. GODWIN: [interjecting] Whether or not it was signed, you promulgated and stood for it, and you stand for it now?

FDR: [continuing] And sent for the radio man and said put this on the air.
That's all.

Q: Have you, since that time, Mr. President, wished that you had a formal
document which was signed, sealed and attested?

FDR: No, except from the point of view of sightseers in Washington. I
think that they will—they will like to see it, perhaps not so much as the
Declaration of Independence or the Constitution of the United States.
Well, if you wanted to exhibit it, there isn't any good reason we can't.[75]

A notable aspect of this exchange (besides its "Who's on first?" quality) is the rare glimpse it affords of FDR the lawyer alongside FDR the genial statesman. After the contretemps broke, the Roosevelt-hating journalist John Flynn scornfully explained that another reporter had returned
to the museum hoping to inspect the display copy of the Atlantic Charter,
"And lo! The great Charter was gone. An attendant told him it had been
ordered off the wall twenty minutes before. Thus ended the story of this
wretched fraud. The fake document which was never signed . . . was
nothing more than a publicity stunt."[76]

It is unlikely that Flynn would have been much more enthusiastic
about the legitimacy of a notarized Atlantic Charter etched onto stone
tablets. Yet the charter's status as just a press release was meant to suggest something significant, as far as Flynn and other critics were concerned, by epitomizing the phony qualities of Roosevelt's entire administration.[77]

Unexplored by participants in this public relations kerfuffle was the
question of why the Atlantic Charter's humble physical status should
matter at all. The charter was of course widely reprinted and quoted.
Moreover, in devising it, Roosevelt had been clear that the more informal
the document was, the better. He certainly did not want a treaty that
would be subject to Senate approval, nor did he want to inflame isolationist opinion by suggesting a military alliance.[78]

Nevertheless, after the Atlantic Charter's exposure as a mere telegram,
it was no longer eligible to be fetishized as an object. Pauline Maier, a historian of the American revolutionary era, describes this cultural response
to original documents as having deep roots in Anglo-American traditions: "The original, signed texts of the Declaration of Independence and,
to a lesser extent, the Constitution have become for the United States
what Lenin's body was for the Soviet Union, a tangible remnant of the

revolution to which its children can still cling." Over time, the Declaration of Independence "began to assume the quasi-religious attributes later institutionalized without a shadow of subtlety at the 'shrines' in the Library of Congress and, more recently, the National Archives." The Atlantic Charter, by contrast, had been kicked out of its Washington museum.[79]

In a sense, the Atlantic Charter's humble physical status—as "nothing more than a publicity stunt"—marks a kind of turning point for the modern conduct of foreign relations. Diplomacy by press release, sound bite, and photo-op has since become the norm. In this first major diplomatic summit for FDR since the advent of scientific public opinion polling, we may see a harbinger of things to come. Despite FDR's skittishness about permitting newsreel cameras and even still photography at the conference—a sensitivity not shared by Churchill—these negotiations nevertheless inaugurated a recognizably modern, outward-looking, image-conscious diplomacy, where leaders disseminated their views through a variety of media outlets. As FDR indicated in his circular, almost comic exchange with the press, the Atlantic Charter initially met its public not as a posted piece of parchment, as a "duly attested" document, or even as a reprint in the newspapers, but rather via "the radio man" who "put this on the air."

The debate about the charter's physical qualities might also be seen as a proxy for a deeper anxiety about its underlying legal status. After the January 1942 Declaration by United Nations established a formal military alliance with Britain and with the twenty-six other nations then at war with the Axis, American diplomats became interested in enhancing the Atlantic Charter's legal status rather than downplaying it. Subsequent international agreements accordingly featured repeated references to the charter. For example, a somewhat defensive 1945 United Nations pamphlet spelled out how the Atlantic Charter was "explained and interpreted by responsible statesmen of the United Nations speaking on behalf of their governments . . . Thus, it has become both a part of the treaty law of the world and a part of the philosophical background against which the peace is being planned." This pamphlet earnestly traced how the charter was transmitted to Congress on August 21, 1941, referred to the Committee on Foreign Affairs in the form of a message from the president, and incorporated into a lengthy series of official international agreements.[80] *These* agreements presumably bristled with duly attested signatures.

This device of citing a long chain of subsequent ratifications offers a snapshot of the international legal codification process during this period. By American lights, international law in the absence of a supranational sovereign was first and foremost a question of consent—a product of explicit, often bilateral, treaty agreements. Such treaties were ratified by the Senate and ideally included specific arbitration clauses for differences of opinion regarding interpretation. Agreements between states were generally held to bind only those parties who had signed and ratified them, and the most important quality in creating a binding international agreement was an explicit intent to be bound, analogous to the creation of a contract under domestic law.[81]

By contrast, piling up evidence of additional adherences and ratifications was a way of laundering the Atlantic Charter's status as international law under a theory analogous to the growth of Anglo-American common law. This technique of incorporating the Atlantic Charter by reference was a step in the direction of a more amorphous, customary law approach rather than the explicit intent-to-be-bound approach, also known as legal positivism. Custom was of course a respected *source* of international law, but was more troubling to American commentators as actual *evidence* of such law, again because even widely prevalent state practices did not necessarily correlate with the requisite sense of legal obligation.[82]

American legal authorities publishing in the 1940s, such as Charles Cheney Hyde, professor of international law and diplomacy at Columbia, accepted the hierarchy of the sources of international law derived from the famous Article 38 of the Permanent Court of International Justice statute (though this was not a standard that would have been officially recognized by the United States in 1941, since it had repeatedly rejected membership in the World Court, most recently in 1935). According to the provisions of Article 38, the sources of international law were "international conventions [treaties] . . . ; international custom, as evidence of a general practice accepted as law; the general principles of law as accepted by civilized nations"; and finally, "as a subsidiary means" of determining the content of law, "judicial decisions and the teachings of the most highly qualified publicists of the various nations." As Americans saw it, the best kind of customary law, in the interwar era, was the kind that had been formally acknowledged by reference as part of the treaty-making process.[83]

Discussions of the Atlantic Charter's legal status borrowed from this tradition, while marking a transition to a looser conception of a growing and changing customary law based more on "general principles accepted by civilized nations" than on specific multilateral agreements. As Hyde put it, by endorsing "practices manifesting a common and sharp deviation from rules once accepted as law," the international community "may in fact modify that which governs its members," even in the absence of specific agreements. In this sense the Atlantic Charter was a precursor to the London Agreement of August 8, 1945, which included the Nuremberg Charter, where an older language of justification legitimized a newer approach to international justice.[84]

Yet another way to look at the question of whether the Atlantic Charter was in any way binding would be to set the question aside as being simply irrelevant. The wartime debate about the Atlantic Charter's legal status was at root a dispute about the legitimacy and influence of the charter's ideas. Critics' derogations of the Atlantic Charter's status—as not being a duly-executed treaty, as not amounting to binding law, as not even existing as a proper document—were ways of downgrading that legitimacy.

To put it another way, *of course* the Atlantic Charter was not "binding," any more than one could call upon domestic or international courts to enforce the preamble to the Declaration of Independence. To say that the Atlantic Charter did not meet Austinian standards of enforceability does not really tell us anything about its influence on wartime political culture, both in the United States and internationally. Nor does the fact that the preamble of the Declaration of Independence is not enforceable in a court of law tell us much about the social, political, or cultural role of that document. According to Thomas Jefferson, for example, the Declaration was intended "to be an expression of the American mind, and to give that expression the proper tone and spirit called for by the occasion." Pauline Maier explains that "as a statement of political philosophy, the Declaration was therefore purposely unexceptional in 1776."[85]

So too with the Atlantic Charter. Harold Ickes was only one of many contemporary commentators who observed that "Roosevelt and Churchill agreed upon eight points, but there was nothing new about them." As with Roosevelt's Four Freedoms, the provisions of the Atlantic Charter were understood as largely aspirational, even by contemporaries. Chinese officials, for instance, in 1943 advocated steps to make the charter "a living reality," but they also recognized that "what gives the Charter life" is that it "crystallizes the deep virtues of the heart and mind of the generations between the two world wars." In a similar way, the Declaration of Independence over time came to be understood as "a statement of values that more than any other expresses not why we separated from Britain, and not what we are or have been, but what we ought to be, an inscription of ideals that bind us as a people."[86]

This quality of distilling pre-existing ideals and injecting them with fresh aspirations is widely shared by other iconic documents, such as Lincoln's Gettysburg Address, which, according to the Civil War historian James McPherson, "betokened [a] transition" in the American national self-image. McPherson traces the use of words such as "Union" and "national" throughout Lincoln's speeches to show how a more unified sense of national identity emerged from the crucible of war, and how terminology can reflect conceptual and political change: "Before 1861 the two words 'United States' were generally rendered as a plural noun: 'the United States *are* a republic.' The war marked a transition of the United States to a singular noun." Similarly, Maier summarizes how "the eloquence of Jefferson's and Lincoln's text depended in part on the resonances they captured, and their messages were convincing because the hearts of their audiences had been—to adopt the language of Lincoln's early New England ancestors, on which he drew so heavily in the dark years of the Civil War—'prepared' to receive it."[87]

The Atlantic Charter was part of an effort on Roosevelt's part to "prepare" the hearts of the American public for an increasingly activist, multilateralist foreign policy. In 1943 he expressed exasperation with what he perceived as his critics' pedantic literalism: "I am everlastingly angry at those who assert vociferously that the four freedoms and the Atlantic Charter are nonsense because they are unattainable," commented FDR, in a peroration he wrote himself for a speech marking the end of the First Quebec Conference in August 1943. The president continued testily: "If those people had lived a century and a half ago they would have sneered and said that the Declaration of Independence was utter piffle. If they had lived nearly a thousand years ago they would have laughed uproariously at the Magna Charta. And if they had lived several thousand years ago they would have derided Moses when he came from the Mountain with the Ten Commandments."[88]

The implicit analogy between the Ten Commandments and the Atlantic Charter left a few reporters rather taken aback when the president deployed it again in a 1944 press conference. Roosevelt lectured, "A great many of the previous pronouncements that go back many centuries, they have not been attained yet, and yet the objective is still just as good as it was when it was announced several thousand years ago . . . There are a lot of people who say you can't attain an objective or improvement in human life or in humanity, therefore why talk about it. Well, those people who come out for the Ten Commandments they will say we don't all live up to the Ten Commandments, which is perfectly true, but on the whole they are pretty good. It's something pretty good to shoot for."[89]

The president's larger point was that general and forceful statements of principle were still worth making, even if the stated objectives remained largely unrealized: "The Atlantic Charter is going to take its place, not—not comparing it with the Christian religion or the Ten Commandments, but as a definite step, just the same way as Wilson's Fourteen Points constituted a major contribution to something we would all like to see happen in the world. Well, those Fourteen Points weren't all attained, but it was a step toward a better life for the population of the world." The sheer historical sweep of this response seems to have rather flummoxed the questioner, who soon asked, "Mr. President . . . did you mean to imply by that that we are as far from attaining the ends of the Atlantic Charter as the world was a thousand years ago?" Offering something akin to a statement of personal philosophy, Roosevelt replied, "Oh, no. Oh, no. The world goes a little bit by peaks and valleys, but on the whole the curve is upward . . . and things are going to get better, if we work for it."[90]

Framed this way, what the legal scholar Edward Laing has called the Atlantic Charter's "flexible constitutional essence" was a source of strength, with its very terseness making that document more capacious. It was this thin, aspirational quality that enabled leaders such as Nelson Mandela and Mohandas Gandhi to hear "the news, not the vehicle that brought it." Writing about the Declaration of Independence, Maier similarly notes that "when the Declaration was read listeners heard mainly what was already in their heads." In the early 1940s, National Resources Planning Board Vice-Chair Charles Merriam explained this less-is-more philosophy in terms that could apply to the Atlantic Charter as well: "The strength of the Constitution was its brevity and its generality in combination. A Constitution ten times as long and detailed would have been far less effective." So too with the Atlantic Charter. Early planning documents for subsequent, detailed blueprints such as the charters of the United Nations, Nuremberg, and Bretton Woods all drew their inspiration, and in many cases their specific provisions, explicitly from the Atlantic Charter, as the drafters of those documents discussed at length.[91]

The nineteenth-century British historian Lord Acton wrote of France's 1789 Declaration of the Rights of Man and Citizen that "it was a single confused page . . . that outweighed libraries and was stronger than all of the armies of Napoleon." In a more limited way, the hastily prepared 376-word telegram we now know as the Atlantic Charter participated in this kind of world-historical dynamic. It became "incalculably more powerful as an instrument of human freedom" than Churchill, Roosevelt, and their aides could ever have imagined, and in the process transformed the role of the United States on the world stage.[92]

The power of the charter's ideas, soon to be embodied in a variety of international institutions, was highlighted all the more by the very unimpressiveness of the physical artifact itself. A comment by Winston Churchill unwittingly captured the dynamic through which the Atlantic Charter became a cultural as well as a political icon. "Unwittingly," because the prime minister's observation was made in a context where he was trying to wriggle out from under the perceived strictures of the charter, by arguing in conversation with Roosevelt that its provisions were not "legally binding." "The Atlantic Charter," Churchill lyrically explained, "is not a law—it is a star."[93] But sometimes it is our stars, more than our laws, that chart our course through history.

CHAPTER 2

FORGING A NEW AMERICAN MULTILATERALISM

Norman Rockwell was feeling rejected. Early in 1942 the well-known American illustrator wanted to make an artistic contribution to the Allied war effort. He hoped to go beyond the sentimental content of his First World War propaganda posters, with their images of well-scrubbed soldiers singing around the campfire, and paint something with a message: "I wanted to do something bigger than a war poster," he later explained, in order to "make some statement about what the country was fighting for."

Accordingly, Rockwell thought he might illustrate the principles of the August 1941 Atlantic Charter, "thinking that maybe it contained the idea I was looking for." But how to paint the ideas in the Atlantic Charter? Rockwell eventually gave up. He noted in his autobiography that not only could he not *paint* the Atlantic Charter; he couldn't even bring himself to *read* it. "I hadn't been able to get beyond the first paragraph," he confessed. The artist then decided that although the ideas in the Atlantic Charter were doubtlessly very noble, he, Rockwell, was "not noble enough" to paint them: "Besides, nobody I know was reading the proclamation either, despite all the fanfare and hullabaloo about it in the press and on the radio."

The Office of War Information officials whom Rockwell solicited were not particularly interested in employing the 48-year-old illustrator anyway. They were seeking someone younger and fresher for a 1942 war bond campaign. They insulted the notoriously thin-skinned Rockwell by suggesting that his realistic style might lend itself to illustrating a calisthenics manual instead.

So what was a patriotic and publicity-hungry artist to do? Instead of illustrating an abstract international agreement, Rockwell went on to paint his famously homespun interpretation of a related initiative: a depiction of Roosevelt's 1941 "Four Freedoms." The illustrator's "salt-of-the-earth" rendition of these wartime ideals, featuring scenes from the daily lives of his Vermont neighbors, were highly popular, and commentators contrasted them favorably with the Office of War Information's "brainy" and "dense" presentation of the Four Freedoms in a 1942 pamphlet. As Rockwell himself put it, "I'll express the ideas in simple, everyday scenes . . . Take them out of the noble language of the proclamation and put them in terms everybody can understand."[1]

Rockwell took the thin and universalist language from the Four Freedoms speech and thickened it by using a local, culturally specific idiom. The artist understood intuitively that concrete images of home and hearth would exert a more powerful grip than discussions of rights and ideas as symbols of "what we are fighting for." Yet Rockwell made the Four Freedoms *so* culturally specific that his rendition was almost incomprehensible even to America's closest allies. Rockwell himself noted that starving, overrun, displaced Europeans "sort of resented" the image of abundance in the "Freedom from Want" poster, which depicted a large, well-fed family sitting around the dinner table anticipating the consumption of an enormous roast turkey.[2]

The contrast between Rockwell's and Roosevelt's visions of the Four Freedoms highlights the difference between a domestic and an international focus for the American war effort. Roosevelt's presentation of the Four Freedoms had percussively stressed the worldwide relevance of each "freedom," pounding out the phrase "everywhere in the world" over and over again. The emphasis in Rockwell's Four Freedoms paintings was almost exclusively domestic, in both senses of that term. The runaway success of Rockwell's vision suggested that national sacrifice was an easier sale when it was expressed in the front-porch imagery of private citizens' everyday lives. Even the initial circulation of these images was privatized: Rockwell ended up selling his paintings to his long-time client the *Saturday Evening Post*. An instant hit, the images were soon picked up by the Office of War Information anyway, as part of a war bond campaign. Repackaged as a series of posters adorning the walls of schools and other government buildings, Rockwell's Four Freedoms went on to become some of the most enduring icons of the war years for many Americans on the home front.[3]

Unlike FDR's Four Freedoms, Rockwell's rendition neatly avoided mixing what might be called the "New Deal content" of the Four Freedoms—that is, economic rights—with more traditional political and civil rights. By setting his image of abundance in a private space—the family dining room—Rockwell steered clear of any implication that ensuring freedom from want was the government's responsibility. The historian Lizabeth Cohen notes how "Rockwell depicted 'Freedom From Want' not as a worker with a job, nor as government beneficence protecting the hungry and homeless, but rather as a celebration of the plenitude that American families reaped through their participation in a mass consumer economy."

By contrast, the government-sanctioned message of the Four Freedoms implied a "reciprocal relationship" between states and citizens around the globe, where each state would be obliged "to provide and protect a minimal level of subsistence for the individuals who comprise it," as the historian Robert Westbrook explains. The framing of the Atlantic Charter echoed this New Deal–inspired synthesis of political and economic provisions.[4]

The Genesis of FDR's Four Freedoms: "Someday it will dawn upon us that all the clauses in the Preamble to the Constitution are worth fighting for"

The evolution of Roosevelt's formulation of the Four Freedoms can be traced back to a press conference on June 5, 1940. Responding to a question about how he might "write the next peace," FDR had offered a checklist for "the elimination of four fears": "the fear in many countries that they cannot worship God in their own way"; "the fear of not being able to speak out"; "the fear of arms"; and "the fear of not being able to have normal economic and social relations with other nations." The following month, another reporter's question elicited a list that added up to five protected freedoms: freedom of information, religion, and expression, as well as freedom from fear and want—although the fifth one was added by the questioner after the president had finished an initial tally:

> Q [MR. HARKNESS]: Well, I had a fifth in mind which you might describe
>   as "freedom from want"—free trade, opening up trade?
> THE PRESIDENT: Yes, that is true. I had that in mind but forgot it. Freedom
>   from want—in other words, the removal of certain barriers between
>   nations, cultural in the first place and commercial in the second place.
>   That is the fifth, very definitely.[5]

A simultaneous set of debates over social welfare in Britain influenced Roosevelt's evolving list of fears and freedoms long before the president's shipboard summit with Churchill. A clippings file maintained for the president on the general topic of an "economic bill of rights," and used for the preparation of the Four Freedoms speech, contained a letter quoting New York Post columnist Samuel Grafton, whose book All Out had been published recently in Britain. The Grafton excerpt explained that "in September of 1940 the better sections of the English press began to debate the need for an 'economic bill of rights,' to defeat Hitlerism in the world forever by establishing minimum standards of housing, food, education, and medical care, along with free speech, free press and free worship." These British initiatives were part of a transatlantic wave of interest in linking domestic social welfare provisions (that is, individual security), to wider war and peace aims (international security).[6]

In Britain, concerns about the economic contours of the postwar world led to the commissioning of extensive surveys in 1941 that would eventually underpin the so-called Beveridge Report, published in late 1942. Named after the British economist and social welfare expert Sir William Beveridge, this report detailed a proposal "designed to abolish physical want" in Britain through "social security," noting that "social security for the purpose of the Report is defined as maintenance of subsistence income." When the report was finally released, a year after the publication of the Atlantic Charter, it mentioned the charter explicitly and used the language of the Four Freedoms, as did the American and British press covering it. The Beveridge Report was "put forward as a measure necessary to translate the words of the Atlantic Charter into deeds," concluded its official summary. But the report cautioned that "freedom from want cannot be forced on a democracy . . . It must be won."[7]

The American press referred to the Beveridge Report as a British "blueprint for [a] postwar New Deal," which would stand as "the first attempt to translate the four freedoms into fact" by giving life to "at least one of the rights specified in the Atlantic Charter—the right to live without hunger or destitution." Freedom from want had evolved from the "fear of not being able to have normal economic and social relations with other nations" in 1940, to offering the key link between individual security and international security in a fresh articulation of national interests.[8]

By 1942, such an expansion of the idea of security was simply assumed in policy statements of the Roosevelt administration as one of the lessons of the Great Depression. A September 1942 pamphlet from the National Resources Planning Board entitled "After the War—Toward Security: Freedom From Want" noted that its own postwar planning efforts were "designed to meet the challenge to our national security caused by lack or inadequacy of jobs or income." Explaining that "without social and economic security there can be no true guarantee of freedom," the agency asserted that these objectives are "indeed a fundamental part of national defense."

Ideas about national security were expanding in the domestic realm, as well. To pressure Roosevelt to sign an executive order prohibiting discrimination by defense contractors, labor leader A. Philip Randolph threatened a march of 100,000 African-American workers on the White House in June 1941, while Thurgood Marshall urged that anti-lynching legislation was "just as important as portions of the National Defense Program" for a nation that was "starved for military personnel, begging for factory workers, and striving for international credibility."[9]

The Four Freedoms, Atlantic Charter, and Beveridge Report were three of the more visible crests in a transatlantic sea of advocacy for a wider government role in establishing individual security by journalists, social welfare activists, academics, professionals, and church leaders as well as elected political leaders and bureaucrats in the early 1940s. The editor of the London *Times,* Robert M. Barrington Ward, wrote an impassioned letter to Churchill in April 1942 proposing additional dramatic public declarations based on the Atlantic Charter: "The fundamental demand on the peace-makers," the editor explained, "from uncounted millions of mankind, will be for welfare and security. These twin aims sum up the essential purpose of the [Atlantic] Charter. They are aims which will more and more obliterate the distinctions once possible between domestic and foreign policy. The realization of the Charter can and must begin at home."[10]

Roosevelt's famous phrase that Dr. New-Deal would have to yield to Dr. Win-the-War as primary physician to America's body politic has led a number of historians to conclude that the New Deal was fading out under the impact of the war. An alternative perspective would highlight the New Deal's transformation from a set of domestic programs into a war aim, which then became infused with an explicit human rights agenda as it was multilateralized through the Four Freedoms and Atlantic Charter. Or as an anti–New Deal *Time* magazine editorialist observed, censoriously, "Dr. Win-the-War has apparently called into consultation Dr. Win-New-Rights." The legal scholar Cass Sunstein observes that "the threat from Hitler and the Axis powers broadened the New Deal's commitment to security and strengthened the nation's appreciation of human vulnerability." In the early 1940s, a new iteration of the New Deal was becoming nothing less than America's vision for the postwar world.[11]

Because of the way analysts commonly write about rights today, discussions of the Four Freedoms and the Atlantic Charter tend to separate these statements' "political" from their "economic" provisions. Skipping ahead to the late 1940s, we can see how political rights—often known as "civil rights" during the interwar era and embodied, for example, in the

US Bill of Rights—came to be anointed by US analysts as essential fundamental freedoms defining the "free world" in opposition to its remaining totalitarian rival, the Soviet Union. By contrast, economic rights, such as a right to food, shelter, medical care, or employment, were denigrated as not merely utopian but affirmatively un-American, because of their association with Marxist doctrine.[12]

Indeed, by 1949 the former State Department official, presidential speechwriter, librarian of Congress, and unofficial poet laureate Archibald MacLeish was warning that American politics operated "under a kind of upside-down Russian veto"—that is, whatever Moscow advocated must by definition be the opposite of liberty-loving American aspirations. By the late 1940s American officials were dismissing economic, social, and cultural rights as anathema to free enterprise and limited government, since these ideas had been tainted by their association with the Soviet system.[13]

But such a polarization had not yet occurred at the pivotal moment in the early 1940s when the realities of oncoming war were converging with the ideologies of a mature New Deal. In another section of his Four Freedoms speech, FDR had spelled out his ideas about the "basic things expected by our people of their political and economic systems." This list served as the basis for a more elaborate "Economic Bill of Rights" devised by the National Resources Planning Board, and widely reprinted as a pamphlet under the title "Our Freedoms and Rights." The Planning Board's vice-chair, Charles E. Merriam, in his 1941 Godkin Lecture on Democracy at Harvard University, offered a summary of these "fundamentals which underlie a democratic program guaranteeing social justice":

> For everyone equal access to minimum security as well as to the adventures of civilization.
> For everyone food, shelter, clothing, on an American minimum standard.
> For everyone a job at a fair wage—if he is in the labor market—and a guaranty against joblessness.
> For everyone a guaranty of protection against accident and disease.
> For everyone a guaranteed education, adapted to his personality and the world in which he lives.
> For everyone a guaranty of protection against old age.
> For everyone an opportunity for recreation and the cultural activities appropriate to his time.[14]

This is an astonishing list—and the degree of our astonishment is one measure of the extent to which our contemporary sensibilities have been formed by Cold War–inspired shifts in America's political discourse of rights. In a commentary that could just as easily be about the Atlantic Charter itself, Merriam explained:

> There are two great objectives of democracies in the field of world relationships:
> I. The security of a jural order or the world in which decisions are made on the basis of justice rather than violence.
> II. The fullest development of the national resources of all nations and the fullest participation of all peoples in the gains of civilization.

The linkage of these two ideas as a matter of public policy was a direct outgrowth of the New Deal. Indeed, Roosevelt speechwriter Samuel Rosenman referred to the 1941 Annual Message as a whole—which included such innovative initiatives as Lend-Lease, the Four Freedoms, and the Economic Bill of Rights—as the president's "renewed summation of the New Deal." Part of what was new about it was its explicit international focus. Merriam framed his own speech with the hope that "some day it will dawn upon us that all the clauses in the Preamble to the Constitution are worth fighting for." As Sunstein observes, New Deal–infused commitments such as the Four Freedoms and their later elaboration in an Economic Bill of Rights offered Roosevelt administration planners "a basis for a broadened understanding of what a nation would do if it were genuinely committed to ensuring the 'security' of its citizens. The threat to security from abroad was a reason to strengthen and rethink the idea of security at home."[15]

A more historically nuanced categorization of the Atlantic Charter than a simple political-economic duality would highlight three sets of approaches: First, updated Wilsonian ideals, including the disavowal of territorial aggrandizement, assertion of self-determination and sovereign rights of peoples, disarmament, and international organization. Second, diluted versions of the free trade provisions that were so dear to Secretary of State Hull, where American negotiators had tried (and largely failed) to seize an opportunity to press a vulnerable Britain on a longstanding American agenda. And third, what might be called Four Freedoms ideals, encompassing the prosaic provisions for "improved labor standards, economic advancement and social security," as well as the more lyrical "freedom from fear and want."

Such a reparsing is more respectful of the complexity of history, and avoids superimposing *post hoc* ideological categories on a messy and contingent past. While the mission of the political theorist may be to "blast a

specific era out of the homogenous course of history" in order to "grasp
. . . the constellation which his own era has formed with a definite earlier
one," as Walter Benjamin has argued, historians tend to be more circumspect about the impact of the present on the past. Daniel Rodgers has
used the image of "passengers being towed along by the locomotive of
history," observing that "when they pull into the station marked '1946,'
they don't turn to each other and say, '1946! This must be the Cold War!'
No—their sensibilities and reactions have been conditioned by the earlier
stops along the way: the Depression, the New Deal, the impact of the
War itself." Such an approach frames the provisions of the Atlantic Charter so as to avoid recapitulating an anachronistic Cold War sensibility,
while also implicitly reframing the Cold War itself, as just one more way-
station from which the locomotive of history has recently departed.[16]

FDR's vision of the Atlantic Charter as a New Deal for the world supplements Winston Churchill's vision of the "Atlantic Charter as press release" and Nelson Mandela's vision of the charter as a manifesto of individual dignity. It included the other two approaches and then went on to
fold in the Four Freedoms to produce an expanded list of rights—human
rights—that included economic security.

"To preserve human rights and justice in their own lands as well as in other lands"

"Human rights" was not a new term born of World War II, but during this period it became a shorthand term readily understood by educated readers and influential commentators both in the United States
and abroad. And as the term entered general use, its meaning gradually
shifted. Before the war, the phrase occasionally appeared as a somewhat
disfavored variation of the much older locution, "rights of man." Human rights also sometimes served as a synonym for the narrower legal
term "civil rights," as part of interwar era controversies relating to the
Bill of Rights or specialized fields such as labor rights. By the end of the
war, however, the term "human rights" was consistently serving as a caption for the so-called fundamental freedoms that differentiated the Allies
from their totalitarian rivals.[17]

These fundamental freedoms included a subset of traditional civil rights,
such as freedom of speech and religion, to which all individuals were entitled "simply by virtue of being human." Hannah Arendt subscribed to
this view, writing that the wartime encounter with totalitarianism "dem-

onstrated that human dignity needs a new guarantee which can be found only in a new political principle, in a new law on earth, whose validity this time must comprehend the whole of humanity." This "resurgence of normative foundationalism," as the legal scholar Richard Primus describes it, soon resulted in "a new vocabulary of 'human rights'" which linked wartime political commitments with "a broader idea rarely seen in the generation before the war but ascendant thereafter: that certain rights exist and must be respected regardless of the positive law." This was the "Mandela vision" of the Atlantic Charter proclamation: the universalist ideal of individual dignity, irrespective of the unjust policies of particular sovereign states.[18]

Measurement of such a rhetorical and conceptual sea-change is necessarily inexact, but it is suggestive of the shift in usage that the *New York Times Index* for 1936 contains no "human rights" heading at all. The term makes a tentative appearance with two articles in 1937, one on property rights and one on labor rights. By 1946 the term is listed as a separate heading, but the reader is referred to "civil rights," where there are approximately 150 articles we would recognize as addressing human rights–related topics. In 1956, the human rights heading is no longer cross-referenced to civil rights, but rather to a whole new conceptual universe, "freedom and human rights," under which heading there are over 600 articles.[19]

Allowing for a time lag in the index of a general-interest newspaper, we can see that a shift in the use of the phrase "human rights" was well under way by the end of the war. Indeed, if there were an exact "moment" when the term "human rights" acquired its modern meaning, a leading candidate would be the signing of the Declaration by United Nations on January 1, 1942. This document was a product of the second major Churchill-Roosevelt summit, codenamed Arcadia, just four months after the Atlantic Conference, in December 1941 and January 1942. Immediately after the December 7th attack on Pearl Harbor, the prime minister proposed a Washington summit to formalize a "Grand Alliance" of Anglo-American military operations. In private at least, Churchill indicated that he no longer saw himself as the hopeful suitor in his relationship with the United States, commenting that "now that she is in the harem, we talk to her quite differently."[20]

Churchill famously took up residence in the White House for fourteen days, keeping Roosevelt up all hours, charming the American press corps and Congress—and having a mild heart attack, kept secret so as not to unsettle Allied morale. In a widely acclaimed address to a joint session of

Congress on December 26, 1941, the prime minister noted bluntly that "if we had kept together after the last war, if we had taken common measures for our safety, this renewal of the curse need never have fallen upon us."[21]

At the urging via cable of Deputy Prime Minister Clement Atlee, the two leaders agreed "that this war is being waged for the freedom of the small nations as well as the great powers," and therefore their resulting statement of alliance should be broadened to include the other nations at war with the Axis. FDR himself coined the term "United Nations" for this anti-Axis coalition: the president liked the way the term stressed common purpose and de-emphasized the military component. (Churchill preferred "Grand Alliance.") Roosevelt was reportedly so taken with his choice of title that he interrupted Churchill's bath to tell the prime minister about it. In this January 1942 Declaration by United Nations, the twenty-six nations fighting the Axis began by affirming the "common program of purposes and principles . . . known as the Atlantic Charter." The United Nations coalition went on to assert that they were fighting to secure "decent life, liberty, independence, and religious freedom" as against the "savage and brutal forces seeking to subjugate the world." These nations pledged to cooperate in order "to preserve human rights and justice in their own lands as well as in other lands."[22]

The term "human rights" had been absent from the December 25 draft of this Declaration by United Nations. It was likely added in response to a memo from Harry Hopkins, who wrote that "another sentence should be added including a restatement of our aims for human freedom, justice, security, not only for the people in our own lands but for all the people of the world." He continued, "I think a good deal of care should be given to the exact words of this and I do not think the reference to the Atlantic Charter is adequate." The Declaration also included a reference to religious freedom, inserted over Soviet objections. Roosevelt insisted that this addition brought the Declaration more into line with the Four Freedoms; he had been severely criticized in the US press for omitting it from the Atlantic Charter.[23]

Incorporating the Atlantic Charter by explicit reference, the final version of the Declaration by United Nations is the first multilateral statement of the four key elements of a new, anti-Axis definition of "human rights." It included: (1) traditional political rights as core values; (2) a broader, "Four Freedoms" vision including references to economic justice; (3) inclusion of individuals as potential beneficiaries of these rights; and (4) discussion of the domestic as well as international relevance of these principles. This was a fresh formulation of a much older term, and all four elements continue to inform our modern conception of the term "human rights."[24]

The heartbreaking irony in the timing of this ringing declaration is that it circulated worldwide during the same month in 1942 as the infamous Wannsee Conference where Heinrich Himmler stepped up his efforts to coordinate the genocide of the European Jews. January 1942 was also the month that US officials decided, with Roosevelt's approval, to "relocate"—under what were effectively POW conditions—some 127,000 persons of Japanese ancestry in the continental United States, roughly two-thirds of whom were American citizens. Such horrifying events emphasize why it is important continually to juxtapose discussions of words and ideas with an examination of lived realities during this period. Mohandas Gandhi's letter to Roosevelt in July 1942 ("I venture to think that the Allied Declaration that the Allies are fighting to make the world safe for freedom of the individual and for democracy sounds hollow, so long as India, and for that matter, Africa are exploited by Great Britain, and America has the Negro problem in her own home") underscores how aware historical actors themselves often were of these yawning gaps between rhetoric and reality.[25]

In part, it is an awareness of such disjunctures—in the examples above, amounting to a cognitive dissonance so strong as to induce near vertigo—that itself constituted a kind of engine of historical change in its own right, as political leaders struggled to narrow the perceived gap between their actions and the words of their own press releases. The transformation of the label "human rights"—from a set of narrow, domestic ideas about civil rights into a broader, internationalized vision of fundamental freedoms—is an unusually clear example of how a conceptual change can be reflected in a rhetorical shift.[26]

Beyond human rights as "an isolated block of concepts"

Contemporary scholarship on the subject of human rights tends to suffer from three interrelated challenges. First, many prominent works are overtly polemical, taking as their starting point the rather narrow intellectual position that "human rights are great and there ought to be more of them." In political science, philosophy, law, and history, where many scholars are also prominent practitioners and activists, such an advocate's stance is natural and often appropriate.[27]

Nevertheless, as unexamined normative assumptions pile up, many discussions of human rights ideas acquire what Judith Shklar has called a "thereness"—a problematic tendency to congeal as "an isolated block of concepts that have no relevant characteristics or functions apart from their possible validity or invalidity within a hypothetical system." Because such concepts are correspondingly isolated from history, they become prone to "intellectual rigidities and unrealities." An unhappy by-product of this polemical turn is to limit the impact, or at least the intellectual reach, of this interesting and important literature.[28]

Second, discussions about human rights tend to suffer from an inability to manage the problem of cultural specificity. Modern human rights ideas grew out of legal traditions stressing individual rights, many of which were rooted in earlier conceptions of property rights and expressed in written instruments or charters such as Britain's Magna Carta, Petition of Right of 1628, and 1689 Bill of Rights.[29] Despite claims to universality expressed in such instruments—notably the 1776 American Declaration of Independence and the 1789 French Declaration of the Rights of Man and Citizen—these antecedents are nevertheless vulnerable to critiques by non-Western scholars, who tend to view them as being too tightly linked to the Western cultural configurations within which they arose.[30]

Recent studies have gone to considerable lengths to fold in non-Western sources and traditions, but such additions often seem tacked-on or artificial. The active debate in policy circles over whether various human rights are culturally specific or universal is recapitulated in the scholarship, often unreflectively. Expressing appropriate respect for cultural specificity while making an argument for the universality of certain "core" human rights is a balance that many theorists and practitioners find hard to strike. The legal historian Stanley Katz argues that "rights-based legal idealism" can only be validated as legitimate by local and relativist political and cultural realities, and not by what he calls a universal "legal/structural/textual checklist." Yet he also agrees with Shklar that beyond a certain point, such respectful cultural relativism results in a race toward the lowest common denominator.[31]

A more deeply contextualist approach might introduce what the legal scholar Ruti Teitel has called "mediating concepts" into this seemingly irreducible duality between universalism and localism. Supranational norms of international law can themselves serve as mediating factors, for example. The field of public international law is by design an evolving synthesis between locally validated positive law and universalist ideas of international law. Indeed, one key feature of the intellectual history of the World War II era was the development, consolidation, and application of pre-existing legal norms on a more universalized basis. For example, soon after the promulgation of the 1941 Atlantic Charter and the 1945 United Nations Charter, the older idea of self-determination and sovereign equality of peoples contributed its moral pedigree to newer and much broader issues of decolonization.[32]

A third challenge to understanding human rights in historical context is that scholarship often simply mirrors the ahistorical conflation of traditions that it detects among historical actors themselves. That historical actors would muddle or misconstrue various schools of thought for their own political ends, or out of ignorance, is hardly surprising. Fashioning rhetorical weapons from the resources that come to hand has always been a familiar maneuver in the American political arena. For example, the historian Bernard Bailyn notes the highly instrumentalist role of classical allusions in Revolutionary-era polemics: "What is basically important in the Americans' reading of the ancients is the high selectivity of their real interests and the limitation of the range of their effective knowledge." The same was true of mid-twentieth-century American politicians and their speechwriters as they reached into the rhetorical quivers marked "Enlightenment Ideas," "Natural Law," or "Common Law" to defend their claims.[33]

But contemporary analysts of human rights ideas must strive for a certain imaginative distance from our subjects, if we are to get a purchase on the specific and highly contingent contexts in which such ideas arose. The legal theorist Paul Kahn, diagnosing a conflation of theory and practice in the study of legal ideas generally, compares the study of rule-of-law ideologies in law schools today to the study of Christianity in universities prior to the twentieth century: such study "was not an intellectual discipline. It was, instead, part of a religious practice."[34] So, too, with the contemporary study of human rights.

Another way of expressing the limitations of these dominant approaches to international human rights would be to say that they exhibit, to varying degrees, what might be called the "plumb line" problem, following the analysis of the historian Eric Foner. In purporting to offer a historical treatment of a political theory or idea, scholars often "tend to give it a fixed definition and then trace how this has been worked out over time." Such treatments "drop a plumb line into the past, seeking the origins of one or another current definition [of an idea] while excluding numerous meanings that do not seem to meet the predetermined criteria."[35]

As contemporary scholars of human rights ransack the past for early expressions of familiar-sounding political concepts, they often distort ideas by divorcing them from context. For instance, up through the early twentieth century, human rights–related ideas were often expressed in terms of group or communal rights. But since current definitions of human rights focus almost exclusively on ideas about the dignity of the individual, the study of group-related rights, such as the Mandates system of the League of Nations, has fallen into desuetude. Similarly, human rights ideas in many non-Western contexts, as well as in Europe before the Enlightenment, were often expressed in terms of linked sets of rights and duties. But again, because elaborating formal lists of duties proved to be a legal and institutional dead end—just as ideas about group rights have proved to be over the last sixty years—traditions emphasizing duties also tend to receive short shrift in contemporary debates. As rights-related discussions in unfamiliar configurations receive scant attention, an already thin intellectual tradition is further impoverished.[36]

In the specific case of the Atlantic Charter, a "plumb-line" approach distorts our understanding of that document by focusing exclusively on how important the charter was. Such a one-dimensional analysis downplays the charter's many critics and overemphasizes its noteworthiness to contemporaries, the vast majority of whom, in America at least, could not recall a single charter provision six months after the Atlantic Conference. Even if, after critical analysis, the Atlantic Charter turns out to have earned a place in the pantheon of influential statements of American ideology, it is still important for scholars to try to understand how a such a small "critical mass" of public and elite opinion could animate these ideas so effectively. If we are truly trying to analyze America's changing global role during World War II, it does not advance our understanding to exaggerate internationalism, or to downplay the depth of indifference or opposition to international engagement.[37]

Framing the plumb-line problem in this way favors (and flatters) historians, since the difficulty can be addressed, in large part, by a more historically nuanced treatment of ideas and institutions. Historical analysis has much to contribute to the burgeoning literature in the several disciplines that actively concern themselves with human rights. For example, the study of what is sometimes called a "culture" of international human rights might fruitfully begin by approaching this subject as a branch of the history of ideas, supplementing the more polemical orientation of the legal, philosophical, and social scientific approaches that currently dominate the field. Approaching human rights ideas as a historical phenomenon—as Shklar has suggested treating legal ideas more generally—could "replace the sterile game of defining law, morals, and politics in order to separate them as concepts both 'pure' and empty, divorced from each other and from their common historical past and contemporary setting." This approach of setting ideas in context is most closely identified with the "Cambridge school" associated with the historian of ideas Quentin Skinner. Rather than a Straussian model characterizing human rights as an immutable set of values that is only gradually uncovered over time, this history starts with the assumption that events shape ideas in important ways, as well as vice-versa.[38]

Another issue in the study of human rights, perhaps in tension with the previous one, concerns the role of language and "discourse." Without doubt, rhetorical manifestations offer important clues to underlying ideas or events. But such discourse is something less than a pure proxy for the ideas or events they represent. Events actually happened and we should study them; somewhat more inferentially, ideas also happened, and had real-world effects. Analyzing texts or discourse is one source of evidence that may be more probative or less, depending on the context, even in language-intensive fields of inquiry such as politics, law, and culture.[39]

The infusion of human rights ideas into traditional American conceptions of the national interest resulted in something new under the sun in the mid-1940s. The human rights ideas embedded in the Atlantic Charter—as well as in the 1942 Declaration by United Nations—reshaped the concept of national interest by injecting an explicitly moral calculus. The historian Carol Anderson describes the Atlantic Charter as a "revolutionary" source of inspiration for many African-Americans, for example, a "bible for [a] religious conversion" that "eloquently supported the principle of self-determination, committed the Allied Powers to improving the quality of life for the world's inhabitants, and promised a peace that would secure for all peoples the Four Freedoms, especially freedom from fear and want." While international initiatives infused with moralistic ideas were hardly a new development in US politics, now mobilized and mainstream constituencies were paying attention and reacting in a way they had not before. These vocal constituencies were quick to shout about the betrayal of the "principles of the Atlantic Charter" when confronted with US policies that ignored British colonialism, protected national sovereignty, and facilitated racial repression.[40]

The prime minister of New Zealand echoed many of America's allies when he repeatedly demanded that "the principles of the Atlantic Charter . . . must be honoured because thousands have died for them." In a 1944 speech to the Canadian parliament linking the Atlantic Charter and the Four Freedoms, he elaborated: "Your boys, boys of New Zealand, South Africa, India, the United States and all the united nations have given their lives that the four freedoms—freedom of speech, freedom of religion, freedom from fear and freedom from want—may be established and the masses of the people given greater opportunities than ever before." He then warned, "Unless we strive to carry out those principles we shall be undoing in peace what has been won on the battlefield."[41]

The ideology of the Atlantic Charter had become a sort of "entangling alliance" in its own right, to use Lloyd Gardner's evocative analogy, by both creating and raising expectations about the justice and legitimacy of any proposed postwar order—much to the inconvenience of the American officials charged with planning for a postwar world.[42]

"Mr. Roosevelt relies upon opposites to coax him first to one side and then the other, believing apparently that this will insure a middle course approximately in line with the temper of the average American"

World War II is rightly viewed as a turning point for American internationalism. But one flaw in the image of a new world order springing whole from the ashes of war is that all of the fundamental ideas about multilateralism and human rights that are attributed to this historical moment had been fully articulated decades earlier.[43]

For example, emphasis on rules-based regulation of wartime conduct was part of a wider nineteenth-century backlash against the carnage of the Crimean War and the US Civil War. This "legalistic" approach contrasted with an alternative, "moralistic" idiom, whose hortatory aspiration was nothing less than to outlaw war itself. A wave of Wilsonian moralism, which crested during the interwar period, had started to swell before the First World War. A third approach, which reached its efflorescence during and shortly after World War II, was firmly grounded in the style and substance of the Depression-era New Deal: a synthetic, institution-based, problem-solving approach that American policymakers projected onto the postwar international arena. During the war, enthusiastic policymakers did not hesitate to draw strategically on the lessons of the Depression and the New Deal, as well as on their more legalistic and moralistic precursors.[44]

THE LEGALISTIC IDIOM

The Hague Conferences of 1899 and 1907, which focused on legitimate ways of making war, were prime examples of the legalist idiom of multilateralist discourse. Appalled by the death and suffering of the Crimean

War and US Civil War, military officials, policymakers, and lawyers responded with a slew of rules and regulations defining appropriate weapons, targets, and tactics for military engagement. Noting that "calamitous events and atrocities have repeatedly driven the development" of the laws of war, the international legal scholar Theodor Meron explains that "the more offensive or painful the suffering, the greater the pressure" for negotiating restraints and controls in the aftermath of armed conflict.[45]

These so-called "Hague laws" were international examples of positivist approaches to law, codifying law by means of conventions and formal treaties, based on an underlying assumption about the nature of law as man-made sets of rules. Positivists, of whom the premier turn-of-the-century example was the international legal scholar Lassa Oppenheim, focused on the "is" and not the "ought" of law, believing that explicit agreement among sovereigns was the only legitimate source of international law. One example of such positivism in the Hague conventions was a provision known as the *si omnes* clause, which held that if one belligerent in a given armed conflict was not a signatory to the convention, the treaty would not apply to any relations between any of the belligerents in the conflict. (This clause threatened to pose quite a problem at the Nuremberg trial, as Germany was not always a party, or had at some time withdrawn as a party, to several of the international legal instruments it was charged with violating.)[46]

The positivist perspective contrasted with the outlook of natural law philosophies, which assumed a higher law, either innate in human nature or of divine origin, capable of being discovered by reason or divine revelation. These contrasting approaches to the legitimate sources of international law in turn supported competing visions of how international law might legitimately change over time.[47]

A legalistic efflorescence of declarations, handbooks, and military codes flowing out of the Hague agreements purported to police the boundaries of wartime conduct. One influential example originating in the United States was a set of regulations developed by Francis Lieber, a German-born Columbia College professor and wartime advisor to President Lincoln. "Lieber's code" was promulgated in 1863 as the General Orders for United States Armed Forces in the Field. It spawned numerous imitators, fulfilling its author's hope that "it will be adopted as a basis for similar works by the English, French and Germans."[48]

One offspring inspired by Lieber's code, the *Oxford Manual of the Laws of War on Land,* illustrates the hallmarks of the legalistic approach: "So long as the demands of opinion remain indeterminate, belligerents are exposed to painful uncertainty and to endless accusations," the manual explained. "A positive set of rules, on the contrary, if they are judicious, serves the interests of belligerents and is far from hindering them, since by preventing the unchaining of passion and savage instincts—which battle always awakens, as much as it awakens courage and manly virtues—it strengthens the discipline which is the strength of armies, it also ennobles their patriotic mission in the eyes of the soldiers by keeping them within the limits of respect due to the rights of humanity." The sober virtues of restraint, predictability, and clarity would best advance these undefined "rights of humanity."[49]

One cultural factor reinforcing the legalist movement in the United States was a rule-oriented sensibility in the latter part of nineteenth century, growing out of the Industrial Revolution and earlier European influences, especially in Germany and Britain. A popular fascination with games, procedures, and mechanization resulted in a cult of efficiency that held US business leaders in its thrall. The Red Cross, YMCA, and Salvation Army developed their military-style organization during this period. At the level of international affairs, this yearning for orderliness fueled a drive for procedures to separate the messiness and randomness of politics from the "science" and certainty of law.[50]

"Arbitrationism" was one expression of this search for order in the legal field, calling for the formal arbitration of international disputes and led to the establishment of a Permanent Court of Arbitration in 1899. Arbitrationism offered an attractive legalist solution to the traditional isolationist/internationalist duality in American foreign policy. Compulsory arbitration of international disputes would enable the United States to take maximum advantage of its increasingly prominent international role without succumbing to the perceived "contamination" of European power politics. The capstone of these legalist developments in the United States was the publication of the inaugural volume of the *American Journal of International Law* in 1907, the first English-language journal dedicated to chronicling, analyzing, and promoting the development of international law on a "scientific" model of progress and advancement.[51]

Far from being woolly-headed peace advocates, these legalist advocates were sober men of affairs, often Republicans, many with international business connections. Leading examples included Henry Stimson, a prominent East Coast lawyer who went on to serve as William Howard Taft's secretary of war, Herbert Hoover's secretary of state, and Franklin Roosevelt's secretary of war, as well as Stimson's even more illustrious mentor, Elihu Root, William McKinley's secretary of war, Theodore Roosevelt's secretary of state, Nobel peace laureate for 1912, and later senator from New York.[52]

Yet the legalist turn was not exclusively, or even primarily, an internationalist impulse. Most advocates of legalist approaches to problems of international order, such as the arbitrationists and peace activists, were also absorbed by the pursuit of other kinds of domestic reforms such as the professionalization of social work, woman suffrage, temperance, or various kinds of responses to the rising tide of immigration from Eastern Europe. Roland Marchand, a historian of the American peace movement, argues persuasively that "these fears and anxieties about domestic disharmony were projected outward into the realm of foreign affairs." Elite "influentials" made earnest efforts "to educate the populace in a respect for law and treaties, and in qualities of self-restraint that would make them less restless and warlike." One example of this improving mission was the American Peace Society's periodical for children, *Angel of Peace,* which was described in advertisements running from 1900 to 1905 as "devoted to peace, temperance, good morals and good manners." Efforts to inculcate such Sunday School virtues may have served as a way for genteel, elite reformers to "compensate for being shut out of local politics" by burgeoning immigrant communities, transferring their reformist impulses to the international arena. The restraint and control so sorely missed in the domestic sphere could, perhaps, be cultivated at the international level.[53]

The legalist turn, with its disdain for sentimentalism and its exaltation of professionalism, might also be analyzed as a chapter in American gender history. The annual Mohonk Arbitrationist Conference, begun in 1895, had its roots in earlier moral and social reform movements such as temperance, religious perfectionism, abolitionism, and Quaker pacifism, all sociocultural movements where women had long held leadership roles. In hiving arbitrationism off from its earlier expressions in the broader American movements of reform, international lawyers captured it for a professionally socialized "guild" that by definition contained no women leaders.[54]

Arbitrationism was part of a larger Progressive-era trend toward professionalization and specialization. Peace societies expanded and, in Marchand's estimation, were "re-energized" by an infusion of lawyers, academics, and social scientists, but not all expressions of this rule-oriented sensibility were particularly pacifist: war-gaming and personal and political philosophies favoring military adventure also enjoyed wide popularity, especially in the United States, Germany, and England. (Again, gender analysis might usefully contribute to an analysis of these developments, as recent studies in the history of "American masculinity" have suggested.) Vulgarizations of Darwinian or Hegelian ideas were stewed together with "belligerent popular literature and folklore" to produce a potent brew of racism and militarism, as an ideological complement to the politics of imperialism. These bellicose developments shared the popular preoccupations of the age with science, order, and hierarchy.[55]

The Hague agreements of 1899 and 1907 and other turn-of-the-century legalist instruments were the first modern expressions of three key underlying assumptions on which modern multilateralism is based: (1) that international law can legitimately regulate the behavior of sovereign states; (2) that the major source of legitimacy for international regulation is explicit agreement among states voluntarily to bind themselves; and (3) implicitly, that such agreements could itemize and strengthen an early, restricted vision of what we would now call human rights provisions. It would be anachronistic to refer to the Hague agreements as "human rights" treaties. But under the Hague regulations, a specific category of persons—members of a state's armed forces—acquired a right to conduct their operations free from a list of prohibited activities, such as the use of banned weapons. Both "lists"—the list of protected categories of persons and the list of prohibited activities—were later lengthened, in subsequent iterations of the Geneva Conventions, to include prisoners of war and civilians. This checklist approach to human rights was legalism's answer to the goal expressed in the *Oxford Manual of the Laws of War on Land*, of protecting "the rights of humanity."[56]

Such an incrementalist approach was a far cry from what this study has been calling "Nelson Mandela's Atlantic Charter"—the idea that each individual should have a direct relationship with protective norms of international law. Yet the Hague regulations contain a kernel of protectiveness that would grow over time to encompass other individuals. They are in some ways analogous to the way that ideas about welfare entitlements in the United States began with soldiers and were later generalized to widows, mothers, and "the deserving poor," before becoming more universal.

The Hague Conferences were a prologue to the more public diplomacy of the later negotiations over the Covenant of the League of Nations and the Charter of the United Nations. Andrew White, US ambassador in Berlin and head of the American delegation at the 1899 Hague

Conference, expressed dismay at the overwhelming "shoal of telegrams, reports of proceedings of societies, hortatory letters, crankish proposals and peace pamphlets from America." One titled German delegate disparaged the way "the Conference has attracted here the political riff-raff of the whole world," including "journalists of the worst sort . . . baptized Jews . . . [and] woman peace activists," as well as Young Turks and socialists.[57]

The Hague approach to the laws of warfare expressed the legalistic idiom's dominant themes of limitation and restraint, with the state of war itself as a neutral context subject to moderate, consensual regulation. The main contribution of this first wave of international regulation to what we now think of as the modern human rights regime was the idea that "the right of belligerents to adopt a means of injuring the enemy is not unlimited." Hague law, concerned with the conduct of belligerents, and Geneva law, concerned with the status and protection of victims of conflict, were also linked to questions of arms control and disarmament. These legalist approaches to the limitation and restraint of armed conflicts are important precursors to contemporary human rights ideas, even though arms control and human rights are now treated as separate fields of law and diplomacy.[58]

THE MORALISTIC IDIOM

The "moralistic" phase of modern multilateralism assumed a more central role on the international scene after the loss of approximately ten million young men in the trenches of the Great War. This second wave marked a conceptual shift, presupposing the existence of an international community that was capable of sitting in judgment on belligerent acts. Broadening the language of legalism, where "war" was posited as a strategic game and the focus was on modifying its rules, interwar agreements spoke the language of moralism, which questioned the underlying legitimacy of the very state of war itself. War, if outlawed, "could no longer be the source and subject of rights," as then-Secretary of State Henry Stimson argued in 1932. Accordingly, wrote Stimson, "when two nations get into conflict, either one or both are wrongdoers—violators of the law of nations. We no longer draw a circle about them and treat them with the punctilios of the duelist's code. Instead we denounce them as ruffians and call the police."[59]

In the moralistic idiom, the new threshold question for analyzing the legitimacy of a belligerent act was whether it was part of a war of aggression (and therefore prohibited), or an act of self-defense (and therefore more likely to be permissible). In the terminology of international legal theorists, such debates dealt with the *jus ad bellum*—the laws about the rights and wrongs of going to war in the first place—rather than the *jus in bello*—the rules regulating the conduct of armed conflict that applied to all belligerents equally.[60]

The Great War had shown the neutral amorality of the positivist approach to be tragically inadequate, strengthening a more moralistic backlash. Interwar pacts and covenants tended toward declarations of principle rather than formal codifications of existing practices. During the boom years of the 1920s, such nonbinding expressions of abiding moral principles suited a noninterventionist American public just fine, dovetailing with the popular assumption that the United States could lead by means of high-sounding proclamations, while avoiding entangling alliances with the Old World. The negotiation of the 1928 Kellogg-Briand Pact illustrates this syndrome. As with other moralistic agreements, the pact was notably thin on enforcement mechanisms. The State Department had been too skittish about the League of Nations to participate in the negotiation of the League-sponsored Locarno treaties of 1925, so it opted instead for the highly publicized gesture of signing the Kellogg-Briand Pact—an "international kiss" that was meant to embody a more ethereal "spirit of Locarno" without formally taking on the burdens of boundary guarantees.[61]

The French Foreign Minister, Aristide Briand, had proposed a Franco-American peace pact to honor the tenth anniversary of America's entry into the First World War. (The gesture was actually the vestige of a promised Franco-American security treaty that was never consummated.) Secretary of State Frank Kellogg upped the ante by proposing to broaden the renunciation of war to include any other nations wishing to sign on. Kellogg's offer proved "as irresistible as it was meaningless," as former Secretary of State Henry Kissinger has described it. Germany, Japan, and Italy all happily signed the pact, along with over one hundred other nations. The historian Denis Brogan, who published mostly during the 1940s and 1950s, offered the analogy that "the United States, which had abolished the evils of drink by the 18th Amendment, invited the world to abolish war by taking the Pact of Paris pledge."[62]

The analogy with temperance activism, while snide, was not specious. The mingling of legalistic and moralistic voices in an ongoing dialogue of reform in the international realm echoed an earlier conversation within the domestic movements for temperance and abolitionism. In both arenas, rule-oriented, legislative strategies favoring courts and traditional political maneuvering alternated with longer-term educational approaches emphasizing "moral suasion" and public opinion. Moral suasion focused on the need to create a receptive audience in order for reform advocacy to garner lasting results. Similarly, for the League of Nations' moralistic idiom to have any impact, as Woodrow Wilson noted, "we are depending primarily and chiefly upon one great force, and that is the moral force of the public opinion of the world." Wilson seemed to assume that such a sympathetic audience was already in place.[63]

Yet by the late 1920s, the convergence of this rather remote and abstract idealism with a complacent "dollar diplomacy" had produced a popular backlash against American participation in World War I. During the 1930s this backlash congealed into opposition to engagement in international politics, beyond the realm of international trade and finance. The 1934 Committee Investigating the Munitions Industry, headed by Senator Gerald P. Nye, progressive Republican from North Dakota, portrayed the earlier American war effort as having been engineered by greedy arms merchants and devious international bankers (benignly personified in the comic strip figure "Daddy Warbucks"). The weak international response to the Manchurian crisis of September 1931 was one example of what happened when ineffectual intellectual moralism met studied American indifference. Speaking about the crises in China in the 1930s, one senior at Rutgers University's School of Agriculture in New Jersey indicated that, for himself and his classmates, "Europe was a place they'd read about, and China was a place they hadn't."[64]

This American inertia did not bode well for other idealistic diplomatic initiatives of this era, including disarmament, the peaceful settlement of international disputes, economic harmonization, and the rationalization of war reparations. Proposals such as Roosevelt's 1935 initiative to encourage the US Senate to accept the jurisdiction of the World Court were similarly doomed. Such retrenchment was not confined to American shores. Gilbert Murray, a League of Nations advocate and retired professor of Greek at Oxford, described an interwar conversation with a "disillusioned" young man whom he later identified as a "Hitlerite." A former idealist, by 1935 this young person was "railing against *idées wilsoniennes*—against constitutional liberalism, internationalism, and the introduction of morality into politics." Murray continued: "For a time, [the young man] said, he had been taken in by President Wilson: 'You told us to put our faith in the Society of Nations, in the World Court of International Justice, in open diplomacy, in constitutional advance by parliamentary methods. We have tried them all. Why are we then so miserable? Is it not better to throw all that stuff to the winds and grab what we can?'"[65]

The major contribution of this much-derided "moralistic" phase of interwar multilateralism to the cause of human rights was the idea of a group of "civilized nations," to which otherwise sovereign polities were ultimately answerable. As a British commentator observed, "Before the League [of Nations], it was held both in theory and in practice that every state was the sole and sovereign judge of its own acts, owing no allegiance to any higher authority, entitled to resent criticism or even questioning by other States. Such conceptions have disappeared for ever: it is not doubted, and can never again be doubted, that the community of nations has the moral and legal right to discuss and judge the international conduct of each of its members." An international community existed and was entitled to pass judgment, however ineffectually it may have acted when called upon to police members' behavior.[66]

During the interwar period, the political figure with the clearest sense of how weak American multilateralist sentiment was and therefore how much caution was required in its promotion was probably FDR himself. After having publicly come out as a strong advocate for joining the League of Nations and World Court, particularly as a vice-presidential candidate in 1920, Roosevelt backtracked dramatically in a 1932 speech to the New York State Grange convention in Albany. He indicated that he no longer favored US participation in the World Court *or* in the League of Nations. FDR's turnabout occurred in his first public speech after a pillorying in the isolationist Hearst press. He explained to a disappointed internationalist associate, "I had hoped you would understand . . . Can't you see that loyalty to the ideals of Woodrow Wilson is just as strong in my heart as in yours—but have you ever stopped to consider that there is a difference between ideals and the methods of obtaining them?"[67]

As late as the 1941 Atlantic Conference, President Roosevelt was still treading lightly around the subject of multilateral commitments. One standard interpretation of FDR's approach is that the shock of the Pearl Harbor attack freed the president to show his true internationalist stripes, because he knew that at last he would be supported by public opinion. But was this shift toward internationalism really due exclusively to the galvanizing effect of Pearl Harbor, four months after the Atlantic Conference? Or were there other factors between the two world wars that prepared the minds of Americans for multilateralism?

THE NEW DEAL IDIOM

The third idiom in the development of modern multilateralism was an internationalization of the New Deal sensibility. The journalist Marquis Childs captured this spirit in wartime Washington when he wrote that the atmosphere in the city was in many ways a reprise of the early New Deal era. Childs had come to DC as a correspondent for the *Saint Louis Post-Dispatch,* describing himself as a "Middle Westerner" with "a deep suspicion of big government and big business." He continued, "I have never been able to see how we could have a democracy if all the orders came from a few men in one city on the Eastern seaboard, whether that city was Washington or New York." To Childs, "the all-inclusive corral that is called for convenience sake the New Deal" was itself "a kind of war": "Thousands of people, some utterly new to Washington, came in its wake. They began the crowding and the pushing, the bursting at the seams. Often they seemed, to the settled inhabitants, like noisy visitors who had suddenly burst into a shrine."[68]

The New Deal was characterized by a certain naive cheerfulness about the efficacy of sweeping, institutional solutions to large-scale social problems. Childs sketches New Dealers themselves as embodying this optimistic orientation: "Some were eccentrics, some were dreamy time-wasters. For the most part, however, they were exceptionally keen and intelligent. Earnest, hard-working, giving off ideas like showers of meteors, they stood on the threshold of a new era, a little tremulous. Theirs was a cozy conspiracy of good will to remake America on a cleaner, truer, more secure pattern." Such enthusiasts shared some of the personal characteristics of the New Deal's mercurial progenitor, Roosevelt himself. Isaiah Berlin described Roosevelt as exuding an "inner élan," as well as an impatience with qualities such as theoretical purity and ideological consistency. The "ghost of Woodrow Wilson" haunted Roosevelt throughout his tenure as president, particularly through what FDR liked to call, disdainfully, "perfectionism." One facet of New Deal–style multilateralism was thus a backlash against the moralistic turn in American diplomacy during the Wilson administration; New Dealers preferred to see themselves as "hardboiled."[69]

In their pragmatic and polyglot New Deal idiom, FDR and his experts attempted to project an activist regulatory state onto the wider world stage. The sheer hubris of this enterprise was reminiscent of the darker side of the domestic New Deal, the New Deal of high-handed bureaucratic blunders and self-satisfied obliviousness to local wisdom or particularity. Childs parodied this smugness: "So much needed doing. People out there didn't seem quite to know that it needed doing. You had to make them understand what you were doing for them. You were a conspirator. Soon, however, an unhappy omission became apparent. The conspirators had neglected to take the American people into their confidence . . . [this oversight] was typical of the effort to superimpose from Washington a ready-made Utopia."[70]

In 1944 and 1945, Treasury Secretary Henry Morgenthau, Jr., a veteran New Dealer himself, tried to be somewhat more discriminating in handing out ready-made Utopias to the rest of the world. This is what he meant when he said scornfully that the State and War Departments were planning to treat defeated Germany like a "nice WPA job." Morgenthau did not want battalions of American GIs to repaint factories, run soup kitchens, and put on shows for the defeated Nazis while self-sacrificing European Allies looked on, half-starved. A one-size-fits-all approach to relief and rehabilitation was inappropriate for a nation that had launched two global conflicts in as many generations, he believed. Yet the treasury secretary's alternative, the so-called Morgenthau Plan for defeated Germany, might itself be described as a kind of New Deal artifact, concerned as it was with a top-down reconfiguration of German politics and society.[71]

What Isaiah Berlin called the "Rooseveltite" orientation outlived its namesake, although not by very long. Multilateralist developments expressing this New Deal ideology included declarations of war and peace aims—especially the Atlantic Charter of 1941, but also the later Teheran, Cairo, and Potsdam declarations—along with institutions for the postwar world such as the United Nations, the World Court, the World Bank, the International Monetary Fund, and the Marshall Plan, as well as UN-sponsored agreements such as the Nuremberg Principles, the Universal Declaration of Human Rights, the Genocide Convention, and revisions of the Geneva Conventions to encompass the protection of civilians. Both the legalistic and moralistic traditions in American foreign policy found strong expression in these multilateral developments, despite Roosevelt's professed disdain for Wilsonian moralism.[72]

Taken all together, these World War II–era proclamations and organizations embodied a key conceptual step at which earlier multilateralist initiatives only hinted: a vision of the individual as the ultimate object of protection by the international community, with individuals in turn having responsibilities to that community. Furthermore, this important breakthrough combined with an essential institutional development be-

queathed by the New Deal: that legitimate international regulatory organizations could have in essence a fragment of sovereignty donated to
them by treaty, both to perpetuate themselves and to develop enforcement mechanisms against member countries. As a 1946 League of
Women Voters pamphlet explained, "If we accept the premise on which
the United Nations Charter is based . . . then we must roll up our sleeves
and go to work to *make* the United Nations Organization work, and to
develop it eventually into a world organization with its own measure of
sovereignty."[73]

The New Deal's more spacious vision of security in turn suggested a
more dynamic reconceptualization of the very idea of sovereignty, somewhat in parallel with the disaggregation of that concept which is part and
parcel of American federalism. The traditional "hard-shell" vision of
state authority depicted sovereignty as a static attribute, as poker chips in
a pile, including such key chips as the ability to control one's borders, authorize currency, and enter into agreements with other states. By contrast, Roosevelt administration planners tended to treat the decision-
making authority inherent in sovereignty as a process divisible among
sovereigns and able to be delegated, if only in small, symbolic ways, to
multilateral institutions. Such sovereignty was also a dynamic process
rather than a static attribute, what international legal scholars Abram
and Antonia Chayes have characterized as the capacity to participate in
the international system. When cooperating sovereigns created an institutional nexus of mutual commitments, they produced a political order that
resembled, in a general way, a domestic constitutional order writ large.[74]

In the domestic realm, Charles Merriam spoke analogously of the evolution "of administrative agencies with wide discretionary powers in recent times—with what are termed sub-legislative powers. Long accepted
in most democratic states, these powers were within the last generation
set up in the United States, and have operated with notable success."
Such powers assumed as a corollary an expansion of executive authority
generally, to the alarm of anti–New Dealers. H. L. Mencken's sarcastic
redrafting of the US Constitution, "A Constitution for the New Deal,"
took a swipe at these new agencies by providing that "the President may
establish such executive agencies as he deems necessary, and clothe them
with such powers as he sees fit. No person shall be a member to any such
bureau who has had any practical experience of the matters he is appointed to deal with."[75]

By contrast, Merriam's 1941 Godkin Lecture was an ode to the virtues
of large-scale planning by administrative agencies. He breathlessly dis-

cussed how "the growth of the administrative process shows little sign of being halted. Instead, [it] still exhibits the vigor that attends lusty youth . . . Yet, its extraordinary growth in recent years, the increasing frequency with which the government has come to resort to it, the extent to which it is creating new relationships between the individual, the body economic, and the state, already have given it great stature." Of course, a fear of Merriam's "sub-legislative powers" taking hold at the international level was precisely what kept isolationist activists and members of Congress awake at night, because of the implications for traditional conceptions of national sovereignty.[76]

The New Deal style of multilateralism was one political expression of a broader cultural shift toward pluralism. One of Merriam's mentors, the constitutional scholar Edward S. Corwin, wrote of "the world of administration" as "a pluralistic rather than a monistic world." Here the New Deal idiom stressed pluralism as the appropriate response to the incommensurability of different value systems. Oxford don Gilbert Murray offered this first-hand comparison of the coherence of the Victorian Era with the fragmentation of the interwar era: "The old progressive Victorian outlook on life, shaped partly by Christian tradition, partly by J. S. Mill and the Utilitarians, was in some ways inadequate," Murray recollected somewhat wistfully, "but it seemed intelligible; it was a real guide to life." The integrity of this system received "a shock," however, by the decentering impact of the theories of Einstein and Freud: "We once had a conception of the physical universe; it has broken down, and we have instead many discoveries, many varying conceptions, culminating in one which Einstein himself says is not perfectly intelligible, and a theory which he regards as probably not correct." Murray concluded, "Where there was once a cosmos, there is now a chaos."[77]

This is not to argue that Einstein and Freud were somehow part of the New Deal. The analysis is more attenuated: that the New Deal idiom was one expression of this transition toward a more pluralistic vision of modernity. New Dealers tended to embrace chaos as a creative force. FDR himself embodied this pluralism, insofar as such a quality was possible in a single individual: "So passionate a faith in the future, so untroubled a confidence in one's power to mould it, when it is allied to a capacity for realistic appraisal of its true contours, implies an exceptionally sensitive awareness, conscious or half-conscious, of the tendencies of one's milieu, of the desires, hopes, fears, loves, hatreds of the human beings who compose it, of what are impersonally described as social and individual 'trends.' Roosevelt had this sensibility developed to the point of genius," wrote Isaiah Berlin. One of Berlin's own biographers asserts that the great historian of ideas himself believed that the "form of social and political organization" that had "historically, proved able to provide both the positive social framework for the maximum flourishing of individuals . . . as well as the best context for trade-offs between values, [was] the New Deal of Roosevelt."[78]

American legal culture shared in this New Deal pluralism, by means of a pragmatic, sociological school of jurisprudence influenced by Progressive-era social scientific approaches. This "legal realist" orientation explained laws as products of the society from which they arose, and saw law generally as a tool for adapting principles and norms in order to improve specific human conditions. The measure of the worth of any given piece of legislation was the extent to which it could "improve man's lot or organize society so that the system better fulfills the needs of men." As Henry Steele Commager described this approach, "Sociological jurisprudence was, however, more than a method. It had substance and an affirmative program. It held that the truth of law, like truth in general, was something to be found through experience, that it was relative, and that it could be created. It asserted that good law was what worked best for society, that law was functional and to be understood in terms of ends rather than origins, and that the actual workings of the law were more important than its abstract legal content."[79]

The intellectual predeliction to treat law as virtually another branch of anthropology was already the subject of active argument in academic legal circles as early as the 1920s. In the 1930s the legal realist approach flowered with an infusion of institutional and policy support from ideologically compatible New Deal programs. By the early 1940s many of these New Deal lawyers were seeking ways to contribute their skills to the war effort; these "boys with their hair on fire" brought their intellectual orientations with them as they participated in wartime planning for the postwar world.[80]

The contribution of this New Deal–style multilateralism, especially in the field of human rights, was twofold. First, such an approach highlighted the idea of universal application, usually expressed as the idea that every person is entitled to be free of certain kinds of oppressions simply by virtue of being human. This orientation was a major leap beyond legalistic Hague law, which recognized sovereign states exclusively and demanded explicit acquiescence for a state to be bound.[81]

Second, multilateralist developments in the immediate aftermath of World War II established the idea that the international community was capable of reaching through a nation's so-called veil of sovereignty, to hold individuals directly accountable under international law. As noted, this vision posited a more porous conception of sovereignty, drawing on American ideas about the division of decision-making authority under federalism. At the Nuremberg and Tokyo trials for example, Axis wartime leaders were not protected by the traditional "act of state" doctrine that would have obviated official responsibility for wartime decisions. Nor could secondary figures exonerate themselves with pleas of superior orders. These developments opened the door to an important corollary, as yet only recently developed in some regional court systems: the idea that an individual might in turn petition an international forum directly to protest local violations of his or her rights.[82]

Of course, any attempt at periodization hides important complexities. For example, many activists who sought to regulate war during the Hague era spoke openly of wanting to see war outlawed. This collapsing of categories worked in the other direction as well: legalists such as Henry Stimson and Elihu Root saw the moralist agenda of outlawing war as one way to ensure greater security for an American-dominated economic empire, one in which legalist and moralist objectives would work in tandem.

The fact that historical developments are rarely tidy does not negate the value of identifying dominant trends. The historian of international relations Martin Wight has characterized much of Western international relations theory as a debate over three major themes: (1) a Machiavellian tendency, correlating roughly with realism; (2) a Kantian tendency, correlating roughly with idealism; and (3) a Grotian tendency, amounting to "a residual category, defined in part as the *via media* between the idealized Machiavellian and Kantian positions." Roosevelt's New Deal was its own kind of *via media,* right down to the chief executive's management style. Childs explained that "Mr. Roosevelt relies upon opposites to coax him first to one side and then the other, believing apparently that this will insure a middle course approximately in line with the temper of the average American."[83]

Wight's critics have complained that "there is a point at which the debate that Wight is describing ceases to be one that has actually taken place, and becomes one that he has invented; at this point his work is not an exercise in the history of ideas, so much as an exposition of an imaginary philosophical conversation." Similar caveats apply here in the attempt to describe an ongoing dialogue expressed in legalistic, moralistic, and New Deal–style idioms. Wight answered his critics by noting that "this difficulty may be met in part if it is possible to single out points of similarity which, though not each shared by all of them, overlap amongst them, much as members of a family resemble each other." Wight himself preferred to think of the categories as "paradigms rather than precise lines of argument to which theorists or policymakers subscribed *in toto*" in the hope that "reflections on [the different categories'] intellectual antecedents may contribute both to the articulation of the issues and the structuring of the analysis of them."[84]

The same applies here to the legalistic, moralistic, and New Deal idioms: they are useful if they help us understand the interplay of politics, ideas, and culture in American planning for postwar multilateralism. They are less useful in analyzing the personal politics of a complex figure such as Henry Stimson, for instance, who was conversant in all three discourses and would pick and choose his rhetoric from each, depending on his particular purpose.

"The war changed our whole idea of how we wanted to live"

The question of why American multilateralism achieved cultural traction after World War II, but not after World War I, is usually greeted with the scholarly equivalent of a shrug. Popular explanations center around how the shock of Pearl Harbor marked the death of American isolationism, or that American economic hegemony accounted for this and virtually every other shift in postwar international relations. But close examination shows these standard approaches to be both overinclusive and underinclusive.[85]

Even Robert Divine's pathbreaking history of American internationalism, *Second Chance: The Triumph of Internationalism in America During World War II*, skirts the "why after World War II but not World War I" question in a tantalizing way. For Divine, elite activists and mobilized pressure groups brought about this transformation by "creating such overwhelming public support that Senate approval of the United Nations Charter was a certainty," for example. Clark Eichelberger was one such advocate, a League of Nations supporter and Chautauqua speaker who was a leader of the internationalist Committee to Defend America by Aiding the Allies and the later Commission to Study the Organization of Peace. Yet organizers and lecturers such as Eichelberger and the equally indefatigable Columbia professor James T. Shotwell were zealously making these very same multilateralist arguments in the wake of World War I, with all the added energy and idealism of youth. Why were the same arguments so much more effective just a generation later?[86]

Divine's conclusion, shared by other respected contemporary historians, seems to be that American public opinion was somehow not ready to support an international leadership role after the First World War. But since World War I led to World War II, one of the lessons for Americans must have been to accept the internationalism they had rejected earlier. As with the Pearl Harbor argument, this assessment is fine as far as it goes—plausibly necessary but probably not sufficient. At a minimum it seems to overstate the role of activist elites who took it upon themselves to explain the meaning of the World War I experience; ordinary Americans play a largely inert role in this formulation, remaining "confused and uncertain about the complexities of foreign policy" while passively waiting to be enlightened and energized by their betters.[87]

This history highlights the supplemental impact of wider developments in American society—particularly the New Deal response to the Great Depression and the transformative effect of America's wartime experiences. The New Deal reshaped American perceptions of the capacity of the central government to tackle seemingly intractable problems with large-scale institutional solutions. America's participation in the war also consolidated a national identity as a problem-solving, "professional," and pragmatic player on the world stage.

The cumulative impact of the Depression and the war on the American generation who became young adults in the 1940s is the missing piece in Divine's argument. America's Great Depression, beginning in 1929 and unfolding in several phases through the beginning of World War II, shattered lives and forever reshaped those who remembered it. Over the course of a decade in which unemployment never fell below 14 percent, and often approached 50 percent in cities such as Detroit and Chicago, nearly half of all white families, and 90 percent of African-American families, lived for some time in poverty. Even the marriage rate declined by almost one-fourth, as pessimistic young people faced an uncertain future.[88]

The Depression assumed a pivotal importance not only for the certainties it shattered and the improvisation and resourcefulness it called forth from so many individuals but also for the scope and variety of institutional responses. As local charities and states with depleted coffers turned helplessly to Washington, it was federally sponsored programs that got the country moving again. The WPA (Works Progress Association, after 1939, Works Progress Administration) employed some eight and a half million of the formerly jobless; the Civil Works Administration employed over four million; the Civilian Conservation Corps put three million more to work on forestry, flood control, and anti-erosion projects. The WPA and other federal programs had an impact far beyond the numbers of those directly employed: for example, over 30 million Americans saw the productions of the Federal Theater Project, while the Federal Music Project sponsored over 200,000 performances by 15,000 musicians.[89]

Millions of Americans responded to the New Deal experiment with fervor. The White House received 450,000 letters during FDR's first week in office; seventy people were hired just to respond to the overwhelming volume of mail. President Hoover had managed with a lone mailroom employee during his entire tenure in office. Berlin wrote of Roosevelt that "he altered the fundamental concept of government and its obligations to the governed" by initiating "a tradition of positive action." This tradition in turn fed new expectations that quickly ossified into perceived entitlements. Security for individuals—the dominant motif of the New Deal—would be permanently associated with "entitled benefits that only the federal government could confer."[90]

For policymakers, the lessons of the New Deal response to the Great Depression were twofold: first, that there was a connection between individual security and the stability and security of the wider polity; and second, that government had "an affirmative responsibility" to help individuals achieve that security. After World War II broke out in Europe in 1939, these lessons were readily extrapolated to the international level by aides in the executive branch as well as by State, War, and Treasury Department planners, many of whom had served as New Deal administrators themselves.[91]

The legal scholar and political scientist Anne-Marie Slaughter has noted specific similarities in regulatory structure, institutional design, and even casts of characters between various New Deal programs and wartime multilateral initiatives. United States security became bound up with the collective security embodied by the United Nations system, in a way that large groups of citizens as well as traditional policy elites could intuitively understand. In the words of a 1946 League of Women Voters pamphlet, "Even before this war had ended this nation had decided that singlehanded it could not ensure its own security, and that the only safety lay in working away from the old system of a world organized into intensely competitive nationalistic states working together for agreed-upon ends." American multilateralism became a way of using rules and institutions to entrench US interests in the global arena beyond the war.[92]

In addition to the Depression and the New Deal, another factor in the acceptance of postwar multilateralism was the actual wartime experiences of American citizens. Over 15 million people—one in eight adults ages 18 to 65—served in the military in some capacity following the attack on Pearl Harbor, and three-quarters of them served overseas. Meanwhile, 15 million Americans, out of a total population of not much more than 130 million, changed their county of residence during the war, almost 8 million of them heading for the Pacific coast. One veteran, asked if the war had "changed his attitude" about the different types of Americans he met while serving, and the many different regions of the United States and the world he saw while training and serving, replied that, no, he had not *changed* his attitude: "I *developed* an attitude. I didn't have any attitude about different parts of the country. It was of no interest to me. I didn't know anything about it. I suddenly became from a very provincial person to a person that was very much internationally oriented. I think that happened to many of us."[93]

This veteran was interviewed as part of the Rutgers Oral History Archives of World War II. Another interviewee, who as a youth had never left the New York/New Jersey area, except for a family trip to St. Louis, received military training in Kansas City, Missouri; Lexington, Kentucky; Dayton, Ohio; Battle Creek, Michigan; and Abilene, Texas. He then shipped out from San Pedro, California, for service as a quartermaster in India and China, and completed his wartime duties as an instructor for British intelligence officers in Karachi. He referred to his life before the war as "when I was still a hick." A Navy officer with a similarly provincial background underwent training at Penn State and Notre Dame and then in Puerto Rico, Miami, and Portland, Oregon, before serving in Hawaii, Korea, China, and the Philippines. He described his most memorable wartime experience as entering a remote Chinese village where the streets were lined with Chinese children waving little American flags. In a 1945 interview published in *Yank*, a popular GI periodical, a "corporal with a rural background" explained that, "I never got much more than fifteen miles from home. The Army's taken me through fifteen countries from Brazil to Iceland and from Trinidad to Czechoslovakia. After where I've been and what I've seen, I couldn't settle down on any farm."[94]

These new "cosmopolitan" experiences were then consolidated, for eight million of these former servicemen, by education and training supported by the "GI Bill of Rights." One veteran explained how overseas service worked together with the GI Bill to change the life trajectory of so many of his generation:

The war changed our whole idea of how we wanted to live when we came back. We set our sights pretty high. If we didn't have the war, in Poughkeepsie, the furthest you'd travel would be maybe New York or Albany. But once people started to travel—People wanted better levels of living, all people . . . Fellas I had gone into the service with, five or six, we all had the same feeling. We all went back to school. One's an engineer today, another one's a pharmacist. We just didn't want to go back and work in a factory in the hometown. The GI Bill was a blessing. It paid for 99 percent of your college expenses and gave you money each week to live on. That's the best thing the government came out with after the war.[95]

Such repercussions from federal programs were all but absent after the First World War. Federal expenditure in 1929 had amounted to a mere 3 percent of the gross national product, compared to 9 percent by 1936 and 16 percent in 1945. As late as 1930, 44 percent of the American public was still classified as "rural." This was the era of which Calvin Coolidge matter-of-factly observed, "If the Federal Government should go out of existence, the common run of people would not detect the difference in the affairs of their daily life for a considerable length of time."[96]

By contrast, about one-quarter of the veterans interviewed in the Rutgers project from the Rutgers class of 1942 had significant contact with New Deal programs or agencies (most had been employed by the National Youth Administration), and over 70 percent had served overseas during World War II (slightly over half in combat situations). After the war, a surprising 63 percent of these veterans expressed explicitly "internationalist" sensibilities, or indicated that the war and its attendant experiences had led them to change paths in their postwar life, such as going to law school or becoming an international business executive rather than a dairy farmer (many of these veterans had been attending Rutgers on scholarships to the university's agricultural college). There was also a high correlation between experiencing disruption from the Depression or having geographically diverse wartime experiences and expressing cosmopolitan, tolerant, or internationalist attitudes after the war.[97]

Participants in the Rutgers sample were by and large veterans from working-class backgrounds who were not selected for their wartime heroics or on the basis of membership in veterans' associations, but rather simply because they were members of the Rutgers class of 1942. As one of the interviewees observed, "Probably the most significant thing that ever happened in my life and probably most of the lives of people of my generation . . . was World War II. It changed your attitude completely. It changed direction completely for many." This trifecta of life-changing experiences—a youth in the Great Depression, wartime service, and benefits under the GI Bill—shaped a key swath of public opinion about "what we were fighting for," both during and in the immediate aftermath of the war.

Furthermore, these seismic shifts in attitudes no longer passed undetected by decision-makers in Washington. The study of public opinion had been systematized in 1935, when George Gallup and Elmo Roper began using statistical sampling in their surveys and widely disseminated the results. Gallup founded the American Institute of Public Opinion in 1935, the same year Roper launched the so-called *Fortune* survey based on scientifically designed national samples. Pre-release data from Gallup, Roper, and Princeton public opinion polls were widely circulated in the Roosevelt White House after that date, and played an influential role in memoranda that were exchanged among aides and sent on to the president, as circulation lists attached to the archived memos show. Indeed, copies of the polls themselves were often appended to the memos and sent directly to FDR.[98]

Policymakers now had a new way to talk about public opinion, and to respond to it. Some polls were devised to sound out certain kinds of policies in advance of promulgation—polls as trial balloons—and then the policies were in turn reshaped to bring them closer to the preferences expressed through the poll numbers—polls as virtual focus groups. On the topic of American participation in multilateral institutions, the Rutgers interviews also mirror larger collections of polling data systematically gathered in the 1940s. Two Princeton public opinion polls of enlisted men taken in April 1945 and in August 1945 showed overwhelming numbers for the following propositions, on postwar international security:[99]

Proposition	April 1945	August 1945
After the war a permanent organization of nations should be set up to settle quarrels between countries and try to prevent wars.	86%	89%
There should be an international police force under the direction of the international organization.	65%	63%
The best way for the United States to try to keep out of wars in the future would be to join a strong permanent international organization.	73%	68%
The United States should join such an organization even if it meant that this organization would have some say about how we deal with other countries.	63%	58%
Number of cases	*1,917*	*3,013*

The Rutgers dataset complements the polling data by suggesting how the very demographic group designated as "the attentive public" had itself changed composition considerably during the war. This heterogeneous group, in between elite "opinionmakers" and mass culture, included people who occasionally read a "middlebrow" periodical such as *Readers' Digest* or *The Saturday Evening Post* in addition to a daily metropolitan newspaper. Just a few percentage points' increase in this group consolidated the critical mass favoring multilateralism—a mass that was either absent or quiescent after World War I. The very term "middlebrow" dates from the early 1940s, although the cultural historian Joan Shelley Rubin traces its roots to the founding of the Book-of-the-Month Club and other developments in the late 1920s. The cultural historian Robert Westbrook has claimed that World War II "was the first American war to follow the consolidation of mass culture and social science," putting policymakers and other elites in a position to act on the systematic "investigation of the reflective life of less articulate men and women."[100]

A voter-information pamphlet advocating individual activism on international issues explained that it is "only with the backing of a majority of its citizens that such policies can be consistent and effective. It was Lincoln who said: 'Public sentiment is everything. With public sentiment nothing can fail; without it nothing can succeed. Consequently, he who moulds public sentiment goes deeper than he who enacts statutes or pronounces decisions. He makes the statutes and decisions possible to be executed.'" Therefore, "the citizen's responsibility then, in the present disturbed state of international relations, is to know clearly what goal he wants his government to pursue, and to urge that specific decisions lead in the direction of that goal."[101]

An image-conscious senator considering how to vote on international issues in the summer of 1945 encountered a very different landscape than the one he would have seen in 1919 or even 1935. But attempting to identify the "difference that makes a difference" between the post–World War I and post–World War II situations risks setting up a sterile debate over the relative impact of the Depression, the New Deal, and World War II. The important thing to note about this cluster of events is the way they worked together. A straight statistical comparison will inevitably emphasize the war's importance. But that cannot explain everything: despite large numbers of Americans serving in combat and support roles during the First World War, interwar America had emphatically turned its back on the politics of international engagement.

By contrast, a typical American who served in the armed forces during the second global conflict had already his world disrupted by the Great Depression and had witnessed the power of the federal government in an active, problem-solving role during the New Deal. Wartime experiences that did not involve combat, such as traveling to different military bases, within the United States or overseas, would additionally have served to break down more provincial perspectives.

One unintended consequence of these cultural shifts was to expose US race relations to heightened domestic and international scrutiny. "Under the pressures of this conflict," observed former Republican presidential candidate Wendell Willkie in the summer of 1942, in an address to the NAACP, "longstanding barriers and prejudices are breaking down. The defense of democracy against the forces that threaten it from without has made some of its failures to function at home glaringly apparent. Our very proclamations of what we are fighting for have rendered our own inequities self-evident. When we talk of freedom and opportunity for all nations the mocking paradoxes in our own society become so clear they can no longer be ignored."[102]

Willkie's subsequent 1942 world tour, suggested by Roosevelt, was replete with "inflammatory" statements of this kind, and elicited a harsh procolonialist reaction from Winston Churchill. It was at least partially in response to criticism from Willkie that the prime minister offered his famous observation that he had "not become the King's first minister in order to preside over the liquidation of the British Empire." The historian Penny Von Eschen notes that debates over the antiracist and anticolonialist meanings of the 1941 Atlantic Charter often appeared in wartime coverage of these issues in African-American communities in the United States by way of stories originating in London, where Churchill's attempts to narrow the scope of the Atlantic Charter and the Churchill-Willkie contretemps were widely covered by West African and South Asian anticolonial journalists.[103]

Many of the white men interviewed as part of the Rutgers Oral History Archive offered observations suggesting that changes in their racial and ethnic attitudes paralleled the transformation of their views about America's role in the world. Race was the quintessential "American dilemma," and domestic issues of racial equality—packaged with broader issues of religious and ethnic tolerance—constitutively shaped the Americans' anti-Nazi crusade: "It was partly because the problem of racial discrimination was already present in American minds that racism was what Americans saw when they looked at Nazi Germany," observes Richard Primus.[104]

The wartime pattern of receiving military training in the South exposed many white, northern GIs to more overtly segregationist attitudes on the part of local whites, and also to greater numbers of African Americans than had been their experience growing up in the North, which was of course highly segregated in its own way in the early 1940s. Of the first sixty-three subjects in the Rutgers database, for example, one-third commented on the existence of racial segregation in the military and one-sixth of them comment specifically on how the racial attitudes they saw as part of their training in the Deep South disgusted them, with several specifically describing a change in attitude about American racial issues as part of their wartime experience.[105]

The widespread wartime message that "World War II was a war against racial and religious intolerance" became a foundation of civil rights litigation and social activism in the late 1940s and early 1950s. One dramatic example is the story of Nicholas deB. Katzenbach, who was appalled by the racism he saw among American inmates of a German POW camp, and referenced those experiences when he served as Lyndon Johnson's attorney general and as one of the primary architects of the Civil Rights Act of 1964.[106] Impossible to measure is the subtler point suggested by the Rutgers interviews: that many northern whites who might otherwise have been expected strongly to oppose postwar civil rights agitation, given their demographic profiles, either refrained from opposition or were mildly supportive, due in large part to their earlier wartime experiences. And while awareness of the contrast between America's ideals and its realities was nothing new to African-American communities, the connection between local activism and a sense of international engagement was a burgeoning development in the 1940s. As civil rights leader Walter White explained, "World War II has given to the Negro a sense of kinship with other colored—and also oppressed—peoples of the world."[107]

The background of the Depression and the New Deal shaped how many US veterans understood their varied wartime experiences. There were of course many exceptions to this sense of international engagement. One GI told the essayist John Hersey that he wanted nothing more for the future than to come home "for a piece of blueberry pie." The internationalist sensibilities of the Rutgers respondents represent just one among several crosscurrents of American political discourse. Grasping the legal and diplomatic culture of this period—in what Clifford Geertz has called "the struggle for the real"—involves identifying and, to a certain extent, constructing pathways through a shifting historical and political terrain. As with virtually all groups of veterans, this group continued to see themselves as a cohort as they moved through their lives, but their world-view had been formed by the convergence of a series of events going back to their childhoods in the Depression, a context that was absent for veterans of the First World War.[108]

The *Zeitgeist* of 1945

The final year of World War II often appears as a high-water mark of American idealism—an ephemeral moment when ideas rather than ideology drove US foreign policy. It has been held up as a time when "wise men" answered policy questions on the merits, before the exigencies of the on-rushing Cold War distorted decisionmaking.

Yet what was new in "the *Zeitgeist* of 1945" was neither the idea of human rights underlying the Atlantic Charter nor proposals for international institutions to pursue them. What was new about the multilateralist developments of the mid-1940s—the Nuremberg trial, the extension of the laws of war to the protection of civilians, the founding of the United Nations, World Bank, and International Monetary Fund—indeed what made these developments possible, was their congruence with the life experiences of many ordinary Americans. The language of international engagement expressed in the Atlantic Charter may have been catalytic, but "to be successful, however, a rhetorical device must capture some aspect of an audience's world-view."[109]

For the majority of World War II veterans, their life experience did not include direct exposure to the atrocities of the Third Reich or imperial Japan, or even to direct combat. What it did include was exposure to the ravages of the Great Depression, and to the perceived success of society-wide programs in dealing with this huge, transnational, and seemingly intractable financial crisis. This was the difference that made a difference in US foreign policy in the wake of the Second World War. Added to these experiences were the life-changing exigencies of wartime service. Participation in World War II did not just involve larger numbers of Americans in the war, it involved a society-wide mobilization on a different order of magnitude.[110]

But how can we be sure of the pivotal role played by these large, amorphous shifts in the attitudes of many ordinary Americans, when faced with the long list of traditional explanations for America's turn toward multilateralism during World War II—the shock of Pearl Harbor, the growing awareness of the Holocaust, the dominance of the US economy, the existence of a permanent class of internationalist elites, the chilling effect of the early Cold War? The answer lies in a two-pronged approach. First, we must evaluate each of these traditional factors on its own terms. For example, recent scholarship suggests that Holocaust awareness was not really much of a consideration in shaping domestic political debates until at least 1949, and possibly as late as the early 1960s. Second, we must ask what given mix of causal factors might adequately explain the consolidation of American multilateralism following World War II, when similar sets of programs had failed so miserably following World War I.[111]

What gave human rights and multilateralist developments their cultural traction in the World War II era was not the legalistic or moralistic coherence of these ideas, so much as a pragmatic willingness of policy-makers and the general public to experiment on a grand scale, as a direct legacy of the sensibility this discussion has been calling the "New Deal idiom." American postwar planners were supported in their faith in institutional solutions by their domestic experience of administering a welter of programs, policies, and personalities summarized broadly as the New Deal. And they were supported by a groundswell of public opinion that had developed internationalist and interventionist sensibilities on an epic scale, by means of direct personal experiences that had been largely absent after World War I. For many ordinary Americans, the New Deal at home and the prospect of victory abroad had kindled optimism and hope, even as their world had been turned upside-down by massive economic suffering and total war. Together, these sets of transformative experiences served to prepare the minds of Americans for expanding the New Deal—with all its contradictions and limitations—to the rest of the world.

PART II

BRETTON WOODS, JULY 1944

There is a curious notion that the protection of national interests and the development of international cooperation are conflicting philosophies—that somehow or other men of different nations cannot work together without sacrificing the interests of their particular nations . . . We have found on the contrary that the only genuine safeguard for our national interests lies in international cooperation.

US Treasury Secretary Henry Morgenthau, Jr., remarks at the closing banquet of the Bretton Woods Conference

CHAPTER 3

THE PERILS OF ECONOMIC PLANNING

Dean Acheson could sense disaster looming. The American assistant secretary of state for economic affairs was preparing to serve as the State Department's chief representative at the upcoming inter-Allied conference on international financial institutions, to be held at Bretton Woods, New Hampshire, in June and July of 1944. The 730 delegates from 44 countries were meeting to refine blueprints for "a rule-based postwar financial order"—an international monetary fund to stabilize and manage currency exchange rates, and an international bank to finance large-scale reconstruction and development projects.[1]

The basic idea was to devise a mechanism for the free convertibility of currencies, rather than allowing weaker currencies to coalesce into mutually exclusive trading blocs around stronger currencies, as had happened in the 1930s. As with other institutions for the postwar world, the Depression-derived watchword was "stability"; freer trade, freely convertible currencies, and reconstruction projects that were not unduly hamstrung by crippling wartime debts were to be the economic ingredients for a more prosperous and stable international system.

Acheson was worried because he could see the outlines of a classic Senate imbroglio taking shape. Treasury Secretary Henry Morgenthau, Jr., who chaired the international financial conference, was planning to assemble a delegation that would be predisposed to favor his own multilateralist designs. And he intended to bypass the ranking Republican on the Senate Banking and Currency Committee, Charles Tobey of New Hampshire, a well-known isolationist, in favor of the next most senior Republican, John Danaher of Connecticut.[2]

To Acheson, the problem with this tactic was obvious: "To have been pointedly excluded from a conference held in his own state when he was running for re-election would have been an insult Senator Tobey could not have overlooked. The sacred rights of seniority would have ranged his [Senate] colleagues on his side and an enterprise that needed all the congressional support it could get would have been launched with a bitter partisan row. This, I told Morgenthau, could prove [the conference's] death warrant."[3]

Acheson had come by this strategic wisdom the hard way. The previous year he had mishandled relations with the Senate when heading up the American delegation at one of the earliest United Nations economic conferences, on relief and rehabilitation. There, in response to a Senate query about whether multilateral economic agreements were in the nature of treaties requiring Senate approval, Acheson had peremptorily answered no. Howls of congressional protest could be heard throughout Washington, based on "highly prized" prerogatives relating to the Senate's formal role in ratifying international agreements and the House's role in funding such commitments. Extricating himself from that "bad mistake" had required Acheson to engage in "some judicious eating of crow," as he put it, doubtlessly a challenge for the supremely confident Groton, Yale, and Harvard-educated diplomat.[4]

By the time the Bretton Woods Conference loomed in 1944, a chastened and wiser Acheson was arguing that planners for the postwar world needed to be more politically canny about just how they would go about translating their ideals into institutional realities. More canny than he had been the previous year, and more canny than the last time the United States had promoted multilateralist principles in the pursuit of peace. One of the cardinal lessons American planners had distilled from the experience following the First World War was to keep the Senate actively involved in shaping plans for the postwar era. Consulting early and often, with putative foes as well as with prospective friends— and dining on crow when necessary—was the key to Acheson's hardheaded approach to keeping economic planning on track.

By his own quietly self-congratulatory account, Acheson persuaded Morgenthau on these points and "reluctantly, he backed away from this folly and Tobey became one of the most effective supporters in the Congress of the international bank and fund." Acheson went on to seal the deal at the Bretton Woods Conference itself: "While we were battling disorganization during the opening weekend at Bretton Woods, Senator Tobey came to me with a request," Acheson wrote. "The Fourth of July and the need for an address at the conference were hard upon us. So was the Republican primary in New Hampshire, where [Tobey] faced opposition. If he could make the Independence Day address, he would receive most gratifying publicity throughout the state . . . [Tobey's speech] was arranged, and our relations were forever cemented."[5]

The very opportunity to make such a high-profile speech may itself have played a role in Senator Tobey's decision to embrace multi-lateralism. The eminent economist John Maynard Keynes, head of the British delegation, wrote in private correspondence that he felt Tobey's "conversion" to multilateralism, though mysterious, was emblematic of how American Republicans would ultimately come around to supporting internationalist measures.

"The case of Senator Tobey is a good illustration," wrote Keynes in a ruminative letter to a friend. "He is a Republican, formerly isolationist . . . Owing to his general attitude the Administration fought hard to keep him off the American Delegation; they did not succeed. By the second day he had come round completely and on the third day he had delivered a public oration, at which the Press were present, calling down the blessings of God on the Conference and saying that we shall be untrue to Christ if we did not put these plans through." Keynes concluded with the dry cross-cultural observation, "All of the above was delivered through a microphone in a voice which shook the largest room, with raised arms and fists and intense conviction and genuine belief. We met him at tea and he was all friendliness and told us that it was quite definitely the duty of everyone concerned to see this matter through. What a strange country!"[6]

Whether Acheson's behind the scenes maneuvers on behalf of Senator Tobey qualify as brilliant negotiation or cynical manipulation depends on the eye of the beholder. The important point is how this staffing move illuminates debates about what had gone wrong on the domestic front after World War I. The volatile and emotional Senator Tobey got kid-glove treatment in 1944 largely because of the disastrously ineffective handling of Senate opposition during the debate over ratification of the League of Nations Covenant in 1919 and 1920. The question that American planners were asking themselves in the early 1940s was this: How can we make sure that the our designs for a new world order are not destroyed, once again, by the contentious currents of partisan politics?

On a tactical level, assembling a felicitous mix of influentials in the American delegation required Morgenthau to take political considerations into account. On a broader, strategic level, selling the ideas of academic economists such as Keynes to their American constituents required the delegates to trim and stuff complicated financial arguments into appealing packages that would attract legislative and public support. Inevitably, some degree of political compromise would be required at this level as well—a reality against which Keynes often railed. Regarding his rejected plan for an international currency "clearing union," the famed economist lamented, "There is nothing more difficult than to continue a controversy with people who admit that your proposal is immeasurably better than theirs but nevertheless hold out on the ground that for obscure psychological reasons only theirs is practical politics."[7]

At the same time that they recognized these political realities, however, the Bretton Woods planners turned to "neutral" experts—economists presumably unsullied by the rough and tumble world of political horse-trading—to design the postwar economic blueprints. The conference papers almost always refer to these economists as "technicians," at least partly in order to distinguish them from partisan advocates. Mirroring this perspective, the American delegates also insisted that the new financial institutions themselves would be rule-based and function in a neutral, evenhanded manner.[8]

The following exchange, from the hearings before the Senate Committee on Banking and Currency on the Bretton Woods charters, illuminates the Roosevelt administration's vision of this elision of partisan politics:

> THE CHAIRMAN [SENATOR WAGNER]: I have just checked with Senator Tobey, and neither one of us heard any politics at all at Bretton Woods.
> MR. MORGENTHAU: The thought was that those countries could come to a world bank and get their financial needs taken care of without having to sell their political souls . . . that is my conception of Bretton Woods. There are to be financial institutions run by financial people, financial experts, and the needs in a financial way of a country are to be taken care of wholly independent of the political connection.[9]

The clinical calculations of these "experts" were meant to insulate the workings of international finance from the petty and partisan considerations of domestic politics. Yet the technical-sounding proposals that emerged from Bretton Woods were inseparably interwoven with traditional diplomatic interests, including blunt, heavy-handed power politics when necessary. In contrast to the enthusiastic Americans, British commentators cast a gimlet eye over the emerging Bretton Woods agreements, portraying Britain's accession to the new economic regime as being "the real price" for Lend-Lease and other American aid. The design of the Bretton Woods charters was thus emblematic of a longer-term shift of financial clout away from London and toward Washington, as a corollary to an attendant transfer of military and political power. The foreign relations analyst Walter Russell Mead has termed this transfer "the most important geopolitical shift of the twentieth century."[10]

The Bretton Woods charters were swept up in the *Zeitgeist* of 1945—a euphoria arising from the approaching victory in Europe and from an energetic determination to avoid the political and economic mistakes of the settlement following the First World War. This new spirit produced a brief vogue for all things multilateral and cosmopolitan, and was seized upon by congressional representatives responsive to this new optimism among their constituencies. The Bretton Woods charters were major beneficiaries of this shift in the broader currents of public opinion in 1944 and 1945, though most citizens had little interest in the specifics of the charters' provisions.[11]

In the short run, Morgenthau's strategy to deploy expertise to elide perceptions of partisanship succeeded in a limited way. The technical details of high-level finance never attracted the same degree of public scrutiny and debate as the later United Nations or Nuremberg charters, even though the Senate was reviewing the results of Bretton Woods at the same time as the drafting and debating of the UN and Nuremberg charters. "The monetary plans were not clearly understood by the public," confirmed an economist serving in the American embassy in London during the war, "and hostile congressmen ready to seize any opportunity to attack the administration were less likely to venture into the mysteries of finance." Ironically, if congressional representatives had understood the Bretton Woods accords well enough to have a more informed debate, they probably would not have approved them.[12]

Keynes's most well-known saying, "In the long run we are all dead," while true for individuals, is not necessarily true for the institutions those individuals create. In the long run, the world's perception of the IMF and World Bank would become just the opposite of the apolitical and technocratic image that Morgenthau promoted at Bretton Woods. Nothing could be more political in practice than the workings of institutions supporting what one political scientist has called an "open world economic order," a fact that the skeptical British and Soviet negotiators at Bretton Woods recognized immediately.[13]

Well before the opening of the Bretton Woods negotiations, Keynes had already come to regret his famous *bon mot*. "I could have said equally well," he wrote in one of his more philosophical editorials, that "in the short run we are still alive. Life and history are made up of short runs."[14] And in the short run, it was the obfuscating details of macroeconomics, not the high-mindedness of an economic and social vision of human rights, that allowed these two nascent financial institutions to survive.

"A deliberate policy of organized plenty"

Keynes saw Bretton Woods above all as a chance for those alive in the short run—especially the generation that had lived through World War I—to get it right this time. This overarching goal meshed very well with that of America's lead negotiator, Harry Dexter White. Despite their colorful clashes of personality, both economists sought to bring predictability to an international economic order and, more specifically, to design organizations that would foster and shelter domestic policies ensuring full employment and other guarantees of individual security. To American negotiators, these two interlocking goals—global economic stability and local individual security—were a logical extension of the New Deal truism that the stabilization of capitalism begins at home. After the First World War, American planners, facing strong opposition on the domestic front, had lacked the leverage to impose their vision of global security on their home population and on their reluctant Allies. This time around, Roosevelt administration negotiators were designing institutions to crystallize a power shift that had already taken place.

Many of the tactical lessons learned from the World War I settlement, such as keeping the Senate involved with postwar planning, applied in the realm of economic negotiations as well. But another set of lessons from the interwar era shadowed discussions of economic policy in the early and mid-1940s. These were the lessons of the Great Depression. Wartime debates among economists amounted to an extended postmortem on what had gone wrong in the previous decade. As Keynes mordantly observed, "In the interval between the Wars the world explored in rapid succession almost, as it were, in an intensive laboratory experiment all the alternative false approaches" to problems of international trade, investment, and currency exchange.[15]

The list of perceived mistakes during the 1930s was long. Industrialized countries had undercut one another's export markets by competitively devaluating their currencies. In an attempt to maintain domestic income in the face of shrinking markets, some countries began to impose trade barriers in the form of tariffs and restrictions on currency convertibility. Out of self-defense, other countries followed suit. A "prisoner's dilemma" dynamic ensued: strategies that were rational for each individual country led to outcomes that left all the players collectively worse off than if they had cooperated. As an IMF publication explained, "There was a growing recognition of the largely self-defeating nature of these 'beggar-my-neighbor' policies at the country level and of their contribution to lower trade and employment and a less efficient allocation of resources at the global level." When regional trading blocs developed around the German and Japanese economies, American planners complained that the US economy could not survive as merely the hub of a regional spoke system. The disastrous results of these quasi-autarkic policies after World War I led American economists in 1944 to advocate developing "an agreed code of conduct in international trade and financial matters."[16]

There were still other Depression-era mistakes. When Britain went off the gold standard in 1931, foreign investment virtually ended. New long-term enterprises became too risky, while widespread defaults on loans made past investments unprofitable. Owners of capital, seeking safety rather than profit, fled from one perceived refuge to another, destroying already strained exchange markets. Unemployed capital meant unemployed labor, leading to reduced consumer buying power. In the opening years of the 1930s, world trade fell to three quarters of its 1929 volume, while prices dropped on average by more than half, so that the total value of trade in 1932 was little more than one-third of its value in 1929.[17]

After the First World War, the European Allies insisted that Germany pay reparations for war damages, as part of taking responsibility for its acts of aggression. During the early 1920s, Germany's inability to meet its payment schedule, which had been fixed in 1921 at the equivalent of roughly $31 billion, contributed to escalating tensions with France and to France's temporary occupation of the Ruhr in 1923. The Allies finally scaled back their unrealistic reparations demands in the second half of the 1920s.[18]

Germany was not the only country to feel the squeeze of war debt. Successive American administrations insisted that their own allies repay the loans extended during the war, amounting to almost $10 billion. To Great Britain, France, and many other smaller nations, German reparations and Allied debts were linked. Reparations were to be used, in part, for paying off the Allies' war debts. At the Paris Peace Conference, for instance, British Prime Minister Lloyd George proposed a plan designed by Keynes that would have enlisted American help in settling Allied debts by, in effect, guaranteeing a percentage of what Germany owed the Allies.[19] President Wilson rejected this three-way financial relationship, highlighting what was to become a continuing philosophical as well as a policy difference over principles of international finance between the United States and the European Allies, especially Britain. The Americans tended to apply principles of domestic fiscal responsibility to international economics, and therefore to interpret the extension of American loans to Europe as being on "business terms." Private lenders supplied the needed funds, with only the lightest public policy guidance from the State and Treasury departments. The European Allies, by contrast, tended to see such international economic arrangements as another expression of international politics. Loan forgiveness, under this interpretation, would be an appropriate vehicle for "thanking" the Allies for the sacrifices they had made in a war effort that had profited the United States handsomely—and to which the United States had contributed little until the final year of conflict. The Harding administration was unsympathetic to this European perspective. "They hired the money, didn't they?" growled Vice President Coolidge.[20]

Ray Stannard Baker, who had been a member of the American Commission to Negotiate the Peace, questioned the logic of British and French demands for such high reparations, which would "practically make it impossible for Germany ever to pay." But he added that if the Allies were going to pursue their own selfish interests, it was hard to see why the United States should assume the "chief burden" of guaranteeing that reparations were actually paid. This was his main justification for Wilson's rejection of the British plan. "We did not see," he later confessed, "how completely political stability and peace depended upon economic stability and peace."[21]

In his influential book *The Economic Consequences of the Peace,* published in 1919, Keynes had presciently made this point already. "The magnitude of the Great Depression of 1930," argued Columbia political science professor James T. Shotwell, who had also served as an advisor to the American delegation in Paris, "was due to two things: the economic cost of the first World War and the acceptance of disastrous economic policies after it, especially the erection of tariff and other barriers against a revival of trade. We were left to ourselves to recover from a situation which could only be cured by a healthy world economy." Writing in 1944, Shotwell concluded, "Fortunately this experience is sufficiently fresh in our memory so that no argument is needed to drive it home."[22] Policymakers concluded that this time around, they must reframe international economic stability as a national security issue.

Economic planners in the first Roosevelt administration had discounted a coordinated, multilateral approach in favor of short-term domestic recovery programs. The memory of the unsuccessful 1933 London Economic Conference, where President Roosevelt had emphatically abandoned multilateralism generally, served as a cautionary tale for the Bretton Woods delegates: "Looking back on that unhappy episode, it seems to have been caused primarily by divided counsel within the Administration and sloppy preparation," wrote Acheson, "which obscured for both the President and the Secretary [of State] the relation between the foreign and domestic issues involved and the essential connection between foreign trade policy and international monetary arrangements." But eleven years later, in 1944, "these issues had been resolved, and brilliant results were achieved at the International Monetary Conference at Bretton Woods."[23] By the end of the 1930s, it was a truism that turning one's back on the international economy would have unfavorable domestic repercussions.

Wartime planners in the United States accordingly tried to see whether policymakers could develop "some system of organized international relations" not only to maintain postwar peace and security, but also to "promote the general welfare," as former State Department official Ruth Russell explained in her magisterial history of the United Nations Charter. As Republican presidential candidate Wendell Willkie wrote in his runaway bestseller, One World, the flawed World War I settlement did not "sufficiently seek solution to the economic problems of the world. Its attempts to solve the world's problems were primarily political. But political internationalism without economic internationalism is a house built upon sand." Continuing on a bipartisan note, he concluded: "For years many in both parties have recognized that if peace, economic prosperity, and liberty itself were to continue in this world, the nations of the world must find a method of economic stabilization and co-operative effort." This new definition of security linked international to domestic economics, and then yoked both to a stable international order.[24]

One popular explanation for the failure of democratic reforms generally—in Germany, the Soviet Union, and the United States during the Depression—was the despair and chaos resulting from economic want. As one multilateralist pressure group claimed in 1944, a "deliberate policy of organized plenty is the only alternative to chaotic economic confusion and a recurrence of war." This emphasis on making economic policies "deliberate" and "organized" expressed what this history has been calling the New Deal idiom, although an infatuation with planning had deep roots in the reform politics of Progressive era America as well. The Roosevelt historian William Leuchtenburg famously distinguished New Dealers from their Progressive predecessors by noting that "unlike the earlier Progressive, the New Dealer shied away from being thought of as sentimental." Furthermore, New Deal reformers had "abandoned—or claimed they had abandoned—the old Emersonian hope of reforming man and sought only to change institutions." As Leuchtenburg hints, however, perhaps the New Deal generation of reformers harbored hopes that the workings of their institutions would nevertheless serve to redeem the men, in the bargain.[25]

Somewhat analogously, the workings of international institutions might also serve to transform participating nations, or even the international system as a whole. The orientation and ideology of the New Deal lawyers and academics drafting, administering, and interpreting the Roosevelt administration's domestic policies in the 1930s carried over into the international planning of the 1940s. More senior New Dealers such as Charles Merriam, Edward Corwin, Robert H. Jackson, and Felix Frankfurter in turn influenced a younger generation, including Benjamin Cohen, Joseph Landis, Telford Taylor, and Tommy Corcoran.[26]

Charles Merriam linked international planning in the economic realm to the very constitutional fabric of American life: "The Constitution itself was an economico-political plan on a grand scale, not only providing a democratic frame of government, but . . . also setting up special plans for dealing with currency, tariffs, interstate commerce, and international relations," he explained. "Justice was the first term in the [Constitution's] preamble and liberty the last, but between them came the general welfare, common defense, and domestic tranquility. The Constitutional Convention itself was a large-scale planning board." The Bretton Woods Conference was a chance to generalize this planning orientation to the international level, even to the level of "constitutional" planning, in the British sense of a constitutional order based on institutions, precedents, and accretions of rules and norms over time.[27]

In late 1937, Roosevelt was busy beating a hasty retreat from the multilateralist themes of his so-called Quarantine speech, in the face of an isolationist backlash. The president had argued that "it seems to be unfortunately true that the epidemic of world lawlessness is spreading. When an epidemic of physical disease starts to spread, the community approves and joins in a quarantine of the patients in order to protect the health of the community against the spread of the disease." Roosevelt speechwriter Sam Rosenman surmised that "if [this speech] had been delivered a year later, it would have been accepted without excitement. But in October, 1937, it caused a sensation." Isolationist reaction was "violently hostile" to the president's analysis, condemning it as "warmongering and saber-rattling." Roosevelt "had made a mistake that he seldom made," concluded Rosenman, "the mistake of trying to lead the people of the United States too quickly . . . Having gone too far out on a limb too fast, he decided . . . that he had better get back."[28]

Throughout the early and middle 1930s, American diplomats tended to treat consultation with other countries on the development of international economics and law as a kind of luxury, readily abandoned in the face of more pressing domestic demands or an unfavorable political climate. Later in the 1930s, the deepening international crisis in Europe and in the Pacific pushed experiments in economics yet further into the background. Roosevelt considered and rejected a 1938 proposal explicitly foreshadowing the provisions of the 1941 Atlantic Charter, calling for an "agreement to support certain principles of international conduct" that would include "the expansion and stabilization of world economy, peaceful revision of treaties, reduction of the burden of armaments, the rights of neutrals, and the laws and customs of warfare," for example.[29]

International tensions mounted with the German annexation of Austria in March 1938, the Munich crisis in September, the November 1938 burning and looting of Jewish homes, businesses, and synagogues in Germany and Austria known as *Kristallnacht*, the German occupation of the rest of Czechoslovakia in March 1939, and the Italian invasion of Albania in April of that year. On April 15, 1939, Roosevelt issued an appeal to the Axis states along the lines of his abandoned conference proposal of 1938, calling on Hitler and Mussolini to demonstrate their sincerity by resolving their international disputes through peaceful methods. Hitler publicly derided this speech, especially the section where Roosevelt proposed that the dictators should assure the other states of Europe and the Near East that they would not be attacked and that broad international discussions should be held "in the resulting peaceful surroundings," in which the United States "would gladly take part."[30]

In another, often overlooked, section of this same speech, Roosevelt explained the "essential problems" he felt these negotiations should cover: "Simultaneously the Government of the United States would be prepared to take part in discussions looking towards the most practical manner of opening up avenues of international trade," Roosevelt argued, prefiguring the economic provisions of the Atlantic Charter, "to the end that every nation of the earth may be entitled to buy and sell on equal terms in the world market as well as to possess assurance of obtaining the materials and products of peaceful economic life." These statements mark the American transition toward blending economic concerns with the politics of collective security. International problems—trade barriers, financial stability, respect for the rule of law generally—were understood as reinforcing one another, so prospective solutions should presumably be integrated, as well.[31]

Early in 1940, before the German onslaught in Western Europe

mooted any further idea of a conference of neutrals, an advisory committee at the State Department drafted a memorandum succinctly presenting
the American position on postwar economic policies. Discussions of the
"best means of strengthening moral and economic cooperation" in the
international sphere were considered suitably uncontroversial by the tim-
orous pre–Pearl Harbor State Department, as was the objective "of securing a stable world order based upon international law and a sound international economic system" in order to prevent future wars.[32]

The approach outlined in the 1940 State Department memo remained
a guide to American thinking throughout the war and formed the basis of
later proposals for postwar economic policies and multilateral organizations. It stressed the interrelationship among economic policies, political
stability, and expenditures for armaments. The memo further concluded
that new international commercial and financial agencies would probably be necessary in order "to restore international trade on a sound basis
after the war . . . to achieve non-discriminatory commercial policies, to
agree on methods of dealing with essential raw materials and foodstuffs,
to re-establish free and stable exchanges, and to restore sound international credit and investment relations."[33]

This is a succinct summary of what would become the Roosevelt administration's wartime agenda in the field of international economics,
though it would acquire a distinct New Deal twist in the hands of Treasury Secretary Morgenthau. He saw the establishment of new financial
institutions as the key to avoiding monetary instability in the future, and
he intended to coordinate monetary policy through agreements among
governments rather than private bankers, whom he perceived as "pursuing selfish ends." Morgenthau wanted international monetary affairs to
be "restructured." In the words of one of his biographers, "From the
first, he envisaged a kind of New Deal for a new world."[34]

"If I get a nice garden hose back, I am in pretty good shape"

In September 1940 President Roosevelt had arranged for the transfer of
fifty "over-age" destroyers to Britain, in exchange for American leases on
British naval bases in Newfoundland and the Caribbean. The largely favorable American press for this destroyers-for-bases swap was due, in
large part, to the administration's "spin" on the parleys: that tough
American negotiators had secured a good deal on favorable terms.[35]

This angle highlighted the legal idea of "consideration," which in US commercial law meant that both parties were bound to an agreement by virtue of the value for which they had bargained. This bargaining for mutual value is what distinguished an (enforceable) contract from an (unenforceable) gift. Throughout the 1940s, it became a touchstone for Anglo-American negotiations over supplies, finance, and the shape of the postwar economic world. The Americans saw the idea of exchanging value as a device for avoiding the public relations disaster of unpaid war loans, while the British continually contested America's narrow, monetized concept of "value." To the British, the American approach seemed to devalue important elements of international politics that were less tangible, such as Britain's lone stand against fascism since 1939.[36]

Three months later, after winning an unprecedented third term, Roosevelt received Churchill's famous "desperate but dignified" letter, which the president pondered as he sat in his deck chair on board the *Tuscaloosa*. This 4,000-word missive requesting the "gift, loan or supply" of material to Britain framed the defense of Britain as the forward line of defense for the United States. In addition to serving as an important impetus for the Atlantic Charter, this letter was also the genesis of Lend-Lease. As Roosevelt explained at a press conference the following week, Lend-Lease would get rid of "the foolish, silly old dollar sign" and permit the United States to lend "a garden hose" to a neighbor whose house was on fire. "If I get a nice garden hose back," explained the president primly, "I am in pretty good shape."[37]

The framing of Lend-Lease was designed as a lawyerly end-run around the entrenched culture of the Neutrality Act of 1935, which Congress had renewed and modified in 1936, 1937, and 1939. American neutrality legislation operated on a "strict" or "impartial" basis, forbidding Americans from supplying any combatants—whether aggressors or victims—with arms, loans, or credits, in addition to other restrictions on travel that were later loosened. Together with the Johnson Act of 1934, which prohibited American loans to nations in default on their World War I debts, this strict approach to neutrality contrasted with a "discretionary" approach that Roosevelt would have preferred, where the chief executive would have been able to designate aggressors and victims and allocate or deny aid accordingly. It meant that Roosevelt was effectively hamstrung in his most assertive efforts to increase aid to Britain throughout the late 1930s, although FDR's aides designed several modifications to the Neutrality Acts to benefit Britain disproportionately. For example, the cash-and-carry provision of the 1939 Neutrality Act meant that belligerents had to pay cash for supplies and carry them away in non-American ships, a provision clearly favoring Britain's naval strength.[38]

According to the terms of Lend-Lease—which the president always insisted on calling the "aid to democracies bill" and which his opponents often called "the dictator bill"—Britain could go on buying supplies under the pre-existing cash-and-carry system and could procure additional supplies that the United States government would lend or lease. On paper, these provisions were always to remain American property, although it was soon clear that their eventual return was a polite fiction. British historian Robert Skidelsky writes of "the supreme psychological importance of this moment" for Britain, with Lend-Lease as "the most adventurous political coup of Roosevelt's presidency. It was the one occasion in the war when he led decisively from the front on Britain's behalf."[39]

Skidelsky also brilliantly captures the wider significance of Lend-Lease, describing it as a measure that "not only bypassed the Neutrality and Johnson Acts, isolating the isolationists; it broke with the whole American tradition of making loans on business terms. It set the precedent for post-war Marshall Aid," thus paving the way in the United States for the shift from private to public sources of international finance. Through wartime economic initiatives, Morgenthau himself candidly indicated that he hoped "to move the financial center of the world from London and Wall Street to the United States Treasury." This was a twofold transition: from London to Washington, symbolizing the passing of the torch from the Old World to the New, but also from Wall Street to Washington, as emblematic of the shift from private to public resources.[40]

As Lend-Lease terms were being debated among administration lawyers such as Benjamin Cohen, Edward H. Foley, Herman Oliphant, and Oscar Cox, a diplomatic spat arose over the proper handling of Britain's pre–Lend-Lease orders. John Winant, the former governor of New Hampshire and the new American ambassador in London, suggested that Keynes should go over to Washington and personally try to clear up this aspect of the financing. "It might be useful and it would certainly be exciting," Keynes rather naively wrote to his mother.[41]

The Lend-Lease Bill, patriotically entitled HR 1776 in order "to confuse the opposition," landed in Congress on January 11, 1941, just five days after FDR's Four Freedoms speech. It authorized the president to make available to belligerents any materials necessary "for the defense of the United States," in return for an undefined, non-cash "benefit." It was important that the Lend-Lease materials not be a gift or a sale, so as not to run afoul of neutrality legislation. The content of what this reciprocal "benefit" would actually be was the essence of the so-called Article 7 negotiations over Lend-Lease. Article 7 was the key "consideration" clause that made Lend-Lease into a contract, according to the flotillas of American lawyers involved.[42]

These extremely contentious Article 7 negotiations, spearheaded by Keynes for the British and Acheson for the Americans, exposed philosophical differences between the two democracies around economic issues to an even greater extent than the later Bretton Woods negotiations did. Article 7 talks were more than just a dry run for Bretton Woods: they were the diplomatic battlefield where the terms of Anglo–American cooperation were thrashed out. According to Skidelsky's somewhat controversial thesis, "The United States demanded that in return for Lend-Lease Britain pledge itself to abandon its imperial preference and sterling area systems, and the way Washington managed the flow of Lend-Lease supplies had the effect, and possibly the intention, of leaving Britain dependent on US help after the war on whatever terms America chose to impose . . . America did not fail its fellow democracy; but also used the occasion to settle old scores, and secure pole position in the post-war international order." Keynes's contemporaneous expression of this assessment, in a March 1941 tirade about Morgenthau, is somewhat more colorful: Morgenthau was treating Britain "worse than we have ever ourselves thought it proper to treat the humblest and least responsible Balkan country."[43]

Although the Lend-Lease Bill became law in March 1941, Congress still had to approve the $7 billion appropriation (equivalent to over $87 billion today), and the "consideration" terms of Article 7 were still serving as what Acheson rather delicately described as "the apple of discord." Acheson downplayed the extent to which this discord also extended to squabbles within the American team, notably between the Treasury and State departments. While FDR and Churchill did not discuss Lend-Lease at the Atlantic Conference, the free trade issues so dear to Secretary Hull were a dominant feature of some of the most spirited sparring on board the *Prince of Wales* and the *Augusta*. Hull's perspective was reflected in a particularly wooden draft of the already notorious Article 7 consideration clause that was circulated to Keynes in July 1941, shortly before the Atlantic Conference began:

> The terms and conditions upon which the United Kingdom receives defense aid from the United States of America and the benefits to be received by the United States in return therefore, shall be such as not to burden commerce between the two countries but to promote mutually beneficial economic relations between them and the betterment of world-wide eco-

nomic relations; they shall provide against discrimination in either the
United States of America or the United Kingdom against the importation
of any product originating in the other country; and they shall provide for
the formulation of measures for the achievement of these ends.[44]

This language (likely drafted by Acheson) must surely have pained the
master stylist Keynes, even leaving aside the actual content of the provision, which also enraged him. The draft prompted Keynes to refer to
the American obsession with free trade as "the lunatic proposals of Mr.
Hull." And it provoked another outburst from Keynes in the course of a
meeting with Acheson, where the American diplomat recounted that
"as coldly as I could—which I have been told is fairly cold," he explained
to Keynes that all the United States was asking from the British was
that, "after the emergency was over and after they had received vast aid
from this country, they would not regard themselves free to take any
measures they chose against the trade of this country but would work
out in cooperation with this country measures which would eliminate
discrimination and would provide for mutually fair and advantageous
relations." ("Next to the Lincoln Memorial in the moonlight," wrote
New York Times columnist James Reston, "the sight of Mr. Dean G.
Acheson blowing his top is without doubt the most impressive view in
the capital.")[45]

The negotiators finally framed Article 7 on February 23, 1942, with a
rephrasing that was somewhat less offensive to the British. The final version linked a commitment by both countries to eliminate discrimination
and reduce tariffs with a commitment that its terms and conditions were
to be "directed to the expansion, by appropriate international and domestic measures, of production, employment, and the exchange and consumption of goods, which are the material foundations of the liberty and
welfare of all peoples." It further committed the United States and the
United Kingdom, "in general, to the attainment of all the economic objectives set forth in the Joint Declaration made on August 12, 1941, by
the President of the United States of America and the Prime Minister of
the United Kingdom"—that is, to the terms of the Atlantic Charter.[46]

In addition to reprising the philosophical differences over finance from
1919–20 (when the United States had insisted on bankers' terms while
the Allies expected moral or political principles to prevail), the Anglo-
American Lend-Lease dispute foreshadowed differences at Bretton
Woods over the extent to which Britain's vulnerable domestic economy
should be sheltered from the rigors of "business" standards in interna-

tional lending and exchange rate flexibility after the war. American negotiators, predictably, saw the provisions of Lend-Lease in much less bullying terms. They continually emphasized the connection between Article 7 and the Atlantic Charter, referring to Article 7 as "Atlantic Charter No. 2" and as "virtually a Magna Charta for postwar economic collaboration." The United States also revised its other Lend-Lease agreements, notably with Latin American countries, to bring them into line with the "consideration" provisions in the revised Anglo-American version, and to include references to the Atlantic Charter. Subsequent Lend-Lease agreements, such as the one with the Soviet Union, also used similar language.[47]

Keynes later sent an apology to Acheson, in which he explained that his reaction "was the result of my feeling so passionately that our hands must be free to make something new and better of the post-war world." Basically, the whole legalistic line of the argument about "consideration" in Article 7 offended the British. To them, the only consideration that seemed fitting—the bargained-for "value" that Britain was contributing—was that "we should go on fighting."[48]

"The Mayflower, when she sailed from Plymouth, must have been entirely filled with lawyers"

These many disagreements between the British and the Americans over financial arrangements reflected cultural as well as substantive differences. The British preferred to work on problems informally, while the Americans were constantly relying on lawyers and detailed contract provisions. Keynes disliked the cautious legalisms and technical jargon of American economists—he referred to such shop-talk disdainfully as "Cherokee." Keynes also observed that, based on how thick lawyers were on the ground in wartime Washington, "the Mayflower, when she sailed from Plymouth, must have been entirely filled with lawyers."[49]

Some of the superficial differences in style were quite amusing. For example, the Americans were always interrupting face-to-face meetings to take telephone calls, which infuriated and puzzled the British negotiators. Keynes once suggested getting up and leaving the meeting in order to call the relevant official back on the phone, thus securing his American counterpart's undivided attention.[50]

The contrasting personalities of Keynes and White seemed to embody these national differences. Keynes was a product of two of the British

Empire's most elite institutions, Eton and King's College, Cambridge. He also served as a fellow on the governing body of Eton and as bursar of Kings, refusing to curtail these and other ancillary roles during the war. A patron of the arts, he was interested in what would now be called quality-of-life issues for ordinary people and served as chair of the Council for the Encouragement of Music and the Arts, founder of the London Artists' Association, and cofounder and chair of the Trustees of the Cambridge Arts Theatre. He had played a prominent part in public policy debates since his role as Treasury representative at the Peace Conference of 1919, when he was in his mid-30s. His 1919 warning that a punitive reparations regime would encourage the growth of a dangerous revanchist sentiment in Germany went largely unheeded by policymakers but soon cemented his image as a prescient interpreter of the influence of economic policy on international politics.[51]

Keynes's *General Theory of Employment, Interest, and Money*, published in 1936, served as a foil for widely discredited approaches to fiscal conservatism in both the United States and United Kingdom. Knighted in 1942—he had impishly requested to be dubbed Baron Keynes of Keynes but settled for Baron Keynes of Tilton, the hamlet where he owned a large country property—he shared the casual anti-Semitism common to his background and social class. Keynes was in fragile health because of weakened valves in his heart (which today we know was caused by a bacterial infection that is now treatable with antibiotics). His glamorous second wife, Lydia Lopokova, a retired Diaghilev ballet dancer, tried to keep her husband from working in the evenings and enforced frequent retreats to the country for rest and recreation. The couple were friendly with leading cultural figures of the day, including such Bloomsbury luminaries as Virginia and Leonard Woolf and Clive and Vanessa Bell. Keynes's 1946 obituary in the London *Times*—he died at 62—noted soberly that "to find an economist of comparable influence one would have to go back to Adam Smith."[52]

If Keynes had "intellectual sex appeal and zing," in the words of one colleague, his American negotiating counterpart, Harry White (he added the "Dexter" himself in high school), stood as a contrast in almost every way—Jewish, short, brusque, and fast-talking, with a quick temper, gravelly voice, toothbrush moustache, and an owlish, blue-eyed gaze. His parents were Lithuanian immigrants who had owned a hardware store in his native Boston; he was the youngest of seven children. Though he had written an award-winning dissertation at Harvard under the supervision of Frank Taussig, he had been unable to secure a permanent offer from a prestigious research university, perhaps in part because of a reluctance to hire Jewish academics in the interwar years. Relegated to a small midwestern teaching institution, White sought a broader audience for his ideas about ways that a domestic economy could be insulated from external disturbances. His indefatigable work habits soon garnered him the attention of Jacob Viner, a prominent New Deal economist. At Viner's request, White joined the Treasury Department in 1934 to assist with a survey of banking and monetary legislation, and within three months he had submitted a 450-page monograph on US monetary standards.[53]

White's quick grasp of statistics and his ability to explain arcane economic ideas to less gifted auditors (such as Morgenthau) led to his rapid promotion. After serving as assistant director of research and statistics, White became director of monetary research, a position Morgenthau created for him in 1938. White was responsible for devising monetary policies and advising Secretary Morgenthau on international economic issues generally, first informally, then in 1941 as the official assistant to the secretary, and later as acting assistant secretary.

After the war, informants and anticommunist investigations exposed White as one of a coterie of second- and third-tier government officials who had been passing classified papers to the Soviets during the war, among them Alger Hiss, Whittaker Chambers, and White's own assistant, Harold Glasser. Although White was among the most highly placed of these covert operatives, he was also one of the least active, and his involvement may have consisted largely in turning a blind eye to the activities of his subordinates. The Soviet Union was America's wartime ally, and sympathetic officials who were disturbed by growing anti-Sovietism in the mid-1940s felt that continuing US-Soviet accord would be the key to peace in the postwar world. Papers originating with White dealt almost exclusively with information that would help Soviet negotiators garner a large loan on favorable terms from the United States as part of the immediate postwar settlement. As Morgenthau's biographer John Morton Blum has observed, White's assistants, "in White's view, were as free to pass along information about treasury policy to the Russians as was Averell Harriman, for example, free to talk to the British." The loan never did go through, and while it may be charitable to describe White's role as merely "naive," still, he seemed genuinely to believe that US interests and Soviet interests were not in conflict, at least on certain issues, and that it would be imperative to integrate the USSR into any postwar international system. The legal historian G. Edward White, in his recent monograph attempting definitively to show Alger Hiss's high level of involvement, refers to Harry White at one point as a Soviet "agent" but then later merely as a "sympathizer," for example.[54]

In 1941 and 1942 Keynes and White, working independently of each other, developed astonishingly parallel plans for postwar international institutions designed to stabilize trade and monetary policy, especially currency exchange rates, while protecting domestic full employment policies. The historian of US foreign relations Lloyd Gardner explains that "the principal contrasts between the White Plan and its coeval Keynes Plan . . . define the basic agreements and disagreements between London and Washington on this subject—and many other related ones." Scholars tend to emphasize contrasts and competition, but it is striking how similar the Keynes and White approaches actually were: together they amount to what Gardner calls the "new New Deal"—applying a broad-brush interventionist and expansionist orientation to the realm of international economics.[55]

In August 1941, the same month that Churchill and Roosevelt negotiated the Atlantic Charter, an exhausted Keynes had just returned from a particularly discouraging round of Article 7 Lend-Lease negotiations. He retreated to his house in the country for several weeks, where he developed the proposal that would eventually be called the Keynes Plan. His approach was based on earlier ideas about how and why equilibrium in the balance of payments had so catastrophically broken down in the interwar era, creating national demands for protectionism and competitive currency depreciation. He sought to deploy the lessons of history by devising activist mechanisms of intervention.

As Keynes put it, "To suppose that there exists some smoothly functioning automatic mechanism of adjustment which preserves equilibrium if only we trust to methods of *laissez-faire* is a doctrinaire delusion which disregards the lessons of historical experience without having behind it the support of sound theory." The plan proposed an International Clearing Union that would link national currencies in a harmonized international system, based on a specially created banking money, to be known as Bancor. The Keynes Plan was revised by many hands as it circulated through the Treasury Department during the winter of 1941–42. The American economic advisor Edward Penrose, serving in London during the early war years as an assistant to the US ambassador, observed that the plan "was unusual among government papers in the distinction of its style, in the form of its presentation, in the breadth of its vision, and in its underlying moral earnestness"—all part of the Keynesian signature. Keynes himself modestly observed that it was merely "an attempt to reduce to practical shape certain general ideas belonging to the contemporary climate of economic opinion . . . born of the spirit of the age."[56]

Keynes hoped to create a system that would "prevent the piling up of credit and debit balances without limit." His vision was to base the system on the principles of domestic banking; that is, each member country would be allocated "overdraft facilities" or drawing rights commensurate with its share of world trade. Credit balances would be available as potential purchasing power, but if left idle they were to be made available to other members in order to circulate liquidity within the system. As Keynes explained it, "No depositor in a local bank suffers because the balances, which he leaves idle, are employed to finance the business of someone else." The limits of these overdraft facilities would be determined by a designated quota derived from the annual value, averaged over a specified period from the interwar years, of the volume of import and export trade of a given country. Countries that had high volumes of foreign trade in the interwar era—led, presumably, by Great Britain, the preeminent nation of shopkeepers—would have the largest quotas and therefore the most flexibility under the system and the most say in how the organization was run. (This as opposed to privileging nations that simply possessed large amounts of gold, such as the United States.)[57]

The workings of the overall system would eliminate contractionist pressures on world trade, much as Keynesianism in domestic economics had promoted expansionist incentives. It would also restore "unfettered multilateral clearing"—aided by freely exchangeable currencies—among members, while eliminating the need for endless bilateral agreements on currency exchange rates. An important feature of the proposal was that member states would be charged interest penalties when their account balances were out of equilibrium, whether they were creditors or debtors. In other words, accounts that were chronically in surplus would also incur interest penalties: debtors and creditors would share responsibility for keeping the system in equilibrium.

British Treasury officials celebrated the Keynes Plan as a tremendous morale-booster. "It would be difficult to exaggerate the electrifying effect on thought" that the circulation of the plan generated in the Treasury, wrote one Treasury Department official. "Nothing so imaginative and ambitious had ever before been discussed as a possibility . . . it became as it were a banner of hope, an inspiration to the daily grind of war-time duties."[58]

Late in 1941, traveling along an entirely separate trajectory, Treasury Secretary Morgenthau had asked Harry White to think about what

Morgenthau was then calling "an international stabilization fund," as well as a possible international unit of currency and a bank for reconstruction and development. From the very beginning, the American emphasis was on stability, not growth. The resulting "White Plan," which went through many iterations but coalesced into a 159-page draft dated April 1942, had three purposes: "to prevent the disruption of foreign exchanges and the collapse of monetary and credit systems; to assure the restoration of foreign trade; and to supply the huge volume of capital that will be needed virtually throughout to world for reconstruction, for relief, and for economic recovery." The White Plan opened with the intention of linking economic stability with peace, as the draft itself explained: "If we are to avoid drifting from the peace table into a period of chaotic competition, monetary disorders, depressions, political disruption, and finally into new wars . . . we must be equipped to grapple with these three problems and make substantial progress toward their solution."[59]

The White Plan emphasized that a new multilateral economic institution would facilitate stability primarily by reining in exchange rate fluctuations, to ensure against competitive depreciations and to make debtor countries behave responsibly. Like the Keynes Plan, White's approach also made advances available to members needing to weather short-term imbalances of payments. The source of these advances was not an overdraft facility, however, but rather a pooled fund of member subscriptions. The subscription quotas were to be allocated "in accordance with an elaborate formula in which arbitrary weights were assigned to gold stocks, gold production, national income, foreign trade, population, foreign investments, and external debts," explained Penrose. He added, in a candid assessment: "This formula, the pseudo-scientific trappings of which covered political motives, would have required the United States to contribute an amount five times as great as that of the next largest contributor and at the same time, since votes would be proportionate to contributions, would have weighted the United States vote in the same proportion."[60]

White's rather nakedly "political" formula highlighted one of the more counterintuitive contrasts in the early plans on both sides of the Atlantic: the Americans were the ones who were more comfortable with the idea of a more interventionist and judgmental board of directors for the new fund, envisaging a perpetual American dominance in decision-making that would ensure that the United States would never be on the receiving end of adjustment pressure. The British, by contrast, wanted a more hands-off directorship for the Fund, one that would provide more scope for national action, with less meddling. Just as the Americans were anticipating a permanent dominance in making Fund decisions, the British were anticipating their own permanent, or at least long-term, indebtedness after the war. The Americans accordingly felt they had little to fear from a more interventionist international institution, while the British found themselves advocating greater scope for considerations of national sovereignty.

Harry White always saw his main constituency as US senators, who in turn would likely be influenced by the assessments of powerful bankers and business professionals. His plan accordingly relied more on traditional banking conceptions than Keynes's approach. This pandering to conventional commercial expectations was not just a question of form but also of substance. White's Plan spelled out an important role for gold, a commodity the United States possessed in great abundance. It set the value of gold at $35 an ounce, to create a standard unit of measurement for valuing other members' currencies, and in the process monetized the Americans' substantial holdings. Pegging dollars to gold also meant that the United States would be less likely to support the highly flexible exchange rates sought by the British. If other countries were allowed to devalue their currencies while the United States had to maintain a set relationship between gold and the dollar, the American export sector would suffer.[61]

"We have to find some way to feed the horse"

Keynes didn't like White, and the antipathy was mutual. Keynes prided himself on being the more sophisticated theorist, while White saw himself as the more practical popularizer. White believed he could reduce any argument to layman's terms; Keynes, though a more elegant stylist, had little patience for people (such as Morgenthau) who couldn't keep up with him intellectually. Negotiations between the two camps were informed by Keynes's perspective that White held all the cards, and by White's perspective that anything they agreed to had to get through the US Senate.

In addition to their different styles and negotiating positions, the two economists were committed to two different conceptions of multilateralism, shaped by their differing national interests: "White, like Morgenthau, was committed to a form of internationalism which would spread the American notion of responsible capitalism abroad and make the dollar the world's top currency," observed the economic historian Alan Dobson, while "Keynes' internationalism was partly devised to help compensate Britain for her lack of economic power."[62]

Keynes and the British Treasury officials were initially the ones pushing for progress in the negotiations, arguing that whatever plan was ultimately synthesized should be inaugurated "in the first energy of victory and whilst the active spirit of united action lasts." At the urging of British diplomats, Keynes and White met in London in the late summer of 1942 (this after White had snappishly insisted that he did not "want to talk with anyone but Keynes"). Their main differences were over the size of the proposed fund—Keynes thought it should be much larger—and whether the capital comprising it should be subscribed by member contributions or created as an international currency in its own right. White insisted that subscribed capital was the only basis for the Fund that could conceivably garner the approval of Congress. Keynes additionally argued that Britain needed the "freedom to act unilaterally" if necessary, and should not be constrained by overly rigid exchange rates or an overly activist directing board of the Fund. While the British negotiators urged continuing Anglo-American consultations, White warned that the talks should include other allies to avoid the appearance "of an Anglo-Saxon gang-up." Keynes objected to broadening the basis of consultation, protesting that "to throw open to a meeting of over fifty nations so complicated a matter . . . would be to throw it into a monkey-house."[63]

Informal sets of meetings nevertheless blossomed, with the British consulting the European governments in exile in London and the Americans consulting with Latin American allies and with Canada. The Canadians contributed their own plan, dubbed "Off-White" due to how close it seemed to the American approach. This informal set of discussions culminated in a series of meetings among representatives of thirty of the allies in Washington in the winter of 1943–44. A happy by-product of these consultations seems to have been Keynes's realization that backing off from some of the specifics of his approach would likely garner a better overall result for Britain. As he observed to another participant, "I now consider that the success of the plan depends on the will to cooperate; without that will, no manipulation of voting powers will help."[64]

These discussions resulted in the Joint Statement by Experts of April 21, 1944. After a preamble that highlighted the terms "technical," "expert," and "practical," the Joint Statement listed the objectives of the future monetary fund: to facilitate cooperation on international monetary policies in order to foster international trade, which would in turn help member countries maintain full employment policies; to provide resources to members to assist them in correcting disequilibria in their balance of payments without resorting to the destructive trade policies of the 1930s; and to foster stability of exchange rates and eliminate foreign exchange restrictions.[65]

Now it was the Americans who wanted to move ahead—urgently. The US Treasury Department in particular was pushing for a multilateral conference to draft a charter for this new international economic organization late in the spring of 1944, that is, before the Republican convention at the end of June. But now it was the British Treasury officials' turn to proceed slowly. They protested that they needed to present the plans to Parliament and to the Dominions before appointing a delegation to an international conference.

The best White could do in the face of what he saw as persistent British foot-dragging was to convene what he termed preliminary negotiations on international financial institutions—still limited to "experts" and "technicians"—in Atlantic City in mid-June 1944, with the main conference scheduled for early July. Seventeen countries participated in the Atlantic City discussions, with seventy-five experts divided into four substantive committees, each of which reported daily to a general session. A separate track of higher-level Anglo-American meetings proceeded in tandem. The only one who could see the whole developing draft at once was White himself. American negotiators would employ this divide-and-conquer strategy, combined with parsimonious sharing of information, again at the forty-four-nation conference at Bretton Woods the following month, and again during the summer at San Francisco, when fifty nations would convene to draft the United Nations Charter.

Representatives of what the American and British negotiators tended condescendingly to call "the smaller powers"—meaning any country lacking in great power status, no matter what its size—felt particularly ignored in Atlantic City: Harry White joked that he had only invited the Cubans because "their main function would be to bring cigars." White's objective was to prepare a draft of the International Monetary Fund charter and to hold focused discussions on the International Bank for Reconstruction and Development, which had so far received little attention. The benign-sounding goal was merely to cut down and then to clarify any remaining differences over the April 21st Joint Statement, in order to present clearer choices for the Bretton Woods delegates. But even this innocuous-sounding agenda was too ambitious for Morgenthau, who found White's procedures entirely too secretive. Morgenthau berated White by telephone for leaving his superior in the dark, complaining, "Look, Harry, you're leaving me completely high and dry, and all the rest of the American delegates and then you expect us to come up there and sign on the dotted line, and it won't work, it just won't . . . supposing I don't like at all what's been agreed to[?]"[66]

Mindful of the principles of international monetary governance that were at stake, the American Bankers Association circulated an influential memo in June 1944, replete with objections to the whole concept of the International Monetary Fund (the International Bank for Reconstruction and Development was less of a threat, apparently). W. Randolph Burgess, president of the Bankers Association and vice-chair of the National City Bank of New York, acted as one of the bankers' spokesmen. He explained to Morgenthau that the bankers "are distrustful of any program for giving away American gold; [and] they are distrustful of all spending programs, especially when sponsored by Lord Keynes."[67]

An American economic administrator offered a reply which might stand as the rationale for American multilateralism more generally in this era: he quoted the aphorism that in every alliance, "one party wears boots and spurs while the other wears a saddle." "We obviously are wearing the boots," he elaborated; yet "if we want to stay in this fortunate position, we have to find some way to feed the horse."[68] The design of the IMF and World Bank, for these American officials, was part of their search for new ways to feed the horse.

CHAPTER 4

INVESTING IN GLOBAL STABILITY

In the spring of 1944, as planning for a "united nations" conference on international financial institutions hastily progressed, John Maynard Keynes urged Harry White not to "take us to Washington in July, which should surely be a most unfriendly act." Acheson noted that the conference venue in New Hampshire "had been chosen both for the beneficent climate of the White Mountains and the availability there of a summer hotel of adequate size and condition." Such a convocation demanded quite formidable facilities, especially for wartime: 730 delegates from forty-four countries, not including at least twice that number in clerical staff, plus representatives of an assortment of international organizations, descended from a series of special trains onto the 350-room Mount Washington Hotel at the end of June. Most had signed on to the hotel's "American plan"—meals included—at a rate of $11 per day, while those few who had been able to wrangle "superior accommodations" paid a surcharge.[1]

It was "a wonderful place in the woods," Keynes wrote to a colleague shortly after arriving at the conference. "The only trouble is that the hotel is only just being opened and reconditioned, having been closed for two or more years, with the result that broadly speaking . . . the hotel is being built around us, whilst we sit on our appointed perches." Keynes's wife, Lydia Lopokova, put it more bluntly: in her opinion, it was "a madhouse." Even Dean Acheson, the chief State Department negotiator at Bretton Woods, was reduced to operating out of what he liked to call a "so-called office," formerly a bar: "Into this spot of happier memories [my secretary] moved her typewriter and used the sink designed for washing glasses as a filing cabinet."[2]

The immediate tasks of the delegates from the United States and the United Kingdom were to finish the synthesis of the Keynes and White currency stabilization plans and somehow to fold the other "united nations"—the common wartime term for the anti-Axis alliance—into this process. By the summer of 1944, finding ways to include the other allies, and planning conferences in a feverish haste, was nothing new to the formerly somnolent Department of State. The Bretton Woods Conference benefited from two important precursor parleys: one on food and agriculture, and one on relief and rehabilitation. Roosevelt's sudden announcement of a conference slated for June 1943 to plan the Food and Agriculture Organization had caught the staff at State by surprise. Both Sumner Welles's planning committees and the "Hull men" under Leo Pasvolsky had been puttering along throughout 1942 and the early spring of 1943, distracted by their turf wars, and making plans on what the veteran peace activist James T. Shotwell diplomatically termed "more of an academic level." But from the very first year of US involvement in the war, international advocacy groups had been quite vocal about the need for immediate relief aid, and Roosevelt had been listening closely.[3]

The president abruptly decided to convene a conference of the united nations on this bread and butter issue, indicating that food was "man's most fundamental concern and a good place to begin postwar planning." The president had attentively reviewed an October 1942 memorandum by an Australian official, Frank McDougall, entitled "United Nations Programme for Freedom from Want of Food." This memo proposed an elaborate, permanent international machinery, and an unofficial working group of Australian, Canadian, British, and American supporters was promoting it within the US Department of Agriculture. While FDR indicated that he preferred something shorter-term and more informal, the proposal had clearly captured his capricious imagination.

Ordinarily, Secretary Hull preferred to start international negotiations with a series of informal bilateral consultations. He used meetings of small groups to sketch out a framework accord, developing a series of increasingly detailed drafts. Any subsequent multilateral conference would serve as little more than the ceremonial ratification of these earlier, behind-the-scenes agreements. In the case of the inaugural Food and Agriculture conference, however, the intense time pressure made this pattern untenable, as the State and Agriculture Departments struggled to transform the president's vague wishes into a workable agenda.[4]

Acheson—ubiquitous as usual—captured some of the frantic atmosphere in his description of an initial briefing by Undersecretary of State Sumner Welles. The imperious senior diplomat abruptly informed Acheson that the president "had decided to call a United Nations conference as soon as the preparatory work could be rushed through. Speed was important. The subject would be food and agriculture. The place was to be the Homestead Hotel in Hot Springs, Virginia, recently vacated by the interned Japanese diplomatic and consular corps. The high wire fence that had been put around it for security purposes was to remain and would continue to be guarded by military police. The press were to be excluded. The president wished to reproduce as nearly as he could the conditions of seclusion and quiet that had so contributed to his confidential discussion with Mr. Churchill during the Atlantic Conference." President Roosevelt seemed to be thinking that the model of a confidential, high-level discussion such as the one that produced the Atlantic Charter might usefully apply to this very different agenda. "When this seemed to complete Welles's instructions," Acheson dutifully "asked what the President wanted done about food and agriculture." The pith of Welles's reply was that this was now Acheson's problem.[5]

"Whatever schemes our New Deal crystal-gazers might desire"

When an official attached to the American Embassy in London explained the president's "nebulous ideas" to Keynes, the great economist scoffed that "what you are saying is that your President with his great political insight has decided that the best strategy for post-war reconstruction is to start with vitamins and then by a circuitous route work round to the international balance of payments!" In fact, this seems to have been quite a succinct summary of the American chief executive's overall approach: Roosevelt was a master at timing, and his almost perfect pitch for public opinion suggested to him that the American public wanted to "do something" to relieve European misery right away.[6]

In addition to the other united nations, Hull's staff also invited those states known as the "associated nations." For the most part, these were Latin American republics that had severed relations with the Axis but had not declared war. The overt rationale for including them in the FAO conference was a longstanding State Department attempt to maintain Latin American support for the war effort. Presumably it did not hurt that expanding the list of invitees in this way also boosted the numbers in the pro-US camp.[7]

Economic programs for the united nations were to be New Deal projects writ large. As plans for the Food and Agriculture conference accelerated, American administrators reached for handy, pre-existing programs, often internationalizing New Deal initiatives such as the Commodity Credit Corporation, an organization designed to shore up low prices by purchasing surplus commodities and then selling them when prices were higher. Devising such an entity for international markets in turn suggested a need for more comprehensive and integrated agreements about production and trade in primary products. Proposals such as these, which were very close to the American New Dealers' hearts, held no fascination at all for Prime Minister Churchill, however. Economic issues bored him; Churchill refused even to discuss a proposal on setting up a program for "buffer stocks" of commodities, grumbling "What's all this about butter scotch?" to the British War Cabinet.[8]

Welles's original instructions for the Hot Springs conference had included barring the press. Military police controlled access to the hotel, with the press headquartered in a nearby casino. Members of the fourth estate complained incessantly ("Is this what we are fighting for?"), leading to a series of concessions: conference receptions would include invitations to journalists who could then "talk with delegates on the golf course and tennis court." The need for all this secrecy was not clear to the conference's organizers, much less to the delegates or the press. The delegates felt "cooped in" by the fortress-like security arrangements, observed Acheson, who candidly observed that "since the only secret within a hundred miles was what they were there for and no one seemed to know the answer to that, they could see no purpose in the elaborate security."[9]

Supposedly the main reason for excluding the press was that Axis propaganda might exploit any public disagreements in order to weaken Allied morale. "Bitter charges were made that the United Nations were using the technique of the old [secret] diplomacy with all that that implied," wrote James Shotwell. "As a matter of fact, the only reason for hesitancy in opening the meetings to the press was a fear that the Conference might fail and even break up in disagreement." At his next press conference, on May 18, 1943, President Roosevelt testily observed that the press "might just as well ask to sit at Cabinet meetings or attend secret conferences in his office, or even to watch him take his bath, as to attend the FAO meetings." The organizers on the State Department staff later concluded that the presence of the military police had been a gratuitous provocation, and that at future UN conferences it would be better to allow the press to "see or hear anything they chose." American planners were apparently still digesting this lesson a full year later, however, when it came time for a planning conference for a postwar collective security organization at Dumbarton Oaks in Washington, DC.[10]

Unsurprisingly, multilateralist pressure groups assessed the results of the FAO conference favorably: "It is important to note that this [FAO]

Conference concentrated on getting things done rather than upon setting up an elaborate machinery for international management. No constitution was drafted but only a series of recommendations for doing this and that." Keynes's skeptical biographer, Robert Skidelsky, demurred; as far as he was concerned, the "delegates of the Allied and associated nations gathered at Hot Springs, Virginia in May and emitted a suitable blast of hot air."[11]

In a sense, both assessments were correct: implementing the broad, sweeping principles of the Atlantic Charter through small, practical measures had indeed proved an effective approach—the smaller and more practical the better. Nor did the fact that this first united nations conference was as much a public relations exercise as anything else diminish the efficacy of this strategy. The conference's immediate results amounted to a set of rather general recommendations—Ruth Russell of the State Department characterized them as "obvious"—on such issues as long-term problems of nutrition, agricultural production, and distribution.

The experience of the FAO negotiations was also a lesson in just how difficult it was to proceed from broad principles to specific practices. It took more than two years for the interim commission established in June 1943 to finish drafting a constitution for a permanent UN Food and Agriculture Organization. Delegates had problems agreeing on the scope and authority of the international machinery they were designing. What was true for the relatively low-stakes, low-profile subject of food and agriculture proved doubly true for higher-profile conferences on international finance and collective security. The FAO served as a practice round for the Bretton Woods and United Nations charter negotiations, in large part because it educated participants not to expect easy answers.[12]

Another result of the Hot Springs conference was to stimulate additional American planning for economic aid. Wartime discussions of aid usually divided the topic into three categories: relief, rehabilitation, and reconstruction. The logic underlying these divisions was apparently to separate short-term emergency aid from longer-term assistance, but definitions and boundaries remained somewhat mysterious, even to the planners themselves. For example, shortly after the FAO conference, draft proposals for an international relief agency, to be called the United Nations Relief and Rehabilitation Agency (UNRRA), circulated to the countries that had attended the FAO forum. "I have assumed that the relief organization was to be concerned only with relief," a perplexed John Winant, US ambassador to Britain, cabled to the relevant authorities at the State Department. "I note, however, that the word 'rehabilitation' is added to relief in the new draft . . . I would be interested to know the definition given the word in this context." Acheson later commented: "A good question it was, but never answered. To us the word had no definition . . . UNRRA would have done its work and passed away before we were to know what 'rehabilitation' really required from us, and General Marshall was to outline the task at Harvard."[13]

Acheson was referring to George C. Marshall's June 1947 Harvard commencement speech, in which Marshall, then serving as President Truman's secretary of state, unveiled the European Recovery Program, quickly labeled the Marshall Plan. Already, the 1947 plan was an artifact of a deepening Cold War chill. It embodied American policymakers' understanding that Western Europeans could not become consumers again without the rehabilitation of their own infrastructure and productive capacity, and that stable economies were essential for keeping vulnerable Europeans out of the Soviet orbit. But back in 1943, policy planners were still striving to separate relief, rehabilitation, and reconstruction from trade, finance, and currency policies, and from more overtly "political" considerations as well. It was through the experiences of the united nations conferences of mid-1943 to mid-1944 that these planners learned just how interrelated these various fields actually were.[14]

In planning UNRRA, Secretary Hull was able to adhere to the negotiation pattern that he preferred, starting with an extended process of informal exchanges among the most important players, followed by fairly expeditious agreement on a formal text. Shotwell, who had served as a member of President Woodrow Wilson's "Inquiry" at the end of the First World War, contrasted the UNRRA approach with the World War I relief experience: "There was no such organization as UNRRA at the end of the first World War, for the American organizations for relief, the greatest of which was under Mr. Hoover's direction, were never officially coordinated and the organizations of other nations, especially the Dutch and Scandinavian, ran independent courses. This was inevitable so long as the governments, as well as private organizations, still thought in terms of charity." This transition from the private to the public realm in relief and rehabilitation marked a further internationalization of New Deal–style problem-solving.[15]

The European governments in exile in London played a major role in accelerating the pace of American and British planning by developing their own competing drafts. And as early as January 1942 the Soviets were also circulating a draft plan for a relief agency. American proposals for postwar institutions often evolved as a way of short-circuiting the planning efforts of other countries, which by American lights were potentially dangerous. The Soviet draft, for instance, called for all countries to participate "on the basis of equality" with all decisions adopted unanimously. To American planners, this was a reprise of the dreaded "rule of unanimity" that had hamstrung the League of Nations; it would have meant in practice that the organization would be held hostage to a Soviet veto.[16]

Acheson explained the special role the UNRRA conference played in educating American diplomats about how to negotiate with the Soviets: "At our first meeting Litvinov uncovered the classic Soviet positions toward international institutions." Pointing particularly to the Soviet insistence on unanimity, Acheson explained how "one can recognize the now familiar pattern by which the Soviet Union has sought in the quarter century since the war to protect itself from foreign penetration and to insure its power to negate any international action uncongenial to Soviet designs. We were present, so to speak, at the creation of the pattern." Realistically, as even Acheson acknowledged, the resulting quick agreement on UNRRA was likely due in large part to "the Soviet desire for relief assistance" rather than the superior skills of American negotiators. Acheson's use of the phrase "present at the creation"—the title of his Pulitzer Prize–winning memoir—had two meanings in the politics of the postwar order: the genesis of an American-dominated system of multilateral organizations, and the creation of a pattern of Cold War–style US–Soviet confrontations.[17]

In June 1943 the Senate Committee on Foreign Relations discovered that the State Department expected the administration to promulgate the UNRRA charter as an executive agreement, not requiring Senate approval. Senators Tom Connally and Arthur Vandenberg, the committee chairman and senior minority member respectively, correctly interpreted this proposed procedure as an attempt to by-pass the Senate. "Without warning a hurricane struck," according to Acheson, who was at the eye of the storm. "The word is used advisedly to describe a severe cyclonic disturbance caused by hot air revolving counterclockwise . . . Its center was filled with a large mass of cumulonimbus cloud, often called Arthur Vandenberg, producing heavy word fall." Vandenberg saw the attempt to sneak UNRRA past the Senate as "a preview of the method by which the president and the State Department intend [to settle] every possible war and postwar issue." Connally, though a Democrat, agreed that such unwarranted executive autonomy would set "a dangerous precedent." Even worse, in Vandenberg's opinion, the original draft of the UNRRA agree-

ment "pledged our total resources to whatever illimitable schemes for relief and rehabilitation all around the world our New Deal crystal gazers
might desire to pursue." This epithet soon became a badge of honor, as
Roosevelt's aides began gleefully referring to themselves as "New Deal
crystal-gazers."[18]

Secretary Hull emerged with a suitable compromise after enduring a
"stormy session" with the Senate Foreign Relations Committee. Congress would be asked to consider the draft UNRRA agreement in the
form of a joint resolution; US diplomats would negotiate changes in the
draft that Congress wanted, most notably by inserting a right of withdrawal and giving Congress control over US contributions. Fortunately,
the other signatories accepted these American modifications, and in the
end Congress passed the agreement without trouble. And Connally and
Vandenberg were right to be vigilant about the UNRRA approval
process. The earlier palaver with Congress ultimately produced closer
consultations between Congress and the executive over postwar policies
which proved an important deposit of goodwill heading into congressional hearings on the Bretton Woods and United Nations charters. Hull
and Acheson were not interested in eating any more congressional crow.
The UNRRA approval process also set a precedent for congressional approval of similar agreements going forward.[19]

On November 9, 1943, the representatives of forty-four nations met
with FDR in the East Room of the White House for a formal signing ceremony of the UNRRA agreement. In his remarks upon signing, the president offered a pragmatic vision that foreshadowed his perspective on the
United Nations organization as a whole: "Nations will learn to work together only by actually working together."[20]

**"In Washington Lord Halifax / Once whispered to Lord Keynes: / It's true
they have the money bags / But we have all the brains."[21]**

"Agriculture and relief were simple matters compared to international
monetary arrangements," noted Acheson. "The period of gestation of
the latter about doubled that of elephants." Keynes, for his part, professed not to understand why the American approach to the negotiations
was so very time-consuming. After having read an American newspaper
report that the Bretton Woods conference was slated to last "several
weeks," Keynes wrote to British Treasury officials Sir David Waley and
Sir Wilfred Eady in May 1944 that, "unless this is a misprint for several

days, it is not easy to see how the main monkey-house is going to occupy itself. It would seem probable that acute alcohol poisoning would set in before the end."[22]

The overarching goal of the Bretton Woods accords remained agreement on what Shotwell called a "workable international monetary mechanism" that could encourage the growth of trade by making currencies interchangeable at stable rates and by making short-term credit available, with a focus on facilitating the rebuilding of Europe after the war. Evolving plans for an international monetary fund addressed this stabilization goal in three specific ways. First, the Fund would administer a "code of conduct" regarding exchange rate policies. Second, it would support members with financial help in correcting or avoiding payments imbalances. Third, it would convene regular sessions for members to consult and collaborate on international monetary matters.[23]

The code of conduct on exchange rate policies reflected the hope "of avoiding both the disruptive fluctuations that had occurred in the 1930s and the rigidity of rates that had prevailed under the gold standard," in the words of one IMF publication. Prospective economic solutions, in other words, were meant to be the mirror image of the perceived economic problems of the 1930s. The Atlantic City synthesis of the Keynes and White plans sought a sustainable balance between stability and flexibility that could make international transactions more predictable and shelter domestic programs aimed at full employment and expansive social programs.[24]

The conference work continued day and night for almost four weeks. "The pressure of work here has been quite unbelievable," wrote Keynes in a July 21 letter to Sir John Anderson, chancellor of the Exchequer, "carried on in committees and commissions numbering anything up to 200 persons in rooms with bad acoustics, shouting through microphones, many of those present, often including the Chairman, with an imperfect knowledge of English." Keynes collapsed at least once during the conference. Although he later denied it, he confessed in private correspondence that "I have resolutely refused to go to any committees after dinner (except once only against orders which promptly led to a heart attack, so that I suffered from guilt not less than bodily discomfort!)."[25]

The economic historian Richard Gardner described the daily routine of the negotiations between Keynes and White, based on an eyewitness account by Gardner's dissertation advisor, Roy Harrod. Every day, Keynes and White could be seen "sitting together at the head of a long table, the other members of the British and American delegations on either side. Occasionally interventions were made by these other delegates; but it was Keynes and White who led the discussion, controlling its subject-matter and setting its tone."

> "Well, Harry," Keynes would say, "what shall it be to-day—passivity, exchange stability, or the role of gold?" With this informal beginning the two of them would exchange observations on some theoretical issue. Occasionally bitterness would creep in. Keynes would take White out of his depth; White would feel, but not admit, his intellectual inferiority; he would say something to remind Keynes that he, not Keynes, represented the stronger party in the negotiations. There would be angry words; papers would be thrown on the floor; one of them would stalk out of the room. The other negotiators would stay to patch up the quarrel. The next day the same procedure would be repeated.[26]

The outstanding issues on the design of the IMF centered on the questions of who would contribute how much to the Fund and on what terms this money would be made available. Another open question was within what range and on what terms members would be allowed to alter their currency exchange rates. On the exchange rate question, the goal was to find a formula that combined stability and predictability without ruling out a certain amount of flexibility.

Building in *too* much flexibility, however, would conflict with the equally important objective of discouraging members from devaluing their currencies. Trading partners sought stability at a systemic level, and businesses benefited from predictability; but any given country facing a weak domestic economy would want the maximum flexibility to inflate or depreciate its currency with minimal outside interference. Devaluation was a tempting way to support struggling domestic industries, since it made a country's exports less expensive in foreign markets. To White, the devaluation issue was paramount. He instructed the US delegation at a strategy session shortly after the conference opened that the primary purpose of the IMF was "to prevent competitive depreciation of currencies and a race for lower rates and cut-throat competition in the international field"—one of the major international financial problems of the 1930s.[27]

One of the issues that the preliminary negotiations at Atlantic City had left open was the question of "quotas"—how much a given member would be expected to contribute to the Fund (and the Bank), and the linked question of how much they would be allowed to borrow. Harry White started from the position that the IMF would be supported by a fixed aggregate pool, that the United States would be the main contributor, and that other countries would in effect need to fight it out with one another about their relative quota rankings (with the United States serving as the final arbiter). As the economic historian Armand van Dormael explained it, "When the individual quotas were announced at Bretton Woods, each country would also know that, if it wanted its quota increased, something would have to be taken away from another country. Thus, instead of fighting the American delegation which had set the quotas, they would have to fight each other." These spats over quota allocations took up a large percentage of the actual negotiating time at the conference, and became a kind of proxy for the relative international prestige and influence of the participants.[28]

White sought to cap the American contribution at $2–3 billion, which appears from his papers to have been a rather arbitrary figure, "large enough to convince foreign states that the Fund and the Bank would be capable of improving postwar economic conditions, while it would be limited enough to convince American bankers that he was not planning to set up an international superbank." The United States quota was roughly on a par with that of the entire British Commonwealth. China and France each wanted the fourth largest quota. India wanted a quota larger than China's in recognition of its higher volume of international trade. White noted dismissively that "the smaller countries all want larger quotas," complaining that Australia was "the most troublesome" due to its insistence on "participating to an extent far beyond the proper role of a country of her size and importance." Since national prestige was implicated, "There is not too much logic in any of this," conceded State Department economist Emilio G. "Pete" Collado. White's rather cynical negotiating tactic was to reserve an extra, unallocated slush fund of about $400 million, so that when petitioning countries made "strong arguments," the United States could then "add a little something," and then "they feel that they have negotiated . . . and I think they will feel better."[29]

By way of putting these numbers in perspective, *Time* magazine explained that "the proposed World Stabilization Fund is small change, an $8 billion fund into which the US may put two and a half billions, the equivalent of what the nation now spends every ten days on the war." The American delegation also wanted to ensure that loan money was made available in proportion to the amount that a borrowing country had contributed to the Fund. This "contributory" model was offered as an alternative to the "overdraft" model from the earlier Keynes Plan.[30]

In rejecting the Keynes approach, the American negotiators explained that Congress would never swallow the overdraft concept, with its vast loan facilities, including a potential American liability of a stratospheric $26 billion. Acheson, mindful of his 1943 trip to the congressional woodshed and thinking perhaps of Senator Vandenberg's earlier attack on "illimitable schemes for relief and rehabilitation all around the world," argued that an overdraft principle would violate the exclusive constitutional authority of Congress to authorize federal spending.[31] Another casualty of the negotiation process, from the British perspective, was the Keynes Plan's emphasis on placing part of the responsibility for exchange rate adjustments onto creditor nations as well as debtors. Even the 1943 White Plan had featured a provision directing the IMF to issue a report to the creditor country with recommendations for restoring equilibrium, but this provision did not make it into the final charter. Negotiators accordingly also deleted a provision instructing members in such a situation to "give immediate and careful attention to recommendations made by the Fund."[32]

The American delegation had never been comfortable with the concept of creditor responsibilities. Just as America's insistence on bankers' terms for war loans during the First World War was an international projection of a domestic financial model, so too was America's image of debtors as being somehow morally suspect. The legal historian Bruce Mann traces the longstanding American attitude toward what he calls "the moral economy of debt" back to deeply rooted ideals "that presupposed the dependence of debtors and the omnipotence and inherent justness of creditors." As a cautious Congress for the second time in less than thirty years looked out over an international landscape littered with debtor nations and shattered economies, this ethos surfaced once again. Such differences could be expressed in biblical terms, wrote Skidelsky in an essay on "Keynes's Road to Bretton Woods," with the American orientation having "Old Testament overtones: Justice demanded that the profligate should be punished for their extravagance," while the British orientation was in more of a New Testament vein: "Debts, like sins, should be forgiven."[33]

During the weeks of intense negotiations at Bretton Woods, the proposed charter for a World Bank did not receive nearly as much attention as did the IMF charter. This was probably because the British were not interested in it at all until quite late in the game—Keynes first began to see the Bank's potential just a few months before the Bretton Woods conference opened. Their lack of interest in this American proposal was understandable: the British did not anticipate being eligible for reconstruction aid from the World Bank, nor did they have the resources to contribute much toward setting it up.

Another tactical move on White's part was to put Keynes in charge of the negotiations on the Bank, as a way of neutralizing his influence over the more politically sensitive IMF. Perhaps unsurprisingly, it turned out that Keynes was a difficult chairman to follow. Dr. Emanuel A. Goldenweiser, an American "expert" at Bretton Woods who was also director of research and statistics of the Board of Governors of the Federal Reserve system, recalled that "the outstanding personality at Bretton Woods was Lord Keynes. He shone in two respects—in the fact that he is, of course, one of the brightest lights of mankind in both thinking and expression and in his ability to influence people, and he shone also by being the world's worst chairman." Acheson elaborated: "Meetings on the Bank, which are conducted by Keynes, are being rushed in a perfectly impossible and outrageous way . . . He knows this thing inside out so that when anybody says Section 15-C he knows what it is. Nobody else in the room knows. So before you have an opportunity to turn to Section 15-C and see what he is talking about, he says, 'I hear no objection to that,' and it is passed. Well, everybody is trying to find Section 15-C. He then says, we are now talking about Section 26-D. Then they begin fiddling around with their papers, and before you find that, it is passed."[34]

The role of the Bank was to make it easier to mobilize economic resources for longer-term reconstruction and development projects which, unaided, might not attract private investment. While there was no link between a member's contribution to the Bank and its right to draw funds, the Bank had strict limits on its direct lending. Rather than making loans itself, the Bank was designed to operate primarily on the basis of loan guarantees to encourage additional private investment. It was able to make some loans from its original resources, and it could also raise capital by issuing securities. Nevertheless, the provisions concerning the payment of member subscriptions suggested severe limitations on the Bank's role as an independent lender.[35]

Over the course of the Bretton Woods negotiations, for example, the maximum amount of the Bank's loans and guarantees was reduced from a multiple of its total capital to just 100 percent of that capital. That is to say, the potential impact of the Bank's resources was constricted by virtue of not being "leveraged." This retrenchment from more expansive proposals was specifically in anticipation of congressional objections to "risky loan authorizations." Yet the first article of the Bank's charter still reflected the earlier idea that one of the institution's major functions was to facilitate reconstruction, "including the restoration of economies destroyed or disrupted by war." The Bank was also supposed to "assist in bringing about a smooth transition from a wartime to a peacetime economy." Hobbled by the numerous modifications negotiated at Bretton Woods, the Bank, even more than the Fund, was manifestly unequal to its paper mandate.[36]

The Bretton Woods Conference culminated in an emotional banquet on the evening of July 22, 1944. A British delegate described Keynes's dramatic entrance, after most of the other delegates were seated: "As he moved slowly toward the high table, stooping a little more than usual, white with tiredness, but not unpleased at what had been done, the whole meeting spontaneously stood up and waited, silent, until he had taken his place. Someone of more than ordinary stature had entered the room." Keynes accepted the World Bank and IMF charters on behalf of Britain in an effusive after-dinner speech, with the delegates standing for him again as he rose to speak. He thanked everyone from the Boy Scouts who had served as messengers to the "good temper and humor" of the notoriously abrasive Harry White. There were even uncharacteristic kudos for the lawyers, "who have turned our jargon into prose and our prose into poetry," although he qualified this uncharacteristically generous comment by including the jab that he still wished that the lawyers "had not covered so large a part of our birth certificate with such very detailed provision for our burial service, hymns, and lessons, and all."[37]

Keynes also highlighted the work ahead, noting that "we have reached this evening a decisive point. But it is only a beginning. We have to go out from here as missionaries, inspired by zeal and faith. We have sold all this to ourselves. But the world at large still needs to be persuaded." He concluded by citing the inspiring example of forty-four nations cooperating, despite many obstacles: "If we can continue in a larger task as we have begun in this limited task, there is hope for the world. At any rate we shall now disperse to our several homes with new friendships sealed and new intimacies formed. We have been learning to work together." His peroration summed up the Roosevelt rationale for international organization generally, whether political, legal, or economic.[38]

"Less trouble, and less expensive than building a bomb shelter"

Treasury Secretary Morgenthau was determined to have CBS broadcast his own remarks "live" from the closing ceremony at Bretton Woods. He rearranged the order of speakers and then halted the procession of speeches entirely for a short interlude just before he was due to address the assembly, to fit in with the radio network's schedule. He was aiming his presentation primarily at the general public, rather than at the exhausted convocation of economists, diplomats, and lawyers assembled in front of him. His folksy language suggested as much: "I am gratified to announce that the Conference at Bretton Woods has successfully completed the task before it . . . The actual details of an international monetary and financial agreement may seem mysterious to the general public. Yet at the heart of it lie the most elemental bread and butter realities of daily life. What we have done here in Bretton Woods is to devise machinery by which men and women everywhere can freely exchange, on a fair and stable basis, the goods which they produce through their labor."[39]

Morgenthau also began preemptively to address potential opposition: "There is a curious notion that the protection of national interests and the development of international cooperation are conflicting philosophies—that somehow or other men of different nations cannot work together without sacrificing the interests of their particular nations. There has been talk of this sort—and by people who ought to know better—concerning the international cooperative nature of the undertaking just completed at Bretton Woods." He pointed to the concrete experience of the conference as refuting this zero-sum reasoning: "Yet none of us has found any incompatibility between devotion to our own countries and joint action. Indeed, we have found on the contrary that the only genuine safeguard for our national interests lies in international cooperation."

His presentation was a Rooseveltian reformulation of the very concept of the US national interest, in explicitly multilateralist terms: "We have come to recognize that the wisest and most effective way to protect our national interests is through international cooperation—that is to say, through united effort for the attainment of common goals. This has been the great lesson taught by the war, and is, I think, the great lesson of contemporary life . . . Today the only enlightened form of national self-interest lies in international accord."[40]

Early in 1945 President Roosevelt optimistically appealed to Congress for quick approval of the Bretton Woods charters, while the Treasury Department expanded Morgenthau's publicity campaign to garner support for the two institutions. Morgenthau had retained a professional public relations firm to help educate the US public. One of its representatives, Randolph Feltus, in presenting his strategy to British Foreign Office officials in February 1945, explained that "the American left" was already solidly behind the Bretton Woods program. Accordingly, the main job would be "to impress the center." The most promising angle would be "that Bretton Woods is good business for the US, good business for American business, good hard-headed business, good Yankee trading business." Also, that the Bretton Woods institutions would not stand on their own but would "be fitted into the San Francisco [UN] conference picture." It was important that the institutions not be too closely associated in the public mind with the US Treasury, however, because "the Treasury is suspect. The Treasury is New Deal looney."[41]

At first glance, the Bretton Woods charters did not appear to be the kind of program that Congress would easily ratify. Underlying the whole Bretton Woods approach was what the isolationist Senator Robert A. Taft, Republican of Ohio, considered to be a violation of a cardinal rule of sovereignty—as he put it, that "no international body should have any jurisdiction over the domestic policies of the United States."[42]

The American Bankers Association expressed dismay, in their February 1945 review of the Bretton Woods charters, that the IMF's liquidity arrangements were based on what they argued were "financially unsound" provisions, employing "lending methods that are unproved and impractical." In the private sector, they explained, the lender was always appropriately in the driver's seat, whereas under the provisions of the IMF, "we should be handing over to an international body the power to determine the destination, time, and use of our money." It would be especially unwise to sign on to policies that smacked of a "super-government" at a time when there were "large amounts of private United States dollars ready to go abroad."[43]

These representatives of the American banking community believed that the United States should instead use its lending policies to express its national interests, "represented by such concepts as those in the Atlantic Charter." These leading bankers—who opposed the IMF—nevertheless attempted to co-opt Rooseveltian rhetoric and ideas. The authors of the bankers' review also observed at another point that "we need freedom from fear of war and freedom from hampering trade barriers, subsidies, and other economic weapons." This language suggests that the Atlantic Charter and Four Freedoms had a cultural traction to which even those with major doubts about New Deal–style American multilateralism had to pay heed. The bankers suggested that the United States should highlight instead the general applicability of its own economic model, for "one of the greatest contributions the United States can render to the world is to make available to other countries the virility and productiveness of our system of private enterprise."[44]

Senator Taft amplified the bankers' concerns in Senate hearings in

June 1945: "I think it is outrageous, because I think in this case this is a question of creditors and debtors . . . And in this case we are giving our money to a board which is controlled by the debtors, by the very fellows who are going to borrow . . . I do not think anybody has ever proposed to give away American money as this Fund proposes to give it away, to people who will themselves control its disposition." The following month the senator's assessment was even more succinct: participation in such a multilateral institution would be "pouring money down a rat hole."[45]

British critics were no more charitable. In parliamentary debates, the Bretton Woods charters were whipsawed between two powerful constituencies. Old-style imperialists such as Lord Beaverbrook, in 1945 the Lord Privy Seal, favored a sterling bloc as a counterweight to American power. Meanwhile, British socialists and other critics on the left favored policies that would create domestic employment, even though the additional taxes would likely slow any postwar recovery. These unlikely bedfellows both refused to sacrifice their maneuvering room in the domestic economy for the sake of abstract ideas about multilateralism, which would likely benefit only the selfish Americans anyway. The response of the British left, in particular, was based on assumptions about the postwar American economy that proved completely inaccurate, including confident predictions of high unemployment and long-term economic instability.

Two qualities rescued the Bretton Woods charters from this transatlantic barrage of criticism: first, the Bretton Woods agreements were too technical to elicit widespread public interest, despite Secretary Morgenthau's efforts; and second, the charters benefitted from the reflected glow of the *Zeitgeist* of 1945, with its spirit of multilateralism, especially in the United States. The essayist E. B. White, writing editorials anonymously for the *New Yorker,* observed early in 1945 how "the year is already clothed in a certain historical radiance like that of stars of the first magnitude." He analogized the new multilateralist moment to the successful model of America's pluralist, polyglot, overpopulated cities, which were able to function only by dwelling under one unwritten law, "and the law is: *Thou shalt not push thy neighbor around.*" White noted the theme of Roosevelt's Fourth Inaugural Address, where the president "said that we had learned to be citizens of the world." He lamented wryly, "but he did not tell us where we might apply for our first papers. The world's department of justice is still a long subway ride from any given point, but to go forever unnaturalized, in so promising a land, is unthinkable." White thought the most promising prospects for this new sense of global stewardship were the ordinary folks in the armed services, "the young soldiers who have got far enough from our shores to see the amazing implications of a planet."[46]

The decidedly unpoetic Bretton Woods charters were swept along in this surge of internationalist goodwill (although nations not designated as great powers—and even some that were—were already cynical about E. B. White's "no-pushing" rule). "Such a conjunction of power and idealism in economic affairs was entirely unprecedented in American history," argues Gardner, nothing short of "a political miracle." Timing alone played a large role in this "miracle." The internationalist spirit was reaching its very apogee during the congressional committee hearings for the Bretton Woods Act, in July 1945, immediately after the signing of the United Nations charter. The administration's successful arguments in favor of the UN charter spilled over somewhat indiscriminately into testimony in favor of Bretton Woods. These powerful debating points hit home with congressional representatives, who were sensitive to the question of how future generations might remember their role in such self-consciously historic times:

> Mr. Smith: Do you think that we must have this fund?
> Mr. White: I think we would make a very serious error if we do not have
> it. I think history will look back and indict those who fail to vote the
> approval of the Bretton Woods proposals in the same way that we now
> look back and indict certain groups in 1921 who prevented our adher-
> ence to an international organization designed for the purpose of pre-
> venting wars.[47]

Administration officials knew they had a winner with this argument. Harry Dexter White's confident presentation was emblematic of the substantial sea-change in the public mood. The caution over specific multilateralist commitments that had befogged President Roosevelt's Atlantic Charter diplomacy in 1941 was burning away by 1944. The following verbal duel at the Bretton Woods hearings between two Republican senators captures the opposing forces in this transformative process:

> Senator Tobey: We have a world that is prostrate. If we are going to live
> in it ourselves we have got to make some effort to get it back on its
> feet. There has to be an element of faith, an element of confidence
> somewhere. That is what we are trying to do here. We can afford to
> take some chances. I am willing to do it. The risks are small compared

to the benefits that will come from this. The world is in extremis. We
have got to do something.

SENATOR TAFT: Well, I say that is baloney. It will ruin this country, that
kind of doctrine. Every cent we give away must come from the American working man.[48]

Both senators were well-known isolationists from the interwar and early
war years, but while Robert Taft clung to his original views, Charles
Tobey had undergone a Bretton Woods conversion during his service as
an American delegate.

The Bretton Woods charters expressed a kind of global Keynesianism—the paradoxical view that "in a depression the attempt to save
more will make a community poorer, but that a community which invests
enough will never be short of saving." Similarly, in the international
arena, governments had to spend to save; that is, they had to invest in
the weaker members of the community in order to save the whole system
from instability. What Taft repeatedly called "giving away" American resources was construed by more imaginative decisionmakers—even recent
isolationists such as Senator Tobey—as an American investment in global
stability and predictability.[49]

By 1945, supporters of Bretton Woods had no trouble explaining to
the general public what the United States was getting for its money.
Echoing the themes of Secretary Morgenthau's CBS broadcast, a pamphlet from the Writers' War Board argued that "less trouble, and less expensive than building a bomb shelter would be a letter or wire to your
Senators and Representatives urging ratification of Bretton Woods." This
expansive conception of the US national interest contrasts sharply with
earlier lawyerly disputes over appropriate "consideration" for America's
largesse in the Lend-Lease program.[50]

Late in 1941, Keynes had received a letter from an old friend, a British
banker based in Washington, who tried to explain why he believed that
Americans would never accept plans for the supranational regulation of
currency values: "I remember during my education always learning that
the control of currency was an especial attribute of sovereignty. This is of
course the difficulty that faces all schemes of international cooperation."
Yet multilateralist precepts proved more persuasive than even these venerable arguments about sovereignty as state control of resources, at least
for a brief, transitional moment in American history.[51]

This multilateralist moment reconfigured the very idea of sovereignty.
Taft's conception of sovereignty suggested a stack of poker chips that

must be hoarded, guarded, augmented, and certainly not squandered. Sovereignty resided in a checklist of controls over currency, territory, or military resources. Responsible officials served their nation's interest by not giving away any item on their checklist, at least not without getting something of obviously comparable value in return, in a kind of geopolitical version of the "consideration" argument. But underlying the approach of Roosevelt administration officials and other internationalists in 1945 was a vision of sovereignty not as an attribute but as a process. Spreading decisionmaking authority around, through multilateralist institutions such as Bretton Woods, strengthened the system as a whole, reconceptualizing sovereignty in a more instrumentalist way, as the capacity to participate in the international system.[52]

What was "given away," in terms of decisionmaking authority, earned returns in the form of increased security and stability. At one point in the Senate hearings, a witness started making old-style, Taft-like arguments about sovereignty. Senator William Fulbright of Arkansas answered this witness as follows: "The movements you have suggested are the traditional movements that were utilized in the past 20 to 25 years. There is a general feeling not only in the financial but in the political field that we have tried that system and look at the trouble we are in. Now you are suggesting the traditional way . . . There is a feeling that we must do something a little different . . . There is a tendency to say we must take a chance."[53]

Keynes used to enjoy pointing out that after World War I, everyone had wanted to get back to the simpler, idyllic world of 1913. But in the wake of World War II, "no one wants to go back to the world of the 1930s."[54] It was time to try something new.

"Why should we give a quart of milk a day to every Hottentot?"

Plans for the International Monetary Fund and the World Bank were integral to an American wartime vision that extended far beyond economic recovery and financial stability. The Bretton Woods institutions were part of a wider planning effort meant to institutionalize the human rights ideology of the Four Freedoms and Atlantic Charter. One internationalist pressure group analyzed the United Nations economic conferences of 1943 and 1944 (the FAO, UNRRA, and Bretton Woods) as efforts to design "the international mechanisms that will be needed to achieve what the great Chinese leader Sun Yat-sen once described as 'the principle of livelihood'—what we now call 'freedom from want.'" These institutions were meant to offer a path away from the prewar status quo, using economic rights as a tool to realize a broader, transformative agenda. These goals encompassed New Deal ideas about "the development of the human personality," as well as Keynesian terms such as "well-being" and "the good life" for ordinary people, and ultimately, human rights ideas about the dignity of man.[55]

The design of the World War II multilateral institutions reflected these ideas about economic rights. These institutions defined and pursued international justice in a way that the more static premises underlying the League of Nations had been unable to conceive. In 1944 a leading multilateralist advocacy group wrote that discussions about international economic institutions could now confidently be "built upon the assumption that a determined and sustained attempt will be made by the United Nations not to restore the *status quo,* but to concert policies designed to improve the well-being of the world's peoples." This kind of language betokened a larger transition, away from what the historian Alan Brinkley calls "the reform liberalism of the first third of the twentieth century" and toward the "rights-based liberalism that succeeded it."[56]

Transcendence of the status quo involved connecting economic programs to what we would today describe as human rights ideas, with their emphasis on the "dignity of man." New Dealer Charles Merriam highlighted the connection: "The root problem of democracy in our day is to see that the gains of our civilization are fairly distributed and translated into terms of the common good without undue delay." He explained that "these gains are not material alone; they consist of goods, but also of services and opportunities for the development of the human personality in many ways, some calculable and others imponderable. In a democracy they are set in the framework of the dignity of man and the consent of the governed as essential to the protection and development of the general welfare." Economic security was an integral part of human dignity; multilateral economic institutions would generalize this essential security to the international level.[57]

As with the Atlantic Charter itself, the Bretton Woods vision was meant to serve both as an improvement on the old status quo League of Nations approach and as an embodiment of a specifically anti-Nazi alternative to world order. Arthur De Souza Costa, chair of the Brazilian delegation at Bretton Woods, observed in an address to the other delegates that the conference itself was evidence that "human solidarity is not a result of racial unity, that it does not depend on the language one speaks but rather on a community of feeling." To De Souza, Bretton Woods stood as a testimonial "against the Nazi claim that a supposed racial superiority gives the right to rule the world." Instead, "Bretton Woods offers a way for the guidance of human destinies through the development of human brotherhood, attained by concerted effort, inspired by a single ideal—that happiness be distributed throughout the face of the earth." This human welfare framing of international security had an affirmative dimension: while it was fundamentally about freedom from fear, it was also about augmenting "happiness," a perspective Keynes shared with the American New Dealers.[58]

The Bank and the Fund were two specialized mechanisms for implementing this vision of a transformed postwar world. Percy E. Corbett, a professor of law and political science, wrote of the importance of integrating political and economic war aims as early as September 1941: "The desire to put an end to aggression, to establish the rule of law, to deliver peoples from fear, finds expression in most declarations of war aims. Coupled with this in many instances is the hope . . . that a more equitable distribution of the necessities and amenities of life may be achieved." Linking the outlawry of aggression to a social justice agenda under the umbrella of ideas about the rule of law was the essence of a "new New Deal"—the elusive "third phase" of the New Deal that Alan Brinkley indicates "continued to develop as an idea" well into the 1940s, particularly in its international dimension.[59]

Just a month after its publication, the Atlantic Charter was already exerting a major influence on activist academics such as Corbett, who highlighted the contrast with the postwar order following World War I: "One of the principal reasons why the League [of Nations] failed was its lack of effective jurisdiction in economic matters. It has become a commonplace that nations must surrender part of their 'economic sovereignty,' and accept some measure of supranational control, if they wish to avoid major depressions and recurrent wars." The interdependence of global economics with domestic security mirrored the new convergence of economic and political rights.[60]

In his 1943 State of the Union address, Roosevelt continued to fill in the content of "Freedom from Want" as an explicit war aim:

> The people at home, and the people at the front, are wondering a little about the third freedom—freedom from want. To them it means that when they are mustered out, when war production is converted to the economy of peace, they will have the right to expect full employment . . .

but that with the opportunity for employment they want assurance against the evils of all major economic hazards—assurance that will extend from the cradle to the grave. And this great Government can and must provide this assurance.[61]

By 1943 Roosevelt and his advisors were treating such a synthetic recasting of national interests as simply obvious. A passage deleted from this speech reveals how Roosevelt yearned to go on the offensive regarding the linkage between international development and domestically sensitive trade issues. The president's aides thought that the paragraph came across as too defensive, and they prevailed on him to edit it out. Still, this paragraph, which FDR dictated in January 1943, shows his clear conception of the connection between economic and political considerations, as well as the linkage between the domestic and international realms:

> Some snob asks glibly "Why should we give a quart of milk a day to every Hottentot?" First of all that type of man would have you people think that this is the great American aim in life. Secondly, he deliberately omits the fact that if the population of Dakar, and the population of Morocco and the population of Algiers and even the Hottentots could be helped to get a better standard of living, each one of them would have greater capacity to participate more greatly in the trade of the world and by that create employment needs among nations and, incidentally, assure greater markets for producing for the manufacturing nations of the world, including the people of the United States of America.[62]

Roosevelt framed economic rights as a supplement to a more traditional foundation of political rights. Both layers would work together to secure justice as well as security in a pluralistic society.

Roosevelt's Four Freedoms speech had included a short, general checklist itemizing "the basic things expected by our people of their political and economic systems." This list was a preliminary version of what he and his aides later elaborated as an "Economic Bill of Rights." The phrase was popular in the United States and in Britain in the wake of the 1942 Beveridge Report. Secretary of the Interior Harold Ickes, for instance, proposed a bill of rights in 1943 that must "of necessity" be underpinned by sixteen "elementary principles." Four of his principles were either specifically economic or had predominantly economic implications, including "the right to security—to financial security and to physical security, including the right of preventative and of curative medicine."[63] On the domestic front, this analysis had influential allies both inside and outside of government. A group of American economists around Alvin Hansen of Harvard, known as the "American Keynesians," had been attacking the idea of "pump-priming" since the late 1930s— the theory that encouraging private spending could sustain the economy when government spending contracted. They accordingly advocated programs of public spending, redistributive taxation, and full employment. Supporters of this approach within government included Federal Reserve Chair Marriner S. Eccles (later to serve as a delegate to the Bretton Woods Conference), Eccles's former assistant Lauchlin B. Currie, after 1939 an important Roosevelt aide on economic policy, as well as early support from the Columbia University economist and "brain truster" Rexford Tugwell. As the historian Lizabeth Cohen shows in her portrait of the "citizen consumer," during World War II civic-minded individuals also understood that they could legitimately expect safeguards from the state even as they acted on the presumption that their private and domestic consumption would support a wider network of national and even international prosperity.[64]

This orientation received its most forceful articulation in FDR's State of the Union Address of 1944: "We have come to a clear realization of the fact that true individual freedom cannot exist without economic security and independence . . . In our day these economic truths have become accepted as self-evident. We have accepted, so to speak, a second Bill of Rights under which a new basis of security and prosperity can be established for all—regardless of station, race, or creed." The president explicitly called for "a second Bill of Rights . . . an economic bill of rights." Listing the familiar goals that would lead to "protection from economic fears," Roosevelt concluded that "all of these rights spell security."[65]

FDR's language is at once familiar and strange to twenty-first-century sensibilities. On the one hand, his phrases about pluralism ("regardless of . . . race or creed") have become platitudinous through repetition over the last sixty years. On the other hand, the Cold War and considerations of racial politics in the Senate would soon eclipse the president's confidently expressed economic precepts. The historian James MacGregor Burns has argued that discussions of economic rights had already been overtaken by events in 1944, since such proposals were based on outdated assumptions drawn from Depression-era economics. This grounding in the recent past is precisely the point, however: early 1940s pronouncements about rights, including economic rights, drew upon the immediate experiences of Depression and war; they did not prefigure a Cold War orientation. The Economic Bill of Rights created a bridge between the economic aspirations of the Four Freedoms and wartime attempts to institutionalize a developing culture of human rights by means of New Deal–style institutional planning.[66]

The GI Bill of Rights, which Roosevelt signed in June 1944, was a pale vestige of the full-blooded Economic Bill of Rights that FDR and his planners had imagined. As with the idea of an Economic Bill of Rights, the GI Bill also grew out of Depression-era anxieties about massive unemployment, as government officials confronted the prospect of huge waves of veterans returning home, only to face joblessness and frustration. A widely cited 1942 government pamphlet, Alvin Hansen's "After the War—Full Employment," began its analysis of postwar aims with a section entitled "The Expected Post-War Slump." Factors holding back Keynesian programs in the domestic realm after 1944 included the fact that these dire predictions of postwar joblessness were simply wrong: postwar prosperity undermined support for more expansive social welfare programs, even as it vindicated the basic Keynesian analysis of how defense spending would buoy and expand the wartime economy.[67]

A key factor militating against the domestic program of a "new New Deal" was the so-called southern veto. Roosevelt had long been beholden to a restive "Dixiecrat" constituency in Congress—hence the president's unwillingness to push for strong anti-lynching legislation and his inconstant support for the Fair Employment Practices Committee. The constitutional scholar William Forbath points out that southerners had been natural allies of the New Deal in its early years, as populists hailing from an impoverished region, but were becoming increasingly disillusioned by the late 1930s. Southern representatives viewed the expansion of federal police powers and executive authority as intrusive, and were especially vocal in opposing any federal role that might threaten their traditional prerogatives of extracting abundant and cheap labor from the region's African-American population.[68]

Southern committee heads in Congress accordingly "stripped all the main pieces of New Deal legislation of any design or provision that threatened the separate southern labor market," according to Forbath, including cutting the predominantly black sectors of agricultural and domestic workers out of social insurance programs. This same southern veto was at work in downsizing wartime labor legislation. What Forbath calls the Keynesian promise of the American "social citizenship tradition" ultimately foundered on the shoals of this southern resistance.[69]

Part of this Dixiecrat backlash included the way an increasingly conservative Congress in 1943 terminated the National Resources Planning

Board, responsible for disseminating and promoting many of these ideas, by cutting off its funding and mandating that its functions could not be reallocated to other agencies. The framing of the GI Bill of 1944 grew out of this more constricted perspective, as did the Employment Act of 1946, designed to promote "maximum employment, production, and purchasing power." The historian John Jeffries calls attention to the Employment Act's careful phrasing, pointing out that the Act "called for 'maximum' rather than 'full' employment, lacked explicit Keynesian prescriptions for compensatory fiscal policy, [and] guaranteed no 'right to work.'" In the end it amounted to more a "symbolic consensus statement" than a "binding commitment."[70]

Framed more as a reward than as an entitlement, the GI Bill offered job placement services, unemployment compensation, home and business loans, and subsidies for education, with roughly eight million veterans taking advantage of benefits from the educational programs alone. The historian David Kennedy observes that "GI Bill beneficiaries . . . dramatically raised the educational level and hence the productivity of the workforce, and in the process unimaginably altered their own lives." The spectacular success of the GI Bill was tempered by a similar set of limitations to the domestic New Deal as a whole, however; its passage came at the cost of all but excluding comparatively powerless constituencies such as women or African-Americans.[71]

While the southern veto severely downsized the domestic realization of an economic rights agenda, the international vision remained surprisingly expansive. The policies the Bretton Woods charters and the GI Bill embodied were a high-water mark for economic rights as human rights in mainstream American politics, and the international expression was in many ways more robust than the domestic one, perhaps because it was not so explicitly bound up with questions of race. When institutional innovations of the "multilateralist moment" of the 1940s did implicate decentralized state control over discriminatory racial policies—as in the domestic jurisdiction provisions of the United Nations Charter or the "crimes against humanity" provisions of the Nuremberg Charter— southern vigilance and resistance was much more evident.

The negotiation of international financial institutions thickened the thin, glittering abstractions of the Atlantic Charter. Together with the United Nations (designed to pursue collective security) and Nuremberg (to pursue international justice), Bretton Woods was meant to be one of the three great building blocks upon which nations could collaboratively build a more just, durable, and legitimate postwar order. In the words of the 1944 report of the Commission to Study the Organization of Peace, "It is the will of the United Nations to construct out of the chaos of the bombed and twisted aftermath of war, more spacious and more gracious, as well as more secure, ways of living for the ordinary man." This populist vision of well-being amounted to a third strand woven through Nelson Mandela's universalist interpretation of the Atlantic Charter and Winston Churchill's more focused and instrumental one. Harold Ickes called it "a just peace, a people's peace, a resources-sharing peace."[72] It was Franklin Roosevelt's Atlantic Charter, the New Deal for the world.

1. Churchill and Roosevelt aboard HMS *Prince of Wales* for the Atlantic Conference, August 1941, Placentia Bay, Newfoundland. FDR is supported by his son Elliott. (© Corbis)

2. Controversy raged over the presumed beneficiaries of the Atlantic Charter: the European governments-in-exile (Churchill's intent) or "all humanity," as this image suggests. (Fred O. Seibel, *Richmond Times-Dispatch*, reprinted in *New York Times*, October 29, 1942)

3. Roosevelt and Churchill (seated upper left) attend Sunday religious service aboard HMS *Prince of Wales*. Over 1500 sailors joined their leaders on deck. (AP/Wide World Photos)

4. A framed copy of the Atlantic Charter is the centerpiece of an Office of War Information exhibit in Rockefeller Plaza, New York, March 1943. (Marjory Collins, Library of Congress)

AUGUST 14—"TWO YEARS AGO TODAY, PRESIDENT ROOSEVELT AND PRIME MINISTER CHURCHILL SIGNED THE ATLANTIC CHARTER."... NEWS ITEM

"A SECOND EMANCIPATION PROCLAMATION!!"

5. A vision of the spirit of Lincoln supporting the signing of the Atlantic Charter suggests the document belonged to a tradition of historic covenants. The original Charter was, however, an informal, unsigned agreement. (Charles Alston, 1943. Courtesy National Archives)

6. Unemployed during the Great Depression. The widespread dissemination of such images fueled a heightened awareness of the link between individual economic security and stability at the national—even international—level. (Courtesy Franklin D. Roosevelt Library)

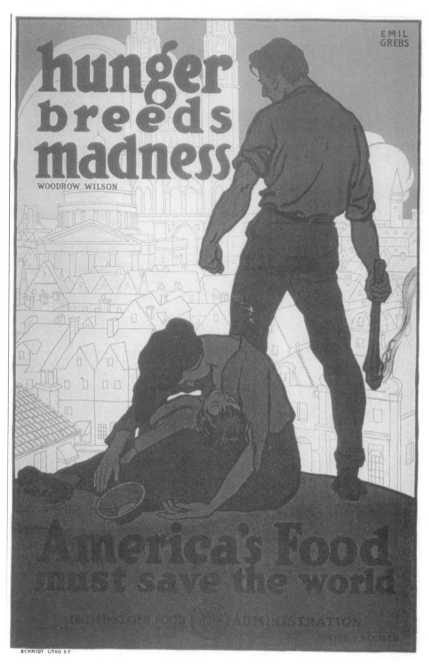

7. This government poster from the World War I era highlights the connection between political stability and international security, emphasizing America's global role. (Courtesy National Archives)

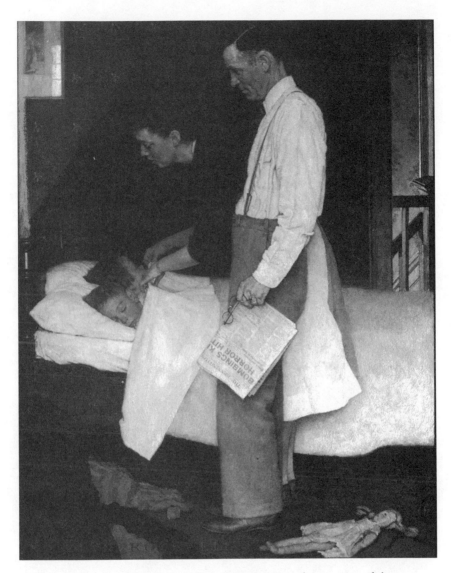

8. Norman Rockwell's *Freedom from Fear* contrasts the security of the American family with the bombing of London as shown in the newspaper headline. (The Norman Rockwell Art Collection Trust, The Norman Rockwell Museum at Stockbridge, Massachusetts. Reprinted by permission of the Norman Rockwell Family Agency. Copyright © 1943 the Norman Rockwell Family Entities)

9. *Freedom from Want* illustrates the contrast between Rockwell's domestic
vision of security and FDR's international emphasis in his 1941 Four Freedoms
speech. (The Norman Rockwell Art Collection Trust, The Norman Rockwell
Museum at Stockbridge, Massachusetts. Reprinted by permission of the
Norman Rockwell Family Agency. Copyright © 1943 the Norman Rockwell
Family Entities)

10. Titled *Uncomfortable Grandstand*, this British cartoon depicts American leaders in a rickety and unstable observation post labeled "neutrality." (David Low, *Evening Standard*, September 22, 1939/Solo Syndication)

11. This cartoon protests the extension of Lend-Lease aid to the Soviet Union, where the "Four Freedoms" lie buried while presidential aide Harry Hopkins talks to Stalin. (Joseph Parrish, *Chicago Tribune*, August 4, 1941. Copyright Tribune Media Services, Inc. All rights reserved. Reprinted with permission.)

12. Part of a Lend-Lease shipment, cases of American spare parts are unloaded at a British ordnance center. (Courtesy Franklin D. Roosevelt Library)

There's No Price on Liberty!

$6000000000

13. Uncle Sam extends Lend-Lease aid worth $6 billion in the interest of "liberty." Some British negotiators interpreted parts of the Lend-Lease Act as a demand for the dismantling of the British Empire. (Bruce Russell, September 21, 1941, copyright 1941 *Los Angeles Times*. Reprinted with permission.)

14. An American soldier looming over a devastated European landscape emphasizes the outsized U.S. responsibility for maintaining peace. The headstone notes the world's failure to secure peace after World War I. (Bruce Russell, November 11, 1944, copyright 1944 *Los Angeles Times*. Reprinted with permission.)

15. British economist John Maynard Keynes and U.S. Treasury official Harry Dexter White at the international monetary conference at Savannah, Georgia, March 1946. (Thomas D. McAvoy/Time Life Pictures/Getty Images)

"THIS TIME WE'LL LOCK THE BARN DOOR"

Smith in The Lynchburg News

16. This cartoon shows the "World Money Control Plan," as embodied by the IMF and World Bank, protecting currency stabilization to thwart the thugs representing 1930s problems. The charters for the two financial institutions were under debate in the Senate. (Dorman H. Smith, *Lynchburg News*, reprinted in *New York Times*, July 15, 1945)

18. A diminutive and overburdened American taxpayer carries a dispropor-
tionate share of the global financial load in a cartoon critical of the Bretton
Woods plans. (Carl Somdal, *Chicago Tribune*, July 19, 1945)

17. *(facing page)* The Bretton Woods conference, New
Hampshire, July 1944. Despite the egalitarian alphabetical
arrangement of nations, the most important decisions had
been made at a preliminary conference in Atlantic City,
New Jersey the previous spring. (© Bettmann/Corbis)

19. Lord Halifax, British ambassador to the United States, signs the Bretton Woods charters at the State Department, January 1, 1946. (Hulton Archive/ Getty Images)

20. British Permanent Undersecretary of Foreign Affairs Sir Alexander Cadogan is flanked by American diplomats Edward Stettinius (left) and W. Averell Harriman. (Courtesy Franklin D. Roosevelt Library)

21. A favorite rhetorical device of New Deal planners and American internationalists was to use mechanical imagery to indicate that a properly designed mechanism would make the machinery of peace function smoothly. (Edwin Marcus, *New York Times*, October 1, 1944)

23. A bombed-out Berlin is contrasted with San Francisco, where hope shines brightly as the United Nations Conference gets underway, April 1945. (Edwin Marcus, Library of Congress)

22. *(facing page)* In a 1945 town hall meeting in East Kingston, New Hampshire, town citizens voted 25-1 to support U.S. membership in the world peace plans outlined at the Dumbarton Oaks conference. (© Bettmann/Corbis)

24. Meeting of the United Nations' "Big Four": Edward Stettinius, Lord Halifax, Andrei Gromyko, and V. K. Wellington Koo in San Francisco. (© Hulton-Deutsch Collection/Corbis)

26. Thousands fill San Francisco's Civic Auditorium to pray for the success of the UN Conference in progress. Many religious groups advocated increased U.S. involvement in the multilateral plans for the postwar world. (Library of Congress)

25. *(facing page)* This example of the American isolationist sentiment depicts the globe as a ball and chain with which the "Dumbarton Oaks plotters" planned to shackle a free and patriotic United States. (Carey Orr, *Chicago Tribune*, March 14, 1945)

27. This cartoon suggests the UN Conference, rather than liberating colonized people around the world, served merely to reinforce imperial powers, Britain in particular. (Joseph Parrish, *Chicago Tribune*, May 28, 1945. Copyright Tribune Media Services, Inc. All rights reserved. Reprinted with permission.)

28. Mexican delegate Ezequiel Padilla signs the United Nations Charter. Padilla was one of the leaders of the "smaller" nations at the conference who argued for strengthening human rights and international law provisions. (Thomas D. McAvoy/Time Life Pictures/Getty Images)

The Mighty Oak and the New Acorn

29. Published on July 4, 1945, this image portrays the UN Charter as an organic offshoot of the Declaration of Independence. (Bruce Russell, copyright 1945, *Los Angeles Times*. Reprinted with permission.)

30. One of twelve witnesses who testified against the UN Charter during the Senate hearings, W. E. B. DuBois argued that the charter did not adequately protect colonial peoples. (Marie Hansen/Time Life Pictures/Getty Images)

31. Opponents argued that the UN Charter betrayed Atlantic Charter principles, especially that of self-determination, and that the Big Three—Britain, U.S. and Soviet Union—sank the ideals of the earlier agreement. (Carl Somdal, *Chicago Tribune*, July 26, 1945)

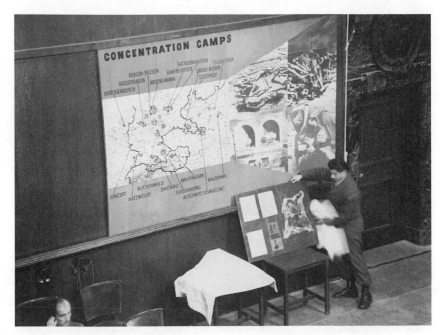

32. Prosecutors at the Nuremberg war crimes trial display a map of the major concentration camps. (© *Corbis*)

33. This 1945 cartoon suggests that the choice between force and law for the postwar world was linked to the cause of "world government," a sentiment eschewed by the U.S. administration because it played directly into opponents' worst fears. (Charles G. Werner, *Chicago Sun*)

34. German defendants in the dock at Nuremberg. Front row, left to right: Hermann Goering, Rudolf Hess, Joachim von Ribbentrop, Wilhelm Keitel. (Courtesy National Archives)

35. Published during the early phase of the Nuremberg proceedings, this cartoon suggests the trial will mete out "victors' justice" under retroactively enacted laws. (Carl Somdal, *Chicago Tribune*, October 24, 1946)

36. Chief U.S. prosecutor Robert H. Jackson at Nuremberg. Jackson was also the chief U.S. negotiator of the London Agreement, to which the Nuremberg Charter was annexed. (© Bettmann/Corbis)

37. Investigators at the Katyn mass grave of Polish soldiers, 1952. In a dispute that helped undercut the Nuremberg trial's legitimacy, the Soviet Union tried to blame the Nazis for the massacre but prosecutors, suspecting the Soviets, refused to charge the Germans with it. (© Bettmann/Corbis)

38. Two leading isolationist Republican senators, Arthur Vandenberg and
Robert A. Taft, are depicted jumping on a foreign aid steamroller in recognition
of the futility of opposition to the European Recovery Program, or the Marshall
Plan. (Clifford K. Berryman, *Washington Evening Star*, December 2, 1947.
From the U.S. Senate Collection, Center for Legislative Archives)

39. Marshall Plan aid at work in the rebuilding of Berlin. A year before the aid was scheduled to end, Germany had surpassed its prewar industrial production level. (Courtesy National Archives)

40. Eleanor Roosevelt holds up the Universal Declaration of Human Rights in Spanish. As chair of the UN's Human Rights Commission, the former first lady oversaw the committee that drafted the declaration. (Courtesy Franklin D. Roosevelt Library)

SAN FRANCISCO, JUNE 1945

The ideal, once it is embodied in an institution, ceases to be an ideal and becomes the expression of a selfish interest, which must be destroyed in the name of a new ideal. This constant interaction of irreconcilable forces is the stuff of politics. Every political situation contains mutually incompatible elements of utopia and reality, of morality and power.

E. H. Carr, The Twenty Years' Crisis: 1919–1939

CHAPTER 5

THE CHIMERA
OF COLLECTIVE SECURITY

Dumbarton Oaks is a spacious Georgetown estate above Rock Creek Park that the Robert Woods Bliss family donated to Harvard University in 1940. On August 21, 1944, the main mansion, which ordinarily housed a center for Byzantine studies, became the site for the first Big Four negotiations to plan a postwar organization for collective security. The proposal that came out of this meeting between the United States, Britain, the Soviet Union, and, belatedly, China was the first multilateral draft of what would become the United Nations Charter.

The estate's tree-shaded, high-ceilinged conference rooms, picturesque lily ponds, and sixteen acres of formal gardens would keep the proceedings from getting too overheated, or so the State Department hoped. But the inscription on the 1801 mansion, *Quod severis metes*—Reap what you sow—may have had a chilling effect as well. Still, "it was devilish hot," recalled one War Department staffer; and in a concession to the stifling heat, the thirty-nine diplomats paid a visit to the White House in "seersucker suits and tropical woolens" rather than the usual black swallowtailed morning coats.[1]

The Dumbarton Oaks planners believed they had learned the essential lessons from the First World War on how to devise a postwar multilateral order: start planning while hostilities are still continuing; make the plan identifiably and organically American-led; use "experts" and "technicians" to make the process appear less political; and separate the actual peace treaty from the machinery for resolving later disputes. But the proposal that emerged from Dumbarton Oaks was remarkably similar to the plan for the League of Nations from twenty-five years before. Almost ten months later in San Francisco, negotiators of the final UN Charter would modify the Dumbarton Oaks draft in favor of a more expansive set of references to the Atlantic Charter's human rights orientation, after lobbying from Roosevelt's aides, domestic and international public opinion, and FDR himself. But the genealogy of these ideas was clear from the beginning, even in the perfunctory reference to human rights in the Dumbarton Oaks proposals. Carlos Romulo, who would serve as chief delegate from the Philippines at the UN conference and would become an important advocate for anticolonial interests and the interests of the "smaller countries," was sorely disappointed in the Dumbarton Oaks proposals, but even he noted that "the outline of the [UN] Charter as drafted at Dumbarton Oaks was more or less an echo of those four principles of the Atlantic Charter. The essence of the Atlantic Charter was in the draft."[2]

The story of the human rights provisions in what would become the UN Charter is in some ways emblematic of a larger human rights story during the fluid and transitional "multilateralist moment" of the mid-1940s. Explicit human rights language in the UN Charter was initially edited out and even derided by the Dumbarton Oaks negotiators, only to be folded in later, in an intentionally unenforceable gesture which was at loggerheads with other explicit provisions relating to the prerogatives of national sovereignty. Yet as with the Atlantic Charter itself, the UN Charter ultimately became surprisingly influential as a standard of achievement—and measure of hypocrisy—in an increasingly divided world.

"A Conference not so much of Idealists (though idealism was not lacking) as of technicians"

The State Department had billed the Dumbarton Oaks discussions as an informal and exploratory exchange among military and foreign affairs experts. This focus on professional expertise was meant to stand in stark contrast with the 1919 proceedings of the Paris Peace Conference which had produced the infamously unsuccessful Treaty of Versailles. At Paris—or at least in the Paris negotiations that inhabited the popular imagination in 1940s America—cynical politicians and amateurish idealists had based their decisions on naked power politics or pious utopian aspirations rather than on a dispassionate analysis of the facts. "I have forgotten how many experts we took to Versailles at that time," commented Franklin Roosevelt dismissively in a 1943 press conference, "but everybody who had a 'happy thought,' or who thought he was an expert got a free ride." Roosevelt himself was among those happy free-riders headed to France at the end of World War I. But this time around, in San Francisco, the professionals were going to handle the details.[3]

From the earliest days of postwar planning, Allied advisors had stressed a split in planning functions between high-level summit meetings and lower-level consultations of experts and technicians, such as at

Dumbarton Oaks. Harvard history professor Sydney Fay wrote during the meeting that it "was a Conference not so much of Idealists (though idealism was not lacking) as of technicians . . . Their preoccupation was less with principles and more with a practicable and quick-working machinery."[4] Oft-repeated terms such as "technician" and "machinery" were meant to foster perceptions of a neutral, or at least nonpartisan, execution of collective security functions, just as the discussion of the role of experts at the Bretton Woods Conference had helped sanitize the topic of international monetary problems the month before. The contrast with the "politicized" 1919 experience was meant to be clear, despite the fact that at least six of the forty or so Dumbarton Oaks "technicians" were themselves veterans of the Paris peace process.[5]

The Dumbarton Oaks meetings were officially captioned as "conversations" in order "to convince the small states that this meeting would be very informal and that nothing would be decided without them," according to the journalist and historian Frank Donovan. Whether any small states were reassured by this packaging is doubtful; indeed, many Latin American states were so alarmed at being shut out of the process that they scheduled their own conference four months later to critique the Dumbarton Oaks draft. Nevertheless, Undersecretary of State Edward Stettinius, Jr., was trying to modernize the State Department by paying unprecedented attention to public relations. As head of the American contingent, Stettinius was in his element presiding at Dumbarton Oaks, his first high-profile role since succeeding the scandal-ridden Sumner Welles in late 1943.[6]

Undersecretary of State Welles had resigned in August of that year under pressure from his petulant boss, Cordell Hull, and with the reluctant assent of President Roosevelt. An intelligent and able internationalist, the imperious Welles had never been on good terms with Hull, a down-to-earth Tennessean who resented the way his condescending subordinate seemed able to exclude his boss from high-level decisions (one example being the 1941 Atlantic Conference itself, where an ailing Hull had been left behind in favor of the ambitious Welles). The occasion for Welles's ouster was an alleged indiscretion unusually scandalous by 1940s standards: the divorced and remarried Welles, in a drunken episode, had reportedly propositioned an African-American porter on board the presidential train. A series of strange and rather defensive asides about Welles's earlier diplomatic career in a biography by his elder son seems to suggest that the rumor had some substance. (For example, during a stint in Africa, Welles had acquired a taste for amorous adventures with black people, according to his son, and during Welles's tour in Argentina, it was understood that cosmopolitan diplomats often took young boys as lovers.) Welles's many enemies, led by the former US ambassador to France (and the Soviet Union) William Bullitt, told Roosevelt repeatedly that the rumor was well-known in the Senate and was bound to leak out to the public. By 1943, when the administration could anticipate seeking Senate ratification of peace treaties and other multilateral instruments, anti-Welles officials argued successfully that such a scandal could be used to blackmail the whole administration.[7]

The 43-year-old Stettinius—who had "gone far with comparatively modest equipment," in Dean Acheson's caustic assessment—had already served as the chairman of the board at US Steel, as a vice president of General Motors, and as the chief Lend-Lease administrator before his appointment to the State Department in the wake of Welles's abrupt departure. Internationalists and New Dealers were suspicious of Stet's big-business background, while old-line diplomats dismissed him as a lightweight.[8] Yet he was skilled at putting people at ease. For example, Stettinius's advance men had thoughtfully removed a painting of the Polish statesman and pianist Ignace Jan Paderewski from the music room at Dumbarton Oaks, which would be serving as the main meeting room, in case such graphic evidence of Polish nationalism might be disturbing to the Soviets.[9]

The State Department had decided against including congressional representatives in the American contingent, in part because they would not be perceived as "experts." Behind the scenes, however, Hull was continually updating a core group of eight senators with whom he had been meeting for postwar planning purposes for the past four months. In addition to Stettinius, the American group—even the word "delegation" was avoided as denoting too official an imprimatur—comprised most of a State Department subcommittee on international organization, along with six representatives of the military. The inclusion of Henry P. Fletcher, general counsel for the Republican National Committee and a former undersecretary of state, sounded the requisite bipartisan note. The proceedings were dominated by the genial Stettinius, senior British diplomat Alexander Cadogan, permanent undersecretary of foreign affairs and a principal player in the 1941 Atlantic Charter negotiations, and the Soviet ambassador to Washington, Andrei Gromyko, only 35 years old and already dour and impassive.[10]

In light of the general public mood of "hopeful expectancy" about postwar planning and the high-profile location in Washington DC, the

State Department's decision to exclude the press from all but the most ceremonial occasions at Dumbarton Oaks was "rather naive on the part of the planners," in Donovan's understated phrase. Using military police to bar reporters from the grounds seemed particularly pointless after *New York Times* reporter James "Scotty" Reston began publishing leaked position papers virtually verbatim, for which the American team initially blamed Cadogan. Reston's series on Dumbarton Oaks, which garnered him a Pulitzer prize, was in fact informed by a junior member of the Chinese delegation who had once worked as an apprentice reporter at the *Times*.[11]

Reston gleefully referred to the *Times*'s decision to publish the conference's confidential papers over several days, instead of all at once, as "the Chinese torture treatment" for his competitors, who were "absolutely on the warpath" at what they perceived as the State Department's spoon-feeding of the *Times*. Packs of aggressive journalists (who outnumbered the delegates four to one) even besieged the negotiators on what was supposed to be a secret tourist junket to New York City, which included a stop at Radio City Music Hall. But no reporter managed to capture the straight-laced Cadogan's response when Stet took him backstage and asked the British aristocrat if he might like to explain the significance of the Dumbarton Oaks meetings to the Rockettes.[12]

Three weeks into the negotiations, Stettinius arranged another outing for the delegates, to show off the historic sites of Virginia. Stettinius treated these getaways as negotiating tools, acting on Roosevelt's optimistic advice that even the most intractable conflicts could be resolved if the negotiators had a chance to relax together. The neophyte Stettinius seems to have taken FDR's guidance to heart. According to Stettinius's diary, many major decisions were made on these outings, as well as during meals, coffee breaks, and quiet strolls through the Dumbarton Oaks grounds. Stet carefully arranged for the mutually wary Soviet and Chinese representatives to be attached to separate touring parties, and while Gromyko stayed behind in sweltering Washington the other participants toured the presidential estates of Monticello and Montpelier, sipping mint juleps at Monroe's Ash Lawn. They also toured the Skyline Drive of the Blue Ridge mountains, the University of Virginia, and the Civil War battlefield at Bull Run.[13]

Using what Cadogan drily described as a "showman manner," the animated Stettinius threw himself into the role of guide to the bucolic Virginia scenery "as if he not only owned it but had painted it." In fact the American diplomat did own a rather hefty swath of it, and the tour concluded with an informal evening meal at Stet's own estate, Horse Shoe. "An astonishing scene," the world-weary Cadogan wrote in his diary. The entertainment was a "negro quartet" singing spirituals. "Admirable food . . . unlimited butter," noted Cadogan, "which one collected and took to an armchair or sofa. Flashlight photographers followed one— also the negro 'spirituals.' And meanwhile the motor-bike police strolled about the house smoking cigarettes. All very pleasant but unintelligible." In a letter to his wife, the British career diplomat summarized the experience with the cross-cultural *aperçu* that Americans were "extraordinary people . . . in some ways rather like ourselves but (as you can see) so utterly different." It may have been an ominous harbinger for international understanding, however, if an upper-class English-speaking diplomat found such an elite country-house scene to be "unintelligible."[14]

Back in the nation's capital, a sweaty and sour press corps was reduced to covering the homespun views of various citizen protesters. The Reverend Gerald L. K. Smith, a rabble-rousing advisor to the late Governor Huey Long of Louisiana, was preaching outside the iron gates of Dumbarton Oaks with his wife. The Smiths were in Washington to argue that Roosevelt should be impeached for, among other things, setting up a "superstate" that would serve as a "world police force," as well as the shocking crime of conducting a conference of foreigners on American soil while a war was going on. In their stingy distribution of genuine news, the State Department planners repeated the mistake they had made at the Food and Agriculture Conference in Hot Springs, Virginia, in June. By isolating and embittering the press corps, they guaranteed increased coverage of dissenting perspectives.[15]

Stettinius and Secretary Hull seemed genuinely taken aback by the volume of carping cables and editorials from both left and right, criticizing the secrecy policy, the exclusion of smaller countries, the great power orientation of the conference, the absence of agenda items on human rights, and the composition of the American delegation (as including no women and too many millionaires), among other complaints. "The cure for a dangerous isolation is not a more dangerous membership in an international gang of exploiters," scoffed the Socialist presidential candidate Norman Thomas about the Dumbarton Oaks proposals. One of the key lessons the Roosevelt administration had drawn from the First World War was that any postwar commitments must be widely perceived by Americans as being deeply congruent with US national interests—the American people must "own" the peace. In the summer and early autumn of 1944, this sense of ownership was being taken rather more literally than the patrician technicians at the State Department had expected, by wartime pressure groups, the press, Congress, assorted high-profile individuals, and even ordinary Americans.[16]

Meanwhile, in the splendid isolation of Dumbarton Oaks, the sequestered diplomats were earnestly discussing how earlier organizations for collective security had foundered for want of public understanding and support. That their own process for reaching consensus in many ways replicated the very element of remoteness that they sought to avoid apparently went unremarked by these insiders. Or at least, they did not remark on it enough to change their behavior. But an increasingly vocal cohort of outsiders had definitely noticed the disjuncture between the rhetoric of democracy, inclusion, and sovereign equality and the reality of deference to "experts," exclusivity, and perceived great power arrogance. This gap between rhetoric and reality became an engine of change in its own right, as the Dumbarton Oaks draft made its way across the continent to San Francisco.

"It is no longer a question of whether perpetual peace is really possible . . . we must simply act as if it could really come about"

Early efforts at international organization date from a time before there were actual nation-states to organize. Rulers and merchants in Italian city-states and other emergent polities in what is today Western Europe often sent emissaries to foreign courts. Over time, customs developed for the safe passage of these "diplomats," a title derived from the term for one who carries a diploma, or confidential message folded in two. Mutually honored privileges and immunities smoothed the way for the day-to-day operations of commerce and statecraft and helped maintain useful alliances, or at least orderly coexistence.[17]

In practice, however, such norms were quite minimal, and orderly procedures were more the exception than the rule. A good example of the inconvenience and chaos resulting from the absence of widely observed diplomatic norms was the conduct of the Congress of Westphalia, the six-year-long peace conference that ended the Thirty Years' War in 1648. Settlement of this conflict was delayed for years because of haggling over procedural details, which were ironed out at later conferences and soon came to be considered standard practice. The wastefulness and futility of this war, and the frustration and inefficiency of its settlement, spurred jurists and philosophers to new thinking on the nature of war and peace.

This pattern—of a burst of reformist activity following a particularly destructive armed conflict—would recur in the Western world, shaping and reshaping its ideas and institutions for collective security.[18]

Theorists and philosophers of war and peace writing in the fifteenth and sixteenth centuries, such as the Spanish Dominican friar Francesco de Vitoria, the Spanish Jesuit Francesco Suarez, and the Italian Protestant Alberico Gentili, had been developing theories of aggression, self-defense, and the legitimacy of defense of third parties since the time of Saint Augustine and Saint Thomas Aquinas. These scholars elaborated on the ideas about "just war" they had drawn from the Catholic tradition as well as classical Greek and Roman ideas about the nature of law and war.[19] But it was not until the Thirty Years' War that a writer emerged who could unite the abstractions of theologians with concrete lessons drawn from historical practice. The work of Hugo Grotius was a confluence of the ideas he had drawn from philosophy, theology, and diplomacy. This synthesis is reflected in the eclecticism of Grotius's own career as a theologian, poet, and theorist who was also a diplomat, bureaucrat, and advocate for the Dutch East India Company.[20]

Commentators often use Grotius's life and work to symbolize the leap from the medieval to the modern (and indeed what could be more modern than a stint as a corporate lobbyist between diplomatic posts?). The Dutch jurist is sometimes invoked as the father of international law, a moniker with which analysts of the arguably more pathbreaking work of other scholars often take issue. The point to make about Grotius's writings is not their originality or brilliance but rather their perceived relevance to their immediate political context, the negotiation of the Peace of Westphalia. When a theorist is able to frame ideas in such a way as to support evolving practice, the resulting analysis tends to gain an influence denied to earlier ruminations lacking such connections. "Grotius's achievement," according to an international lawyer writing in 1940, "was that he synthesized what had gone before him and set up a framework of law within which the practice of states could be codified." Contemporary scholars of international relations use the term "Grotian moment" to refer to any such transformative shift in the "modus operandi of international life." The end of the Second World War was such a Grotian moment—a concentrated era when dramatic events catalyzed pre-existing ideas.[21]

By the early nineteenth century, European diplomats had developed a body of agreed-upon practices for parleys over peace, trade, and mutual defense, inaugurated by the Congress of Vienna of 1814–1815.[22]

The victors of the Napoleonic wars—England, Austria, Russia, and Prussia—formed an alliance which stood for stability, the status quo, and "legitimacy," meaning the purity and continuity of the bloodlines of Europe's ruling class. The conservative ideology of this "Concert of Europe" stood in stark opposition to what Charles Webster, a British delegate at Dumbarton Oaks, called "the continued excesses" of revolutionary France, especially its tendencies toward liberal democracy and popular nationalism. Largely because of the erratic participation of England, the Concert's balance of power was short-lived. But within Europe, a more durable and concrete outcome was the convening of periodic conferences among high-level diplomats. The basic idea of keeping interstate relations on an even keel by having regular discussions at the ambassadorial level—as opposed to staging emergency meetings in response to specific crises—was an important impetus for the overarching concept of the League of Nations, as well as the United Nations.[23]

As far as American diplomacy was concerned, the main legacy of the Concert of Europe was the way this "Old World" approach served as a useful foil for the unfolding theme of American exceptionalism in the nineteenth century. The idea of America's self-proclaimed "special mission" in the New World only becomes comprehensible when American ideas and institutions are studied in comparative perspective with Europe. As the sociologist Seymour Martin Lipset has explained, the idea of "American-ness" had always been based on a creed embedded in the Declaration of Independence and other iconic charters. This grounding in beliefs and ideology explains why an American-born individual could become "un-American" by failing to subscribe to what Lipset calls the American creed of "liberty, egalitarianism, individualism, populism and laissez-faire." By contrast, one could not become un-Swedish or un-English based on one's political beliefs, since Europeans drew their national identities from historically delineated communities rooted in immutable accidents of birth, blood, soil, and class.[24]

Consistent with this ideological faith in rules, processes, and institutions, American approaches to "international peace"—what we would today call collective security—tended to feature either a more practical, commercial, legalist orientation or a more utopian, idealistic, moralist approach based on religious ideas. The origins of the more hard-headed legalist orientation trace back to transnational efforts to end piracy, while the more moralistic and utopian approach was rooted in the international abolitionist movement. The legalists sponsored numerous arbitration and arms control congresses, while the moralists tended to favor international labor, women's rights, or peace movements. What the approaches had in common was a tendency to favor the slow accretion of norms and practices such as international congresses and cultural exchanges, and both owed much to Immanuel Kant's famous dictum: "It is no longer a question of whether perpetual peace is really possible or not . . . we must simply act as if it could really come about."[25]

Whether legalist or moralist, American policymakers quite consciously stood aloof from the shifting alliances and Byzantine secret protocols of European power politics. Nineteenth-century American scholars of international law, such as Henry Wheaton, dismissed European balance-of-power machinations as based on a "primitive idea" belonging "rather to the science of politics than of public law," that is, the very antithesis of Lipset's "American creed" of a government of laws and not of men. Whether policymakers envisaged the American experiment as a practical and generalizable blueprint for the world or as a millennial city on a hill, they tended to portray Europe as a source of contamination and decay. Woodrow Wilson's close friend and first biographer, Ray Stannard Baker, wrote of his own young adulthood in 1890s Chicago: "I knew something of European history—the old tyranny of kings, the absurdity of aristocracy, the futility of feudal wars—out of which America, the wonderful, had stepped proudly into the enlightenment of the Bill of Rights and the Declaration of Independence." This kind of imagery was alive and well in the mid-1940s and contributed to the debate over what any proposed post–World War II security organization should look like.[26]

For example, a witness from a right-wing citizens' group, testifying against the "San Francisco Charter" (the United Nations Charter), inquired of the Senate Foreign Relations Committee in 1945, "How can there be peace with two-thirds of the people of the world held in thrall to the wishes of a Big Five? It has been tried before and it failed, and it will ever fail as long as liberty lives in the hearts of men. The Holy Alliance of 1815 was the San Francisco Charter of its time." This witness's choice of language underlined her opinion that the proposed UN Charter was nothing more than an undemocratic great power cartel. Provisions of the UN Charter violated "that immortal document, the Declaration of Independence," because it would "have the power to regulate the intimate details of the lives of our people." She further lamented the passing of the Monroe Doctrine, which "has protected the Western hemisphere and its people from the old world gang for over 100 years . . . The [UN] Charter is the final chapter in the long series of secret commitments by world politicians and financiers, who have planned wars and depressions."[27]

This strand of American isolationism was both anti-imperial and anti-multilateral, complicating standard left–right antinomies about the agenda of those who opposed Roosevelt's wartime foreign policy. The comparison of the newly drafted United Nations Charter to the Holy Alliance, the "old world gang" that was part of the Concert of Europe, was here intended as the worst possible insult, a way of labeling the proposed organization as definitively un-American.

"Had [President Wilson] lived, he would have seen the League concept rise again from this second blood bath of mankind under the name of the United Nations"

The Covenant of the League of Nations was an attempt to strengthen and weave together these legalistic and moralistic strands of what contemporaries often called "intergovernmental unions." International conferences often inaugurated such unions, where high-level diplomats negotiated a charter or constitutional document, setting up an organization that continued under the administration of a permanent secretariat and reconvened at regular intervals, sometimes with ambassadorial-level delegates.

Sometimes portrayed as a feeble emanation from the fevered brain of an ailing Woodrow Wilson, the initial design for the League of Nations incorporated a number of these established nineteenth-century approaches to transnational organization. Early sketches of the League's mission supplemented a mission to suppress armed conflict with articles aimed at disarmament, arbitration of commercial disputes, cultural exchange, suppression of the narcotics trade, and codification of labor standards. These supplemental goals grew out of pre-existing transnational organizations that today we would call NGOs (non-governmental organizations), although many had state support as well. The strongest of these older approaches embodied the interests of merchants who regularly handled situations with some international dimension. The maintenance and regulation of international rivers in Europe, for example, was governed through a well-developed body of "riparian law" that stressed rights to free navigation and equal treatment of all users of the river.[28]

The Paris negotiations trimmed many of these economic, cultural, and legal dimensions from the design of the League, reducing it to a debating society focused on sterile security issues, as British League of Nations advocate Alfred Zimmern summarized in 1936. During the interwar era, the workings of the League were hobbled by the way the organization reflected what Zimmern called "the world situation" existing at the time the organization was set up: "The League was preeminently a league of victor nations and . . . its character in practice would largely be determined by their special interests and concerns." The League as a great power club meant there was "from the beginning, a constant emphasis on the security function of the League."[29]

By the late 1930s and throughout the early 1940s, the League was serving explicitly as a checklist of how *not* to design a mechanism for international peace and security. "While the Covenant makers of 1919 had to build from scratch," explained Amherst political scientist Karl Loewenstein in 1945, "the bricks being mainly the utopian schemes poets, philosophers and visionaries have dreamed through the ages," the drafters of the United Nations Charter "have before their eyes and on their fingertips twenty years and more of the bitter and tale-telling experience of the League of Nations."[30]

Analysis of the League's shortcomings was endlessly fascinating to those 1940s critics we would now call policy wonks, of both legalist and moralist persuasion. They catalogued the League's flaws as including the paralysis-inducing unanimity rule; the absence of teeth to enforce provisions; the lack of truly universal membership; the League's limited economic, social, and cultural mission; and its deliberately weak chief executive. These shortcomings were starkly demonstrated in the organization's ineffectual responses to Japan's invasion of Manchuria in 1931, Italy's invasion of Abyssinia (Ethiopia) in 1935, and Germany's reoccupation of the Rhineland, annexation of Austria, and occupation of Czechoslovakia in the late 1930s.[31]

As a 40-year-old vice-presidential candidate in 1920, Roosevelt had given more than 800 speeches in support of the League of Nations, telling his audiences that if the United States stayed out, the organization would soon degenerate into a new Holy Alliance, dominated by European states. In 1923, as a private citizen recovering from the failure of his election bid, as well as coping with the devastating onset of paralytic polio in 1921, Roosevelt devised a "Plan to Preserve World Peace" (for a contest attracting over 22,000 entries), the most notable feature of which was dispensing with unanimity in decisions involving sanctions and the use of collective force. While unanimity may have made sense when applied to conferences that often had only five or six participants, it would lead to hopeless deadlocks in an organization of forty or fifty members. "Common sense," wrote Roosevelt, "cannot defend a procedure by which one or two recalcitrant nations could block the will of the great majority."[32]

The unanimity rule was an artifact of the legalist view that interstate conflicts are amenable to structured, rule-bound approaches similar to those used to resolve disputes within states. But the use of formal legal procedures was not confined to the League Covenant's conciliation protocols and its affiliated tribunal, the confidently captioned Permanent Court of International Justice. Many of the ordinary functions of the League resembled legal hearings, with interstate issues framed as "disputes" on an implicit model of two opposing litigants. Yet the major conflicts of the interwar period—Germany's resentment of the strictures of the Treaty of Versailles, the demands of Italy and Hungary for further territorial gains, the expansionist ambitions of Japan, and many other conflicts between supporters of the status quo and those soon to be called the "revisionist powers"—did not lend themselves to such judicial-style processes. On the contrary, these disputes were rooted in basic disagreements about the legitimacy of the existing international order itself. As the historian Evan Luard observed, "Legal procedures must depend on some general consensus on what represented a 'just' legal system. At the very least it demanded respect for the 'law' and some agreement as to its content. And none of these existed." By the late 1930s, John Maynard Keynes had taken to calling the revisionist nations "the brigand powers," invoking images of international piracy.[33]

In addition, there were no ultimate sanctions through which an international security organization could impose its judgments. Members papered over what they called "gaps in the Covenant," such as enforcement authority, actual internationalized military forces, arms control provisions, boundary guarantees, and vigorous social and economic agencies, with a patchwork of supplemental pacts and accords. These supplemental agreements were sometimes more technical and legalistic than the Covenant provisions, as in the case of the Washington Arms Control treaties of 1921 and 1925 and the Locarno Treaties of 1925, and at other times more overtly moralistic and aspirational, such as the 1928 Pact of Paris.[34]

A slew of portentious-sounding but ultimately unratified agreements also littered the legal landscape of the interwar era, such as the various iterations of the Geneva Protocol for the Pacific Settlement of International Disputes, starting in 1924. Historians tend to ignore these unratified agreements because the accords were "unenforceable," while legal scholars tend to overestimate the significance of unconsummated agreements as building blocks in a growing edifice of international common law. At a minimum, the lack of official ratification was emblematic of a gap in understanding between international lawyers and diplomats, on the one hand, and educated public opinion within the League member states, on the other, and it was evidence of the absence of multilateral accord on both the substance and process of international law.[35]

This lack of solidarity on collective measures to resist aggression was the main obstacle to the League's success, many contemporaneous analysts believed, and it was rooted primarily in domestic politics. "The textual weaknesses [of the League Covenant] might not have mattered so much if the spirit had been strong," argues Luard. The overarching lesson of the League experience was that the powers of any multilateral organization "depended utterly on a willingness to use them: that is, on the policies and attitudes of individual members. If these lacked resolution to resist aggression, no organisation, whatever its constitutional structure, could preserve the peace." Commentators from the 1940s agreed. The most "serious criticism of the League," wrote political scientists Max and Edna Lerner in an educational pamphlet in 1943, "was that its whole conception of international relationships was a narrowly political one." Such an approach "ignored the psychological and economic realities" of growth and change on the international scene, and unsuccessfully "superimposed a static political building on a shifting economic quicksand."[36]

Despite its flaws, over the two decades of its existence the League of Nations enjoyed several notable successes, and American planners hoped to learn from those "wins" as well as from the many losses. They included the management of specific international controversies not involving the great powers, such as a stubborn frontier dispute between Finland and Sweden; the innovative mandates system, ostensibly for the protection and advancement of dependent territories (although in practice its workings hardly differed from prewar colonialism); the League's most active affiliated agency, the International Labor Organization; and the League's architecture itself, based on an assembly, a council, a secretariat, and an international court.[37]

In drafting the UN charter, delegates looked to the League of Nations as a cautionary tale about the domestic pitfalls of multilateralism and as an example of traps to avoid—but also, in very limited ways, as a model worth emulating. The UN draft and the Covenant of the League seemed so similar to former President Herbert Hoover that he noted, in his sympathetic account of the negotiation of the Treaty of Versailles, *The Ordeal of Woodrow Wilson*, that, had Wilson lived, "he would have seen the League concept rise again from this second blood bath of mankind under the name of the United Nations."[38]

"Asking a man whether he wants an international police force is like asking him whether he wants the Rockettes"

In the spring and summer of 1941 few Americans had any opinion about "what should be done to maintain world peace after the present European war is over," in the phrasing of a Gallup poll of the day. Only 34 percent of respondents had devoted any thought to this issue. As far as most Americans were concerned, European wars were for Europeans. Those who responded in the affirmative ranked prescriptions for peace in the following order: "An international federation; moral, social, and political reform based on toleration and Christian principles; divide Germany among the victors."[39]

Not quite a year and a half later, Gallup asked again, this time specifically about a collective security organization. Pearl Harbor, military conscription, and a deluge of war news—much of it featuring sobering analyses of setbacks in the Pacific or heroic portraits of America's allies—had intervened. Now 73 percent of respondents wanted to see the United States join what the pollsters were still calling a "postwar League of Nations." These extraordinary numbers held steady over the following year. When asked in March 1943 whether they believed that "the United States should stay out of world affairs, or take an active part in world affairs" in the postwar era, 76 percent thought that the United States should take an active part. Even more specifically, in the summer of 1943, 76 percent agreed that the countries fighting the Axis should "set up an international police force after the war is over to try to keep peace throughout the world." These numbers were all the more impressive after wartime public opinion analysts explained that a consensus of greater than 70 percent meant virtual unanimity in such a heterogeneous society.[40]

But what were these scientifically sampled citizens of Main Street really favoring? "Doctor Gallup, the asker, has asked people whether they favor an international police force, and three out of four have said they do," noted the essayist E. B. White in an anonymous editorial published in the *New Yorker* in the spring of 1943. "That is very nice," he continued, "it is also quite misleading. Asking a man if he wants an international police force is like asking him if he wants the Rockettes"—desirable in the abstract, perhaps, but totally unrealistic when it comes down to specifics. It is unsurprising that a wide spectrum of wartime public opinion favored some mechanism for making the postwar world safe for Americans. The surprise is, rather, that large numbers across the regional and political spectrum seemed to be taking it for granted that such solutions would be implemented through League-like multilateral institutions with independent enforcement powers.[41]

A combination of factors had opened the American mind to the desirability of collective security. Opinion leaders and internationalist pressure groups were one part of the story. After Vice President Henry Wallace gave a little-noticed speech to one such group in New York City in May 1942, his utopian phrases were publicized by the liberal newspaper *PM* and soon came to represent the internationalist vanguard of American public opinion. Wallace argued that the world conflict was part of a "long-drawn-out people's revolution" that would mark the twentieth century down as "the century of the common man." In a phrase drawing on the heritage of the Civil War, Wallace spoke of World War II as "a fight between a slave world and a free world," a caption that enjoyed an enduring afterlife in the Cold War. The columnist Raymond Clapper labeled the speech "the Gettysburg Address of World War II," while the federal Office of Facts and Figures published it as a pamphlet and distributed hundreds of thousands of copies.[42]

Meanwhile, Wendell Willkie, Roosevelt's vanquished Republican rival from the 1940 election, wrote a polemic about the international tour he had undertaken in August 1942 at FDR's suggestion. *One World* was published in the spring of 1943, in an initial print run of 40,000 copies. The first printing sold out in forty-eight hours, and almost 200,000 copies had sold by the end of the first week. Two printing plants ran their presses around the clock to keep up with the demand for 25,000 copies a day over the ensuing weeks. *One World* became the best-selling work of nonfiction in every city the *New York Times* surveyed for its weekly ranking.

"Continents and oceans are plainly only parts of a whole, seen, as I have seen them, from the air," Willkie wrote, "and it is inescapable that there can be no peace for any part of the world unless the foundations for peace are made secure throughout all parts of the world." One reviewer described Willkie as at least "128 years ahead of the State Department," which was unflatteringly described as "still planning in terms of the Congress of Vienna." This utopian strand of internationalist thinking was still gaining momentum in 1944, with a series of popular speeches by Sumner Welles (now a private citizen) arguing explicitly that Wilsonian ideals should be reaffirmed, and a widely publicized 1944 film, *Wilson,* produced by Darryl F. Zanuck, which made for emotional viewing by State Department policy planners, among others.[43]

Robert Divine calls Wallace, Willkie, and Welles the "three prophets," but implies that they were prophets without honor, both for publicly failing in their career ambitions and for being too far in the vanguard of even the most liberal wing of American public opinion. Even Breckinridge Long, a free-trade internationalist in the Hull camp at the State Department, referred to Wallace as one of the "Post War Dream Boys." While the books, articles, and speeches of these three publicists often garnered dramatic public support, anti–New Dealers and anti-internationalists saw the Wallace, Willkie, and even Welles proposals as particular targets of invective.[44]

Henry Luce, publisher of *Time* magazine, and several other high-profile Republican internationalists resented the attempt by fellow-Republican Willkie to out-Roosevelt Roosevelt. Luce's internationalism was a sort of globalized version of the Frederick Jackson Turner "frontier thesis" from the late nineteenth century. In its twentieth-century iteration, "the American frontier now encompassed the world, one which hungered for food and hope and American know-how," in the words of one Luce biographer. Feeding and equipping the world would in turn boost the productivity of America's farms and factories. To Luce, the twentieth century was the "American Century" (the title of the famous essay he published in *Time*'s February 1941 issue). He objected to what he saw as the antibusiness, collectivist slant of the New Deal, and he also disliked and distrusted Roosevelt personally. But the publishing mogul was equally critical of Republicans who would have America turn its back on its global responsibilities. (It so happened that Luce also disliked Senator Robert A. Taft, one of the Republicans' principal isolationist leaders, and had used his magazine empire to ridicule the senator's presidential aspirations.)

For Luce, the US Constitution and Bill of Rights were best understood as "our free gift to all peoples," while American values centering around free enterprise and individualism would serve as a "powerhouse from which the ideals spread throughout the world." The *Reader's Digest* and *Washington Post* reprinted Luce's "American Century" essay, and Luce himself distributed thousands of free copies to schoolchildren; he also bought space for the essay to be excerpted in the *New York Times*. Stanley Hornbeck, one of the State Department's experts on Asia, circulated excerpts within the State Department. In his crusading zeal, Luce resembled his own missionary father, who at the turn of the last century had set out to spread the blessings of Christianity in China, as one Luce family member pointed out. Luce's vision of America in the world came to dominate the field during the Cold War, combining the moralism of Wilson with the trade-oriented dollar diplomacy of Theodore Roosevelt and William Howard Taft.[45]

The real significance of popular commentators such as Welles, Wallace, Willkie, Luce, and the journalist and essayist Walter Lippmann was not their direct influence on policy so much as their role as gadflies. Dramatic outpourings of support for their views tended to evoke strong counter-reactions. Responding specifically to Wallace's Common Man speech, for example, the president of the National Association of Manufacturers famously pointed out that "I am not making guns or tanks to win a 'people's revolution.' I am making armament to help our boys save America . . . I am not fighting for a quart of milk for every Hottentot, or for a TVA [Tennessee Valley Authority] on the Danube."[46]

Republican isolationists—who might more accurately be described as anti-interventionists or unilateralists—objected to what they saw as America's attempt to take Britain's place as the policeman of the world. Senator Robert A. Taft of Ohio, son of President William H. Taft and himself a perennial presidential aspirant, strenuously protested Luce's American Century argument, seeing it as nakedly imperialistic. "Our fingers will be in every pie," Taft lamented, rather presciently. "Our military forces will work with our commercial forces to obtain as much of the world trade as we can lay our hands on. We will occupy all the strategic points in the world and try to maintain a force so preponderant that none shall dare attack us. How long can nations restrain themselves from using such force . . . Potential power over other nations, however benevolent its purpose, leads inevitably to imperialism." The United States should instead focus on the fact that "the only effective way in which we can spread the four freedoms throughout the world is by the force of our own example." In a 1943 address to the American Bar Association in Chicago, Taft dismissed the possibility of turning the resources of sovereign states over to "President Whoozis of Worlditania," a program which, he observed scornfully, "may appeal to the do-gooders who regard it as the manifest destiny of America to confer the benefits of the New Deal on every Hottentot."[47]

Such colorful invective sparked debate, increasing overall public awareness. While liberals favored the positions of Welles or Willkie, droves of more conservative respondents supported the positions of Henry Luce or Walter Lippmann, and a plurality converged over the free trade internationalism of Cordell Hull. The 1941 Atlantic Charter itself reflected this synthetic middle ground: an article titled "An American Program for Joint Action" appeared in the May 1942 edition of *Fortune* magazine, pointing to the Atlantic Charter as a demonstration that "in permanent collaboration with our allies lies a way to greater freedom than the world has ever seen" and featuring a photograph of Roosevelt and Churchill at the joint Anglo-American church service aboard the *Prince of Wales*. And the nation as a whole had shifted farther out along an internationalist trajectory than it probably would have without such vociferous public debate.[48]

Published poll results on international topics often broke the responses down by region, based on the assumption that the Midwest was more isolationist than the coasts. (One impetus for this assumption was voting patterns in the Senate during the First World War, when midwestern senators had voted along more isolationist lines.) In fact, Gallup and other polls from the 1940s consistently reflected only the most minor regional variations. The stereotype of the Midwest as stubbornly isolationist persisted, however, and an internationalist pressure group, the Commission to Study the Organization of Peace, accordingly designed an unintentionally hilarious pamphlet aimed specifically at selling multilateralism to midwestern farmers. "Neighboring is a two-way proposition," the pamphlet explained in as folksy a manner as its Manhattan-based authors could muster, and "this is just as true with nations as it is with individuals . . . Just as pigs need to huddle together on a cold night, the world's many nations need to stick together."[49]

At least these academic activists considered farmers to be capable of reading connected prose. Women were another story. *Ladies' Home Journal* published a seven-page cartoon version of Walter Lippmann's best-selling *US Foreign Policy: Shield of the Republic*, discussing a promised postwar era of order, security, and well-being—the same qualities one hoped to find in a good marriage. An advertisement for Eureka vacuum cleaners explained to women consumers that by "fighting for freedom and all that means to women everywhere, you're fighting for a little house of your own, and a husband to meet every night at the door" (a little house that would, presumably, need constant vacuuming).[50]

Public opinion in the American constitutional system is expressed most concretely through the workings of the people's representatives in Congress. This always-messy process became a somewhat more direct expression of popular will—or the dominant competing strands of the popular will—after the advent of public opinion polling in 1935. The transition to internationalism of one of the Senate's most ardent isolationists, Arthur Vandenberg, Republican of Michigan and senior minority representative on the Senate Foreign Relations Committee, was a case in point. Vandenberg represented a state with a large Polish population and thus had every incentive to become a grandstanding anti-Soviet demagogue. As US officials debated plans for the postwar world, the vain and verbose Vandenberg had a chance to act as the Henry Cabot Lodge of his day. But he chose not to travel this path. Instead, he accepted informal appointments from the secretary of state in a Democratic administration to serve on an assortment of postwar policy planning panels. In addition, he served on an advisory panel of senators working behind the scenes at Dumbarton Oaks; he made one of the most widely acclaimed internationalist speeches ever offered on the Senate floor; he offered his own amendments to the Dumbarton Oaks proposals advocating an increased role for international law and "adjustments to the status quo in line with principles of international justice"; and went on to serve as one of the most effective American delegates to the 1945 San Francisco Conference founding the United Nations.[51]

Contemporaries often described Vandenberg's dramatic *volte-face*, whether admiringly or contemptuously, as a "conversion." The obvious question is what motivated it. In addition to having the advantage of witnessing the opprobrium history was already heaping on his predecessor, Henry Cabot Lodge (and the stratospheric levels of adulation for Lodge's nemesis, Woodrow Wilson), Vandenberg was differently situated from World War I–era isolationist senators in two other important ways. He had a chance to see specific and detailed public opinion polls, often broken down by region, age, or education, as a supplement to the impressionistic process of reviewing his mail and talking with constituents. And he could see how the Roosevelt administration had absorbed one of the fundamental lessons of the interwar League fight: that it was important to lay the groundwork for bipartisan support of any prospective postwar multilateral commitments and to shore up such groundwork early and often, especially with the Senate.

Vandenberg was the biggest individual beneficiary of this policy, as his roster of appointments suggests. By contrast, Assistant Secretary of State Dean Acheson recalled cynically that these talking-shops for postwar planning were a big waste of time, as embodying "a sort of mechanistic idealism." Acheson himself had chaired one of these innumerable planning committees, most of which were based in the State Department, though he later confessed he could not recall any of the many meetings he attended. "Paging through the printed report, the whole effort, except for two results, seems to have been a singularly sterile one, uninspired by gifts of either insight or prophecy." And what were these two bright spots? "One of these was the foundation work for the United Nations Charter; the other, which laid an even broader foundation, [was] the education of Senator Arthur Vandenberg to understanding that beyond the borders of the United States existed a vast external realm which could and would affect profoundly our interests and our destiny."[52]

In autumn of 1943, congressional debates over two high-profile resolutions on the American commitment to a postwar international security organization induced a jolt of presidential leadership. Representative William Fulbright of Arkansas sponsored a short, straightforward resolution expressing Congress's favorable view of "the creation of appropriate international machinery with power adequate to maintain a just and lasting peace, among the nations of the world" and advocating "participation by the United States" in such an organization. Senator Tom Connally of Texas, chair of the Senate Foreign Relations Committee, sponsored the other resolution, focusing on staking out a role for "constitutional processes"—meaning Senate approval—before the United States would assume a role in an international organization. The more assertive Connally resolution, which passed the Senate in November 1943 with a vote of 85 to 5, also put in a plug for the protection of the sovereignty of individual member states, while conceding that the "establishment and maintenance of international authority with power to prevent aggression" should be "established at the earliest practicable date." The Senate resolution was so unexceptionable that even Taft voted for it.[53]

This active public debate also catalyzed the continuing but somewhat desultory State Department planning that had earlier fallen victim to turf wars between Hull and Welles. Public opinion was the engine driving this revitalization of the administration's interest in planning. Roosevelt was well aware that 78 percent of Americans polled by Gallup in the summer of 1943 had indicated that they supported the Fulbright resolution's call for a postwar international security organization.[54]

"No charter is required to put the great powers on top of the heap. They are there already"

At the beginning of 1944 the governments of the United States, Great Britain, and the USSR had started regular consultations about their proposals for a postwar security organization, as their foreign ministers had agreed at Moscow in 1943. British Foreign Minister Anthony Eden believed that the United States should take the initiative in this process, and a preoccupied Soviet Union did not object. In February President Roosevelt gave preliminary approval to the ideas set out in one of the elaborate State Department plans. After a protracted Soviet silence, the principals signed off on State Department policy planner Alger Hiss's suggestion that the United States convene an informal planning meeting in the summer of 1944 at Dumbarton Oaks. Sino-Soviet relations were virtually nonexistent, and the Soviets objected to Chinese participation in the planning conversations, insisting that a virtually prostrate China, dependent on US aid, should not be considered a great power. American planners proposed the rather stilted compromise that the Soviet Union would participate in the first round of the talks and China immediately join thereafter in a second round. British negotiators agreed, although they too doubted that China belonged in the first tier of great power planners. (Churchill famously referred to the Chinese "pigtails" as "a faggot vote for the United States.")[55]

Document collections and educational pamphlets published by the State Department and other internationalist sources during World War II tended to start with the 1941 Atlantic Charter as the fountainhead of modern planning for collective security, as opposed to the more relevant Covenant of the League of Nations (or even the precepts of Immanuel Kant). The editors of these publications had absorbed FDR's own position that the world was making a fresh start, with a founding document that was simultaneously multilateral and truly American. But in fact, this fresh start was more for public consumption than for the experts behind the scenes. The Dumbarton Oaks draft that emerged in the autumn of 1944 was most remarkable for how much it resembled the old League Covenant, protests to the contrary notwithstanding.[56]

The opening sessions of the Soviet phase of the Dumbarton Oaks conversations focused on nomenclature. The Soviets proposed that the new organization be called the International Security Organization. They accepted an American counterproposal that security would be adequately emphasized by renaming the Executive Council of the great powers the Security Council. The Soviets then proposed World Union as the title of the general organization. The Americans objected on the grounds that a World Union was exactly what unilateralist American opponents of the whole project most feared. The others finally deferred to the American proposal to call the new organization the United Nations—a name Roosevelt had devised in late 1941 for the anti-Axis alliance. The term had been in continuous use since 1942 by both European and American postwar planners, and the Dumbarton Oaks drafters adopted it despite the Soviet insistence that it had no acceptable Russian translation.[57]

American negotiators also argued for the term "charter" as the name of the UN's constitutional document because "from Magna Carta to the Atlantic Charter this term has meant liberty and freedom under law, which is the essence of this instrument." The term struck the perfect note as far as State Department planners were concerned—more legalistic and less evangelical than a covenant and less formal (and presumably less binding) than a constitution.[58]

Despite some initial Soviet resistance, the delegates gravitated toward the detailed proposals of the Americans as a basis for discussion. There was little inclination to challenge a League-like structure for the UN: a General Assembly with representatives from every member state; a Security Council consisting of four or five permanent great power members as well as several other rotating members, which would have the main responsibility for considering questions of peace and security; an International Secretariat under a chief executive; and an International Court of Justice to rule on legal disputes arising between states.

Delegates agreed that the most powerful nations, which was to say themselves, must take an active role in enforcing any kind of world peacekeeping scheme. Roosevelt's idea of the "Four Policemen" was the starkest expression of this orientation. And they further agreed that the unanimity rule, bane of the League's existence, should be abolished for all except the permanent members. Where the use of force seemed likely, the Security Council could "take any measures necessary for the maintenance of international peace and security." It could start with sanctions or breaking off communications (a direct import from the League); but if such measures failed, it could take action through air, naval, or land forces, including blockades. Each member of the organization would "obligate" itself to accept and carry out the Security Council's decisions.[59]

The two major areas of disagreement among the Dumbarton Oaks planners were the scope of the four nations' veto power and the voting process in the Security Council. Both touched on the extent of great power dominance. Minor disagreements included criteria for membership, both in the Security Council and in the General Assembly; lingering British proposals favoring more regional approaches; the precise type of military force that would be at the Security Council's disposal; and the role of economic and social appendages, if any.

The intractable controversy over the veto continued to plague negotiators right through the drafting of the final UN Charter and was only resolved by the personal intervention of Stalin, after Harry Hopkins and others prevailed upon him to issue new instructions to his negotiators. The Dumbarton Oaks negotiators had no difficulty agreeing on the general principle that they themselves should enjoy the right to prevent any unacceptable decision. The controversy erupted over the way the system would operate when one of the great powers was itself involved in a dispute or a complaint. The Soviet Union insisted on blanket veto, holding that a great power should be able to prevent any action by the Security Council—even including measures of peaceful settlement—when it was itself involved. American and British analysts eventually concluded that any enforcement action against a major power would necessarily mean that the organization had already failed in its core mission of preventing armed conflict, possibly resulting in "all-out war, probably World War III. In such a case, the peacekeeping organization would be out of business anyway, so they might as well agree on the need for unanimity."[60]

Other controversies swirled around the relative weight of the great powers vis-à-vis one another, as expressed through several differences over voting and membership provisions. The United States had originally wanted a system of weighted voting in the General Assembly for decisions on financial questions, somewhat along the lines of the system of voting adopted at Bretton Woods for the World Bank. But this was unacceptable to the others, as it would have given a large proportion of the votes to the United States. An eventual consensus was found for having a simple majority rule apply for most questions in the Assembly, with a two-thirds majority needed only for "important" questions, including budgetary matters.

Regarding membership in the General Assembly, "Gromyko exploded a bombshell by demanding that each of the sixteen Soviet republics should be an individual member," wrote Stettinius in his diary. "FDR said the idea was 'absurd' and told me that it would be just as logical for the United States to demand forty-eight memberships, one for each state." Fearing the effect of this proposal on American public opinion, "Roosevelt ordered that it be kept as quiet as possible . . . Within the American delegation it was referred to as the 'X matter,' and was the only aspect of the meeting that did not leak to the press." Well aware that communist states would be a tiny minority in the new organization, the Soviets came up with this device to help redress the imbalance. Other negotiators record being quite shocked at the Soviet proposal—although, when set against the US trial balloon exploring an overall weighted voting system, it might seem somewhat less illegitimate. Stalin sent FDR a telegram arguing that the republics enjoyed autonomy under the newly adopted Soviet constitution and that some had far larger populations than many independent states.[61]

With no resolution in sight, the diplomats agreed to shelve the X-matter for the moment. (It was later the subject of a controversial secret protocol at the February 1945 Yalta Conference.) In addition, there was no agreement about whether the "associated states" not formally at war with the Axis powers but committed to the Allied cause (mainly Latin American states) should be members from the start and invited to the initial conference establishing the organization. Turning to the less controversial topic of membership in the Security Council, the British wanted to include France as a counterweight to a possible resurgence of Germany, and Secretary Hull (who was constantly being consulted behind the scenes) agreed. But Roosevelt preferred Brazil, supposedly for wider geographical distribution, although this proposal seems more likely to have been motivated by FDR's personal dislike of Charles de Gaulle. In general, whenever the opportunity arose, the Soviets pursued a policy of concentrating authority in the Security Council, where they held a veto, and would cling to this position until the USSR's dissolution in 1991.[62]

There were also differences between the Soviet Union and all the rest on economic and social provisions. The non-communist powers felt that the absence of these provisions had hamstrung the League of Nations, and they wanted the new organization to take on considerably more responsibilities in these arenas. The Soviet Union, concerned about minimizing pretexts for interference in the domestic affairs of member states, wanted to restrict the organization to matters of peace and security. Both the Soviets and the British objected to an American proposal that the General Assembly should be able to make recommendations "for the promotion of the observance of basic human rights," concerned that such a provision might allow the UN to intervene in domestic affairs, in violation of national sovereignty. They even resisted a revised draft that merely mentioned the responsibility of each state "to respect the human rights and fundamental freedoms of all its people," arguing that the domestic policies of states were not the organization's concern.

Stettinius, however, continued to press "our hope" that a reference to human rights and fundamental freedoms "can be included in some place in the document," urged on by his most active advisors on human rights and domestic jurisdiction, Leo Pasvolsky and Ben Cohen. (A handwritten correction in the unpublished version of Stettinius's diary alters the original typescript, which read "Promise of respect for human rights and fundamental freedoms." Stettinius substituted "Promotion" of respect for human rights above the crossed-out "Promise.") After Roosevelt expressed his personal interest in the matter, the Soviet representative negotiated for instructions from Moscow to make a concession on the point, inducing the British representative to do the same. The diplomats finally agreed that the organization would "promote respect for human rights and fundamental freedoms," a development which "gratified" Roosevelt, according to Stettinius, since the president "felt the inclusion of the human rights sentence was extremely vital."[63]

The Soviet phase of the Dumbarton Oaks conversations dragged out over five weeks. For the Chinese phase, Stettinius was careful to re-stage the opening ceremony in the Dumbarton Oaks music room, complete with welcoming statements of good will and high hopes. However, Cadogan, the head of the British contingent, left town immediately after delivering what he briskly termed "my usual little speech." The Chinese were then presented with the American-British-Soviet draft and told that if they had any quibbles they should submit them in a separate paper. Otherwise it would interfere with the schedule for producing a completed draft in a prearranged press release in only a week's time.[64]

Wellington Koo, the urbane, Columbia-educated head of the Chinese delegation, suggested supplementing the existing draft with a statement of moral principles that could serve as a touchstone for the rest of the document, as well as arguing that "the Charter should provide specifically that adjustment or settlement of international disputes should be achieved with due regard for principles of justice and international law." The Chinese delegation also advocated that the organization "should be responsible for initiating studies and making recommendations with respect to the development and revision of the rules and principles of international law"—in other words, that the UN should build in some mechanisms for adjusting to a changing status quo, rather than merely serving as one more ossifying force in international politics. The British and Americans dismissed these concerns as too "idealistic" to be particularly valuable.[65]

On October 9, 1944, the State Department published its press release as planned, cabling the Proposals for the Establishment of a General International Organization simultaneously to Washington, Moscow, London, and Chungking. Belying the initial framing as the product of informal "conversations," the US administration immediately began pointing to the Dumbarton Oaks proposals as evidence of a deep and abiding Big Four consensus. When a reporter asked why the Soviet phase had taken so long, Roosevelt replied, "We are trying to work out a world that will probably be free from wars, and you don't just call a conference in the morning and solve that largest of human problems by four o'clock in the afternoon." FDR added that the delegates had agreed on 90 percent of the issues, "what we used to call in the old days a darned good batting average."[66]

Part of this 90 percent consensus—Stettinius's assessment in his diary was 75 percent—was an agreement to disagree on highly contentious issues such as the veto question and separate representation for individual Soviet republics. The negotiators had also set aside other questions for later consideration, such as a proposed trusteeship system to replace the League of Nations mandate system and the extent of any modifications to the International Court of Justice. Above all, the Dumbarton Oaks proposals showed that "the great powers had decided that their own interests were too important to entrust to an international body." Or, as an analysis by an eminent study group at Yale observed succinctly, "No charter is required to put the great powers on top of the heap. They are there already."[67]

CHAPTER 6

LEARNING TO
WORK TOGETHER
BY WORKING TOGETHER

In a public affairs radio broadcast in early 1945, a lower-level State Department official from the Office of Special Political Affairs remarked, somewhat disingenuously, that "the articulate will of the masses of our people [had] provided a constant guide" for the cloistered experts at Dumbarton Oaks. "This reciprocal relationship between the government and the people is a major aspect of democracy," he added helpfully. Editorialists generally interpreted the fact that the much-anticipated Dumbarton Oaks proposals pleased no one completely as a sign that the draft was probably a fair compromise, given a world "still ruled by selfish powers." Another editorial in *The New Republic* reasoned, "It is a practical device, suited to the realities of the situation, rather than an idealistic dream put on paper. As long as these characteristics are maintained, we need not worry too much about the details."[1]

Prominent internationalists duly logged their endorsements, such as Columbia University President Nicholas Murray Butler, Justice of the Permanent Court of International Justice Manley O. Hudson, President of the American Society of International Law Frederic Coudert, President of the Congress of Industrial Organizations Philip Murray, and foreign affairs analyst Walter Lippmann. The ubiquitous James T. Shotwell, Columbia University historian and director of numerous internationalist pressure groups, was one of the most enthusiastic commentators, effusing that the "Dumbarton Oaks agreement . . . seems almost too good to be true."[2]

Some internationalist commentators put the best face on the absence of detailed provisions for specific problems of collective security in the Dumbarton Oaks draft, describing these silences as sources of flexibility that might serve to make the draft less controversial. Vera Micheles Dean, research director of the Foreign Policy Association, commented favorably that "the Dumbarton Oaks proposals, unlike the League [of Nations] Covenant, did not contain a long list of fundamental principles about international problems such as disarmament, treatment of back-ward peoples, [and] labor or health conditions," thus making the result-ing organization "more adaptable to changing circumstances." But other commentators expressed concern about key omissions, reasoning that the relevant provisions would need to be negotiated later.[3]

"Our [new] League needs a soul"

For American observers, the two most important gaps in the proposals included the absence of voting procedures in the Security Council, and unresolved implications for domestic politics, such as whether the Senate would need to approve the use of American troops each time, or only approve the executive branch's initial commitment to an organization that was authorized to send troops. Arguments about these two items be-came issues in the 1944 US presidential election, held less than a month after the publication of the Dumbarton Oaks draft. FDR apparently became worried after his Republican opponent, Governor Thomas E. Dewey of New York, began attacking "Washington wasters" who "talk glibly of an American WPA [Works Projects Administration] for all the rest of the world." While this remark was presumably aimed at Vice Pres-ident Henry Wallace, it stung Roosevelt as well.[4]

Other Republicans tried to make a campaign issue of Roosevelt's age (62) after photos appeared of the president looking tired and ill in pub-lic. "Well, here we are together again—after four years," remarked a la-conic Roosevelt during a speech at a Teamsters Union dinner in Septem-ber 1944, "and what years they have been! You know, I am actually four years older, which is a fact that seems to annoy some people." The presi-dent proceeded, rather more pointedly, to paint his Republican oppo-nents as isolationists "who first woke up to the facts of international life a few short months ago—when they began to study the polls of public opinion." In a speech to the Foreign Policy Association in October 1944, Roosevelt explained that "the [Security] Council of the United Nations must have the power to act quickly and decisively to keep the peace by force, if necessary." He then vividly elaborated on these "facts of interna-tional life": "A policeman would not be a very effective policeman if, when he saw a felon break into a house, he had to go to the town hall and call a meeting before the felon could be arrested. If we do not catch the international felon when we get our hands on him . . . then we are not do-ing our share to prevent another world war."[5]

Undisputed master of the homespun image since well before his Lend-Lease-as-fire-hose days, FDR then linked his argument to the debate over Senate authorization for using US troops in UN operations: "So to my simple mind it is clear that, if the world organization is to have any reality at all, our American representative must be endowed in advance by the people themselves, by constitutional means through their representatives in the Congress, with authority to act." The unacceptable alternative was "to let a criminal escape because the town meeting has not passed an ordinance for his arrest." Once again, the polls—both election and opinion polls—supplied what was widely interpreted as a definitive response. The Democrats garnered an additional thirty seats in the House and maintained their Senate majority, while prominent isolationists of both parties lost their posts. "The election results have announced to the world that 1944 is not 1920!" proclaimed *The Nation*.[6]

Secretary Hull, ailing and disillusioned, resigned shortly after the 1944 election and was replaced by the energetic, 44-year-old Edward Stettinius. The new secretary then put the noted internationalist Archibald MacLeish, poet and former librarian of Congress, at the head of an unusually creative publicity campaign in favor of the Dumbarton Oaks proposals. Still, some constituencies on both left and right expressed outright dismay with the proposals. In the pages of *The New Yorker*, E. B. White sarcastically noted that the "Fifty Sovereign Nations of the World Solemnly Sworn to Prevent Each Other from Committing Aggression" had all the cohesion of marbles in a dish: "Put your toe in the dish and the marbles will scatter, each to its own corner." The socialist presidential candidate Norman Thomas observed caustically that "the cure for a dangerous isolation is not a more dangerous membership in an international gang of exploiters." Senator Burton Wheeler, an isolationist, concurred, asserting that "Dumbarton Oaks is a grim hoax . . . designed to put the United States in the position of holding the draw strings of an international grab bag while Britain and Russia connive or fight for the spoils."[7]

Administration proponents of the proposals and press advocates alike countered by calling on the general public to avoid the Versailles-era sins of "perfectionism." Freda Kirchwey, editor of *The Nation*, was one among many arguing along the lines that "the alternative to an unsatisfactory international order is not generally a satisfactory international order; it is uncontrolled power politics, international anarchy, and everything thrown into the lap of the nation with the fiercest appetite and most brutal arrogance."[8]

Many of the "smaller states"—small by the criterion of great power status—expressed disappointment in the timidity of the Dumbarton Oaks draft. On the initiative of Mexican Foreign Minister Ezequiel Padilla, members of the Pan American Union met at Chapultepec castle, near Mexico City, in February 1945 to offer a critique of the Dumbarton Oaks draft in advance of the full United Nations Conference on International Organization (UNCIO) slated for later that spring. As Vera Dean phrased it, the Latin American states believed that the Dumbarton Oaks proposals "left much to be desired in the way of adequate guarantees and stronger representation for the small nations."[9]

This Chapultepec conference was part of a venerable tradition of inter-American relations dating back to nineteenth-century expressions of pan-American solidarity, institutionalized and extended after 1890. These periodic conferences involved a series of multilateral statements pledging cooperation and mutual respect, informed by the perspective of trying to temper the interventionism of "the colossus to the North." In 1945 the Pan American Union invited members who were "united and associated American states cooperating in the war effort"—that is, excluding Argentina, where the fascist-leaning government of General Edelmiro Farrell had seized power in 1944. The nineteen Latin American participants aired their longstanding concerns about non-intervention and preservation of sovereignty. But in the waning months of the war, these representatives were just as worried about the United States abandoning regional security in favor of an all-encompassing commitment to an untested UN system—a system run by a Security Council with no Latin American member.[10]

Pledging to support and expand FDR's "Good Neighbor" policy, the convenors framed the Chapultepec meeting as internationalizing the Monroe Doctrine, making it into a regional collective security pact. Other agenda items included: approving provisions for wartime security measures; discussing the appropriate circumstances under which Argentina might rejoin the Union; negotiating an "Economic Charter of the Americas"; and approving a series of declarations on coordinated policies for war criminals, freedom of information, and control of enemy property.[11]

But the key agenda item for the Latin American delegates was their detailed and trenchant critique of the Dumbarton Oaks draft, with an eye to developing points which "should be taken into consideration in the formulation of the definitive charter" at San Francisco, in the words of the conference's final statement. Their two main concerns related to a stronger voice for Latin American countries and broadening the charter's vision of human rights. The delegation from Nicaragua admonished that "the peace and security of the world" now depended on "all nations, large and small, adopting in their international relations . . . solid principles of equality and justice, of liberty and law, principles that find their most faithful expression in the [1941] Atlantic Charter," while the Bolivian representatives proposed that language about self-determination should be strengthened by drawing from the Atlantic Charter example.[12]

Conference President Padilla, who had formerly served as Mexico's attorney general and as a revolutionary leader under Pancho Villa, explained that wartime solidarity needed to be converted "into a solidarity of peace; a solidarity that considers the poverty of the people, its social instability, its malnutrition." His proposals included inserting more specific human rights provisions in the principles and purposes of the organization, creating an international agency charged with promoting "intellectual and moral cooperation" among nations, and expanding the jurisdiction of the international tribunal associated with the organization.[13]

Padilla also offered an overarching analysis from the perspective of all the countries excluded by the Dumbarton Oaks process: that "the small nations do not pretend to equal participation in a world of unequal responsibility. What they do desire is that, in the hour in which injustice may strike at the doors of small nations, their voice may be heard: that they may appeal to the universal conscience, and that their complaints and protests against injustice shall not be shrouded in the silence and blind solidarity of the great powers." In addition to the Chapultepec critique, other "small" countries offering human rights–related comments on the Dumbarton Oaks proposals included the members of the British Commonwealth, who met in April 1945 in London, as well as Egypt, Greece, Lebanon, and Turkey, among others, all of which asked for more expansive language on the role of international law in the new institution. Australia and New Zealand met in Wellington in November 1944 and similarly developed a joint proposal calling for a greater role for smaller powers and expanded human rights provisions, particularly regarding social and economic rights.[14]

The comparatively restrained reception of the Dumbarton Oaks draft, even among its supporters, was "perhaps due to the over-legalistic phraseology of a document devoid of any literary appeal, and to its lack of idealism and ideological courage," wrote the Amherst political science professor Karl Loewenstein in April 1945, who concluded, "emotionally the [Dumbarton Oaks] proposals have been a dud." The economic historian Broadus Mitchell concurred, noting regretfully that "the Atlantic Charter and the Four Freedoms promised America and the world a much more courageous plan than Dumbarton Oaks turned out to be." This kind of ideological courage was exactly what the Chinese negotiators had sought at their truncated phase of the Dumbarton Oaks talks, and what many of the modifications proposed by other nations not invited to Dumbarton Oaks had sought to introduce. As Senator Vandenberg concluded in his own proposed amendments, "In a word, our League needs a 'soul.'"[15]

"We cannot jump to what we consider perfection if the other fellow does not go the whole way"

Senator Vandenberg had been reading the polls, too, and in the winter of 1944 the well-known isolationist had been reconsidering his position. The Roosevelt administration was dismayed to learn that Vandenberg would be making a major foreign policy address in the Senate on January 10, 1945. To the astonishment of many of his colleagues, the senator rose and opened with the following invocation: "Mr. President, there are critical moments in the life of every nation which call for the straightest, the plainest, and the most courageous thinking of which we are capable. We confront such a moment now." After warning against disunity among the united nations fighting the Axis, he called for "maximum American cooperation, consistent with legitimate American self-interest . . . to make the basic idea of Dumbarton Oaks succeed."[16]

Although Vandenberg emphasized the depredations of Soviet policies in Eastern Europe, especially in Poland, he refrained from condemning the Soviets. He then offered his own proposal for a treaty among the major Allies "to keep the defeated Axis powers permanently demilitarized and thus ensure a lasting peace . . . at the moment when enlightened civilization is our common stake." The editors of *Time* magazine argued that the senator's unexpected testimonial "might well prove to be the most important speech made by an American in World War II," and the liberal *New Republic* agreed that it was "a turning point in world affairs." A poll by the Associated Press showed that sixty-seven senators supported Vandenberg's proposals, and even the White House asked for reprints of the speech. The ambitious senator's name began to appear on Gallup poll lists of possible Republican presidential contenders in the 1948 election. The most important result of the speech, however, was to maroon the genuine isolationists in the Senate. Coming just one week later, Senator Burton Wheeler's attack on Dumbarton Oaks as a "grim military alliance to underwrite tyranny" suddenly looked like the fulminations of a fringe element.[17]

The "soul" that Vandenberg sought was not to materialize at the Yalta Conference. Churchill, Roosevelt, and Stalin had agreed to meet on the Crimean coast in the Soviet Union in early February 1945. Although the leaders had been negotiating over the scheduling of this summit since the Teheran Conference in November 1943, high on the agenda was a face-to-face resolution of some of the outstanding disagreements that had surfaced at Dumbarton Oaks. President Roosevelt's itinerary included a brief stop at Malta en route, prompting a cable from Prime Minister Churchill, "No more let us falter! From Malta to Yalta! Let nobody alter!" Privately, Churchill noted to Harry Hopkins that "ten years of research could not have unearthed a worse place to meet," but Stalin had insisted, dragging the ailing Roosevelt many thousands of miles, much of it over difficult terrain.[18]

Agreements at Yalta included establishing the new collective security organization as soon as possible—that is, before the end of the war—even if this meant courting the appearance as well as the reality of a glorified alliance of the victorious powers. Initiating machinery for collective security in advance of any armistice or peace settlement was one of the cardinal lessons of the Paris Peace Conference a generation before. The principals further agreed that the United States would host the organization's founding conference a brief two and a half months later, at the end of April 1945. Prompted perhaps by his shabby accommodations in Livadia Palace, particularly the shared bathroom, Secretary Stettinius awakened in the night with a vision of clean, modern San Francisco as the site of the conference. "I saw the golden sunshine, and as I lay there on the shores of the Black Sea in the Crimea, I could almost feel the fresh and invigorating air from the Pacific," he wrote in his diary.[19]

The three leaders reviewed the outstanding questions of the veto and membership in the new organization. Stalin initially stood by the Soviet position at Dumbarton Oaks, that a Security Council veto meant veto power over agenda items, precluding even the discussion of undesirable topics. Churchill, like Roosevelt, doubted whether it was advisable to press the Soviets too hard, but both Stettinius and British Foreign Secretary Anthony Eden felt strongly that if a great power could veto even the discussion of a peaceful means of resolving a dispute in which it was involved, some of the most important postwar issues might be excluded altogether from the ambit of the new organization. In addition, small states would doubtlessly feel aggrieved if the great powers were uniquely protected in this way and might decline to join altogether. Eventually, this combined pressure seemed to have some effect. Soviet Foreign Minister Vyacheslav Molotov—colloquially known as "Old Stone Ass" for his negotiating stamina—declared that the Soviet Union would be satisfied with the latest American formula, which provided that there should be no veto available if nothing more than the peaceful settlement of a dispute was under discussion.

Dumbarton Oaks' top-secret "X-problem," the USSR's request for individual membership for all sixteen Soviet republics, persisted at Yalta. Using the analogy of the British Commonwealth countries, which had acquired independence over time and thus would be entitled to separate voting rights at the outset, Molotov announced that the Soviet government would be prepared to accept, as a first step, that only two or three of the Soviet republics should be given individual membership. Roosevelt and Churchill were actually inclined to accept this, but other members of the US delegation were unhappy at the president's concessions, fearing American public opinion.

Roosevelt's advisors urged the president at least to ask the other two leaders to commit in writing to giving the United States parity in seats with the Soviet Union, to which Churchill and Stalin agreed. This weighted voting formula would have given the United States at least three seats at the UN, on the theory that its status as the preeminent great power meant that it should appropriately act as a counterweight to the augmented number of Soviet votes. Roosevelt and his advisors did not foresee the public relations disaster this proposal would become, suggesting as it did that the United States was just another cynical player in a great power game, rather than a principled advocate of the sovereign equality of all states in a new democratic world order.[20]

The Yalta negotiators also agreed in principle that the proposed UN Charter should include a system of trusteeship, a touchy topic the Dumbarton Oaks negotiators had decided to leave for the principals to explore. Churchill initially rejected the concept outright, fearing that the system might be extended to the whole of the British Empire. This was indeed what Roosevelt personally would have liked to see. When Stettinius explained that the proposal would cover only former enemy territories, territories that were already mandates, and territories voluntarily offered, Churchill relented. The prime minister was prepared to accept a general reference in the conference report to the need for such a system. An undisclosed American agenda also informed this new and quite limited formula about what territories should be administered as trusteeships: US military officials had indicated that they wanted the United States to continue to occupy the Pacific islands it had seized from Japan as strategic assets, free from multilateral supervision.[21]

Other parts of the Yalta agreement included statements relating to the postwar treatment of Germany and a fatally vague declaration on the reorganization of Poland's Soviet-directed government of so-called "Lublin Poles" (as opposed to the "London Poles," the non-communist government in exile). The Yalta declaration designated the Lublin government as merely provisional and called for a "reorganized" government "on a broader-based democratic basis," including democratic leaders "from Poles abroad." However, FDR and Churchill must have known that the Soviet Union, which was then occupying Poland, would retain that beleaguered nation firmly in its orbit, in the absence of any monitoring or enforcement measures. "It's the best I can do" for Poland, a resigned Roosevelt reportedly observed later to an aide.[22]

As part of the Yalta discussions, Stalin also extracted an agreement that all Soviet citizens should be repatriated to the USSR, whether they wished to return or not. In practice the workings of this provision proved incredibly harsh. Soviet secret police fanned out through the European continent and swept up many thousands of Soviet prisoners of war, now suspect due to their surrender and capture, and simply because of the time they had spent outside the purview of the Soviet system. This mandate also ensnared thousands of Russians who had formerly served as anti-Bolshevik partisans, many of whom had resettled elsewhere in Europe and no longer held Soviet passports. The Soviet specialist Anne Applebaum in her account of the USSR's "Gulag" system estimates that over 400,000 repatriated Soviets were detained in Soviet "filtration" camps at the end of the war in Europe, many of them serving long sentences at forced labor.[23]

Roosevelt had directed that certain provisions of the Yalta accords be kept secret and held back for later release. Upon his return, the exhausted president personally presented a meandering report to Congress—which he delivered sitting down, making a rare reference to the "ten pounds of steel" on his legs. FDR focused on Yalta's two public purposes: to hasten Germany's defeat and to "build the foundation for an international accord which would bring order and security after the chaos of war." The controversial weighted membership formula was not released until a month later, and generated outrage among FDR's critics and bewilderment among his supporters. The details of the Polish declaration and the trusteeship arrangements were also not included in the public protocols. Senator Vandenberg (representing a large Polish constituency) fulminated that the arrangement for Poland was "totally unsatisfactory," before observing philosophically that "manifestly America will not go to war with Russia to settle such an issue."[24]

Another major provision not released until seven months later included the bargain whereby the Soviets would enter the Pacific War on a two-to-three-month timetable after the German capitulation and in exchange for specified Japanese territories. UN specialist Stephen Schlesinger speculates that "Roosevelt's anxiety about the United Nations soon overrode his usually sound political instincts about how he would announce the Yalta results . . . Roosevelt was so determined to mold the US response to the UN that he stayed silent about controversies he considered unnecessary distractions." If this was FDR's strategy, it certainly backfired, in that the secrecy itself generated tremendous anxiety. The very label "secret protocols" tapped into deep American fears about the entanglements of "Old World" diplomacy.[25]

This dark side of Yalta amounted in effect to a betrayal of key principles of the Atlantic Charter, notably the idea of self-determination. Where was self-determination for the Poles? Or for Pacific Islanders, who would be exchanging Japanese for US occupation? Or for subnational groups such as the forcibly repatriated Russians, or, for that matter, the soon-to-be-defeated Germans? The three leaders' reaffirmation of "their faith in the principles of the Atlantic Charter" and "the right of all people to choose the form of government under which they will live" occurred in the subsection on Poland, where the hypocrisy of such a statement would soon become glaringly apparent.[26]

Churchill may have viewed the Yalta agreements as little more than great power horse-trading at the end of an exhausting global conflict, taking into account realities on the ground, such as the outsized Soviet sacrifice and occupation by the Red Army. Complementary analyses of the negotiations have examined the role of Roosevelt's failing health, or the president's faith in the power of personal diplomacy, in leading him to yield to Stalin's single-minded brutality and even paranoia. As the end of the European phase of the war was coming into view, the American negotiators were also very eager to secure Stalin's commitment to enter the ongoing war in the Pacific, then projected to proceed to a costly endgame. The Soviet leader's continuing anger over the Anglo-American failure to make good on FDR's promise to open a second front in western Europe in 1942, or even in 1943, may also have led Churchill and Roosevelt to feel that they had little moral capital to use as leverage.[27]

But squandering moral capital was precisely the problem at Yalta. Across the Allied political spectrum, reactions of outrage and dismay to the full panoply of Yalta protocols suggested, in a backhanded way, the power of idealistic statements such as the Atlantic Charter and Four Freedoms. People who genuinely believed that they were fighting for Atlantic Charter ideals felt let down, even duped. General Carlos Romulo, who would serve as delegation chief from the Philippines at the UN conference and who had served with MacArthur on Bataan and Corregidor, admitted to coming to San Francisco "starry-eyed" about the prospect of negotiating the UN Charter. But Romulo later wrote with great bitterness that the optimistic delegates had not fully understood the strict limits on what they could accomplish in San Francisco, because "the goose was cooked at Yalta." FDR's critics who had doubted these ideals all along felt vindicated, or argued that Roosevelt should have driven a harder bargain.[28]

Roosevelt may also have believed that the upcoming San Francisco Conference would offer his negotiators a second bite at the apple—that the Yalta concessions had been necessary to ensure Soviet attendance at the UN conference in the first place, where Americans and their allies might yet work out a better deal. Two months after the Yalta Conference, on April 9, President Roosevelt wrote to the internationalist Senator Claude Pepper, Democrat of Florida, with some ruminations on the art of negotiation: "We cannot jump to what we consider perfection if the other fellow does not go the whole way . . . He might think that his point of view was just as good or better than ours." Roosevelt concluded with the hope that he would see Pepper after returning from "the San Francisco parley." Three days later the president died suddenly, only ten days before the conference was to begin.[29]

Within an hour of formally taking office, Harry Truman declared that the UN conference would go ahead as planned. The historian Arnold Offner has recently cast doubt on Truman's internationalist credentials, emphasizing the new president's parochial background, personal insecurity, and lack of creativity. A former haberdasher from Independence, Missouri, Truman occasionally expressed racist views and exhibited little interest in foreign affairs before becoming a senator, despite serving in France during World War I. By contrast, Stephen Schlesinger emphasizes what he sees as Truman's natural internationalist inclinations, including the way he had carefully preserved in his wallet, throughout his career, a copy of Tennyson's poem "Locksley Hall," describing "a Parliament of Man, the Federation of the World." Harry Hopkins indicated that Roosevelt had chosen Truman in the first place in large part because FDR had "wanted somebody that would help him when he went up there [to Capitol Hill] and asked them to ratify the peace." Whatever the verdict on Truman's overall performance, it seems clear that the new president perceived his own mandate on United Nations issues to be a continuation of Roosevelt's multilateralist agenda.[30]

On April 16, the day after Roosevelt's funeral, Truman gave his first major speech as president, addressing a joint session of Congress. Members gave their former colleague an emotional standing ovation as he entered the House chamber. "The responsibility of great states is to serve and not to dominate the world," said Truman, calling on "every American, regardless of party, race, creed, or color, to support our efforts to build a strong and lasting United Nations organization."[31]

"We must build a new world—one in which the eternal dignity of man is respected"

The UN Conference on International Organization opened at the Opera House in San Francisco on April 25, 1945. Secretary of State Stettinius presided at the first meeting, and the 282 delegates surveyed a scene of muted exaltation—muted by design, because the war was still continuing in the Pacific. There were no processions, concerts, parades, or public festivals. The main hall featured an elevated stage with four gold columns symbolizing Roosevelt's Four Freedoms, with the flags of the United Nations floodlit against a vivid blue background the design team had dubbed "Stettinius blue." President Truman addressed the delegates via radio from Washington, having decided to attend the closing ceremonies rather than the opening. "We must build a new world," he urged, "a far better world—one in which the eternal dignity of man is respected."[32]

By far the toughest job description at San Francisco was that of the conference's secretary-general, Alger Hiss of the State Department's Office of Special Political Affairs. Among many other responsibilities, Hiss was in charge of allocating hotel rooms, an all-but-impossible task for a conference with thousands of consultants, observers, support staff, and an additional two thousand press representatives flocking into town, over and above the hundreds of credentialed delegates. The Soviet contingent had taken over the entire tenth floor of the St. Francis Hotel but were concerned enough about confidentiality that they relayed their official communications from a ship moored in San Francisco Bay. Stephen Schlesinger speculates that a ship full of such sensitive, state-of-the-art equipment was most likely being used for monitoring purposes, as well as for secure transmissions.[33]

Indeed, everyone's security concerns were probably well founded, as Schlesinger explores in his analysis of a set of documents declassified in the 1990s and obtained through the Freedom of Information Act. The US Army Signal Security Agency and FBI were industriously spying at the San Francisco Conference, not only on foreign delegations but also on American observers and consultants, notably African-American and labor groups. They were not able to intercept Soviet transmissions, however. Hiss himself would be forced out of the State Department the following year under suspicion of spying for the Soviets, and Harry Dexter White—also active at the San Francisco Conference as well as at Bretton Woods—would be called to testify before the House Un-American Activities Committee in 1948. With regard to Hiss's role, Schlesinger notes that there was "no hint" of impropriety at San Francisco; Hiss had also advised Stettinius at the Yalta Conference and had argued against Soviet proposals there, such as allocating UN seats to additional Soviet republics.[34]

General Carlos Romulo, as one of few Asian delegates himself, observed that the UN assemblage was notably exotic in 1945 San Francisco. Riding in an elevator with Prince Faisal of Saudi Arabia, Romulo recounted, an American teenager was inspired by the novelty of the prince's burnoose to speculate aloud what he might be wearing underneath. "Young lady," the prince spoke up imperiously, "it is a BVD."[35]

Four main commissions steered discussions on general provisions, the General Assembly, the Security Council, and a judicial organization. Twelve working committees oversaw negotiations on specific substantive areas such as the peaceful settlement of disputes or regional arrangements. Each of these groups was an unwieldy committee consisting of representatives from every state. On paper at least, a steering committee was the designated forum for deciding all major questions of procedure and organization, but in practice a more compact executive committee, including the heads of fourteen delegations, served as a sort of court of appeals for intractable issues forwarded by the commissions.

The real center of gravity of the conference, however, was Stettinius's penthouse suite at the Fairmont Hotel, where the heads of the Big Four delegations met each evening to discuss what changes they would permit in the blueprint agreed upon at Dumbarton Oaks. They referred the more technical issues to an informal group of advisors headed by Leo Pasvolsky of the State Department's policy planning staff. On May 4

France was invited to join the group as well, and the Big Four became the Big Five. (France had declined to serve as one of the convening powers of the San Francisco Conference, because of the offense General de Gaulle took at not having been invited to Yalta.)[36]

Even what had seemed in February to be relatively uncontroversial provisions of the Yalta accords blew up into disagreements once the conference got underway. At Yalta the Allies agreed that all countries which had declared war against the Axis powers by March 1, 1945, were qualified to take part in the UN's founding conference. The United States was especially eager to include the six Latin American nations which, as of February, had broken off relations with the Axis states but not declared war. By March 1, Chile, Ecuador, Paraguay, Peru, Uruguay, and Venezuela as well as Turkey, Egypt, Lebanon, Syria, and Saudi Arabia had all declared war and so had become eligible to receive invitations.

But Argentina did not declare war until March 27, 1945, weeks past the deadline. The other Latin American delegations nevertheless strongly urged the seating of Argentina, especially after the USSR seated two of its republics as separate delegations. Averell Harriman and other US diplomats worried, correctly, that the Soviets would use an invitation to Argentina as an excuse to lobby for the seating of the Lublin (now Warsaw) Poles. The UN executive committee and the steering committee each voted separately on April 30 to seat Argentina over vociferous objections from the Soviets. And although the Warsaw Poles were never seated at the San Francisco Conference, the Allies recognized a Soviet-dominated government just eleven days after the signing of the San Francisco charter, retroactively designating them as among the UN's "founding members."[37]

Additional East–West spats erupted early and often. The formidable Vyacheslav Molotov opened by demanding that each of the four sponsoring powers should hold the presidency of the conference in rotation, an unusual request much resented by the United States and its allies. British Foreign Minister Anthony Eden offered a complicated face-saving formula by which the presidency of the public sessions would rotate among the four sponsoring powers, while Stettinius would continue to preside over the steering and executive committees.[38]

Controversy continued over the use of the Security Council veto, with the Soviets maintaining that a Security Council member should be able to veto even the proposal to discuss a matter. In practice, this would mean that any one party would hold veto power over the council's agenda. The United States, Britain, and France had categorically rejected the Soviet interpretation of the veto power at Yalta and now indicated that they were prepared to risk the breakdown of the entire conference rather than yield on this point. Fortuitously, the intrepid Harry Hopkins was once again in Moscow, this time as Truman's special emissary, trying to resolve the increasingly snarled difficulties over Poland. In desperation, Stettinius wired Hopkins and begged him to lobby Stalin personally about the veto question and to warn the Soviet leader that the entire UN conference threatened to collapse over this issue. When Hopkins and the US ambassador to Moscow, Averell Harriman, saw Stalin on June 6, the Soviet leader seemed surprised about the controversy and blithely accepted the Western position that the veto could not be used to prevent discussion of a matter. To their astonishment, Stalin indicated that he thought the point was trivial.[39]

Delegates from smaller nations banded together at the conference, taking offense at great power arrogance, particularly on the part of the British and the Soviets. The British delegate Alexander Cadogan wrote smugly to his wife, "I generally sit next to the American . . . I tell him he's our heavy artillery and I am the sniper. It works quite well and we wiped the floor with a Mexican last night." A disgruntled Romulo wrote how the Soviets "acted as if they owned the world: they considered us small nations as pygmies subject to their wishes, and they strutted around the Veterans Memorial Building like conquerors in their ill-cut suits with bell-bottom trousers." Molotov had mocked Mexican Foreign Minister Padilla at one of the first sessions, after Padilla supported the US position on the host nation serving as chair. Molotov publicly stated that he suspected that Padilla's speech must have been written by the US State Department, sarcastically noting that he admired Padilla's good memory for reciting it so well. All the Latin American nations took offense at this attack, noted Romulo, "and became anti-Russian to a man."[40]

States completely lacking great power status, such as Australia, Canada, India, New Zealand, and a concert of various Latin American countries, found they could "punch above their weight" in influencing the negotiations. By portraying themselves as selfless contributors to the Allied war effort, these countries were able to leverage the quality that Senator Vandenberg had referred to as "moral authority," enhanced by their articulate arguments, frequent press conferences, and a sense of solidarity based on extensive behind-the-scenes consultations. These so-called smaller powers at San Francisco made valiant efforts to enhance the role of the General Assembly, in line with their criticisms of this aspect of the Dumbarton Oaks proposals. New Zealand demanded that the assembly should be able to consider "any matter within the sphere of international relations." Eventually, and somewhat unwillingly, the Big Five relented.

The American delegation introduced a new article declaring that the General Assembly could recommend measures for the peaceful adjustment of any situation "which it deems likely to impair the general welfare or friendly relations among nations." These changes had to be worked out by a subcommittee of Stettinius, Gromyko, and Herbert Evatt, the Australian foreign minister. Evatt and Stettinius then offered that the General Assembly's competence should be extended to any question within the "scope of the Charter," a masterful elision to get around Soviet objections to perceived meddling by the General Assembly. Again the unresolved dispute traveled all the way up the chain of command to Moscow. The UN Charter accordingly provided that the assembly could discuss "any questions or any matters within the scope of the present Charter," with the exception of matters being considered by the Security Council.[41]

The San Francisco charter was in most ways an echo of its Dumbarton Oaks predecessor, however. It maintained the dominant role accorded to the Security Council, although it significantly augmented the powers of the General Assembly. Changes at San Francisco were at the margins and tended to focus on areas where perceived flaws in the League of Nations Covenant had not been adequately addressed at Dumbarton Oaks. For example, the Security Council was authorized to take "provisional" measures to deal with a threat to the peace before reaching a final decision on enforcement action. (This revision actually strengthened the powers of the Security Council.) Its genesis was in the wartime experience of China in the 1930s, when the League had dithered for a year in deciding what to do about Japanese aggression in Manchuria.[42]

Part of the transformation from the Dumbarton Oaks draft to what would become the UN Charter was to add enhanced human rights provisions, even though they contradicted existing language about national sovereignty, self-defense, or the nature of trust territories. In the end, what might loosely be called human rights provisions—language, structure, revisions to the trusteeship committee, the creation of an additional substantive committee—amounted to the most significant changes from the Dumbarton Oaks proposals.[43]

"We fought for freedom, not for one country, but for all peoples and for all the world"

Perhaps stung by criticism of the lack of lyricism in the Dumbarton Oaks proposal—which had, after all, been drafted by "technicians"—the drafters of the final United Nations Charter included the kind of inspirational preamble for which the Chinese had argued in vain at Dumbarton Oaks. The charter began by invoking its ultimate legitimating authority, which would ordinarily have been the member states by means of their authorized plenipotentiaries. A drafting committee revised it to read, in a deliberate echo of the US Constitution: "We the Peoples of the United Nations . . ." The preamble continued:

> Determined to save succeeding generations from the scourge of war, which twice in our lifetime has brought untold sorrow to mankind, and
>
> To reaffirm faith in fundamental human rights, in the dignity and worth of the human person, in the equal rights of men and women and of nations large and small, and
>
> To establish conditions under which justice and respect for the obligations arising from treaties and other sources of international law can be maintained, and
>
> To promote social progress and better standards of life in larger freedom . . .
>
> Have resolved to combine our efforts to accomplish these aims.[44]

As with the Atlantic Charter, the preamble's short, vague, and uplifting phrases crystallized expectations worldwide and elicited a predictably rapturous reception. But such high-flown rhetoric also served to expose hypocrisy, and generated a great deal of cynical or dismissive commentary among human rights activists. The lofty language provided an ironic counterpoint to actual state practice, including the behavior of states that had most actively advocated strengthening the charter's human rights provisions.

Article 1 of the charter also received an injection of idealism, cataloguing the organization's four purposes as:

> 1. To maintain international peace and security, and to that end: to take effective collective measures for the prevention and removal of threats to the peace, and for the suppression of acts of aggression or other breaches of the peace, and to bring about by peaceful means, and in conformity with the principles of justice and international law, adjustment or settlement of international disputes or situations which might lead to a breach of the peace;
>
> 2. To develop friendly relations among nations based on respect for the principle of equal rights and self-determination of peoples, and to take other appropriate measures to strengthen universal peace;
>
> 3. To achieve international cooperation in solving international problems of an economic, social, cultural, or humanitarian character, and in

promoting and encouraging respect for human rights and for fundamental freedoms for all without distinction as to race, sex, language, or religion; and

4. To be a center for harmonizing the actions of nations in the attainment of these common ends.[45]

The Dumbarton Oaks draft had similarly featured collective measures for peace and security, friendly relations, and cooperation for economic, social, and humanitarian (but not "cultural") problems. Notably absent from the earlier version, however, were references to equal rights, self-determination, human rights, and fundamental freedoms, as well as the language about distinctions of race, sex, language, and religion.[46]

The moment had clearly passed for old-fashioned imperialism, even though it had been barely fifty years since Rudyard Kipling was writing odes to the "white man's burden." Negotiations over the charter's trusteeship system revealed most starkly the contradictions between Atlantic Charter idealism and great power *realpolitik*. The trusteeship story also suggests that wartime planning for collective security was not the happy tale of humanitarian progress sometimes on display in the human rights literature and elsewhere. From a human rights point of view, the UN trusteeship regime was arguably a step backward from the League of Nations' system of mandates. At least the mandated territories could not be used for military purposes, for example.[47]

Trusteeship was the major feature of the charter that earlier proposals had not clearly sketched out. While Churchill, Roosevelt, and Stalin had discussed some general principles at Yalta, FDR's advisors deliberately kept those negotiations from getting too specific—an agenda with which Churchill was only too happy to collude. Roosevelt had expressed his hope on several occasions that the new organization would be given special responsibilities for overseeing *all* dependent territories and assisting their progress toward independence. However, the first State Department proposals to this effect had run afoul of the expectations of the armed forces. The US Navy in particular was anxious to maintain unfettered American control of conquered Japanese Pacific territories, which it viewed as essential to American security. Naval planners were dismissive of any proposal that might make the United States internationally accountable for any of these territories. As part of the resolution of this internal disagreement, American officials hit on the plan of establishing two types of trust territories: the normal type, similar to the old League mandates, to be supervised by a new Trusteeship Council; and a set of "strategic trust territories," to be supervised directly by the Security

Council. It was left to the member exercising physical control of each territory to say which kind of trusteeship would apply.[48]

American delegates presented this proposal to the rest of the Big Five consultative group at the opening session of the San Francisco Conference. For the so-called strategic trust territories in the Pacific, the US government refused to accept any specific provisions for receiving petitions, for creating annual reports, or even for accommodating visits of inspection. Britain strongly opposed the idea of a special status for strategic trust territories, arguing that the general aim of protecting the interests of the inhabitants through international supervision applied just as much to the strategic territories as to others. The Soviet Union and China agreed with Britain and offered their own proposals. State Department aide Ruth Russell notes briskly that "none of these proposals, for obvious political reasons, was acceptable to the United States."[49]

The other four of the Big Five yielded the point, extracting only the minimal concession that the strategic territories should come under the general objectives of the trusteeship system, namely, promoting the advancement and progressive development of the territories' inhabitants (including "respect for human rights and for fundamental freedoms"). Critics of the UN Charter negotiations, such as the African-American historian and foreign affairs commentator Rayford Logan, noted how the strategic trust approach amounted to a "distinct retreat from the anticolonialism of Roosevelt." In practice, this new system would mean that "America would forfeit its moral claim to oppose colonialism elsewhere in the world." The cost of US insistence on the strategic trust territory concept did indeed become apparent immediately: other nations administering their own trust territories soon lobbied to remove restrictions on military recruiting or military fortifications of those territories, and the United States had no choice but to acquiesce.[50]

The Big Five had an easier time reaching agreement about the nonstrategic trust territories. A Trusteeship Council would oversee the metropolitan power's administration and would send visiting missions as well as receive regular reports. The Trusteeship Council could not, however, alter or amend existing agreements about administering the territory without the metropolitan power's consent, suggesting that the council lacked the power to deprive an unwilling metropolitan power of its responsibilities. "These Europeans were colonial masters and they carried their colonialism with them to the United Nations consciously or unconsciously," observed Romulo, a representative on the Trusteeship Committee. Some of the white delegates clearly had problems dealing with the newly visible sense of agency among representatives of colonized peoples. Among the worst offenders, according to Romulo, was Francis B. Sayre, grandson of Woodrow Wilson and a US representative on the Trusteeship Committee, who was "so patently unwilling to listen to the views of developing countries."[51]

A section of the charter concerning all "non-self-governing" territories supplemented the trusteeship provisions. Britain accepted the idea that there should be some kind of general declaration whereby the colonial powers would undertake to protect the interests of the inhabitants of these territories and to promote their political, economic, and social advancement. The British presented their own proposal along these lines to the Big Five, specifying that it was a "sacred trust of civilization" to promote to the utmost the well-being of dependent territories and to "develop self-government in forms appropriate to the varying circumstances of each territory." Conspicuous by its absence was any language about leading the territories to actual independence, however, although both the Soviet Union and China demanded that this function should be included in the list of responsibilities. The Soviet–Chinese demand was particularly unacceptable to France, which at this time did not accept independence as a goal for its dependent territories.[52]

The question of the eventual independence of dependent territories was a subject of vociferous debate in San Francisco. Even the much-maligned Covenant of the League of Nations had referred to the eventual aim of independence, at least for the mandates. China, the Soviet Union, the Philippines, Egypt, and Iraq made forceful arguments that dropping independence as a goal from the UN Charter would lower its aspirations below those of the League's Covenant. The traditional colonial powers, backed by the United States, initially closed ranks to resist demands for language about eventual independence. Lord Cranborne of the British delegation indicated that: "I do not believe that the situation is so simple as it appears. Many of these territories are small, poor, and defenceless and could not stand on their own feet. Many of them are extremely backward and need a helping hand. Take away that helping hand and such territories would rapidly relapse into barbarism."[53]

As a compromise, the United States finally proposed that a declaration on non-self-governing territories would refer only to the goal of "self-government," but the objectives of the trusteeship system as a whole would be broadened to include independence, the protection of human rights, and consideration of the wishes of the people concerned. In the end, the Declaration Regarding Non-Self-Governing Territories committed administering authorities to vague goals of "political, economic, social and educational advancement" without committing them to the aim of independence, which most delegates regarded as the heart of the matter. Included with the declaration, however, was a little-noticed requirement to "transmit regularly to the Secretary-General . . . information relating to economic, social and educational conditions in the territories." This rather minimalist-sounding commitment eventually became the focal point for heated debates in the General Assembly over colonial questions, quite contrary to the wishes of the colonial powers.[54]

Small nations had objected to the omissions of more explicit human rights language in the Dumbarton Oaks proposals, but so had internationalist, religious, labor, and African-American activist groups within the United States. In a strategic move, the State Department had taken the unprecedented step of inviting forty-two non-governmental "pressure groups" to San Francisco, ostensibly to serve as consultants but also to help with publicizing and advocating for the charter among their home constituencies after the conference was over. The British were alarmed by this gambit, which included bestowing an official role on the League of Women Voters, the Congress of Industrial Organizations, the NAACP, and others, but later admitted that it had been a masterful exercise in public relations acumen.[55]

The American Legion, the American Bar Association, and the US Chamber of Commerce also sent delegates, along with the National Lawyers Guild and Americans United for World Organization. Civic groups such as the Rotary Club, Lions, and Kiwanis participated enthusiastically, side-by-side with representatives of religious groups, women's groups, and veterans' organizations. Many of these NGOs had long been developing agendas focused on strengthening the human rights content of any postwar international security organization, and they became vectors for petitions from additional groups that had not been invited. For example, the NAACP—the only group representing African-Americans —brought in petitions and commentary from the National Council of Negro Women, the US-based Council on African Affairs, as well as the African-American press.[56]

NAACP co-founder W. E. B. DuBois, who had returned to serve as the organization's director of special research after a forced retirement from Atlanta University, was one of three NAACP representatives at the conference. DuBois had represented the NAACP as an observer at the Paris Peace Conference in 1919, the same year he began serving as one of the chief organizers of the Pan-African movement. He made a point of linking domestic racism with transnational colonialism, noting that "what was true of the United States in the past is true of world civilization today—we cannot exist half slave and half free." Leading editorialists in the African-American press echoed this sense of connection with international movements, asserting that "the World Security Conference in San Francisco has but one meaning to the Negro people—that is, how far democratic principles shall be stretched to embrace the rights of our brothers in the colonies and to what extent the American Negro's own security at home shall be guaranteed."[57]

DuBois and NAACP Executive Director Walter White noted that their presence at the conference served merely as "window dressing," in White's phrase. While the same could be said of the other NGOs, they all nevertheless took their roles quite seriously and came away from the conference feeling they had made a significant contribution to the human rights provisions of the charter. As the representative for the American Jewish Committee, Judge Joseph Proskauer, recalled, it was the passion of the American NGOs that stiffened the spine of Stettinius to insert or strengthen key human rights provisions in the charter, at a crucial and emotional meeting on May 2 at the Fairmont Hotel. "I said that the voice of America was speaking in this room," recalled the judge in a 1950 memoir, "as it had never before spoken in any international gathering; that this voice was saying to the American delegation: 'If you make a fight for these human rights proposals and win, there will be glory for all. If you make a fight for it and lose, we will back you up to the limit. If you fail to make a fight for it, you will have lost the support of American public opinion—and justly lost it.'"[58]

A brilliant and textured analysis of this specific scene by the human rights specialist Kirsten Sellars suggests that we treat these self-aggrandizing accounts with great caution. This NGO meeting lasted half an hour, for one thing; its transcript suggests no such emotional tone; Stettinius was already committed to the human rights–related provisions in question and likely did not change any instructions based on this encounter. As with the 1941 Atlantic Charter, however, there is another, symbolic layer to the NGO meeting. Over time, the encounter has come to represent the birth of the modern NGO movement, and the capacity of organized groups of citizens to speak truth to power.

William Korey begins his analysis of the role played by NGOs in modern human rights politics with an account of the May 2 meeting, arguing that the UN's human rights provisions would barely exist "without the commitment, determination and pressure of a group of American nongovernmental organizations." A plaque on the Garden Room at the Fairmont Hotel commemorates the NGO role in the charter provisions for human rights. On one level, it is ahistorical and even a little silly to mythologize an ordinary committee meeting. But the role of energized NGOs was one of the biggest developments for postwar human rights politics to come out of the UN conference, along with a more virulent pattern of US–Soviet confrontation and the increasing pressure for de-colonization and racial justice. The State Department may not have ap-preciated this role at the time, but then again they did not appreciate the significance of the other two transformations either.[59]

"The world has waited in vain for a way out of the vicious circle"

In addition to the rather obvious limitations on the human rights goals built into the trusteeship system, further qualifications, exceptions, and omissions offset many of the changes promoting human rights. In evalu-ating the earlier Dumbarton Oaks proposals, Karl Loewenstein lamented that "what is offered here with the right hand is forthwith taken away with the left." These internal contradictions were, if anything, sharpened in the final UN Charter. Notable among these "clawback" provisions was a capacious clause in article 2 of the charter regarding domestic ju-risdiction—matters that would be sheltered from the international com-munity as the internal affairs of a particular sovereign state. Opening with the sweeping assertion that "nothing contained in the present Char-ter shall authorize the United Nations to intervene in matters which are essentially within the domestic jurisdiction of any state," the clause tem-pered this yawning exemption with the minimalist qualifier that the ex-ception did not apply to matters affecting threats to international peace.[60]

But many quite egregious human rights violations might not necessar-ily interfere with "international peace." Two months later, as the Allies negotiated the terms of the Nuremberg Charter, they debated this very concept—whether a transborder impact was strictly necessary to create a right of intervention. What, beyond generating refugees, was the threat to international peace when Germany persecuted its domestic population of German Jews in the 1930s? And what about persecution of minority populations that did not generate mass waves of refugees, such as the Af-rican-American population in the United States?

The domestic jurisdiction provision transparently aimed to help with the politics of US Senate ratification as well as Soviet sensitivities to foreign scrutiny or intervention. John Foster Dulles, advising the Republican members of the US delegation, indicated that domestic jurisdiction was "a basic principle of the organization" and drew an analogy with "federalism in the United States." The analogy was quite apt. American federalism promoted local control and governance that was responsive to popular sovereignty. But in the southern states in particular, it also sheltered racist regimes from the reach of the US Constitution. Philip C. Jessup, who served as one of the "technical experts" on international law at San Francisco, drew the international parallel: that in protecting domestic jurisdiction, diplomats "thereby have built a Maginot line against the invasion of new ideas in the international world, and behind that rampart the demagogue and the reactionary are enthroned."[61]

Another limiting provision in the charter was article 51, purporting to protect "the inherent right of individual or collective self-defense." This exemption started as a compromise with pre-existing regional arrangements such as the Latin American Chapultepec agreement and the Soviet system of security pacts. States that were already part of regional security networks wanted the flexibility to respond to an attack without having to wait for the imprimatur of an untested UN Security Council. In practice, however, article 51 served as the basis for future growth of military alliances outside the UN system, notably NATO and the Warsaw Pact. It legitimized just the kind of spheres-of-influence diplomacy that the charter as a whole was created to obviate.[62]

Commenting on the charter negotiation process, Loewenstein observed that "the world has waited—and waited in vain—for a way out of the vicious circle created by the irreconcilability of an international organization with internal sovereignty." The UN Charter's timid enforcement language did not help square this circle. As the human rights scholar Paul Gordon Lauren has pointed out, drafting committees rejected firm language demanding that charter adherents "safeguard," "preserve," "protect," "guarantee," "implement," "assure," or "enforce" human rights provisions, consistently choosing such locutions as "should facilitate," "may discuss," "initiate studies," "consider," "make recommendations," "assist," "encourage," or "promote." The charter did not even include working definitions of terms such as "human rights and fundamental freedoms," "just treatment," or, for that matter, "political, economic, social and educational advancement."[63]

W. E. B. DuBois offered a sustained critique of the Dumbarton Oaks draft and final UN Charter, before, during, and after the San Francisco Conference. Speaking of the Dumbarton Oaks draft in testimony before the State Department in 1944, the aging activist observed that the proposed charter's "emphasis on nations and states and the indifference to races, groups or organizations" were among the new organization's weakest points. So many of the world's problems, he presciently observed, were simply "beyond the jurisdiction" of the new system, especially those of non–self-governing peoples. The optimistic and effusive Carlos Romulo proclaimed upon signing the UN Charter that the document was "not an Atlantic Charter, nor a Pacific Charter; it is a World Charter; it is the Spiritual Bill of Rights."[64] But as DuBois understood, individuals with human rights grievances and no state to turn to would have to settle for spiritual rather than actual relief for some time to come.

PART IV

NUREMBERG, AUGUST 1945

The Nuremberg trial was an immense revolutionary effort to give utterance to a collective human conscience, to bring into being a collective standard by which gross violations of that conscience can be punished. Some may gibe that I am speaking of a human conscience and a moral sense that are vague and formless, things on which no body of law can be built. I submit that they are the only things that a body of law ever rests on. The surest basis of a future world society lies in the sense of our common plight.

Max Lerner, 1948

CHAPTER 7

THE LIMITS OF LAW

Major Airey Neave, famous at age twenty-nine for his multiple escapes from Nazi prisons, noticed the unusually brilliant shine on Colonel Burton Andrus's helmet, as the two officers stood waiting outside the prison wing of the Palace of Justice at Nuremberg on the afternoon of October 19, 1945. Neave was a German-speaking London barrister whose wartime heroics with the clandestine British intelligence service MI-9 had involved disguising himself variously as a Dutch electrical worker, a German corporal, and a German artillery lieutenant.[1] The afternoon before, Francis Biddle, former US attorney general and the American judge at Nuremberg, had cavalierly informed Neave that the young major was to serve copies of the Nuremberg Charter, along with a detailed criminal indictment, on the Nazi leaders incarcerated in the Palace of Justice.[2]

Major Neave's initial assignment in post-surrender Germany had been to gather evidence on the Krupp family's wartime use of slave laborers in its armaments factories. When this project was stalled due to questions about the declining health of the Krupp patriarch, Neave was reassigned as an aide to the justices at Nuremberg. "You look remarkably young," the nasal-voiced Biddle observed in passing. Upon receiving these instructions, the young British war hero recalled, "I had several moments of unreasoning panic. I felt as if I were suddenly invited to sing at Covent Garden. It was like a nightmare in which I was endeavouring to lecture on higher mathematics."[3]

Disgusted by the abundant evidence he had already reviewed in connection with his Krupp assignment, not to mention his own wartime imprisonment and interrogation at the hands of the Gestapo, Neave dreaded his imminent personal encounter with what he called the "high priests of Nazism."[4]

"The victor will always be the judge and the vanquished the accused"

The Nuremberg Charter that Neave was to deliver spelled out the charges against twenty-four individual defendants and seven "defendant organizations" under three counts: crimes against peace, war crimes, and crimes against humanity. Crimes against peace encompassed both the "planning, preparation, initiation, or waging of a war of aggression" and "participation in a common plan or conspiracy" to wage such a war, in violation of treaties and international agreements such as the 1928 Kellogg-Briand Pact. In other words, the Nazi leaders were being charged with waging an illegal war, since the international community had outlawed aggressive war during the interwar era. The second count, alleging war crimes, referred to violations of the traditional laws of war, such as battlefield atrocities and mistreatment of prisoners, as codified in the Hague and Geneva Conventions of 1907 and 1929 and other international agreements.[5]

The Nuremberg Charter defined the third and final count, crimes against humanity, as "murder, extermination, enslavement, deportation, and other inhumane acts committed against any civilian population, before or during the war, or persecutions on political, racial, or religious grounds . . . in connection with any crime within the jurisdiction of the tribunal, whether or not in violation of domestic law of the country where perpetrated." Crimes against humanity was the most innovative and controversial of the three counts. Its plain language suggested that it could be employed to indict Nazis for mass atrocities against German Jews—a domestic civilian population—going back to the early 1930s, before the outbreak of international armed conflict in 1939.[6]

The Nuremberg Charter offered a concrete example of how the interaction among politics, ideas, and institutions pushed American diplomacy toward multilateral solutions as World War II drew to a close, even where such multiparty approaches imposed constraints or had awkward implications for the future projection of American power. The charter was the product of a contentious drafting process. The two key issues under debate were: (1) could charges be designed to assign individual guilt for the waging of aggressive war, in order to "establish the initiation of aggressive war as a crime under universally applicable international law," as one assistant prosecutor put it; and (2) would it be feasible, or indeed desirable, to prosecute prewar anti-Jewish atrocities and harassment, even though these depredations were directed against a domestic population within Germany before the outbreak of war? Holding the leaders of a nation-state responsible for transgressions of human rights— even atrocities as outrageous as those suffered by German Jews under the Nazi regime—could have uncomfortable implications for any country with a minority population that regularly endured harassment and discrimination.[7]

The charter's broad wording allowed the tribunal to answer yes to both of these questions—yes to prosecuting individuals, and yes to a count capacious enough to include domestic as well as international crimes. But while the tribunal agreed to criminalize aggression for individuals, it ultimately declined to hold the defendants responsible for prewar atrocities against domestic populations, even though the charter gave it scope to do so. Controversies over these issues were both internal, within the US government, and external, among the charter's signers (Britain, France, the USSR, and the United States).

The Nuremberg Charter used general language and offered fairly abstract guidelines, somewhat similar to the Atlantic Charter. In addition, the prosecutors drafted a rambling sixty-seven page indictment to apply the charter's principles in a specific way to each individual defendant. This indictment was diplomatically described by one of its authors as "a polygenetic document." Opening with a virtually incoherent narrative of Germany's wartime transgressions, the indictment cross-referenced the charter provisions and then reparsed the three charges into four, spelling out the alleged responsibility of each defendant. It concluded by listing each treaty or agreement alleged to have been violated by Germany's wartime leaders.[8]

For the ceremonial serving of the Nuremberg Charter and indictment on the defendants, Major Neave's entourage included the prison warden, Colonel Andrus; the general secretary of the Tribunal, Harold B. Willey, who was on leave as the chief clerk of the United States Supreme Court; one of the two prison psychiatrists, Dr. Douglas M. Kelley; as well as an interpreter and two guards armed with revolvers and small, leather-wrapped cudgels known as blackjacks. As Colonel Andrus opened the iron doors at the end of the low-ceilinged corridor connecting the court building to the prison wing, Neave intoned under his breath the beginning of the brief speech that Harold Willey had helped him draft the night before over Spanish brandies in the bar of the Grand Hotel: "I am Major Neave, the officer appointed by the International Military Tribunal to serve upon you a copy of the indictment in which you are named as a defendant."[9]

Nuremberg's Palace of Justice complex included a courthouse, an office building, and three prison wings, capable of accommodating a total of about 1200 prisoners. The court building was the former Court of Appeals for the Nuremberg region, and had somehow evaded severe damage from the numerous Allied bombing sorties which had all but leveled the rest of the old city. The whole complex filled two acres; the main building was a dusty warren of marble hallways, with 650 rooms.

Roughly half of the remaining cells were occupied by potential future defendants, including a number of women concentration camp guards, detainees awaiting interrogation who might serve as possible witnesses, as well as some ordinary German felons. Some Nazi wardens were still serving as guards for the ordinary criminals; Allied forces were short of military police to replace them. The main courtroom for the Nuremberg trial was created by knocking down a wall between two of the twenty or so courtrooms on the second floor of the main building. Trial officials and journalists often commandeered vacant rooms for unofficial purposes, including the room American journalist Victor Bernstein claimed for his office, for which he made a facetious official-looking placard reading "Ministry of Ruritania."[10]

The incarcerated Nazi leaders were confined to separate cells on the ground floor of a three-tiered structure designed to accommodate about one hundred prisoners. Each thirteen-by-nine-foot cell contained a steel bed bolted to the floor, a chair, and a toilet, with a small, perpetually open observation grille in the heavy oak door. As a precaution against suicide, the chair was removed at night, and its companion cardboard desk was designed to collapse if anyone attempted to stand on it; none of the furniture was allowed within four feet of any wall with a window in it. After the Nazi labor leader Robert Ley nevertheless found a way to hang himself, the guard detail was quadrupled and a sentry was permanently stationed at each door, with instructions to shine a light through the perpetually open grille on the defendant at night. The prisoners were ordered to sleep with their hands visible outside their bedding. Before the start of the trial, the defendants were allowed to talk to one another only during their twenty-minute exercise period in a grim treeless courtyard. Rudolf Hess insisted on goose-stepping, wild-eyed, around the courtyard at exercise time.[11]

Colonel Andrus was the American chief of security at the Nuremberg prison, director of a staff of guards made up of "extremely tough-looking and suspicious" gum-chewing American GIs who couldn't wait "to go home to Wisconsin and Cincinnati." To raise morale, Andrus had personally designed a flashy insignia for the guards' uniforms: a heraldic-looking shield of azure with a key at the top, symbolizing prison security, a rendering of the scales of justice in the center, and a broken Nazi eagle at the bottom. This insignia was painted on Andrus's helmet, to which the prison warden had applied layers of shellac to give it a high shine. Modeling his appearance on his idol and former commander, fellow cavalryman General George Patton, Andrus also often carried a leather riding crop. German inmate Hermann Goering, at one time Hitler's second in command, would sneeringly refer to Andrus as "the Fire Brigade Colonel," apparently a reference to the warden's shiny helmet.[12]

The legendary vanity of Reichsmarschall Goering—"part Machiavelli, part Falstaff"—was of course more than a match for the self-regard of the lowly Colonel Andrus. Goering's titles since 1933 included president of the Reichstag, Reich minister for air, president of the Council of Ministers for the Defense of the Reich, supreme leader of the SA, general in the SS, minister of the Interior of Prussia, chief of the Prussian Police and the Prussian Secret State Police, trustee of the Four Year Plan, head of the Hermann Goering Industrial Combine, successor designate to Hitler, and, for good measure, Germany's chief forester. Once the trial was under way, the 53-year-old Goering, lacking a mirror in his cell, would instruct his dark-suited defense counsel to stand behind the glass partition separating them during their consultations, to make the glass more reflective so he could style his receding brown hair. Such vanity was not, apparently, entirely misplaced. Several weeks into the proceedings, women correspondents covering Nuremberg voted Goering their "overwhelming choice" as the defendant they would most like to sleep with.[13]

Having duly surrendered on V-E Day to the commander of the US 36th Infantry Division in the Austrian Alps, "Goering still believed that he would be treated like a captured emperor and confined to some convenient palace," in Neave's assessment. The reichsmarschall was initially incarcerated with other top-ranking Nazis in an improvised detention center at the Palace Hotel in Bad Mondorf near the Luxembourg border. Hitler's former number two man arrived at the detention center, codenamed "Ashcan" by American service personnel, with a private valet, sixteen pieces of monogrammed ostrich skin luggage, and a red hatbox in tow. Cached in the luggage was evidence of two of his more portable addictions: a trove of looted jewelry and over twenty thousand tablets of a "morphine substitute." Goering took forty of these pills a day. The impression of a dissolute voluptuary—"infinitely corrupt . . . recall[ing] the madam of a brothel . . . a sexual quiddity"—was enhanced by his red lacquered fingernails and toenails and the 340 pounds he carried on his five-foot-six-inch frame. General Carl Spaatz, commander of the American Strategic Bombing Force, promptly threw a party for Goering, who presented Spaatz with an autographed photograph inscribed: "War is like a football game, whoever loses gives his opponent his hand, and everything is forgotten."[14]

Given this initial handling, Goering was understandably slow to realize that the post-surrender exigencies of total war would be different, even for "gentlemen" officers and high-ranking political figures, than the aftermath of combat in the First World War. During that conflict, as a flying ace and successor commander of Baron Manfred von Richthofen's legendary "flying circus," the young Hermann Goering would famously dip his wings to disabled opponents and fly on, rather than administer an unsporting *coup de grace*.[15]

Goering most likely first became aware of this new post-surrender ethos at his interrogation in Augsburg in June 1945. At this session, US General Alexander Patch, commander of the Seventh Army, unceremoniously demanded the reichsmarschall's jeweled marshal's baton, inlaid with twenty golden eagles. "General, I can't give this to you," snapped Goering, offended by what he perceived as an impertinent request. "It is a symbol of my authority." "You have no more authority," came the sharp reply from Patch. "Hand it over!" Goering wrote promptly to General Eisenhower, as supreme commander of the Allied Forces in Europe, insisting that the baton be returned to him and asking to keep his valet. Both requests were refused.[16]

Major Neave's first stop was at Goering's cell, where he served the indictment and charter on the former reichsmarschall. Neave then handed Goering a third document, a list of names and addresses of German lawyers who might serve as defense counsel. Neave recalled feeling surprised that anyone in devastated Germany still had a home address. Judge Biddle and others had impressed upon Neave the importance of urging the defendants to choose defense counsel.[17] Goering commented that he knew no one on the list and asked if he could defend himself. "I think you would be well advised to be represented by someone," Neave persisted. Goering shrugged his shoulders. "It all seems pretty hopeless to me." He continued, "I must read this indictment very carefully, but I do not see how it can have any basis in law."

Goering next requested his own private interpreter, and Colonel Andrus reportedly could not suppress a smile at yet another request for special treatment. After Neave had left Goering's cell, Dr. Gustave M. Gilbert, the prison psychologist, asked the former reichsmarschall to autograph a copy of the indictment. Goering obliged—he was used to Americans asking for his autograph. He wrote, "The victor will always be the judge and the vanquished the accused."[18]

The rather astonishing fact that the prison psychologist asked Goering to record his reactions to the indictment—there were also two prison psychiatrists—highlights one pervasive American vision of the trial as a kind of social science experiment that would serve as national therapy for the German people. In a delightful cross-cultural vignette, British Major Neave observed that "the two psychiatrists and the psychologist were essential to the American way of life at Nuremberg. They constantly interviewed the prisoners about the evidence against them." He continued in this deadpan mode: "In the eccentric atmosphere of Nuremberg, they seemed to be necessary. They supplied learned reports about tensions, blocks and depressions regarded as necessary for understanding the Nazi mind."[19]

Lieutenant Colonel Murray C. Bernays, the brilliant attorney and War Department official who drafted the original memo outlining the conspiracy theory for the trial and punishment of Nazi leadership, wrote in a June 1945 letter to his wife that "not to try these beasts would be to miss the educational and therapeutic opportunity of our generation." The defendants were considered to be singularly psychotic exemplars of a deeply disturbed dystopia, and discussion of their crimes was replete with imagery of disease and dementia.[20]

These details from Goering's initial incarceration capture several related themes of the Nuremberg trial as a legal, political, and even cultural event. The bizarre eccentricity of the atmosphere of the trial in the gutted provincial city was evoked most vividly by British author Rebecca West, whose three essays on the trial, published in *The New Yorker,* were collected in the volume *A Train of Powder.* Of the British delegation, which numbered some 170 people, West wrote colorfully: "Anybody who wants to know what [the British] were like in Nuremberg need only read the early works of Rudyard Kipling. In villas set among the Bavarian pines, amid German modernist furniture, each piece of which seemed to have an enormous behind, a triple feat of reconstitution was performed: people who were in Germany pretended they were people in the jungle who were pretending they were in England."[21]

The overwhelming amount of work necessary to prepare and present the trial intensified this hothouse atmosphere. "The entire preparatory work for the Nuremberg proceedings was attended by a kind of frenetic madness," writes Nuremberg chronicler Robert Conot, "as if the lunacy of the Nazi regime were a virus that had lingered in the atmosphere and infected those who had come to Germany."[22]

Once the trial was under way, however, Nuremberg rapidly became something of "a citadel of boredom" for its foreign visitors, who exhibited a pronounced tendency to drink excessively. One young American interpreter, Edith Simon, ascribed the pervasive loosening of peacetime standards of personal conduct to "a very strange mentality, the mentality of the conquerors." Neave concluded that, for the Soviet contingent especially, frequent "public drunkenness was part of the Nuremberg scene. It was intended to express the triumph of the Soviet peoples over Hitler and bid defiance to bourgeois convention." Simon and Rebecca West described another pervasive practice at Nuremberg, namely how cadres of middle-aged married men, who tended to populate the more senior echelons of the Nuremberg community, were notorious for seeking comfort in the arms of various female members of the administrative staff and press corps, many of whom were young and single.[23]

The Palace of Justice's very location, in bomb-blasted Nuremberg, where the stench of thirty thousand bodies entombed in its ubiquitous rubble was still pervasive, highlighted the way the trial was for many allied personnel an unwelcome reversion to wartime conditions. The American prison staff imposed numerous idiosyncratic security measures that only enhanced these feelings of constriction. West noted dryly that the ever-vigilant Colonel Andrus had noticed one of the so-called "VIP" observers in the gallery who "had crossed her ankles and was showing her shins and a line of petticoat, and he conceived that this might upset the sex-starved defendants, thus underestimating both the length of time it takes for a woman to become a VIP and the degree of the defendants' preoccupations. But, out of a further complication of delicacy, he forbade both men and women to cross their ankles . . . These rules were the subject of general mirth in Nuremberg" where "eccentricity prevailed."

Beyond these quotidian factors, part of the eccentric atmosphere was linked to the trial's anomalous position as an event on the cusp of the transition from war to peace. The trial staff saw themselves as striving to lay the juridical groundwork for a future peace. As West put it in a stark metaphor: "A machine was running down, a great machine, the greatest machine that had ever been created: the war machine . . . It was a hard machine to operate; it was the natural desire of all who served it, save those rare creatures, the born soldiers, that it should become scrap. There was another machine which was warming up: the peace machine, by which mankind lives its life . . . All over the world people were sick with impatience because they were bound to the machine that was running down, and they wanted to be among the operators of the machine that was warming up."[24]

The proceedings were an example of what some legal scholars and political scientists call "transitional justice"—an event simultaneously marking the end of the war and attempting to lay useful juridical ground-work for the peace. The Nuremberg Charter lies at the intersection of three different sets of contexts in the international law and relations of the postwar world. These contexts link the trial's legal ideas to the content and texture of the highly contingent and "eccentric" world of the negotiations that established the Nuremberg trial's parameters and its day-to-day operations.

The first relevant context for the trial was the political question of how the Allies wished to handle defeated Germany as a whole. This broader Allied policy debate implicated key legal issues such as individual accountability, debates over reparations, disarmament, and especially "denazification"—the re-education and rehabilitation of ordinary Germans and their leaders. One perspective on Nuremberg would be to view it as part of the political history of the treatment of defeated states in wartime.

The next relevant context for the trial was the development of its legal ideas. As an instrument of international law, the Nuremberg Charter attempted to accomplish three goals at once. First, it sought to outlaw aggressive war and hold individuals responsible for violations of this emerging norm. Second, it sought to draw global attention to "crimes against humanity," a landmark innovation in international law addressing the kind of mass atrocities itemized in the charter. Third, the charter served as a treaty in its own right, consolidating and building on traditional treaty law regarding the laws of war. Nuremberg's many architects differed over the relative priorities of these three major legal ideals.[25]

The final important context for understanding the Nuremberg trial was institutional. The trial was designed to play a significant role in a wider postwar international order of multilateral organizations. Many contemporaries saw it as a first step on a road to a permanent International Criminal Court. The contours of the Nuremberg Charter emerged from a series of informal negotiations at the San Francisco Conference of June 1945, itself convened to finalize the United Nations Charter. The Nuremberg Charter, the United Nations Charter, and the Bretton Woods charters collectively embodied the ideology of the Atlantic Charter's declaration of war and peace aims. The architects of Nuremberg saw themselves as contributing to a new, integrated idea of "security," encompassing all four of President Roosevelt's Four Freedoms. Together with proposals for comprehensive disarmament, Nuremberg was designed primarily to ensure freedom from fear of aggressive war.[26]

Each of these three contexts—overall treatment of defeated Germany, legal ideas about crimes against humanity, and postwar multinational institutions—offer insights into the "transitional justice" embodied in the Nuremberg Charter and subsequent trial. The rest of this chapter develops the Nuremberg story embedded in the first two contexts; the next chapter takes up the Nuremberg idea as one of several multilateral institutions meant to establish rules and norms for the postwar era. Nuremberg in context was a projection of a peculiarly American, New Deal–style approach onto the international stage.

"The hard facts of defeat and of the need for political, economic and social reorientation must be the teachers of the German people"

"Dear Winston," wrote President Franklin Roosevelt to Prime Minister Churchill in February of 1944, "I have been worrying a good deal of late on account of the tendency of all of us to prepare for future events in such detail that we may be letting ourselves in for trouble when the time arrives." The president was objecting to "detailed instructions and appendices" regarding planning for the postwar world in general, and the prospective defeat of Germany in particular, which he regarded "as prophecies by prophets who cannot be infallible." FDR continued, "Now comes this business of what to do when we get into Germany. I understand that your Staff presented a long and comprehensive document . . . My people over here believe that a short document of surrender terms should be adopted [instead]" that would conform more to "general principles."[27]

One of the lessons 1940s American policymakers learned from the planning experience of the First World War was "do not wait until the war is over to plan the peace." The ordeal of Woodrow Wilson in Paris suggested this insight, where pre-existing secret agreements among the European allies had constrained the American president's idealistic efforts. Yet many students of FDR's decision-making style have noted that Roosevelt's usual response to bureaucratic controversy "was almost invariably to procrastinate, usually by either promising all things to all parties or by quietly putting off any decision." The cabinet's push for prior planning accordingly tended to produce proposals that were quite abstract and general, often based on competing philosophies. Combined with the Rooseveltian tendency to back off in the face of controversy, it was the negotiating skills and agendas of second- and third-tier administration officials that usually dictated the early drafts of the resulting directives.[28]

Bureaucratic controversy in great abundance confronted Roosevelt in late 1944 and early 1945 around the initial post-surrender plans for Germany. This debate distilled into three competing approaches. State Department planners advocated an economically sound and self-supporting Germany as essential to the economic rehabilitation of Western Europe and as a bulwark against communism. Post-surrender planning memos embodied Secretary Hull's longstanding emphasis on economic issues, especially trade—an emphasis that continued even after the ailing Hull's resignation three weeks after the November 1944 election.[29]

By contrast, the War Department, under the venerable Republican Henry L. Stimson, focused on the immediate problems of administering the postwar occupation of Germany. The War Department's *Handbook of Military Government,* circulated in late August 1944, stressed reliance on existing authority structures within Germany to maintain order. The handbook's avowedly short-term approach would likely have longer-term ramifications, however, favoring a "soft peace." A third approach to denazification was centered in the Treasury Department, under New Dealer and Roosevelt confidant Henry Morgenthau, Jr. Treasury's approach aimed at eliminating a future resurgence of German militarism and aggression by demolishing Germany's military and industrial capabilities and imposing policies aimed at thoroughgoing social and even psychological reform.[30]

Historians have ascribed the vehemence of these disputes within the executive branch to a variety of factors, such as differences in the ideology or organizational culture of the various departments; personality clashes among the respective cabinet members; or strains and uncertainties in their personal relationships with Roosevelt. Recent commentators have tended to emphasize the personal social attitudes and background of the cabinet members as well: Stimson's patrician anti-Semitism, for instance, or Morgenthau's German-Jewish heritage. The case of Treasury Secretary Morgenthau, however, illustrates the dangers of armchair psychologizing about motives. Morgenthau's views about the "pastoralization" of Germany—the term was actually Churchill's—and the peace-loving virtues of the yeoman farmer were just as likely to stem from his experience as a gentleman farmer who idealized Jeffersonian values as from his ethnicity. Also, Roosevelt, of a distinctly different heritage, often expressed complete accord with Morgenthau's outlook on the treatment of defeated Germany, particularly his social worker–style focus on cultural transformation of the German people as a whole rather than exclusively on the Nazi party.[31]

Debate over the postwar treatment of Germany spilled over into an acrimonious public dispute shortly after Roosevelt, together with Churchill, publicly supported the so-called Morgenthau Plan at the Quebec Conference of September 1944. The proposal emphasized social and educational "reform of the German character," complemented by complete disarmament, deportations of Nazi officials to help rebuild countries they had devastated, and the partition of industrial areas of the country into internationalized zones so they could no longer serve as "the caldron of wars."[32]

Although this plan called for the trial of the vast majority of accused war criminals, Allied firing squads were summarily to execute a top layer of arch-criminals upon capture and identification. In the autumn of 1944 Roosevelt himself favored summary execution quite explicitly. An aide's notes of a September 9, 1944, conversation indicate that "war criminals, the President hoped might be dealt with summarily. His principal preoccupation was that they be properly identified before being disposed of, but he expressed himself as very much opposed to long, drawn-out legal procedure."[33]

The Morgenthau Plan shared a certain reformist sensibility with the New Deal. This assessment is unsurprising, in light of the fact that Morgenthau's deputy, Harry Dexter White, was the chief drafter of early iterations of the plan. In the immediate aftermath of the Bretton Woods Conference, White turned his attention to a series of State Department memoranda developing occupation policies for the prospective defeat of Germany. He did not like what he saw: plans to reconstruct the German industrial plant in order to generate reparations, but without regard for the fact that while Europe would likely become dependent on a Germany strong enough to pump out reparations, a reconstructed Germany would not be similarly dependent on Europe. Such a scenario contributed to, rather than solved, what White saw as the more basic political problem: how to reshape the German economy, society, and culture so that it would not make a third attempt in as many generations to dominate Europe. Morgenthau agreed. The treasury secretary explained for a popular audience how, "in discussions of what to do with Germany, she has been compared to a mental patient, a problem child . . . a case of retarded development, a young girl led astray, a slab of molten metal ready for the molder and much else besides." These similes, Morgenthau explained, merely emphasized how thoroughgoing was "the educational or evolutionary problem that must be faced." The Treasury program concluded that "the hard facts of defeat and of the need for political, economic and social reorientation must be the teachers of the German people."[34]

As the Roosevelt historian Warren Kimball argues, Morgenthau exemplified "the belief of many New Dealers in the efficacy of grand plans as the solution to problems," and he assumed "that an entire nation could be restructured and redirected by outside agents." In a diary entry referring to Germans over the age of twenty who had been thoroughly inculcated with Nazi ideology, Morgenthau wrote, "I am convinced that you could change them [although] you may even have to transplant them out of Germany to some place in Central Africa where you can do some big TVA project."[35]

While Secretary of War Henry Stimson grumbled privately that the Treasury Department's plan was "Semitism gone wild for vengeance," his public response was much more canny. The day after the Quebec Conference, he sent an influential memo to Roosevelt arguing that the Treasury program violated American principles. Explicitly invoking the Atlantic Charter, the secretary of war asserted that "the proposed treatment of Germany would, if successful, deliberately deprive many millions of people of the right to freedom from want and freedom from fear." Stimson pointedly reminded Roosevelt that "under the Atlantic Charter victors and vanquished alike are entitled to freedom from economic want." He elaborated that it would be "a crime against civilization" to force poverty on the "educated, efficient, and imaginative" German people.[36] Perhaps coincidentally, the controversy simultaneously leaked from an administration source to allies in the press, Drew Pearson and Arthur Krock of the *New York Times*.[37]

Stimson's approach was really a short-term version of the equally conciliatory State Department approach and was favored by such State officials as the young George Kennan, then serving as aide to John Winant, ambassador to Britain. Kennan opposed even the mildest denazification programs as eliminating "the people upon whom Germany had to depend for future leadership" and as likely to promote "disharmony." Stimson and his assistant secretary, John J. McCloy, insisted that their plans were focused only on establishing law, order, and efficiency. Irate Treasury Department staff responded that the complementary War and State Department approaches were predicated on the Allies' assuming responsibility for the quality of life in Germany. The inevitable result would be a higher standard of living among the defeated Germans than in the hard-bitten Allied European nations, which had sacrificed so much for victory.[38]

Of the two approaches, Morgenthau's was the one that more closely approximated American public opinion in autumn 1944. A Gallup poll in November showed that 34 percent of Americans wanted to destroy Germany as a political entity, 32 percent wanted continuing supervision and control over Germany, and 12 percent wanted to "rehabilitate" Germany. But after the cabinet controversy was leaked to the press, public opinion began to shift and the Treasury proposals never again regained the initiative.[39]

The dynamics of this shift in mid-1940s America illustrate the complex workings obscured by the label "public opinion." In the wake of the initial *New York Times* coverage, the influential *Wall Street Journal* and then the nationally syndicated Associated Press quickly took up the Morgenthau story. Newspapers across the political spectrum soon concurred with the *Washington Post*'s assessment that the Morgenthau Plan was "the product of a feverish mind from which all sense of reality had fled." The Treasury plan would ensure that Germany remained "a festering sore . . . in the heart of Europe, and there would be installed a chaos which would assuredly end in war." The *Post* further emphasized that Nazi propaganda minister Josef Goebbels was already using the story "as a threat to spur Germans to greater resistance against the Allies." Stories about the Morgenthau controversy ran in the press alongside parallel columns with stories of a serious Allied setback around Arnheim, in the lower Rhine, due to a rallying of German resistance. Commentators at the time emphasized the coincidence. By the end of September, legislators on Capitol Hill were attacking the Treasury Department plan, and the White House was receiving quantities of unfavorable mail. "Prior to the announcement [of the Morgenthau Plan]," noted Senator Edwin Johnson, "the Germans were surrendering in droves; now they are fighting like demons."[40]

With the presidential election seven weeks away, an embattled and annoyed Roosevelt withdrew his support for the Treasury proposal, favoring the "middle road" of the short-term War Department approach almost by default. The president fired off a memo to the secretary of state: "Somebody has been talking out of turn to the papers on facts which are not fundamentally true. No one wants to make Germany a wholly agricultural nation again, and yet somebody down the line has handed this out to the press. I wish we could catch and chastise him."[41]

The aggregate term "public opinion" is a shorthand caption for this dynamic relationship among activist public officials, press leaks, down-to-the wire electioneering, journalistic editorializing, and congressional and citizens' advocacy for self-serving interpretations of public events. In saying that the Treasury Department's approach was defeated by public opinion, it is important to realize that, on the eve of an election, decision-makers had every reason to be especially sensitive to such opinion.

The British and even the Soviet leadership never took a particularly hard line about post-surrender partition, deindustrialization, or summary execution of war criminals in Germany, although they favored all three policies at one time or another. For example, at the Teheran Conference of November–December 1943, Stalin famously remarked to Churchill at a formal dinner that the Allies ought summarily to execute between 50,000 and 100,000 Germans. Roosevelt apparently tried to turn the comment into a joke by counterproposing the execution of only 49,000 members of the German General Staff. The British were more concerned about extension of Lend-Lease loans, and the Soviets about arrangements for Eastern Europe, than about the details of handling postwar Germany. In the quaintly gendered terms of the historian Warren Kimball, "Conflicts between the Americans and the British were more on the order of family quarrels; quarrels which could, if necessary, be resolved almost peremptorily by the Americans—the breadwinner." Uncertainty over even the broad outlines of war crimes policies still reigned among the so-called Big Three as late as the February 1945 Yalta Conference, just two months before Roosevelt's death.[42]

A statement released for public consumption at Yalta very closely resembled the Morgenthau approach: "It is our inflexible purpose to destroy German militarism and Nazism and to ensure that Germany will never again be able to disturb the peace of the world," the Yalta statement began. "We are determined to disarm and disband all German armed forces; break up for all time the German General Staff that has repeatedly contrived the resurgence of German militarism; remove or destroy all German military equipment; eliminate or control all German industry that could be used for military production; bring all war criminals to just and swift punishment and exact reparation in kind for the destruction wrought by the Germans; wipe out the Nazi party, Nazi laws, organizations and institutions, remove all Nazi and militarist influences from public office and from the cultural and economic life of the German people; and take in harmony such other measures in Germany as may be necessary to the future peace and safety of the world."[43]

The main difference between this statement and the original Treasury Department proposal was that the Yalta language explicitly distinguished between Nazis and the German people—a distinction underlined by the concluding sentence on war criminals: "It is not our purpose to destroy the people of Germany, but only when Nazism and Militarism have been extirpated will there be hope for a decent life for Germans, and a place for them in the comity of nations." This distinction between Nazis and Germans was one that FDR consistently refused to make himself, however. Roosevelt often expressed his opinion "that all Germans, and not just the Nazis, were guilty of aggression and crimes against humanity." The president added numerous handwritten notes to his own copy of the Treasury Department plan aimed at the cultural reform of ordinary Germans, including a proposed prohibition of the goose-step march. At Yalta, Roosevelt commented that he was feeling "more bloodthirsty in regard to the Germans than he had been a year ago," having learned more about Germany's systematic devastation of the areas it had occupied.[44]

Even the most basic outline of Allied denazification policy remained fuzzy until after Roosevelt's death. In May 1944, officials in charge of implementing these policies soon found themselves at sea among overlapping committees. General Lucius Clay, soon to be in charge of the American sector of a quadripartite Allied Control Authority for the administration of Occupied Germany, lamented the proliferating post-surrender bureaucracy. In a letter to a War Department official, Clay saw a bumpy ride ahead for more ambitious Allied approaches to multilateralism. "We understand here that consideration is being given to separate Commissions for Restitutions, for the Trial of War Criminals, for the Internationalization of the Ruhr and for other purposes," he wrote resignedly. Administering these occupied areas was a kind of microcosm of broader cooperative projects: "We are going to face many difficulties in making the Allied Control Authority work. To me it seems clear that if it doesn't work we might as well throw the idea of a United Nations out the window."[45]

By early spring 1945, the State Department position had prevailed on questions of economic policy, that is, against the dismemberment and deindustrialization of Germany and in favor of the rapid rebuilding of productive resources as a bulwark against communism. The moderate positions of the War Department won out on political, legal, and administrative questions, including policies relating to the treatment of war criminals. In sum, the Allies had three options for handling high-ranking Axis authorities as part of implementing their "unconditional surrender" policy. They could deal with leading war crimes suspects by executive fiat (which would have involved shooting them upon identification, as per the Morgenthau Plan, or confining them in political imprisonment); they could let them go free under an amnesty policy; or they could put them on trial.[46]

All three choices were problematic. Summary execution without trial would have been ideologically awkward for the democracies in light of the Allies' pronouncements on the nascent United Nations and the rule of law. The Allies rejected as politically unworkable the option of confinement in a remote area by executive fiat, along the lines of the Elba solution for Napoleon. And given the rhetoric (and reality) of Nazi leaders as enemies of civilization, the Allies never seriously considered granting any kind of outright amnesty either, as it ran the risk of suggesting that the sacrifices of millions of Allied soldiers and civilians had been in vain.[47]

As with the resonant phrases of the Atlantic Charter—resonant because they echoed with people's aspirations and in turn helped shape their expectations—Allied leaders' own propaganda and rhetoric served as a constraint on their policies. A widely publicized pronouncement from the Yalta Declaration linked multilateral action on war crimes to the principles of the 1941 Atlantic Charter itself: "By this declaration we affirm our faith in the principles of the Atlantic Charter, our pledge in the [1942] Declaration by the United Nations, and our determination to build in cooperation with other peace-loving nations a world order under law, dedicated to peace, security, freedom and the general well-being of mankind." Ambiguous public pronouncements on the future treatment of war criminals, as well as the Atlantic Charter's own language that its terms would apply to both victor and vanquished, had already contributed to a vision of the future that proved difficult simply to abandon.[48]

One perspective on the ensuing legal disputes over what to do with war criminals is thus to see them primarily as diplomatic donnybrooks, microcosms of this wider denazification debate, rather than as arguments over the intrinsic merits of abstract legal theories. We might frame the Nuremberg process itself, at least as regards the symbolic role of the Nuremberg defendants as surrogates for wider groups of Nazis in German society, as a vestigial and largely symbolic embodiment of the Morgenthau Plan, with the plan's focus on "reform of the German character."[49] Whatever our assessment, we may best understand the choice to stage a high-profile trial for selected Nazi leaders when we set that decision in the context of possible alternative approaches.

"There are just and unjust wars and . . . unjust wars are illegal"

The ideas about international law embodied in the Nuremberg Charter were a new combination of older conceptions regarding just and unjust wars, mixed with positivist ideas from previous treaties about traditional crimes of war. Allied legal experts then combined these precedents with innovative arguments about the scope of a "living" international customary law, through analogy to the growth of Anglo-American common law. The negotiators and their aides saw themselves as harnessing the pre-existing legitimacy of persuasive legal precedents in order to create something new, even as they explained the precise contours of this synthesis as primarily a political negotiation.[50]

The Nuremberg trial and charter were designed to mark "the reestablishment of the principle that there are just and unjust wars and that unjust wars are illegal," in the words of the chief American negotiator of the charter, Supreme Court Justice Robert H. Jackson, who would later serve as the US Chief Prosecutor. In his June 1945 report to the president on "Atrocities and War Crimes," Jackson explained that "doubtless what appeals to men of good will and common sense as the crime which comprehends all lesser crimes is the crime of making unjustifiable war." He continued, "War necessarily is a calculated series of killings, of destructions of property, of oppressions. Such acts unquestionably would be criminal except that International Law throws a mantle of protection around acts which otherwise would be crimes, when committed in pursuit of legitimate warfare." The report concluded that if the underlying conflict were an illegitimate use of force, however, this mantle of protection would be removed, and the killings, destructions, and oppressions would revert to their normal status as ordinary crimes.[51]

The Jackson Report's reasoning captures the Nuremberg Charter's conception of a war crime, as a label referring to an act which remained criminal even though committed in time of war, and which presupposed the existence of laws of war. The whole concept of "civilized warfare" rested on the assumption that multilateral agreements could mitigate the ravages of battle as far as possible by prohibiting needless cruelties. Legal scholars have traced the practice of regulating the conduct of war to the emergence of knightly chivalry in Europe, and back before that to the *jus fetiale* of ancient Rome.[52]

The early Christian conception of a war crime was linked to the moral status of the conflict as a whole—whether it was just or unjust. In their writings that touched on war, Saint Augustine, Saint Thomas Aquinas, Francisco Suarez, and other scholars and theologians, as well as the jurist Hugo Grotius, were largely concerned with establishing criteria for just and unjust wars. They tended to concur that the situations that might justify forcible resistance were the defense of life, property, or of a third party unjustly attacked.[53]

As the temper of international law became increasingly laicized during the eighteenth century, a more pragmatic, rule-oriented vision of warfare in which the state of war itself was assumed to be a neutral context for actions that could be subject to regulation (the *jus in bello*) came to overshadow the older, moralistic just war tradition, known as the *jus ad bellum*. The Hague Conventions, army field manuals, and Geneva protocols of 1925 and 1929 were legalistic outgrowths of the central premise that "the right of belligerents to adopt means of injuring the enemy is not unlimited." The aftermath of the First World War encouraged a revival of the moralistic tradition of folding the *jus in bello* into the *jus ad bellum*, as part of the wider agenda of outlawing aggressive war. The two concepts, in practice never entirely distinct, became increasingly intertwined.[54]

This trend toward synthesis was particularly pronounced in the wartorn countries of Allied Europe, largely because of the general public's moral outrage at World War I atrocities such as the well-publicized German execution of British nurse Edith Cavell, the destruction of French and Belgian towns such as Lille and Louvain by rampaging German troops, the Zeppelin bombing of British cities, and civilian deaths from German U-boat attacks on the high seas. At the 1919 Paris Peace Conference, British Prime Minister Lloyd George and French Premier Georges Clemenceau had insisted that "war crimes" be the very first agenda item at the conference's first official session. A commission of fifteen prominent international lawyers took up this question and concluded two months later that the Central Powers had "premeditated" the war. A subcommittee of this group then recommended that "for the future, penal sanctions should be provided for such outrages." In other words, the commission determined that Germany should be held responsible, not just for violations of specific laws regarding the conduct of the war but for the very state of war itself.[55]

Yet the phrase "for the future" is quite telling as well, expressing the legalist hesitations of the commission's chair, US Secretary of State Robert Lansing. Lansing and the other American member of the commission, international legal scholar James Brown Scott, refused to sign the commission's report. They submitted a minority report objecting to the proposal to treat as grounds for legal liability "violations of the laws of humanity, as to which there was no fixed and universal standard, but it varied with time, place, circumstance and conscience of the individual judge." The American duo also doubted the feasibility of pursuing penal sanctions because of the "difficulty of finding whether the act was in reality one of aggression or defense." The political scientist Gary Bass explains succinctly that these legalist objections "were not based on a lack of faith in law, but on an excess of it"—a positivist rigidity born of a direct generalization of domestic legal standards to the international level.[56]

Popular pressure played a large role in these developments, as shown by Lloyd George's 1918 election year cry that "the Kaiser must be prosecuted"—sometimes summarized in the press as "Hang the Kaiser!" The prime minister's election polemic continued, "The war was a hideous, abominable crime, a crime which has sent millions of the best young men of Europe to death and mutilation, and which has plunged myriads of homes into desolation. Is no one responsible? Is no one to be called to account?"[57]

Article 227 of the Treaty of Versailles explicitly provided that "a special tribunal will be constituted to try Wilhelm II . . . It will be guided by the highest motives of international policy, with a view to vindicating the solemn obligations of international undertakings and the validity of international morality." The Allied plan proved abortive, however, because the kaiser fled to the Netherlands, which refused to surrender him for trial. Some of the putative backup plans for addressing the kaiser's act of impunity seemed to have been drawn from the libretto of a comic opera. None was successfully implemented, including a proposal that the British government officially urge him to commit suicide; plans for banishment to less familiar venues such as Chile, Java, and the Falkland Islands, presumably after a kidnapping; and an actual abduction attempt by a team of American veterans. Encouraged by his advisors to feign illness in order to garner public sympathy, the former monarch bought a castle twenty-five miles from the German border where he lived in comfortable exile until his death from old age in 1941.[58]

Article 228 of the Versailles Treaty called for prosecution of those Germans who had "committed acts in violation of the laws and customs of war." Belgium, France, Britain, and Italy each produced a list of suspects, totaling about three thousand names. Even allowing for group arraignments for crews of particular U-boats or staffs of individual POW camps, these numbers still suggested close to a thousand separate trials. By 1920 British politicians in particular were worrying about the destabilizing effects of so many trials on Germany's shaky Weimar government, particularly where suspects would need to be handed over to an Allied tribunal by the already unpopular German authorities. "Trying very large numbers," according to meeting minutes paraphrasing Lloyd George, "would create great difficulties for the German Government, which he believed to be better than either a Bolshevist Government or a Militarist Government." Perhaps it would be better to try to prosecute a smaller number, just to "make an example."[59]

The United States, as an Associated rather than an Allied power in the First World War, had not submitted a list of suspected criminals. President Wilson, in particular, felt that the war crimes provisions of the Versailles Treaty were a "weak spot" in that agreement and distracted from the more important work of the League of Nations in establishing the rule of law worldwide. Even after the joint Allied list was boiled down to just over four hundred defendants, plans for trials under the so-called war guilt clauses of the Treaty of Versailles served as flashpoints for popular resentment in Germany. In 1920 German Chancellor Hermann Muller approved a secret fund to pay the expenses of the defendants, while German diplomats in Paris warned that no police force in Germany would be willing to execute the warrants. Confronting these difficulties, the Allies reluctantly accepted a German suggestion to try forty or so suspects before the German Supreme Court (Reichsgericht) sitting at Leipzig, in a series of test cases grouped by the victims' country of origin.[60]

By the time the trials got under way in May 1921, a number of suspects had mysteriously escaped. The German court issued perfunctory sentences to others who did stand trial, often of less than a year; others of these convicts escaped from jail, with wardens of these escapees receiving public congratulations. Still other defendants, including some accused of torturing Belgian children, were acquitted completely, usually on the grounds that they were only following orders. French and Belgian witnesses withdrew from Leipzig in protest, amid jeering German crowds. In 1922 France sought to impose sanctions under the Treaty of Versailles, in large part over German noncompliance on war crimes provisions, and in early 1923 France reoccupied the Ruhr to protest violations of additional articles of the Versailles Treaty.[61]

Continuing Allied demands for legitimate trials precipitated widespread protest demonstrations in Germany, while public celebrations greeted German Chancellor Josef Wirth's announcement in 1922 that no further suspects would stand trial. The dashing young flying ace and decorated war hero Hermann Goering attended one of these protest meetings and was particularly impressed by the electrifying speech of a rumpled and sweaty Adolf Hitler. Goering made a point of introducing himself. Alexander Cadogan, later to serve as the British permanent undersecretary for foreign affairs during World War II, concluded tersely that "the experiment [of the Leipzig trials] has been pronounced a failure."[62]

In the interwar era, a number of diplomatic efforts attempted to reassert the moralistic principle of the *jus ad bellum*, seeking a determination as to whether the underlying conflict was "just" or not. The Covenant of the League of Nations asserted that governments could wage war unjustly, and the Havana Anti-War Resolution of 1928 stated that "the American Republics desire to express that they condemn war as an instrument of national policy in their mutual relations." Using war as an instrument of policy meant the aggressive or discretionary use of armed force; a defensive use of force was still understood as a justified response to attack. The 1925 Locarno treaties banned aggression among their signatories, and the 1928 Pact of Paris also explicitly condemned war. After 1928, "war was no longer to be the source and subject of legal rights, and in that sense became an illegal thing," argued a 1946 article in the *South Atlantic Quarterly,* further asserting that "an aggressor and a victim were no longer equals in law." By implication, then, legal rights in wartime could become dependent, at least in part, on the side for which one fought, with the aggressor responsible not just for individual atrocities but also for the state of war itself.[63]

The Nuremberg approach was an innovation in the world of legal ideas, but the trial's design was also an attempt to learn from the historic failure of the World War I–era approaches. To Nuremberg's proponents, the development of the Nuremberg Charter was a search for a pragmatic, New Deal–style middle way that could support a conception of the progressive development of international law, while avoiding the pitfalls of the past.

To Nuremberg's critics, however, the revival of the just war framework suggested another, and in their view more alarming, corollary: that victims of "illegal" aggression could now be presumed to have virtually unlimited rights, including the right to resort to atomic weapons. The international legal scholar Richard Falk points out that the very day of the signing of the Nuremberg Charter was the same day the United States deployed an atomic weapon against the largely civilian population of Nagasaki, killing tens of thousands and leading to what he calls "the irony of August 8, 1945." The Rooseveltian synthesis of legalism and moralism produced what were in effect twin symbols of American exceptionalism for the postwar era: Nuremberg and Nagasaki.[64]

CHAPTER 8

INTERNATIONALIZING
NEW DEAL JUSTICE

The 1943 Moscow Declaration is the traditional departure point for many accounts of the negotiation of the Nuremberg Charter, mainly because the jurists assembling in London in the summer of 1945 described their task as implementing this Moscow Declaration. At the November 1943 meeting in Moscow between the chief foreign affairs officers of the Big Three, the Allies called for the punishment of those who would later be called "conventional" war criminals—"those who have been responsible for, or who have taken a consenting part in . . . atrocities, massacres, and executions." Significantly, the leading diplomats then officially broadened the term to include "the major criminals, whose offences have no particular geographical localisation." Whatever the meaning of this phrase, it signaled that the Allies would be enlisting legal ideas regarding wartime culpability as part of their larger postwar policy edifice.[1]

Moscow was not the first high-level evocation of Axis criminality, however. Earlier examples included a 1942 statement by Roosevelt, warning that "the time will come when [perpetrators of atrocities] shall have to stand in courts of law in the very countries which they are now oppressing and answer for their acts." In January 1942 the nine governments in exile in London issued the Inter-Allied Declaration of St. James's Palace, asserting that they would "place among their principal war aims the punishment, through the channels of organized justice, of those guilty and responsible for these [war] crimes, whether they have ordered them, perpetrated them, or in any way participated in them."[2]

The Declaration of St. James's Palace also repudiated the idea that "acts of vengeance on the part of the general public" could appropriately punish perpetrators of atrocities against civilians. The signers relied on "the sense of justice of the civilized world" for their authority. One product of this Declaration was the establishment of a United Nations War Crimes Commission (UNWCC) in London in October 1943, an evidence-gathering organ that specifically excluded Holocaust-related atrocities from its purview. The Soviet Union, although a victim of massive German atrocities, refused to participate in the UNWCC, complaining that the commission was dominated by former British colonies. This London-based War Crimes Commission was not under American control either, and one of the factors shaping US war crimes policies throughout 1944 was the effort to fend off unwelcome proposals by the UNWCC as that organization became more assertive.[3]

Warning statements to Germany before late 1944 were deliberately framed in rather vague terms in order to avoid creating a propaganda tool that might stiffen Axis resistance. Nevertheless, fear of reprisals alone cannot explain the astonishingly perfunctory public discussion of Axis atrocities in 1942, 1943, and throughout most of 1944. Prime Minister Churchill, for instance, believed that Allied threats about inevitable future punishments might actually *discourage* atrocities, if they served to "make some of these villains reluctant to be mixed up in butcheries now [that] they realize they are going to be defeated." Given that credible evidence in the United States had verified the outlines of the Final Solution as early as autumn 1942, other factors were probably at work as well.[4]

Forces shaping American attitudes toward information about mass atrocities during World War II included lingering skepticism induced by inflated atrocity stories from the First World War, which some World War II–era commentators had come to see as having manipulated the American public to favor involvement in the Great War. Fears of an influx of refugees who might take newly available jobs and dilute the stock of "native" workers strengthened anti-immigrant sentiment in the United States in the early 1940s. Anti-Semitism likely played a role in these native-stock arguments. Yet the United States was also just emerging from a decade-long Depression where unemployment had skyrocketed. Even plentiful wartime jobs had failed to erase relatively recent memories of bread lines and soup kitchens. Wartime public opinion polls often showed that a majority of Americans predicted another economic depression after the war, with unemployment spiking as millions of young people left the armed forces and tried to rejoin the civilian workforce. The prospect of government programs admitting floods of destitute immigrants played into these fears of higher postwar joblessness, whatever the likely ethnic background of those immigrants.[5]

In addition, State Department officials such as Breckinridge Long argued that waivers of US immigration quotas would be especially undesirable in the case of Jewish refugees and that a deliberate policy of delay would better accomplish State Department objectives. Most unsettling of all, perhaps, was the role played by highly assimilated American-Jewish leaders such as presidential advisor Samuel I. Rosenman, who consistently sought to water down the president's public statements on war crimes and even insisted that FDR refuse meetings with groups advocating on behalf of Holocaust victims. A charitable interpretation of Rosenman's behavior is that American pluralism, for him, meant denying the relevance of ethnicity in every context. He may also have believed that large cohorts of manifestly alien-seeming co-religionist refugees would encourage the growth of American anti-Semitism.[6]

Government officials of Jewish background were sensitive to the accusation that they might use their professional positions for special pleading on behalf of their persecuted co-religionists. Nor were these concerns imaginary: Treasury Secretary Henry Morgenthau recorded an encounter with FDR where the president, a long-time family friend, casually remarked to Morgenthau and to an aide of Catholic background, "You know, this is a Protestant country, and the Catholics and Jews are here under sufferance." Roosevelt does not seem to have elaborated on this observation, concluding only that it was therefore "up to you" to "go along with anything I want." Antisemitic commentators regularly pilloried Roosevelt as being under the sway of Jewish advisors, notably Morgenthau himself, Supreme Court Justice Felix Frankfurter, and the unofficial advisor Bernard Baruch. Perhaps for this reason, Morgenthau in his 1945 book, *Germany Is Our Problem*, did not refer to his own religious background, nor—more astonishingly, given the book's subject and date of publication—did it mention Jews at all. While representatives of Jewish groups were active and persistent, they failed to influence policymakers in any executive department except the Treasury, let alone to penetrate mainstream American consciousness.[7]

The innate human tendency simply to deny the reality of such shocking news as mass slaughters likely played a role as well. Even the November 1943 Moscow Declaration referred to what would become known as the Holocaust incredibly obliquely, as "the slaughters inflicted on the people of Poland." Nuremberg assistant prosecutor Telford Taylor remembered that the establishment of the War Crimes Commission in London "made astonishingly—indeed shamefully—little impact on the public mind. I myself did not become aware of the Holocaust until my exposure to the relevant documents and witnesses at Nuremberg."[8]

After the Moscow Declaration, officials in the War Department developed several general plans, starting with the *Handbook on Military Government for Germany*, which included an annex on war criminals. The *Handbook* included a table listing "categories of Nazi officers" to be "arrested and detained upon the Allied Occupational Forces' entry into Germany," estimated to add up to well over 100,000 potential detaineees in the Western Zone of occupation alone. In the summer of 1944, however, with overall denazification policy still unsettled, it was not possible to be more specific about the fate of those detained. Plans for their processing would most likely have grown out of the guiding principles of this War Department handbook, as summarized by its admonition to occupation authorities that "your main and immediate task, to accomplish your mission, is to get things running, to pick up the pieces, to restore as quickly as possible the official functioning of the German civil government in the area for which you are responsible . . . The first concern of military government will be to see that the machine works and works efficiently."[9]

In large part, the War Department's approach of "treating defeated Germany like a nice WPA job"—that is, like a New Deal project or agency—was what had sparked Treasury Secretary Morgenthau to develop his famously divisive alternative. This dynamic of stimulus and response continued through the autumn and winter of 1944, as controversy over the Morgenthau Plan became a major impetus for the War Department to develop its own plans regarding Germany's suspected war criminals.[10]

"However much a man loved the law, he could not love so much of it as wound its sluggish way through the Palace of Justice at Nuremberg"

Lieutenant Colonel Murray C. Bernays was the thoughtful and bookish chief of the Special Projects Office in the Personnel Branch of the War Department. Bernays had developed a plan for prosecution of war criminals that turned on charging the leaders of the Nazi regime with "conspiracy . . . to commit murder, terrorism, and destruction of peaceful populations in violation of the laws of war." Traditionally an Anglo-American legal doctrine, the conspiracy approach would also criminalize "everything done in furtherance of the conspiracy . . . including domestic atrocities induced or procured by the German Government to be committed by other Axis nations against their respective nationals." Groups as well as individuals could be conspirators, and Bernays envisioned an initial trial of the top echelon of Nazi leaders along with representatives of groups such as the Gestapo and German General Staff.[11]

Once a tribunal had declared a group criminal, it would merely be a matter of showing whether any given individual was a member of that group, thus purging large numbers of Nazis using judicial processes rather than summary execution. Other War Department attorneys, notably Colonel Ammi Cutter, refined the Bernays Plan before Secretary of War Henry Stimson enthusiastically endorsed it in late October of 1944. The criminal conspiracy approach was especially appealing, Stimson later told associates, because as a young lawyer he himself had litigated some trust-busting conspiracy cases against sugar combines and had found the doctrine to be both rigorous and efficient.[12]

American planning for Axis war crimes trials bogged down in the winter of 1944–45 in the face of interdepartmental opposition, mostly from the offices of the judge advocate general and, later, the State Department legal advisor. Officials in these offices, as well as Herbert Weschler in the Justice Department (who would become a supporter and advisor at Nuremberg) objected to the concept of including prewar atrocities against a domestic population, since the strictures of the laws of war were presumably triggered only by an underlying international armed conflict. They also expressed concerns about guilt-by-association problems presented by the conspiracy scheme. But in late January 1945 an unexpected infusion of popular fervor dramatically cut through these bureaucratic debates, galvanizing plans for an ambitious and high-profile trial of Nazi leaders.

On December 17, 1944, during the Battle of the Bulge, the First SS Panzer regiment had machine-gunned seventy American prisoners at Malmédy, Belgium. This was the event that convinced then-Attorney General Biddle—later to serve as the American judge at Nuremberg—that the Nazis were indeed perpetrating a criminal conspiracy to violate the laws of war. "Malmédy fever" started slowly in late December but heated up through January and February. The Malmédy syndrome is a stark vindication of the central thrust of political scientist Gary Bass's thesis that countries are only motivated to pursue the remedy of war crimes trials when enemy atrocities are directed against their own nationals. While the slaughter of these seventy military prisoners was doubtlessly very shocking to American sensibilities, it is equally shocking that the slaughter of millions of noncombatant European Jews of all ages and both genders over the preceding three years had failed to generate even a fraction of this outrage.[13]

The Bass thesis is at root a commentary on the limits of empathy and the links between empathy, mobilization, and policy. Malmédy fever gave the proponents of the modified Bernays Plan the advantage they needed to push through their model of the trial of Axis leaders and organizations. It also gave administration officials charged with negotiating war crimes policy enough confidence to promote their plans over British objections that the proposed trials would be too innovative and complicated. American attitudes toward Axis atrocities thus shaped how such atrocities came to be defined and prosecuted at Nuremberg. Similarly, as the human rights specialist Kirsten Sellars has noted, the American focus on crimes against peace (aggression), rather than crimes against humanity (atrocities), reflected the particular American experience of World War II: "Despite genuine disgust at Nazi atrocities, Washington believed that the regime's most heinous crime had been to draw the Allies into a ruinous global conflict."[14]

Recalled from his diplomatic mission in London to impose an American-style war crimes policy by the unexpected death of President Roosevelt, Sam Rosenman continued refining blueprints for what became the Nuremberg Charter in a series of informal negotiations at the UN San Francisco Conference. He was joined in some of these discussions by the recently appointed chief prosecutor for Axis criminality, Supreme Court Justice Robert H. Jackson. A consummate New Dealer since his days as a small-time practitioner in upstate New York, "Robert H. Jackson was not one of the legal Brahmins typical of the Stimson group," a junior colleague observed. Jackson had not attended college, and after a year at Albany Law School he "read articles" in a law office before sitting for the New York Bar. Telford Taylor noted that Jackson was "probably the last nationally prominent lawyer to gain admission to the bar by serving an apprenticeship rather than by a law school degree"—a common nineteenth-century practice for impecunious aspiring attorneys.[15]

In the 1930s this self-made professional had attracted the attention of leading New York State politicians such as Franklin Roosevelt, Herbert Lehman, and Henry Morgenthau, Jr. Jackson was soon serving ably in a series of increasingly prestigious legal posts in the first three Roosevelt administrations, first as general counsel of the Bureau of Internal Revenue in 1934, then as assistant attorney general in 1936, solicitor general in 1938, attorney general in January 1940, before being nominated as associate justice of the Supreme Court in July 1941.

Jackson had been a supporter of the idea of individual responsibility for war crimes since the so-called Nazi Saboteurs' Case had come before the Supreme Court in 1942, piquing his interest in the laws of war. He had also made several speeches expressing his belief that the 1928 Kellogg-Briand Pact had outlawed international aggression. So when Sam Rosenman appeared in his chambers in April 1945 to ask, on behalf of President Truman, if Jackson would serve as the US representative and chief counsel for war crimes, "he was talking to a man who already had a considerable public record on the subject and who would be a strong advocate of a charge based on the illegality of aggressive war," explained Taylor.[16]

An excerpt from one of these after-dinner speeches offers a window into Jackson's vision of a growing and changing role for multilateral organizations generally, which would later parallel his vision of a dynamic "common law" theory of public international law at Nuremberg. Of the inadequacy of the interwar League of Nations system, Jackson observed: "We now see that such an instrumentality, if it is to compose the world's discord, must have flexibility. Neither maps nor economic advantages nor political systems can be frozen in a treaty. Peace is more than the fossilized remains of an international conclave. It cannot be static in a moving world. Peace must function as a going concern, as a way of life with a dynamic of its own." In these comments, Jackson espoused a common anti-imperialist orientation which he shared with many other New Dealers, such as Harold Ickes. Jackson continued his history lesson: "Unfortunately, however, the internal structure of the League loaded the dice in favor of the perpetuation of the *status quo* which was also the policy of the dominant powers and the governing classes within them. Any peace that is indissolubly wedded to a *status quo*—any *status quo*—is doomed from the beginning. The world will not forego movement and progress and readjustments as the price of peace." This suspicion of the status quo was part of the New Dealer's creed, along with the confidence that experts and activists could make a new and better world.[17]

This November 1941 speech also mentioned the international security provision of the Atlantic Charter—that one of the Atlantic Charter peace aims was to be the "establishment of a wider and permanent system of general security"—while warning that "such happy days wait upon great improvement in our international law and in our organs of international legislation and adjudication. Only by well considered steps toward closer international cooperation and more certain justice can the sacrifices which we are resolved to make be justified."[18]

Negotiations over the provisions for trying Nazi leaders spawned three main legal controversies. Legal delegations from Britain, France, the Soviet Union, and the United States finalized what was soon known as the Nuremberg Charter at a conference in London in the summer of 1945. Jackson was the head of the American group, and Taylor argued that his bombastic style and inability to manage a team made each of these controversies even more contentious. The Nuremberg historian Bradley

Smith noted delicately that "amateur negotiating teams, such as Jackson's, tended to embody . . . national characteristics undilutedly; and with little experience in diplomacy, they plunged forward recklessly."[19]

The first question was whether aggressive war was *already* illegal under a traditional, positivist approach to legal analysis. The jurists agreed that the 1928 Kellogg-Briand Pact had outlawed aggressive war, even though that treaty did not provide specific sanctions for violations of its provisions. Critics of the Nuremberg approach often noted that this argument was significantly weakened by the inability of the charter's drafters to agree on a definition of aggression. The drafters rejected the idea that they were charging the defendants under a retroactive, *ex post facto* charge, since—as Jackson had explained in an earlier memorandum—they were charging the defendants with crimes that had been recognized since the time that Cain slew Abel. The judgment noted that the prohibition on *ex post facto* legislation had its origin in principles of equity, and it did not seem reasonable to the Allies that the Axis leaders could not have known they were doing wrong before they were actually indicted. Still, the unusually blunt language in the American draft of the charter about the pre-existing illegal status of aggressive war troubled the cautious and legalistic British and French delegates.[20]

The second major controversy at London, which continued through the trial, was the scope of application of the conspiracy charge. Was the legal doctrine of conspiracy the new broom that would sweep up thousands of Gestapo members, as Murray Bernays and his boss, Henry Stimson, had hoped in the autumn of 1944? At the charter negotiations, this controversy assumed the form of a cross-cultural issue, since conspiracy was a purely Anglo-American legal doctrine. While the French were particularly unenthusiastic, the British were also suspicious of a theory that would apply a conspiracy charge against groups. The Nuremberg court later expressed its continuing discomfort with the concept by making sure that no defendant was convicted for the crime of conspiracy alone. It also threw out the charge against particular groups it considered to be lacking the requisite cohesion and decision-making integrity to function as a criminal organization, or whose membership had thoroughly changed over time, such as the German General Staff.[21]

The third major legal issue the Nuremberg Charter needed to address was the rationale and legitimacy for treating "murder, extermination, enslavement, deportation, and other inhumane acts committed against any civilian populations" as an indictable category of criminal activities known as "crimes against humanity." The genesis of this term is somewhat obscure. Most commentators depict the idea as originating with Nuremberg itself, but this is clearly not the case. In his 1904 State of the Union Message, President Theodore Roosevelt had explained that "there are occasional crimes committed on so vast a scale and of such peculiar horror as to make us doubt whether it is not our manifest duty to endeavor at least to show our disapproval of the deed and our sympathy with those who have suffered by it . . . in extreme cases action may be justifiable and proper." TR was using this rationale to justify American intervention in Panama and Cuba. Interestingly, he also mentioned "intolerable conditions" suffered by Armenians and Jews in his catalogue of "systematic and long-extended cruelty and oppression."[22]

Theodore Roosevelt was one of the initiators of the 1907 round of Hague conferences, convened to revise and extend the multilateral treaties known as the Hague Conventions of 1899. The Hague Conventions on the Laws and Customs of War on Land of both 1899 and 1907 had the following clause in their preambles: "Until a more complete code of the laws of war has been issued, the High Contracting parties deem it expedient to declare that, in cases not included in the Regulations adopted by them, the inhabitants and the belligerents remain under the protection and rule of the principles of the laws of nations, as they result from the usages established among civilized peoples, from the laws of humanity, and the dictates of the public conscience." This was the famous Martens clause, named after its drafter and advocate, the Russian legal scholar Feodor Martens, and designed to cover both the kind of unconscionable but nontraditional situation TR described in his 1904 speech, as well as the development of weaponry with new and unanticipated capacities.[23]

Another provision of this same treaty, however, contained a clause that seemed radically to restrict the expansive implications of the Martens clause. This was the so-called *si omnes* clause, specifying that "the provisions [of the convention] do not apply except between contracting Powers, and then only if all belligerents are parties to the Convention." In other words, if two nations were at war and only one was a signatory to the Hague Conventions, then that treaties' provisions would not apply to either party, and if several warring countries are at war at once, the conventions would not apply to any of them unless all were signatories.[24]

One framing of the competing legal theories of prosecution and defense at Nuremberg is as a struggle between the expansive, organic Martens approach to legal interpretation—extending protections drawn from the "principles of the laws of nations . . . the usages established among civilized peoples . . . the laws of humanity, and the dictates of the public conscience" to situations where no formal law yet applied—and the narrow, positivist *si omnes* approach. German defense counsel made good use of the *si omnes* clause at Nuremberg, arguing that several of the combatant nations in World War II had not signed the Hague Conventions, for example, and so none of the combatants, including Germany, could appropriately be bound by Hague rules.

In its judgment, the Nuremberg court "brushed aside this contention," as Taylor put it. The tribunal determined that "by 1939 those rules laid down in the [Hague] Conventions were recognized by all civilized nations, and were regarded as being declaratory of the laws and customs of wars which are referred to in Article 6(b) of the [Nuremberg] Charter." The tribunal recognized the 1907 Hague Conventions as declaratory of customary international law, and framed its judgment on innovative charges such as crimes against humanity on the flexible basis of the Martens clause.[25]

The leading French negotiator at the August 1945 London Conference, Robert Falco, had initially doubted the existence of a separate category of "crimes against humanity," preferring to construe German atrocities as an extreme example of the more traditional concept of conventional war crimes. But by the time the French prosecutor, François de Menthon, came to present his case, the French team had undergone a philosophical shift. Crimes against humanity, de Menthon now argued, were "crimes against the spirit," and the source from which all the other crimes in the charter flowed: "I propose to prove to you that all this organized and vast criminality springs from what I may be allowed to call a crime against the spirit. I mean a doctrine which, denying all spiritual, rational, and moral values by which the nations have tried, for thousands of years, to improve human conditions . . . This monstrous doctrine is that of racialism." De Menthon then linked institutionalized racism to violations of individual human dignity. "Race is the matrix of the German people; proceeding therefrom this people lives and develops as an organism . . . National Socialism ends in the absorption of the personality of the citizen into that of the state and in the denial of any intrinsic value of the human person."[26]

. In his opening statement, Jackson drew an analogy with the growth of Anglo-American common law, harking back to his 1941 speech to the Bar Association of Indianapolis, with its image of law as an evolving, organic entity: "The real complaining party at your bar is Civilization. In all our countries it is still a struggling and imperfect thing. It does not plead that the United States or any other country has been blameless . . .

Civilization asks whether law is so laggard as to be utterly helpless to deal with crimes of this magnitude by criminals of this order of importance. It does not expect that you [the tribunal] can make war impossible. It does expect that your juridical action will put the forms of international law, its precepts, its prohibitions, and most of all, its sanctions, on the side of peace." The tribunal agreed, explaining in its judgment that "the law of war is to be found not only in treaties, but in the customs and practice of states which gradually obtained universal recognition, and from the general principles of justice applied by jurists and practiced by military courts. This law is not static, but by continual adaptation follows the needs of a changing world."[27]

Another contentious aspect of the idea of crimes against humanity was the scope of its application. Would this charge apply to prewar atrocities inflicted on Germany's own domestic population? The text of the judgment reflected the Nuremberg court's decision not to address prewar atrocities against domestic minorities despite some ambiguous language in the charter. The prosecution at Nuremberg argued that, under the terms of the charter, the count of crimes against humanity should indeed encompass German atrocities committed within Germany and against German nationals. Even before the German invasion of Poland in 1939 transformed the status of this state-sponsored violence into an international armed conflict, crimes against humanity, wherever committed, ought to be considered a violation of international law. What the prosecution argued, in effect, was for the conspiracy charge in 6(a) to be applied to all three sections of the charter—an especially plausible contention given the last sentence of Article 6. The prewar atrocities would be considered an early part of the "conspiracy" phase of waging aggressive war or committing crimes against humanity.[28]

But the British prosecution team overreached in arguing that this conspiracy stretched back to the creation of the Nazi Party in 1919. The French judge, Donnedieu de Vabres, had not been comfortable with the conspiracy charge to begin with, and he balked at the prospect of an international court applying this strange Anglo-American concept to twenty additional years of German national life.

The tribunal's decision on prewar atrocities was a compromise awkward even by legal standards, based on a very strict reading of Article 6. The judgment held that the atrocities mentioned in section 6c were only meant to include acts that were carried out "in connection with any crime within the jurisdiction of the Tribunal," meaning the provisions described in sections 6a and 6b, for which the specified starting date was

September 1, 1939. Before the invasion of Poland, in other words, it "had not been satisfactorily proven that [these atrocities] were done in execution of, or in connection with, the crimes against peace specified in section 6a." The tribunal therefore declared itself as having no jurisdiction over these "domestic" German atrocities: "The Tribunal cannot make a general declaration that the acts before 1939 were Crimes Against Humanity within the meaning of the Charter."[29]

The Nuremberg judges were apparently troubled by some of the same domestic jurisdiction issues that had alarmed American critics of the original Bernays conspiracy approach. Jackson himself best articulated this cautious view at the London Conference, when he was speaking as a representative of the Roosevelt administration and was not yet serving as an active prosecutor: "It has been a general principle of the foreign policy of our Government from time immemorial that the internal affairs of another government are not ordinarily our business; that is to say, the way Germany treats its inhabitants, or any other country treats its inhabitants is not our affair any more than it is the affair of some other government to interpose itself in our problems," he explained, articulating the standard US interpretation, reaffirmed during World War I and the interwar era. "The reason that this program of extermination of Jews and destruction of the rights of minorities becomes an international concern is this: it was a part of a plan for making an illegal war."[30]

Jackson thus foreshadowed the Nuremberg judgment's approach to Article 6, which required a tight nexus between crimes against humanity and the aggressive war charge—a nexus not necessarily indicated by the plain language of the article itself. Jackson also went on to offer this unusually candid elucidation: "Ordinarily we do not consider that the acts of a government toward its own citizens warrant our interference. We have some regrettable circumstances at times in our own country in which minorities are unfairly treated. We think it is justifiable that we interfere or attempt to bring retribution to individuals or to states only because the concentration camps and the deportations were in pursuance of a common plan or enterprise of making an unjust or illegal war in which we became involved. We see no other basis on which we are justified in reaching the atrocities which were committed inside Germany, under German law, or even in violation of German law, by authorities of the German state." Prewar atrocities could not be "reached" by the tribunal because of fears over the implications of international bodies sitting in judgment on domestic practices, even when those practices were clearly crimes against humanity by any reasonable criteria. There was no principle available that could capture the crimes of Kristallnacht in Germany and yet spare from legal scrutiny the lynching of thousands of African-Americans in the American South.[31]

In a 1946 letter to *The New York Times,* Raphael Lemkin, a former Nuremberg prosecution advisor who had coined the term "genocide," wrote wonderingly of this lack-of-reach argument: "It seems inconsistent with our concepts of civilization that selling a drug to an individual is a matter of worldly concern"—the regulation of transborder flows of narcotics had long been subjected to international oversight through treaties and multilateral institutions—"while gassing millions of human beings might [merely] be a problem of internal concern."[32]

"The basic difficulty with the whole procedure is that Nuremberg is entirely a civilian show and strictly amateur at that"

The prosecution staff thought it essential that the tribunal base its judgment on the Nuremberg Charter. The charter was a treaty in its own right, they argued, legitimately filling the legal vacuum created by Germany's unconditional surrender. The tribunal agreed, denying all defense motions challenging its jurisdiction. Other types of controversies based on the Nuremberg approach included criticisms of the overall design of the trial; the charter's treatment of conflicting, pre-existing legal ideas such as the "act of state" doctrine; criticism of the trial as an American or Jewish show trial; and how the Nuremberg model was intended to be generalized and applied to other situations following World War II.[33]

The major criticism of the overall design of the main Nuremberg trial related to the conspicuous presence of a uniformed Soviet officer on the bench, sitting in judgment of Axis defendants indicted for the crime of aggression, when the Soviets had themselves invaded Poland in 1939 and Finland a year later. Furthermore, one of the counts of the indictment charged German defendants with the massacre of thousands of Polish officers in the Katyn Forest, an atrocity widely suspected at the time (and subsequently confirmed) to have been committed by Soviet forces. Critics leveled similar charges against the other Allies for using the same type of unrestricted submarine warfare for which the defendants had been indicted; for the Allied use of terror bombing against civilians; and especially for the American use of atomic weapons against civilian targets. Posed starkly, these concerns amounted to an accusation of hypocrisy—of "unclean hands," or what in international legal parlance is known as *tu quoque*—"you did it, too." Another facet of this charge of hypocrisy was the only slightly less virulent criticism that the trial lacked legitimacy because only victor nations were represented on the bench.

The *tu quoque* objection to the Nuremberg proceedings was stated most clearly by the perennial US presidential candidate, the socialist Norman Thomas, writing in 1947. "Our socialist principles never precluded the trial and punishment of those guilty of atrocities against civilians and prisoners of war"—that is to say, for conventional war crimes—"for that [crime] there was sufficient law already recognized." But, Thomas continued, such principles "did preclude trials of the sort that are dragging along in Nuremberg and Tokyo as this is being written. Aggressive war is a moral crime but this will not be established in the conscience of mankind by proceedings such as those at Nuremberg, where Russians sit on the bench and exclude evidence of Hitler's deal with Stalin. What was the latter's war against Finland, Poland and the Baltic states but aggression?" He continued, "Indeed, what major power had not in comparatively recent years been guilty of acts of aggression? Mr. Justice Jackson makes much of the analogy of the growth of common law to justify the Nuremberg proceedings. The very composition of the court by victors who are at once judges and prosecutors refutes his analogy."[34]

It did not help when US Admiral Chester Nimitz provided a deposition to the German defense team in support of Admiral Karl Doenitz, attesting that the Germans' conduct of submarine warfare was the same as the Americans'. The prosecution's unsatisfactory response was that simply because some robbers went unpunished did not mean that stealing wasn't a crime. More to the point was Jackson's poetic vow about the future legitimacy of such charges, which would go on to become the trial's most hollow legacy: "We must never forget that the record on which we judge these defendants today is the record on which history will judge us tomorrow. To pass these defendants a poisoned chalice is to put it to our own lips as well."[35]

The traditional legal idea of sovereign immunity, in this context sometimes known as the "act of state" doctrine, protected heads of governments and other high officials from individual liability for their political decisions. Lower level officials, especially soldiers and other military subordinates, relied on a complementary legal tradition to insulate themselves from personal culpability—the doctrine of "superior orders." The combination of the two doctrines negated the responsibility of all actors high and low, and left no one responsible.[36]

Unsurprisingly, given the deaths of the top echelon of Reich officials, defenses claiming incontrovertible superior orders were extremely popular at Nuremberg. This was true even though, for any given defendant, asserting a defense of superior orders inevitably involved listening to defense attorneys downplay one's personal influence, authority, access to Hitler, and overall competence. The psychologist Gilbert noted in his diary that "the innocence of the 'white lambs' was beginning to become a sort of joke" in the defendants' lunchroom. It was apparent that "nobody had anything to do with anything," he noted wearily. "The Foreign Minister was only an office boy; the Chief of Staff of the High Command of the Wehrmacht was only an office manager; the rabid anti-Semites were all in favor of chivalrous solutions to the Jewish problem and knew nothing about the atrocities, including Gestapo Chief Kaltenbrunner."[37]

The Nuremberg Charter had explicitly discarded the act of state doctrine, as part of its mission to bring the idea of individual responsibility into the purview of international law. But the discounting of sovereign immunity made American and other Allied military officers nervous; they were unenthusiastic about the possible precedent that the Nuremberg prosecution staff was laying down, which would presumably restrict the scope of future claims of superior orders. Senator Burton K. Wheeler, an isolationist, as well as Admiral William Leahy, chief of staff under Roosevelt and Truman, raised concerns that congressional representative George A. Dondero of Michigan expressed succinctly. Citing a section of the Nuremberg judgment to the effect that a subordinate was bound to obey only the *lawful* orders of a superior, Dondero urged his listeners to "follow the implications of this statement through to a logical conclusion. In effect, it encourages mass disobedience to superior officers within our armed forces."[38]

The trial's defenders were particularly impatient with these arguments. In July 1946 the political scientist Nicholas Doman wrote, "No responsible military leader can contend that his role is merely that of a concierge or custodian of the war machine under his command and that he bears no responsibility for the use to which that machine is put . . . [The defendants] are on trial not because they lost the war but because they started it. And if recognition is given to the claim of the prosecutors, then this will mean that the collective security of world society attained supremacy over the personal security of the militarists." Military commentators remained skeptical, however, explaining that civilian lawyers could never understand the dynamics of battlefield decisions. Lieutenant Colonel P. F. Gault argued that "the basic difficulty with the whole procedure is that Nuremberg is entirely a civilian show and strictly amateur at that."[39]

Not only was Nuremberg a civilian show, it was also a show produced and directed almost entirely by Americans. One American journalist proudly explained how, "from the very beginning of this joint effort, the United States carried the ball. Although the cooperation of other nations was genuine and sincere, there is ample proof to show that Nuremberg was a 100 per cent American concern. It was American initiative, American persistence, and American idealism that produced the final result in the face of serious difficulties . . . Starting from a shoestring, American enterprise has produced a powerful machine, well equipped to hand down the historic verdict and to open a new age in international good conduct."[40]

The Nuremberg show was also a Robert H. Jackson production. It was Jackson who told Francis Biddle that he, Biddle, should stand aside in the election of chief judge of the tribunal, in favor of the British judge, Sir Geoffrey Lawrence, so that the trial would not be perceived as being so totally dominated by the United States.[41]

Jackson also fretted about the appearance of having "too many Jews" on the prosecution staff, as a public relations problem that the American jurist believed would further reduce the trial's legitimacy for both German and American public opinion. Jackson's efforts on this score were of little avail. Many of the defendants as well as large numbers of ordinary Germans believed that Jews were running the trial anyway. Defendant Streicher, the Nazi propagandist, explained to Gilbert, the American psychologist, that "the prosecution is made up almost entirely of Jews." When Gilbert asked how he knew this, Streicher replied that there were distinctive Jewish physical characteristics, "although there were many exceptions, and it took a real expert like himself to detect them." When pressed, he mentioned that "one could frequently tell by the eyes," and that "more significant than Jewish eyes, however, was the Jewish behind, he had discovered."[42]

Isolationist elements in Congress also suggested that Nuremberg was about Jewish vengeance. Representative John E. Rankin, Democrat of Mississippi, speaking of the so-called secondary Nuremberg trials, drew a parallel between the defeated Nazis and the American South, when he urged the United States to "put a stop to the racial persecution of the people of Germany who are now helpless at out feet . . . If we people of the Southern States had been treated in the same manner after the War between the States as those people have been treated under pressure of a certain racial minority, you would not have heard the last of it until doomsday." He urged that the United States should "treat the people of

Germany . . . with humanity and decency and [do] not permit racial minorities to vent their sadistic vengeance upon them and charge it up to the United States."[43]

The other flagship international criminal trial staged in the name of the Allies was the International Military Tribunal for the Far East, commonly known as the Tokyo trial. Meant to serve as Nuremberg's Far Eastern counterpart and based on an almost identical charter, the Tokyo Tribunal sat from June 1946 until April 1948, reading out its verdict over the course of nine days in early November 1948. The Tokyo trial presented additional cross-cultural challenges, based on differing Western and Japanese legal conceptions, ideas about procedures such as the proper role of the defense attorney, as well as more difficult translation problems. One reason why the Tokyo trial took twice as long as Nuremberg, for example, was that the Tokyo assize could not take advantage of IBM simultaneous translation technology, used to great effect at Nuremberg.[44]

Another important difference with Nuremberg was the number of separate and dissenting opinions at Tokyo. Three of the eleven judges—Radhabinod Pal of India, Henri Bernard of France, and Bernard Röling of the Netherlands—filed full or partial dissents. Pal maintained in his 1,235-page dissenting opinion that the distinction between just and unjust war belonged to the theory of legal philosophers and that the rule concerning the crime against peace—that aggression was illegal—was *ex post facto* legislation. Röling, on the other hand, stated that crimes against peace were not real legal crimes, but they could nevertheless be used as political safety measures to eliminate persons who were dangerous for world peace. Bernard argued that the verdict could not be valid because the procedure was defective and that the Japanese emperor should also have been punished.[45]

Justice Pal, in addition, offered the fascinating anti-imperialist argument that had been foreshadowed by the so-called revisionist powers at the Paris Peace Conference in 1919: that indicting leaders for "crimes against peace" served only to protect an unjust international order, if there were no other workable provisions for peaceful adjustment of the status quo. Two additional judges, including the tribunal's chief justice, filed separate opinions. Chief Justice William Webb of Australia called for a trial of the emperor and commutation of the death sentences to life imprisonment, while Delfin Jaranilla of the Philippines, himself a survivor of the Bataan Death March, argued alternatively for harsher sentences.[46]

The twenty-five Tokyo defendants were known as Class A war criminals, meaning that part of their indictment was for crimes against peace. Class A defendants were tried separately from Class B and C suspects, who were arraigned for violations of the conventional laws of war. From 1945 to 1951, approximately 5,700 Japanese were tried as conventional war criminals—for perpetrating, allowing, or ordering atrocities. Of this number, 1,000 were executed and 3,000 were imprisoned. Most controversially, a US Army court in Manila convicted and hanged the Japanese commanding general of the Philippines, Yamashita Tomoyuki. Yamashita's conviction was based on a theory of "negative criminality"—that he "unlawfully disregarded and failed to discharge his duty as commander to control the operations of the members of his command, permitting them to commit brutal atrocities." The decision was controversial in large part because Yamashita's American opponents had successfully disrupted the general's lines of communication, only to hold him accountable later for having failed to control his troops.[47]

For nationals of European Axis countries, there were also 2,116 known military tribunal hearings of lower-level defendants, not including those conducted in the Soviet Union. All told, more than 5,000 Nazis were condemned by all the Allied war crimes tribunals taken together, with 806 death sentences ordered. The United States Supreme Court held that the writ of habeas corpus did not apply for appellants from these war crimes trials. In addition, over 13,000 people were tried in hearings before German national courts (Spruchkammern), with 86 given life terms and 5,178 given very limited prison terms. While the German courts applied German national law, the new postwar penal codes had incorporated legal ideas from the Nuremberg Charter regarding individual responsibility and absence of an obligation to obey orders that were illegal under international law.[48]

International legal scholar Robert Woetzel has noted that "all these tribunals show a uniformity of approach to the substantive rules of international law involved. This was undoubtedly due to the lead given by the Charter of the International Military Tribunal at Nuremberg which can be regarded as the pre-eminent tribunal in the history of modern war crimes trials." This assessment, written in 1962, is double-edged: Nuremberg was "pre-eminent" because it was the first successful synthesis and application of a wide variety of pre-existing legal ideas and political impulses. It continued to be pre-eminent, however, because it was also the last such attempt, at least until a revival of multilateral criminal prosecutions after the Cold War ended.[49]

"Perhaps this is New Deal Justice . . . transferred to the international scene"

The Nuremberg Charter is an example of the *Zeitgeist* of 1945, the multilateralist sensibility that briefly gripped the United States as World War II drew to a close. "Security, welfare, and justice are the pillars of the world order for which we fight," argued the Commission to Study the Organization of Peace, a multilateralist advocacy group, in 1944. These aspirations "embody the hopes and dreams of countless millions of ordinary folk who yearn for a world in which their children may grow up free from the fears (and from the costs and consequences) of recurrent wars. This is what is meant by Security—freedom from the fear of aggressive war." The Atlantic Charter and the United Nations Charter formed the ideological context for the Nuremberg Charter.[50]

It was largely a matter of chance that the preliminary negotiations over the provisions of the Nuremberg Charter took place at the San Francisco Conference in April–June 1945, where the United Nations Charter was being finalized. "But the coincidence is meaningful," wrote assistant prosecutor Taylor in his memoirs, quoting Robert H. Jackson's son William, himself a lawyer and aide at Nuremberg. The younger Jackson later explained that "it is perhaps not commonly apprehended that the principles of Nuremberg . . . go hand in hand with the organization of the United Nations as the twin foundations of an international society ordered by law."[51]

The Nuremberg Tribunal asserted that its charter was contributing to a broad historical trend affirming the universal value of international moral and legal sanctions, which had been a growing force in international affairs since at least the end of the First World War and which had achieved the status of positive law with the promulgation of the 1928 Kellogg-Briand Pact. President Truman expressed his hope that "we have established for all time the proposition that aggressive war is criminal and will be so treated." The authors and implementers of the Nuremberg Charter explained that the document had been conceived as a means of lifting international justice to a new and higher level. Shortly after the judgment was announced, Judge Biddle wrote that "[Nuremberg's] judgment has formulated, judicially and for the first time, the proposition that aggressive war is criminal and will be so treated . . . Now that it has been so clearly recognized and largely accepted, the time has come to make its scope and incidence more precise . . . I suggest that the time has now come to set about drafting a code of international criminal law."[52]

Even more lyrically, the usually circumspect Walter Lippmann weighed in with a rapturous assessment, pointedly withheld from "thinner" multilateralist statements such as the Atlantic Charter: "For my own part, I do not think it rash to prophesy that the principles of this trial will come to be regarded as ranking with the Magna Charta, the *habeas corpus* and the Bill of Rights as landmarks in the development of law. The Nuremberg principle goes deeper into the problem of peace, and its effect may prove to be more far-reaching than anything else that has yet been agreed to by the peoples of the world."[53]

Attorney General Tom C. Clark echoed Lippmann in observing that "the Ten Commandments, Magna Carta, and the Constitution of the United States have been giant forward steps on the slow and dreadful path to human justice. This age has just given us the judgment at Nuremberg." The historian Eugene Davidson explained the sources of this hyperbolic rhetoric: "The [Nuremberg] trials were intended, not only to bring the guilty to justice . . . In addition, the trials, especially as the Americans saw them, were to be a projection of the new world order that would justify the universal suffering [of wartime] . . . [this was what] the Allies had been fighting for." Here were war and peace aims made real: Nuremberg as embodying and institutionalizing the Atlantic Charter.[54]

Few others were quite so enthusiastic. Critics argued that the trial's controversial design, basis in law, and "streamlined" procedures so undermined the enterprise's legitimacy that the assize itself was an exercise in hypocrisy. Theologian Reinhold Niebuhr worried that the trial might plunge the defeated Germans into existential despair. Others noted with disfavor the likely effect of the trial on the victors themselves: "For the plain citizens of every country, [the trial] serves to reduce the vast and infinitely complex tragedy of the Second World War to the simple abstraction of a movie melodrama, so that with the final titillating scene on the gallows or before the firing-squad, he can relax in an untroubled glow, confirmed in his abiding faith that 'crime never pays,' that his own country is the fount and citadel of all the virtues."[55]

Legal positivists, who understood "law" as growing exclusively from the formal consent of sovereigns to be bound, also understood the Nuremberg Charter and the tribunal's verdict as challenging traditional ideas about sovereignty. The legal scholar Quincy Wright argued that "[Nuremberg's] principles if generally accepted may reduce the unity of the state, increase the difficulties of maintaining domestic order, and deter statesmen from pursuing vigorous foreign policies when necessary in the national interests." Another widely respected authority on international legal affairs, Manley O. Hudson of the interwar Permanent Court of International Justice, noted in 1943 that international judicial agencies set up to deal with war criminals probably had few prospects for developing "a continuing character," at least until some future time when "the need for international action is clearly demonstrated."[56]

Journalist Ernest O. Hauser saw a link between Nuremberg's legal innovations and the loose New Deal approach to problem solving. Early in 1946 he explained how "the ambitious project of creating rather than merely applying international law, and of setting a new standard for good conduct in the family of nations, is essentially Rooseveltian. It can be traced directly to the late President, and it is fascinating to observe how the grandiose concepts as well as the vagueness characteristic of Franklin Roosevelt, are in evidence at Nuremberg." The military historian Alfred A. Vagts developed a similar analogy in his later, more clearly unfavorable assessment: "Perhaps this is New Deal justice," he wrote, roughly a decade after the trial; "the overriding of precedent, the fight against the 'nine old men' who successfully stood out for precedent against administrative absolutism—transferred to the international scene, where no carefully administered law stood in its way. It is also New Deal jurisprudence without the tempering of justice with humanitarianism in which it usually prided itself."[57]

These criticisms highlight how the Nuremberg Charter might also be seen as a New Deal–style institution—an example of a Rooseveltian synthesis of the legalistic and moralistic idioms of American multilateralism. At first glance—and perhaps even at second—the Nuremberg trial hardly seems like an internationalization of the New Deal. Yet a fresh take on Nuremberg might portray the trial as a pragmatic administrative pastiche—an innovation in international organization as well as in international law.[58]

The Nuremberg Charter, in particular, appeared to many contemporary commentators as a concrete realization of the hitherto unsupported moralistic ideas of the post–World War I era, while also serving as an expression of the positivist strain of legalism from the earlier Hague era. Nuremberg was an attempt to express moralistic ideas in a legalistic manner, and in so doing it teemed with internal contradictions. In true pragmatic New Deal style, however, the trial also got the job done, while generating a minimal level of legitimacy denied to both the sterile Hague approach and the sentimental Pact of Paris approach. On a visit to Nuremberg to observe the trial, Senator Claude Pepper, Democrat of Florida, toasted Robert Jackson as "America's international district attorney." Sending the defeated Nazis up the river was to be the international version of busting trusts and tackling American organized crime.[59]

Signature snafus of the New Deal—ham-handed attempts to export domestic norms, personality clashes from unclear lines of authority, and haphazard, ideologically incoherent but ultimately pragmatic legal theories—were abundantly present at the trial as well. Indeed, the colloquial term "snafu" was on everyone's lips at Nuremberg. Major players designing, administering, and advising behind the scenes were prominent New Dealers—Jackson himself, of course, as well as Biddle, Rosenman, and more peripheral advisors such as Harry Dexter White, Harry Hopkins, and Felix Frankfurter. Many of the second-tier participants designing and implementing the trial had served as aides and assistants to New Deal bureaucrats. Examples included Taylor, Bernays, former general solicitor of the Southern Railway Sidney B. Alderman, Columbia law professor Herbert Weschler, Adrian S. Fisher (a Harvard Law graduate who had clerked for Justices Frankfurter and Brandeis), and James H. Rowe (former confidential assistant to FDR and another Harvard Law graduate who, like Biddle, had clerked for Justice Oliver Wendell Holmes).[60]

While the jurisprudence underlying Nuremberg's charter was an unstable amalgam of natural law, common law, and traditional positivist reasoning, the tribunal's main contribution to postwar multilateralism was arguably through its quasi-administrative, fact-finding role—another cherished objective of New Deal–style institutions. It told the truth about the Nazis, even if it fell short of serving as "the greatest history seminar ever held in the history of the world."[61]

"I am a human being, and I believe that nothing that is human is alien to me"

In his memoir of the Nazi concentration camps, *If This Is a Man,* the Italian chemist Primo Levi recounted how he sought to escape the grueling outdoor labor brigade that was slowly killing him in the winter of 1943–44. A low-level position had opened up in one of the chemical laboratories that supported the forced-labor factory system at Auschwitz. Having earned a doctorate in chemistry from the University of Turin only two years before, Levi desperately hoped to secure one of these coveted laboratory jobs, guaranteeing indoor work and exemption from monthly selections for the gas chambers.[62]

In a famously vivid scene, the director of the chemical department, a

German "Doktor Ingenieur" named Pannwitz, interviewed the young Italian-Jewish partisan. In his filthy inmate uniform, Levi stood awkwardly in Pannwitz's shining office, fixating on the German's manicured hands and feeling "that I would leave a dirty stain whatever I touched." After a few moments, the seated scientist stopped writing and raised his eyes to look at Levi. It was a gaze which Levi would remember all his life, the author later said, "because that look was not one between two men; and if I had known how completely to explain the nature of that look, which came as if across the glass window of an aquarium between two beings who live in different worlds, I would also have explained the essence of the great insanity of the [Third Reich]."

Human rights expert Michael Ignatieff has written brilliantly of this scene: "Here was a scientist, trained in the traditions of European rational inquiry, turning a meeting between two human beings into an encounter between different species." Ignatieff continues: "Progress may be a contested concept, but we make progress to the degree that we act upon the moral intuition that Dr. Pannwitz was wrong: our species is one, and each of the individuals who compose it is entitled to equal moral consideration."[63]

Nuremberg embodied the first institutionalized, multilateral attempt to use the ideals of the rule of law to give voice to this moral intuition. It was the flagship event of what Ignatieff calls "the juridical revolution in human rights since 1945." While the bare language of the Nuremberg Charter was not phrased using modern human rights terminology, the trial's context of genocide and atrocity transformed how the proceedings came to be understood in the postwar era. How contemporary planners saw the trial and how commentators received their efforts in the short term is one way to understand the purposes and results of the trial. However, an important paradox of Nuremberg as a human rights institution is the gap between what the architects of Nuremberg thought they were doing and how the perceived human rights lessons of the trial have changed over time.[64]

Law professor Martha Minow describes as "devastating" the yawning gap "between the capacity of the trial form with its rule of law and the nature of mass atrocities." The existence of such a gap may go a long way toward explaining the paradox of the Nuremberg legacy. One of the factors limiting the trial's human rights legacy is the strange divergence between what the Nuremberg Charter purported to be about (primarily, the outlawry of aggressive war) and what the trial is remembered for today (the landmark delineation of crimes against humanity in a context of holocaust and genocide). As late as 1970, the historian William Bosch offered the assessment that "the Tribunal's most significant legal innovation was its legal definition of aggression as the 'supreme crime.'" Yet this now sounds like a singularly off-key summary of what was going on beneath the trial's rhetorical surface.[65]

Recent commentators sometimes express surprise that the word "genocide" does not appear in the Nuremberg Charter, although the term does appear in some of the supporting court papers, including the indictment—the first use of that term in an international legal instrument. As with the 1941 Atlantic Charter (a document that does not use the phrase "human rights"), the Nuremberg Charter was instrumental in crystallizing a pre-existing concept in a new way, for which a modern vocabulary rapidly developed.[66]

An advisor to the American prosecution staff, the Polish-Jewish refugee and Yale international legal scholar Raphael Lemkin, coined the term "genocide" in the course of his wartime research, writing, and advocacy on behalf of victims of the Third Reich. Lemkin's formulation first appeared in his massive 1944 volume, *Axis Rule in Occupied Europe,* published by the Carnegie Endowment for International Peace. Lemkin defined genocide as an intentionally "coordinated plan of different actions aiming at the destruction of essential foundations of the life of national groups with the aim of annihilating the groups themselves. The objectives of such a plan would be the disintegration of the political and social institutions of culture, language, national feelings, religion, economic existence, of national groups and the destruction of the personal security, liberty, health, dignity and even the lives of the individuals belonging to such groups . . . the actions involved are directed against individuals, not in their individual capacity, but as members of the national group."[67]

The New York Times Book Review featured a full page on Lemkin's dense and technical tract on the cover of its January 21, 1945, issue. "Out of its dry legalism," wrote reviewer Otto Tolischus, "there emerge the contours of the monster that now bestrides the earth." Lemkin commented in a draft of his next book, which he began in 1944 but never published, that acceptance and use of a new term can happen only "if, and so far as, it meets popular needs and tastes."[68]

Part of the impetus for developing this new vocabulary was the experience of actually litigating the trial itself, exposing flotillas of articulate young attorneys to the numbing details of mass atrocities. The evidence underlying the charge of crimes against humanity at Nuremberg was simultaneously vivid to the point of luridness and so unimaginable that, ordinarily, the mind needed to draw a veil over their particulars. Such a psychologically self-protective response was not always possible for the prosecution staff at Nuremberg, as well as for those members in charge of prisoners, documents, and exhibits. The French doctor in charge of the trial exhibits relating to atrocities fingered a set of decorative objects made out of flayed, tattooed human skin—exhibits which have since become iconic symbols of Nazism—and observed ruminatively to Rebecca West: "These people where I live send in my breakfast tray strewn with pansies, beautiful pansies. I have never seen more beautiful pansies, arranged with exquisite taste. I have to remind myself that they belong to the same race that supplied me with my exhibits, the same race that tortured me month after month, year after year, at Mauthausen."[69]

It was this deep substratum of horror, as much as the superficial atmospherics of legal improvisation, administrative chaos, and ersatz "colonialism," that underpinned the eccentric atmosphere at Nuremberg. Even at a remove of three generations, it induces a kind of mental short-circuit to ingest even the smallest quantities of this kind of evidence. In a 1946 letter to Karl Jaspers, Hannah Arendt wrote that the Nazi crimes exposed the limits of law, for no punishment could ever be sufficient. Arendt speculated that this is why the Nazis in the dock seemed so smug. As the historian Lawrence Langer has recently written, "The logic of law will never make sense of the illogic of genocide."[70]

Yet this substratum of horror itself became an engine of cultural transformation, reshaping the dominant interpretations of the trial's legal ideas. British barrister and human rights advocate Geoffrey Robertson vividly elaborates how "the spontaneous drama of the [Nuremberg] courtroom provided the defining moment of de-Nazification on the afternoon when the prosecutor showed newsreels of Auschwitz and Belsen and the defendants, spotlit for security in the dock, averted their eyes." While the charges of waging aggressive war were the focus of the Nuremberg Charter on paper, in practice it was the evidence regarding crimes against humanity that soon became what the political theorist Judith Shklar termed "the moral center of the case."[71]

Human rights legacies of Nuremberg that were immediately apparent included legitimating the idea of individual responsibility for crimes against international law; offering a jurisprudential underpinning for political or philosophical assertions of the dignity of the individual irrespective of local, domestic laws; and providing an example of the importance of documenting and narrating the specifics of atrocities to create a detailed and enduring record. Even the trial's least successful legacy, its attempt to consolidate the status of aggression as an international crime, moved human rights law away from policing the political context of armed conflict and more toward the protection of civilians.[72]

Another important facet of the trial's rule of law legacy was procedural: those facing criminal charges had the opportunity to be heard individually, to defend their actions, and to be confronted with the specific evidence against them. Robertson argues that "the most astonishing feature of Nuremberg" was in fact the German defendants' own evolving perception of this procedural fairness, the gradual process through which "the adversary dynamics of the Anglo-American trial sucked in the defendants, who played an earnest and polite, [and] at times desperate, part in making it work."[73]

Robertson explains the link between principles of individual dignity and Nuremberg's development of the pre-existing, although somewhat inchoate, idea of crimes against humanity: "[Nazi atrocities] were crimes that the world could not suffer to take place anywhere, at any time, because they shamed everyone. They were not, for that crucial reason, crimes against Germans . . . they were crimes against humanity, because the very fact that a fellow human could conceive and commit them diminishes every member of the human race." He argues that Nuremberg earned its status as a human rights landmark "for this precedent alone."[74]

Ideas about individual dignity also had a collective element, elaborating this sharper sense of the shared qualities of all humanity. Max Lerner, writing for the liberal daily PM, saw Nuremberg as a kind of public ritual, where the international community could attempt, through "an immense and revolutionary effort to give utterance to a collective human conscience, to bring into being a collective standard by which gross violations of that conscience can be punished." Lerner continued, "Some may gibe that I am speaking of a 'human conscience' and a 'moral sense' that are vague and formless, things on which no body of law can be built. I submit that they are the only things that a body of law ever rests on. The surest basis of a future world society lies in the sense of our common plight. When a Negro is lynched, all of us are strung upon that rope. When the Jews were burned in the Nazi furnaces, all of us were burned."[75]

Law professor Thomas Franck explains how the Nuremberg ideas have served to reconfigure the individual's relationship to national law: "The international war crimes trials which followed the demise of Hitler's Evil Empire gave powerful impetus to the notion that there is a global-system-based duty to disobey positive law when it serves demonic ends," he explained succinctly. "This episode briefly succeeded in focusing attention on an international rule system which is the repository of inalienable rights, rights that may even have the capacity to invalidate the duty to obey national laws." The Nuremberg judges themselves explained that "the very essence of the Charter is that individuals have international duties which transcend the national obligations of obedience imposed by the individual state." This idea of the supranational quality of certain rights was incorporated into the constitution of the Federal Republic of Germany: under Article 25, general rules of international law took precedence over German federal law, while Article 26 decreed it unconstitutional to prepare for acts of aggression. These human rights legacies "sit at the foundation of the rule of law," as they reinforce norms that constrain governments against arbitrary conduct, a notion that Minow terms "fundamental fairness."[76]

The idea of an individual owing obedience to laws based on Martens-clause standards—laws that may or may not be codified, that are constantly changing, and that stand in for ideas of "civilization" which have alarming racialized antecedents—troubles many commentators. The philosopher Peter Haas notes that "one area of human endeavor that claims to stand above individual choices and institutional vagaries is the law . . . but what about a law that transcends individual political structures? Can an 'international law' be invoked that might pass judgment on national legal questions that have run amok?" Haas is doubtful: "Like individual state laws, international law no more than any other law can transcend its origins." He continues: "The assumption behind the [Nuremberg] trials was apparently that 'international law' could somehow establish a reference point that would provide the fulcrum needed to prevent similar events. It is also probably true that the trials were motivated at least in part by an attempt ex post facto on the part of the Allies to distance themselves, after years of silence and inaction, from the deeds of the Nazis."[77]

This search for such a fulcrum remains the central problem of modern human rights theory. The philosopher Michael Perry has recently argued that religious cosmologies must ultimately support ideas about human rights based on theories of innate human dignity. Other scholars, such as the Kantians Alan Gewirth and Christine Korsgaard and the legal theorists Ronald Dworkin and Eric Blumeson, have developed ideas about human dignity based on secular arguments about the human capacities for reason, suffering, or empathy. Several of these theorists have argued that another such secular base for the unique sanctity of the human might indeed be simple intuition.[78]

Whatever the competing merits of these arguments, at some point our philosophical spade is turned before striking the satisfying bedrock of what Richard Primus skeptically calls "the true grounds underlying a claim of rights." Recent work in the new field of "transitional justice" suggests that it may be fine simply to stop digging. As Judith Shklar observed, "In fact, although it is philosophically deeply annoying, human institutions survive because most of us can live comfortably with wholly contradictory beliefs." Scholars arguing for transitional justice approaches use ideas about value pluralism to do an end run around static foundationalist debates about rights. Instead, they emphasize the importance of history, specifically the context of fluid political moments that highlight how "the social understanding behind a new regime committed to the rule of law" can be created. In the case of Nuremberg, part of the political context was the inevitable chaos involved in the transition from war to peace.[79]

The emerging transitional justice paradigm posits an alternative way of thinking about the relation of law to political transformation. This school of thought asserts that justice is distinctive in times of transition— partial, contingent, and shaped by social understandings of prior injustice rather than by abstract, idealized conceptions of the rule of law. An approach emphasizing the transitional nature of Nuremberg would suggest resituating the trial in a political and cultural context of broader denazification programs, and not just as an isolated event in the world of legal ideas.

The Nuremberg criminal trial might best be understood as an alternative to competing schemes such as the Morgenthau Plan, which emphasized the reparatory justice approach of disassembling industrial plants and exporting German labor to rebuild war-torn Allied countries. The transitional justice perspective sees international legal institutions as mediating "between facts and norms," that is, between the horrifyingly concrete realities of wartime events and aspirational abstractions such as "justice" and "security." The legal scholar Ruti Teitel sees international law itself as a "bridge" in transitional situations, "grounded in positive law, but incorporating values of justice associated with natural law."[80]

Nuremberg as a human rights institution is one example of this value pluralism. Along with the internally contradictory beliefs that Shklar found so annoying is the irritating fact that one of the more compelling sources of legitimacy for Nuremberg has always been the unappealing nature of the alternatives. While some commentators such as Robertson saw vindictiveness or hypocrisy in the use of the death penalty, this outcome was surely less vindictive than the alternatives of drumhead court martials or summary executions. Such an argument freely concedes the flaws embedded in the controversial issues such as the victors' justice and *tu quoque* arguments. A contemporary editorial in *The Christian Century* explained, "The court was itself a guilty court and the prosecution was a guilty prosecution. This terrible fact has to be admitted. The trial at Nuremberg was an angel born in a brothel . . . the plain truth is that if justice of any kind is to be done anywhere in the world it will have to be done by the guilty."[81]

In his opening statement, Sir Hartley Shawcross, British chief prosecutor at Nuremberg, confidently expressed a widely held aspiration for what Nuremberg would come to represent: "This Tribunal" he asserted, "will provide a contemporary touchstone and an authoritative and impartial record to which future historians may turn for truth and future politicians for warning." While this "impartiality" was certainly contested, Rebecca West noted with uncharacteristic plainness that "we had learned what they did, beyond all doubt, and that is the greatest achievement of the Nuremberg trial."[82]

Goering himself acknowledged the importance of the seemingly modest objective of getting the facts out, as Gilbert recounted. "Brooding in his cell Goering admitted that his attempts to build a heroic legend had been a failure. 'You don't have to worry about the Hitler legend any more,' he told me. 'When the German people learn what has been revealed at the trial it won't be necessary to condemn him. He has condemned himself.'"[83]

Yet Nuremberg was more than a catalogue of facts. It was an attempt, however flawed, to approach William Butler Yeats's ideal of holding "reality and justice in a single vision." A trial itself is a kind of dialogue, and the essayist Elie Wiesel has argued that this act of dialogue has intrinsic value. "What emerges from Wiesel," writes Haas, "is the recognition that true comfort and reconciliation come only when the victim is able to share the pain with others . . . [Only in] dialogue with fellow human beings is there any foundation for hope and reconstruction." For Wiesel, "acquiescence is the greatest danger, the silent onlooker the most troubling character."[84]

The alternative of amnesty, "silence," as Minow terms it, would have been similarly unconscionable, itself "an unacceptable offense, a shocking implication that the perpetrators in fact succeeded, a stunning indictment that the present audience is simply the current incarnation of the silent bystanders" who had been complicit in the Nazi regime. President Truman overstated the case in 1946 when he indicated that the trial had realized his "high hopes that this public portrayal of the guilt of these evildoers will bring wholesale and permanent revulsion on the part of the masses of our former enemies against war, militarism, aggression, and notions of racial superiority." But the essence of the human rights point about Nuremberg was that through measured judicial retribution—not silent amnesty or indiscriminate vengeance—"the community correct[ed] the wrongdoer's false message that the victim was less worthy or valuable than the wrongdoer."[85]

PART V

AMERICA IN THE WORLD

There exists in the world today a gigantic reservoir of good will toward us, the American people . . . As I see it, the existence of this reservoir is the biggest political fact of our time.

1940 US Republican presidential candidate
Wendell L. Willkie, One World (1943)

CHAPTER 9

FORGOTTEN LEGACIES
OF THE ATLANTIC CHARTER

The postwar story of the international institutions generated by the World War II settlement is in many ways a tale of declension. Contemporary commentators rarely evoke, much less explore, the heady multilateralist *Zeitgeist* of 1945, a moment so full of what the economic historian Richard Gardner called "the wartime spirit of idealism and solidarity." Instead, most narratives tend to fast-forward to the somber specter of Winston Churchill's March 1946 speech at Fulton, Missouri, where the seasoned statesman offered his ominous assessment that "an iron curtain has descended" between Eastern and Western Europe. This dark Cold War vision was deepened by American diplomat George Kennan's July 1947 analysis, published under the pseudonym "X." The cautious young Soviet specialist warned that the Soviet system was both inherently rapacious and fundamentally unreformable, and could only be contained by a consistent and vigilant global counterforce.[1]

In telling the story after our story—that is, what happened to America's "multilateralist moment" and its human rights–related legacies after 1945—the newsreel labeled "Cold War" then skips ahead to scenes in which the Truman administration adopted and extended its containment doctrine through a new set of international institutions. But the wave of multilateralism initiated by the Truman and Eisenhower administrations conveyed a message very different from the wartime ideology of the Atlantic Charter institutions. Under the Marshall Plan, for example, multilateralism morphed into a kind of Cold War regionalism, stabilizing Europe while isolating the Soviets. And in the years leading up to the McCarthyite culture of the 1950s, America's "military industrial complex" (in President Eisenhower's famous phrase) focused almost exclusively on security-related initiatives, such as the National Security Act (1947), the Berlin airlift (1948–49), the creation of NATO (1949), National Security Council Paper 68 (1950), and of course the Korean War.

Presenting the story of the Atlantic Charter's legacy as a Cold War declension has the effect of bracketing the multilateralist moment of the early 1940s as a naive aberration. Maybe, it suggests, the international institutions inaugurated between 1941 and 1945 were merely pet projects on the addled agenda of a dying president, supported by a too-trusting American public's respect for the Soviet Union's enormous wartime sacrifice. Many US history textbooks, if they mention the negotiation of the postwar order at all, use just such a cursory treatment of the "war's end" to fish around for—and inevitably find—early harbingers of the Cold War mentality to come.[2]

To frame the Atlantic Charter's vision as a brief sojourn in what Churchill called the "broad, sunlit uplands" of history, before the inevitable descent into the clouded valley of the Cold War, is not the only way to tell the story of the postwar era, however. This study has suggested the outlines of a counter-narrative—a competing vision of how the institutions associated with America's multilateralist moment generated the staying power to outlast the Cold War. Such a competing narrative emphasizes the lasting sources of legitimacy for international policies that expanded, rather than contracted, American conceptions of national security and the rule of law, and refreshed and reconfigured conceptions of human rights around the world. In this interpretation, the *Zeitgeist* of 1945 saw an America ascendant in the world but also willing to limit the returns to power; firmly entrenching its own interests but also voluntarily constraining its influence through institutional channels; coercing smaller countries but also consolidating their consent through robust policies of aid, trade, and consultation.[3]

Such a counter-narrative reframes the Cold War itself as a kind of historical aberration, an anomalous and temporary bipolar deep freeze that distorted great power diplomacy. Human rights specialist Kirsten Sellars has analyzed a pattern in the postwar world whereby human rights issues have tended to take the stage at junctures where "other ideals were exhausted or ineffective." Hence the brief surge of interest in the 1940s—due in part to the shocking atrocities attendant upon World War II, as well as the way fascist ideologies served to discredit formerly popular Western ideas about racial hierarchies. After the war, explains Sellars, the centrality of human rights ideas "waxed and waned inversely with the Cold War, always assuming a more prominent role when anti-communism—the other great Western ideology of our times—lost its momentum." Human rights are a response to human wrongs, as the saying goes, but also a product of the domestic political culture within the promulgating nations, especially the United States.[4]

The Legacy of Bretton Woods

The Bretton Woods institutions were in many ways the Atlantic Charter's most innovative multilateral artifact, embodying a Keynesian vision of a global New Deal. Yet in the postwar world, the International Monetary Fund and the World Bank quickly became one more Cold War arena for promoting anti-Soviet ideologies through monetary, trade, finance, and development policies. When they functioned poorly, the Bretton Woods institutions helped discredit these Western economic policies. But in their successful projects, the IMF and the Bank offered their own counter-narrative to the Cold War stalemate. Despite their many problems, these institutions were occasionally able to short-circuit crises, undermine repressive regimes, and set the stage for some of the more positive aspects of globalization. At other junctures, where these institutions *contributed* to crises and supported authoritarianism, they were least true to their original mission.

At the 1944 Bretton Woods Conference, all the horse-trading about the size of the Soviet quota was resolved in the USSR's favor, but in the end the Soviet Union chose not to join the Bank and the Fund. One Soviet official remarked how "at first sight" the Bretton Woods institutions "looked like a tasty mushroom, but on examination they turned out to be a poisonous toadstool." During the conference, other delegations had speculated that the Soviets would likely balk at having to open their financial records to international scrutiny, as the IMF charter required. Stalin had also been offended by the abrupt ending of Lend-Lease in May 1945, which he called "unfortunate and even brutal." This imbroglio came to a head during the tense days of the UN San Francisco Conference, just at the time when the other Bretton Woods participants were debating the terms of their respective ratifications. Formal economic cooperation among the great powers was widely perceived as one of the earliest casualties of the Cold War.[5]

Fencing the Soviets out of Bretton Woods was probably unintentional, given the role of US chief negotiator and Soviet sympathizer Harry Dexter White. During the Bretton Woods Conference and after, he continued to promote the increasingly quixotic cause of a $10 billion loan and reconstruction aid program for the Soviets. By contrast, the design of the $13 billion Marshall Plan for the reconstruction of Europe was never intended to include the Soviet Union. When Secretary of State George Marshall initially outlined the European Recovery Program, also known as the Marshall Plan, in June 1947, he explained that the program was open to all and "not directed against any country." But he may have protested too much; the recent experience at Bretton Woods had already suggested that the Soviets would likely walk away from preconditions that included opening their books to foreign inspectors. And in any event, American policy planners understood that an aid program with significant provisions for the USSR would never make it through the US Senate.

Charles Bohlen, an advisor on Soviet issues, bluntly commented that "we gambled that the Soviets would not come in and therefore we could gain prestige by including all Europeans and let the Soviet Union bear the onus for withdrawing." Kennan himself described the Marshall Plan as a form of containment: the program was designed so that the Soviets would, in effect, contain themselves. Even Senator John Bricker, Republican of Ohio and a virulent unilateralist, voted for the Marshall Plan.[6] One consequence was to marginalize both the IMF and the World Bank in the reconstruction and stabilization of Europe. Richard Gardner has argued that adoption of the Marshall Plan marked the end of the multilateralist dream in the realm of international economics and signaled the shift to a Cold War focus on regional development.[7]

The European Recovery Program had its roots in the wartime laments of American business groups that Europe's lack of postwar buying power would precipitate another sharp economic slump for the US economy. At the State Department, in an atmosphere of crisis over political events in Poland, Greece, Iran, Turkey, and Berlin, Kennan and Paul Nitze saw danger in an economically unstable Europe tilting further toward socialism. President Truman encapuslated both of those concerns early in 1947, when he explained that "throughout history, freedom of worship and freedom of speech have been most frequently enjoyed in those societies that have . . . a considerable measure of freedom of enterprise." In this new Cold War version of the Four Freedoms, freedom from want was recast as freedom of enterprise, and freedom from fear was nowhere to be found.[8]

As these forces promoting the development of regional blocs were gathering strength, a preparatory commission convened in Geneva in the spring of 1947 for first-stage discussions on an International Trade Organization. The Bretton Woods negotiators had envisioned it as a complement to the Bank and the Fund, with the mission of drastically reducing tariffs and other barriers to free trade. An ITO that would encourage the free flow of goods addressed one of the lessons Cordell Hull and others had drawn from the Depression, where tariff walls designed to protect domestic industry and screen out foreign competition merely shrank contracting economies still further.

The process for creating an ITO began with the negotiation of a General Agreement on Tariffs and Trade (GATT) to reduce tariffs and preferences on an interim basis, leading up to a conference to negotiate changes to a draft ITO. At the Geneva negotiations over the terms of GATT, the Americans argued with renewed zeal for the immediate elimination of Britain's imperial trade preference system. Republican victors in the 1946 congressional elections were pressing for this result, hoping to realize, at long last, the obligations Britain had undertaken as part of the notorious Article 7 negotiations of the Lend-Lease Agreement. Republicans went so far as to insist that there would be "no point in the Charter" of the ITO without the immediate elimination of imperial preferences. President Truman indicated that these terms in the ITO Charter were "necessary to achieve the objectives of the Atlantic Charter and of Article 7."[9]

But the beleaguered British were in no mood to agree. A pro-preference member of Parliament even offered a strange echo of Churchillian wartime rhetoric, warning those who would eliminate the preference that "we will attack them in the market place, in the towns and in the cities, we will arouse the whole country against them in such a crusade as will overcome this Government." Meanwhile, the United States undercut its own position by negotiating the equivalent of imperial preference arrangements with the Philippines and Cuba.[10]

The absence of Anglo-American accord clouded GATT from the beginning and risked breaking up the 1947 meeting, which in turn would have jeopardized congressional support for the Marshall Plan. A contentious drafting session for the ITO Charter at Havana in autumn of 1947 yielded a complicated draft that offended nearly everyone, and a coalition of smaller states attacked it for paying insufficient attention to the special problems of underdevelopment. Anglo-American opposition watered down but could not dissolve a provision on foreign investment that permitted all kinds of restrictions on the free flow of capital.

The United States never ratified the final version of the ITO Charter negotiated in the spring of 1948, despite the negotiators' arguments that "the ITO would establish the rule of law in international economic relations" and would result in "nearly universal acceptance of America's economic philosophy." The British Parliament also declined to ratify the ITO Charter, prompting one MP to note that "paragraphs 4 and 5 of the famous Atlantic Declaration [Atlantic Charter] which thrilled the world and brought all the democracies together to fight for an ideology" were now definitively "dead."[11]

Nevertheless, the informal, ad hoc process of periodic GATT negotiations coordinated commercial policy reasonably effectively. Explaining that it is often the temporarily expedient measure that proves the most enduring, Gardner and others have emphasized the practical results of the GATT format, which provided a useful forum for resolving trade problems and negotiating tariff concessions. Its very informality proved to be an advantage, and GATT rounds in the 1960s and 1970s generated significant reductions in tariff rates.

In 1995 GATT member states created a successor institution to the ITO, the World Trade Organization, designed to retain some of the informality of its predecessor. Unlike the IMF and World Bank, the WTO was envisaged as a forum for negotiations rather than a rule-making agency, although it does encompass binding dispute resolution mechanisms.[12]

By contrast, as early as 1947 the IMF and the World Bank began to establish funding "rules" based on ever more overtly ideological criteria. For instance, the Bank denied a loan to Poland on the grounds that the Soviet satellite was not a good credit risk. During the Nixon administration the United States formally decoupled its exchange rate from the Bretton Woods regime, in an effort to brighten international financial news in the face of the oncoming election in 1972 and also in a desperate bid for more flexibility in dealing with the cumulative expenses of Vietnam. The Bank and the Fund's missions increasingly overlapped, with both institutions pressuring developing nations to adopt free market practices. The World Bank now has 181 member countries, and its resources for development assistance are the most extensive in the world, lending roughly $30 billion annually. The IMF also lends to countries that meet its requirements, giving the Fund great influence over the domestic policies of many developing countries.[13]

Critics at both ends of the political spectrum offer harsh assessments of the workings of the Bretton Woods institutions in the postwar world. Conservative critics in the United States have long argued that the IMF, World Bank, and WTO are an unconstitutional giveaway of American sovereignty and resources—a polemic stemming from Senator Robert Taft's 1945 objection that supporting international economic institutions was like pouring money down a "rat-hole." This argument regularly resurfaced during the Cold War, despite evidence that when the United States has spent money to stabilize the global economy, even in the form of direct aid (such as the Marshall Plan), it has ultimately benefited US businesses by creating more purchasing capacity for American goods in foreign markets. But conservatives have not been the only critics of the Bretton Woods institutions. As the IMF and World Bank increasingly turned their attention to the developing world, a trenchant critique of their impact began to emerge on the political left as well. By pushing market-driven policies on fragile developing economies, these critics argued, the IMF in particular exacerbated the kinds of societal problems that New Deal–style interventions had been created to ameliorate, such as inequality, corruption, pollution, and unemployment.[14]

One of the New Dealers' central insights was that government policies could foster markets, wealth, and well-being. This affirmative vision of the state's role grew from a key lesson of the Great Depression—that an absence of government did not necessarily produce "freedom." In the throes of the Depression "it seemed a kind of cruel joke to maintain that free markets were sufficient to ensure either liberty or prosperity," writes the constitutional scholar Cass Sunstein. The most basic protections of property rights depend on the rule of law, for example, and "these forms of law represent large-scale 'interventions' into the economy," even though Americans are often unaware of "the omnipresence of government help for those who are well-off." In other words, there has never been a binary choice in the economic realm between a hands-off, laissez-faire regime and some kind of meddling "nanny state." Government policies play a decisive role either way, by protecting and augmenting the resources of those who already possess great wealth, or by expanding opportunities and resources for all citizens, including the less well-off.[15]

So too at the international level. "It is governmental factors—a climate of public safety, a working financial system, courts to enforce business contracts, security against economic predation, governmental or private . . . that we've belatedly learned are the most important factors in permitting economic conditions to improve," summarizes the *Washington Post* reviewer and columnist Ken Ringle, in discussing prospects for reform of the World Bank. In pushing standardized free-market solutions for almost every economic problem, the Bretton Woods institutions soon cemented their reputations for ignoring the human impact of policies at the local level. The emergence at the end of the 1980s of the so-called Washington Consensus—a policy orientation within the IMF, the World Bank, and the US Treasury promoting open markets, deregulation, and privatization for developing countries—meant that, in practice, Fund assistance became contingent on policies such as reducing deficits or raising taxes and interest rates. Such contractionist structural adjustments have further destabilized already fragile economies, leading to hunger and riots in some countries, according to the development economist Amartya Sen.[16]

Sen's analysis has contributed to a parallel "Third World" critique of international economic institutions that has been developing since the 1950s. These approaches have filled in the substantive content of stalled ideas about "freedom from want" from more radical vantage points. Urging a reframing of development "as a process of expanding the real freedoms that people enjoy," Sen has offered statistical measures of development that would "place the human person at the centre of the development paradigm," defining these substantive freedoms as sets of capabilities. Examples include an ability to avoid deprivations such as malnourishment, starvation, or premature illness and death, as well as Rawlsian ideas about more affirmative capabilities such as literacy, free speech, and participation in political processes.[17]

Sen advocates this vision over what he terms "narrower views of development" limited to growth rates, gross domestic product targets, or rates of industrialization. In an echo of Roosevelt's New Deal perspective that "economic laws are not made by nature, they are made by human beings," Sen has emphasized that hunger and deprivation are a result of conscious policy choices. These ideas about "capabilities" build on and contribute to a larger institutional movement, sometimes captioned the "right to development." Such Four Freedoms–style social and economic aspirations draw on general provisions in the UN Charter and the 1948 Universal Declaration of Human Rights, notably the UDHR provision that "everyone is entitled to a social and economic order in which the rights and freedoms set forth in this Declaration can be fully realized."[18]

The establishment in 1964 of the United Nations Conference on Trade and Development (UNCTAD), a permanent intergovernmental body, offered an additional forum for Third World advocacy of fairer terms of trade and more liberal terms for financing development. The so-called nonaligned nations expressed their disappointment in the economic dimensions of Cold War power politics through proposals for a "new international economic order," also emphasizing development and economic rights. The NIEO functioned primarily as a rallying cry against postcolonial economic exploitation and role of the IMF and World Bank in facilitating it.[19]

These substantive criticisms have combined with other, more procedural concerns about the governance of the Bretton Woods institutions. Conservative critics have tended to focus on corruption as a justification

for denying resources and legitimacy to multilateral institutions generally, while critics on the left have focused on the transparency issue of
"who decides." As the former chief economist at the World Bank, Joseph
Stiglitz, explains the concern, "The institutions are dominated not just
by the wealthiest industrial countries but by commercial and financial interests in those countries . . . The problems also arise from who *speaks*
for the country. At the IMF, it is the finance ministers and the central
bank governors. At the WTO, it is the trade ministers. Each of these ministers is closely allied with particular [elite] constituencies *within* their
countries." Stiglitz's criticism that the IMF in effect amounts to a system
of "taxation without representation" applies to governance problems
within the "three main institutions that govern globalization"—the
World Bank, the IMF, and the WTO. The WTO in particular became a
target of antiglobalization protests during the late 1990s for not being
democratically accountable, being driven by corporate interests, and dis-
tributing its meager benefits disproportionately to wealthy elites.[20]

Critics also point out the hypocrisy of the industrialized nations themselves failing to follow the rules they enforce against weaker, developing
nations by means of these international financial institutions. The farmers of the developed world receive subsidies in amounts approaching
$1 billion each day, according to one recent review of the economic liter-
ature—subsidies that shelter overproduction of commodities and suppress prices in poor countries. At the stalemated September 2003 WTO
talks in Cancún, for example, twenty-one lesser developed countries,
spearheaded by Brazil, China, India, and South Africa, insisted on drastic
reductions in these subsidies as a precondition for further discussions.
WTO critics attacked "the hypocrisy of pretending to help developing
countries by forcing them to open up their markets to the goods of
the advanced industrial countries while keeping their own markets protected, policies that make the rich richer and the poor more impoverished—and increasingly angry."[21]

Some of the problems these large, locally unaccountable international
institutions suffer are analogous to those that contributed to the demise
of the domestic New Deal. Critics suggest that the architecture of multilateral economic organizations is in need of serious renovation, including
reform of the most basic rules of operation, to address concerns about
substantive fairness, procedural inclusiveness, corruption, and inertia.
These institutions might also "democratize" by agreeing to make themselves more publicly accountable, publishing more information, undergo-
ing periodic and publicly available assessments, and setting up mecha-

nisms to enable them to hear from NGOs and other groups in civil society that are affected by their policies. More open procedures might address some of the disadvantages of relying on what political scientists call an "epistemic community" of behind-the-scenes experts; in the words of the political scientist David Held, "Those who are significantly affected by a global good or bad should have a say in its provision or regulation." Or, in the even more succinct slogan of antiglobalization protesters, "More World, Less Bank!"[22]

Yet, also in parallel with the New Deal, the international economic institutions established at the end of World War II have transformed global expectations on some very deep level. Isaiah Berlin wrote of Roosevelt's New Deal legacy that "it is not too much to say that he altered the fundamental concept of government and its obligation to the governed." Similarly, part of what gave international economic institutions their staying power—what some political scientists have called their "stickiness"—is a change in attitudes, worldwide, toward international economic stability and toward the responsibility of the great powers to help achieve it. As Roosevelt emphasized to his speech-writers when he argued that the Four Freedoms applied "everywhere in the world": "The world is getting so small that even the people in Java are getting to be our neighbors now."[23]

And like the domestic New Deal, multilateral economic institutions have helped capitalism preserve itself. Despite criticism from the left that they embody the antithesis of universalist claims for distributive justice, the IMF, World Bank, and WTO give concrete form to the principle that we all help ourselves when we help the worst cases to get back on their feet. Many of the institutions' harshest critics share this perspective, even as they argue for internal reforms.

In the post–Cold War era, the many cheerleading commentators on "globalization" have tended to see trends toward economic, political, and cultural connections across borders in almost theological terms, as inevitable and largely beneficial by-products of modernity. Those who emphasize the negative effects of globalization have pointed to disturbing countertrends: a strengthening of nationalism and religious fundamentalism, along with accelerating pollution, drug trafficking, terrorism, exploitation, and disease. A condescension reminiscent of the disdain that advocates of laissez-faire in 1920s America held for naysayers sometimes greets these more cautious voices. But in the first half of the twentieth century, unregulated markets needed the countercyclical stabilization of Keynesianism, and domestic capitalism needed the ballast of the New Deal regulatory regime. Similarly, today, globalization requires a transnational analogue to the New Deal—a twenty-first-century Keynes to tame its excesses, leaven it with social justice, and save it from itself.[24]

Stiglitz mordantly observes that "Keynes would be rolling over in his grave were he to see what has happened" to the international economic institutions he helped conceive in the early 1940s. The International Monetary Fund and World Bank were "founded on the belief that markets often worked badly," and were explicitly designed to use public resources for action to prevent depressions, protect domestic employment rates, and ensure the stability necessary to create security. In the interwar era, the acute external threat of communism and fascism served as an important impetus for the domestic New Deal. At the same time, the Depression contributed to a sharp discrediting of business and financial communities at home, reducing internal barriers to reform.[25]

In twenty-first-century America, commentators such as Stiglitz and the labor expert Robert Reich argue that if we do not take some basic, moderate, New Deal–type steps to buffer the impact of globalization, we pave the way for an alternative which the historian John Lewis Gaddis tersely captions as "something worse." Amy Chua, a legal scholar, sketches a dire scenario of what this something worse might look like. She argues that "the universalization of Western liberalism, democracy, and human rights . . . is a long way from happening," and suggests that America's missionary zeal for the spread of democracy and free markets is "fomenting ethnic envy and hatred" in developing countries, and generating eversharper contrasts between winners and losers in volatile environments where the winners are disproportionately wealthy and members of unpopular ethnic minorities. In this dark vision, America's naive advocacy of democratization without commensurate attention to problems of inequality, corruption, and social safety nets will serve only to channel "the anger of the damned" in America's direction, increasing terrorism, instability, and ethnic strife.[26]

Rather than pushing for the removal of the state from the economy, Paul Martin, the former Canadian finance minister, has offered an alternative Montreal Consensus favoring "a more balanced vision of how developing countries and poor countries can share in the benefits of the global economy." Similarly, Latin American nations swept up in that region's "pink tide"—a movement one Washington analyst recently described, without irony, as "concerned with social justice and other leftist causes"—are making a point of breaking with the assumptions underlying the contractionist Washington Consensus. Brazil and Argentina have presented their own alternative, a reformist Buenos Aires Consensus calling for "a far more active role for public institutions that encourage sustainable growth and equitable distribution of its benefits."[27]

Early on in the domestic New Deal, Keynes wrote in an open letter to FDR that "you have made yourself the trustee for those in every country who seek to mend the evils of our condition by reasoned experiment within the framework of the existing social system. If you fail, rational change will be gravely prejudiced throughout the world, leaving orthodoxy and revolution to fight it out." Just as even the boldest policies of the New Deal were on some level fundamentally conservative, serving as the "savior of capitalism," so too might the international economic institutions that grew out of the Atlantic Charter yet save globalization—if they are bold enough.[28]

The Legacy of the United Nations

The dream of collective security in a postwar world order was grounded in two important assumptions, most clearly revealed in the Dumbarton Oaks conversations of 1944. One assumption was that the great powers would continue to dominate the new United Nations. Even if the four Dumbarton Oaks principals were not configured into the regionalist "Four Policemen" of FDR's original vision, they would continue to behave as such, in a functional solidarity with one another and as monitors of other states lacking great power status. This assumption proved to be ill-founded. Great power solidarity was an early casualty of the Cold War. The second assumption, that the smaller states would continue to acquiesce in the dominance of the local cop on the beat, also proved a completely incorrect prediction of the course of postwar international relations.

The Cold War's destruction of great power solidarity and the rapid postwar processes of decolonization, which augmented the numbers of smaller states, meant that the genteel collective security envisioned at San Francisco would remain what Kant had called a "chimera." International politics developed along radically different lines than those the San Francisco framers had planned. In practice, for example, a deadlocked Security Council meant much more power for the General Assembly, the specialized agencies, and nongovernmental organizations generally. Just as the model of international relations as a series of two-party legal disputes did not work for the League of Nations in the interwar era, so too the basic UN rulebook for a great power club did not address the political realities of the second half of the twentieth century—much less the twenty-first.[29]

The course of the negotiations extending through the 1940s for an explicit "international bill of rights" reflects the failure of both of these assumptions. A discussion group meeting under the auspices of the American Law Institute in 1943 touched on the subject of whether the catalogue of rights they were developing should apply to all peoples, even non–self-governing peoples. Karl Loewenstein, a professor of political science and jurisprudence at Amherst College, expressed doubts: "Such a bill of political rights could not and should not be applied indiscriminately to all nations and peoples. For several countries and peoples a period of education and preparation would be necessary." Warren Seavey, a professor at Harvard Law School, agreed: "I don't believe that the peoples of at least half the world are now ready for the democratic form of government." But Ricardo Alfaro, a Panamanian international lawyer who had briefly served as that country's president in 1931, articulated a different perspective.

As one of three non-American participants quoted in the summary report (out of twenty-one), Alfaro went beyond the Bill of Rights–based catalogue of political safeguards that many of the participants (Judge Learned Hand among them) were advocating. "The International Bill of Rights must not be restricted to a redefinition of old rights," Alfaro insisted. "I believe the Bill should recognize that man may be oppressed not only by political power but also by economic power." Alfaro argued that an international bill of rights reflecting social and economic rights should serve "as an expression of the conscience of civilization" and should apply to all people equally.[30]

Think-tank projects on the idea of an international bill of rights continued throughout the war, both inside and outside the US government. Hersch Lauterpacht helped convene a British International Law Committee in 1944, after he found the efforts of the relevant committee within the American Society for International Law, under the direction of Harvard legal scholar Manley O. Hudson, to be "rather timid and uninspired." But Hudson's approach if anything proved too bold as far as the State Department was concerned: American negotiators at Dumbarton Oaks could barely shoehorn in a few isolated references to human rights, given the strong British and especially Soviet resistance, much less a full-blown "bill of rights" checklist. The United States was happy to add any additional provisions relating to human rights to the list of bracketed items, such as trusteeships, on which detailed discussion was postponed.[31]

By the spring of 1945, such a potentially contentious catalogue had no great power advocate at all: State Department officials had decided that while the final UN charter "should contain fuller provisions than those contained in the Dumbarton Oaks Proposals" relating to human rights, the proper approach would be to postpone the specifics yet again, by ensuring "that a Commission on Human Rights and Fundamental Freedoms should be one of the commissions established under the authority of the Economic and Social Council" of the United Nations. Accordingly, Secretary of State Stettinius announced at the San Francisco Conference that the UN would establish a Human Rights Commission to "promptly undertake to prepare an International Bill of Rights." (A British diplomat indicated dismissively that this "sudden statement" was meant as a "sop" to the Latin American governments, who had asked for an international declaration on the rights of man as part of the February 1945 Chapultepec Conference.)[32]

At its very first session in 1946, the UN General Assembly approved a proposal to develop "an international bill of rights," and delegated this task to the newly formed Commission on Human Rights, soon to be chaired by Eleanor Roosevelt. A number of prominent men in US public life had objected to President Truman's appointment of the former First Lady to represent the United States at the United Nations. These included John Foster Dulles, who felt that ER was too liberal; Democratic Senator William Fulbright, who felt she was too inexperienced; and such high-profile lawyers as Frank E. Holman, soon to serve as president of the American Bar Association, who complained that "she was not in any sense a person trained in legal concepts or in the legal effect of language"—that is, she was not a lawyer.[33]

In 1946 the young diplomat Dean Rusk was heading up the Office of Special Political Affairs at the State Department (succeeding Alger Hiss in that role). He recorded this reminiscence of working with Ambassador Roosevelt: "My job at SPA put me in touch with Eleanor Roosevelt, known to all of us as the grandmother of the United Nations. As Head of the UN Human Rights Commission she did a brilliant job in producing the Universal Declaration of Human Rights. Eleanor Roosevelt was indefatigable, one of the hardest workers I ever saw. She often began her morning discussing UN matters with delegates over breakfast and went right through her day at full speed until midnight, when she would come home and dictate her column, 'My Day.' We assigned a staff officer to each member of our delegation, but to her we assigned two; one could not possibly keep up with her . . . people just adored her. She and John Foster Dulles were the two best vote getters we ever had."[34]

Drawing on what may have been a rather limited repertoire of images of women in power, Rusk elaborated that Mrs. Roosevelt "repeatedly took the Russian delegates over her lap and spanked them for human rights violations, and everybody enjoyed it, including the Russians." Contemporary awareness of ER's role endures not because of her theoretical contributions to the field or, for that matter, for the wisdom or durability of her solutions to specific problems. Ambassador Roosevelt herself understood and apparently acquiesced in the theory that her appointment was meant to serve a largely symbolic function. The historian Joseph P. Lash attributes to her the opinion that "because of her connection with FDR," Truman was wise to think that her presence "would remind delegates of [FDR's] hopes for the new organization and would help to keep the Assembly's sights high."[35]

ER was also the driving force behind the strategic decision to draft the Declaration of Human Rights as an Atlantic Charter–style document rather than as a detailed and "binding" treaty. Ambassador Roosevelt, as well as the phalanx of State Department advisors assigned to her, was concerned that a detailed and complex instrument would risk ridicule or irrelevance for what would inevitably be its lack of enforcement powers (or for the inability of delegates to agree on anything at all). One State Department analysis indicated that the relevant analogy for the human rights document was not the US Bill of Rights at all but rather the US Declaration of Independence, "because our Declaration of Independence was only a declaration of principles and not intended to be a legal document."[36]

Two years later, in 1948, the Universal Declaration of Human Rights emerged from a contentious drafting process to serve as a kind of Atlantic Charter of the human rights movement. In other words, it was toothless in the way the Declaration of Independence is toothless—unenforceable in any court of law but having a moral, cultural, and even political grip that resisted attempts by the great powers, especially the United States and the USSR, to wriggle free. As its preamble indicated, the Universal Declaration was intended as a "common standard of achievement for all peoples and all nations," a way-station on the path toward more detailed and binding provisions on human rights.[37]

Not surprisingly, given the inhospitable political climate of 1948, more detailed elaborations were not forthcoming for some time. The historian

David Fromkin has described the Universal Declaration as "the last train out of the station" of New Deal–style multilateralism before the full force of the Cold War descended on the international community. Members of the Human Rights Commission soon disagreed about the scope and appropriateness of including economic and social rights in future conventions that were meant to be binding, and in 1952 the General Assembly bifurcated the process to create separate documents for economic and social rights on the one hand, and civil and political rights on the other. These two human rights instruments were opened for signature in 1966, and approximately 140 states now adhere to each.[38]

Nevertheless, the 1948 Universal Declaration remains the more influential document. Many of its provisions have been incorporated into the national constitutions of the numerous UN member states which drafted their foundational documents after 1948. The Declaration is also widely used as a yardstick to measure achievement—or to highlight hypocrisy. One popular legal treatise suggests that "the Universal Declaration is, after the UN Charter, the most influential instrument of the second half of the twentieth century." Others criticize the document's pragmatic and pluralistic style for its conceptual incoherence and unprincipled compromise. But as the legal scholar Mary Ann Glendon argues, the Universal Declaration has proved more appealing and influential as a "beacon" than did the two subsequent detailed, technical UN treaties, the Covenant on Civil and Political Rights or the Covenant on Economic, Social, and Cultural Rights. Today, the human rights provisions of the UN Charter, the Universal Declaration, and the two UN human rights covenants are now sometimes captioned collectively as "the International Bill of Rights."[39]

The two key developments of the postwar years—a full-blown Cold War and rapid decolonization—pushed any potential for a less diffuse, unitary bill of rights even further into the background. Any multilateral commitment that might have enabled a UN agency to impose norms or to act on petitions from aggrieved individuals seemed especially threatening to influential American unilateralists as the proportion of US-controlled votes in the UN General Assembly dwindled. The international legal scholar José Alvarez has noted the irony of how "the United Nations, intended to institutionalize an effective collective security system, [became] the greatest state-producing device in the history of the world." Twenty-five years after the signing of the UN Charter, poorer, developing countries represented about two-thirds of the organization's membership.[40]

A significant second-order effect of 1940s multilateralism had been to provide a forum for elite representatives and experts from developing countries to encounter their peers, often repeatedly, at a variety of wartime conferences, especially those organized by the United Nations. Patronized, ignored, and sometimes scorned by their counterparts from the "developed" world, these representatives learned to consult with one another and to band together in order to pressure more powerful players. Their growing sense of solidarity within the UN served as an important impetus for decolonization, self-determination, and self-government. In 1952 the French demographer Alfred Sauvy coined the term "Third World" to refer to what in the 1940s had been known as less-developed, backward, colonized, or captive peoples in Africa, Asia, and Latin America who were beginning to organize to press their own concerns. Analogizing them to the French "third estate"—the residual category for commoners not included in the nobility or clergy—Sauvy wrote that the Third World was "nothing," yet it "wants to be something." The Third World label also suggested nonalignment with either the "first world" of industrialized, capitalist countries or a "second world" of socialist states.[41]

Third World representatives became more vocal and assertive at the 1955 Bandung Conference, a convocation of Asian and African delegates who proudly referred to themselves as speaking for the majority of mankind. Convenors Burma, Ceylon (Sri Lanka), Egypt, India, Pakistan, and twenty-four other participating countries sought to augment African and Asian economic, cultural, and political cooperation and to oppose colonialism or neocolonialism on the part of the great powers. The United States, in order not to dignify what the State Department dismissed as communist-dominated proceedings, refused even to send observers.

Conference participants spoke of a "spirit of Bandung" and negotiated a ten-point "declaration on promotion of world peace and cooperation" incorporating principles of the UN Charter. The Bandung principles began with an affirmation of "respect for human rights." The conference, which also adopted the brand of Third World solidarity identified with Jawaharlal Nehru, fostered the establishment of the Nonaligned Movement in 1961. Originally intended to serve as a counterpart to NATO and the Warsaw Pact, the Nonaligned Movement was in practice a much looser affiliation of over one hundred states focusing on a Bandung-based agenda of support for nations struggling to gain independence and the eradication of poverty through development.[42]

While the advent of the Cold War and the rise of Third World states altered the 1945 model of collective security in unexpected ways, the frequent hortatory statements of principles and purposes emanating from nonaligned leaders highlighted the limits of aspirational rhetoric in the absence of geopolitical muscle. Promotional declarations divorced from any enforcement capacities—or from realities on the ground, in the case of egregious human rights violators signing on to a variety of high-sounding human rights conventions—served to attenuate and discredit the whole Atlantic Charter/Universal Declaration approach. While rhetoric could inspire hope, highlight hypocrisy, and offer a benchmark, it also engendered cynicism as the list of hollow declarations grew longer.[43]

Over the course of the Cold War, the idea of collective security as embodied in the United Nations disintegrated into regionalism—but not in the way Roosevelt had anticipated, as a hub-and-spoke system coalescing around powerful countries. While dominant state actors remained at the center, a variety of groupings around regional, ideological, or substantive interests grew up alongside or within the UN as it became increasingly clear that the organization could not live up to its mandate.

In 1947–48, the UN's growing independence from an American-dominated agenda was of grave concern to the new Republican-dominated US Congress. In addition, many Republican senators and their Democratic colleagues in the South worried that international human rights standards might penetrate the state and federal court system and establish precedents there that might affect racial issues. These constituencies were especially alarmed by a pair of Supreme Court cases where litigants offered arguments relying at least in part on international instruments such as the UN Charter or the Universal Declaration, or where Supreme Court justices commented on these charters, though without necessarily relying on their standards as the basis of the decision.[44]

In 1948 the American Bar Association, under the leadership of Frank Holman of Utah, carried a resolution condemning the new Universal Declaration of Human Rights. Holman also strenuously opposed the 1948 UN Convention on the Prevention and Punishment of Genocide, arguing in one publication that, under the convention's provisions, a white driver who had accidentally run over a black child could be charged with genocide. Holman found a promising collaborator in Senator John Bricker, Republican of Ohio. As a vice-presidential candidate, Bricker had run against Roosevelt on a ticket with Governor Thomas Dewey of New York in the presidential election of 1944. Bricker's identity as an anti–New Deal, anti-multilateralist midwesterner was meant to balance Dewey's Republican internationalism. Dewey and Bricker lost their presidential bid but nevertheless garnered the most votes of any ticket opposing FDR.[45]

Bricker successfully ran for a Senate seat in 1946, where in 1949 he proposed a constitutional amendment, with Holman's support behind the scenes. The Bricker amendment would have restricted the application of treaties, subordinating them to the US Constitution, while virtually eliminating the capacity of the president to enter into executive agreements without Senate approval. Support for this initially popular amendment collapsed in 1953 in the face of a coordinated attack from the Eisenhower administration, masterminded in the Senate by Lyndon B. Johnson. The amendment's powerful opponents disliked the way the proposed language would have constrained executive discretion. (LBJ may have had his eye on a future stint in the Oval Office himself, even at this early date.) Bricker lost the battle, but he won the war. John Foster Dulles, by 1953 serving as Eisenhower's secretary of state, testified before the Senate that the executive did not intend to submit UN human rights treaties such as the Genocide Convention or the Covenant on Civil and Political Rights to the Senate in any event.[46]

A more diffuse Brickerite sensibility persisted in the law and politics of US foreign relations until at least the Vietnam era and possibly beyond, even though the 1957 Supreme Court decision in *Reid v. Covert* addressed one of Bricker's main concerns by denying that treaties could confer power "free from the restraints of the constitution." One of the after-effects of the Bricker controversy was to encourage the executive simply to sidestep possible tussles with Congress over multilateralist commitments, based on "a lasting impression in the American polity that human rights treaties were so controversial they were best left alone," in the words of political scientist David Forsythe.[47]

Nevertheless, congressional leaders who were so inclined could sometimes lead the executive branch on human rights and collective security. Forsythe has argued that it was congressional leaders in the 1970s who established the groundwork for a new wave of American multilateralism through their opposition to the Nixon administration, and particularly to Secretary of State Henry Kissinger, who strongly resisted congressional pressure to incorporate human rights perspectives into American foreign policy. For example, in 1974 Kissinger fired off missives to the US ambassador to Chile to "cut out the political science lectures" on human rights issues that might embarrass the Pinochet regime. Though Kissinger later responded to his many critics by revising and sanitizing his views in order to appear more supportive of human rights policies, he consistently argued against such support both in his academic publications on international relations history and theory and in his diplomatic practice during the most influential phases of his long career.[48]

In 1973, reacting to the US-supported overthrow of the democratically elected Allende government in Chile, Democratic congressional representatives started arguing for cutting off US military aid to chronic human rights violators. Congressional representative Donald Fraser, chair of a subcommittee on International Organizations and Movements, initiated hearings on human rights conditions in countries receiving American aid. These hearings and their accompanying research reports supported a spate of legislation such as a "sense of the Congress" resolution in 1973 that denied both military and other economic aid to countries that detained political prisoners, and a 1974 amendment denying certain trade benefits to socialist countries that restricted emigration (such as the Soviet Union, which strictly limited the emigration of Jews). In 1977, leaders in Congress prodded a sympathetic but wavering Carter administration to link human rights standards to US economic and military assistance, as well as to US support in the UN, the IMF, and the World Bank. Kirsten Sellars offers the insightful analogy that "like John Bricker's campaign of the fifties, these [congressional] activists sought to wrest control of foreign policy from the White House," although this time around, "with human rights being kicked onto the agenda, rather than off of it." Expanding congressional influence was one agenda on which liberals and conservatives could agree.[49]

The late 1970s saw renewed congressional attacks on multilateral institutions more generally, resulting in legislation which would hold America's UN dues hostage to a variety of US substantive and procedural concerns—or would stop or drastically reduce such dues altogether. This movement, which shows no signs of slowing down, represents what José Alvarez, no starry-eyed one-worlder, calls "unilateralism at its worst." The unwieldy and deliberately decentralized and duplicative UN system has always presented publicity-seeking American officials with a soft target. These developments also fell into line with the Reaganite orientation of the 1980s, which viewed the UN as overly influenced by its delegates from communist countries. Reagan-era officials such as Jeane Kirkpatrick preferred a more selective deployment of human rights-driven sanctions, confining human rights criteria to situations where they could be used as a stick to beat the Soviet Union, while increasing support to noncommunist "friends," however repressive their regimes.[50]

US official John Bolton famously observed that "if you lost ten stories today" off of the UN Secretariat building in New York, "it wouldn't make a bit of difference. The United Nations is one of the most inefficient intergovernmental organizations going." At least this 1994 critique started with the premise that reform of the UN is desirable and possible. Bolton's more recent comments suggest the less-flexible premise that perhaps the UN is simply unreformable: "If I were redoing the Security Council today, I'd have one permanent member because that's the real reflection of the distribution of power in the world." Here the underlying concern is not so much waste, fraud, and abuse as a more root-and-branch suspicion of international law and multilateralism generally—and the perspective that the world's lone superpower simply does not need the legitimacy or the allies that multilateralism provides.[51]

The UN has successfully supported decolonization, contributed to an influential body of human rights law (notably through the Universal Declaration, the Human Rights Covenants, and specialized treaties such as the Conventions on Torture and Genocide), and helped resolve international disputes in the over seventy judgments and twenty-four advisory opinions of the International Court of Justice (the 1945 tribunal that is one of the six principal organs of the UN). United Nations sanctions and denunciations helped to end racially invidious regimes in South Africa and the former Rhodesia, and its sporadic sponsoring of peacekeepers, particularly on the African continent, has often proved successful. Yet Alvarez points out the obvious: that "the UN collective security system, designed in the wake of the Holocaust, has prevented neither intrastate disputes nor repeated mass atrocities." Periodic bursts of external pressure and internal reform have failed to overhaul a structure that can support neither effective peacekeeping nor nation-building on a sustained basis.[52]

UN Secretary-General Kofi Annan's latest reform-oriented report, *In Larger Freedom: Towards Development, Security, and Human Rights for All,* soberly notes that the most fundamental reforms could not come from within but rather would require the consent and active, constructive engagement of member states. In a summary discussion of his report published in the journal *Foreign Affairs,* Annan calls for "a new San Francisco moment" for designing and enacting these revisions, because "we cannot just muddle along and make do with incremental responses," particularly to threats posed by non-state actors such as terrorists, organized criminals, and traffickers in weapons and illegal drugs, as well as epidemics spread by human behavior, such as AIDS. Annan also proposes replacing the Human Rights Commission with a more powerful Human Rights Council able to bar UN member states that are egregious human rights violators.[53]

Clearly, the original UN vision, so redolent of the political compromises of the 1940s, is in need of revision. The essayist E. B. White and other "world federalists" of the 1940s expressed disappointment at the abandonment of more ambitious plans for an integrated collective security system with its own air force, lawmaking capacity, and courts capable of issuing binding decrees. But even if the Cold War had not intervened, Eleanor Roosevelt's instincts about the Universal Declaration were correct: attempts to make detailed and binding covenants can in practice produce the opposite effect, strengthening unilateralist visions of state authority, as the Bricker backlash in the United States demonstrated.[54]

Recent analyses, including a bipartisan congressionally mandated task force chaired by Newt Gingrich and George Mitchell reporting in June 2005, argue that the UN might do more by concentrating on fewer activities. Stressing that the UN should revamp its management procedures and focus on major human rights violations, the task force urges that the UN develop a "rapid deployment force" to prevent genocide and mass killings. While such a focus would mark a retrenchment from the economic and social aspects of the UN's mission, it is nevertheless well beyond Eleanor Roosevelt's minimalist assessment of the UN role as "a bridge on which we can meet and talk."[55]

The Kantian dream of collective security may have to yield to more pluralist visions of how nations and peoples might best manage their differences. Looking beyond a monolithic collective security organization focused on nation-states, Amitai Etzioni, Michael Walzer, and other political theorists argue that a pluralist vision holds the most promise for protecting the cluster of values we call international human rights. Multiple sets of decision-making centers—not just the UN—and "an increasingly dense web of social ties that cross state boundaries" would mean giving up on tightly integrated "new world orders" while developing a skein of international political arrangements "that most facilitates the everyday pursuit of justice." Among other drawbacks, such a layered and messy architecture would embody a variety of internal tensions and contradictions. In arguing for this pluralist vision, Walzer asserts that "other regimes are worse," echoing Churchill's famous assessment of democracy itself.[56]

Etzioni has argued that transformations in the direction of what he calls "a global normative synthesis" are already evident in such divergent realms as "shared opposition to land mines, sex slaves, whale hunting, trade in ivory, the degradation of the environment, and much else." He concedes that not everyone shares such values—and, moreover, that "not everyone adheres to values that are shared." Nevertheless, Etzioni's main point is that such shifts in attitude become possible through argument and contestation in a variety of arenas—the EU, OSCE, other regional or trade organizations, NGOs—and that these shifts in outlook lead to transformative processes. Walzer elaborates: "The solution is to build on institutional structures that now exist, or are slowly coming into existence, and to strengthen them, even if they are competitive with one another."[57]

Such a welter of uncoordinated regulatory agencies, activists, and experts would inevitably lead to duplication of effort and to bloated bureaucracies, and possibly paralysis. But it could also generate creative, pragmatic approaches to intractable problems, respectfully engage with local forums, and ground activism in effective, legitimate commitments. A guiding orientation might be the principle of "subsidiarity"—the idea that whatever jurisdiction is closest to the local level ought to be the vanguard that addresses any given problem (a perspective conspicuously absent from the American New Deal). Walzer's multivalenced, pluralist vision is a more powerful and pragmatic action program than simply another call for reform of the UN; and in its untidy creativity, it is reminiscent of both the strengths and weaknesses of the American New Deal as well as the Atlantic Charter ideology that gave rise to the United Nations in the first place.[58]

The Legacy of the Nuremberg Trial

In the post–Cold War era, the iconic stature of Nuremberg has a great deal in common with that of Franklin Roosevelt himself. FDR's early reputation as a controversial and somewhat amateurish figure has become steadily more burnished with the passage of time. So too with the Nuremberg trial: what was in many ways a dubious and controversial set of innovations has become, over the ensuing decades, a touchstone in the development of human rights ideas and institutions.

The very location of the Nuremberg proceedings was intended to serve a symbolic function. An American-led Allied council chose Nuremberg as the site of the flagship trial in large part because the facilities at the Palace of Justice were intact, but also because this particular city had lent its name to the infamous anti-Semitic laws of 1935. In the heyday of the Nazi regime, Nuremberg's enormous Zeppelin stadium was widely identified with fanatical National Socialism because of the huge Nazi Party rallies held there each September, several of which were famously filmed by Leni Riefenstahl in widely distributed and influential documentaries.[59]

British Colonel Airey Neave, a junior lawyer at Nuremberg, highlighted the symbolic value of the location this way: "South of the town was the great Party rally ground, where Speer's searchlights once played on huge swastika banners, as thousands cried '*Sieg Heil!*' The great arena was quiet and empty [during the trial]. Instead of the massed Brownshirts on parade, a few GIs played baseball. It was this victory of the Common Man that the Western Allies sought to impress upon the world."[60]

This basic level of transformative symbolism succeeded in the postwar era. As Nuremberg prosecutor Telford Taylor noted in the early 1990s, "Ask the passerby what the words 'war crimes' bring to his mind, and the chances are that the reply will be 'Nuremberg.'" Holding the trial at Nuremberg, legal scholar Martha Minow explains, "began to transform the associations with that place, and thus symbolized how law can turn horror into hope."[61]

What Minow terms "the spirit of the Nuremberg trials" had an even longer-term impact on human rights–related culture, far beyond the confines of the city itself: "Nuremberg launched a remarkable international movement for human rights founded in the rule of law; inspired the development of the United Nations and of nongovernmental organizations around the world; encouraged national trials for human rights violations; and etched a set of ground rules about human entitlement . . . Ideas, notably ideas about basic human rights, spread through formal and informal institutions . . . The Nuremberg trials inspired even their critics to develop conceptions of law that might begin to assure human dignity, even when nations failed to do so." In Minow's view, Nuremberg illustrated the power of ideas and institutions to reshape attitudes.[62]

The format of the Nuremberg trials has served as a template for subsequent trials following mass atrocities, such as the 1961 Eichmann trial in Israel. More informal examples combined politics with law and theater. Lord Bertrand Russell, the mathematician, philosopher, and peace activist, staged a mock international tribunal in 1967 in order to publicly condemn American political and military leaders for the conduct of the war in Vietnam. The court's president, French philosopher Jean-Paul Sartre, observed in opening the proceedings, "It is true: we have neither the power to condemn, nor the power to acquit anyone . . . But the judges are everywhere. They are the people of the world, and particularly the American people. It is for them that we are working."[63]

The Nuremberg Charter exemplified a broader struggle to give juridical life to the Atlantic Charter's ideal of equal dignity for all persons. And the trial's focus on the individual was a prerequisite for the 1948 Universal Declaration whose short preamble described the essential "foundation of freedom" as the "recognition of the inherent dignity and of the equal and inalienable rights of all members of the human family." The Universal Declaration noted that "disregard and contempt for human rights have resulted in barbarous acts which have outraged the conscience of mankind," which is now collectively seeking "the advent of a world in which human beings shall enjoy freedom of speech and belief and freedom from fear and want," protected by "the rule of law." This language is an expansion of the abstract ideas of the Atlantic Charter by way of the concrete experience of Nuremberg.[64]

At the conclusions of the Nuremberg and Tokyo trials, the United Nations took up the task of "codifying" international criminal law, to incorporate the verdicts into a consistent body of law defining war crimes that international tribunals could apply in the future. Ideally, "crimes against peace" and "crimes against humanity" would grow beyond their status as a set of violations that could only, by their initial formulation, be committed by representatives of the defeated Axis regimes. In practice, this meant a two-pronged approach: approving a general set of so-called Nuremberg Principles and drafting a Convention on the Crime of Genocide.

In 1947 the UN General Assembly approved a resolution spelling out "the principles of international law" that had guided the Nuremberg tribunal in reaching its judgment. These principles included the idea that individuals as well as states have obligations under international law and that the demands of international law take precedence over national laws. The Nuremberg Principles also asserted that the Nuremberg crimes had transcended the status of treaty law (laws created by specific, state-to-state agreements) and had entered the generally applicable realm of *jus cogens* (laws that are universally valid whether or not a particular state has agreed to them).[65]

On paper at least, the Nuremberg Principles represented a breakthrough for the ideas informing what this study has been calling "Mandela's Atlantic Charter"—the idea of a direct relationship between individual human dignity and some set of supranational legal norms, not dependent on the intervening layer of a possibly capricious or repressive sovereign state. This is a key component of our contemporary conception of international human rights. The international legal scholar Richard Overy has observed that "what is striking about the summer of 1945 is . . . that so much was achieved in the chaos of post-war Europe in building the foundations for contemporary international law on war crimes, and contemporary conventions on human rights. The International Criminal Court established in 2002 is a direct descendant of the Nuremberg Military Tribunal, as were the European Convention on Human Rights signed in 1950 and the Genocide Convention signed two years earlier."[66]

The Convention on the Prevention and Punishment of the Crime of Genocide garnered UN General Assembly approval on December 9, 1948. It defined genocide as acts, including killing, "committed with intent to destroy, in whole or in part, a national ethnic, racial or religious group, as such," and declared that persons charged with genocide shall be tried "by a competent tribunal of the State in the territory of which the act was committed, or by such international penal tribunal as may have jurisdiction." The General Assembly then delegated the task of generating a more detailed and enforceable legal framework to one of its subsidiary organs, the International Law Commission, which began work on a set of "draft articles" for a proposed Code of Crimes against the Peace and Security of Mankind. But the draft articles quickly foundered on the shoals of sovereignty, specifically the question of who decides which side is the aggressor in an armed conflict, and on the question of whether to establish a permanent International Criminal Court.[67]

As its title indicates, the Draft Code of Crimes against the Peace and Security of Mankind limited its scope to major offenses, what one of its articles termed "systematic or mass violations of human rights." It elaborated on one of the major Nuremberg Principles, that the "characterization of an act or omission as a crime against the peace and security of mankind is independent of internal law." But the draft did not even receive its formal "first reading" until after the end of the Cold War, in 1991.

The Nuremberg Principles and the Genocide Convention were examples of a certain kind of "fundamental law" approach to advancing the cause of human rights during armed conflicts. Determining who was the aggressor under the Nuremberg Principles would be a highly politicized process, dependent on an underlying commonality of interests among the great powers who would inevitably be sitting in judgment. As with the *jus ad bellum* tradition, it would involve passing judgment on the underlying "legality" of the war itself. But in the polarized environment of the

Cold War, approaches premised on accord among the great powers were doomed: one side's aggression was inevitably the other camp's defensive action.

Another, more bounded approach proved to be much more fruitful. Incremental, measured additions to pre-existing accords, such as the 1949 expansion of the Geneva Conventions to include measures for the protection of civilians, followed the *jus in bello* tradition of evenhanded laws regulating the conduct of armed conflicts, no matter how such conflicts began or who was in the right in taking up arms. In addition to the 1949 Geneva Conventions, these *jus in bello* analogues included such practical international instruments as the Convention against Torture and Other Cruel, Inhuman, or Degrading Treatment or Punishment, adopted by the UN General Assembly in 1984, as well as additional protocols to the Geneva Conventions added in 1977.[68]

Ratifying states often adopted the Geneva standards into their own national military codes, for example, internalizing them as part of domestic law. The 1949 Geneva Conventions are "among the most widely-ratified of international treaties," according to a recent international law treatise, with all 191 UN member states adhering (in addition to non-member Switzerland). While there will always be examples of rule-breakers, the Geneva Conventions' "stickiness" comes from the powerful incentive of reciprocity. States have a built-in incentive to adhere to these provisions, because developing an international reputation as a scofflaw ultimately puts one's own service members at greater risk.[69]

In 1998 and 1999 the UN Security Council authorized the creation of international tribunals to respond to mass atrocities in the former Yugoslavia and in Rwanda. The prosecutor of the International Criminal Tribunal for the former Yugoslavia (ICTY) indicted President Slobodan Milosevic of the Federal Republic of Yugoslavia for atrocities that were part of the conflict in Kosovo in May 1999. This marked the first time an international tribunal had ever called a still-serving head of state to account. The Hague and Rwanda tribunals were "the first international tribunals since Nuremberg," according to international lawyer Cherie Booth, although the principle of individual accountability before international law had been supported by the October 1998 arrest in London of former president of Chile Augusto Pinochet on charges of crimes against humanity, under a request for his extradition to Spain.[70]

The Rwanda and Yugoslav tribunals "provided the strongest support for the idea that a permanent international criminal court was desirable and practical," in Booth's assessment. At a meeting in Rome in 1998,

120 nations approved the Rome Statute of the International Criminal Court (ICC), partially realizing the Nuremberg-era vision of a permanently sitting tribunal with jurisdiction to prosecute individuals under international law. UN Secretary-General Kofi Annan indicated that the Rome Statute was a "prodigious achievement," given that "divergent and sometimes diametrically opposed national criminal laws and procedures had to be reconciled. Small states had to be reassured that the Statute would not give more powerful ones a pretext to override their sovereignty. Others had to be convinced that the pursuit of justice would not interfere with the vital work of making peace."[71]

The Rome Statute highlights the issue of the relationship of domestic law to international law, what international lawyers call "complementarity," where a particular individual crime or set of crimes might fall under the jurisdiction of domestic and international legal regimes simultaneously. But it offers mechanisms to reassure member states that the tribunal is meant to address only the most "serious violations of international humanitarian law," limited to charges of genocide, crimes against humanity, and war crimes, and also that the tribunal is a forum of last resort, authorized to make inquiries only where a member state refuses to act or proceeds merely to shield a potential defendant from accountability.[72]

The ICC Statute entered into force on July 2, 2002. The United States had initially signed the statute under the Clinton administration, with the caveat that the "flawed" treaty would not be presented to the Senate for ratification (where it clearly had no chance of garnering the requisite two-thirds support in any event). In an unprecedented diplomatic maneuver, the George W. Bush administration later "unsigned" the treaty, citing concerns about excessive prosecutorial discretion, the specter of unsympathetic foreigners second-guessing decisions by US courts, and the vulnerability of American members of the armed forces to prosecution while serving overseas. An assessment by the Federalist Society soberly noted in 2002 that "one needs only to observe the rash of criticism directed against the United States for its treatment of the detainees at Guantanamo Bay to realize the scope of the threat the ICC poses." As one American journalist commented: "International justice is for broken-down states, Washington seems to assume, not for the one superpower."[73]

Although progress in establishing institutions to address international justice was very limited until after the end of the Cold War, the Nuremberg process built an important bridge from the Atlantic Charter idea of the individual's relationship with international law to the practical reality that an individual is actually answerable to international standards, whether on an ad hoc basis, as in the Rwanda and other tribunals, or under the auspices of a continuously functioning institution, such as the ICC. And in a more attenuated way the ICC is also a legacy of the iconoclastic New Deal sensibility of the Atlantic Charter, in that "the Rome Statute recognizes the need to change the international status quo." The example Booth cites is how gender issues are now acknowledged as a topic of concern for human rights—a perspective that was totally alien to the cultural moment of the Atlantic Charter and Four Freedoms, which long pre-dated the expansion of human rights issues into what we would now call identity politics.[74]

Most of the action in the realm of multilateral institutions focusing on international justice has been through developments in Europe, both through specific innovations such as the ICC and European Convention, leading to the European Court of Human Rights, but also through more amorphous processes of norm creation. The Helsinki Final Act of 1975, for example, contained an influential set of provisions known as the "third basket," addressing such qualities as human rights and democratization and affirming the human rights provisions of the UN Charter and the Universal Declaration. The third basket emphasized particular sets of rights that were conspicuously not being respected by the Soviet Union. The Final Act also generated ongoing machinery for consultation and monitoring: the thirty-five member Conference on Security and Cooperation in Europe (now the OSCE, with fifty-five members), and Helsinki human rights monitoring groups in Moscow, Ukraine, Lithuania, Georgia, and Armenia. This "Helsinki effect" was a major factor in undermining communism before its implosion fifteen years later, argues the political scientist Daniel Thomas, through the support it offered to previously isolated dissidents.[75]

These institutions and norms, however fully realized, will never signal the end of human rights violations. Nor will they even contribute much to "the beginning of the end," to paraphrase Churchill. But such institutions and norms may mark the end of what human rights advocates call "impunity." As Primo Levi observed, the option of silence, of shrugged shoulders, of turning away "means that the man of yesterday—and so also the man of today—can act against all reason, with impunity. He can state obvious errors as fact, and be believed and applauded. He can order senseless massacres and be obeyed."[76]

Skeptics about the very idea of international law claim that the whole concept is nothing more than a rhetorical mask for power politics. One concrete counter-example might be the recent trend of suspected Serbian war criminals to give themselves up for trial. Since the Security Council established the ICTY in 1993, the Serbian government had been turning over to the Hague only those suspects who gave themselves up voluntarily—and, unsurprisingly, there were very few takers. But toward the end of 2004, the Serbian government began to change its policy.

Serbian police surrounded the house of Ljubisa Beara, accused of genocide as a participant in the Srebrenica massacre. Beara "was told to either surrender or be arrested," according to a BBC news report, and then after Beara's arrest, "all of them realized there was no more hiding. And the government would fulfill all its [international] obligations." The government had sent a message that led to a change in behavior: over the course of the next few months, the news report continued, "indictee after indictee either contacted the Serbian government directly or sent emissaries in their place, trying to negotiate as good a deal as possible." Serb officials responded with incentives, offering the accused war criminals government guarantees so they could be released on bail, as well as financial support, airline tickets, and even spending money for family trips to the Hague. "The basic thing was that the government sent a clear message that it would no longer tolerate Hague indictees," explained Rasim Ljajic, government minister responsible for Serbian and Montenegrin relations with the Hague.

But why would the sovereign Serbian government decide to send such a message in the first place? The answer suggests a relationship between emerging norms for the rule of law, international institutions, and the power of public opinion to promote human rights: "They're not going to be able to join the EU or NATO, which is where their stability and future prosperity lie, until they hand in all these war criminals," explains General David Leakey, director of EU peacekeepers in Bosnia, "and that pressure is really, really beginning to tell." Ordinary Serbs could see for themselves how the EU had recently denied Croatia's application for membership because of a failure to cooperate with the Hague tribunal. "Underpinning the international pressure and change in policy of the Serb government has been a change in Serbian public opinion," explained the BBC analyst. The Serbian people cared more about improving their economic situation and surviving day to day, and "these economic pressures mean that people have more important things on their minds than supporting those accused of war crimes."[77]

This change in behavior goes beyond the familiar story of a small, weak country being pushed around. Or rather, it is that story and something more besides: an example of the way reputational costs in the international arena can have real-world impacts.

An Integrated Vision of "Security"

The core idea in international diplomacy to emerge from World War II for American policy planners was the conviction that security was indivisible: political, legal, and economic developments supported (or undermined) one another in myriad direct and indirect ways. President Roosevelt's Four Freedoms elegantly expressed the assumption that economic security supported political stability, in an international projection of the ideology and values that had underpinned the domestic New Deal. On the home front, the New Deal had saved American free enterprise by sanding the roughest edges off that system, and by articulating a more inclusive vision for the one-third of the nation that was not being well served by the economy in its time of crisis. The historian Jennifer Klein reminds us that "the politics of the New Deal put security at the center of American political and economic life" and that New Deal economic programs stabilized capitalism even as they "legitimized the modern state."[78]

This New Deal orientation explicitly involved a shoring-up of the old way of doing things, however, rather than the advent of a revolutionary new order. In historian William E. Leuchtenburg's terms, the New Deal was a "halfway revolution": FDR was saving capitalism from its own worst excesses, not building something new. So too with the international dimensions of the Four Freedoms: an integrated view of political and economic rights that advocated minimum standards applying worldwide did not present an alternative vision of international relations but rather sought to smooth the edges off the harshest workings of older approaches.[79]

The 1941 Four Freedoms and Atlantic Charter internationalized this New Deal sensibility by explicitly embedding it in the inspirational rhetoric of Allied war aims. "We cannot hope to prosecute a sustained crusade against Nazism unless it is part of an adequately organized ideology," argued the political scientist Harold D. Lasswell in 1941, invoking "organization" as a typical New Deal ideal. "Symbols that release the energy of millions must be connected with a unified view of the world, a comprehensive ideology that stands out against every rival." Atlantic Charter and Four Freedoms rhetoric envisioned an international order that internationalized the qualities of what political theorists call a "decent" society. It was meant to shine out as the antithesis of Nazism, rallying the British to fight on and the Americans to step away from neutrality and toward further moral and material commitment to the anti-Axis cause. It transformed the domestic New Deal into an Allied fighting faith.[80]

In his 1941 essay "War Aims and Post-War Plans," the legal scholar Percy Corbett warned that the inspirational ideals of the Atlantic Charter and Four Freedoms "cannot be spread throughout the world by mere words, or even by mere agreements. They can be realized, if at all, only by the creation of agencies having the authority and the means of executing joint decisions even when they run counter to the will of a state." In other words, ideas needed to be translated into institutions. But it is one thing to devise institutions, and another thing to make them binding. Why would a newly minted hegemon such as the United States ever agree to fetter itself, especially given its traditional response to perceived threats, which had historically been to seek enlargement of the zone where the United States exercised freedom of action?[81]

Bretton Woods offers an important clue: the United States sought to entrench its postwar influence, to make its leadership role both more legitimate and more durable, but "in seeking the institutional commitment of less powerful states—locking them into the postwar order—the leading state has to offer them something in return: some measure of credible institutionalized restraint on its own exercise of power," explains the political scientist John Ikenberry. The end of a major armed conflict presents a "rare strategic moment" for the negotiation of a new deal, in Ikenberry's analysis, where there are "opportunities and incentives for states to confront each other over the establishment of new principles and rules of order." A powerful state can choose to dominate, abandon, or transform the new order into a configuration most favorable to its long-term interests. In the nineteenth century, the United States rejected the imperial model of domination as incompatible with its national creed. In the wake of the First World War, the nation experimented with abandonment—washing its hands of the Byzantine diplomacy of the Old World. By the end of the Second World War, that experiment from the previous generation was widely considered a cautionary tale. Actively engaging and shaping the new world order seemed to be the strategy most compatible with a new and more integrated vision of national security.[82]

The American multilateralists who sought to "organize" the postwar peace along broadly New Deal lines—however imperfectly realized or cynically implemented—reconfigured the idea of national security. The historian John Lewis Gaddis has shown how the United States has historically broadened its security perimeter in response to perceived threats or security shocks such as Pearl Harbor. But during World War II the United States expanded this security perimeter in another way as well—conceptually, to synthesize all four of FDR's Four Freedoms and encompass economic and well as political rights.[83]

After the fall of the Berlin Wall in 1989, the United States seemed once again on the verge of a multilateralist moment, this time in response to the exigencies of the more fluid, transborder phenomenon of globalization. Developments in technology, communications, corporate governance, and the regulation of trade and finance had intertwined with geopolitical developments to tighten economic, political, and cultural bonds across borders. Globalization was "the most dramatic idea to emerge from the collapse of communism and the end of the Cold War," according to one recent analysis. "Suddenly, it seemed, there was 'one world.'"[84]

The Atlantic Charter's ideology of trade liberalization, collective security, and the rule of law underpinned by respect for individual rights and tempered by modest social welfare provisions seemed to offer the most promising framework for taming the excesses of globalization while reaping its benefits. After 1989, some commentators even suggested that American multilateralism would do best simply to pick up where it had left off in 1945, by tapping into long-dormant strains of an American foreign policy tradition.

But by the 1990s, as the historian Norman Naimark reminds us, "the great hopes of 1989" were already beginning to dissipate. Early factors dispelling the initial optimism included the unfounded nature of early assessments regarding the "end of history"—with "history" meaning the Cold War's ideological stand-off—as well as severe structural impediments in the transition away from centrally run economies. As the "fires of hatred" raged across the former Yugoslavia in the form of renewed ethnic conflict, "Once again, war on the European continent had disgorged tens of thousands of haggard refugees, telling horrific stories of rape, torture, and death," writes Naimark. And as a genocidal mania burned through the former French colonial possession of Rwanda in 1994, the international community folded its hands, unwilling to intervene forcefully to stop the slaughter.[85]

At the turn of the new century, the incoming US administration sought to revamp and retrench American policy toward multilateral initiatives in the realms of the environment (Kyoto Accords), security (North Korea), justice (the draft charter for an International Criminal Court), and even disarmament (through unilateral withdrawal from the Anti-Ballistic Missile Treaty and stratospheric levels of funding for space-based weaponry). As evidence mounted that the Strategic Defense Initiative was having a destabilizing effect on US relations with China, creating an impetus for the PRC to build ever more nuclear weapons in an accelerated program to overwhelm the "shield" functions of such a weapons system, one American journalist struggled to explain the continuing appeal of SDI for unilateralist policymakers. Its main selling point grew out of the "promise of replacing politics with mechanics," the journalist explained; "an expert at the Heritage Foundation informed me when I was working there that 'if we have SDI, we won't need allies.'" The hard task of learning to work together "only by actually working together," in FDR's words, required too much effort in an era of overwhelming American power. Why waste time cultivating recalcitrant allies, when threats, force, or space-based hardware could do the job instead?[86]

But even overwhelming power has its limits. Such unilateralist assumptions about the parameters of power in international affairs might have been severely shaken by the shock of the terrorist attacks of September 11, 2001. Within hours, America's NATO allies invoked Article 5 of NATO's Washington Treaty, the collective defense provision, for the very first time, and on September 12, 2001, an editorial in France's *Le Monde* memorably asserted "We are all Americans now." A worldwide outpouring of sympathy and solidarity with America's injury created an unprecedented moment for the United States to reinforce the values, goals, and interests that it shared with other nations, in the struggle against transborder terrorism.[87]

Instead of capitalizing on this refreshed reservoir of goodwill, however, a reactive US administration chose instead to turn inward, restricting civil liberties, and to lash outward, embracing unilateralism in the use of armed force, abrogating international standards in detaining suspects, and eventually engaging in systematic, state-sponsored human rights violations of its own. This approach turned the emerging post–Cold War maxim for international problem-solving upside down: "multilateral if possible, unilateral if necessary" became "unilateral if at all possible, multilateral only if absolutely necessary."[88]

The key crisis, as many analysts have recently observed, centers on the concept of "legitimacy"—the moral right to lead—and the links between that idea and the workings of multilateralism. The "sticky" Atlantic Charter institutions—the IMF and World Bank, the UN and the

Nuremberg-inspired International Criminal Court—possessed a modicum of legitimacy that enabled them to outlast the Cold War. For all their limitations, they produced a set of promising legacies for the transborder problems of the post–Cold War era. But such stickiness is not enough: to retain their influence in the new millennium, such institutions will need to generate some glue of their own.[89]

At the conclusion of his round-the-world speaking tour in 1943, Wendell Willkie observed, "There exists in the world today a gigantic reservoir of good will toward us, the American people . . . as I see it, the existence of this reservoir is the biggest political fact of our time." Willkie's assessment has taken on a fresh resonance in twenty-first-century America, where questions about the United States' role in the world, as well as perceptions of that role, are once again in a state of flux and the subject of intense public debate. To be successful, institutions dedicated to reconciling liberty with security need to draw on the kind of qualities that created a "moral right to lead" in the first place—the wellsprings that first filled the "reservoir of good will toward the American people."[90]

CHAPTER 10

AN EXPANDING VISION OF THE NATIONAL INTEREST

The design of the multilateral institutions near the end of World War II transformed the American conception of the national interest. By 1945 the equation included an integrated, New Deal–style vision of security that relied in part on the fresh conception of legitimacy known as international human rights.

While the term "human rights" long pre-dated World War II, its mobilization as part of an arsenal of wartime rhetoric transformed its meaning. By the end of the war, human rights was regularly serving as a shorthand caption for an Atlantic Charter ideology of individual human dignity. This new synthesis highlighted traditional political and civil rights as core values, while incorporating a more expansive vision of so-called Four Freedoms rights, including basic conceptions of economic justice. It filled in the content of an older term in a new way, suggesting that the subjects of this vision included individuals as well as sovereign nation-states, and emphasizing that these principles applied domestically as well as internationally. "Freedom means the supremacy of human rights everywhere," President Roosevelt declared in his Four Freedoms address of 1941. It was "no vision of a distant millennium. It is a definite basis for a kind of world attainable in our own time and generation."[1]

Such lofty sentiments served the Allies well as a weapon in their fight against fascist powers in Europe and Asia, and they also played well on the domestic front. But as the legal scholar Percy Corbett foresaw in 1941, the inflated expectations fostered by Allied wartime rhetoric would themselves become a future constraint on policy. While "people versed in the ways of diplomacy may heavily discount such expressions of generous intent," he wrote, "by some sections of the public . . . they are likely to be regarded as promises. On them may be built expectations which it will be politically inexpedient to disappoint when the time for settlement arrives."[2]

As Corbett predicted, the power of such expectations soon became a catalyst for change in its own right. The necessity of placating public opinion or blocking more radical plans from other quarters often spurred the most productive planning for postwar international institutions in the State, War, and Treasury departments of the United States. The inspirational impetus of what I have been calling "Nelson Mandela's Atlantic Charter" helped to generate powerful, and ultimately transformative, expectations in constituencies far from Roosevelt and Churchill's targets, such as subjects of colonial regimes the world over, as well as African-American communities and a variety of nongovernmental organizations in the United States. These and other groups in several cases dramatically reconfigured their ideas about what they were fighting for, rearticulating why sacrifices were worth making, how mistakes of the past could be rectified, and why domestic ideals about ways of expressing values of freedom and justice were worth sharing with the wider world.

America's Multilateralist Moment

While the war was still raging, Roosevelt administration planners backed up the president's inspirational statements of ideology with concrete plans for international institutions, in part by promoting the Bretton Woods, UN, and Nuremberg charters. This policy architecture was designed to entrench the Atlantic Charter ideology on a multilateral basis. Their mechanisms constrained the behavior of member states, including the United States, while at the same time clearing a new path for the projection of US influence. The contentious negotiations that ensued—often analyzed simply as early expressions of Cold War power politics—may be reframed more positively as struggles by the Roosevelt administration to project America's New Deal values and regulatory state onto the wider world stage.

The legal and diplomatic infrastructure, blueprints for transnational institutions, and moral instincts essential to modern multilateralism were all present after World War I, but these elements were not synthesized in a way that could connect with US culture and public opinion until after the Second World War. Cold warriors and their neorealist successors have sometimes sneered at how ineffectual and unrealistic the progenitors of modern multilateralism were. Liberal internationalists, by contrast, sometimes try to portray these wartime innovations as more thoroughgoing and relevant to domestic policy than history supports. But a third way to orient ourselves toward these developments, as thoughtful readers and as citizens, is by contextualizing them historically and culturally, as part of Roosevelt's vision of a New Deal for the world.

This New Deal orientation inevitably shared some of the flaws of its domestic analogue, such as ideological inconsistency, the privileging of highly organized, pre-existing constituencies, a premium on large-scale bureaucracy, and a heavy-handed, one-size-fits-all philosophy of reform. Even given its limitations, the historian of ideas Isaiah Berlin found the ideology of the American New Deal to be the best way concretely to realize a pluralistic and pragmatic politics, for which FDR himself stood in as a figurehead. "Roosevelt believed in flexibility, improvisation, the fruitfulness of using persons and resources in an infinite variety of new and unexpected ways; his bureaucracy was somewhat chaotic, perhaps deliberately so," Berlin explained. "His moral authority—the degree of confidence which he inspired outside his own country, and far more beyond America's frontiers than within them at all times—has no parallel."[3]

Especially when the flaws of this New Deal perspective are acknowledged and openly addressed, America's multilateralist moment amounted to a kind of global Keynesianism; just as a society needed to "spend to save" at home—to reflate its economy in order to protect priorities such as domestic employment—so too powerful states had to "give to get" in order to garner the benefits of a stable international system, by spreading not just resources but also decision-making authority around, at least a little bit. For Karl Polanyi, another commentator in 1940s America who had his origins in Europe, "it had been the New Deal, and only the New Deal, that extended the hope that liberty and security might be reconciled effectively." The idea that political and cultural pluralism might be a source of societal strength was of course the very antithesis of the Nazi ideology of cultural decay through demographic mixing.[4]

If American multilateralism at the end of World War II was a Keynesian moment, it also marked a fluid and transitional "constitutional" moment, in the literal sense of that term. In inaugurating a new configuration of ideas, interests, and institutions, the constitutionalism of this era "has both an explanatory and a justificatory aspect to it," explains international legal scholar Veijo Heiskanen, at once defining a societal ideal and serving as a standard of that ideal against which a society's accomplishments might be measured. The 1941 Atlantic Charter itself was constitutional in just this sense, generating rules, norms, and institutional frameworks. Successful constitutional orders serve to constrain the powerful, at least minimally, and to give a voice to the weak so that everyone has an incentive to keep playing and no one gains by kicking over the table. To US policymakers, the longer-term benefits of entrenching American interests through channels that other players would have perceived as

at least minimally legitimate made the attendant constraints an acceptable cost of doing business.[5]

Functional constitutional orders promote shared values and reciprocity, even in the face of pointed differences of interest: California and Ne-
vada do not wage war over water rights, after all. And looser federal
structures protect national and local particularities by addressing the so-
called democracy deficit of multilateral institutions, refreshing them by a
forced proximity to the wellsprings of popular sovereignty. But decentralized constitutional designs have their downside, as students of American federalism have explored, as when states' rights ideology was used to
shelter racially invidious practices from federal intervention. The domestic jurisdiction provisions of the UN Charter reflected this same tension
at the international level, gutting the charter's human rights promise in
the same way that states' rights arguments gutted the promise of equal
citizenship in the US Declaration of Independence.[6]

America's multilateralist moment was also what the legal scholar
Richard Falk has called a "Grotian" moment: "a time when old ways of
thought and old institutional arrangements were so obviously inadequate—as they had been in the 17th-century legal scholar Grotius's
time—that something different was required." Senator Charles Tobey,
Republican of New Hampshire, articulated this sensibility during the
hearings over the Bretton Woods charters in the summer of 1945: "We
have a world that is prostrate," the former isolationist explained. "If we
are going to live in it ourselves we have got to make some effort to get it
back on its feet. There has to be an element of faith, an element of confidence somewhere. That is what we are trying to do here. We can afford
to take some chances. I am willing to do it."[7]

For many commentators in the 1940s, such a seismic shift in sensibility replicated the "urgently obvious" need that Grotius had addressed, by
offering a new framework for thinking about international relations. Politics and social life at home were inextricably bound up with the conduct
of international affairs, as reflections of national integrity and even personal morality, because in the Grotian vision, "the individual is the ultimate unit of all law . . . in the double sense that the obligations of international law are ultimately addressed to him and that the development,
the well-being, and the dignity of the individual human being are a matter of direct concern to international law," as British legal scholar Hersch
Lauterpacht wrote in 1946. In part because of its extraordinary timeli-
ness in showing how international legal standards were "essential to civilized life," Lauterpacht explained, Grotius's major international legal

treatise was not so much a book as a "wide-spreading act" in and of itself.[8]

Through the Depression, New Deal, wartime service, wartime mobility and—for eight million veterans—the GI Bill, the World War II brand of American multilateralism became more firmly congruent with other aspects of American society and culture than its World War I era counterpart had been able to do. The narratives of the Rutgers Oral History Archive suggest the importance of a concrete connection of international events with the lived experience of a critical mass of ordinary Americans. As the historian John Lewis Gaddis has pointed out, "For most of us most of the time historical and personal experiences don't intersect"— and indeed the luxury of being able to insulate domestic life and personal choices from the brutal vagaries of geopolitics is sometimes analyzed as a peculiarly American perspective on foreign policy. But times of extraordinary strain break down these comfortable barriers between the personal and the political, the domestic and the international.[9]

Veterans in the Rutgers survey had not thought much about the US role in the world before the shock of the Pearl Harbor attack. Yet many members of this cohort, shaped by these dramatic departures from "normalcy," continued to be engaged with international affairs after the war's end, at a level that would not have been imaginable had they not personally experienced the Depression, the New Deal, and the war. Congressional representatives, after 1935 more precisely apprised of their constituents' wishes through the new developments in the science of public opinion polling, responded accordingly at the war's end when it was time to vote on the United Nations and Bretton Woods charters.

In the aftermath of World War I, American planners may simply have lacked the leverage to implement this more expansive vision of the national interest. Consider, for example, the role that Columbia University historian James T. Shotwell played in the interwar era as well as in the 1940s, as a behind-the-scenes advisor and activist in planning for both the 1919 and 1945 postwar settlements. Contemporary accounts often portrayed Shotwell and fellow activists such as Clark Eichelberger as enlightened voices in the isolationist wilderness of interwar America, as political actors who "woke up" the American people with the sheer forcefulness of their ideas. But the contrast between the new world orders following World Wars I and II, at least in the American case, suggests that new ideological configurations based on pre-existing ideas do not tend to take hold when they are confined to the realm of elite polemicists.

In the seventeenth century, Grotius had argued for the ultimate congruence of the internal and external realms, tracing the integration of domestic and international politics. This history suggests the mirror image of Grotius's point: that the more the conduct of diplomacy is isolated from the rest of domestic politics and social life, the less legitimacy any resulting multilateral innovations will likely have. Woodrow Wilson and Franklin Roosevelt embodied this contrast between an aloof leader who did not speak for his people and an engaged one who did, particularly in their negotiations with Congress over America's postwar international role.

Wilson had excluded his Republican opposition from any meaningful role in the design of a postwar world order, claiming that a Democratic victory at the polls was the only road to international security. Roosevelt liked to see himself as having learned from Wilson's mistakes, and pointedly included influential Republicans on negotiating teams at the United Nations and Bretton Woods conferences, in behind-the-scenes planning groups for postwar policies, and even in his own cabinet. Roosevelt understood intuitively that education and exposure—not merely to additional information but also to situations where one's experience is valued and one's contribution is respected—would serve to smooth the way for attitude change. Not only did internationally minded Republicans such as John Foster Dulles and Wendell Willkie end up supporting Roosevelt's New Deal for the world, but so did several prominent former isolationists, such as Senators Arthur Vandenberg and Charles Tobey—in both cases, as a likely by-product of their inclusion in the decision-making process.[10]

While ideas, experts, and the policy architecture of particular institutions played a role in crafting America's multilateralist moment, these forces also needed to resonate within a larger environment of values, culture, and lived experience. This was Grotius's great insight: that legal and institutional ideas could be synthesized into a framework which might itself contribute to a transformative shift in the organization of international relations. The salience of this proposition accounts in part for the revival of interest in the seventeenth-century jurist's life and thought in the 1940s, among scholars and policymakers alike.[11]

So too with the 1941 Atlantic Charter and its more practical progeny, the Bretton Woods, United Nations, and Nuremberg charters. The provisions of these charters animated a lost vision of America's role in the world: the idea that "the rule of law in the global arena serves America's interests and reflects its most fundamental values," in the words of the international legal scholar Anne-Marie Slaughter. They were not so much documents as "wide-spreading acts" in the Grotian sense.[12]

Values and the National Interest

World War II–era attempts to remake the world in the image of the United States replicated some of the gaps between ideals and institutions, rhetoric and reality, already present on the domestic American scene. "The predicament of American democracy resides not only in the gap between our ideals and institutions, but also within the ideals themselves, and within the self-image our public life reflects," writes the political theorist Michael Sandel. These gaps have featured, most notoriously, the space between commitments to formal political equality and the lived reality of economic and racial inequality.[13]

How could the United States "fight a war for freedom," asked NAACP executive secretary Walter White in 1945, with a Jim Crow army? In the wake of a spate of especially vicious torture-lynchings in the 1940s, White observed that "as long as human beings are shot, hanged, and roasted to death . . . without the federal government lifting a finger to do anything about it," then the United States had no business offering "Sunday school lectures to other nations" which only highlighted "this hypocritical thing called democracy." But the outrage hypocrisy generates can be energizing: just as the cauldron of wartime mobilization highlighted internal contradictions and tensions over racial issues on the US home front, so too did Allied human rights rhetoric intersect with and catalyze postwar struggles for self-determination and national liberation in the international realm.[14]

These gaps between rhetoric and reality highlighted some of the least attractive features of "American exceptionalism"—the contested concept that America's particular culture, geography, or values set it apart from other nations. American exceptionalism is a notoriously two-edged idea, with a dark side reflecting a penchant for double standards. The hypocrisy African-American leaders such as Walter White were decrying in the 1940s served to weaken US moral authority. It encouraged American officials to withdraw from their leadership role in advancing human rights in the postwar world, for example, partly as a response to the fears of southern senators that international rights covenants "might affect the Colored question."[15]

The paradox of America in the world has been the way the United

States simultaneously led the world and dragged its feet in the areas of human rights, respect for the rule of law, and the design and functioning of international institutions. As the international legal scholar Harold Hongju Koh explains, a continuing double standard about the universality of rules only "diminishes US power to persuade through principle," and even worse, "can end up undermining the legitimacy of the rules themselves, not just modifying them to suit America's purposes." He continues, "the irony, of course, is that by doing so, the United States disempowers itself from invoking those rules, at precisely the moment when it needs those rules to serve its own national purposes."[16]

Equally compelling, however, is the vision of what Koh calls America's "good exceptionalism": the way US leadership during World War II vaulted the country into the role of human rights leader as part of its very war aims. Roosevelt "did not simply call America to war. Instead, he painted a positive vision of the world we were trying to make," giving the United States "a claim to lead globally through moral authority." Central to such leadership was the idea that the rhetoric of the Four Freedoms and Atlantic Charter had an important congruence with the reality of multilateral institutions such as Bretton Woods, the UN, and Nuremberg. Under Roosevelt's wartime leadership, the United States struggled mightily, if not always successfully, to narrow the gap between its words and deeds. And even the glaring exception of the Allies' disappointing wartime record on racial issues served to highlight America's hypocrisies for all the world to see, galvanizing many ordinary citizens at home and abroad to press for political equality and self-rule.[17]

The chapters of this history have woven together some of the connections among foreign policy, national culture, and public opinion in a democracy, in the specific historical context of mid-1940s America. It is a story of how a variety of factors worked in tandem to effect a particular kind of transformation, linking a new, integrated definition of human rights to the realization of a fuller, more robust vision of the national interest. A work of historical fiction, the 1961 film *Judgment at Nuremberg,* written and produced at the height of the Cold War, expresses with great economy and elegance how we might define the national interest in terms of values—including the values that we now group under the rubric of human rights.

In one of the most moving perorations in modern film, the American chief judge announced the tribunal's verdict in one of the so-called secondary Nuremberg trials of Nazi judges. The three American judges on this tribunal had recently come under political pressure by Occupation authorities to go easy on the German defendants—after all, it was 1947, the war was over, and early Cold War considerations were militating against harsh treatment of influential members of the old regime. In reading out the verdict, the chief judge began by spelling out a traditional conception of the national interest, based on notions of *raison d'état:* "There are those in our own country too who today speak of the protection of country, of survival. A decision must be made in the life of every nation at the very moment when the grasp of the enemy is at its throat. Then it seems that the only way to survive is to use the means of the enemy, to rest survival on what is expedient."[18]

The judge then highlighted what was lacking from such a reactive vision, in a response that resonates with today's debates about the scope of the national interest: "Only, the answer to that is, 'Survival as what?' A country isn't a rock; it's not an extension of oneself. [A country] is what it stands for. It's what it stands for when standing for something is the most difficult." He then articulated what the postwar United States and its allies ought to be "standing for," in terms that make sense only in light of the human rights–related transformations growing out of the Atlantic Charter ideology: "Before the people of the world, let it now be noted that here in our decision, this is what we stand for: Justice, truth, and the value of a single human being."

The poignant image of a single human being seeking justice by direct appeal to a supranational legal authority harks back to the iconic sixth point of the Atlantic Charter, describing a postwar order that would "afford assurance that all the men in all the lands may live out their lives in freedom from fear and want." This focus on an individual's direct relationship with international human rights norms invokes the image of the young South African lawyer who in 1941 was so inspired by the Atlantic Charter's "faith in the dignity of each human being" that he helped revise the Charter of the African National Congress to bring it into line with Atlantic Charter principles.[19]

Such transformative moments in a nation's vision of the world are rare, fleeting, and multifaceted processes that do not lend themselves to one-dimensional analyses. A richer and more textured historical perspective might offer some food for thought with respect to our own time: first, that broad-gauge shifts in the values of a nation are usually not under the exclusive control of elites; second, that such shifts must intersect in some meaningful way with the lives of ordinary people to have any real staying power; and third, that such transitions will inevitably have unpredictable but significant second-order effects, such as the rise of anticolonialism in the immediate aftermath of World War II or the later flowering of the civil rights movement in the United States.

Multilateralism and Legitimacy

This history suggests a correlation between multilateralism—solving problems in tandem with allies—and a globalized, integrated vision of human rights that applies within national boundaries as well as across them. But in the contemporary world, the shadowy outline of a new and disturbing correlation is emerging on the international scene: an axis linking *unilateralism* with a *lack* of respect for human rights. This link has a certain intuitive traction; that decency itself might become a casualty of discarding what the US Declaration of Independence calls "a decent respect for the opinion of mankind."

Lack of comprehension of these dynamic processes of transformation may well be the pith of what is lacking from neoconservative and "realist" analyses of international politics. Such approaches are too static. They tend to discount the prospects for transformation that emerge through the workings of institutions, activism, ideas, education, technology, and reactions to local or international events. The late twentieth-century wave of what the international legal scholar Jonathan Greenberg calls "rule of law revolutions" in Eastern Europe, the Philippines, Chile, South Africa, South Korea, and Taiwan was a set of developments that realist analysis completely failed to predict, for example. These revolutions drew much of their power from international human rights ideas and institutions. Astonishingly, they also unfolded without the cataclysmic violence one would have expected, given the entrenched regimes they overthrew or drastically modified. But no realist-dominated mode of inquiry has been able to explain this phenomenon.[20]

Equally important, standard realist approaches unrealistically discount the possibility of transformation in *unwelcome* directions, such as the creation of additional terrorists and the alienation of allies through poorly planned, unilateral interventions. A worldview which assumes that the pool of "evildoers" is fixed is just as erroneous as one which assumes that a good process is the same thing as a good result.

Grotius was especially concerned to attack what had, by the seventeenth century, already become a common reason for disparaging international law: the Machiavellian critique that, for a leader or for a polity, "nothing is unjust which is expedient . . . might makes right." Grotius confronted this idea of *raison d'état* on its home turf of effectiveness and rejected it. "Reason of state" meant the absence of constraints on action and the idea that "one does violence to his own interests if he consults the advantage of others." But this is simply not true, Grotius pointed out: "There is no state so powerful that it may not sometime need the help of others outside itself."

In the process of rethinking what is truly meant by expediency, the Dutch jurist conjured a longer-term vision of what we would now call the national interest: "Just as the national, who violates the law of his country in order to obtain an immediate advantage, breaks down that by which the advantages of himself and of his posterity are for all future time assured," Grotius explained, "so the state which transgresses the laws of nature and of nations casts away the bulwarks which safeguard its own future peace." In other words, some superficially appealing short-cuts are simply not worth taking. Morally compromised means may be so corrupting that they are themselves transformative.[21]

In 1941 the political scientist Harold Lasswell expressed his concern that, as a democracy mobilized to fight its enemies, it might transform itself into a "garrison state." He feared the emergence of a technocratic dystopia where "the specialists on violence are the most powerful group in society," having usurped legislators and other representative groups who were merely "specialists on bargaining." In Hannah Arendt's analysis of the origins of totalitarianism, the first, fatal step on this downward path was the advent of the device of "protective custody" for so-called "undesirable elements . . . whose offenses could not be proved and who could not be sentenced by ordinary process of law." Repression of traditional civil rights at home, combined with the creation of what Arendt called "a condition of complete rightslessness" in occupation zones abroad, created one kind of Grotian congruence between internal and external policies.[22]

Wartime political theorists also understood that the process of administering such a garrison state, at home and abroad, would have a transformative effect on individual citizens. The lawyer and sociologist David Riesman worried in 1942 that a kind of authoritarian politics might be possible even in America: "Like a flood," he wrote evocatively, such a collapse of democratic institutions "begins in general erosions of traditional beliefs, in the ideological dust storms of long ago, in little rivulets of lies, not caught by the authorized channels." The ends—order, elite control, and military mobilization—would somehow serve to justify the means—repression, squelching of civil liberties, and the sowing of suspicion among citizens.[23]

In the twenty-first century, we are starting to see that transforming one's polity into an occupying power can have dramatic and deleterious effects on the people called upon to do the actual occupying. The cultural critic Susan Sontag examined how individuals take their moral cues from the system in which they are embedded. The US torture scandal beginning in 2004 was "not an aberration," she explained, but rather "a direct consequence of the with-us-or-against-us doctrines of world struggle with which the [US] administration has sought to change, change radically, the international stance of the United States and to recast many domestic institutions and prerogatives." Such an impact also translates transnationally: the international relations specialist Rosemary Foot has noted how arrests under Malaysia's internal security act have spiked since 9/11, as has internal repression against separatists in Indonesia, with officials in those countries justifying repressive measures against internal opponents specifically on the basis of America's handling of its own detainees in the war on terror.[24]

Here again, the human rights politics of the 1940s have something to tell us. Seeking a different kind of congruence between the internal and the external, Roosevelt in his Four Freedoms address explained that "just as our national policy in internal affairs has been based upon a decent respect"—note the deliberate echo of the Declaration of Independence—"for the rights and the dignity of all our fellow men within our gates, so our national policy in foreign affairs has been based on a decent respect for the rights and dignity of all nations, large and small." While FDR's assessment may have been excessively optimistic, he captured a dynamic through which rhetoric can reshape reality. Legally unenforceable ideals, such as those embodied in the Declaration of Independence or Atlantic Charter, might nevertheless serve "both as personal aspiration and as effective political fulcrum," in the words of legal scholar David Martin, offering an impetus for positive changes.

By contrast, cultivating a reputation as a bully who fails to show decent respect—who scorns the permission slip of multilateral legitimacy for interventionist policies—may turn out to be especially costly and ineffective when imprudently devised plans go awry. The veteran American journalist Walter Cronkite observed in the waning months of the formal US occupation of Iraq that "in the appalling abuses at Abu Ghraib prison and the international outrage it has caused, we are reaping what we have so carelessly sown. In this and so many other ways, our unilateralism and the arrogance that accompanies it have cost us dearly." Rather than "draining the swamp of terrorism," in the imagery of today's political strategists, such policies have instead drained the "gigantic reservoir of good will toward the American people"—the increasingly parched resource that Wendell Willkie in the 1940s termed "the biggest political fact of our time."[25]

As Grotius argued in rejecting the ethical rationalizations and compartmentalization of Machiavelli, the external almost inevitably reflects the internal. Congruence between internal and external realms is what creates legitimacy, and legitimacy in turn is what generates the consent necessary for effective governance. Leadership that thrusts ahead without legitimacy and in the absence of consent will eventually fall back on coercion and bullying—certainly a more expensive and, ultimately, a weaker strategy. As the foreign affairs analyst Thomas Friedman observed at the height of the prisoner abuse scandal, "We have ceased to export hope, and are now exporting fear." This new reality is the very opposite of the forgotten Atlantic Charter vision, of people everywhere able to "live out their lives in freedom from fear and want."[26]

Perhaps a growing sense of what even the realist political scientist Robert Kagan acknowledges is a crisis of legitimacy for the United States will in time provoke a new Grotian moment. Contentious times, not interludes of tranquility, have historically given rise to fundamental shifts in America's vision of its role in the world—including a venerable tradition of increasingly expansive conceptions of national security. Arguments by the Bush administration that the American chief executive is somehow above the law, able to create what one legal scholar has called "constitutional black holes" where the Geneva Conventions do not apply, represent a significant shift in the national narrative. "How can we uphold the rule of law if we break the rules ourselves?" asks a law school dean pictured in a recent advertisement for the American Civil Liberties Union.[27]

This is not to say that rights are always trumps and that a free society can never take steps to protect itself, including bounded curtailments of liberties, as the human rights specialist Michael Ignatieff has recently argued. But Ignatieff also shows that it is a significant blow to a free society—a win for the bad guys—when the very institutions underpinning a free society are reframed as a source of weakness. This dystopian narrative, the narrative of Lasswell's 1940s "garrison state," deflates the spacious concept of the national interest, by disparaging and diminishing those very values and principles that other peoples might admire about the United States and even wish to emulate.[28]

Joseph Nye has coined the term "soft power" for what he describes as "the ability to get what you want through attraction rather than coercion or payments. It arises from the attractiveness of a country's culture, political ideals, and policies." Nye's premier example of this phenomenon is "the impact of Franklin Roosevelt's Four Freedoms in Europe at the end of World War II"—a classic instance "when our policies are seen as legitimate in the eyes of others."[29] His analysis is even more pointed in an era where human rights have once again become a vector for transformations in America's self-image and its role in the world. A sense that the United States is on the wrong path, that a nation which once served as a beacon of hope is now pervasively "exporting fear," may serve as the impetus to inspire the next Grotius.

The Grotius of tomorrow is unlikely to be a diplomat, scholar, or man of affairs, as the original "miracle of Holland" was, quietly synthesizing the wisdom of the ancients to prick the conscience of the moderns. Tomorrow's Grotius will likely be an organizer, a videographer, a web-logger—think of the Iraqi electronic diarist Salam Pax or the anti-landmine activist and Nobel laureate Jody Williams.[30] Alternatively, tomorrow's Grotius might not even be an individual. In the ultimate tribute to the transformative power of institutions, the postmodern Grotius might be an NGO—a network, association, or "virtual community" of like-minded activists. The list of forty-two nongovernmental organizations playing a novel, consultative role at the 1945 United Nations Conference in San Francisco may inadvertently have served as a model for what the political theorist Hedley Bull has called "international society." Although the machinery of international action, as it was known in the 1940s, will continue to be dominated by states, nonstate actors with interests that cross national borders will increasingly shape international affairs, for good or ill. Similarly, transborder concerns will continue to penetrate the ever-more-porous boundaries of the nation-state, shaping domestic politics, local associations, and even personal life.[31]

The Power of Ideas

But a postmodern Grotian moment premised on "connectivity" would still, at root, be propelled by individuals, and individuals are still inspired to positive action by principled ideas. Ideas do affect behavior, even if they "can never be an engine of history in the way that power is an engine of history," in the words of the political scientist Rogers Smith. The force of compelling ideas helps to determine which tracks the engine of history travels along, even if they do not actually serve as the coal that fires the engine of historical change.[32]

Or to use another image, ideas can serve as convenient hooks on which policy choices might hang. In a universe of competing options, policies seem more compelling and legitimate when pre-existing and easily recognizable principles are supporting them. For example, the demise of the draconian plan for denazification, popularly known as the Morgenthau Plan, was attributable in part to the powerful principles explicitly stated in the Atlantic Charter. The plan failed for a number of interlocking reasons—untimely leaks to a hostile press, a war-weary American public that viewed the plan as bolstering a desperate Nazi resistance, internal opposition from other cabinet members (which probably accounted for the press leaks), and uncertain support from the chief executive himself, who was facing a presidential election in less than two months' time. But if one particular moment sealed the doom of the Morgenthau Plan, it was when FDR read a memo from his secretary of war, Henry Stimson, arguing that the dismantling of German heavy industry, the division and "pastoralization" of German territory, and forced labor and reeducation for former Nazis and their families violated the principles of the Atlantic Charter.

Freedom from want and fear, Stimson argued, applied to the vanquished as well as the victors, according to the terms of the charter. Roosevelt had staked a great deal of his own legitimacy as a leader on an internationalized vision of the Atlantic Charter and Four Freedoms, intended to apply "everywhere in the world," and these Atlantic Charter ideals were integrally linked to America's assertion of what the war was fundamentally about. Stimson's reframing helped Roosevelt see this specific political decision about the administration of defeated Germany in a new light. Of course, Stimson was clearly working hard to manipulate FDR here, and arguments based on the power of ideas do not automatically lead to optimal answers. But the skillful deployment of ideas themselves can have an impact on policy.

The words and ideas that make up the medium of politics are themselves composed of "historically mutable meanings" which shift at a seemingly "glacial" pace, as the historians of ideas Terence Ball and J. G. A. Pocock have shown. Sometimes, however, "such shifts in meaning and reference occur at a remarkably rapid rate, yielding unforeseen and often radical results for political thought and action." A list of such eras might include early sixteenth-century Florence, the English Civil War and Glorious Revolution, and the French and American revolutions. Similarly seismic shifts took place in the United States during the World War II era, when the meaning of ideas about security, sovereignty, the national interest, and especially international human rights dramatically changed. The modern idea of human rights—as expressed through institutional architecture or individual activism—is emblematic of this conceptual shift.[33]

Eleanor Roosevelt observed that court decisions, statutes, administrative regulations, and foreign policies are merely external reflections "of the way people progress inwardly." She elaborated that, "The basis of success in a Democracy is really laid down by the people. It will progress only as their own personal development goes forward." In a similar vein, Grotius wrote that an individual accomplishes justice "when you call back to life laws that are on the verge of burial, and with all your strength set yourself against the trend of an age which is rushing headlong to destruction."[34]

The classical heroine Antigone refused to consider violating her ancestral traditions, even when admonished that it would be a hopeless project to try to bury her slain brother in violation of an unjust local decree. She considered the burial to be the principled expression of a higher law. "That much, at least, I can do," she offered simply, as explaining why she chose to proceed, in peril of her own life. "And what a person can do, a person ought to do."[35] Finding new ways to aggregate this individual resolve may be all we need to go forward. Churchill's "sunlit uplands" of history may still await.

ATLANTIC CHARTER
NOTES
BIBLIOGRAPHY
ACKNOWLEDGMENTS
INDEX

ATLANTIC CHARTER, AUGUST 12, 1941

[Full text of the telegram headed, in President Franklin Roosevelt's hand-writing, "For delivery to press and radio at 0900 EST on Thursday August 14." Atlantic Charter proper begins after the heading "Joint Declaration."]

The President of the United States and the Prime Minister, Mr. Churchill, representing His Majesty's Government in the United Kingdom, have met at sea.

They have been accompanied by officials of their two Governments, including high-ranking officers of their Military, Naval and Air Services.

The whole problem of the supply of munitions of war, as provided by the Lend-Lease Act, for the armed forces of the United States and for those countries actively engaged in resisting aggression has been further examined.

Lord Beaverbrook, the Minister of Supply of the British Government, has joined in these conferences. He is going to proceed to Washington to discuss further details with appropriate officials of the United States Government. These conferences will also cover the supply problems of the Soviet Union.

The President and the Prime Minister have had several conferences. They have considered the dangers to world civilization arising from the policies of military domination by conquest upon which the Hitlerite Government of Germany and other Governments associated therewith have embarked, and have made clear the steps which their countries are respectively taking for their safety in the face of these dangers.

They have agreed upon the following Joint Declaration:

JOINT DECLARATION

The President of the United States of America and the Prime Minister, Mr. Churchill, representing His Majesty's Government in the United Kingdom, being met together, deem it right to make known certain common principles in the national policies of their respective countries on which they base their hopes for a better future for the world.

First, their countries seek no aggrandizement, territorial or other.

Second, they desire to see no territorial changes that do not accord with the freely expressed wishes of the people concerned.

Third, they respect the right of all peoples to choose the form of government under which they will live; and they wish to see sovereign rights and self-government restored to those who have been forcibly deprived of them;

Fourth, they will endeavor, with due respect for their existing obligations, to further the enjoyment by all states, great or small, victor or vanquished, of access, on equal terms, to the trade and to the raw materials of the world which are needed for their economic prosperity.

Fifth, they desire to bring about the fullest cooperation between all nations in the economic field, with the object of securing for all improved labor standards, economic advancement, and social security.

Sixth, after the final destruction of the Nazi tyranny, they hope to see established a peace which will afford to all nations the means of dwelling in safety within their own boundaries, and which will afford assurance that all the men in all the lands may live out their lives in freedom from fear and want.

Seventh, such a peace should enable all men to traverse the high seas and oceans without hindrance.

Eighth, they believe that all the nations of the world, for realistic as well as spiritual reasons, must come to the abandonment of the use of force. Since no future peace can be maintained if land, sea, or air armaments continue to be employed by nations which threaten, or may threaten, aggression outside of their frontiers, they believe, pending the establishment of a wider and permanent system of general security, that the disarmament of such nations is essential. They will likewise aid and encourage all other practicable measures which will lighten for peace-loving peoples the crushing burden of armaments.

Franklin D. Roosevelt
Winston S. Churchill
[Both signatures in Roosevelt's handwriting]

NOTES

Introduction: Charting a New Course for Human Rights

1. Conference at Sea Folder, FDR, Papers as President, OF 463-C, FDRPL; Elliott Roosevelt, *As He Saw It*, 33ff; Transcript of Winston Churchill's BBC broadcast, Sunday, Aug. 24, 1941, in CHAR, Group 9:176.

2. FDR, "Memorandum of Trip to Meet Winston Churchill, Aug., 1941," dated Aug. 23, 1941, 2, Papers as President, PSF, Safe File, Atlantic Charter (1), Box 1, FDRPL; Eleanor Roosevelt, *This I Remember*, 224.

3. FDR, "Memorandum," 3–4; "Log of the President's Cruise on Board the USS *Potomac* and USS *Augusta*, 3–16 Aug., 1941," dated Sept. 5, 1941; "Presidential Cruise, Aug. 1941, Press Release of Aug. 10, 1941," FDR, Papers as President, PSF, Safe File, Atlantic Charter (2), Box 1, FDRPL; Grace Tully, *FDR My Boss*, 247; Elliott Roosevelt, *As He Saw It*, 19–20.

4. Theodore A. Wilson, *The First Summit: Roosevelt and Churchill at Placentia Bay, 1941*; British High Commissioner Brian Fall, "Commemorative Remarks at Placentia Bay," in Douglas Brinkley and David R. Facey-Crowther, eds., *The Atlantic Charter*, xiv.

5. Walter H. Thompson, unredacted typescript, "I Guarded Winston, 1939 to 1945," n.d. but completed by May 20, 1945, CHUR, Group 494A, 95ff; edited version later published as *I Was Churchill's Shadow* (London: C. Johnson, 1951), 72; "Log of the President's Cruise on Board the U.S.S. *Potomac* and U.S.S. *Augusta*, 3–16 Aug., 1941," FDR, Papers as President, PSF, Safe File, Box 1, Atlantic Charter (1), FDRPL, 6–7; Wilson, *First Summit*, 78ff; David Robinson, "The Atlantic Charter Meeting: An Eyewitness Account," in Brinkley and Facey-Crowther, eds., *The Atlantic Charter*, 173–188; Robert E. Sherwood, *Roosevelt and Hopkins: An Intimate History*, 365.

6. Letter dated Aug. 3, 1941, signed "George R.I." to FDR, Papers as President, Atlantic Charter (1), FDRPL; Henry V. Morton, *Atlantic Meeting: An Account of Mr. Churchill's Voyage in H.M.S.* Prince of Wales *in August, 1941, and the Conference with President Roosevelt which Resulted in the Atlantic Charter*, 78; Sir John Martin, *Downing Street: The War Years*, entry for Aug. 10, 1941; "Order of Divine Service, Aug. 10, 1941," Conference at Sea Folder, FDR, Papers as President, OF, 463-C, FDRPL.

7. I thank James Vernon, of University of California, Berkeley's Center for British Studies, for the image of "Roosevelt as bride." Several of the American sailors who kept diaries or wrote memoirs observed how moved they were by this Sunday service, and commented on the sense of brotherhood they felt with their British counterparts. They were especially saddened to learn that the *Prince of Wales* had been sunk by Japanese torpedo planes near Singapore four months later, just three days after Pearl Harbor, with a loss of 327 lives (roughly 20 percent of those on board). See also Churchill, *Grand Alliance*, 431; David Robinson, "The Atlantic Charter Meeting: An Eyewitness Account," in Brinkley and Facey-Crowther, eds., *The Atlantic Charter*, 173–188; Martin Middlebrook and Patrick Mahoney, *Battleship: The Loss of the* Prince of Wales *and the* Repulse, 3; Martin, *Downing Street*, Aug. 10, 1941, entry; Morton, *Atlantic Meeting*, 107. "Order of Divine Service, Aug. 10, 1941," Conference at Sea Folder, FDR, Papers as President, OF 463-C, FDRPL; Elliott Roosevelt, *As He Saw It*, 33.

8. Winston Churchill, transcript of BBC broadcast of Sunday, Aug. 24, 1941, in CHAR, Group 9:176; Morton, *Atlantic Meeting,* 153; Jon Meacham, *Franklin and Winston: An Intimate Portrait of an Epic Friendship;* Atlantic Charter, untitled telegram headed in Roosevelt's handwriting, "For delivery to Press and Radio at 0900 EST on Thursday, Aug. 14," FDR, Papers as President, PSF, Safe File, Atlantic Charter (1), Box 1, FDRPL; "Obituary: Arthur Webb: Retired British Newsman," *Washington Post,* Apr. 23, 1973, FDRPL clippings file.

9. The terms "thick" and "thin" are drawn from the cultural anthropology of Clifford Geertz, who famously advocated "thick description" in the struggle to understand diverse societies from the position of an outsider. On "thick and thin" in the context of ethics and politics, see Kenneth Cmiel, "Review Essay: The Recent History of Human Rights," *American Historical Review* 109 (Feb. 2004): 117, 126 n.26; Michael Walzer, *Thick and Thin: Moral Argument at Home and Abroad* (Notre Dame: University of Notre Dame Press, 1964); Clifford Geertz, *The Interpretation of Cultures: Selected Essays;* Avishai Margalit, *The Ethics of Memory* (Cambridge: Harvard University Press, 2002), 7–8, 14, 37–38; Geertz, "Found in Translation: On the Social History of the Moral Imagination," in Geertz, *Local Knowledge.*

10. The proposal for the Lend-Lease Act of Mar. 1941 was initially introduced by Roosevelt in his Annual Message to Congress of Jan. 6, 1941, the same speech in which he also announced his Four Freedoms as well as an early version of what would become known as his Economic Bill of Rights. FDR, "Annual Message to Congress, Jan. 6, 1941," *PPA,* 1940, 672; Rosenman, *Working with Roosevelt,* 261–262, 271–272.

11. Seymour Martin Lipset, *American Exceptionalism: A Double-Edged Sword,* 14.

12. FDR explicitly sketched these ideas as applying "everywhere in the world" even before Four Freedoms aspirations were endorsed in multilateral statements of war aims such as the Atlantic Charter and the 1942 Declaration by United Nations. FDR, "Annual Message to Congress, Jan. 6, 1941," *PPA,* 1940, 672, 673. On earlier efforts to establish multilateral institutions, see Hans von Mangoldt and Volker Rittberger, eds., *The United Nations System and Its Predecessors,* vol. 2; Martti Koskenniemi, *The Gentle Civilizer of Nations: The Rise and Fall of International Law, 1870–1960,* and A. W. Brian Simpson, *Human Rights and the End of Empire: Britain and the Genesis of the European Convention.*

13. Marquis W. Childs, *I Write from Washington,* 32. For a traditional approach to the New Deal, see Rexford G. Tugwell, *The Democratic Roosevelt* (Garden City: Doubleday, 1957); Arthur M. Schlesinger, Jr., *The Age of Roosevelt: The Politics of Upheaval,* 392. For skeptical commentary on this bifurcated approach, see William E. Leuchtenburg, *Franklin D. Roosevelt and the New Deal, 1932–1940,* 162–164; Daniel T. Rodgers, *Atlantic Crossings: Social Politics in a Progressive Age,* 410. See also Conrad Black, *Franklin Delano Roosevelt: Champion of Freedom;* Freda Kirchwey, "A Program of Action," *The Nation* 158 (Mar. 11, 1944): 300. The label "New Deal" was of course widely used by contemporaries as a term of opprobrium. See, for example, discussions of the New Deal in Sherwood, *Roosevelt and Hopkins;* Rosenman, *Working with Roosevelt,* 50; Childs, *I Write from Washington;* and, more colorfully, Childs, *They Hate Roosevelt!* (pamphlet circulated by the Democratic National Committee, Hotel Biltmore, New York, 1936).

14. FDR, Press Conferences (Dec. 28, 1943), *PPA,* 1943, 569–575. The historian John W. Jeffries finds a "new" New Deal extending from 1937 to 1945; similarly, the historian Alan Brinkley sees a transformed New Deal in the turn toward social Keynesianism that New Dealers pursued after what Brinkley calls "the end of reform" in 1937. John W. Jeffries, "The 'New' New Deal: FDR and American Liberalism," *Political Science Quarterly* 105 (1990): 397–418; Alan Brinkley, *The End of Reform: New Deal Liberalism in Recession and War,* 3–10.

15. The policy historian Ira Katznelson's forthcoming book, *The Southern Cage: New Deal Democracy and the Origins of Our Time*, posits the international dimensions of the New Deal as enduring well into the Truman administration.

16. On the New Deal as a turning point in the "social politics" of the relationship between the United States and Europe, see Rodgers, *Atlantic Crossings*, 409–446. On cosmopolitanism see David A. Hollinger, "Not Universalists, Not Pluralists: The New Cosmopolitans Find Their Own Way," *Constellations* 8 (2001): 236–248.

17. On the New Deal's redefinition of security for individual Americans, see David M. Kennedy, *Freedom from Fear: The American People in Depression and War, 1929–1945*, chap. 12, "What the New Deal Did." On the limits of this transformation, see especially Barton J. Bernstein, "The Conservative Achievements of Liberal Reform," in Bernstein, ed., *Toward a New Past: Dissenting Essays in American History* (New York: Pantheon, 1968); and Michael Sandel, *Democracy's Discontent: America in Search of a Public Philosophy*.

18. At root, debates about the extent of FDR's internationalism tend to center around whether Roosevelt was a true Wilsonian, despite a patina of pragmatism, or whether he was in fact a "thoroughly disenchanted Wilsonian idealist" who "had become an advocate and exponent of realpolitik," as Townsend Hoopes and Douglas Brinkley argue in *FDR and the Creation of the UN*, 11. For FDR as true Wilsonian, see Sherwood, *Roosevelt and Hopkins*, 266. For postwar examples of the relationship between morally inspirational rhetoric and foreign policy realities, see Leslie H. Gelb and Justine A. Rosenthal, "The Rise of Ethics in Foreign Policy: Reaching a Values Consensus," *Foreign Policy*, May/June 2003, 2–7.

19. Gandhi to Roosevelt, July 1, 1942, US Department of State, *FRUS, 1942*, 1: 678–679; Sherwood, *Roosevelt and Hopkins*, 362–363.

20. On the relationship between domestic political concerns and foreign affairs in the US, specifically in the area of race relations and anticolonialism, see Carol Anderson, *Eyes off the Prize: The United Nations and the African-American Struggle for Human Rights, 1944–1955*; Mary L. Dudziak, *Cold War Civil Rights: Race and the Image of American Democracy*; Penny M. Von Eschen, *Race against Empire: Black Americans and Anticolonialism, 1937–1957*; "Symposium: African Americans and U.S. Foreign Relations," *Diplomatic History* 20 (Fall 1996): 531; Brenda Gayle Plummer, *Rising Wind: Black Americans and U.S. Foreign Affairs, 1935–1960*.

21. I am grateful to Jeremi Suri for his formulation of the "new international history," on which this summary is based. See also Thomas Bender, ed., *Rethinking American History in a Global Age*; Suri's review of *Rethinking American History*, "The Significance of the Wider World in American History," *Reviews in American History* 31 (Mar. 2003): 1–13.

22. On transitional justice, see Chandra Lekha Sriram, review essay, "Transitional Justice Comes of Age: Enduring Lessons and Challenges," *Berkeley Journal of International Law* 23 (Summer 2005); Ruti G. Teitel, *Transitional Justice*; Eric A. Posner and Adrian Vermeule, "Transitional Justice as Ordinary Justice," *Harvard Law Review* 117 (Jan. 2004): 761–825; Carla Hesse and Robert Post, eds., *Human Rights in Political Transitions: Gettysburg to Bosnia*; Neil Kritz, ed., *Transitional Justice: How Emerging Democracies Reckon with Former Regimes*; John Herz, ed., *From Dictatorship to Democracy: Coping with the Legacies of Authoritarianism and Totalitarianism* (Westport, CT: Greenwood Press, 1982). On the possibility of political and personal reconciliation after mass atrocities, see Martha Minow, *Between Vengeance and Forgiveness: Facing History after Genocide and Mass Violence*; Roy L. Brooks, ed., *When Sorry Isn't Enough: The Controversy over Apologies and Reparations for Human Injustice*; Antjie Krog, *Country of My Skull: Guilt, Sorrow, and the Limits of Forgiveness in the New South Africa*.

23. Teitel, *Transitional Justice*, 3. On the role of international regimes in the transition

from war to peace, see Paul Kennedy and William I. Hitchcock, eds., *From War to Peace: Altered Strategic Landscapes in the Twentieth Century;* Thomas W. Zeiler, *Free Trade, Free World: The Advent of GATT;* Goldstein and Keohane, eds., *Ideas and Foreign Policy.* On regime theory, see the essays in John G. Ruggie, *Constructing the World Polity: Essays on International Institutionalization,* and in Ruggie, ed., *Multilateralism Matters: The Theory and Praxis of an Institutional Form* ; Stephen D. Krasner, ed., *International Regimes;* Anne-Marie Slaughter, review of *Regime Theory and International Relations,* ed. V. Rittberger and P. Mayer, *AJIL* 89 (1995): 454. For a treatment of the entire twentieth century, including a rare historicization of the important term "globalization," see Akira Iriye, *Global Community: The Role of International Organizations in the Making of the Contemporary World.*

24.   See Jürgen Habermas, *Between Facts and Norms: Contributions to a Discourse Theory of Law and Democracy.* For thoughtful criticism of *Between Facts and Norms,* see William E. Forbath, "Habermas's Constitution: A History, Guide and Critique," *Law & Social Inquiry* 23 (Fall 1998): 969–1016, concluding that Habermas's analysis would have been strengthened by greater attention to historical context and a stronger conception of the role of international institutions.

25.   Gelb and Rosenthal, "The Rise of Ethics in Foreign Policy," 3.

26.   Judith Shklar, *Legalism: Law, Morals, and Political Trials,* 18, 117–118, 146, 156; Max Weber, "Social Psychology of the World's Religions," in *From Max Weber: Essays in Sociology,* ed. H. H. Gerth and C. Wright Mills, 280.

27.   G. John Ikenberry, "Creating Yesterday's New World Order: Keynesian 'New Thinking' and the Anglo-American Postwar Settlement," in Goldstein and Keohane, eds., *Ideas and Foreign Policy,* 59.

28.   FDR, "Fourth Inaugural Address, Jan. 20, 1945," *PPA,* 1944–45, 524; Rosenman, *Working with Roosevelt,* 517.

1. The Ghost of Woodrow Wilson

1.   See John B. Whitton, ed., *The Second Chance: America and the Peace,* esp. Gordon A. Craig, "American Foreign Policy: Retrospect and Prospect," 8–29. See also Robert Divine, *Second Chance: The Triumph of Internationalism in America During World War II.*

2.   "Life's Reports: Target for Tomorrow," by a British airman who was "asked by *Life* to contribute his views on the future world which he is helping to create"; *Life,* May 11, 1942, 12.

3.   G. John Ikenberry, *After Victory: Institutions, Strategic Restraint, and the Rebuilding of Order after Major Wars,* 4.

4.   Ibid., 3–5. See also Rosemary Foot, S. Neil MacFarlane, and Michael Mastanduno, eds., *U.S. Hegemony and International Organizations: The United States and Multilateral Institutions;* G. C. A. Junne, "International Organizations in a Period of Globalization: New (Problems of) Legitimacy," in Jean-Marc Coicaud and Veijo Heiskanen, eds., *The Legitimacy of International Organizations,* 189–220.

5.   Isaiah Berlin, "Winston Churchill in 1940," in Berlin, *The Proper Study of Mankind: An Anthology of Essays,* 617, 616, 608, 625; see also "President Franklin Delano Roosevelt" in ibid., 628–637.

6.   Berlin, "The Hedgehog and the Fox: An Essay on Tolstoy's View of History," in ibid., 436. Hopkins quoted in Sir John Kennedy, *The Business of War: The War Narrative of Major-General Sir John Kennedy,* 155.

7.   On Hopkins's pivotal role as gatekeeper and confidant for FDR, see Marquis W. Childs, "The President's Best Friend," *Saturday Evening Post,* Apr. 19, 1941, 9–11, 126–128. Hopkins quoted in Lord Moran (Charles McMoran Wilson), *Churchill at War, 1940–*

45, 4–5. Hopkins's quotation is a paraphrase from the Old Testament parable of joined fates in the Book of Ruth, 1:16–17.

8. Moran, *Churchill at War*, 5; Harold L. Ickes, *Diaries*, Saturday, Feb. 11, 1941, 5205, Ickes Papers, LC (hereafter *Ickes Diaries*). See also Ickes, *The Secret Diary of Harold L. Ickes: The Lowering Clouds, 1939–1941*, 3: 429.

9. Sherwood, *Roosevelt and Hopkins*, 350.

10. Warren F. Kimball, ed., *WSC-FDR: Alliance Emerging, Oct. 1933–Nov. 1942*, 1: 23; Wilson, *First Summit*, 14–15. This first meeting was supposedly still a sore point twenty years later for the image-conscious Roosevelt. Sherwood, *Roosevelt and Hopkins*, 350–351.

11. Harriman noted that he was drawn aside by Churchill several times so that the prime minister could inquire whether the president liked him. W. Averell Harriman and Elie Abel, *Special Envoy to Churchill and Stalin, 1941–1946*, 75.

12. Sir John R. Colville, *The Fringes of Power: Downing Street Diaries, 1939–1955*, entry for May 2, 1948, 624; perhaps a feminized United States and US president served, on some level, as a device for managing British anxieties about growing US power—American wiles were nothing a stalwart "John Bull" couldn't handle. See Jonathan Rutherford, *Forever England: Reflections on Race, Masculinity, and Empire*; D. Cameron Watt, *Succeeding John Bull: America in Britain's Place, 1900–1975* (Cambridge: Cambridge University Press, 1984).

13. Winston S. Churchill, *The Second World War: The Grand Alliance*, 427; Martin Gilbert, *Winston S. Churchill: Finest Hour, 1939–1941*, 6: 1160; Sherwood, *Roosevelt and Hopkins*, 362.

14. *Ickes Diaries*, Sunday, May 12, 1940, 4380, LC; Ickes, *Secret Diary*, 3: 176. On Churchill's putative alcoholism, see Lord Halifax, *Secret Diary*, Feb. 17, 1941, as quoted in Robert Skidelsky, *John Maynard Keynes: A Biography*, vol. 3: *Fighting for Freedom*, 92. See also Christopher Hitchens, "Churchill Takes a Fall," *Atlantic Monthly* 289 (Apr. 2002): 118–137; Sherwood, *Roosevelt and Hopkins*, 362.

15. Sumner Welles, *The Time for Decision*, 171ff; Churchill to Roosevelt, Dec. 7–8, 1940, in Kimball, ed., *WSC-FDR*, 1: 102–109, and described further by Churchill in *The Second World War: Their Finest Hour*, 3: 360, 362–367, 494. Britain's strategic situation and its relationship to the Atlantic Charter are discussed in R. A. Humphrey, "The Atlantic Charter: Symbol of United Democracy," *Public Affairs Bulletin* No. 9: 2; Fiorello H. LaGuardia, "Interpreting the Atlantic Charter: Its True Intent and Meaning," rpt. in LaGuardia, *Vital Speeches of the Day*, 555–556.

16. Churchill before the House of Commons, June 4, 1940, rpt. in *Winston S. Churchill: His Complete Speeches, 1897–1963*, 6231.

17. See entry for the Battle of Britain in Norman Polmar and Thomas B. Allen, *World War II: The Encyclopedia of the War Years, 1941–1945*.

18. Warren F. Kimball, *The Most Unsordid Act: Lend-Lease, 1939–194*, 22, 32, 33, 34; Joseph Alsop and Robert Kintner, *American White Paper: The Story of American Diplomacy and the Second World War*, 81; Lord Lothian (Philip Kerr) quoted in Skidelsky, *John Maynard Keynes*, 3: 96; David Dimbleby and David Reynolds, *An Ocean Apart: The Relationship between Britain and America in the Twentieth Century*. See also Walter Russell Mead, "In the Long Run: Keynes and the Legacy of British Liberalism," *Foreign Affairs*, Jan./Feb. 2002, 199–204.

19. Churchill to Roosevelt, Dec. 7–8, 1940, in *WSC-FDR*, 106–108; Skidelsky, *John Maynard Keynes*, 3: 100.

20. FDR, Press Conferences, No. 702 (Dec. 17, 1940), *PPA*, 1940, 607.

21. The term "arsenal of democracy" was coined by French diplomat Jean Monnet, the future advocate of European integration who was serving as a representative of the Free

French in Washington during the war. Monnet used the phrase in 1940, in conversation with Justice Felix Frankfurter, who sometimes acted informally as an advisor to FDR. Recognizing that the phrase captured the essence of the next important role for the United States, Frankfurter asked that Monnet refrain from using the term in public so that Roosevelt could be the one to give it "world currency." Rosenman, *Working with Roosevelt*, 260–261. See "Fireside Chat on National Security," Dec. 29, 1940, *PPA*, 1940, 633–644; Kimball, *Unsordid Act;* William L. Langer and S. Everett Gleason, *The Undeclared War, 1940–1941*, 237; and David Reynolds, *The Creation of the Anglo-American Alliance, 1937–41: A Study in Competitive Cooperation*, 150ff.

22. Sherwood, *Roosevelt and Hopkins*, 360, 227. On foreign policy advice, see "Memorandum Concerning the Meeting of May 3, 1941" (May 31, 1941), FDR, PPF, 1920, FDRPL; Adolf Berle, "The Uses of Victory," Typed Memorandum, Sept. 19, 1942, State Department Subject File, Post-War Plans, 1939–1944, Adolf Berle Papers, FDRPL, 5ff; see also Harley A. Notter, *Postwar Foreign Policy Preparation, 1939–1945*, Department of State Publication 3580, General Foreign Policy Series 15, 22ff.

23. FDR, "Annual Message to Congress, Jan. 6, 1941," *PPA*, 1940, 672.

24. Sumner Welles testimony before Congress, Nov.–Dec. 1945, *Report of the Joint Committee Investigating the Pearl Harbor Attack*, Part 2, 536ff. See also Welles, *Where Are We Heading?* 6.

25. Hadley Cantril, letter of Mar. 20, 1941 (to Anna Rosenberg for the President), PPF, 1820, Box 5, FDRPL. See also Sherwood, *Roosevelt and Hopkins*, 231.

26. "Memorandum Concerning the Meeting of May 3, 1941" (May 31, 1941), FDR, Papers as President, PPF, 1820, FDRPL; Primus, *Language of Rights*, 177–179, 192. US Ambassador Laurence Steinhart to Secretary of State Cordell Hull, Aug. 1, 1941, in *FRUS, 1941*, 1: 814; Harry Hopkins, "The Inside Story of My Meeting with Stalin," *American Magazine*, Dec. 1, 1941, 35; Memorandum by Hopkins of Conference with Premier Stalin, July 31, 1941, in *FRUS, 1941*, 1: 805–814. Only seven weeks had passed since Hitler's invasion of the Soviet Union. Hopkins joined the American delegation to the Atlantic Conference with 90 pages of notes from these meetings in his luggage. Churchill to Atlee, "Most Secret" Telegram, Tudor No. 23, Aug. 12, 1941, CHAR 20/48: 15; "1st British Draft" in FDR's handwriting, on otherwise untitled typescript dated Aug. 10, 1941; FDR, Papers as President, PSF, Safe File, Box 1, Atlantic Charter (1), FDRPL.

27. The structure of this brief and formal ceremony spoke to the fact that Roosevelt, unlike Churchill, was head of state as well as the leader of his government. Sherwood, *Roosevelt and Hopkins*, 351; David Dilks, ed., *The Diaries of Sir Alexander Cadogan, O.M., 1938–1945*, 397 (hereafter *Cadogan Diaries*); see also Morton, *Atlantic Meeting*, 23–28; Undersecretary Welles's Memorandum of Conversation with Sir Alexander Cadogan, Aug. 9, 1941, in *FRUS, 1941*, 1: 346–354.

28. Irwin F. Gellman, *Secret Affairs: Franklin Roosevelt, Cordell Hull, and Sumner Welles*, x, 59. See also Benjamin Welles, *Sumner Welles: FDR's Global Strategist*, 7–41; *Cadogan Diaries*, 399; Walter H. Thompson, *Assignment: Churchill*, 271.

29. "Dinner in Honor of the Right Honorable Winston Churchill, Prime Minister of Great Britain, and his Staff, Given by the President of the United States, FDR, on Board the United States Flagship *Augusta* (Saturday, Aug. 9, 1941)" (Menu card autographed by participants), FDR, Papers as President, PSF, Safe File, Atlantic Charter (1), Box 1, FDRPL. Most of the dinner conversation centered around Harry Hopkins's recent meetings with Stalin.

30. Although Welles had supposedly written up an earlier draft in Washington, according to his son's later account, Welles merely used it for talking points in his negotiations with Cadogan. B. Welles, *Sumner Welles*, 300–304. For a depiction of the entire document originating with the British, see Sherwood, *Roosevelt and Hopkins*, 350; "1st British

Draft" in FDR's handwriting, dated Aug. 10, 1941; FDR, Papers as President, PSF, Safe File, Box 1, Atlantic Charter (1), FDRPL.

31. "1st British Draft," dated Aug. 10, 1941.

32. The 1932 Ottowa Agreements on trade preferences granted special privileges to Commonwealth countries in their trade with Britain and were a particular bugaboo of Cordell Hull. See Welles, *Where Are We Heading?* 9.

33. Sherwood, *Roosevelt and Hopkins*, 320. Senator Robert A. Taft of Ohio, in particular, was a magnet for isolationist correspondence from all over the country. As the son of former president William Howard Taft, he had a nationwide base of supporters, many of whom felt that he should be the next president. Taft Papers, Correspondence Files, LC. The portrait of the America First Committee is drawn from Justus D. Doenecke, *The Battle against Intervention, 1939–1941*, 9. See also Manfred Jonas, *Isolationism in America, 1935–1941*; James T. Patterson, *Mr. Republican: A Biography of Robert A. Taft*; Welles, *Where Are We Heading?* 10. On isolationism in the early 1940s, see Isaiah Berlin, *Washington Despatches, 1941–1945: Weekly Political Reports from the British Embassy,* ed. H. G. Nichols; Robert A. Divine, *Foreign Policy and the US Presidential Elections, 1940–1948.*

34. Elliott Roosevelt, *As He Saw It*, 35–37.

35. Welles's draft rpt. in Welles, *Where Are We Heading?* 10.

36. Memorandum by Welles of Conversation, Aug. 11, 1941, *FRUS, 1941*, 1: 362.

37. Ibid., 363. See also Robert Dallek, *Franklin D. Roosevelt and American Foreign Policy, 1932–1945*, 283–284.

38. Prime Minister to Lord Privy Seal, "Most Secret" Telegram Tudor No. 15, Aug. 11, 1941, CHAR 20/48: 5; see also Churchill, *Grand Alliance*, 441.

39. Atlantic Charter, Point 8.

40. Wheeler quoted in Kimball, *Unsordid Act*, 154. See also Rosenman, *Working with Roosevelt*, 273. On FDR's internationalism, see James MacGregor Burns, *Roosevelt: The Soldier of Freedom*, 213–217, 266–268.

41. Herbert Feis, *Churchill, Roosevelt, Stalin: The War They Waged and the Peace They Sought,* 21; Gaddis Smith, "Roosevelt, the Sea, and International Security," in Brinkley and Facey-Crowther, eds., *The Atlantic Charter,* 33.

42. See also Gilbert, *Finest Hour,* 1163.

43. Feis, *Churchill, Roosevelt, Stalin,* 22. See also Arthur W. Schatz, "The Anglo-American Trade Agreement and Cordell Hull's Search for Peace, 1936–1938," *Journal of American History* 57 (June 1970): 85–103.

44. Churchill, "Most Secret" Telegram, Tudor No. 16, Aug. 11, 1941, CHAR 20/48: 7; Gilbert, *Finest Hour,* 1163.

45. Churchill, Speech to the Allied Representatives, St. James's Palace, June 12, 1941, CHAR 9 (Speeches) 182A: 56, 64.

46. Nelson Mandela, *Long Walk to Freedom,* 83–84.

47. Hersch Lauterpacht, "The International Protection of Human Rights," *Académie de Droit International, Recueil des Cours,* 1947 (1): 11; Koskenniemi, *Gentle Civilizer of Nations,* 353–413.

48. Mandela, *Long Walk to Freedom,* 83–84; Francis Meli, *South Africa Belongs to Us: A History of the ANC* (Harare, Zimbabwe: Zimbabwe Publishing House, 1988); Edwin W. Smith, *Events in African History; or, The Atlantic Charter and Africa from an African Standpoint;* Joseph Sulkowski, "The Atlantic Charter and the Principle of Self-Determination," *New Europe,* Aug. 1942; Julius Stone, *The Atlantic Charter: New Worlds for Old;* Stanislaw Stronski, *The Atlantic Charter: No Territorial Guarantees to Aggressors, No Dictatorships.* Secondary sources addressing the Atlantic Charter's reception among colonized peoples include Penny M. Von Eschen, *Race against Empire: Black Americans and Anticolonialism, 1937–1957;* Thomas Borstelmann, *Apartheid's Reluctant Un-*

cle: The United States and Southern Africa in the Early Cold War; and Kenneth R. Janken, *Rayford W. Logan and the Dilemma of the African-American Intellectual* (Amherst: University of Massachusetts Press, 1993).

49. Sherwood, *Roosevelt and Hopkins,* 362–363; see also *India's Right to Freedom* (pamphlet), Nov. 1944, G.P.D. 506/4, Widener Library, Harvard University, stamped "specimen of British war literature supplied for record purposes only," chapter headed "Does the Atlantic Charter 'Not Apply' to India?"; Taraknath Das, *The Atlantic Charter and India* (pamphlet).

50. Churchill speech of Sept. 9, 1941, extract from *Hansard* of Sept. 9, 1941, cols. 68–69, in Prime Minister's Official Papers, NA-Kew, 4/43A/3: 86. See also Das, *Atlantic Charter,* 4–5.

51. Sherwood, *Roosevelt and Hopkins,* 363.

52. David Reynolds, "The Atlantic 'Flop': British Foreign Policy and the Churchill-Roosevelt Summit," *London Chronicle* 1 (Aug. 15, 1941): 1129–1150; James Leutze, ed., *The London Journal of General Raymond E. Lee, 1940–1941* (Boston: Little, Brown, 1971), entry for Aug. 14, 1941, 368–369; see also Angus Calder, *The People's War: Britain 1939–45* (London: Cape, 1969), 264.

53. "Katzenjammer in London und Washington," *Der Völkische Beobachter,* Aug. 17, 1942, 1; "Komödie auf See," *Der Angriff,* Aug. 16, 1941, 1; "Weltbetrug der Kriegsverbrecher," *Der Völkische Beobachter,* Aug. 16, 1941, 1; "Politische Offensive — um Amerika," *Frankfurter Zeitung,* Aug. 16, 1941, 1; "Eine schreckliche Kollektion frommer Platitüden," *Frankfurter Zeitung,* Aug. 17, 1941, 2.

54. "Der amerikanische Anspruch," *Frankfurter Zeitung,* Aug. 17, 1941, 1; "Die Erkärungen in London und Washington," *Frankfurter Zeitung,* Aug. 16, 1941, 2; "Onkel Sam will kassieren, aber nicht bluten," *Der Angriff,* Aug. 16/17, 1941, 2.

55. Ickes, *Secret Diary,* 3: 601; Tully, *FDR My Boss,* 152. Early was upset that "the Prime Minister, contrary to the understanding of the President, had brought three correspondent-authors in faint disguise among his staff and the conference and its charter of principles was first revealed under London's dateline." Ibid., 247. Dallek, *Franklin D. Roosevelt and American Foreign Policy,* 284; British War Cabinet Minutes, No. 84 (Aug. 19, 1941, 11:30 a.m.), Secretary's File, Cabinet Papers 65/19(41), as quoted in Gilbert, *Finest Hour,* 1168; Welles testimony before Congress, Nov.–Dec. 1945, *Report of the Joint Committee Investigating the Pearl Harbor Attack,* Part 2, 536ff.

56. Sherwood, *Roosevelt and Hopkins,* 382. See Dallek, *Franklin D. Roosevelt and American Foreign Policy,* 70–72,75–77, 85–86, 101–110, 117–121; see also Robert A. Divine, *The Illusion of Neutrality* (Chicago: University of Chicago Press, 1962).

57. William A. Lydgate, *What America Thinks,* 42–43; Lawrence S. Wittner, *Rebels against War: The American Peace Movement, 1941–1960* (New York: Columbia University Press, 1969), 120. In 1942, "nine out of ten Americans could not name any provisions of the Atlantic Charter," as cited in John M. Blum, *'V' Was for Victory: Politics and American Culture during World War II,* 46; B. Welles, *Sumner Welles,* 308; Gardner, "The Atlantic Charter: Idea and Reality, 1942–1945," in Brinkley and Facey-Crowther, eds., *The Atlantic Charter,* 45–81.

58. Sherwood, *Roosevelt and Hopkins,* 367.

59. Stewart Alsop, "Wanted: A Faith to Fight For," *Atlantic Monthly,* May 1941, 594–597; Harold Lavine, "Why the Army Gripes," *The Nation,* Aug. 30, 1941, 179–180; Forrest C. Pogue, *George C. Marshall: Global Commander.*

60. Sherwood, *Roosevelt and Hopkins,* 355–358.

61. Churchill to Atlee, Aug. 12, 1941, "Most Secret" Telegram, Tudor No. 25, CHAR 28/48: 16; see also Winston S. Churchill, "Prime Minister's Broadcast, Sunday 24th Aug.,

1941, 9 p.m." (discussing the Atlantic Conference), CHAR 9/182B: 164; Gilbert, *Finest Hour,* 6: 1165; Eleanor Roosevelt, *This I Remember,* 7.

62. David Reynolds, "The Atlantic 'Flop': British Foreign Policy and the Churchill-Roosevelt Meeting of Aug. 1941," in Brinkley and Facey-Crowther, eds., *The Atlantic Charter,* 130.

63. For Asian—specifically Chinese—and Latin American interpretations, see Chapters 5 and 6, below.

64. "Mr. Atlee on Increasing Self-Government for West Africans," extract from *West Africa* of Aug. 23, 1941, in PREM 4/43A/3:82, 83. Attlee was responding to a speech by student leaders.

65. Prime Minister's Personal Telegram, "From Nigeria" (Governor Sir B. Bourdillon to Secretary of State for the Colonies, forwarding Cable No. 1129 of Nov. 15, 1941, from the Editor of the *West African Pilot* to Mr. Winston Churchill), PREM 4/43A/3: 85. See George Padmore, "Nigeria Questions Intent of Atlantic Charter," *Chicago Defender,* Jan. 31, 1942, 12, as quoted in Von Eschen, *Race against Empire,* 26.

66. Das, *Atlantic Charter* pamphlet, 6, 14.

67. Timothy Garton Ash, *Free World: America, Europe, and the Surprising Future of the West,* 7; David Reynolds, "The Atlantic 'Flop,'" 130.

68. See Judith Shklar's definition of ideology, as the political preferences or attitudes that arise as "a series of personal responses to social experiences which come to color, quite insensibly often, all our categories of thought." Shklar, *Legalism,* 41, 4, 5. See also Nancy Chodorow, *The Power of Feelings,* 1, 2.

69. Roosevelt, *Press Conferences,* No. 762 (Aug. 19, 1941), 18: 93–94; Frankfurter's original letter of Aug. 18, 1941, was worded slightly differently, but the quoted language is what FDR actually said at the press conference. For the original wording, see Max Freedman, ed., *Roosevelt and Frankfurter: Their Correspondence, 1928–1945,* 612–613.

70. LaGuardia, "Interpreting the Atlantic Charter," 556; "Wanted: An African Charter," *Pittsburgh Courier,* Dec. 19, 1942; "What about a World Charter?" and "Asiatics Seeking a Pacific Charter," *Pittsburgh Courier,* May 16, 1942, as cited in Von Eschen, *Race against Empire,* 198 n.14, 200; Borstelmann, *Apartheid's Reluctant Uncle,* 13; Herbert Evatt speech, Canberra, Sept. 3, 1942, excerpts rpt. in United Nations Information Office, "The Atlantic Charter: Some Notes on Background and on United Nations Agreements and Resolutions," 4.

71. Quoted in Sherwood, *Roosevelt and Hopkins,* 407. See also Welles, *Where Are We Heading?* 288; "'Atlantic Charter Applies to All,' Says Roosevelt," *Pittsburgh Courier,* Nov. 7, 1942, 7.

72. George M. Elsey, "Some White House Recollections, 1942–53," *Diplomatic History* 12 (Summer 1988): 359; "Roosevelt Says Nobody Signed an Atlantic Charter Document," *New York Herald Tribune,* Dec. 20, 1944, 1; Warren E. Leary, "Nation's Vital Documents Get Checkups," *New York Times,* Feb. 14, 1995, C1, C14, as quoted in Pauline Maier, *American Scripture: Making the Declaration of Independence,* ix.

73. William Shakespeare, "I must have liberty withal, as large a Charter as the winde." *As You Like It,* II, vii, 48; Thomas Hobbes, *Leviathan* (London: Printed for Andrew Crooke, 1651). See also Lynn Hunt, ed., *The French Revolution and Human Rights: A Brief Documentary History* (Boston: Bedford, St. Martin's, 1996); Lucién Jaume, ed., *Les Déclarations des Droits de l'Homme: Du Débat 1789–1793 au Préambule de 1946* (Paris: Flammarion, 1989); William Blackstone, *The Great Charter and Charter of the Forest* (Oxford: Clarendon, 1759).

74. John T. Flynn, *The Roosevelt Myth,* 385–386.

75. In this press conference excerpt, very little has been edited out; the entire exchange

is substantially intact. The many dashes appear in the original. FDR, *Press Conferences,* No. 984 (Dec. 19, 1944), 24: 266–270.

76. Flynn, *Roosevelt Myth,* 386.

77. Ibid., 385, 386.

78. See also *Textes de la Liberté: Déclarations officielles faites au cours de l'histoire des États-Unis,* OWI Library Services Division, US Office of Education, 1944, featuring "La Charte de l'Atlantique" along with such venerable examples as "La Pacte du Mayflower."

79. Maier, *American Scripture,* xiii, xviii, ix. I thank James Kloppenberg for the suggestion that I analyze the Atlantic Charter as a physical artifact.

80. United Nations Information Office, *Atlantic Charter Background Notes,* 1; this document includes a sampling of multilateral instruments explicitly referencing the Atlantic Charter.

81. Charles Cheney Hyde, *International Law, Chiefly as Interpreted and Applied by the United States,* 8; Robert W. Wilson, "International Law in the Treaties of the United States," *AJIL* 31 (1937): 271–289; J. Mervyn Jones, *Full Powers and Ratification: A Study in the Development of Treaty-Making Procedure;* see also Anthony Aust, *Modern Treaty Law and Practice,* 14–24; Detlev Vagts, "Taking Treaties Less Seriously," *AJIL* 92 (1998): 458–462.

82. On customary international law, see Lazare Kopelmanas, "Custom as a Means of the Creation of International Law," *BYIL* 18 (1937): 127–151; Maurizio Ragazzi, *The Concept of International Obligations Erga Omnes;* Oscar Schachter, "The Twilight Existence of Non-Binding International Agreements," *AJIL* 81 (1977): 296–304; see also Edward A. Laing, "Relevance of the Atlantic Charter for a New World Order," *Indian Journal of International Law* 29 (July–Dec. 1989): 298–325, 323.

83. Wilson, "International Law in the Treaties of the United States," 275 (emphasis in original; quoting *Opinions of the Attorney General* [1855]). Article 38, Statute of the Permanent Court of International Justice, quoted in Hyde, *International Law,* 1: 10–12; (the content of Article 38 remained the same in the 1945 Statute of the International Court of Justice, itself incorporated by reference into the UN Charter); see Vaughan Lowe and Maglosia Fitzmaurice, eds., *Fifty Years of the International Court of Justice;* Michael Dunne, *The United States and the World Court, 1920–1935* (London: Pinter, 1988).

84. Hyde, *International Law,* 1: 9; Lawrence Douglas, *The Memory of Judgment: Making Law and History in the Trials of the Holocaust;* Robert Woetzel, *The Nuremberg Trials in International Law;* Antonio Cassese, *International Law,* 123–124.

85. Thomas Jefferson to Henry Lee, May 8, 1825, quoted in Richard B. Bernstein, *Thomas Jefferson,* 32; Maier, *American Scripture,* xvii.

86. Ickes, *Secret Diary,* 3: 601; see also Laura Crowell, "Building of the 'Four Freedoms' Speech," 269; statement of T. V. Soong, former Chinese Minister for Foreign Affairs, New Haven, June 9, 1944; and statement of T. F. Tsiang, director of the Department of Political Affairs of the Executive Yuan, on the second anniversary of the signing of the Atlantic Charter, Chungking (Aug. 14, 1943), as quoted in UN Information Office, *Atlantic Charter Background Notes,* 7; Maier, *American Scripture,* xix.

87. James M. McPherson, *Battle Cry of Freedom: The Civil War Era,* 859. I am grateful to David Kennedy for calling my attention to McPherson's argument. See also Maier, *American Scripture,* xx; Garry Wills, *Lincoln at Gettysburg: Words That Remade American History,* 38.

88. Quoted in Rosenman, *Working with Roosevelt,* 387.

89. Roosevelt, *Press Conferences,* No. 985 (Dec. 22, 1944), 24: 276–277; on world-historical significance for the charter, see LaGuardia, "Interpreting the Atlantic Charter," 555–556; Philippe Drakidis, *La Charte de l'Atlantique, 14 août 1941: Source Permanente de Droit des Nations-Unies;* Julius Stone, *The Atlantic Charter: New Worlds for Old.*

90. Roosevelt, *Press Conferences*, No. 985 (Dec. 22, 1944), 24: 277–278.

91. Laing, "Relevance of the Atlantic Charter," 298; Maier, *American Scripture*, 160. Charles E. Merriam, *On the Agenda of Democracy*, 19. George B. Galloway, *Postwar Planning in the United States*, 100.

92. Lord Acton (John E. E. D. Acton) as quoted in Hersch Lauterpacht, *International Law and Human Rights*, 126; and in Arthur H. Robertson and J. G. Merrills, *Human Rights in the World: An Introduction to the International Protection of Human Rights*, 4. See also Dale Van Kley, ed., *The French Idea of Freedom: The Old Regime and the Declaration of Rights of 1789*; Acton, *History of Freedom*; Robert E. Sherwood, *White House Papers of Harry L. Hopkins: An Intimate History*, vol. 1 (London: Eyre and Spottiswoode, 1948–1949), 364.

93. Churchill, *Triumph and Tragedy*.

2. Forging a New American Multilateralism

1. Norman Rockwell, *My Adventures as an Illustrator*, 338–341; Stuart Murray and James McCabe, *Norman Rockwell's Four Freedoms*, 8, 37–38, 40; OWI pamphlet, "The United Nations Fight for the Four Freedoms: The Rights of All Men—Everywhere." See also Robert B. Westbrook, "Fighting for the American Family: Private Interests and Political Obligation in World War II," in Richard Wightman Fox and T. J. Jackson Lears, eds., *The Power of Culture: Critical Essays in American History*, 194–221, rpt. in Westbrook, *Why We Fought: Forging American Obligations in World War II* (Washington: Smithsonian, 2004).

2. Benedict Anderson, *Imagined Communities: Reflections on the Origins and Spread of Nationalism*, 10; Rockwell, *Adventures*, 343. An Oct. 11, 1943, advertisement for Wilson Sporting Goods equipment in *Life* magazine asked Americans to dedicate themselves "to the proposition that all men everywhere are entitled to Freedom from Fear, Freedom from Want, Freedom of Speech and Freedom of Worship. *But* let us also be a *Nation of athletes*—ever ready, if need be, to sustain our rights by the might of millions of physically fit sports-trained, freedom-loving Americans."

3. Murray and McCabe, *Rockwell's Four Freedoms*, x. The only reference to international affairs in Rockwell's Four Freedoms series is an oblique one: the partially obscured headline describing the bombing of London, in a newspaper held by a concerned and loving father, as he watches his children being safely tucked in bed. Westbrook, "Fighting for the American Family," 203.

4. Lizabeth Cohen, *A Consumers' Republic: The Politics of Mass Consumption in Postwar America*, 56; Westbrook, "Fighting for the American Family," 204. See also Cass R. Sunstein, *The Second Bill of Rights: FDR's Unfinished Revolution and Why We Need It More Than Ever*, 9–30.

5. FDR, *Press Conferences*, No. 649-A (June 5, 1940), 498–499; Laura Crowell, "The Building of the 'Four Freedoms' Speech," *Speech Monographs* 22 (1955): 268; FDR, *Press Conferences*, No. 658 (July 5, 1940), 18–22.

6. Rosenman, *Working for Roosevelt*, 263–264; Frances Perkins, *The Roosevelt I Knew* (New York: Viking, 1946), 279–284; Samuel Grafton, *All Out! How Democracy Will Defend America, Based on the French Failure, the English Stand, and the American Program*, 60. See also Louis Minsky, "Religious Groups and the Post-War World," *Contemporary Jewish Record* 5 (Aug. 1942): 357–372; Sunstein, *Second Bill of Rights*, 9–30.

7. "Social Insurance and Allied Services, Report by Sir William Beveridge," Papers of William H. Beveridge (1st Baron Beveridge), Archives of the London School of Economics and Political Science, Part 8, File 46, "Summary and Guide to [Beveridge] Report and Related Papers, 1941–44," 7–8; Edward A. Laing, "Relevance of the Atlantic Charter

for a New World Order," *Indian Journal of International Law* 29 (July–Dec. 1989): 307; Rodgers, *Atlantic Crossings*, esp. "London, 1942."

8. American Division, Ministry of Information, "Beveridge Report: American Survey" by cable from the British Press Service, New York, Report of Friday, Dec. 4, 1942, quoting the *Louisville Courier Journal* of Dec. 3, 1942, and Report of Saturday, Dec. 5, 1942, quoting the *Atlanta Constitution* of Dec. 3, 1942, in Beveridge Papers, Part 8, File 49, part 2. 1940 examples of statements linking individual and international security include the Philadelphia Conference of the Federal Council of the Churches of Christ in America, establishing the Commission to Study the Bases of a Just and Durable Peace, as well as Roosevelt's Annual Message to Congress of Jan. 3, 1940, and Radio Address of Jan. 19, 1940, *PPA, 1940*, 1, 53; Minsky, "Religious Groups and the Post-War World," 362.

9. National Resources Planning Board, "After the War—Toward Security: Freedom from Want," Sept. 1942, FDRPL, PSF, Postwar Planning, Box 157, Introductory Note, 1, 8; Anderson, *Eyes off the Prize*, 11, 14. FDR signed the highly controversial Executive Order 8802, setting up the Fair Employment Practices Commission, but declined to present antilynching legislation during the war; Randolph cancelled the March on Washington.

10. On the British side, see Deputy Prime Minister Clement Atlee's speech notes for the International Labor Organization, Nov. 16, 1941, CHAR 20/23: 86, 87. Robert M. Barrington-Ward to Churchill, Apr. 14, 1942, CHAR 20/62: 9–10; Rodgers, *Atlantic Crossings*, 485–501.

11. FDR, Press Conferences, Dec. 28, 1943, *PPA 1943*, 569–575; *Time*, Jan. 24, 1944, 13, quoted in Sunstein, *Second Bill of Rights*, 15, 1; Ira Katznelson, *The Southern Cage: New Deal Democracy and the Origins of Our Time* (forthcoming).

12. See Stuart J. Little, "The Freedom Train: Citizenship and Postwar Political Culture, 1946–1949," *American Studies* 34 (1979): 35–67, 40ff, 48.

13. Archibald MacLeish, quoted in Studs Terkel, *"The Good War": An Oral History of World War Two*, 13. See also Arthur M. Schlesinger, Jr., *A Life in the 20th Century: Innocent Beginnings, 1917–1950*, esp. chap. 14, "Blowup at OWI"; Sherwood, *Roosevelt and Hopkins*, 215; Anderson, *Eyes off the Prize*, 5; Les K. Adler and Thomas G. Patterson, "Red Fascism: The Merger of Nazi Germany and Soviet Russia in the American Image of Totalitarianism, 1930's-1950's," *American Historical Review* 75 (Apr. 1970): 1046–1048.

14. FDR, "Annual Message to Congress, Jan. 6, 1941"; Rosenman, *Working with Roosevelt*, 262–265; and Crowell, "The Building of the 'Four Freedoms' Speech," 266–283; Merriam, *Agenda of Democracy*, 98–99; National Resources Planning Board, "After the War—Toward Security: Freedom From Want," Sept. 1942, in PSF, Subject File: Postwar Planning, Box 157, FDRPL, esp. 19–28; National Resources Planning Board, *National Resources Development: Report for 1942*, 3, as discussed in Rosenman, *Working with Roosevelt*, 53–54; Merriam, "The National Resources Planning Board: A Chapter in the American Planning Experience," *American Political Science Review* 38 (Dec. 1944): 1075, 1079.

15. See Merriam, *Agenda of Democracy*, 52–53, 9, 78; Sunstein, *Second Bill of Rights*, 4; Rosenman, *Working with Roosevelt*, 264.

16. Walter Benjamin, "Theses on the Philosophy of History," in *Illuminations: Essays and Reflections*, ed. Hannah Arendt (London: Pimlico, 1999), 263; Daniel Rodgers, comments on a paper by Elizabeth Borgwardt, "The World the War (and Depression) Made: Projecting the New Deal Regulatory State in the Post–World War II Era," Society of Historians of American Foreign Relations Annual Conference, Princeton, NJ, June 25, 1999. See also Bernard Bailyn, *The Ideological Origins of the American Revolution*, v.

17. Paul Gordon Lauren, *The Evolution of International Human Rights: Visions Seen*, 21, speculates that the term "human rights" originated with Thomas Paine's "sensational and provocative best seller," *The Rights of Man* (1791). See also Kenneth Cmiel, "Review Essay: The Recent History of Human Rights," *American Historical Review* 109 (Feb.

2004): 117, 129; Risa Goluboff, "The Work of Civil Rights in the 1940s: The Department of Justice, the NAACP, and African-American Agricultural Labor" (PhD diss., Dept. of History, Princeton University); and Anderson, *Eyes off the Prize*, 1–2, 7, 18.

18. Lauren, *Evolution of International Human Rights*, 1; Hannah Arendt, *The Origins of Totalitarianism*, xxvii; Primus, *Language of Rights*, 179, 178; Hersch Lauterpacht, "The International Protection of Human Rights," *Académie de Droit International de la Haye, Recueil des Cours* 70 (1947): 1–108. See also Peter Novick, *The Holocaust in American Life*, 1999.

19. These 600 articles are limited to articles pertaining to human rights in the United States; additional human rights articles focusing on other countries are found under the separate country headings.

20. Churchill quoted in Arthur Bryant, *The Turn of the Tide, 1939–1943*, 282.

21. Winston S. Churchill, *The Unrelenting Struggle: War Speeches by the Right Hon. Winston S. Churchill*, 360; Lord Moran, *Churchill at War, 1940–1945*, 17; Sherwood, *Roosevelt and Hopkins*, 444.

22. Atlee cable quoted in Sherwood, *Roosevelt and Hopkins*, 446; Tully, *FDR My Boss*, 305. It seems to have been rather commonplace for Churchill to have visitors during his twice-daily baths. Declaration by the United Nations, Jan. 1, 1942, *FRUS, 1942*, 1: 25–26; see also US Department of State, *Cooperative War Effort: Declaration by United Nations, Washington, D.C., Jan. 1, 1942, and Declaration Known as the Atlantic Charter, Aug. 14, 1941*, 3. Forty-six countries ultimately adhered to this Declaration. Roosevelt himself insisted that India and other Dominion countries sign as independent entities, and not under Great Britain's signature. Roosevelt, Papers as President, PSF, Safe File, Box 1, Atlantic Charter (1), FDRPL. John Milton Cooper traces the phrase "united nations" to a 1915 speech given by Woodrow Wilson's nemesis, Senator Henry Cabot Lodge, an apparent coincidence. Lodge, "Force and Peace," speech of June 9, 1915, in Henry Cabot Lodge, *War Addresses, 1915–1917*, 12. On Roosevelt's coining the term "united nations," see Churchill, *The Grand Alliance*, 575, 577.

23. Sherwood, *Roosevelt and Hopkins*, 448. The phrase "in their own lands as will [*sic*] as in other lands" was added by Roosevelt and appears in his own handwriting in an undated draft of the Declaration. Declaration of the United Nations draft, PSF, Box 1, Atlantic Charter (1), FDRPL.

24. See Lauren, *Evolution of International Human Rights*; Henry J. Steiner and Philip Alston, *International Human Rights in Context: Law, Politics, and Morals*; Richard Pierre Claude and B. H. Weston, eds., *Human Rights in the World Community*.

25. Richard Breitman, *The Architect of Genocide: Himmler and the Final Solution*; Ian Kershaw, "Improvised Genocide? The Emergence of the 'Final Solution' in the Warthegau," *Transactions of the Royal Historical Society*, 6th ser., 2 (1992): 51–78, although more recent scholarship paints a more nuanced picture. See Christopher R. Browning, *The Origins of the Final Solution: The Evolution of Nazi Jewish Policy, September 1939–March 1942* (Lincoln: University of Nebraska Press, 2004), which notes that Himmler commissioned concentration camps with gas chambers for mass killings three months earlier, in Oct. 1941. On the US internment of ethnic Japanese, see Greg Robinson, *By Order of the President: FDR and the Internment of Japanese Americans*; Roger Daniels, *Prisoners without Trial: Japanese Americans in World War II* (New York: Hill and Wang, 1993); Eugene V. Rostow, "The Japanese American Cases—A Disaster," *Yale Law Journal* 54 (1945): 489–533. Gandhi to Roosevelt, July 1, 1942, *FRUS, 1942*, 1: 678–679. See also Ronald Takaki, *Double Victory: A Multicultural History of America in World War II*; Michael Kammen, *A Machine That Would Go of Itself: The Constitution in American Culture*, 344.

26. See Lloyd Gardner, "The Atlantic Charter: Idea and Reality, 1942–1945," in Brinkley and Facey-Crowther, eds., *The Atlantic Charter*, 48; Primus, *Language of Rights*,

7–8. A similar shift, including the time lag, is mirrored in the more detailed and specialized *Index to Legal Periodicals* for this era.

27. The quotation is from a law student who had recently taken an introductory course on human rights at Columbia Law School, responding to a question about what he had learned (William Covington Jackson interview with the author). On human rights scholarship in the service of advocacy, see Lauren, *Evolution of International Human Rights;* Thomas Buergenthal and Dinah Shelton, *Protecting Human Rights in the Americas;* Richard Pierre Claude and B. H. Weston, eds., *Human Rights in the World Community;* Louis Henkin, ed., *The International Bill of Rights: The Covenant on Civil and Political Rights;* Myres H. L. McDougal, Harold D. Lasswell, and Lung-chu Chen, *Human Rights and World Public Order: The Basic Policies of an International Law of Human Dignity.* See also Lynn M. Maurer, "Activist Note: Democracy, Harmony, and Human Rights in the Twenty-First Century," *Peace & Change,* 25 (July 2000): 407–412. There are also, of course, numerous exceptions to this "polemical" syndrome. See the essays in *Historical Change and Human Rights,* ed. Olwen Hufton, esp. chaps. by Robert Darnton, Emmanuel Laudrie, and Orlando Patterson; see also Kenneth Cmiel, "Recent History of Human Rights."

28. Shklar, *Legalism,* 11, 34, 80–81, 112.

29. Forrest McDonald, *Novus Ordo Seclorum: The Intellectual Origins of the Constitution.* See also Zechariah Chafee, Jr., *Documents on Fundamental Human Rights;* Chafee, *How Human Rights Got into the Constitution;* Jonathan Clark, *The Language of Liberty, 1660–1832: Political Discourse and Social Dynamics in the Anglo-American World* (Cambridge: Cambridge University Press, 1994); and Felix Gilbert, *To The Farewell Address: Ideas of Early American Foreign Policy.*

30. Abdullah An-Na'im, ed., *Human Rights in Cross-Cultural Perspectives: A Quest for Consensus;* Frank Snyder and Surakiarat Sathirathai, eds., *Third World Attitudes toward International Law: An Introduction;* Thomas M. Franck, *Human Rights in Third World Perspective;* David A. Hollinger, "Cultural Relativism," in *The Cambridge History of Science,* 708–720.

31. Stanley N. Katz, "Constitutionalism and Civil Society," Jefferson Lecture, University of California at Berkeley, Apr. 25, 2000.

32. Teitel, *Transitional Justice,* 19–22. See also Robert H. Jackson (no relation to the Nuremberg chief prosecutor), "The Weight of Ideas in Decolonization: Normative Change in International Relations," in Goldstein and Keohane, eds., *Ideas and Foreign Policy,* 111–138.

33. Bailyn, *Ideological Origins of the American Revolution,* 25.

34. Paul W. Kahn, *The Cultural Study of Law: Reconstructing Legal Scholarship,* 6, 2; Michael Ignatieff, *Human Rights as Politics and Idolatry,* ed. Amy Gutmann.

35. Eric Foner, *The Story of American Freedom,* xiv.

36. On group rights and minorities treaties, see Stephen D. Krasner, *Sovereignty: Organized Hypocrisy,* 73–96; Carole Fink, *Defending the Rights of Others: The Great Powers, the Jews, and International Minority Protection, 1878–1938.* On traditions emphasizing duties as well as individual rights, see the discussion in Kenneth Cmiel, "Freedom of Information, Human Rights, and the Origins of Third World Solidarity," in Mark P. Bradley and Patrice Petro, eds., *Truth Claims: Representation and Human Rights,* 107–130; Cmiel, "Review Essay: The Recent History of Human Rights," 119.

37. Jerome S. Bruner, "Public Opinion and the Peace," in Whitton, ed., *Second Chance,* 181.

38. Shklar, *Legalism,* 3; Quentin Skinner, "Political Philosophy: The View from Cambridge," *Journal of Political Philosophy* 10 (2002): 1–19; Melissa Lane, "Why History of Ideas at All?" *History of European Ideas* 28 (2002): 33–41.

39. See John R. Searle, *The Construction of Social Reality.*

40. New Zealand Prime Minister Peter Fraser addressing the Canadian Parliament, Friday, June 30, 1944, *Debates,* House of Commons, Session 1944, vol. 5, 4424; Anderson, *Eyes off the Prize,* 16–17.

41. See *Christian Century* 62 (Jan. 3, 1945): 3–4; Horace R. Clayton, "That Charter: We Seem to be Reneging on the Principles of the Atlantic Charter," *Pittsburgh Courier,* Nov. 28, 1942, 12, as cited in Von Eschen, *Race against Empire,* 198 n.15; Fraser Address to the Canadian Parliament, Friday, June 30, 1944.

42. Gardner, "The Atlantic Charter: Idea and Reality, 1942–1945," in Brinkley and Facey-Crowther, eds., *The Atlantic Charter,* 45–81.

43. Any World War II-era legal or institutional "innovation," from an expansion of international humanitarian law to a collective security organization for maintaining peace, had existed as a well-defined and much-debated reality during the interwar era, and indeed, several dated from well before the turn of the century. World War I-era examples include: the Covenant of the League of Nations, with its attendant Permanent Court of International Justice; the so-called Leipzig Trials that were held for 28 of the 411 accused German war criminals (and administered by the Germans themselves); and, later, the 1928 Kellogg-Briand Pact purporting to outlaw war. Earlier examples from the late nineteenth and early twentieth centuries include the St. Petersburg Declaration of 1868 where the parties renounced certain prohibited weapons and limited the weight of other types of weapons, as well as the Hague Conventions of 1899 and 1907.

44. This study uses the term "legalism" much the way that Judith Shklar does, as both "an ideology internal to the legal profession," and, more broadly, "as the extremity of rule-oriented thinking." This is in contrast to more recent uses of the term as either a shorthand way of contrasting "law" with "politics" or as a synonym for a more hardheaded sect of liberal internationalists. See Shklar, *Legalism,* vii, viii; Gary J. Bass, *Stay the Hand of Vengeance: The Politics of War Crimes Tribunals;* Boyle, *Foundations of World Order.*

45. Well-publicized impetuses included the experiences of Florence Nightingale in the Crimea and the publication of Red Cross founder Henri Dunant's *Un Souvenir de Solferino,* reporting on his experiences at the 1859 Battle of Solferino. See also Robert B. Edgerton, *Death or Glory: The Legacy of the Crimean War;* Theodor Meron, "The Humanization of Humanitarian Law," *AJIL* 94 (Apr. 2000): 243.

46. Lassa Oppenheim spelled out the positivist creed in his "The Science of International Law: Its Task and Method," *AJIL* 2 (1908): 373. The iconic positivist was John Austin (1790–1859). Hague Convention No. 4 on the Laws and Customs of War on Land (Oct. 18, 1907), article 2, states that its provisions "do not apply except between contracting powers, and then only if all the belligerents are parties to the Convention"; rpt. in Adam Roberts and Richard Guelff, eds., *Documents on the Laws of War;* this clause was based on a provision in the 1856 Declaration of Paris outlawing privateering among European nations, which asserted that "the present Declaration shall not be binding except upon those Powers which have acceded, or shall accede to it." Quoted in Hyde, *International Law* 1: 8 n.2.

47. On natural law and natural rights, see Brian Tierney, *The Idea of Natural Rights: Studies on Natural Rights, Natural Law, and Church Law, 1150–1625;* John Finnis, *Natural Law and Natural Rights;* Brian Bix, "Natural Law Theory," in Dennis Patterson, ed., *A Companion to Philosophy of Law and Legal Theory,* 223–240.

48. On Lieber's impact on the development of nineteenth-century legalism, see James Farr, "The Americanization of Hermeneutics: Francis Lieber's *Legal and Political Hermeneutics,*" in Gregory Leyh, ed., *Legal Hermeneutics: History, Theory, and Practice* (Berkeley: University of California Press, 1992); Francis Lieber letter to General Halleck, quoted in Thomas E. Holland, *The Laws of War on Land,* 72; "Instructions for the Government of

the Armies of the United States in the Field, General Orders No. 100" (Apr. 24, 1863), excerpts rpt. in Dietrich Schindler and Jiri Toman, eds., *The Laws of Armed Conflicts,* 3. Similar codes were promulgated by Prussia (1870), the Netherlands (1871), France (1877), Russia (1877 and 1904), Serbia (1878–9), Argentina (1881), Spain (1882), Great Britain (1883 and 1904), Portugal (1890), and Italy (1896); a more complete treatment with documents may be found in Dietrich Schindler and Jiri Toman, eds., *Droits des Conflits Armés: Recueil des Conventions, Résolutions et Autres Documents.*

49. *Oxford Manual of the Laws of War on Land,* as quoted in Schindler and Toman, eds., *Laws of Armed Conflicts,* 25.

50. See Robert Wiebe, *The Search for Order, 1877–1920;* William M. Wiecek, *The Lost World of Classical Legal Thought: Law and Ideology in America, 1886–1937* (New York: Oxford University Press, 1998); Morton J. Horwitz, *The Transformation of American Law, 1870–1960: The Crisis of Legal Orthodoxy;* Gerard W. Gawalt, ed., *The New High Priests: Lawyers in Post–Civil War America* (Westport, CT: Greenwood, 1984); Robert W. Gordon, "Legal Thought and Legal Practice in the Age of American Enterprise, 1870–1920," in Gerald L. Geison, ed., *Professions and Professional Ideologies in America* (Chapel Hill: University of North Carolina Press, 1983), 70–110.

51. A group within the annual Lake Mohonk Conference on International Arbitration, a mainstream American peace movement founded in 1895, wished to professionalize that organization and focus on more "scientific" approaches to international peace and security, leading to the foundation of the American Society for International Law. See *Report of the Thirteenth Annual Meeting of the Lake Mohonk Conference on International Arbitration,* 116; Edwin D. Mead, *The Literature of the Peace Movement* (Boston: World Peace Foundation, 1912); George A. Finch, "The American Society for International Law, 1906–1956," *AJIL* 50 (1956): 293, 295–298; Boyle, *Foundations of World Order,* based on his 1983 dissertation for the Harvard Government Department, "Realism, Positivism, Functionalism and International Law"; Elizabeth Borgwardt, book review of Boyle's *Foundations of World Order* in *Peace & Change* 27 (Oct. 2002): 647.

52. On Root, see Jonathan Zasloff, "Law and the Shaping of American Foreign Policy: From the Gilded Age to the New Era," *New York University Law Review* 78 (2002): 239–373; Philip C. Jessup, *Elihu Root* (New York: Dodd, Mead, 1938); James Brown Scott, *Elihu Root's Services to International Law* (Worcester: Carnegie Endowment for International Peace, 1925); Sean Malloy, "The Reluctant Warrior: Henry L. Stimson and the 'Crisis of Industrial Civilization'"; Jonathan Zasloff, "Law and the Shaping of American Foreign Policy: The Twenty Years' Crisis," *Southern California Law Review* 77 (2004): 583–682; David F. Schmitz, *Henry L. Stimson: The First Wise Man* (Wilmington, DE: SR Books, 2001); Godfrey Hodgson, *The Colonel: The Life and Wars of Henry Stimson, 1867–1950;* Elting E. Morison, *Turmoil and Tradition: A Study of the Life and Times of Henry L. Stimson* (Boston: Houghton Mifflin, 1960).

53. C. Roland Marchand, *The American Peace Movement and Social Reform, 1898–1918,* ix, xiv, 13, 9.

54. Marchand, *American Peace Movement,* 16; Jean Bethke Elshtain, *Meditations on Modern Political Thought: Masculine/Feminine Themes from Luther to Arendt* (University Park: Pennsylvania State University Press, 1992).

55. On "masculinity" see Hoganson, *Fighting for American Manhood;* Rutherford, *Forever England.* See also Geoffrey Best, *Humanity in Warfare: The Modern History of the International Law of Armed Conflicts,* 136.

56. Later Geneva Conventions expanding protected categories of persons were: 1949 Geneva Convention I for the Amelioration of the Condition of the Wounded and Sick in Armed Forces in the Field; 1949 Geneva Convention II for the Amelioration of the Condition of Wounded, Sick, and Shipwrecked Members of Armed Forces at Sea; 1949 Geneva

Convention III Relative to the Treatment of Prisoners of War, and especially 1949 Geneva Convention IV Relative to the Protection of Civilian Persons in Time of War. See also the 1977 Geneva Protocol I Additional to the Geneva Conventions of 12 Aug. 1949, and Relating to the Protection of Victims of International Armed Conflicts; and the 1977 Geneva Protocol II Additional to the Geneva Conventions of 12 Aug. 1949, and Relating to the Protection of Victims of Non-International Armed Conflicts, 6 UST 3115ff, 75 UNTS 85ff, rpt. in Adam Roberts and Richard Guelff, eds., *Documents on the Laws of War.*

57. Quoted in Alfred E. Zimmern, *The League of Nations and the Rule of Law, 1918–1935,* 103.

58. John B. Porter, *International Law,* 12; Article 22, Fourth Hague Convention Respecting the Laws and Customs of War on Land (1907), rpt. in James B. Scott, ed., *The Hague Conventions and Declarations of 1899 and 1907,* 100–127; Best, *Humanity in Warfare,* 150.

59. See Niall Ferguson's estimate ("revised death figures") of 9,450,000 soldiers killed and his "best estimate" of 32,780,048 military casualties overall (killed, taken prisoner, and wounded). Of these figures, he estimates total casualties for the United States at 324,170 wounded, 114,000 killed. Ferguson, *The Pity of War: Explaining World War I,* 295–296; Henry L. Stimson, "Outline Analysis of the Kellogg Pact," n.d. [1932], Reel 131, Stimson Papers.

60. Literature on the *jus ad bellum* is traditionally traced to the writings of St. Augustine and St. Thomas Aquinas. This just war tradition also finds expression in a late-medieval flowering of writing about "natural law," the most prominent exponents of which were Francisco Suarez (1548–1617), Samuel Pufendorf (1623–1694), and of course, Hugo Grotius (1583–1645). By contrast, the *jus in bello* or laws of war were generally held to be outgrowths of medieval chivalric traditions and found their purest expression in nineteenth-century military manuals. See David W. Kennedy, "Primitive Legal Scholarship," *Harvard International Law Journal* 27 (1986): 12; Deryck Beyleveld and Roger Brownsword, "The Practical Difference between Natural-Law Theory and Legal Positivism," *Oxford Journal of Legal Studies* 5 (1985).

61. Statement of Senator Clyde Martin Reed, Republican of Kansas, *Congressional Record,* 70th Cong., 2d sess., 1186; Treaty of Mutual Guarantee between Germany, Belgium, France, Great Britain, and Italy, Locarno, Oct. 16, 1925 (Locarno Treaty), *League of Nations Treaty Series* (1926): 291; Robert H. Ferrell, *Peace in Their Time: The Origins of the Kellogg-Briand Pact* (New York: Norton, 1969).

62. The American draft of the Pact of Paris was accompanied by an explanatory note further eviscerating the agreement, which read: "There is nothing in the American draft of an anti-war treaty which restricts or impairs in any way the right of self-defence. That right is inherent in every sovereign state and is inherent in every treaty. Every nation is free at all times and regardless of treaty provisions to defend its territory from attack or invasion and it alone is competent to decide whether circumstances require recourse to war." Rpt. in *Proceedings of the American Society of International Law* (1928): 143; James T. Shotwell, *War as an Instrument of National Policy and Its Renunciation in the Pact of Paris;* Henry A. Kissinger, *Diplomacy,* 280; Denis W. Brogan, *The French Nation, 1814–1940: From Napoleon to Pétain;* Frederick Alexander, *From Paris to Locarno and After: The League of Nations and the Search for Security 1919–1928;* Zimmern, *The League of Nations and the Rule of Law.*

63. See John R. McKivigan, "Series Introduction," *History of the American Abolitionist Movement: A Bibliography of Scholarly Articles;* Woodrow Wilson, "An Address to the Third Plenary Session of the Peace Conference, Feb. 14, 1919," rpt. in Arthur S. Link, ed., *Papers of Woodrow Wilson,* Feb. 8–Mar. 16, 1919 (Princeton: Princeton University Press, 1966–1994), 175; David Hunter Miller, *The Drafting of the Covenant.*

64. On the Nye Committee, see Manfred Jonas, *Isolationism in America, 1935–1941*, 144–148. See also Akira Iriye, *The Globalizing of America, 1913–1945*, 124–126. The veteran's quotation is from an interview in the Rutgers Oral History Archives of World War II with Judge Mark Addison, a former signal corps officer who served in the Far East during the war. Interview of Apr. 13, 1994.

65. Alan Brinkley, *Voices of Protest: Huey Long, Father Coughlin and the Great Depression*, 135–137; Gilbert Murray, "Then and Now: The Changes of the Last 50 Years," in Murray, *From League to U.N.*, 24–25.

66. Francis P. Walters, *A History of the League of Nations*, 1–2.

67. See FDR, "Address before the New York State Grange [Excerpts], Albany, N.Y.," Feb. 2, 1932, *PPA*, 155–157; James MacGregor Burns and Susan Dunn, *The Three Roosevelts: Patrician Leaders Who Transformed America*, 226.

68. Childs, *I Write from Washington*, 32, 9, 3–4.

69. Ibid., 12; Isaiah Berlin, "Winston Churchill in 1940," rpt. in Berlin, *Proper Study of Mankind*, 616; Sherwood, *Roosevelt and Hopkins*, 360, 227; Leuchtenburg, *Franklin D. Roosevelt and the New Deal*, 338.

70. Childs, *I Write from Washington*, 13.

71. US Senate, 1944, Committee on the Judiciary, Subcommittee to Investigate the Administration of the Internal Security Act and Other Internal Security Laws, Statement by Henry A. Morgenthau, Jr., 90th Cong., 1st sess., Aug. 17, 1944, in *Morgenthau Diary (Germany)*, 1: 414.

72. Atlantic Charter, untitled telegram headed, in Roosevelt's handwriting, "For delivery to Press and Radio at 0900 EST on Thursday, Aug. 14," FDR, Papers as President, PSF, Safe File, Atlantic Charter (1), Box 1, FDRPL; Potsdam Declaration, rpt. in *The Axis in Defeat: A Collection of Documents on American Policy Toward Germany and Japan;* United Nations Charter, 1, *United Nations Treaty Series* (UNTS) xvi, *United States Treaty Series* (USTS) 999, 59 Stat. 1031 (June 26, 1945); Nuremberg Principles, Affirmation of the Principles of International Law Recognized by the Charter of the Nuremberg Tribunal, UN GAOR, GA Res. 95(1), UN Doc. A/64/Add.1 (1947); see also Principles of International Law Recognized in the Charter of the Nuremberg Tribunal and in the Judgment of the Tribunal, adopted Aug. 2, 1950, princ. 1, UN Doc. A/1316, rpt. in *Yearbook of the International Law Commission* 2 (1950): 374; Universal Declaration of Human Rights, adopted Dec. 10, 1948, GA Res. 217A (III), UN Doc. A/810 (1948), 71; Convention on the Prevention and Punishment of the Crime of Genocide, 78 UNTS 277, UN GAOR 260 (III)A (Dec. 9, 1948).

73. National League of Women Voters, "Memorandum: The United Nations: The Road Ahead," 4.

74. Abram Chayes and Antonia Handler Chayes, *The New Sovereignty: Compliance with International Regulatory Agreements*, 27. See also Daniel Philpott, *Revolutions in Sovereignty: How Ideas Shaped Modern International Relations;* Stephen D. Krasner, *Sovereignty: Organized Hypocrisy;* Georges Abi-Saab, "The Changing World Order and the International Legal Order," in Yoshikazu Sakamoto, ed., *Global Transformation: Challenges to the State System* (Tokyo: United Nations University Press, 1994), 439; Hendrik Spruyt, *The Sovereign State and Its Competitors: An Analysis of Systems Change* (Princeton: Princeton University Press, 1994); Leo Gross, "The Peace of Westphalia 1648–1948," *AJIL* 42 (1948): 20.

75. Merriam, *Agenda of Democracy*, 36–37; H. L. Mencken, "A Constitution for the New Deal," *Reader's Digest* 31 (July 1937): 27–29.

76. Merriam, *Agenda of Democracy*, 37.

77. Edward S. Corwin, *The President: Office and Powers, 1787–1984: History and*

Analysis of Practice and Opinion (New York: New York University Press, 1984), 359, as quoted in Merriam, *Agenda of Democracy,* 37; Murray, *From League to U.N.,* 26, 33.

78. Isaiah Berlin, "Winston Churchill in 1940," rpt. in Berlin, *Proper Study of Mankind,* 615; Roger Hausheer, "Introduction," in ibid., xxxv.

79. Roscoe Pound, *Interpretations of Legal History* (Holmes Beach, FL: Gaunt, 1986), 163–164; Henry Steele Commager, *The American Mind: An Interpretation of American Thought and Character since the 1800s,* 379. On the legal realists, see Barbara Fried, *The Progressive Assault on Laissez Faire: Robert Hale and the First Law and Economics Movement* (Cambridge: Harvard University Press, 1998); Louis Menand, *The Metaphysical Club: A Story of Ideas in America;* William W. Fisher, ed., *American Legal Realism* (New York: Oxford University Press, 1993); Horwitz, *The Transformation of American Law;* Laura Kalman, *Legal Realism at Yale, 1927–1960.*

80. An important intellectual influence on legal realists and New Deal lawyers generally was Oliver Wendell Holmes, Jr., for whom many of them had clerked (including Francis Biddle, the American judge at Nuremberg). See Holmes, "The Path of the Law," *Harvard Law Review* 10 (1897): 457; Jerome Frank, *Law and the Modern Mind;* Karl Llewelyn, "Some Realism about Realism—Responding to Dean Pound," *Harvard Law Review* 44 (1931): 222; George Peek, quoted in Peter H. Irons, *The New Deal Lawyers.*

81. See Michael Ignatieff, "Human Rights: The Midlife Crisis," *New York Review of Books* 46 (May 20, 1999): 58.

82. See Rosalyn Higgins, "The European Convention on Human Rights," in Theodor Meron, ed., *Human Rights in International Law: Legal and Policy Issues* (Oxford: Clarendon, 1984), 538; Henry Steiner, "Individual Claims in a World of Massive Violations: What Role for the Human Rights Committee?" in Philip Alston and James Crawford, eds., *The Future of UN Human Rights Treaty Monitoring* (Cambridge: Cambridge University Press, 2000), 19; Optional Protocol to the International Covenant on Civil and Political Rights (Dec. 16, 1966), 999 *United Nations Treaty Series* 171, rpt. in 6 *International Legal Materials* 383 (1967); American Convention on Human Rights, Pact of San José, Nov. 22, 1969, rpt. in *ILM* 9 (1970): 673.

83. See Charles S. Maier, "I paradossi del 'prima' e del 'poi': Periodizzazioni e rotture nella storia," *Contemporanea* 2 (Oct. 1999): 715–722; Daniel T. Rodgers, *Contested Truths: Keywords in American Politics since Independence,* 13, 179; Hedley Bull, "Martin Wight and the Theory of International Relations," *British Journal of International Studies* 2 (1976): 111. The characterization of Wight's approach is from Benedict Kingsbury and Adam Roberts, "Introduction: Grotian Thought in International Relations," in Hedley Bull, Benedict Kingsbury, and Adam Roberts, eds., *Hugo Grotius and International Relations,* 55; Martin Wight, *International Theory: The Three Traditions,* ed. Gabrielle Wight and Brian Porter (London: Leicester University Press, Royal Institute of International Affairs, 1996); Childs, *I Write from Washington,* 22.

84. Bull, "Martin Wight," 111. "Introduction," in Bull, Kingsbury, and Roberts, eds., *Hugo Grotius,* 56, 58.

85. Henry Brady, "Causal Explanation in Social Science." See also John Lewis Gaddis, *The Landscape of History: How Historians Map the Past,* chap. 4, "The Interdependency of Variables."

86. Divine, *Second Chance,* 4; see also Eichelberger's memoir, *Organizing for Peace: A Personal History of the Founding of the United Nations,* which is a remarkably impersonal treatment of Eichelberger's activism.

87. Divine, *Second Chance,* 23.

88. US Department of Commerce, *Historical Statistics of the United States, Colonial Times to 1970s.* See also Paul Webbink, "Unemployment in the United States, 1930–1940,"

Papers and Proceedings of the American Economic Association 30 (Feb. 1941): 250; Leuchtenburg, *Franklin D. Roosevelt and the New Deal*, 1–3.

89.   *HSUS*; FDR, "Three Essentials for Unemployment Relief," Mar. 21, 1933, *PPA, 1933,* 80–81; Harry A. Hopkins, *Spending to Save: The Complete Story of Relief* (Seattle: University of Washington Press, 1972), 114, 117, 120; Leuchtenburg, *Franklin D. Roosevelt and the New Deal*, 128.

90.   Louis M. Howe, "The President's Mailbag," *American Magazine,* June 1934, 22; Leuchtenburg, *Franklin D. Roosevelt and the New Deal*, 331; Leila A. Sussman, *Dear FDR: A Study of Political Letter-Writing* (Totowa, NJ: Bedminster, 1963); Isaiah Berlin, "President Franklin Delano Roosevelt," rpt. in Berlin, *Proper Study of Mankind*, 636; Michael Ignatieff, *Isaiah Berlin: A Life*, 132; Kennedy, *Freedom from Fear*, 27.

91.   See Anne-Marie Burley (now Anne-Marie Slaughter), "Regulating the World: Multilateralism, International Law, and the Projection of the New Deal Regulatory State," in John G. Ruggie, ed., *Multilateralism Matters: The Theory and Praxis of an Institutional Form,* 125, 126; Childs, *I Write from Washington*, 23.

92.   Burley, "Regulating the World"; Eichelberger, *Organizing for Peace*, 197; National League of Women Voters, "Memorandum: The United Nations: The Road Ahead," 3–4.

93.   *HSUS*; Henry S. Shyrock, Jr., and Hope I. Eldridge, "Internal Migration in Peace and War," *American Sociological Review* 12 (Feb. 1947): 27–39; Lee Kennett, *G.I.: The American Soldier in World War II*, 236, The Rutgers Oral History Project Archives contained 225 interviews as of Aug. 2004, and more are being added all the time, up to a projected database of about 300 subjects; interview with William H. Barr, Oct. 7, 1994, Rutgers Oral History Archives,

94.   Interview with Mark Addison, Apr. 13, 1995; Interview with John F. Ambos, Sept. 13, 1994, Rutgers Oral History Archives; "Separation," *Yank,* Sept. 1945, quoted in Kennett, *G.I.*, 231.

95.   Burns and Dunn, *The Three Roosevelts*, 492. See also Keith W. Olson, *The G.I. Bill, The Veterans, and the Colleges* (Lexington: University Press of Kentucky, 1974). Interview with Jack Short, as quoted in Terkel, *"The Good War,"* 144–145.

96.   *HSUS*; Coolidge quoted in Schlesinger, *The Age of Roosevelt,* 1: 57. See also Lizabeth Cohen, *Making a New Deal: Industrial Workers in Chicago 1919–1939*, 253–254.

97.   Christina Koningisor, "Rutgers Summary" (Sept. 2004), unpublished report on file with the author.

98.   Rutgers Oral History Archives, Bauer Interview. After the founding of the American Institute of Public Opinion in 1935, the Gallup organization established a series of international affiliates, including the British Institute of Public Opinion (1936), the Canadian Institute of Public Opinion (1941), Australian Public Opinion Polls (1942), the Swedish Gallup Institute (1943), the Danish and Finnish Gallup Institutes (1945), the Norwegian Gallup Institute (1946), and the Brazilian Institute of Public Opinion (1946). Hadley Cantril and Mildred Strunk, eds., *Public Opinion, 1935–1946,* vii; Sarah Igo, "Constructing American Community: Social Science and the Popular Imagination, 1920–1950," PhD diss., Department of History, Princeton University, 2002; Jean Converse, *Survey Research in the United States;* H. Schuyler Foster, *Activism Replaces Isolationism: US Public Attitudes, 1940–1975* (Washington, DC: Foxhall, 1983); Steven Kelman, "The Political Foundations of American Statistical Policy," in William Alonso and Paul Starr, eds., *The Politics of Numbers* (New York: Russell Sage Foundation, 1987). For a published reference to the way Roosevelt used polls, see Sherwood, *Roosevelt and Hopkins*, 943 n.127.

99.   See FDR, PSF, Subject File: Public Opinion, Public Opinion Polls 1935–1942 and 1942–1944, FDRPL; Papers of Adolf Berle, State Department Subject Files, Post-War Prob-

lems, *Summary of Opinions and Ideas* (typescripts, new editions circulated roughly fortnightly); Division of Special Research, 1938–1945, FDRPL; Papers of Sumner Welles, Postwar Foreign Policy Files 1940–1943, Summary of Opinions, FDRPL; Arthur A. Lumsdaine, *The American Soldier: Combat and Its Aftermath*, 2: 591. On these numbers as "overwhelming," see Lydgate, *What America Thinks*, note preceding page 1.

100. For a discussion of the concept of the attentive public, see Gabriel Almond, *The American People and Foreign Policy*, 139–143, 150–152, 233. See also Eugene R. Wittkopf, *Faces of Internationalism: Public Opinion and American Foreign Policy* (Durham: Duke University Press, 1990); William L. Rivers, *The Opinionmakers*. On the idea of "middlebrow" culture in America, see Joan Shelley Rubin, "Between Culture and Consumption: The Mediations of the Middlebrow," in Fox and Lears, eds., *Power of Culture*, 162–191, 163; Virginia Woolf, "Middlebrow," in Woolf, *The Death of the Moth* (New York: Harcourt Brace Jovanovich, 1974), 180–184; Russell Lynes, "Highbrow, Lowbrow, Middlebrow," *Harper's*, Feb. 1949: 19–28.

101. "The United Nations: The Road Ahead," 3.

102. "Willkie Says War Liberates Negroes," *New York Times*, July 20, 1942, 28.

103. Churchill quoted in the context of a response to Willkie in Von Eschen, *Race against Empire*, 26–27. For commentary in the African-American press, see George Padmore, "Nigeria Questions Intent of Atlantic Charter," *Chicago Defender*, Jan. 31, 1942, 12; "Twenty Million Africans Ask Churchill to Explain Atlantic Charter Meeting," *Pittsburgh Courier*, Feb. 7, 1942, 12, quoted in Von Eschen, *Race against Empire*, 26.

104. Primus, *Language of Rights*, 186; Gunnar Myrdal, *An American Dilemma: The Negro Problem and Modern Democracy* (New Brunswick, NJ: Transaction, 1996). See also Gary Gerstle, *American Crucible: Race and Nation in the Twentieth Century*, esp. chap. 5, "Good War, Race War, 1941–1945."

105. Interview with Tom A. Kindre, June 28, 1994, Rutgers Oral History Archive.

106. Nicholas deB Katzenbach Oral History, Lyndon Baines Johnson Library and Museum, Interviews I and III; John Katzenbach, *Hart's War* (New York: Ballantine, 1999); Thomas Borstelmann, *The Cold War and the Color Line: American Race Relations in the Global Arena*.

107. White, "Kinship of Colored Peoples: People, Politics, and Places," *Chicago Defender*, Mar. 3, 1945, quoted in Von Eschen, *Race against Empire*, 7–8. Membership of the NAACP grew from 50,000 to 400,000 during the war years. Jonathan Rosenberg, "'How Far Is the Promised Land?' World Affairs and the American Civil Rights Movement from the First World War to Vietnam," PhD diss., Harvard University, 1997, 273; Borstelmann, *Cold War and the Color Line*, 29; Takaki, *Double Victory*, 130.

108. John Hersey, *Into The Valley: A Skirmish of the Marines*, 137; Geertz, *Interpretation of Cultures*, 316. On the problem of shaping amorphous cultural practices to fit legal and historical categories, see James Clifford, "Identity in Mashpee," in his *The Predicament of Culture: Twentieth-Century Ethnography, Literature, and Art* (Cambridge: Harvard University Press, 1988).

109. Author interview with Kurt Steiner (Tokyo War Crimes Trial Prosecutor), Aug. 1999. See Charles H. Haskins, *Some Problems of the Peace Conference*; Edward M. House and Charles Seymour, eds., *What Really Happened at Paris: The Story of the Peace Conference, 1918–1919*; David Hunter Miller, *My Diary at the Conference of Paris*; James W. Headlam, *A Memoir of the Paris Peace Conference, 1919* (London: Methuen, 1972); Primus, *Language of Rights*, 186.

110. Murray, *From League to U.N.*, 8–9; Eleanor Roosevelt, *This I Remember*, 239; Jason Berger, *A New Deal for the World: Eleanor Roosevelt and American Foreign Policy*.

111. Novick, *Holocaust in American Life*, 128.

3. The Perils of Economic Planning

1. The IMF and the World Bank are collectively referred to as the Bretton Woods institutions in this chapter. Other, related institutions were proposed as part of the negotiation process leading up to Bretton Woods that were either not enacted, partially enacted, or enacted later, such as an International Clearing Union, an International Trade Organization, an International Development Authority, or the later General Agreement on Trade and Tariffs (as an ad hoc substitute for the ITO). Proposals for these ancillary institutions are touched on in this history, but a detailed consideration of them is beyond the scope of the present chapter. See Skidelsky, *John Maynard Keynes,* 356; Louis Menand, "Buried Treasure: The Impish Brilliance of John Maynard Keynes," *New Yorker,* Jan. 28, 2002, 82–88.

2. Acheson, *Present at the Creation,* 82; James Chace, *Acheson: The Secretary of State Who Created the American World;* David S. McLellan, *Dean Acheson: The State Department Years* (New York: Dodd, Mead, 1976); Gaddis Smith, *Dean Acheson,* vol. 16, *The American Secretaries of State and Their Diplomacy,* ed. Samuel Flagg Bemis and Robert H. Ferrell (New York: Cooper Square, 1963); Oral History Interview of Dean G. Acheson, HSTPL, Independence, Mo.

3. Acheson, *Present at the Creation,* 82.

4. Ibid., 71–72.

5. Ibid.

6. Keynes to Lord Catto, July 4, 1944, War Files, Keynes Papers, King's College Archive Center, Cambridge, UK. Catto and Keynes were friends—they referred to themselves as "Catto and Doggo"—and shared a certain outsider status as Treasury office officials without portfolio in the early war years. See Skidelsky, *John Maynard Keynes,* 3: 544.

7. Keynes to Sir Wilfred Eady, Oct. 3, 1943, in John Maynard Keynes, *The Collected Writings of John Maynard Keynes,* 25: 357.

8. Some of the economists at Bretton Woods interpreted the term "technician" or even "expert" as a put-down, meaning someone who worked at too low a level to be responsible for making policy. But highlighting the technical expertise of the delegates and their advisors was clearly meant to insulate the results of Bretton Woods from partisan criticism. See the precursor document to the charter of the IMF, pointedly titled "Joint Statement by Experts on the Establishment of an International Monetary Fund of the United and Associated Nations" (Apr. 21, 1944), which begins, "For more than a year, the technical experts of the United and Associated Nations have been considering tentative proposals . . . " T160/1281/F18885/11, NA-Kew; statement rpt. in US Department of State, *Proceedings and Documents of United Nations Monetary and Financial Conference, Bretton Woods, New Hampshire, July 1–22, 1944,* 2: 1629.

9. US Senate, Committee on Banking and Currency, *Bretton Woods Agreements Act,* Hearings on HR 3314, 79th Cong., 1st sess. (June 1945): 14–15.

10. Dimbleby and Reynolds, *An Ocean Apart,* 178–179; Walter Russell Mead, "In the Long Run: Keynes and the Legacy of British Liberalism," *Foreign Affairs* 81 (Jan./Feb. 2002): 202.

11. Although the Bretton Woods charters were negotiated in the summer of 1944, they were not approved by the Senate until the summer of 1945.

12. The constitutions of the IMF and World Bank as agreed to at Bretton Woods are variously described in the documents as agreements, accords, or charters—this study uses "charters" for purposes of symmetry with the other charters under consideration. See Richard N. Gardner, *Sterling-Dollar Diplomacy: The Origins and Prospects of Our International Economic Order,* 143, for an economic historian's use of the term "charters" to describe the products of the Bretton Woods conference. Gardner's trenchant analysis is still widely acknowledged as the definitive account of the conference, although I believe he inap-

propriately downplays the significance of the Lend-Lease negotiations and overemphasizes Anglo-American competition in describing the negotiations. Gardner's account of the Senate ratification process led me to four of the quotations I use from the *Congressional Record* regarding debates over the Bretton Woods charters in the Senate. Penrose, *Economic Planning*, 51; for the full text of the Bretton Woods charters see *Proceedings*, 1: 942–1014.

13. On the inadvisability of taking testimony or documentation generated by the legislative process at face value, see Mildred L. Amer, *The Congressional Record: Content, History and Issues*, CRS Report for Congress 93–60 GOV, 1993, 1–9; Howard N. Mantel, "The *Congressional Record*: Fact or Fiction of the Legislative Process," *Western Political Quarterly* 12 (Dec. 1959): 981–995; and the remarks of Karl E. Mundt, *Congressional Record*, June 10, 1942, 2182–2185. I am grateful to Williamjames Hoffer for directing me to these sources. G. John Ikenberry, "Creating Yesterday's New World Order: Keynesian 'New Thinking' and the Anglo-American Postwar Settlement," in Goldstein and Keohane, eds., *Ideas and Foreign Policy*, 57. The Soviets also ultimately decided not to ratify the Bretton Woods charters and later withdrew from both the Bank and the IMF.

14. John Maynard Keynes letter to the *New Statesman*, July 1937, quoted in Skidelsky, *John Maynard Keynes*, 3: 33.

15. Keynes, "Proposal on Postwar Currency Policy," Sept. 8, 1941, T247/116, NA-Kew.

16. On the origins and evolution of the IMF, see David D. Driscoll, ed., *The International Monetary Fund: Its Evolution, Organization, and Activities*; J. Keith Horsefield et al., *The International Monetary Fund, 1945–1965: Twenty Years of International Monetary Cooperation*; *Chronicle* 1: 4–10; Driscoll, *International Monetary Fund*, 1; Leo Pasvolsky, "The Necessity for a Stable International Monetary Standard"; Nicholas John Spykman, *America's Strategy in the World: The United States and the Balance of Power.*

17. See Alfred E. Eckes, *A Search for Solvency: Bretton Woods and the International Monetary System, 1941–1971*; Horsefield, *International Monatry Fund*, 1: 4. For statistics broken down by country, see Barry Eichengreen, *Elusive Stability: Essays in the History of International Finance, 1919–1939*, 154ff; Skidelsky, *John Maynard Keynes*, 183–184.

18. Eichengreen, *Elusive Stability*, 125; Ray Stannard Baker, *Woodrow Wilson and World Settlement*, 2: 271, 275; Eckes, *Search for Solvency*, 8–10.

19. John Maynard Keynes, "Proposal for the Reconstruction of Europe, 1919," in his *Collected Writings*, 9: 14–32.

20. The United States was not an Allied power in World War I— it kept its semantic distance as an "associated" power. Coolidge quoted in Edward M. Lamont, *The Ambassador from Wall Street: The Story of Thomas W. Lamont, J. P. Morgan's Chief Executive* (Lanham, MD: Madison, 1994), 192; see also Robert H. Ferrell, *The Presidency of Calvin Coolidge* (Lawrence: University Press of Kansas, 1998). On the interwar shift from private money to public money, see Michael R. Adamson, "Inventing U.S. Foreign Aid: From Private to Public Funding of Economic Development, 1919–1941."

21. Baker, *Woodrow Wilson and World Settlement*, 2: 290, 326; 3: 346.

22. John Maynard Keynes, *The Economic Consequences of the Peace*; James T. Shotwell, *The Great Decision*, 153.

23. Acheson, *Present at the Creation*, 10.

24. Russell, *History of the United Nations Charter*, 1. Russell was a former aide to Leo Pasvolsky of the State Department's Division of Special Research. George B. Galloway, *Postwar Planning in the United States*, 100–101. Russell also served as an aide to one of the Technical Commissions at the Bretton Woods Conference. *Bretton Woods Proceedings*, 2: 1132; Wendell L. Willkie, *One World*, 168–169.

25. Commission to Study the Organization of Peace, *Fourth Report*, rpt. in *International Conciliation: Documents for the Year 1944* (New York: Carnegie Endowment for In-

ternational Peace, Dec. 1944), 396: 69; Leuchtenburg, *Franklin D. Roosevelt and the New Deal*, 338. William Lasser, *Benjamin V. Cohen, Architect of the New Deal* (New Haven: Yale University Press, 2002), ix, xi.

26. Lasser, *Benjamin V. Cohen*, ix, xi.

27. Merriam, *Agenda of Democracy*, 78; Philip Allot, "Intergovernmental Societies and the Idea of Constitutionalism," in *Legitimacy of International Organizations*, ed. Coicaud and Heiskanen, 69–103; Jose E. Alvarez, "Constitutional Interpretation in International Organizations," in ibid., 104–154. See also the succinct comparison of British and American conceptions of constitutionalism in Richard B. Bernstein, *Thomas Jefferson*, 23.

28. FDR, *PPA*, 1937, 406. The "quarantine" passage was FDR's own embellishment on the draft the State Department had prepared, according to Cordell Hull. See Hull, *The Memoirs of Cordell Hull*, 1: 545; Samuel I. Rosenman, *Working with Roosevelt*, 165–167; Russell, *History of the United Nations Charter*, 13.

29. Quoted in Russell, *History of the United Nations Charter*, 13. See also Sumner Welles, *The Time for Decision*, 251–255.

30. FDR, Speech of Apr. 15, 1939, *PPA*, 1938, 201–205.

31. Ibid.

32. Sumner Welles Memorandum of Jan. 12, 1940, FDR, Papers as President, PSF, Box 24, FDRPL.

33. Text of State Department Memorandum in US Department of State, *Postwar Foreign Policy Preparation, 1939–1945*, 458–460.

34. Blum, *Morgenthau Diaries*, 228–229.

35. These base areas included Argentia, on the coast of Newfoundland in Canada, the coastal waters of which provided the site of the 1941 Atlantic Conference. Another part of this agreement involved a British promise to transfer the Royal Navy to the United States in case of a German invasion. See Robert Dallek, *Franklin D. Roosevelt and American Foreign Policy*, 245–247.

36. See Peter Benson, "Contract," in *A Companion to Philosophy of Law and Legal Theory*, ed. Dennis Patterson, 31–32, 48. See also James Gordley, *The Philosophical Origins of Modern Contract Doctrine* (Oxford: Clarendon, 1991).

37. Skidelsky, *John Maynard Keynes*, 3: 99; FDR, Press Conferences, No. 702 (Dec. 17, 1940), *PPA*, 1940, 608.

38. On the executive-congressional struggles over neutrality legislation, see Dallek, *Franklin D. Roosevelt and American Foreign Policy*, 102–103, 120, 137, 212.

39. Skidelsky, *John Maynard Keynes*, 3: 100.

40. Ibid.; *New York Herald Tribune*, Mar. 31, 1946, quoted in David Rees, *Harry Dexter White: A Study in Paradox*, 133.

41. Quoted in Skidelsky, *John Maynard Keynes*, 3: 105.

42. Acheson, *Present at the Creation*, 22; Skidelsky, *John Maynard Keynes*, 3: 104.

43. Skidelsky, *John Maynard Keynes*, 3: xiv-xv. Skidelsky's thesis is controversial primarily because it posits a more competitive, zero-sum relationship than other recent scholars have presented of these Anglo-American financial negotiations. See G. John Ikenberry, "Creating Yesterday's New World Order"; Keynes, *Collected Writings*, 23: 46.

44. Acheson, *Present at the Creation*, 29. The value of 7 billion 1941 US dollars translates to 87,619,002,003 dollars using the Consumer Price Index Inflation Calculator at www.jsc.nasa.gov (consulted Aug. 18, 2004). Rpt in Keynes, *Collected Writings*, 23: 173.

45. Acheson, *Present at the Creation*, 22, 30; Roy F. Harrod, *The Life of John Maynard Keynes*, 512; *FRUS, 1941*, 3: 12; Douglas Brinkley, *Dean Acheson: The Cold War Years, 1953–71* (New Haven: Yale University Press, 1992), 82.

46. "Mutual Aid Agreement with Great Britain," *USDSB* 6 (1942): 190–192; quoted

with commentary in Edward R. Stettinius, Jr., *Lend-Lease: Weapon for Victory* (New York: Macmillan, 1944), v, 371.

47. "Memorandum on Progress of Lend-Lease Agreements," Apr. 10, 1942, Harley Notter files 14, RG 59, NARA; *FRUS, 1942,* 6: 139–141; Edward A. Laing, "Relevance of the Atlantic Charter for a New World Order," *Indian Journal of International Law* 29 (July–Dec. 1989): 315; Alan Dobson, "Economic Diplomacy at the Atlantic Conference," *Review of International Studies* 10 (1984): 143–148.

48. Keynes, *Collected Writings,* 23: 177; Blum, *Morgenthau Diaries,* 2: 243.

49. Blum, *Morgenthau Diaries,* 2: 244–245; Keynes, "Closing Remarks," 1: 1109. (Keynes refers to the *Mayflower* as sailing *from* Plymouth, the English port from which the Pilgrims embarked; later they named their New World landing-point Plymouth, as a tribute.)

50. Keynes, *Collected Writings,* 24: 195.

51. John Maynard Keynes, *The Economic Consequences of the Peace;* see also Keynes, *A Revision of the Treaty: Being a Sequel to the Economic Consequences of the Peace* (London: Macmillan, 1971); Keynes, "Reparations and Inter-Allied Debt," in *Essays in Liberalism* (London: W. Collins Sons, 1922).

52. Alan Booth, "The 'Keynesian Revolution' in Economic Policy-Making," *Economic History Review* 36 (1983); on the American Keynesians, see William J. Barber, *Designs within Disorder: Franklin D. Roosevelt, the Economists, and the Shaping of American Economic Policy, 1933–1945,* 128–129. In a casual aside that may well have actually been about Harry White, Keynes disparaged "the gritty Jewish type" of American civil servant as "perhaps a little too prominent" in Roosevelt administration circles, even while conceding that they were "exceptionally capable and vigorous." He also organized a wartime ballet gala in Cambridge, as a benefit performance to aid Jewish refugees, Skidelsky, *John Maynard Keynes,* 3: 116, 51; *Times* (London), Apr. 22, 1946, quoted in Skidelsky, *John Maynard Keynes,* 3: 472.

53. Armand Van Dormael, *Bretton Woods: Birth of a Monetary System,* 40–42; Rees, *Harry Dexter White,* 20–22; Skidelsky, *John Maynard Keynes,* 3: 240–241.

54. Blum, *Roosevelt and Morgenthau,* 461; Rees, *Harry Dexter White;* Allen Weinstein and Alexander Vassiliev, *The Haunted Wood: Soviet Espionage in America—The Stalin Era* (New York: Random House, 1999); John Earl Haynes and Harvey Klehr, *Venona: Decoding Soviet Espionage in America* (New Haven: Yale University Press, 1999); G. Edward White, *Alger Hiss's Looking-Glass Wars: The Covert Life of a Soviet Spy,* 48, 227.

55. Lloyd C. Gardner, *Economic Aspects of New Deal Diplomacy* (Boston: Beacon, 1971), 285.

56. Keynes, *Collected Writings,* 9: 358; Penrose, *Economic Planning,* 41–42.

57. Penrose, *Economic Planning,* 41–42; Keynes, "Postwar Currency Policy," T247/116 (Sept. 8, 1941), NA-Kew.

58. Lionel Robbins, *Autobiography of an Economist* (London: Macmillan, 1971), 196.

59. Harry D. White, "Proposal for United Nations Stabilization Fund and a Bank for Reconstruction and Development of the United and Associated Nations," Apr. 1942, Treasury Department folder, Papers of Bernard Bernstein, HSTPL. White often backdated his drafts.

60. Penrose, *Economic Planning,* 45.

61. Ibid., 45, 46; "Discussions Regarding Postwar Economic and Financial Arrangements, *FRUS, 1942,* 1: 163–242; Alan P. Dobson, *The Politics of the Anglo-American Economic Special Relationship,* 52.

62. Dobson, *Economic Special Relationship,* 52, 53.

63. Keynes Plan, para. 41, T247/116, NA-Kew. The American economist Edward F. Penrose was present at this informal meeting, and although neither side kept official records, the quotations are drawn from his account of the discussions, published in 1953. Penrose, *Economic Planning*, 49.

64. Penrose, *Economic Planning*, 52, 54.

65. "Joint Statement by Experts on the Establishment of an International Monetary Fund of the United and Associated Nations," Apr. 21, 1944, T160/1281/F18885/11, NA-Kew.

66. Van Dormael, *Bretton Woods*, 53; Morgenthau Diary, 746, FDRPL, 133, 139.

67. Blum, *Morgenthau Diaries*, 253.

68. John S. Fischer, an American official with the Foreign Economic Administration, quotes an adage that he very possibly did not realize is widely attributed to the British general and statesman John Churchill, the first Duke of Marlborough and Winston Churchill's most illustrious ancestor. John S. Fischer letter to Lauchlin Currie, July 20, 1944, quoted in Robert M. Hathaway, *Ambiguous Partnership: Britain and America, 1944–1947* (New York: Columbia University Press, 1981), 316–317.

4. Investing in Global Stability

1. Quoted in Skidelsky, *John Maynard Keynes*, 3: 339; Acheson, *Present at the Creation*, 82; US Department of State, *Proceedings and Documents of the United Nations Monetary and Financial Conference, Bretton Woods, New Hampshire, July 1–22, 1944*, 2: 1129.

2. Keynes to Richard V. N. Hopkins (British Treasury official responsible for bringing Keynes into the Treasury Department in 1940; permanent secretary 1942–1945), July 1, 1944, T247/65/74, NA-Kew; Lydia Lopokova letter of July 12, 1944, quoted in Skidelsky, *John Maynard Keynes*, 3: 347; Acheson, *Present at the Creation*, 84.

3. Shotwell, *Great Decision*, 176.

4. Frank McDougall, "United Nations Programme for Freedom from Want of Food," Oct. 1942, rpt. in United Nations Food and Agriculture Organization, *The McDougall Memoranda: Some Documents Relating to the Origins of the FAO and the Contributions Made by Frank L. McDougall* (Rome: Food and Agriculture Organization of the United Nations, 1956); see also Penrose, *Economic Planning*, 118–119; Russell, *History of the United Nations Charter*, 65, 66; Acheson, *Present at the Creation*, 73.

5. Acheson, *Present at the Creation*, 73.

6. Penrose, *Economic Planning*, 120, 119.

7. These "associated nations" also included a few other non-American neutrals. The forty-four participants at the conference included twenty-six original signers of the 1942 UN Declaration, five later adherents (Brazil, Ethiopia, Iraq, Mexico, and the Philippines), and the thirteen "associates": Bolivia, Chile, Colombia, Ecuador, Paraguay, Peru, Uruguay, and Venezuela in the Western Hemisphere; and Egypt, Iceland, Iran, Liberia, and representatives of what Russell delicately calls "the so-called 'Free French.'" These early decisions about whom to include served as "a precedent for all subsequent UN economic conferences, and in the end was to give rise to some contention with the Soviet Union over the states to be invited to the San Francisco Conference." Russell, *History of the United Nations Charter*, 67.

8. Commission to Study the Organization of Peace, *Fourth Report*, rpt. in *International Conciliation: Documents for the Year 1944*, 396: 76; Skidelsky, *John Maynard Keynes*, 3: 238.

9. Acheson, *Present at the Creation*, 74.

10. Shotwell, *Great Decision*, 166–167; Acheson, *Present at the Creation*, 75.

11. Shotwell, *Great Decision,* 168; Skidelsky, *John Maynard Keynes,* 3: 300.

12. Russell, *History of the United Nations Charter,* 68–70; Shotwell, *Great Decision,* 168; *USDSB* 13 (Oct. 21, 1945): 619.

13. Winant cable quoted in Acheson, *Present at the Creation,* 68, 69.

14. The text of Marshall's speech is rpt. in *USDSB* 16 (June 15, 1947): 1160.

15. Shotwell, *Great Decision,* 171.

16. This dynamic, of Allies pushing the Americans to develop alternative plans almost as a defensive maneuver, would also prove true in the development of the Nuremberg and UN charters; Acheson, *Present at the Creation,* 66.

17. Ibid, 69; *USDSB* 9 (Sept. 25, 1943): 211–216; George Woodbridge, *UNRRA: The History of the United Nations Relief and Rehabilitation Administration.*

18. Acheson, *Present at the Creation,* 71; Arthur H. Vandenberg Jr., ed., *The Private Papers of Senator Vandenberg,* 67, 70; Tom Connally, *My Name is Tom Connally,* 262–263; Rosenman, *Working with Roosevelt,* caption and ill. preceding p. 337.

19. Russell, *History of the United Nations Charter,* 70–71. Senator Connally noted that "I could have insisted on a treaty, but since UNRRA was chiefly a matter of the United States appropriating billions for relief abroad, I thought it best to bring the House of Representatives into the picture, too." Connally, *My Name Is Tom Connally,* 262.

20. Shotwell, *Great Decision,* 171; see also *USDSB* 9 (Nov. 11, 1943): 319.

21. Gardner, *Sterling-Dollar,* xvii; Gardner cites "a yellowing piece of paper salvaged from the Anglo-American financial negotiations [of 1944]."

22. Lord Keynes to British Treasury officials Sir David Waley and Sir Wilfred Eady, May 30, 1944, T247/28, NA-Kew.

23. Acheson, *Present at the Creation,* 81; Shotwell, *Great Decision,* 176.

24. Driscoll, ed., *The International Monetary Fund,* 2.

25. Keynes to Anderson, July 21, 1944, T160/1375/F17942, NA-Kew.

26. Harrod, a British economist and Keynes's first biographer, was present at several of the sessions; see Gardner, *Sterling-Dollar,* 111–112.

27. American Delegation at Bretton Woods, Minutes of Meeting, July 1, 1944, Morgenthau Diaries, 749: 25, FDRPL.

28. Van Dormael, *Bretton Woods,* 166.

29. White and Collado, quoted in Van Dormael, *Bretton Woods,* 170, 176, 181.

30. *Time,* July 10, 1944, 80; Georg Schild, *Bretton Woods and Dumbarton Oaks: American Economic and Postwar Planning in the Summer of 1944.* See also White memoranda reproduced in the Morgenthau Diaries, 657: 132ff.

31. John Parke Young, "Developing Plans for an International Monetary Fund and a World Bank," *USDSB* 23 (1950): 778.

32. "White Plan," Apr. 1942, Section 3, para 6, Harry Dexter White Papers, Box 8, Seeley Mudd Library, Princeton University.

33. Bruce Mann, *Republic of Debtors: Bankruptcy in the Age of American Independence,* 2, 3; Skidelsky, "Keynes's Road to Bretton Woods: An Essay in Interpretation," in Marc Flandreau, Carl-Ludwig Holtfrerich, and Harold James, eds., *International Financial History in the Twentieth Century: System and Anarchy,* 127.

34. Goldenweiser and Acheson, quoted in Van Dormael, *Bretton Woods,* 174, 198–199.

35. Of the Bank's authorized capital of $10 billion, only 20 percent was immediately subject to call, and only 2 percent had to be paid over in gold or US dollars. Bank Articles of Agreement, article 2, sections 5 and 7.

36. Bank article 3, section 3; Eckes, *Search for Solvency,* 158; see Bank article 3, section 4(v); Bank article 1, section 1; Bank article 1, section 5.

37. Sir Wilfred Eady, second secretary of the Treasury 1942–1952, account published

in the *Listener*, June 7, 1951, quoted in Skidelsky, *John Maynard Keynes*, 355; "Verbatim Minutes of the Closing Plenary Session," *Bretton Woods Proceedings*, 1: 1109–1110.

38. "Verbatim Minutes of the Closing Plenary Session," *Bretton Woods Proceedings*, 1: 1109–1110.

39. Ibid., 1116.

40. Ibid., 1117.

41. Memorandum of Feb. 16, 1945, FO 371/45663, NA-Kew.

42. US Congress, Senate Committee on Banking and Currency, *Bretton Woods Agreements Act*, Hearings on HR 3314, 79th Cong., 1st sess. (June 1945): 371.

43. American Bankers Association, *Practical International Financial Organization through Amendments to Bretton Woods Proposals* (Feb. 1, 1945) (copy sent to British treasury officials by W. Randolph Burgess, vice chair of the National City Bank of New York and president of the American Banker's Association), T-230, 50, summary, 12, 18, 24, NA-Kew; Robert M. Collins, *The Business Response to Keynes, 1929–1964* (New York: Columbia University Press, 1981).

44. American Bankers Association, *Practical International Financial Organization*, 20–21.

45. US Congress, Senate Committee on Banking and Currency, *Bretton Woods Agreements Act*, 125–126; "rat hole" comment from *Congressional Record* 91 (July 16, 1945): 7573, quoted in Gardner, *Sterling-Dollar*, 130.

46. Gardner, *Sterling-Dollar*, 129; E. B. White, *The Wild Flag: Editorials from The New Yorker on Federal World Government and Other Matters*, 54, 56, 72, 16.

47. Gardner, *Sterling-Dollar*, 142, 13; US Congress, House Committee on Banking and Currency, *Bretton Woods Agreements Act*, 1: 155.

48. US Congress, Senate Committee on Banking and Currency, *Bretton Woods Agreements Act*, 37.

49. Skidelsky, *John Maynard Keynes*, 3: 12. Richard Nixon famously observed in 1972 that "We are all Keynesians now." Quoted in Robert B. Reich, "John Maynard Keynes" in *Time 100: The Most Important People of the Century* (Mar. 29, 1999), www.time.com/time/time100.

50. Writers' War Board, "Recipe for World War III," rpt. in US Congress, House Committee on Banking and Currency, *Bretton Woods Agreements Act*, 2: 1331.

51. Robert H. Brand (then an official with the British Food Mission in Washington, later the UK Treasury representative in Washington and a delegate at Bretton Woods) to John Maynard Keynes, Oct. 11, 1941, Keynes Papers, Letters Files, King's College Archive Center, Cambridge, UK (the third volume of Skidelsky's biography of Keynes first guided me to this quotation, which Dr. Skidelsky found in the Brand papers at Oxford and I found among the Keynes papers at Cambridge).

52. See my earlier formulation of sovereignty as process in "The Modern Machiavelli: Legitimacy, Conflict, and Power in the International Legal Order," *UCLA Law Review* 43 (Oct. 1995): 139; 153–158; Chayes and Chayes, *The New Sovereignty*; Anne-Marie Slaughter, "Disaggregated Sovereignty: Towards the Public Accountability of Global Government Networks," *Government and Opposition* 39 (Apr. 2004): 159–190.

53. US Senate, Committee on Banking and Currency, *Bretton Woods Agreements Act*, 314.

54. Keynes, *Collected Writings*, 25: 56.

55. Commission to Study the Organization of Peace, *Fourth Report*, 68.

56. Ibid., 69; Brinkley, *The End of Reform*, 10.

57. Merriam, *Agenda of Democracy*, 100.

58. De Souza Costa credits Roosevelt as the "great inspirer" of this perspective. Address by the Honorable Arthur De Souza Costa, chairman of the Brazilian Delegation,

at the Closing Plenary Session, July 22, 1944, 9:45 p.m., Doc. no. 535, *Bretton Woods Proceedings*, app. 2: 1231–1232. See also John Kenneth Galbraith, "How Keynes Came to America," in Galbraith, *A Contemporary Guide to Economics, Peace and Laughter* (Boston: Houghton Mifflin, 1971), 43–53.

59. Percy E. Corbett, "War Aims and Post-War Plans," 4. (Corbett mentioned the Four Freedoms several times in this seven-page conference paper, and attached the Atlantic Charter as an appendix, noting that it was announced after he had completed his essay); Brinkley, *The End of Reform*, 3; Jeffries, "The 'New' New Deal," *Political Science Quarterly* 105 (1990): 397–418. Jeffries traces the expression "new New Deal" to an article by Kenneth C. Crawford, "From Pump-Priming to Pumping," *Nation*, May 27, 1939, 607. On a third phase for the New Deal, see also Dean L. May, *From New Deal to New Economics: The American Liberal Response to the Recession of 1937* (New York: Garland, 1981).

60. Corbett, "War Aims," 4; Commission to Study the Organization of Peace, *Fourth Report*, 78.

61. FDR, "State of the Union Message to Congress, Jan. 7, 1943," *PPA*, 1943, 34.

62. Deleted speech excerpt rpt. in Rosenman, *Working with Roosevelt*, 376.

63. Harold L. Ickes, *Autobiography of a Curmudgeon*, 335–336. Interestingly, one of Ickes's sixteen principles was "the right to bring international criminals before the bar of an international court," supporting the contention that what would later become known as the Nuremberg trial was an echo of a more integrated vision of what was originally intended to be an ongoing international institution.

64. On Hansen's ideas and his influence, see the bestselling *Economic Program for American Democracy*, Richard V. Gilbert, George H. Hildebrand, Jr., and Arthur W. Stuart, eds. (New York: Vanguard, 1938); Alvin H. Hansen, *Fiscal Policy and Business Cycles* (New York: Norton, 1941); Richard Lee Strout, "Hansen of Harvard," *New Republic*, Dec. 29, 1941, 888–890; Hansen, "The Postwar Economy," in Seymour E. Harris, ed., *Postwar Economic Problems* (New York: McGraw-Hill, 1943). On the American Keynesians generally, see Barber, *Designs within Disorder*; Byrd L. Jones, "The Role of Keynesians in Wartime Policy and Postwar Planning, 1940–1946," *American Economic Review* 62 (May 1972): 125–133. Cohen, *Consumers' Republic*, esp. chap. 2, "War: Citizen Consumers Do Battle on the Home Front."

65. FDR, "Unless There Is Security Here at Home, There Cannot Be Lasting Peace in the World—Message to Congress on the State of the Union, Jan. 11, 1944," *PPA*, 1944, 42, 41. For background on this speech and FDR's earlier iterations of this agenda, in addition to the Four Freedoms and Atlantic Charter, see the discussion in Rosenman, *Working with Roosevelt;* on the role of the National Resources Planning Board, as well as FDR's speech in Chicago as part of his 1944 presidential campaign, see Rosenman, 417–427, 492–498.

66. Burns, *Roosevelt: The Soldier of Freedom*, 424–426.

67. Alvin H. Hansen, "After the War—Full Employment," Washington, DC: National Resources Planning Board, 1942, 1 (pamphlet in Keynes's Personal Files, NA-Kew); on social planning in the New Deal era see Edwin Amenta and Theda Skocpol, "Redefining the New Deal: World War II and the Development of Social Provision in the United States," in Margaret Weir, Ann Shola Orloff, and Theda Skocpol, eds., *The Politics of Social Policy in the United States* (Princeton: Princeton University Press, 1988), 81–122; Margaret Weir and Theda Skocpol, "State Structures and the Possibilities for 'Keynesian' Responses to the Great Depression in Sweden, Britain, and the United States," in Peter B. Evans, Dietrich Rueschemeyer, and Theda Skocpol, eds., *Bringing the State Back In* (New York: Cambridge University Press, 1985).

68. William E. Forbath, "Caste, Class, and Equal Citizenship," *Michigan Law Review*

98 (Oct. 1999): 1, 76–77; Gavin Wright, *Old South, New South: Revolutions in the Southern Economy since the Civil War* (New York: Basic Books, 1986), 219; V. O. Key, Jr., *Southern Politics in State and Nation* (New York: Knopf, 1949).

69. William E. Forbath, "Caste, Class, and Equal Citizenship," 1.

70. Forbath, "Caste, Class, and Equal Citizenship," 1; Cohen, *Consumers' Republic,* 118; Jeffries, "The 'New' New Deal," 415, 417; Forbath, "The New Deal Constitution in Exile," *Duke Law Journal* 51 (2001): 165; Margaret Weir, "Full Employment as a Political Issue in the United States," *Social Research* 54 (Summer 1987): 377–402; Marion Clawson, *New Deal Planning: The National Resources Planning Board* (Baltimore: Johns Hopkins University Press, 1981); Stephen K. Bailey, *Congress Makes a Law: The Story Behind the Employment Act of 1946* (New York: Columbia University Press, 1950).

71. Kennedy, *Freedom from Fear,* 786–787. On the GI Bill, see Michael J. Bennett, *When Dreams Came True: The GI Bill and the Making of Modern America* (Washington, DC: Brassey's, 1996); Harold G. Vatter, *The US Economy in World War II* (New York: Columbia University Press, 1985). Some studies of the effects of the GI Bill have highlighted how these dramatic, transformative benefits were disproportionately restricted to white male veterans. See, for example, June A. Wilentz, *Women Veterans: America's Forgotten Heroines* (New York: Continuum Press, 1983); David H. Onskt, "First a Negro . . . Incidentally a Veteran: Black World War II Veterans and the GI Bill of Rights in the Deep South, 1944–1948," *Journal of Social History* 31 (Spring 1998): 517–544.

72. Ickes, *Autobiography of a Curmudgeon,* 333.

5. The Chimera of Collective Security

1. For descriptions of preparations and the meeting's opening, see *Time,* Aug. 21, 1944, 19, and Aug. 28, 1944, 14; *Newsweek,* Aug. 21, 1944, 37; *New York Times,* Aug. 22, 1944; *USDSB* 9 (Aug. 27, 1944): 199. Murray C. Bernays recalling the weather during Dumbarton Oaks, letter of June 10, 1945, American Heritage Center, University of Wyoming. See also Robert C. Hilderbrand, *Dumbarton Oaks: The Origins of the United Nations and the Search for Postwar Security,* 67–70; Divine, *Second Chance,* guided me to many of the sources for this and the following chapter.

2. Carlos P. Romulo, *Forty Years: A Third World Soldier at the UN,* 7.

3. FDR, *Press Conferences,* No. 888 (Mar. 30, 1943), 21: 250; see also Rosenman, *Working with Roosevelt,* 402. As assistant secretary of the Navy, FDR's official task in France at the end of World War I was to supervise naval demobilization. Although Roosevelt prided himself on negotiating several advantageous contracts with the French, it is clear that his presence was unwelcome to the US naval officers already on the spot, who considered him superfluous. While FDR personally was very interested in the peace negotiations that were unfolding simultaneously, he was relegated to the role of "spectator at Paris," as historian Frank Friedel titled the chapter on Roosevelt's role in 1919. Frank Burt Freidel, *Franklin D. Roosevelt,* vol. 2, *The Ordeal* (Boston: Little, Brown, 1952), 3, 5, 7–9.

4. Sidney B. Fay, "The Dumbarton Oaks Conference: How Can We Organize for Postwar Peace?" *Current History* 7 (Oct. 1944): 257–264.

5. Dumbarton Oaks delegates who had participated in the 1919 Paris Peace talks included president of Johns Hopkins University Isaiah Bowman (designated as Special Advisor to the Secretary of State for the purposes of Dumbarton Oaks); Director of the State Department's Office of Far Eastern Affairs and former Ambassador to Japan Joseph Grew; British delegate and professor of international history at the London School of Economics Charles K. Webster; head of the Chinese delegation V. K. Wellington Koo; and head of the British delegation Sir Alexander Cadogan. Cadogan had also served as the chief of the League of Nations section at the British Foreign Office since 1923. Also, US policy planning

chief Leo Pasvolsky had covered the Paris Peace Conference for the internationalist *New York Herald Tribune.*

6. Frank Donovan, *Mr. Roosevelt's Four Freedoms: The Story behind the United Nations Charter,* 104.

7. B. Welles, *Sumner Welles,* 2–3, 33, 57–58, 341–349, 379; Gellman, *Secret Affairs.*

8. Acheson, *Present at the Creation,* 88; *Cadogan Diaries,* 656; Memorandum, Stettinius to Roosevelt, Aug. 21, 1944, *FRUS,* 1944, 1: 713–714; Memorandum from Division of International Conferences, Aug. 12, 1944, in Notter, *Postwar Foreign Policy Preparation,* 301; Hilderbrand, *Dumbarton Oaks,* 69–70. This history uses two versions of Stettinius's diary: a published version, Thomas M. Campbell and George C. Herring, eds., *The Diaries of Edward R. Stettinius, Jr., 1943–1946* (hereafter *Stettinius Diaries*), and an unpublished version, "First Draft of Dumbarton Oaks Diary," in the Edward R. Stettinius, Jr., Papers of the Albert and Shirley Small Special Collections Library, University of Virginia. *Stettinius Diaries,* entry for Aug. 21, 1944.

9. In summer 1944 the Soviets were setting up a communist "Lublin Government" in Poland, correctly regarded as a puppet organization, to usurp the Polish government in exile based in London. Polish nationalism was thus a touchy subject for the Soviets.

10. This bipartisan group included Tom Connally (D-Texas), chair of the Senate Foreign Relations Committee; Walter F. George (D-Georgia); Alben W. Barkley (D-Kentucky); Guy M. Gillette (D-Iowa); Arthur H. Vandenberg (R-Michigan); Warren R. Austin (R-Vermont); Wallace H. White, Jr. (R-Maine); and one member of the Progressive party, Robert M. LaFollette, Jr., of Wisconsin. In mid-1944, Vandenberg, Gillette, and LaFollette were well-known isolationists; only Austin had any kind of reputation as an internationalist. The State Department's International Organization Group had been known as the Informal Political Agenda Group before June 1944. See Russell, *History of the United Nations Charter,* 220–221. For an engaging narrative of the work of this group, and preparations for the negotiation of the United Nations Charter generally, see Stephen C. Schlesinger, *Act of Creation: The Founding of the United Nations: A Story of Superpowers, Secret Agents, Wartime Allies and Enemies, and Their Quest for a Peaceful World.*

11. Donovan, *Roosevelt's Four Freedoms,* 195; *Cadogan Diaries,* 657; James Reston, *Deadline,* 134; *New York Times,* Aug. 23–28, 1944; *New York Herald Tribune,* Aug. 24, 1944.

12. For the Manhattan junket, see *Time,* Sept. 4, 1944, 21, 22–23; *New York Times,* Aug. 28, 1944; *Cadogan Diaries,* 659.

13. *Time,* Sept. 4, 1944, 23; *Stettinius Diaries,* entry for Sept. 10, 1944.

14. *Cadogan Diaries,* 662–663.

15. For the Smiths' trip to Washington, see *Stettinius Diaries,* entry for Aug. 25, 1944; Memorandum of telephone conversation, Breckinridge Long and Mrs. L. K. Smith, and Smith to Hull, Aug. 23, 1944, Breckinridge Long Papers, LC. For Isaiah Berlin's alarmed reaction to how much attention fringe elements such as the Smiths were receiving, see Berlin, *Washington Despatches,* ed. Herbert G. Nicholas, 407–408; Conrad Black, *Franklin Delano Roosevelt: Champion of Freedom,* 326.

16. See Berlin, *Washington Despatches,* 413–415, 431 (noting that most reactions, however, were praising the Conference), 438; Monthly Report, Division of Public Liaison, "The Dumbarton Oaks Proposals," Nov. 1944, in *Dumbarton Oaks Proposals—Reactions,* Box 4, Green Hackworth Papers, LC.

17. A thirteenth-century author explained how diplomats "should normally be the greatest and most eloquent citizens . . . naturally this meant frequent calls on the families of aristocratic descent." Quoted in Daniel Waley, *The Italian City-Republics,* 3rd ed. (London: Longman, 1988), 96. Such a selection criterion is not so far removed from that of the pre-World War II US State Department. See Acheson, *Present at the Creation,* "The 'Old'

State Department." On the origins of the term "diplomat," see Zimmern, *The League of Nations and the Rule of Law*, 13.

18. See, for example, Derek Croxton, *Peacemaking in Early Modern Europe: Cardinal Mazarin and the Congress of Westphalia, 1643–1648* (Selinsgrove, PA: Susquehanna University Press, 1999), 160, 181, 259; Stephen J. Lee, *The Thirty Years War* (London: Routledge, 1991); Kenneth Colegrove, "Diplomatic Procedure Preliminary to the Congress of Westphalia," *AJIL* 13 (1919): 450–482.

19. Representative writings on these topics include, for example, St. Augustine, *De Civitate Dei Contra Paganos*, bk. 24, sec. 7; St. Thomas Aquinas, *Summa Theologiae*, Secunda Secundae, Quaestio 40; Francesco de Vitoria, *De Indis et de Jure Belli Relectiones*; Francesco Suarez, *Selections from Three Works, De Triplici Virtute Theologica: Charitate*, Disputation 13, sec. 4, part 3; Alberico Gentili, *De Jure Belli*, Book 1, sec. 6. For classical influences, see Coleman Philipson, *The International Law and Custom of Ancient Greece and Rome*; David W. Kennedy, "Primitive Legal Scholarship," *Harvard International Law Journal* 27 (1986): 12.

20. Grotius's best-known work of international law is *De Jure Belli ac Pacis* (*On the Laws of War and Peace*). On changing assessments of Grotius's achievement, see Peter Haggenmacher, *Grotius et la Doctrine de la Guerre Juste* (Paris: Presses Universitaires de France, 1983), 629; Roger Labrousse, "Il problèma della originalità di Grozio," *Revista internazionale di filosofia del diritto* 28 (1951): 1–20; Maurice Bourquin, "Grotius est-il le pere du droit des gens?" in *Grandes figures et grandes oeuvres juridiques*; Pieter Geyl, "Grotius," *Transactions of the Grotius Society* 12 (1926): 81–97; and Bull, Kingsbury, and Roberts, eds., *Hugo Grotius*.

21. A revival of interest in Grotius was a feature of the intellectual history of the first half of the twentieth century, especially (and unsurprisingly) during and just after the two world wars. Hamilton Vreeland, *Hugo Grotius: The Father of the Modern Science of International Law*; Durwood V. Sandifer, "Rereading Grotius in the Year 1940," *AJIL* 34 (1940): 459–472, 471; Hersch Lauterpacht, "The Grotian Tradition in International Law," *British Year Book of International Law* 23 (1946): 43; Robert H. Jackson, "The Grotian Moment in World Jurisprudence," *International Insights, Special Issue: The International System in a Grotian Moment* 13 (Fall 1997): 35. On the early 1940s as a new "Grotian moment," see, for example, Richard Falk's introduction to Charles S. Edwards, *Hugo Grotius: The Miracle of Holland*, xiii–xxi; Falk, "A New Paradigm for International Legal Studies: Prospects and Proposals," in Richard Falk, Friedrich Kratochwil, and Saul H. Mendlovitz, eds., *International Law: A Contemporary Perspective*, 651–702; Jackson, "The Grotian Moment in World Jurisprudence"; Leo Gross, "The Peace of Westphalia, 1648–1948," *AJIL* 42 (1948): 20; Dorothy V. Jones, *Toward a Just World: The Critical Years in the Search for International Justice*.

22. Robert B. Mowat, *The Concert of Europe*; Harold G. Nicolson, *The Congress of Vienna: A Study in Allied Unity, 1812–1822*, and William Penn Cresson, *The Holy Alliance: The European Background to the Monroe Doctrine*; Henry A. Kissinger, *A World Restored: Metternich, Castlereagh and the Problems of Peace, 1812–22*. For a critique of Kissinger's idealization of the Concert of Europe's approach to international law and organization, see Elizabeth Kopelman, "The Modern Machiavelli: Legitimacy, Conflict and Power in the International Legal Order," *UCLA Law Review* 43 (Oct. 1995): 139–158.

23. Memorandum of Lord Castlereagh, Aug. 12, 1815, quoted in Sir Charles K. Webster, ed., *British Diplomacy, 1813–1815* (London: G. Bell and Sons, 1921), 361–362. Webster, a professor of international history who later helped draft the Dumbarton Oaks proposals, researched the Congress of Vienna at the request of the British Foreign Office, as a background study for the 1919 Paris Peace talks. Webster, *The Congress of Vienna, 1814–1815*; P. A. Reynolds and E. J. Hughes, *The Historian as Diplomat: Charles Kingsley Web-*

ster and the United Nations, 1939–1946. Alfred Vagts and Detlev F. Vagts, "The Balance of Power in International Law: A History of an Idea," *AJIL* 73 (1979): 555–580, 565; Alfred Vagts, "The Balance of Power: Growth of an Idea," *World Politics* 1 (1948): 82, 89–92; Quincy Wright, "International Law and the Balance of Power," *AJIL* 37 (1943): 97.

24. Lipset, *American Exceptionalism,* 31; Rodgers, *Contested Truths,* 13.

25. See, for example, the opening chapter of Akira Iriye's *Cultural Internationalism and World Order;* Immanuel Kant (1724–1804), *The Metaphysics of Morals* (1797), sec. 3: 62, "Cosmopolitan Right," rpt. in Micheline R. Ishay, ed., *The Human Rights Reader: Major Political Essays, Speeches, and Documents from the Bible to the Present,* 172. See also Kant, "The Principle of Progress considered in connection with the Relation of Theory to Practice in International Law" (1793), in Kant, *Eternal Peace and Other International Essays,* trans. W. Hastie (Boston: World Peace Foundation, 1914), 65; Kant, *Perpetual Peace,* with an introduction by Nicholas Murray Butler (New York: Columbia University Press, 1939); Carl J. Friedrich, ed., *Inevitable Peace* (Cambridge: Harvard University Press, 1948), includes Kant's essay "Eternal Peace."

26. Henry Wheaton, *Elements of International Law,* 76, 78. Ray Stannard Baker, *American Chronicle* (New York: C. Scribner's Sons, 1945), 83. On American perceptions of the "old world" of Europe as corrupt and decayed, see also Rodgers, *Atlantic Crossings,* 1, which led me to Baker's useful quotation.

27. The witness, Lyel Clark Van Hyning, was president of an advocacy group called "We the Mothers Mobilize for America, Inc." of Chicago, speaking at the Hearings on the UN Charter to the Senate Foreign Relations Committee. US Senate, 1945, Committee on Foreign Relations, *The Charter of the United Nations for the Maintenance of International Peace and Security, Submitted by the President of the United States on July 2, 1945: Hearings.* 79th Cong., 1st sess., part 5 (unrevised), July 13, 1945: 507–509. Note that left-liberal commentators also used the image of European power politics in their rhetoric. "It is really the old alliance and balance of power theory that has failed over and over again down the centuries," wrote a disappointed UN advocate quoted in Divine, *Second Chance,* 126.

28. On the development of international technical cooperation, see Leonard Woolf, *International Government* (New York: Brentano's, 1916), 153ff; Paul S. Reinsch, *Public International Unions* (Boston: World Peace Foundation, 1911); Lyman C. White, *International Non-Governmental Organizations* (New York: Greenwood, 1968).

29. Zimmern, *The League of Nations and the Rule of Law,* 85; Willard Range, *Franklin D. Roosevelt's World Order* (Athens: University of Georgia Press, 1959), 162–170; Sumner Welles, *Seven Decisions That Shaped History,* 176; Eleanor Roosevelt, *Autobiography* (New York: Harper, 1961), 101.

30. Karl Loewenstein, "The Serpent in Dumbarton Oaks: What Is a Peace-Loving State?" *Current History* 8 (Apr. 1945): 310–316, 310; Sidney B. Fay, "The Dumbarton Oaks Conference: How Can We Organize for Postwar Peace?" *Current History* 7 (Oct. 1944): 257–264, 258.

31. See John Milton Cooper, Jr., *Breaking the Heart of the World: Woodrow Wilson and the Fight for the League of Nations,* 405–408.

32. Franklin Roosevelt, "Plan to Preserve World Peace," rpt. in Eleanor Roosevelt, *This I Remember,* 353–366. FDR did not enter the Peace Prize contest in the end, sponsored by Edward Bok, a former editor of the *Ladies' Home Journal,* because Eleanor Roosevelt was one of the jurors. Secretary of the New York Peace Society and retired professor of history at MIT Charles H. Levermore won with an essay calling for the "progressive cooperation with the organized world, sustained by the moral force of public opinion and by developing law." Esther Everett Lape, ed., *Ways to Peace* (New York: C. Scribner's Sons, 1924), 447.

33. Evan Luard, *A History of the United Nations: The Years of Western Domination,*

1945–1955, 1: 5–6, 15; Keynes correspondence, quoted in Skidelsky, *John Maynard Keynes,* 3: 30, 32, 34.

34. See Acheson, *Present at the Creation,* 12.

35. See the excellent discussion of international legal scholar Hersch Lauterpacht's thought on issues of the relationship of international law to politics in Koskenniemi, *Gentle Civilizer of Nations;* Zimmern, *The League of Nations and the Rule of Law,* 358; Oscar Schachter, "The Twilight Existence of Non-Binding International Agreements," *AJIL* 81 (1977): 296.

36. Luard, *History of the United Nations,* 1: 5–6; "International Organization after the War," rpt. in Robert E. Summers, ed., *Dumbarton Oaks,* 86.

37. Robert E. Asher, et al., *The United Nations and Promotion of the General Welfare* (Washington: Brookings Institution, 1957), chap. 1; Mangoldt and Rittberger, eds., *United Nations System.*

38. Herbert Hoover, *The Ordeal of Woodrow Wilson,* 302.

39. Poll published Mar. 5, 1941 (usually the questions were posed the preceding month). George H. Gallup, ed., *The Gallup Poll: Public Opinion 1935–1971,* v. 1, 1935–1948 (New York: Random House, 1972), 267.

40. Poll published July 6, 1942, "Postwar League of Nations," in *Gallup Poll,* 1: 340; poll published Mar. 24, 1943, "Postwar Role for the United States," in *Gallup Poll,* 1: 377; poll published June 5, 1943, "International Police Force," in *Gallup Poll,* 387–388. Lydgate, *What America Thinks,* designated as "overwhelming" a 60 percent majority for a proposition, with a majority between 55 and 60 percent considered "substantial." Lydgate was an editor with the American Institute of Public Opinion.

41. *New Yorker,* May 15, 1943, 11.

42. Henry A. Wallace, "The Price of Free World Victory," May 8, 1942; "The Reminiscences of Henry Agard Wallace," Columbia University Oral History, 1550; for an excellent discussion of the ideas of Wallace, Wendell Willkie, and Sumner Welles see Divine, *Second Chance,* 105–109.

43. Sales statistics quoted in Divine, *Second Chance,* 105; Willkie, *One World,* 12; Stettinius Papers, "First Draft of Dumbarton Oaks Diary," Box 241, Folder Sept. 19–30 1944, Tuesday, Sept. 19, 1944, 7; Thomas Knock, *To End All Wars: Woodrow Wilson and the Quest for a New World Order* (Princeton: Princeton University Press, 1995), 272; Welles, *The Time for Decision,* 3. On the continuing influence of Wilsonian ideals see, for example, David Steigerwald, *Wilsonian Idealism in America* (Ithaca: Cornell University Press, 1994); Frank Ninkovich, *The Wilsonian Century: US Foreign Policy since 1900* (Chicago: University of Chicago Press, 1999); David M. Kennedy, "What 'W' Owes to 'WW,'" *Atlantic Monthly,* Mar. 2005, 36–40.

44. See John C. Culver and John Hyde, *American Dreamer: A Life of Henry A. Wallace,* 123.

45. Luce and Luce correspondence quoted in Robert E. Herzstein, *Henry R. Luce: A Political Portrait of the Man Who Created the American Century* (New York: C. Scribner's Sons, 1994), 178, 179, 180.

46. The "quart of milk for every Hottentot" contretemps is described in Culver and Hyde, *American Dreamer,* 279–280; the phrase was so widely repeated by contemporaries that FDR apparently thought the line was actually part of Wallace's original speech.

47. Taft quoted in James T. Patterson, *Mr. Republican: A Biography of Robert A. Taft,* 288–289. As with many of Roosevelt's opponents, Taft tried to co-opt the language of the New Deal by framing his critique in the idiom of the Four Freedoms.

48. Editors of *Fortune, Time,* and *Life,* "An American Program for Joint Action," *Fortune* 28 (1942): 59–63. Henry Luce owned all of these magazines.

49. "Winning the War on the Spiritual Front," undated pamphlet, Commission to Study Organization of Peace files, Hoover Institution.

50. "Can U.S. Have Peace after This War?" *Ladies' Home Journal*, Aug. 1943, 24; advertisement for Eureka vacuums quoted in Cohen, *Consumer's Republic*, 74. See also Westbrook, "Fighting for the American Family."

51. Vandenberg, ed., *Private Papers of Senator Vandenberg*, 143.

52. Acheson, *Present at the Creation*, 88, 64.

53. U.S. House of Representatives Resolution No. 114, Introduced by Representative J. W. Fulbright (Arkansas), passed Sept. 21, 1943, by a vote of 360 to 29; U.S. Senate Resolution No. 192, Introduced by Senator Tom Connally (Texas), passed Nov. 5, 1943, by a vote of 85 to 5; rpt. in *The Reference Shelf: Dumbarton Oaks*, 18: 97, 99–100.

54. *Gallup Poll* of June 27, 1943; Stettinius, "First Draft of Dumbarton Oaks Diary," Sept. 20, 1944, 21, describing the American Group at Dumbarton Oaks explicitly discussing poll results.

55. Churchill quoted in Dallek, *Franklin D. Roosevelt and American Foreign Policy*, 223.

56. For an explicit linkage of the terms and objectives of the United Nations Charter and the 1941 Atlantic Charter, see the introduction to Stettinius's official report on the results of the UN Charter negotiations at San Francisco, "Charter of the United Nations: Report to the President on the Results of the San Francisco Conference by the Chairman of the United States Delegation, the Secretary of State" (June 26, 1945), HST Papers, PSF Folder, Trips 1945, 21–22 (President's personal copy signed by Stettinius): After quoting the Atlantic Charter, Stettinius explains that it became the State Department's task during the war "to devise ways and means by which the United States could make its contribution toward the translation of these high purposes and ideals into an institutional structure of organized international relations."

57. Schild, *Bretton Woods and Dumbarton Oaks*, 141.

58. Donovan, *Roosevelt's Four Freedoms*, 106.

59. "Proposals for the Establishment of a General International Organization (The Dumbarton Oaks Proposals)," rpt. in "Texts of Statements on Dumbarton Oaks and Documents Giving Tentative Security Plans," *New York Times*, Oct. 10, 1944, 12.

60. Donovan, *Roosevelt's Four Freedoms*, 100.

61. *Stettinius Diaries*, 227, 238.

62. Donovan, *Roosevelt's Four Freedoms*, 97.

63. Stettinius, "First Draft of Dumbarton Oaks Diary," Wednesday, Sept. 20, 1944, 1914; Wednesday, Sept. 27, 1944, 9. Louis Henkin, "Human Rights from Dumbarton Oaks," in *The Dumbarton Oaks Conversations and the United Nations, 1944–1994*, ed. Ernest R. May and Angeliki E. Laiou, 97.

64. *Cadogan Diaries*, 669, noting that the speech was drafted by historian Charles K. Webster.

65. "Chinese Proposals on Dumbarton Oaks Proposals," *Documents of the United Nations Conference on International Organization, San Francisco, 1945*, vol. 3, *Dumbarton Oaks Proposals: Comments and Proposed Amendments*, 200; Hilderbrand, *Dumbarton Oaks*, 236–237. Wellington Koo had earned a doctorate at Columbia in 1912 and served as Nationalist China's Ambassador to Britain 1941–1946, ambassador to the United Nations 1944–1946, and ambassador to the United States 1945–1946.

66. Press Conference of Sept. 22, 1944, in Rosenman, *Working with Roosevelt*, 127; Stettinius, "First Draft of Dumbarton Oaks Diary," Friday, Sept. 22, 1944, 1.

67. Stettinius, "First Draft of Dumbarton Oaks Diary," Tuesday, Sept. 19, 1944, 4; Hilderbrand, *Dumbarton Oaks*, 243; Percy E. Corbett, Yale Institute of International

Studies Confidential Report, "The Dumbarton Oaks Plan," Nov. 25, 1944, Memorandum No. 13, 6.

6. Learning to Work Together by Working Together

1. Andrew W. Cordier, Division of International Security Affairs, Office of Special Political Affairs, Department of State, "A General Peace and Security Organization: Analysis of Its Major Functions," from a radio speech broadcast on the Southwest Radio Forum, Tulsa, Oklahoma, Feb. 17, 1945, rpt. in *USDSB* 12 (Feb. 18, 1945): 253–255; Editorial, "America and Dumbarton Oaks," *New Republic*, Mar. 12, 1945, 350–351; Editorial, "The Dumbarton Oaks Plan," *New Republic*, Oct. 23, 1944, 510–511.

2. Shotwell quotation and list of endorsers from "The Dumbarton Oaks Proposals," *World Affairs* 107 (Dec. 1944): 237–251; see also Walter Lippmann, "Pacification for Peace," *Atlantic Monthly*, Dec. 1944, 46–52.

3. Vera Micheles Dean, *The Four Cornerstones of Peace*, 6–7. The "four cornerstones" of the book's title were the Dumbarton Oaks, Chapultepec, Yalta, and San Francisco conferences.

4. Robert Divine indicates that Dewey's speech, delivered in Louisville, Kentucky, on Sept. 18, 1944, had been written by John Foster Dulles. Dewey quoted in Divine, *Second Chance*, 235.

5. Franklin Roosevelt, 1944, *PPA*, 13: 284–285; 290.

6. *PPA*, 1944, 13: 344–345, 348–350; prominent isolationists losing seats in 1944 included Senator Gerald P. Nye of North Dakota and Representatives Hamilton Fish of New York and Stephen A. Day of Illinois. Newly elected internationalist politicians included William Fulbright of Arkansas (elected to the Senate for the first time) and Leverett Saltonstall of Massachusetts. The Roosevelt administration was mindful of the World War I–era contrast with Woodrow Wilson, who had asked for the "mandate" of a Democratic Congress (and had not received it) to help him negotiate and ratify the Paris peace negotiations. Editorial in the *Nation,* Nov. 11, 1944, 573–574.

7. E. B. White essay of Oct. 21, 1944, rpt. in his *Wild Flag*, 40; Norman Thomas, "Something Better than Dumbarton Oaks," speech broadcast over CBS radio network on Mar. 10, 1945, excerpts rpt. in Summers, ed., *Dumbarton Oaks*, 131; *Congressional Record*, Jan. 6, 1945; Archibald MacLeish, "Popular Relations and the Peace," address at the annual meeting of the Association of American Colleges, Atlantic City, New Jersey, Jan. 10, 1945 (Washington, DC: US GPO 1945).

8. Editorial, *Nation*, Oct. 21, 1944, 451.

9. Dean, *Four Cornerstones*, 47; Dana G. Munro, "The Mexico City Conference and the Inter-American System," *USDSB* 12 (Apr. 1, 1945): 525; Leo S. Rowe, "Report on the Inter-American Conference on Problems of War and Peace," *Bulletin of the Pan American Union* 79 (May 1945): 249.

10. First International Conference of American States, Washington DC, 1890 (advocating the adoption of an arbitration model for regional dispute resolution); Second Conference, Mexico City, 1901–2 (adhering to the Hague Conventions of 1899 for pacific adjustment of international disputes); Third Conference, Rio de Janeiro, 1906 (adopting conventions on the codification of international law); Fourth Conference, Buenos Aires, 1910 (adopting the title of "Pan American Union" for the ongoing conference system); Fifth Conference, Santiago, 1923 (establishing a commission of inquiry for intractable conflicts); Sixth Conference, Havana, 1928 (censuring US interventions); Seventh Conference, Montevideo, 1933 (condemning intervention by one state in the internal affairs of another); Eighth Conference, Buenos Aires, 1936 (Additional Protocol Relative to Non-Intervention); Havana Declaration of 1940 (directed against a non-American aggressor). Pan Amer-

ican Union Notes, "Reply to the Request of the Argentine Government," *Bulletin of the Pan American Union* 79 (Mar. 1945): 153; R. A. Humphries, *The Evolution of Modern Latin America* (New York: Oxford University Press, 1946).

11. Pan American Union, *Inter-American Conference on Problems of War and Peace*; Olive Holmes, "The Mexico City Conference and Regional Security," *Foreign Policy Reports* 21 (May 1, 1945): 44–45; David Green, *The Containment of Latin America: A History of the Myths and Realities of the Good Neighbor Policy* (Chicago: Quadrangle, 1971).

12. "Synopsis of Essential Observations Made by the Mexican Delegation on the Dumbarton Oaks Proposals," Inter-American Conference on Problems of War and Peace (Conference of Chapultepec), Feb. 25, 1945, Box 9, Conference File, Papers of Leo Pasvolsky, LC; Editorial in *El Universal* (Mexico), Feb. 28, 1945, 8; US Department of State, *Report of the Delegation of the United States of America to the Inter-American Conference on Problems of War and Peace, Mexico City, Mexico, Feb. 21–Mar. 8, 1945* (Washington, DC: US GPO 1945). See also *FRUS, 1945*, 9: 29, 51.

13. Pan American Union, *Inter-American Conference*, 5; Dean, *Four Cornerstones*, 39–52.

14. Pan American Union, *Inter-American Conference*, 9–10; Holmes, "The Mexico City Conference"; British Commonwealth Conference, *Yearbook of the United Nations 1946–1947*, Department of Public Information, United Nations (Lake Success, NY: 1947), 10; *United Nations Conference on International Organization (UNCIO): Selected Documents*, Department of State Publication No. 2490 (Washington, DC: USGPO, 1946), 94–99; Lauren, *Evolution of International Human Rights*, 168–169.

15. Karl Loewenstein, "The Serpent in Dumbarton Oaks: What Is a Peace-loving State?" *Current History* 8 (Apr. 1945): 310, 315; Broadus Mitchell, "Statement on Dumbarton Oaks," rpt. in *International Conciliation* 409 (Mar. 1945): 166; "Text of Senator Vandenberg's Oaks Memorandum," *New York Times*, Apr. 2, 1945, 11.

16. *Congressional Record*, Jan. 10, 1945, 164–167.

17. *Time*, Jan. 22, 1945, 15; *New Republic*, Jan. 22, 1945, 103. Vandenberg, ed., *Private Papers of Senator Vandenberg*, 139; *Congressional Record*, Jan. 15, 1945.

18. A. Merriman Smith, *Thank You, Mr. President: A White House Notebook* (New York: Harper, 1946), 160, 165–166.

19. Quoted in Edward R. Stettinius, Jr., *Roosevelt and the Russians: The Yalta Conference*, 123.

20. Vladimir O. Pechatnov, "The Big Three after World War II: New Documents on Soviet Thinking about Post War Relations with the United States and Britain," Working Paper No. 13, Cold War International History Project (July 1995); Diane Shaver Clemens, *Yalta* (New York: Oxford University Press, 1970); Russell, *History of the United Nations Charter*, 515–551.

21. See *FRUS, Malta and Yalta, 1945*: 969–973.

22. Jan Karski, *The Great Powers and Poland, 1919–1945: From Versailles to Yalta* (Lanham: University Press of America, 1985), 525–531; Dallek, *Franklin D. Roosevelt and American Foreign Policy*, 513.

23. Norman N. Naimark, *The Russians in Germany: A History of the Soviet Zone of Occupation, 1945–1949* (Cambridge: Harvard University Press, 1995); Anne Applebaum, *Gulag* (New York: Random House, 2003), 436–437; see also Elena Zubkova, *Russia after the War: Hopes, Illusions, and Disappointments, 1945–1957* (New York: M. E. Sharpe, 1998), 105–106.

24. Text of Roosevelt's address, *USDSB* 12 (Mar. 4, 1945): 321–326; Vandenberg quoted in Russell, *History of the United Nations Charter*, 544–545.

25. S. Schlesinger, *Act of Creation*, 61–62.

26. *FRUS, Malta and Yalta, 1945*: 970.

27. On Churchill's hardheaded approach to "horse-trading" with Stalin, see Albert Resis, "The Churchill-Stalin Secret 'Percentages' Agreement on the Balkans, Moscow, Oct. 1944," *American Historical Review* 83 (Apr. 1978): 368–387. Churchill and Stalin had informally negotiated an arrangement over "spheres of influence" four months before the Yalta conference, whereby the British would exercise a 90 percent influence in Greece while the Soviets would by design have 90 percent of the influence over Romania, 75 percent over Bulgaria, and 50 percent in Hungary and Yugoslavia. See also Warren F. Kimball, *Forged in War: Roosevelt, Churchill, and the Second World War* (New York: W. Morrow, 1997), 290.

28. Romulo, *Forty Years*, 41, 7, 15. Romulo went on to serve as the Philippine foreign minister and as the first Asian president of the UN General Assembly. He had garnered a Pulitzer prize for a 1941 series of journalistic essays predicting the end of colonialism. On criticism of FDR "selling out" at Yalta, see Sherwood, *Roosevelt and Hopkins*, 875.

29. Roosevelt to Pepper, Apr. 9, 1945, FDR, Papers as President, OF 3575, FDRPL.

30. Arnold A. Offner, *Another Such Victory: President Truman and the Cold War, 1945–1953*, xii, 4–5, 7, 23; S. Schlesinger, *Act of Creation*, 4–6; Sherwood, *Roosevelt and Hopkins*, 881–882.

31. *New York Times*, Apr. 15, 1945, 1; *USDSB* 12 (Apr. 22, 1945): 722.

32. Oliver Lundquist of the Office of Strategic Services and the Broadway designer Jo Mielziner staged the Opera House for the opening ceremony. (Mielziner was at the same time designing the sets and lighting for the musical *Carousel*.) *New York Times*, Apr. 26, 1945, 1; Nicholas J. Cull, "Selling Peace: The Origins, Promotion, and Fate of the Anglo-American New Order during the Second World War," *Diplomacy and Statecraft* 7 (Mar. 1996): 22.

33. S. Schlesinger, *Act of Creation*, 102–103.

34. The Signal Security Agency intercepted diplomatic cables and staffed a listening post at the US army base at the Presidio while the FBI focused on American lobbying groups; see S. Schlesinger, *Act of Creation*, 93–110; David Alvarez, *Secret Messages: Code-Breaking and American Diplomacy, 1930–1945* (Lawrence: University Press of Kansas, 2000); for accounts supporting Hiss's guilt, see White, *Alger Hiss's Looking-Glass Wars*, and Allen Weinstein, *Perjury: The Hiss-Chambers Case* (New York: Random House, 1997). For materials supporting skepticism about Hiss's guilt, see the NYU-hosted website "The Alger Hiss Story: Search for Truth," http://homepages.nyu.edu/~th15/home.html. On Harry White, who testified before the House Un-American Activities Committee shortly before his death in 1948, see R. Bruce Craig, *Treasonable Doubt: The Harry Dexter White Spy Case* (Lawrence: University Press of Kansas, 2004), concluding that the most serious charges against White cannot be substantiated.

35. Romulo, *Forty Years*, 1, 8, 34, 63.

36. Russell, *History of the United Nations Charter*, 542–543.

37. The UN convenors did not invite Iceland, on the other hand, which decided not to declare war. Nor did they at first invite Denmark, which, unlike most West European countries, had no government-in-exile. But when Denmark was liberated during the conference, it was immediately admitted. Ibid., 508, 537, 626. See also Luard, *A History of the United Nations*, 1: 41.

38. The presidency of an international conference traditionally would go to the host state. It may also in some cases be allocated to the initiating country, as in the Hague Conferences of 1899 and 1907. Russell, *History of the United Nations Charter*, 634–638. On East-West contretemps generally at the UN conference, see S. Schlesinger, *Act of Creation*, 93–243.

39. Russell, *History of the United Nations Charter*, 732–733.

40. Alexander Cadogan, letter of May 15, 1945, *Cadogan Diaries*, 742; Romulo, *Forty Years*, 9, 21–22.

41. Russell, *History of the United Nations Charter*, 771–772; "Text of Senator Vandenberg's Oaks Memorandum," *New York Times,* Apr. 2, 1945, 11; New Zealand Department of External Affairs, *United Nations Conference on International Organization: Report on the Conference held at San Francisco, 25 Apr.–26 June 1945*, Publication No. 11 (1945), 28.

42. Russell, *History of the United Nations Charter*, 666–668; 675–676.

43. See *UNCIO: Selected Documents*, append. 2, Table of Correspondence between the [UN] Charter and Dumbarton Oaks Proposals, 989–991.

44. Charter of the UN preamble, in *UNCIO: Selected Documents*, 1035. Contrast the UN preamble with the more traditional opening of the Covenant of the League of Nations: "The High Contracting Parties, in order to promote international co-operation and to achieve international peace and security . . . agree to this Covenant of the League of Nations." League of Nations Covenant reprinted in *UNCIO: Selected Documents*, 978–989.

45. UN Charter, Article 1 in *UNCIO: Selected Documents*, 1036.

46. Dumbarton Oaks draft proposals, in *UNCIO: Selected Documents*, 375.

47. Ibid. On the role of anticolonial activists in discrediting colonialism by positing alternative norms of self-determination, see Robert H. Jackson, "The Weight of Ideas in Decolonization," in Goldstein and Keohane, ed., *Ideas and Foreign Policy*, 111–138.

48. *UNCIO: Selected Documents*, 382. On Roosevelt's attitudes toward trusteeship, which he liked to extrapolate from the Philippine model of progress toward self-government over the first half of the twentieth century, see the discussion in Mark Philip Bradley, *Imagining Vietnam and America: The Making of Postcolonial Vietnam, 1919–1950* (Chapel Hill: University of North Carolina Press, 2000), 74–81.

49. Russell, *History of the United Nations Charter*, 834.

50. United Nations Charter, article 76, in *UNCIO: Selected Documents*, 1047–1048; Russell, *History of the United Nations Charter*, 834, 836; Rayford Logan critique summarized in Von Eschen, *Race against Empire*, 82.

51. *UNCIO: Selected Documents*, 808–822; Romulo, *Forty Years*, 33.

52. *UNCIO: Selected Documents*, 808–822.

53. *UNCIO* Commission II, General Assembly Committee 4 (Trusteeship System), May 27, 1945.

54. United Nations Charter, articles 73 and 74, in *UNCIO: Selected Documents*, 1047.

55. Chairman of the United States Delegation, the Secretary of State, *Charter of the United Nations: Report to the President on the Results of the San Francisco Conference*, June 26, 1945, Appendix C, 264, Truman Papers, President's Secretary's File, HSTPL; for British reactions, see Kirsten Sellars, *The Rise and Rise of Human Rights*, 9–10.

56. *Charter of the United Nations: Report to the President*, Appendix C, 262–266; Von Eschen, *Race against Empire*, 79.

57. DuBois quoted in Paul Gordon Lauren, *Power and Prejudice: The Politics of Diplomacy and Racial Discrimination* (Boulder: Westview, 1988), 157; Metz T. P. Lochard, "Parley May Skip over Hot Issue of Colonies," *Chicago Defender,* May 5, 1945, 2, quoted in Von Eschen, *Race against Empire*, 78. Only one individual from each NGO with "consultant" status at San Francisco served as the actual consultant or head of delegation, and NAACP Executive Director Walter White served as the official consultant for the NAACP. DuBois and the educator and NAACP Vice-President Mary McLeod Bethune served as the "associate" consultants. *Charter of the United Nations: Report to the President*, Appendix C, 264.

58. Walter White quoted in Sellars, *Rise and Rise*, 10; Joseph M. Proskauer, *A Segment of My Times* (New York: Farrar, Straus, 1950), 225.

59. *Charter of the United Nations: Report to the President*, 27–31; Sellars, *Rise and*

Rise, 1–5; William Korey, *NGOs and the Universal Declaration of Human Rights: A Curious Grapevine*, 29.

60. Loewenstein, "Serpent in Dumbarton Oaks," 314–315; United Nations Charter, article 2(7).

61. Dulles quoted in Bruno Simma et al., eds., *The Charter of the United Nations: A Commentary*, 2nd ed., 2 vols. (New York: Oxford University Press, 2002) 1: 150; Jessup quoted in Lauren, *Evolution of International Human Rights*, 192. See also Louis Henkin, "Human Rights and Domestic Jurisdiction," in *Human Rights, International Law and the Helsinki Accord*, ed. Thomas Buergenthal (Montclair: Universe Books, 1977), 21–40.

62. United Nations Charter, article 51, in *UNCIO: Selected Documents*, 1043–1044; for an excellent analysis of the genesis of this provision, see Offner, *Another Such Victory*, 38–40.

63. Loewenstein, "Serpent in Dumbarton Oaks," 315; Lauren, *Evolution of International Human Rights*, 191.

64. "Dumbarton Oaks Proposals Exclude Colonies—DuBois" *Baltimore Afro-American*, Oct. 28, 1944, 3, as quoted in Von Eschen, *Race against Empire*, 75. See also W. E. B. DuBois, *Color and Democracy: Colonies and Peace* (New York: Harcourt Brace, 1945); David Levering Lewis, *W. E. B. DuBois: The Fight for Equality and the American Century, 1919–1963* (New York: Henry Holt, 2000), 503–509; Romulo, *Forty Years*, 51–52.

7. The Limits of Law

1. Major Neave had escaped from the supposedly escape-proof Nazi prison in Colditz Castle, Saxony, a feat which so impressed the senior members of London's Middle Temple that they waived his final Bar examinations. He had learned German as an exchange student in Berlin in 1933, when he had unwittingly participated in a Nazi youth march. His memoir, although not published until the late 1970s, was based on his contemporaneous notes and on a memo he filed with the Nuremberg Tribunal in 1945. Airey Neave, "Memorandum for the General Secretary of the International Military Tribunal," Oct. 24, 1945, PRO/LCO 2 2982 x/LO6978. See Neave, *Nuremberg: A Personal Record of the Trial of the Major Nazi War Criminals in 1945–6*, 17–18, 21.

2. Throughout this study, "Nuremberg" refers to the trial of 22 top-ranking Nazi leaders held in the Palace of Justice at Nuremberg in 1945–46; for published transcripts, see *IMT*. In addition, between 1946 and 1948, 12 other US-sponsored war crimes trials were held at Nuremberg; roughly 200 so-called second-tier Nazis, such as judges, industrialists, police, doctors, and scientists were prosecuted, resulting in 18 executions and 38 acquittals, with the remainder receiving lesser sentences. The transcripts of these later trials are published as *Trials of War Criminals before the Nuremberg Tribunals under Control Council Law No. 10, October 1946–April 1949*; see also Germany (Territory under Allied Occupation, 1945–1955: US Zone), Office of Military Government, Office of the Chief of Counsel for War Crimes, *Final Report to the Secretary of the Army on Nuremberg War Crimes Trials under Control Council Law No. 10*. With minor variations, these "secondary" Nuremberg trials were governed by the same charter as the main trial. In the Far Eastern theater, the Tokyo trial of 28 Japanese leaders was also governed by a charter virtually identical to the one at Nuremberg.

3. Neave, *Personal Record*, 49, 53.

4. Major Neave's perception of the defendants was clearly influenced by his preliminary Krupp investigation, which indicated that the Krupp family and its business directors had enthusiastically abused over 70,000 foreign-born workers, many of them Hungarian-Jewish children. Neave was especially shocked to learn that the exploitation of this forced

labor had been voluntary—"even Hitler was surprised that a company like Krupp would insist on doing so"—and that the Krupp family and its senior employees "expressed no regret for anything" at any time. Neave, *Personal Record,* 58, 39–41. Gustav Krupp von Bohlen und Halbach had been named as a defendant at the main Nuremberg trial but did not appear due to ill health. "Motion on behalf of Defendant Gustav Krupp von Bohlen for postponement of the Trial as to him, and action taken thereon," *IMT,* 1: 124ff. Krupp's son, Alfried, was ultimately tried and convicted of crimes against humanity at one of the later Nuremberg trials, in 1947–48.

5. The Nuremberg Charter is appended to the London Agreement of Aug. 8, 1945 (Agreement by the Government of the United States, the Provisional Government of the French Republic, the Government of the United Kingdom of Great Britain and Northern Ireland, and the Government of the Union of Soviet Socialist Republics for the Prosecution and Punishment of Major War Criminals of the European Axis), *IMT,* 1: 8–16. "Criminal Organizations" was intended to denote identifiable groups with voluntary membership, such as the Geheime Staatspolizei (Gestapo), the Schutzstaffeln der Nationalsozialistischen Deutschen Arbeiterpartei (SS), and, most controversially, the German General Staff and High Command of the German Armed Forces.

6. Nuremberg Charter, article 6.

7. Telford Taylor, *The Anatomy of the Nuremberg Trials: A Personal Memoir,* 76. Taylor was an assistant prosecutor at Nuremberg and later the chief prosecutor of the "secondary" Nuremberg trials.

8. Taylor's characterization of the indictment refers to the astonishing lack of coordination among that document's four drafting committees. Taylor, *Anatomy,* 116–117; see also his description of the vicissitudes of the indictment's drafting process, ibid., 79–118. The New Deal lawyer and former intelligence officer's main criticism concerned not so much the text of the indictment itself as his sense that the underlying "task of selecting the defendants was hastily and negligently discharged." Ibid., 90, 92, 116–117; Indictment in *IMT,* 1: 27–92. Of the 24 individual defendants listed in the indictment, former leader of the Labor Front Robert Ley committed suicide, and Hitler's Deputy for Nazi Party Affairs Martin Bormann, who was never captured, was tried in absentia. Krupp, as noted, was declared unfit to stand trial.

9. Neave, *Personal Record,* 62.

10. Robert E. Conot, *Justice at Nuremberg,* 21, 60, 35; Neave, *Personal Record,* 70, 77; author interview with Nuremberg interpreter Edith Simon Coliver, Apr. 24, 1998.

11. Ley, an alcoholic, had shredded his towel into a rope and attached it to the pipe above the toilet in his cell. See prison psychologist Gustave M. Gilbert's *Nuremberg Diary,* entry for Oct. 24, 1945, 8; Taylor, *Anatomy,* 65, 132, 229–230; Ronald Smelser, *Robert Ley: Hitler's Labor Front Leader.* Rudolf Hess, Hitler's deputy for Nazi Party matters, had famously flown himself across the English Channel in a stolen Messerschmidt on May 10, 1941, and crash-landed in Scotland. Hess claimed he had undertaken his daring flight in order to broker a behind-the-scenes peace, after he became convinced that Germany's situation was hopeless. British officials discounted his story and confined him to house arrest in Britain for four years before turning him over to Allied captors at Nuremberg for trial. British lawyers and doctors advised the American warden that Hess was "as crazy as a Betsy bug." Hess insisted that the British had been trying to poison him and that he was unable to remember events more than two weeks in the past from any given present day. Neave, *Personal Record,* 45; Psychiatrists' Report and accompanying Petition in *IMT,* 1: 155–167; Robert G. Storey, *Final Judgment: Pearl Harbor to Nuremberg,* 141–146. This idiosyncratic memoir by the US executive trial counsel and document chief at Nuremberg, although published in 1966, was compiled from notes taken at the time, according to its author.

12. Neave, *Personal Record*, 19, 59, 70, 76; "Memorandum to Justice Jackson, Sept. 28, 1945," papers of Colonel Burton Andrus, privately held by Joseph E. Persico, cited in Persico, *Nuremberg: Infamy on Trial*, 57; see also Taylor, *Anatomy*, 230.

13. Eugene Davidson, *The Trial of the Germans: An Account of the Twenty-Two Defendants before the International Military Tribunal at Nuremberg*, 59. See also Gilbert's article, "Hermann Goering, Amiable Psychopath," *Journal of Abnormal and Social Psychology* 46 (Apr. 1948): 211; Victor H. Bernstein, *Final Judgment: The Story of Nuremberg*, 3. Regarding the unusual plebiscite, Bernstein, an American journalist who covered the Nuremberg trial for the liberal New York newspaper *PM*, went on to observe dryly that "the competition is not great, it is true." *Final Judgment*, 4.

14. Neave, *Personal Record*, 75, 71; Rebecca West, *A Train of Powder*, 6, 67. Colonel Andrus, who had also been the commandant of the Bad Mondorf prison, immediately put Goering on a diet and weaned him off his addiction to codeine. By the end of the trial he had lost 160 pounds. "Goering Cured of Drugs as Trial Nears: In Perfect Health for Ordeal at Nuernberg," United Press Wire Service, clipping from the *Rocky Mountain News*, Saturday, Sept. 8, 1945, 2, Katharine Fite Letters File, HSTPL; Storey, *Final Judgment* 137, 140. Conot, *Justice*, 31, 32–33.

15. Goering had been awarded the coveted *Pour le Mérite* for his service in the First World War, Germany's highest wartime honor. See Edwin P. Hoyt, *Angels of Death: Goering's Luftwaffe* (New York: Forge, 1994), 34–36. Nor was this "courtliness" confined to the air war; see generally, Stanley Weintraub, *Silent Night: The Story of the World War I Christmas Truce*; Ronald Smelser and Rainer Zitelmann, ed., *The Nazi Elite*.

16. Persico, *Infamy*, 50–51; Burton C. Andrus, *The Infamous of Nuremberg*, 29–31, 34; Neave, *Personal Record*, 75.

17. See "Minutes of the Opening Session of the Tribunal at Berlin, 18 Oct. 1945," in *IMT*, 1: 24–26. The preliminary session of the Tribunal had been held in Berlin as a sop to the Soviet delegation, which had unsuccessfully lobbied both for Berlin to serve as the seat of the entire proceedings and for the presidency of the Tribunal to rotate among the four judges. The Soviet representative on the Tribunal, Major General Ion Timifeevich Nikitchenko, an army judge advocate and vice president of the Soviet Supreme Court, served as Tribunal president for this lone session in Berlin, while Lord Justice Lawrence, the British judge, served as president for the duration of the actual trial in Nuremberg; Neave *Personal Record*, 74–75; Taylor, *Anatomy*, 64–65, 98–99, 123–126.

18. "I asked each of the defendants to autograph my copy of the indictment with a brief statement giving his opinion of it" in order to "crystallize . . . their first spontaneous reactions." Gilbert, *Nuremberg Diary*, 2.

19. Neave, *Personal Record*, 59–60, 76.

20. Papers of Murray C. Bernays, Box 1, Bernays to his wife, June 10, 1945, University of Wyoming, American Heritage Center. "The Nazis were maniacs who plastered history with the cruelty which is a waste product of man's moral nature, as maniacs on a smaller scale plaster their bodies and their clothes with excreta." West, *Train of Powder*, 69. This language is reminiscent of Nazi language about the role of Jews in German society. See entries relating to Nazi propagandist Julius Streicher, in Gilbert, *Nuremberg Diary*, 9–10, 38, 41, 73–74, 117, 125–126. For a more sensationalist treatment, see Randall L. Bytwerk, *Julius Streicher* (New York: Stein and Day, 1983).

21. West, *Train of Powder*, 9. The French and Soviet delegations were smaller than the British one; but the American delegation numbered over 600 people, including 150 lawyers, and totaled well over a thousand, counting the military personnel. Telephone Directory, International Military Trials, Nürnberg, Dec. 1945, Katharine B. Fite Letters, HSTPL; Taylor, *Anatomy*, 213; Conot, *Justice*, 60. Assistant prosecutor Taylor also described what he saw as the "colonialism" of the atmosphere of the Nuremberg enclave, an evanescent interna-

tional community of judges, lawyers, interpreters, secretaries, journalists, military officials of all ranks, a local German population, and of course the defendants themselves, with a smattering of visiting VIPs thrown in for good measure. Taylor, *Anatomy*, 208. West explained that among the Allied forces at all levels, "eccentrics . . . were replacing the more normal types as they were demobilized," *Train of Powder*, 33. West spent only the equivalent of about two weeks at the yearlong trial. Nevertheless her evocative accounts of the trial's atmosphere are unsurpassed.

22. Conot, *Justice*, 58. Katharine Fite, a State Department lawyer specializing in "Nazi criminality" at Nuremberg, educated at Vassar and Yale Law School, wrote to her parents about how "we are in a wild rush with briefs due a week from tomorrow . . . I don't see how we can be ready for the 20th . . . we are carrying the mammoth share." Letter of Nov. 3, 1945, Fite Letters, HSTPL; Taylor similarly wrote of the "frenetic madness" of the trial's preparatory work, *Anatomy*, 174.

23. Both Simon and West drew on personal experience: Simon had an affair with Victor Bernstein, a married American journalist twenty-one years her senior; she ghostwrote large portions of his book, *Final Judgment*. West had an affair with Francis Biddle, former US attorney general and the American judge at Nuremberg. Edith Simon Coliver, interview with the author, Apr. 24, 1998; Edith Helga Simon, unpublished diary, "Judgment Day: Justice: My Trip to the Nuremberg Trials," entries for Oct. 21, 1945, 9; Oct. 27, 1945, 16; Nov. 10, 1945, 26; Nov. 12, 1945, 27; unpub. ms. on file with the author; West, *Train of Powder*, 13–14; Taylor, *Anatomy*, 547; Neave, *Personal Record*, 54.

24. West, *Train of Powder*, 43–44, 11, 10, 45.

25. Political scientist Gary Bass has argued compellingly that the term "crimes against humanity" was first formulated as an indictable offense at the abortive 1920 British-run courts martial of so-called Young Turks for massacres of Armenians in 1915. Bass, *Stay the Hand*, 106. None of the preparatory legal memos I have reviewed for the Nuremberg Charter mention this precedent (including the British materials), and Bass notes as much in his own analysis of Nuremberg. It seems more likely that the Nuremberg legal advisors believed they were deriving the term directly from the so-called Martens clause of the Fourth Hague Convention of 1907, which invoked "the principles of the law of nations, as they result from the usages established among civilized peoples, from the laws of humanity, and the dictates of the public conscience." *Fourth Hague Convention Respecting the Laws and Customs of War on Land* (1907), rpt. in Adam Roberts and Richard Guelff, ed., *Documents on the Laws of War*, 45.

26. On the Atlantic Charter and Four Freedoms as touchstones for US wartime propaganda regarding war aims and postwar aspirations, both within the United States and internationally, see, for example, OWI pamphlet series, *Textes de la Liberté: Declarations officielles faites au cours de l'histoire des États-Unis*, Library Service Division, US Office of Education, 1944 (featuring "Les Quatres Libertés" and "La Charte de l'Atlantique"); N. Ben-Horim, *The American Soldier's Moral Guide* (New York: Printed by Shulsinger Bros., 1943), "as endorsed by the War Department and the Vice-President," and including both the Atlantic Charter and the Four Freedoms speech among its seven reprinted documents. Brigadier-General J. H. Morgan, *The Great Assize: An Examination of the Law of the Nuremberg Trials* (London: J. Murray, 1948), 1; Taylor, *Anatomy*, 639; John Gange, *American Foreign Relations: Permanent Problems and Changing Policies* (New York: Ronald, 1959), 258.

27. Roosevelt to Churchill, Feb. 29, 1944, *FRUS, 1944*, 1: 188–189.

28. Hoover, *Ordeal of Woodrow Wilson*, 191. Warren F. Kimball, *Swords or Ploughshares? The Morgenthau Plan for Defeated Nazi Germany, 1943–1946*, 44. See also Cooper, *Breaking the Heart of the World*.

29. Although Hull had indicated to FDR that he wished to retire earlier, the president

had prevailed on his longest-serving cabinet member to stay at least until after the election. Hull accordingly announced his resignation on Nov. 27, 1944.

30. War Department Handbook of Military Government for Germany, Aug. 1944, attached to Morgenthau's Memorandum for the President, Aug. 25, 1944, in Presidential Diaries Files, Morgenthau Papers, FDRPL, 1394–1396. See also FDR, "Memorandum to the Secretary of War," Aug. 26, 1944, noting that "this so-called 'Handbook' is pretty bad." *Morgenthau Diary (Germany)* 1: 443; Morgenthau, *Germany Is Our Problem*; Kimball, *Morgenthau Plan*, xxiii, 4.

31. Even after publicly backing away from Morgenthau's approach as the 1944 election neared, Roosevelt still encouraged the treasury secretary privately, even urging him to write a book on the subject. In his forthcoming biography of Henry Stimson, Sean Malloy argues that FDR's support was so wholehearted that the so-called "Morgenthau Plan" should more accurately be known as the "Roosevelt-Morgenthau Plan." Malloy, "The Reluctant Warrior: Henry L. Stimson and the Crisis of 'Industrial Civilization'"; Morgenthau, *Germany Is Our Problem*.

32. US Treasury Department, "Program to Prevent Germany from Starting a World War III," Sept. 9, 1944, in *FRUS, Quebec, 1944:* 131–140; this document also elaborated on a Sept. 5, 1944, memorandum from Morgenthau to FDR entitled "Suggested Post-Surrender Policy for Germany," in ibid., 101–106.

33. Robert Murphy, "Memorandum of Conversation with President Roosevelt" (Sept. 9, 1944), Papers of Robert Murphy, Roosevelt File, Box 52, Hoover Institution Archives. Robert Murphy was a State Department official who later became the political and diplomatic advisor to General Lucius D. Clay, chief administrator of the US Occupation Zone in post-surrender Germany. See also Blum, *Morgenthau Diaries*, 3: entry for Sept. 2, 1944, 397; Robert D. Murphy, *Diplomat among Warriors*.

34. Rees, *Harry Dexter White*, 239–265; Morgenthau, *Germany Is Our Problem*, 144; US Treasury Department, "Program to Prevent Germany from Starting a World War III," Sec. 7, "What To Do about German Education."

35. Kimball, *Morgenthau Plan*, 31; Morgenthau Diary, entry for Sept. 2, 1944, quoted in Blum, *Morgenthau Diaries*, 3: 353. The premise of a thoroughgoing restructuring of society by outside agents was in fact largely realized in the case of the US occupation of Japan. See John W. Dower, *Embracing Defeat: Japan in the Wake of World War II* (New York: Norton, 1999).

36. Henry L. Stimson Diaries, entry for Sept. 16–17, 1944 (hereafter *Stimson Diaries*). Stimson was likely the first to refer to Morgenthau's approach as "Carthaginian," an adjective that clung to the plan thereafter and was an evocation of John Maynard Keynes's assessment of the peace provisions of the First World War in Keynes's *Economic Consequences of the Peace*. *Stimson Diaries*, Sept. 16–17, 1944; "Memorandum from Stimson to Roosevelt," Sept. 15, 1944, in *FRUS, Quebec, 1944,* 482–485.

37. Drew Pearson broke the story on Sept. 21, 1944; see "Morgenthau Plan on Germany Splits Cabinet Committee," *New York Times*, Sept. 24, 1944, 1, 8. There is some debate about the identity of the leaker: leading contenders include Stimson himself, Cordell Hull, or head of the Office of War Mobilization and "assistant president," former Supreme Court Justice James F. Byrnes. See, for example, Kimball, *Morgenthau Plan*, 41, 43, suggesting it was most likely Byrnes. Steven Casey believes that it was most likely Hull, while Gary Bass seems to find the circumstantial case against Stimson to be more than suggestive. Steven Casey, *Cautious Crusade: Franklin D. Roosevelt, American Public Opinion, and the War against Nazi Germany*, 183; Bass, *Stay the Hand*, 168–169; Fred Smith, "The Rise and Fall of the Morgenthau Plan," *United Nations World* (Mar. 1947), clipping in Box 12, Bernstein Papers, HSTPL. Stimson biographer Sean Malloy believes that the leaker was un-

likely to have been Stimson personally but could have been a War Department subordinate such as John J. McCloy.

38. George F. Kennan, *Memoirs, 1925–1950,* 175.

39. The material in this paragraph and the next closely follow the excellent analysis of American public opinion in Casey, *Cautious Crusade,* 184–187, which also guided me to useful sources. I thank Susan Ferber, editor with Oxford University Press, for calling my attention to Casey's important work.

40. Arthur Krock, "Why Secretary Morgenthau Went to Quebec," *New York Times,* Sept. 22, 1944; Alfred F. Flynn, "Post-War Germany," *Wall Street Journal,* Sept. 23, 1944. Casey notes that "The AP article was a page-one lead story on Sept. 24 in a number of papers, including *Baltimore Sun, Chicago Tribune, New York Herald Tribune,* and *Washington Evening Star,*" *Cautious Crusade,* 263–264n. Editorial, "Samson in the Temple," *Washington Post,* Sept. 26, 1944; see also, Editorial, "Morgenthau's Plans for Germany," *Washington Times-Herald,* Sept. 26, 1944; "The German Industrial Machine," *PM,* Sept. 27, 1944; "Germans Are Aroused by Morgenthau Proposal," *Washington Post,* Sept. 26, 1944. Johnson quoted in Ted Lewis, "Morgenthau Plan Blamed for Stiffening of Nazis," *Washington Times-Herald,* Sept. 30, 1944; see also Ernest Lindley, "Future of Germany: Reaction to the Morgenthau Plan," *Washington Post,* Sept. 29, 1944. On presidential mail, see Casey's assessment in *Cautious Crusade,* 184–185.

41. FDR, "Memorandum for the Secretary of State," Sept. 29, 1944, Box 52, Murphy Papers. As late as Oct. 20, 1944, the president forwarded a memo to the secretary of state arguing that, as regards "the treatment of Germany . . . speed on these matters is not essential at the present moment . . . I dislike making detailed plans for a country we do not yet occupy." FDR, "Memorandum for the Secretary of State," Oct. 20, 1944, Murphy Papers.

42. See "Minutes of Tripartite Political Meeting, Dec. 1, 1943" in *FRUS, Teheran,* 600, 602–604; Kimball, *Morgenthau Plan,* 17. Note that all the major decision makers, including Stalin, also supported trials at one time or another. See, for example, document headed "Excerpts from a Telegram sent by Prime Minister Churchill to the President (Telegram No. 801, Oct. 22, 1944, received informally from British Embassy)," Murphy Papers, where Churchill notes, "On major war criminals Uncle Joe [Stalin] took an unexpected ultra-respectable line. There must be no executions without trial otherwise the world would say that we were afraid to try them. I pointed out the difficulties in international law but he replied that if there were no trials there must be no death sentences but only life-long confinements."

43. "Report of the Crimea Conference, Feb. 11, 1945," in *FRUS, Yalta,* 970–971. In addition, parallel secret protocols, not released until years later, apparently envisioned a dismemberment almost as thoroughgoing as that in the Treasury Department proposal, along with high reparations. Confidential provisions reprinted as "Protocol of the Proceedings of the Crimea Conference, Feb. 11, 1945," in *FRUS, Malta and Yalta,* 978–979.

44. Kimball, *Morgenthau Plan,* xiv; Robert Murphy, "Memorandum of Conversation with President Roosevelt, Sept. 9, 1944," Murphy Papers; Henry Morgenthau, "Memorandum of Conversation with Roosevelt, Aug. 19, 1944," Presidential Diaries, Morgenthau Papers, FDRPL, 1386–1388; "Memorandum of Conversation with Roosevelt and State Department Officials," in *FRUS, 1943,* 1: 542; "Roosevelt-Stalin Meeting, Feb. 4, 1945," *FRUS: Yalta,* 571. According to the minutes of this meeting, Roosevelt continued that "he hoped that Marshal Stalin would again propose a toast to the execution of 50,000 officers of the German Army."

45. General Lucius D. Clay to General John Hilldring (director of the War Department's Civil Affairs Division), May 7, 1945, in Jean Edward Smith, ed., *The Papers of General Lucius D. Clay, 1945–1949* (Bloomington: Indiana University Press, 1974), 1: 12. See

also Lucius D. Clay, *Decision in Germany*; Clay, "Proconsuls of a People, by Another People, for Both People," *Americans as Proconsuls: United States Military Government in Germany and Japan, 1944–1952*, ed. Robert D. Wolfe, 103–113.

46. Roosevelt had called for the "unconditional surrender" of the Axis regimes at a Jan. 24, 1943, press conference in the aftermath of the Casablanca Conference with Churchill. See Dallek, *Franklin D. Roosevelt and American Foreign Policy*, 373–376; see also Brian L. Villa, "The U.S. Army, Unconditional Surrender, and the Potsdam Proclamation," *Journal of American History* 63 (June 1976): 92.

47. Former US Secretary of State Henry Kissinger has written approvingly of Tsar Alexander's decision to banish Napolean to Elba: in Kissinger's estimation, the tsar and his fellow architects of the Concert of Europe system successfully "resisted the temptation of a punitive peace. This may have been due to the very quality which is usually considered their greatest failing: their indifference to popular pressures." Kissinger, *World Restored*, 139. Napoleon escaped from his initial banishment and was not truly exiled until he was dispatched to St. Helena. See Charles K. Webster, *The Foreign Policy of Castlereagh, 1812–1815: Britain and the Reconstruction of Europe*, and *Congress of Vienna*.

48. *FRUS, Yalta*, 971. See Gary Bass's argument about how domestic norms in liberal states also constrain international action in *Stay the Hand*, 21–23.

49. See Morgenthau's own defense of his approach published with Roosevelt's encouragement for a popular audience in *Germany Is Our Problem*, which Morgenthau published commercially in 1945.

50. A later section of this history summarizes some of the political maneuvering around finalizing the contours of the Nuremberg Charter, but a variety of secondary sources, both scholarly and popular, tell this story well and in greater detail. See, for example, Arieh J. Kochavi, *Prelude to Nuremberg: Allied War Crimes Policy and the Question of Punishment*; Conot, *Justice*; Ann Tusa and John Tusa, *The Nuremberg Trial* (Birmingham, AL: Notable Trials Library, 1990); Bradley F. Smith, *The American Road to Nuremberg: The Documentary Record, 1944–1945*. See also accounts by participants, such as Taylor, *Anatomy*, and Sydney S. Alderman, "Negotiating the Nuremberg Trial Agreements, 1945," in Raymond Dennet and Joseph E. Johnson, eds., *Negotiating with the Russians*; Peter Calvocoressi, *Nuremberg: The Facts, the Law, and the Consequences* (London: Chatto and Windus, 1947).

51. Robert H. Jackson, "Atrocities and War Crimes: Report from Robert H. Jackson to the President," June 7, 1945, Harry S. Truman Official File, HSTPL, War Crimes File, Document 1–2, at 6.

52. The *jus fetiale* constituted a part of the unwritten law of the Roman constitution whereby a special group of priests would determine whether a foreign nation had waged unjust warfare against the Romans. See Arthur Nussbaum, *A Concise History of the Law of Nations* (New York: MacMillan, 1962), 17; Coleman Phillipson, *The International Law and Custom of Ancient Greece and Rome*.

53. See St. Augustine's assessment that while every war is lamentable, particular kinds of wrongs suffered at the hands of adversaries resulted in "the necessity of waging just wars." St. Augustine, *De Civitate Dei Contra Paganos*, Book 19, sec. 7, trans. W. Greene, 6: 150–151. See also St. Thomas Aquinas, *Summa Theologiae*, Quaestio 40: 80–83; Francisco Suarez, *Selections from Three Works, De Triplici Virtute Theologia: Charitate*, Disputation 13, sec. 4, trans. G. Williams, 2: 817; Hugo Grotius, *De Jure Belli ac Pacis*, Book 2, sec. 23, 13, trans. F. Kelsey, 2: 565–566.

54. Hague Convention No. 4, Respecting the Laws and Customs of War on Land, Annex, article 22 (Oct. 18, 1907).

55. See Ebba Dahlin, *French and German Public Opinion on Declared War Aims, 1914–1918* (Stanford: Stanford University Press, 1933); Pierre Miquel, *La Paix de Ver-*

sailles et l'Opinion Publique Française (Paris: Flammarion, 1972); James F. Willis, *Prologue to Nuremberg: The Politics and Diplomacy of Punishing War Criminals of the First World War;* Bass, *Stay the Hand.* The Willis and Bass analyses led me to many of the sources in this and the following seven notes. Council of Ten Meeting (Jan. 17, 1919, 3 p.m.) in *FRUS, Paris Peace Conference, 1919,* 3: 169; Carnegie Endowment for International Peace, International Law Division, *Violations of the Laws and Customs of War: Report of the Majority and Dissenting Reports of the American and Japanese Members of the Commission on Responsibilities at the Conference of Paris, 1919,* Pamphlet No. 32: 18–23.

56. *Violations of the Laws and Customs of War,* 58; Bass, *Stay the Hand,* 59. Bass sometimes uses legalism as a synonym for idealism; in his analysis, the legalist position *favored* trying the defeated Germans. By contrast, I see the anti-trial arguments of Lansing and Scott as better expressing Shklar's (and my) conception of legalism—that is, subjecting the kaiser to trial would necessitate too many innovations and disruptions to established expectations, and so legalists such as Lansing and Scott opposed it. On legalism as idealism, see George F. Kennan, *American Diplomacy, 1900–1950* (New York: New American Library, 1951), 95; James Brown Scott, "The Trial of the Kaiser," in House and Seymour, eds., *What Really Happened at Paris,* 231–258. Lansing does not mention his minority report in his own memoir, *The Peace Negotiations: A Personal Memoir* (Boston: Houghton Mifflin, 1921), 33.

57. David Lloyd George speech of Nov. 29, 1918, reported in the *Times* of London, Nov. 30, 1918, 6; David Lloyd George, *Memoirs of the Peace Conference* (New Haven: Yale University Press, 1939), 1: 109.

58. Treaty of Versailles (June 28, 1919), article 227, 225 Consolidated Treaty Series 188, rpt. in Carnegie Endowment for International Peace, *The Treaties of Peace, 1919–1923.* The Netherlands had an "immemorial tradition" of sheltering asylum-seekers Willis, *Prologue,* 67, 101; Alan Palmer, *The Kaiser: Warlord of the Second Reich* (London: Weidenfeld and Nicolson, 1978), 212–213; for a summary of the even less-plausible alternative plans, see Bass, *Stay the Hand,* 77. See also Quincy Wright, "The Legal Liability of the Kaiser," *American Political Science Review* 13 (Feb. 1919): 120–128; T. H. Alexander, "They Tried to Kidnap the Kaiser and Brought Back an Ash Tray," *The Saturday Evening Post,* Oct. 23, 1937, 5.

59. Treaty of Versailles, Article 228; "British French and Italian Meeting, Paris, Jan. 15, 1920," *Documents on British Foreign Policy, 1919:* 886; Five Great Powers Meeting, Sept. 15, 1919, *FRUS, 1919, The Paris Peace Conference,* 8: 214; Bass, *Stay the Hand,* 78, 58.

60. Wilson, Lloyd George, and Clemenceau Meeting, May 5, 1919, *FRUS, 1919, The Paris Peace Conference,* 5: 470–471; Willis, *Prologue,* 134–135; Bass notes how the breakdown of even this small number of test cases was "proportionate to Allied suffering: sixteen from the Belgian list, eleven from the French, seven British, five Italian, and four from smaller countries." Bass, *Stay the Hand,* 80, 89. See also Ernest R. May, *The World War and American Isolation, 1914–1917* (Cambridge: Harvard University Press, 1966), 40–41.

61. See Bass, *Stay the Hand,* 81, 89; "Convicting Itself," *New York Times,* editorial for July 9, 1921, 7. See also W. M. Jordan, *Great Britain, France, and the German Problem, 1918–1939: A Study of Anglo-French Relations in the Making and Maintenance of the Versailles Settlement* (London: Oxford University Press, 1943), 70–71; Claud Mullins, *The Leipzig Trials: An Account of the War Criminals' Trials and a Study of German Mentality* (London: H.F. and G. Witherby, 1921).

62. Willis, *Prologue,* 141; British Foreign Office, Allied-German Negotiations on War Criminals, Dec. 9, 1922, quoted in Bass, *Stay the Hand,* 81.

63. League of Nations Covenant, article 16, appended to the Treaty of Versailles; Sixth

International Congress of American States, Havana (Feb. 18, 1928); Treaty of Mutual Guarantee between Germany, Belgium, France, Great Britain, and Italy, Locarno (Locarno Treaties, Oct. 16, 1925), *League of Nations Treaty Series* 88 (1926): 291; General Treaty for the Renunciation of War as an Instrument of National Policy, Paris (Kellogg-Briand Pact, Aug. 27, 1928), *League of Nations Treaty Series* 94 (1929): 57; Hogan, "War Criminals," *South Atlantic Quarterly* 45 (Oct. 1946): 418.

64. The Indian judge at the 1946–1948 Tokyo trial of defeated Japanese leaders, Radhabinod Pal, made this point with particular poignancy in a fascinating 1,235 page dissent. Pal illustrated the typeset version of his dissent with photographs of what he considered to be the supreme war crime, atomic destruction. See Pal, *International Military Tribunal for the Far East: Dissentient Judgment*, 38–40. ASIL, "Forty Years after the Nuremberg and Tokyo Tribunals: The Impact of the War Crimes Trials on International and National Law: Remarks by Richard A. Falk," *Proceedings* of the 80th Annual Meeting, 1986, 65. See also the headlines on the front page of the *New York Times,* Aug. 9, 1945, where "4 Powers Call Aggression Crime in Accord Covering War Trials" competes unsuccessfully for space with "Atom Bomb Loosed on Nagasaki." American forces bombed Nagasaki on Aug. 8 US time; because of the time difference, in Japan the bombing took place on Aug. 9.

8. Internationalizing New Deal Justice

1. See the Nuremberg Charter, appended to the London Agreement of Aug. 8, 1945, in *IMT,* preamble; Anglo-Soviet-American Conference, Moscow, 1943, "Declaration on General Security" in US Department of State, *The Axis in Defeat: A Collection of Documents on American Policy Toward Germany and Japan,* 4. See also "Declaration of German Atrocities," *USDSB* 9 (Nov. 6, 1943): 311; Cordell Hull, *The Memoirs of Cordell Hull,* 1: 128–129.

2. FDR, *PPA,* 1942, 330; Inter-Allied Information Committee, "Aide-Memoire from the United Kingdom," in *Punishment for War Criminals: The Inter-Allied Declaration Signed at St. James's Palace, London, on Jan. 13, 1942,* 4; and see generally Arieh Kochavi's excellent *Prelude to Nuremberg.*

3. *Declaration of St. James's,* 5–6; UNWCC, *History of the United Nations War Crimes Commission and the Development of the Laws of War.*

4. Churchill to Stalin and Roosevelt, Oct. 12, 1943, in *FRUS, 1943,* 1: 556–557; see David S. Wyman, *The Abandonment of the Jews: America and the Holocaust, 1941–1945,* 42, 72.

5. See, for example, the Aug. 1944 response to a NORC poll asking a sampling of Americans if a "widespread depression" should be anticipated within 10 years, with just over 50% responding "Yes, we will have a depression" and only 35.9% indicating "We will avoid it." When Republicans were asked this same question in Jan. 1945, 62.1% predicted widespread depression between 1945 and 1955. Cantril and Strunk, eds., *Public Opinion,* 1: 65–66.

6. Wyman, *Abandonment,* 189–190, 75, 256. Rosenman's lengthy political memoir does not mention Jews, the Holocaust, or the fact that its author was Jewish. This omission is particularly notable given that over half of the memoir focuses on the shaping of policy in the White House during the years 1941–1945, during which time Rosenman had almost daily access to the president. Furthermore, in Jan. and Feb. of 1945 Rosenman headed a review team of war crimes prosecution policies, and in May and June of 1945 the former state court judge was one of the primary negotiators for the United States of the draft war crimes policy that led to the Nuremberg Charter. Rosenman, *Working with Roosevelt.*

7. Morgenthau Diary, entry for Jan. 27, 1942, quoted in Michael Beschloss, *The Con-*

querors: Roosevelt, Truman, and the Destruction of Hitler's Germany, 1941–1945, 51. See also "Statement on War Criminals Submitted by the American Jewish Conference to the Secretary of State," Aug. 25, 1944, rpt. in B. F. Smith, *American Road to Nuremberg*, 17–20; Abraham J. Peck, ed., *The German-Jewish Legacy in America, 1938–1988: From Bildung to the Bill of Rights* (Detroit: Wayne State University Press, 1989).

8. For example, War Department official John J. McCloy and Supreme Court Justice Felix Frankfurter discounted first-hand evidence of Holocaust-related atrocities as late as the spring of 1944. See the nuanced account of their skepticism in Kennedy, *Freedom from Fear*, 796–797. Frankfurter professed himself "unable to believe" the testimonials, more out of what he readily conceded at the time was a failure of imagination than any doubts as to the witnesses' veracity. Moscow Declaration, in US Department of State, *Axis in Defeat*, 4; Taylor, *Anatomy*, 26.

9. "War Department Handbook of Military Government for Germany," (Aug. 1944), Morgenthau Papers, 1394, Table D, Nazi Police, Party, Para-Military, and Governmental Officers to be Interned.

10. US Senate, 1944, Committee on the Judiciary, Subcommittee to Investigate the Administration of the Internal Security Act and Other Internal Security Laws, "Statement by Henry A. Morgenthau, Jr.," 90th Cong., 1st sess., Aug. 17, 1944, in *Morgenthau Diary (Germany)*, 1: 414.

11. West, *Train of Powder*, 17; Murray C. Bernays, "Memorandum: Subject: Trial of European War Criminals," Sept. 15, 1944, rpt. in Smith, *American Road to Nuremberg*, 36–37.

12. Henry L. Stimson and McGeorge Bundy, *On Active Service in Peace and War* (New York: Octagon, 1971), 586–587.

13. Francis Biddle, "Memorandum re: Punishment of War Criminals," Jan. 5, 1945, rpt. in Smith, *American Road to Nuremberg*, 91–92. Biddle also notes, "I think we should eliminate, at this point at least, any attempt to punish crimes committed *before the war*. We will have our hands full with crimes after the [declaration of] war." See also Smith, Introduction to sec. 2, *American Road to Nuremberg*, 52; James J. Weingartner, *A Peculiar Crusade: Willis M. Everett and the Malmédy Massacre* (New York: New York University Press, 2000).

14. For a fuller and more nuanced version of the Bass thesis, including the important modification that "legalist" societies are most capable of pursuing international justice beyond their borders, see Bass, *Stay the Hand*, 177–190; Sellars, *Rise and Rise*, 27.

15. Taylor, *Anatomy*, 43; on Jackson's early career and service on the Supreme Court see John Q. Barrett, intro. to Robert H. Jackson, *That Man: An Insider's Portrait of Franklin D. Roosevelt*; on Jackson's role at Nuremberg, see Eugene C. Gerhart, *America's Advocate: Robert H. Jackson*; "The Reminiscences of Robert H. Jackson," Columbia University Oral History Research Office, 1955.

16. Francis Biddle argued the Nazi Saboteurs' Case as attorney general. See *Ex Parte Quirin*, 317 US 1 (1942); Louis Fisher, *Nazi Saboteurs on Trial: A Military Tribunal and American Law* (Lawrence: University Press of Kansas, 2003); Robert H. Jackson, "The Challenge of International Lawlessness," Address before the American Bar Association, Indianapolis, Oct. 2, 1941, rpt. in *American Bar Association Journal* 27 (Nov. 1941): 690; Taylor, *Anatomy*, 45.

17. Jackson, "Challenge of International Lawlessness," 691.

18. Ibid., 692.

19. The London Conference began on June 26, 1945, the day the UN Charter was signed in San Francisco, and ended Aug. 7, 1945, the day news reports were published describing the previous day's explosion of an American atomic weapon over Hiroshima. The memoranda and summaries of negotiation sessions of the London Conference are rpt. in

Robert H. Jackson, *Report of Robert H. Jackson, United States Representative to the International Conference on Military Trials*. The other most active negotiators were Professor André Gros, France; Sir William Jowitt and Sir David Maxwell-Fyfe, Britain; and Ion T. Nikitchenko and General Roman A. Rudenko, Soviet Union. (Three of the major negotiators of the Nuremberg Charter, Jackson, Maxwell-Fyfe, and Rudenko, were soon to become prosecutors, while another, Nikitchenko, would soon become one of the judges.) On Jackson's management skills and negotiation style, see Taylor, *Anatomy*, chaps. 6 and 7; Bradley F. Smith, *Reaching Judgment at Nuremberg* (London: Deutsch, 1977), 47.

20. "Atrocities and War Crimes," Report from Robert H. Jackson to the President, June 7, 1945, rpt. in *USDSB* 12 (1945): 1075; *IMT*, 1: 219; "American Draft Revision, June 14, 1945," in Jackson, *Report*, 58.

21. "Morning Session, June 29, 1946," in Jackson, *Report*, 97. See also Ferdinand A. Hermes, "Collective Guilt," *Notre Dame Lawyer* 23 (May 1948): 499; *IMT*, 1: 239.

22. Theodore Roosevelt, "State of the Union Message 1904," excerpts rpt. in *The Human Rights Reader* (New York: New American Library, 1990), ed. Walter Laqueur and Barry Rubin.

23. Hague Convention respecting the Laws and Customs of War on Land (also known as the Fourth Hague Convention, 1907), Preamble, rpt. in Roberts and Guelff, *Documents on the Laws of War*, 45; Scott, ed., *The Hague Conventions*, 100–127.

24. Fourth Hague Convention, Article 2.

25. Taylor, *Anatomy*, 582; *IMT*, 1: 221; "Revised Draft of Agreement and Memorandum Submitted by American Delegation, June 30, 1945," in Jackson, *Report*, 121 (American Memo at the London Conference mentioning the Martens clause).

26. *IMT*, 5: 371ff.

27. Trial of the Major War Criminals by the International Military Tribunal Sitting at Nuremberg, *Opening Speeches of the Chief Prosecutors*, 34; *IMT*, 1: 221.

28. Article 6 of the Nuremberg Charter provided that: "The Tribunal established by the Agreement referred to in Article 1 hereof for the trial and punishment of the major war criminals of the European Axis countries shall have the power to try and punish persons who, acting in the interests of the European Axis countries, whether as individuals or as members of organizations, committed any of the following crimes. The following acts, or any of them, are crimes coming within the jurisdiction of the Tribunal for which there shall be individual responsibility: A. CRIMES AGAINST PEACE: namely, planning, preparation, initiation or waging of a war of aggression, or a war in violation of international treaties, agreements, or assurances, or participation in a common plan or conspiracy for the accomplishment of any of the foregoing. B. WAR CRIMES: namely, violations of the laws or customs of war. Such violations shall include, but not be limited to, murder, ill-treatment or deportation to slave labour or for any other purpose of civilian population of or in occupied territory, murder or ill-treatment of prisoners of war or persons on the seas, killing of hostages, plunder of public property, wanton destruction of cities, towns or villages, or devastation not justified by military necessity. C. CRIMES AGAINST HUMANITY: namely, murder, extermination, enslavement, deportation, or other inhumane acts committed against any civilian population, before or during the war, or persecutions on political, racial, or religious grounds in execution of or in connection with any crime within the jurisdiction of the Tribunal, whether or not in violation of the domestic law of the country where perpetrated. Leaders, organizers, instigators, and accomplices participating in the formulation or execution of a common plan or conspiracy to commit any of the foregoing crimes are responsible for all acts performed by any persons in execution of such plan."

29. *IMT*, 1: 222; see also Taylor, *Anatomy*, 583.

30. "Minutes of the Conference Session of July 23, 1945," in Jackson, *Report*, 331.

31. Ibid., 333; on the obsession of southern senators with protection of domestic jurisdiction for precisely the reasons Jackson articulates here, see Anderson, *Eyes off the Prize*.

32. Raphael Lemkin, Letter to the Editor, *New York Times*, Nov. 8, 1946.

33. *IMT*, 1: 218–219.

34. Norman Thomas, *Appeal to the Nations* (New York: H. Holt, 1947), 68–69.

35. The tribunal acquitted Doenitz on the conspiracy charge but convicted him for crimes against peace (waging aggressive war), and conventional war crimes. He was not charged with crimes against humanity. He garnered a sentence of ten years—the shortest of any of the defendants convicted. See *IMT*, 1: 366; Conot, *Justice*, 68; William J. Bosch, *Judgment on Nuremberg: American Attitudes toward the Major German War Crime Trials*, 168–169; Howard Ball, *Prosecuting War Crimes and Genocide: The Twentieth-Century Experience*, 58; *Opening Speeches of the Chief Prosecutors*, 5.

36. L. C. Green, *Superior Orders in National and International Law* (Leyden: A. W. Sijthoff, 1976); Guenter Lewy, "Superior Orders, Nuclear Warfare, and the Dictates of Conscience: Dilemma of Military Obedience in the Atomic Age," *American Political Science Review* 55 (Mar. 1961): 19.

37. Gilbert, *Nuremberg Diary*, entry for July 12, 1946, 409.

38. Nuremberg Charter, Article 7; *Cong. Rec.*, 80th Cong., 2d sess., 94: A-2369. See John Foster Dulles, "International Law and Individuals: A Comment on Enforcing Peace," *American Bar Association Journal* 35 (Nov. 1949): 912; Ernest Schneeberger, "The Responsibility of the Individual under International Law," *Georgetown Law Journal* 35 (May 1947): 489; Lawrence Lauer, "The International War Criminal Trials and the Common Law of War," *St. John's Law Review* 20 (Nov. 1945): 24. See also H. K. Thompson, Jr. and Henry Strutz, eds., *Doenitz at Nuremberg, a Reappraisal: War Crimes and the Military Professional* (New York: Amber, 1976).

39. Nicholas Doman, "Political Consequences of the Nuremberg Trial," *Annals of the American Academy* 216 (July 1946): 88; P. F. Gault, *Army and Navy Journal*, Dec. 15, 1945, 522.

40. Ernest O. Hauser, "The Backstage Battle at Nuremberg," *Saturday Evening Post*, Jan. 19, 1946, 18, 138.

41. Taylor, *Anatomy*, 95, 123–124.

42. Streicher elaborated, "You can tell by the way it wobbles when they walk." Gilbert, *Nuremberg Diary*, entry "More Racial Science," July 13, 1946, 411; see also entry for Nov. 21, 1945, 41. An idiosyncratic sampling of ordinary Germans polled informally at the time of the trial agreed with Streicher that the trial was dominated by Jews. See West, *Train of Powder*, 53.

43. John E. Rankin speech of Nov. 28, 1947, *Cong. Rec.*, 80th Cong., 1st sess. 93: 9054.

44. This brief account of the Tokyo trial relies on Borgwardt, "Ideology and International Law: The Dissent of the Indian Justice at the Tokyo War Crimes Trial," rpt. in Gerry Simpson, ed., *War Crimes Law*. The main difference between the Nuremberg and Tokyo charters was that an international team handled the prosecution at Nuremberg, sharing responsibility equally, whereas the Tokyo Charter provided for a single American chief of counsel, chosen by Supreme Commander General Douglas MacArthur, to lead an "International Prosecution Section." Other differences included the fact that the Tokyo Charter provided for eleven judges rather than Nuremberg's four, with no alternates; and the Tokyo Charter provided for review of the sentences by MacArthur, while Nuremberg made no provisions for review of the sentences. The text of the Tokyo trial judgment itself read that "in all material respects the Charters of this Tribunal and the Nuremberg Tribunal are identical." See "Special Proclamation: Establishment of International Military Tribunal for the Far East" (Tokyo Charter), Jan. 19, 1946, in *The Tokyo War Crimes Trial: The Complete*

Transcripts of the Proceedings of the International Military Tribunal for the Far East, 22 vols., ed. R. Pritchard and S. Zaide, 20: Annex No. A-4, 16–18.

45. The Soviet judge at Nuremberg, General Ion Timifeevich Nikitchenko, had dissented on the limited basis that he felt that the sentences were too lenient regarding those defendants who were acquitted or given prison sentences, and that in his opinion the German General Staff and Reich Cabinet were cohesive enough groups to be appropriately deemed "criminal organizations." He concurred in the Tribunal's judgment on its jurisdiction and on points of law, however. Pal, *International Military Tribunal.* (This published version of Pal's Dissent, which includes a number of elaborations and an Appendix not included in the original version, is 735 pages; the original typescript version, reproduced in vol. 21 of the *Transcripts,* is 1,235 pages.)

46. Pal wrote, "The part of humanity which has been lucky enough to enjoy political freedom can now well afford to . . . think of peace in terms of political status quo. But every part of humanity has not been equally lucky, and a considerable part is still haunted by the wishful thinking about escape from political dominations. To them the present age is faced with not only the menace of totalitarianism but the actual plague of imperialism." Pal, *International Military Tribunal,* 115. See also Borgwardt, "Ideology and International Law." Separate and dissenting opinions in the judgment of the Tokyo Tribunal are rpt. in vol. 21 of the *Transcripts.* Richard Minear, *Victors' Justice: The Tokyo War Crimes Trial* (Ann Arbor: Center for Japanese Studies, University of Michigan, 2001), offers a trenchant, if somewhat polemical and oversimplified, critique of the legal basis of the trial; Kirsten Sellars offers a more balanced but still unfavorable assessment in *Rise and Rise,* 47–66.

47. The Tokyo indictment had named 28 Japanese leaders, but during the course of the proceedings two of the defendants had died and the tribunal declared one insane and unfit to stand trial. See Borgwardt, "Ideology and International Law," Appendix A: Defendants, Charges, Verdicts, and Sentences, 442; Philip R. Piccigallo, *The Japanese on Trial: Allied War Crimes Operations in the East, 1945–1951* (Austin: University of Texas Press, 1979), 215 n.10; *In re Yamashita,* 327 US 1, (1946); on appeal to the US Supreme Court, Justice Murphy in dissent noted that "nowhere was it alleged that the petitioner personally committed any of the atrocities, or that he ordered their commission, or that he had any knowledge of the commission thereof by members of his command . . . The only conclusion I can draw is that the charge made against the petitioner is clearly without precedent in international law or in the annals of recorded military history." Ibid., 34, 40. An editorial in the *Army and Navy Journal,* by contrast, applauded the verdict, because the scale of atrocities had been such that the commanding general had "profaned the profession of arms, threatened the very fabric of international society, and failed utterly the soldier's faith." *Army and Navy Journal,* Feb. 9, 1946, 744. See also A. Frank Reel, *The Case of General Yamashita* (Chicago: University of Chicago Press, 1949).

48. See, for example, *Hirota v. MacArthur,* 338 US 197 (1949), (Douglas, J. concurring); Woetzel, *Nuremberg Trials,* 230, 245.

49. Ingo Müller, *Hitler's Justice: The Courts of the Third Reich,* 201.

50. Fourth Report of the Commission to Study the Organization of Peace, rpt. in *International Conciliation: Documents for the Year 1944* (Dec. 1944), 69; the United Nations Charter was drafted Apr.–June 1945; the Nuremberg Charter, part of the London Agreement of Aug. 8, 1945, was being negotiated from June to Aug. 1945 (although formally drafted at the London Conference in Aug.).

51. William Jackson, quoted in Taylor, *Anatomy,* 42.

52. Harry S. Truman, "Prosecution of Major Nazi War Criminals," *USDSB* 15 (Oct. 27, 1946): 954; Francis Biddle, quoted in Gordon Ireland, "Ex Post Facto from Rome to Tokyo," *Temple Law Quarterly* 21 (1947): 27, 54–55. See also Robert H. Jackson,

"Nuremberg in Retrospect: Legal Answer to International Lawlessness," *American Bar Association Journal* 35 (Oct. 1949): 887.

53. Walter Lippmann, "The Meaning of the Nuremberg Trial," *Ladies' Home Journal* 63 (June 1946): 32.

54. Tom C. Clark quoted in the *New York Times,* Oct. 21, 1946, 15; Eugene Davidson, *Trial of the Germans,* 2.

55. Reinhold Niebuhr, "A Report on Germany," *Christianity and Crisis* 2 (Oct. 14, 1946): 13; Waldo Browne, "The Nuremberg Trial," *New Republic* 113 (Dec. 24, 1946): 872; see also Reinhold Niebuhr, "Victors' Justice," *Common Sense* 15 (Jan. 1946), 6; Paul W. Tatage, "The Nuremberg Trials: 'Victor's Justice'?" *American Bar Association Journal* 36 (Mar. 1950): 247.

56. Quincy Wright, "The Law of the Nuremberg Trial," *AJIL* 41 (Jan. 1947), 45. For additional unfavorable comments, see the coverage in the *Chicago Tribune,* such as "The Nuremberg Blunder," *Chicago Daily Tribune,* Oct. 16, 1946, 22; Manley O. Hudson, "International Tribunals in the Post-War World: A Proposed International Criminal Court," ser. 2, Confidential Memo No. 7, Dec. 10, 1943, 7. This memo was prepared as part of a series for an informal wartime working group of American and Canadian lawyers "attempting to arrive at a community of views with reference to the future of international law." Draft invitation, Mar. 1943, container 10, folder: Manley Hudson, International Courts 1942–1945, Benjamin V. Cohen Papers.

57. Alfred Vagts, *Defense and Diplomacy: The Soldier and the Conduct of Foreign Relations* (New York: King's Crown, 1956), 327.

58. See the discussion in Chapter 2.

59. Senator Claude Pepper, quoted in Taylor, *Anatomy,* 216.

60. Edith Helga Simon Diary, entry for Nov. 12, 1945 ("As usual it's snafu . . ."); on the junior New Dealers at Nuremberg, see Taylor, *Anatomy,* 119, 127, 143.

61. Nuremberg assistant prosecutor Robert Kempner, quoted in Ian Buruma, *The Wages of Guilt: Memories of War in Germany and Japan* (London: Vintage, 1995), 145.

62. Sec. heading: Publius Terentius, Rome, c159 BC, favorite saying of Tokyo War Crimes Trial Assistant Prosecutor Kurt Steiner (an interview subject for this history). Primo Levi, *If This Is a Man; The Truce,* 111–112.

63. Levi, *If This Is a Man,* 112; Ignatieff, *Human Rights as Politics and Idolatry,* 3. Such arguments about innate human dignity were the polar opposite of the cultural and scientific orientation of the Third Reich. See, for example, the accounts of Nazi philosophy in Robert Jay Lifton, *The Nazi Doctors: Medical Killing and the Psychology of Genocide* (New York: Basic Books, 1986); James M. Glass, *Life Unworthy of Life: Racial Phobia and Mass Murder in Hitler's Germany* (New York: Basic Books, 1997).

64. Ignatieff, quoted by the ethicist Amy Gutmann in her Introduction to Igantieff, *Human Rights as Politics and Idolatry,* vii; Minow, *Between Vengeance and Forgiveness,* 47; Bosch, *Judgment on Nuremberg,* 14.

66. "[The defendants] conducted deliberate and systematic genocide, viz., the extermination of racial and national groups, against the civilian populations of certain occupied territories in order to destroy particular races and classes of people and national, racial, or religious groups, particularly Jews, Poles, and Gypsies and others." Indictment, *IMT,* 1: 43.

67. See Taylor's account of preparing the indictment, where he notes that over the objections of a member of the British prosecution team, "we used the word 'genocide,' newly coined by Raphael Lemkin." Taylor, *Anatomy,* 103; Lemkin, *Axis Rule in Occupied Europe: Laws of Occupation, Analysis of Government, Proposals for Redress* (Washington: Carnegie Endowment for International Peace, Division of International Law, 1944), 79.

68. Otto D. Tolischus, "Twentieth-Century Moloch: The Nazi-Inspired Totalitarian

State, Devourer of Progress—and of Itself," *New York Times Book Review,* Jan. 21, 1945: 1, 24. See also Waldemar Kaempffert, "Genocide Is the New Name for the Crime Fastened on the Nazi Leaders," *New York Times,* Oct. 20, 1946, E13; Lemkin, draft of "History of Genocide," Lemkin Papers, New York Public Library, quoted in Samantha Power, *"A Problem from Hell": America and the Age of Genocide,* 44, 29–78.

69. West, *Train of Powder,* 21.

70. This exposure took a psychological toll on the Nuremberg staff, possibly contributing to the bizarre suicide of prison psychiatrist Douglas Kelley, who killed himself in the exact manner of Goering. Arendt to Karl Jaspers, Aug. 17, 1946, in *Hannah Arendt–Karl Jaspers Correspondence, 1926–1969,* ed. Lotte Kohler and Hans Saner (New York: Harcourt Brace Jovanovich, 1992), 51, 54; Conot, *Justice,* 9; Lawrence L. Langer, *Admitting the Holocaust: Collected Essays* (New York: Oxford University Press, 1995), 171. See also Naomi Mor, "Holocaust Messages from the Past," *Contemporary Family Therapy* 27 (1990): 371.

71. Geoffrey Robertson, *Crimes against Humanity: The Struggle for Global Justice,* 215; Shklar, *Legalism,* 170. See also Douglas, *Memory of Judgment.*

72. West, *Train of Powder,* 50.

73. Robertson, *Crimes against Humanity,* 216. See also Bejamin B. Ferencz (Nuremberg assistant prosecutor), "Nurnberg Trial Procedures and the Rights of the Accused," *Journal of Criminal Law and Criminology* 39 (July–Aug. 1948): 144.

74. Robertson, *Crimes against Humanity,* 220.

75. Max Lerner, *Actions and Passions: Notes on the Multiple Revolutions of Our Times,* 262–263.

76. Thomas Franck, *The Power of Legitimacy among Nations,* 12; *IMT,* 1: 223; see description of constitutional provisions in Whitney R. Harris, *Tyranny on Trial: The Evidence at Nuremberg* (Dallas: Southern Methodist University Press, 1954), 561. On codification of the so-called Nuremberg Principles at the United Nations level, see the "Report of the International Law Commission Covering Its Second Session, June 5–July 29, 1950," *AJIL Supp.* 40 (Oct. 1950), 125–134; Minow, *Between Vengeance and Forgiveness,* 29.

77. Peter J. Haas, *Morality after Auschwitz: The Radical Challenge of the Nazi Ethic,* 203. Haas's question implicates a fascinating postwar debate in American jurisprudence, between the positivist H. L. A. Hart and the natural law theorist Lon Fuller. Questions at the secondary Nuremberg trials about the validity of defenses resting on prior Nazi laws sparked the Hart–Fuller debate about the nature of law itself. Hart argued that antecedent laws must be construed as valid until replaced, while Fuller argued that the rule of law meant that Germany had to restore "both respect for law and respect for justice" even though "painful antinomies were encountered in attempting to restore both at once." Lon L. Fuller, "Positivism and Fidelity to Law—A Reply to Professor Hart," *Harvard Law Review* 71 (1958): 657. See also Hart, "Positivism and the Separation of Law and Morals," 593.

78. Michael J. Perry, *The Idea of Human Rights: Four Inquiries* (New York: Oxford University Press, 1988); Eric Blumenson, "Who Counts Morally?" *Journal of Law and Religion* 14 vol. 1 (1999–2000): 1–40; Alan Gewirth, *The Community of Rights;* Christine Korsgaard, "Two Distinctions in Goodness," *Philosophical Review* 92 (Apr. 1983): 169; Ronald Dworkin, *Life's Dominion: An Argument about Abortion, Euthanasia, and Individual Freedom* (New York: Knopf, 1993). On the role of intuition, Blumenson cites Thomas Nagel, Pierre Schlag, and of course Ludwig Wittgenstein for the proposition that "the human rights idea might be fully legitimate without any intellectually articulable foundation at all . . . Clearly this is true of some other kinds of knowledge—the kind of intuitive knowledge we draw on when we recognize a family resemblance, anticipate a musical progression, or speak grammatically without knowing the rules." Ibid., n.6. Recent anthropo-

logical evidence also points to certain kinds of universal human reactions that may have moral overtones, such as expressions indicating disgust. See Malcolm Gladwell, "Annals of Psychology: The Naked Face" *New Yorker,* Aug. 5, 2002, 38.

79. Primus, *Language of Rights,* 8; Shklar, *Legalism,* x.

80. See Teitel, *Transitional Justice,* 4–15, 20–21; Forbath, "Habermas's Constitution: A History, Guide and Critique," 969.

81. "Majestic Justice," *Christian Century* 63 (Oct. 16, 1946): 1239–1240.

82. *IMT,* 3: 92; West, *Train of Powder,* 60.

83. Gilbert, "Hermann Goering, Amiable Psychopath," 228.

84. Quoted in James Ryerson, "The Quest for Uncertainty: Richard Rorty's Pragmantic Pilgrimage," *Lingua Franca* (Dec. 2000/Jan. 2001): 48; Haas, *Morality after Auschwitz,* 203. Haas argues further that one of the intellectual underpinnings of this discursive approach is a specifically theological strand of human rights philosophy, which he traces to Jewish traditions of enlightenment through dialogue. "Jewish thinking has always dealt with these tensions through the midrashic method, that is, by creating stories and myths that allow the individual to find meaning within the tensions." Ibid., 223. (Such an approach adds a new layer of irony to Hitler's famously contemptuous reference to "conscience, this Jewish invention.") Hitler quoted in Hermann Glaser, *The Cultural Roots of National Socialism* (Austin: University of Texas Press, 1978), 221.

85. Minow, *Between Vengeance and Forgiveness,* 5, 12; Harry S. Truman, *Public Papers,* Jan. 1–Dec. 31, 1946, 46.

9. Forgotten Legacies of the Atlantic Charter

1. Gardner, *Sterling-Dollar,* xxxiv; Winston S. Churchill, "The Sinews of Peace," address at Westminster College, Fulton, MO, March 5, 1946, rpt. in *Churchill: Complete Speeches,* 7: 7–290; "Long Telegram" excerpted in Kennan, *Memoirs,* 547–559; "X," "The Sources of Soviet Conduct," *Foreign Affairs* 25 (July 1947): 566–582.

2. Akira Iriye notes that very few "volumes on the history of the contemporary world . . . seem to contain more than a passing reference to international organizations generally." Iriye, *Global Community,* 4. Iriye has also objected to the dominance of a "high political" Cold War narrative in analyses of postwar international relations, which, he argues, crowds out other stories related to the development of international order in the second half of the twentieth century.

3. Winston S. Churchill before the House of Commons, June 18, 1940, rpt. in *Churchill: Complete Speeches,* 6: 6–238. See also Paul Alkon, "'Broad, Sunlit Uplands:' An Appreciation of Churchill's Essay," *Winston Churchill Journal: Finest Hour,* 103 (a publication of the Churchill Centre online: www.winstonchurchill.org; consulted Aug. 10, 2004). On using institutions to entrench interests and values, see Ikenberry, *After Victory;* Sellars, *Rise and Rise,* xiii.

5. Raymond F. Mikesell, "Negotiating at Bretton Woods, 1944," in Dennet and Johnson, eds., *Negotiating with the Russians,* 114; Horsefield, *International Monetary Fund,* 1: 117; Walter LaFeber, *The American Age: United States Foreign Policy at Home and Abroad, 1750 to the Present* (New York: Norton, 1994), 460; Offner, *Another Such Victory,* 45.

6. Marshall Plan, *USDSB,* June 15, 1947(speech of June 5, 1947), 1159–1160; George Kennan, "Notes on the Marshall Plan" (December 15, 1947), Box 23, Kennan Papers, Seeley Mudd Library, Princeton University; Charles Bohlen Oral History, HSTPL. See also John Lewis Gaddis, *Surprise, Security, and the American Experience,* 60: "The Marshall Plan was . . . very much an act of Cold War strategy . . . The problem, in this case, was not how to get Stalin to fire the first shot, but *how to get him to build the wall* behind which

he would then be contained . . . The Americans, from that moment on, occupied the moral high ground in Europe, and they never relinquished it." (Emphasis in original.)

7. Gardner, *Sterling-Dollar*, 303–305, 314–315; see also Michael J. Hogan, *The Marshall Plan: America, Britain, and the Reconstruction of Western Europe, 1947–1952*; Anna K. Nelson, ed., *State Department Policy Planning Staff Papers, 1947–1949* (New York: Garland, 1983), 1, PPS/1 (May 23, 1947).

8. Truman, *Public Papers, 1947*, 167–172.

9. Truman, "Statement by the President on the Forthcoming International Conference on Tariffs and Trade" (Nov. 9, 1946), *Public Papers* 7: 475.

10. Gardner, *Sterling-Dollar*, 350.

11. Ibid., 372; House of Commons Debate of Jan. 29, 1948, col. 1906, quoted 371.

12. Ibid., 361; Joseph E. Stiglitz, *Globalization and Its Discontents*, 16.

13. Diane B. Kunz, *Butter and Guns: America's Cold War Economic Diplomacy*, 192; Steiner and Alston, *International Human Rights*, 1334, 1343; David Vines and Christopher L. Gilbert, *The IMF and Its Critics: Reform of Global Financial Architecture* (New York: Cambridge University Press, 2004); United States Congress, "Reform of the IMF and World Bank: Hearing before the Joint Economic Committee, 107th Congress, 1st session, Mar. 6, 2002," Washington, DC: US GPO 2002.

14. Taft, *Congressional Record*, 91 (July 16, 1945): 7573, quoted in Gardner, *Sterling-Dollar*, 130;

15. Sunstein, *Second Bill of Rights*, 27, 21–22, 19; see also Friedrich A. Hayek, *The Road to Serfdom* (1944; Chicago: University of Chicago Press, 1994), 45.

16. Ken Ringle, "Bank Shot," *Washington Post* (June 9, 2002), T4, reviewing William Easterly, *The Elusive Quest for Growth: Economists' Adventures and Misadventures in the Tropics* (Cambridge: MIT Press, 2001); Mary Robinson, "Constructing an International Financial, Trade, and Development Architecture: The Human Rights Dimension," (Speech of July 1, 1999), n.p., www.unhcr.org; Amartya Sen, *Inequality Reexamined*, 39; Amartya Sen, *Development as Freedom*. Policy analysts trace the label "Washington Consensus" to John Williamson's article, "What Washington Means by Policy Reform," in John Williamson, ed., *Latin American Adjustment: How Much Has Happened?* (Washington, DC: Institute for International Economics, 1989).

17. Sen, *Development as Freedom*, 35; Robinson, "Development Architecture," n.p.; Amartya Sen, *Poverty and Famines: An Essay on Entitlement and Deprivation*, 165–166.

18. Sen, "Capability and Well-Being," in Martha C. Nussbaum and Amartya Sen, eds., *The Quality of Life* (Oxford: Clarendon, 1993), 44; FDR quoted in Leuchtenburg, *Franklin D. Roosevelt and the New Deal*, 344. Universal Declaration of Human Rights, article 28; article 56 of the UN Charter commits all member states to take "joint and separate action in cooperation" with UN agencies to realize article 55's objectives for human rights, improving standards of living, and enabling "conditions of social progress and development," including "solutions of international economic, social, health and related subjects."

19. Robert L. Rothstein, *Global Bargaining: UNCTAD and the Quest for a New International Economic Order* (Princeton: Princeton University Press, 1979); Jagdish N. Bhagwati, ed., *The New International Economic Order: The North-South Debate* (Cambridge: MIT Press, 1977); Balakrishnan Rajagopal, *International Law from Below: Development, Social Movements, and Third World Resistance* (Cambridge: Cambridge University Press, 2003); Jack Donnelly, "In Search of the Unicorn: The Jurisprudence and Politics of the Right to Development," *California Western International Law Journal* 15 (1985): 473.

20. Murray Hiebert and John McBeth, "Good Money Gone Bad: The World Bank's Struggle with Corruption" (cover story; article entitled "Corruption: Stealing from the Poor," *Far Eastern Economic Review* (July 29, 2004): 14–20. "Corruption is estimated to

have drained anywhere from 5% to 30% of the roughly 525 billion that the bank has lent over the last six decades," this article explains. The high-end figure was supported by Republican Senator Richard Lugar, chair of the Senate Foreign Relations Committee, in hearings during the spring of 2004, and was vehemently disputed by then–World Bank President James Wolfensohn, who called the numbers "frivolous" and "not soundly based" and very possibly "politically motivated." See also Stiglitz, *Globalization*, 19–20, 10; Ngaire Woods, "Order, Justice, the IMF and the World Bank," in Rosemary Foot, John Lewis Gaddis, and Andrew Hurrell, eds., *Order and Justice in International Relations*, 80–102.

21. Joshi and Skidelsky, "One World?" 20; Stiglitz, *Globalization*, xv.

22. David Held, *Global Covenant: The Social Democratic Alternative to the Washington Consensus*, 97; Carol C. Gould, *Globalizing Democracy and Human Rights* (Cambridge: Cambridge University Press, 2004); "More World, Less Bank!" has been a widely-employed protest chant and poster slogan among antiglobalization activists since the 1990s; www.sinkers.org/posters/moreworld/; see also Mark Weisbrot, "We Need a Lot More World and a Lot Less Bank," *Los Angeles Times* (July 6, 2000), available at www.cepr.net/columns/weisbrot_11/more_world_less_bank.htm; "More World, Less Bank," special issue of the *New Internationalist* (Mar. 2004).

23. Berlin, *Proper Study of Mankind*, 636; Rosenman, *Working with Roosevelt*, 263–264; but see also Adam Cohen, "What's New in the Legal World? A Growing Campaign to Undo the New Deal," *New York Times*, December 14, 2004, A32.

24. Compare, for example, Thomas L. Friedman, *The Lexus and the Olive Tree* (New York: Anchor, 2000), and John Ralston Saul, "The Collapse of Globalism and the Rebirth of Nationalism," *Harper's Magazine* (March 2004), 33–43. For discussions of the implications of globalization, see, for example, Jagdish Bhagwati, *In Defense of Globalization* (Auckland: Oxford University Press, 2004); Anne-Marie Slaughter, *A New World Order*; Robert K. Schaeffer, *Understanding Globalization: The Social Consequences of Political, Economic, and Environmental Change* (Lanham, MD: Rowman and Littlefield, 2003); Pablo De Greiff and Ciaran Cronin, eds., *Global Justice and Transnational Politics: Essays on the Moral and Political Challenges of Globalization* (Cambridge: MIT Press, 2002); Peter Singer, *One World: The Ethics of Globalization*; Stiglitz, *Globalization*; Paul Kennedy, Dirk Messner, Franz Nuscheler, eds., *Global Trends and Global Governance* (London: Pluto, 2002); Symposium issue, "Globalization and Democracy," *AAAPSS* 581 (May 2002); *Globalization, Growth and Poverty: Building an Inclusive World Economy*, a World Bank Policy research report (Washington, DC: World Bank, 2002); Thomas L. Friedman, "The Impact of Globalization on World Peace: The fifth annual Arnold C. Harbenger Distinguished Lecture," University of California at Los Angeles, Burkle Center for International Relations, Working Paper No. 7 (Jan 17, 2001); Richard Falk, *Predatory Globalization: A Critique* (Cambridge: Polity, 1999).

25. Stiglitz, *Globalization*, 11–13.

26. Robert B. Reich, *The Work of Nations: Preparing Ourselves for 21st Century Capitalism* (New York: Knopf, 1991); Gaddis, *Surprise, Security*, 65; Philip Trimble, "Globalization, International Institutions, and the Erosion of National Sovereignty and Democracy," *Michigan Law Review* 95 (1997): 1954; Amy Chua, *World on Fire: How Exporting Free Market Democracy Breeds Ethnic Hatred and Global Instability*, 9, 7. See also Joel Paul, "Cultural Resistance to Global Governance," *Michigan Journal of International Law* 22 (2000):1.

27. Paul Martin, "Notes for an Address by the Honourable Paul Martin to the Royal Institute of International Affairs," London, January 24, 2001, quoted in Slaughter, *New World Order*, 246; Held, *Global Covenant*, 89–93; James Painter, "South America's Leftward Sweep," Feb 3, 2005, BBC News, n.p., (http://news.bbc.co.uk) (Washington analyst quoted is Larry Birns, director of the Washington-based Council on Hemispheric Affairs);

Julian Massaldi, "Buenos Aires Consensus," Nov. 20, 2003, *Zmagazine* (Argentina), n.p. (http://www.zmag.org); see also Jeffrey D. Sachs, *The End of Poverty: Economic Possibilities for Our Time* (New York: Penguin, 2005).

28. Quoted in Leuchtenburg, *Franklin D. Roosevelt and the New Deal*, 337, 336; see also Karl Polanyi's assessment of the New Deal as a response to "the threatening collapse of the international financial system," in Polanyi, *The Great Transformation: The Political and Economic Origins of Our Time* (1944; Boston: Beacon, 2001), 24.

29. Immanuel Kant, "The Principle of Progress considered in connection with the Relation of Theory to Practice in International Law" (1793), in Kant, *Eternal Peace and Other Essays*, trans. W. Hastie (Boston: World Peace Foundation, 1914), 65: "For a lasting universal peace on the basis of the so-called balance of power in Europe is a mere chimera. It is like the house described by Swift, which was built by an architect so perfectly in accordance with all the laws of equilibrium that when a sparrow lighted upon it, it immediately fell."

30. William Draper Lewis, ed., "Report to the Members on the Discussion of the International Bill of Rights Project at the Annual Meeting," American Law Institute (May 12, 1943), 12–15. Important work on Ricardo Alvarez and other "conscience liberals" who were developing a human-rights-related critique of US policies in the mid-twentieth century is forthcoming from the historian Kenneth Cmiel. Cmiel, Roundtable Presentation, "Human Rights at Midcentury: Where the Global and the Local Meet," Annual Meeting of the Law & Society Association, Las Vegas, June 2–5, 2005.

31. Edward R. Stettinius, Jr., "First Draft of Dumbarton Oaks Diary," Wednesday, September 27, 1944, Papers of the Albert and Shirley Small Special Collections Library, University of Virginia; see also Koskenniemi, *Gentle Civilizer of Nations*, 390–391; Henkin, "Human Rights from Dumbarton Oaks," in *Dumbarton Oaks Conversations*, ed. May and Laiou, 97.

32. Alice McDiarmid, "Promotion of Respect for Human Rights and Fundamental Freedoms," (Apr. 7, 1945), Records of the US Delegation to the UN Conference on International Organization, Box 208 RG 59, NARA; Edward Stettinius, US Delegation Press Statement, May 15, 1945; R. H. Hadow, May 17, 1945, FO 371/50716, NA-Kew, as quoted in Sellars, *Rise and Rise*, 4, 8.

33. General Assembly delegation of drafting "international bill of rights": GA Res. 43(I) (Dec. 11, 1946); Mary Ann Glendon, *A World Made New*, 21–22; Frank E. Holman, *Story of the "Bricker" Amendment*, 2.

34. Dean Rusk, *As I Saw It*, 137.

35. Ibid., 137. Joseph P. Lash, *Eleanor: The Years Alone* (New York: New American Library, 1972), 36–37.

36. Holman, *"Bricker" Amendment*, 5.

37. Universal Declaration of Human Rights, GA Res. 217A (III) (Dec. 10, 1948). Histories that tell the story of the negotiation of the Universal Declaration include Glendon's engaging work, *A World Made New*; Johannes Morsink, *The Universal Declaration of Human Rights: Origins, Drafting, and Intent*; Glen M. Johnson, *The Universal Declaration of Human Rights: A History of Its Creation and Implementation* (Paris: UNESCO, 1998); and the early chapters in John P. Humphrey, *Human Rights and the United Nations: A Great Adventure*. Kenneth Cmiel's forthcoming book, mentioned above, will serve as a wide-ranging intellectual history of the Universal Declaration (much as this history aspires to do with the Atlantic Charter); early versions of some of his arguments are available in Cmiel, "Review Essay: The Recent History of Human Rights," *American Historical Review* 109 (Feb. 2004): 117; and Cmiel, "Freedom of Information, Human Rights, and the Origins of Third World Solidarity," in Bradley and Petro, eds., *Truth Claims*, 107–130.

38. David Fromkin, "Drawing a Line, However Thin," book review of Glendon,

World Made New, Sunday New York Times Book Review (Apr. 22, 2001), p. 13; International Covenant on Civil and Political Rights, adopted Dec. 16, 1966, entered into force Mar. 23, 1966, GA Res. 2200A (21); UN Doc. A/6316 (1966), *999 UNTS* 171; International Covenant on Economic, Social and Cultural Rights, adopted Dec. 16, 1966, entered into force Jan. 3, 1976, GA Res. 2200A (21), UN Doc. A/6316 (1966), *993 UNTS* 3.

39. Glendon, *World Made New;* see also Cass Sunstein's review of Glendon's book, where he notes that Glendon "does not explore the complex relationship between the project of 'declaring' the rights that people possess and the very different enterprise of creating institutions." Sunstein, "Rights of Passage," *New Republic* (Feb. 25, 2002; online version); Lori F. Damrosch, Louis Henkin, Richard Crawford Pugh, Oscar Schachter, and Hans Smit, *International Law: Cases and Materials*, 595; David P. Forsythe, "Human Rights in US Foreign Policy: Retrospect and Prospect," *Political Science Quarterly* 105 (1990): 435, 439.

40. José E. Alvarez, "Multilateralism and Its Discontents," *European Journal of International Law* 11 (2000): 395; Von Eschen, *Race against Empire*, 44–95.

41. Alfred Sauvy, "Trois Mondes, Une Planète," *l'Observateur* 118 (Aug. 14, 1952): 14; see also Georges Balandier, ed., *Le "Tiers-Monde," Sous-Développement et Développement* (Paris: Presses Universitaires de France, 1956).

42. *Africa-Asia Speaks from Bandung* (Jakarta: Indonesian Ministry of Foreign Affairs, 1955), 28; Pan Zhenqiang, "Promoting Peace and Development in Asia under the Guidance of the Five Principles of Peaceful Co-existence," China Institute of International Studies Working Paper, available at http://www.ciis.org.cn/item2005-02–23. To mark the fiftieth anniversary of the Bandung Conference, leaders of Asian and African countries attended a new Asian-African Summit in April 2005 in Bandung and Jakarta. The summit participants issued a "Declaration on the New Asian-African Strategic Partnership" with theme of "Reinvigorating the Bandung Spirit." (http://asianafricansummit2005.org/statements_declaration.htm).

43. Adam Roberts, "Order/Justice Issues at the United Nations," in Foot, Gaddis, and Hurrell, eds., *Order and Justice*, 50; Jack Donnelly, "International Human Rights: A Regime Approach," *International Organization* 40 (Summer 1986): 599.

44. Mark Bradley's work in progress on the domestic penetration of international human rights norms discusses *Oyama* and *Shelley* as well as lesser-known cases, and makes the important contribution of analyzing the arguments in the briefs as well as the decisions. Bradley, "Roundtable—Human Rights at Midcentury: Where the Global and the Local Meet," Law and Society Annual Meeting, June 4, 2005; Richard B. Lillich and Hurst Hannum, "Linkages between International Human Rights and US Constitutional Law," *AJIL* 79 (Jan. 1985): 158–163; Murphy and Black concurrences, *Oyama v. California*, 332 US 633 (1948); *Shelley v. Kraemer*, 334 US 1 (1948).

45. Rogers, "The Bricker Wall," 4; *Missouri v. Holland*, 252 US 416 (1920); Duane Tananbaum, *The Bricker Amendment Controversy: A Test of Eisenhower's Political Leadership*, 7, 12–14; Frank E. Holman, *The Life and Career of a Western Lawyer*, 356–357.

46. Text of the amendment in Holman, *"Bricker" Amendment;* Richard O. Davies, *Defender of the Old Guard: John Bricker and American Politics* (Columbus: Ohio State University Press, 1993); John W. Bricker, "Making Treaties and Other International Agreements," *AAAPSS* 289 (Sept. 1953): 134–144; Jay Rogers, "The Bricker Wall: The Fate of Human Rights Treaties in the United States Senate," Seminar Paper, University of Utah Department of History, 2005, 10, 16–17; Tananbaum, *Bricker Amendment Controversy*, 88–89.

47. *Reid v. Covert*, 354 US 1 (1957), plurality opinion of Justice Black. (Note that the underlying legal question in this case was whether a military court could try a civilian American citizen outside the United States. The Court noted firmly that "we reject the idea that when the United States acts against citizens overseas, it can do so free of the Bill of

Rights.") Ibid., 5–6; David P. Forsythe, "Human Rights in U.S. Foreign Policy: Retrospect and Prospect," *Political Science Quarterly* 105 (1990): 436. On "Brickerism," see Natalie Hevener Kaufman, *Human Rights Treaties and the Senate: A History of Opposition* (Chapel Hill: University of North Carolina Press, 1990); Louis Henkin, "US Ratification of Human Rights Conventions: The Ghost of Senator Bricker," *AJIL* 89 (April 1995): 341–350; Vernon Van Dyke, *Human Rights, the United States, and World Community* (New York: Oxford University Press, 1970).

48. Forsythe, "Human Rights in US Foreign Policy," 438–441; Arthur Schlesinger, Jr., "Human Rights and the American Tradition," *Foreign Affairs* 57 (1978): 512. For shifting views reflected in Kissinger's own publications, compare his *American Foreign Policy: Three Essays* (New York: Norton, 1969), arguing that considerations of morality, international law, and human rights were debilitating to more important considerations such as stability, with Henry Kissinger, "Continuity and Change in American Foreign Policy," arguing essentially the opposite. See also Elizabeth Kopelman, "The Modern Machiavelli: Legitimacy, Conflict, and Power in the International Legal Order," review essay on Kissinger's 1994 book, *Diplomacy, UCLA Law Review* 43 (Oct. 1995): 139–158.

49. Congressional Research Service, "Human Rights in the International Community and in US Foreign Policy, 1945–76," Report prepared for the Subcommittee on International Organizations, House Foreign Affairs Committee, July 24, 1977 (Washington DC: US GPO 1977); for summaries of congressional activity, see Forsythe, "Human Rights in US Foreign Policy," 439–440; and Sellars, *Rise and Rise*, 114–115; see also Joshua Muravchik, *The Uncertain Crusade: Jimmy Carter and the Dilemmas of Human Rights Policy* (Latham, MD: Hamilton, 1986).

50. Alvarez, "Multilateralism and Its Discontents," 395; on the Reagan era and the "Kirkpatrick doctrine," which supported close alliances with Chile, Argentina, and apartheid-era South Africa, including sales of electric shock batons and other equipment that could be used for torture to South Africa and Turkey, see Forsythe, "Human Rights in US Foreign Policy," 445–447.

51. John Bolton speaking in New York on Feb. 3, 1994, "Global Structures Convocation"; Bolton Interview with Juan Williams, NPR, 2000, as reported in the *New York Times*, Mar. 9, 2005. For root-and-branch objections to the United Nations, international law, and multilateralism generally, see Jed Babbin, *Inside the Asylum: Why the United Nations and Old Europe Are Worse Than You Think* (Washington, DC: Regnery, 2004); and William F. Jasper, *Global Tyranny . . . Step by Step: The United Nations and the Emerging New World Order* (Appleton, WI: Western Islands, 1992).

52. Roberts, "Order/Justice Issues at the United Nations," 49, 57, 63, 70; Alvarez, "Multilateralism and Its Discontents," 404–407, at 406.

53. Report of the Secretary-General, "In Larger Freedom: Towards Development, Security, and Human Rights for All," Mar. 21, 2005, Doc. A/59/2005 (organized around the three major headings "Freedom from Want," "Freedom from Fear," and "Freedom to Live in Dignity"); Kofi Annan, "'In Larger Freedom': Decision Time at the UN," *Foreign Affairs* (May/June 2005): 65; see also Warren Hoge, "A Report by US, Criticizing UN, Urges Reforms," *New York Times*, June 13, 2005, A1.

54. White, *Wild Flag*.

55. Hoge, "A Report by US, Criticizing UN, Urges Reforms," *New York Times*, June 13, 2005, A1; Eleanor Roosevelt, "The UN and the Welfare of the World," *National Parent-Teacher* 47 (1953): 14. The historian Paul Kennedy's forthcoming intellectual history of the United Nations also urges that the UN retrench to focus on a narrower set of core competencies.

56. Michael Walzer, "International Society: What Is the Best that We Can Do?" Working Paper No. 8, School of Social Science, Institute for Advanced Study, Princeton Univer-

sity (June 2000) 8, 10, 11; a version of this paper appears as ch. 12 of Walzer's *Arguing about War* (New Haven: Yale University Press, 2004); *Hansard* Parliamentary Debates, Nov. 11, 1947, House of Commons Official Report (London: HM Stationery Office, 1947).

57. Amitai Etzioni, *From Empire to Community: A New Approach to International Relations*, 197, 199; Walzer, "International Society," 8; Martha Finnemore, "Norms, Culture, and World Politics: Insights from Sociology's Institutionalism," *International Organization* 50 (1996): 325–348. On NGOs, see Margaret E. Keck and Kathryn Sikkink, *Activists beyond Borders: Advocacy Networks in International Politics*.

58. Kees van Kersbergen and Bertjan Verbeek, "Subsidiarity as a Principle of Governance in the European Union," *Comparative European Politics* 2 (Aug. 2004): 142; Alvarez, "Multilateralism and Its Discontents," 396, 399; Joseph H. H. Weiler, *The Constitution of Europe: "Do the New Clothes Have an Emperor?" and Other Essays on European Integration*. See also the thoughtful critique in David W. Kennedy, *The Dark Sides of Virtue: Reassessing International Humanitarianism* (Princeton: Princeton University Press, 2004).

59. Susan Sontag asserted that Riefenstahl's *Triumph of the Will* (1935), a highly choreographed documentary of the Sixth Nazi Party Congress in 1934, along with Riefenstahl's 1938 film *Olympia*, "may be the two greatest documentaries ever made." She further argued that "*Triumph of the Will* represents an already achieved and radical transformation of reality: history becomes theater." Sontag, *Under the Sign of Saturn* (New York: Farrar, Straus and Giroux, 1980), 95, 83; Siegfried Kracauer, *From Caligari to Hitler: A Psychological History of the German Film* (Princeton: Princeton University Press, 1974); Richard M. Barsam, *Filmguide to* Triumph of the Will (Bloomington: Indiana University Press, 1975). The film is still banned in Germany. See Mary Litch, *Philosophy through Film* (New York: Routledge, 2003).

60. Neave, *Personal Record*, 47

61. Taylor, *Anatomy*, 5; Minow, *Between Vengeance and Forgiveness*, 30.

62. Minow, *Between Vengeance and Forgiveness*, 47–49.

63. In addition to Hannah Arendt's *Eichmann in Jerusalem: A Report on the Banality of Evil* (New York: Penguin, 1965), see also Daphne Eviatar, "The Show Trial: A Larger Justice?" *New York Times*, July 20, 2002, A15, 17; Novick, *Holocaust in American Life*, esp. ch. 6, "Self-Hating Jewess Writes Pro-Eichmann Series"; Anthony Grafton, "Arendt and Eichmann at the Dinner Table," *American Scholar*, Winter 1999, 105; Jacob Robinson, *And the Crooked Shall Be Made Straight: The Eichmann Trial, the Jewish Catastrophe, and Hannah Arendt's Narrative* (New York: Macmillan, 1965). Additional accounts suggestive of the Eichmann trial's cultural role include *6,000,000 Accusers: Israel's Case against Eichmann. The Opening Speech and Legal Argument of Mr. Gideon Hausner, Attorney-General*, trans. Shabtai Rosenne (Jerusalem: Jerusalem Post, 1961); Lord Russell of Liverpool, *The Record: The Trial of Adolf Eichmann for His Crimes against the Jewish People and against Humanity* (New York: Knopf, 1963); and Dewey W. Linze's lurid paperback, *The Trial of Adolf Eichmann* (Los Angeles: Holloway, 1961), the cover of which promises a story "unbelievable, but true—the trial, the evidence, the terror of eyewitness accounts of lust, murder, rape, torture, sterilization—humanity will long remember the trial of Adolf Eichmann!" For additional transcript excerpts, see *Attorney General of Israel v. Eichmann* (unofficial translation) *AJIL* 56 (1962): 85; *Eichmann v. Attorney General of Israel* (appeal), *International Law Reports* 36 (1968), 14. Gosta Julin, "Evidence at Stockholm: The Judges Are Everywhere," *Nation*, June 5, 1967, 712; see also Samuel Rosenwein, "International War Crimes Tribunal: Stockholm Session," *Guild Practitioner* 27 (Winter 1968): 22–29; Jean-Paul Sartre, *On Genocide* (Boston: Beacon, 1968).

64. Universal Declaration of Human Rights, adopted Dec. 10, 1948, GA Resolution 217A(3), UN Doc. A/810, 71. See also Preamble and Article 1; Morsink, *Universal Declaration*. Morsink's chapter entitled "Article 1, Preamble, and the Enlightenment" discusses

the above-quoted language in the context of Enlightenment political theory and in the context of the personal political beliefs of the negotiating delegates, but only touches on the surrounding political, cultural, and legal context. Ibid., 281–328.

65. Nuremberg principles: UN GA Resolution 95(I), UN Doc. A/64/Add.1, (1947).

66. Richard Overy, "The Nuremberg Trials: International Law in the Making," in Geoffrey Wawro and Philippe Sands, eds., *From Nuremberg to the Hague: The Future of International Criminal Justice*.

67. Convention on the Prevention and Punishment of the Crime of Genocide, GAOR 260A(III), UN GAOR 3d Sess. (1)Art IV, UN Doc. A/810 (1948), entered into force Jan 12, 1951; entered into force for the US Feb. 23, 1989; Article 21; Article 2, Draft Code of Crimes against the Peace and Security of Mankind; n.a., *The Work of the International Law Commission*, 2 vols. (New York: United Nations, 2004); Jeffrey S. Morton, *The International Law Commission of the United Nations* (Columbia: University of South Carolina Press, 2000).

68. Geneva Convention for the Amelioration of the Condition of the Wounded and Sick in Armed Forces in the Field, Aug. 12, 1949, 75 *United Nations Treaty Series* (*UNTS*) 31; Geneva Convention for the Amelioration of the Condition of Wounded, Sick, and Shipwrecked Members of Armed Forces at Sea, Aug. 12, 1949, 75 *UNTS* 85; Geneva Convention Relative to the Treatment of Prisoners of War, Aug. 12, 1949, 75 *UNTS* 287; Geneva Convention Relative to the Protection of Civilian Persons in Time of War, Aug. 12, 1949, 75 *UNTS* 287; Convention Against Torture and Other Cruel, Inhuman or Degrading Treatment or Punishment, General Assembly Resolution 39/46 (Dec. 10, 1984), 39 UN GAOR Supp. No. 51 at 197, UN Doc. A/39/51 (1985).

69. Damrosch, Henkin, Pugh, Schachter, and Smit, *International Law*, 1055

70. Cherie Booth, "Prospects and Issues for the International Criminal Court: Lessons from Yugoslavia and Rwanda," in Sands, ed. *From Nuremberg to the Hague*, 159; Philippe Sands, "After Pinochet: The Role of National Courts," in Sands, ed., *From Nuremberg to the Hague*, 68–106; on the shortcomings of the Rwanda Tribunal in particular, see Alvarez, "Multilateralism and Its Discontents," 400–402. On other models, such as South African "Truth and Reconciliation Commissions," see Amy Gutmann and Dennis Thompson, "The Moral Foundations of Truth Commissions," in Gutmann and Thompson, *Why Deliberative Democracy?* (Princeton: Princeton University Press, 2004), 160.

71. Booth, "Prospects and Issues," 159; UN Secretary-General Kofi Annan, address upon receiving an honorary doctorate of law from the University of Witwatersrand, Johannesburg, South Africa, UN Doc. SG/SM/6686, Sept. 1, 1998.

72. See generally James Crawford, "The Drafting of the Rome Statute," in Wawro and Sands, eds., *From Nuremberg to the Hague*, 109–156.

73. Lee A. Casey, Eric J. Kadel, Jr., David B. Rivkin, Jr., and Edwin D. Williamson, "The United States and the International Criminal Court," Federalist Society Working Paper, Feb. 8, 2002, 22; Joseph Lelyveld, "The Defendant: Slobodan Milosevic's Trial, and the Debate Surrounding International Courts," *New Yorker*, May 27, 2002, 82–95.

74. Booth, "Prospects and Issues," 157, 162; subsections dealing with gender issues in Tadeusz Mazowiecki, Special Rapporteur, "Report on the Situation of Human Rights in the Territory of the Former Yugoslavia," UN Doc. A/48/92 and S/25341, Annex pp. 20, 57 (1993); Rhonda Copelon, "Gender Crimes as War Crimes: Integrating Crimes against Women into International Criminal Law," *McGill Law Journal* 46 (2000): 217.

75. Convention for the Protection of Human Rights and Fundamental Freedoms, initially 1950, as amended and with additional protocols, available online from the Human Rights Education Association at http://www.hrea.org/erc/Library/hrdocs/coe/echr.html; n.a., *Human Rights: An Outline Comparison between the European Convention of Human*

Rights and the United Nations International Covenant on Civil and Political Rights (London: British Institute of International and Comparative Law, 1988). The two other "baskets" of Helsinki provisions were Questions Relating to Security in Europe, and Cooperation in the Field of Economics, Science and Technology. See Antonio Cassese, ed., "Papers of the Conference on the Helsinki Final Act, Strasbourg, 9–11 June, s.l., s.n., 1977; Daniel C. Thomas, *The Helsinki Effect: International Norms, Human Rights, and the Demise of Communism*.

76. Marco Belpoliti and Robert Gordon, eds., *The Voice of Memory: Primo Levi, Interviews 1961–1987* (New York: New Press, 2001), 180.

77. Nick Hawton, "Analysis: Serb Surrender Surge," Apr. 29, 2005, BBC News, http://news.bbc.co.uk/2/hi/europe (consulted May 18, 2005).

78. Jennifer Klein, *For All These Rights: Business, Labor, and the Shaping of America's Public-Private Welfare State*, 3; Nelson Lichtenstein, *Labor's War at Home: The CIO in World War II*.

79. Leuchtenburg, *Franklin D. Roosevelt and the New Deal*, 347.

80. Harold D. Lasswell, "Public Opinion and British-American Unity," Document No. 4, American Committee for International Studies, Princeton, New Jersey, Conference on North Atlantic Relations, Prout's Neck, Maine, Sept. 4–9, 1941, p. 6. John Rawls uses the term "decent society" in a limited sense, to describe a polity that is perhaps on the path to becoming a liberal democracy but not there yet, and which meets certain minimum standards of "political right and justice," among which he includes "the right of citizens to play a substantial role, say through associations and groups, in making political decisions," as well as observing "a reasonably just law" for its international law and practice. Avishai Margalit employs a more expansive definition, including criteria for economic well-being and social welfare. See John Rawls, *The Law of Peoples: With "The Idea of Public Reason Revisited,"* 3; Avishai Margalit, *The Decent Society* (Cambridge: Harvard University Press, 1996).

81. Corbett, "War Aims," 5; Ikenberry, *After Victory*, xiii; Yoshikatsu Hayashi, "Discrepancies between Rhetoric and Realities: US Commitments to Its Major Wars during the Last 100 Years," *Japanese Journal of American Studies* 12 (2001): 1–25.

82. Ikenberry, *After Victory*, xi.

83. Gaddis, *Surprise, Security*, ch. 2.

84. Vijay Joshi and Robert Skidelsky, "One World?" *New York Review of Books*, Mar. 25, 2004, 19–28.

85. Norman M. Naimark, *Fires of Hatred: Ethnic Cleansing in Twentieth-Century Europe* (Cambridge: Harvard University Press, 2001), 1, 2; on the failure to intervene in Rwanda, see Power, *"A Problem from Hell,"* and Philip Gourevitch, *We Wish to Inform You that Tomorrow We Will Be Killed with Our Families: Stories from Rwanda* (New York: Farrar, Straus and Giroux, 1998).

86. See Stefan Halper and Jonathan Clarke, *America Alone: The Neo-Conservatives and the Global Order* (Cambridge: Cambridge University Press, 2004), 256; "we won't need allies" quoted in Roger Fisher, Andrea Kupfer Schneider, Elizabeth Borgwardt, and Brian Ganson, *Coping with International Conflict: A Systematic Approach to Influence in International Negotiation* (Upper Saddle River, NJ: Prentice Hall, 1997), 110. For skeptical perspectives, see, for example, Jack L. Goldsmith and Eric A. Posner, *The Limits of International Law* (New York: Oxford University Press, 2005), 13, 6; David Frum and Richard Perle, *An End to Evil: How to Win the War on Terror* (New York: Random House, 2003); Roosevelt quoted in Shotwell, *Great Decision*, 171; see also *USDSB* 9 (Nov. 11, 1943): 319.

87. "NATO after September 11," Speech by Lord Robertson, Secretary General of NATO, to the Pilgrims of the United States, New York, Jan. 31, 2001, www.nato.int (con-

sulted Aug. 16, 2004); Declaration by NATO's North Atlantic Council, ed. version rpt. in *The Guardian*, Sept. 13, 2001, Special Report: Attack on America, www.guardian.co.uk/wtocrash/story; editorial, "We Are All Americans Now," Jean-Marie Columbani, *Le Monde*, Sept. 12, 2001, rpt. in Nov. 2001 issue of *World Press Review*, online at www.worldpress.org.

88. These human rights violations included violations of the traditional protections of the US Bill of Rights such as searches and seizures without probable cause and indefinite detention without charges, rights to counsel, or trial, as well as violations of the Geneva Conventions and the Convention against Torture such as interrogation practices involving torture. See, for example, Anthony Lewis, "Making Torture Legal," *New York Review of Books*, July 15, 2004, 4–8; Ronald Dworkin, "What the Court Really Said," *New York Review of Books*, Aug. 12, 2004, 26–29. In the last days of the formal US occupation of Iraq, according to one poll commissioned by the US-controlled Coalition Provisional Authority itself, only "two percent of Iraqis have great confidence in the Coalition forces, around eighty percent have none at all, and more than half believe that all Americans behave like the abusive jailers at Abu Ghraib." George Packer, "Comment: Wars and Ideas," *New Yorker*, July 5, 2004, 29; Robert Kagan, *Of Paradise and Power: America and Europe in the New World Order*, 125.

89. Coicaud and Heiskanen, eds., *Legitimacy of International Organizations*, 2; G. John Ikenberry, "State Power and the Institutional Bargain: America's Ambivalent Economic and Security Multilateralism," in Foot, MacFarlane, and Mastanduno, eds., *U.S. Hegemony and International Organizations*, 52.

90. Willkie, *One World*, 134, 137.

10. An Expanding Vision of the National Interest

1. FDR, "Annual Message to Congress, Jan. 6, 1941," *PPA*, 1940, 672. This "Four Freedoms" speech may be readily accessed in text and audio formats at history.sandiego.edu/gen/text/us/fdr1941.html.

2. Corbett, "War Aims," 5–6.

3. Berlin, *Proper Study of Mankind*, 625, 631; on the international influence of US rule of law norms more generally, see Louis Henkin and Albert J. Rosenthal, eds., *Constitutionalism and Rights: The Influence of the United States Constitution Abroad* (New York: Columbia University Press, 1990).

4. Karl Polyani quoted in Ira Katznelson, *Desolation and Enlightenment: Political Knowledge after Total War, Totalitarianism, and the Holocaust*, 106.

5. Veijo Heiskanen, "Introduction," in Coicaud and Heiskannen, eds., *Legitimacy of International Organizations*, 18; Ikenberry, *After Victory*, 6. See also Edward A. Laing, "Relevance of the Atlantic Charter for a New World Order," *Indian Journal of International Law* (July–Dec. 1989): 298, 300; Philip Allott, "Intergovernmental Societies and the Idea of Constitutionalism," in Coicaud and Heiskanen, eds., *Legitimacy of International Organizations*, 69.

6. Slaughter, *New World Order*, 254; Robert Howse and Kalypso Nicolaidis, *The Federal Vision: Legitimacy and Levels of Governance in the United States and the European Union* (Oxford: Oxford University Press, 2001); John Valery White, "Federalism and the Challenge for Human and Civil Rights," paper presented at the Conference on Global Sub-National Constitutionalism, Rockefeller Center, Bellagio, Italy, Mar. 23, 2004; see also Patrick R. Hugg, "Transnational Convergence: European Union and American Federalism," *Cornell International Law Journal* 32 (1998): 43–108; Robert F. Nagel, *The Implosion of American Federalism* (New York: Oxford University Press, 2001).

7. On the mid-1940s as a new "Grotian moment," see Falk's introduction to Ed-

wards, *Hugo Grotius*, xiii–xxi; Falk, "A New Paradigm for International Legal Studies: Prospects and Proposals," in Falk, Kratochwil, and Mendlovitz, eds., *International Law*, 651–702; Jackson, "The Grotian Moment in World Jurisprudence"; Leo Gross, "The Peace of Westphalia, 1648–1948," *AJIL* 42 (1948): 20; Jones, *Toward a Just World*, 212–213, describing the years from 1945 to 1948 as a "Grotian moment" (and citing Richard Falk for the term). US Congress, Senate Committee on Banking and Currency, *Bretton Woods Agreements Act*, Hearings on HR 3314, 79th Cong., 1st sess. (June 1945): 37.

8. Lauterpacht, "Grotian Tradition," 17, 24, 19, 27.

9. Gaddis, *Surprise, Security*, 1. Legal historian Lawrence Friedman has suggested that the only two post–Cold War events so far that have encouraged people to break down the barrier between the historical and the personal—to remember "where they were" when they heard the news—were the terrorist attacks of 9/11 and the death of Princess Diana of Wales. Lawrence M. Friedman, *The Horizontal Society* (New Haven: Yale University Press, 1999).

10. See generally, E. Allen Lind and Tom R. Tyler, *The Social Psychology of Procedural Justice* (New York: Plenum, 1988); Christian Reus-Smit, *The Moral Purpose of the State: Culture, Social Identity, and Institutional Rationality in International Relations* (Princeton: Princeton University Press, 1999).

11. Lauterpacht, "Grotian Tradition"; Address of Robert H. Jackson, Attorney General of the United States, Inter-American Bar Association, Havana, Cuba, Mar. 27, 1941, *AJIL* 35 (1941): 348–359 ("Read by the Hon. George H. Messersmith, American Ambassador. Due to weather conditions, the airplane trip of the Attorney General to Havana had to be abandoned."); G. G. Wilson, "Grotius: Law of War and Peace, Prolegomena," *AJIL* 35 (1941): 205–226; Durwood Sandifer, "Rereading Grotius in the Year 1940," *AJIL* 34, (1940): 459–472 (Sandifer served as chief of the division of International Organization Affairs in the State Department during the war, and served as an advisor to the Secretary-General at the United Nations Conference on International Organization in San Francisco in 1945); Bourquin, "Grotius est-il pere du droit des gens?" in *Grandes figures*. See also Bull, Kingsbury, and Roberts, eds., *Hugo Grotius*.

12. Anne-Marie Slaughter, "Leading Through Law," *Wilson Quarterly* 27 (Autumn 2003): 37; see also Jonathan I. Charney, Donald K. Anton, and Mary Ellen O'Connell, eds. *Politics, Values, and Functions: International Law in the 21st Century: Essays in Honor of Professor Louis Henkin* (The Hague: Martinus Nijhoff, 1997).

13. Michael Sandel, "The Political Philosophy of Contemporary Liberalism," quoted in Westbrook, "Fighting for the American Family," 195, 196. See also John Rawls, *Political Liberalism*.

14. Walter White quoted in Anderson, *Eyes off the Prize*, 9, 13.

15. On the idea of American exceptionalism, see Michael Ignatieff, ed., *American Exceptionalism and Human Rights* (Princeton: Princeton University Press, forthcoming), especially Ignatieff's essay and the essay by John Gerard Ruggie, "American Exceptionalism, Exemptionalism, and Global Governance"; Harold Hongju Koh, "On American Exceptionalism," *Stanford Law Review* 55 (May 2003): 1479–1527; Elisabeth Glaser and Hermann Wellenreuther, eds., *Bridging the Atlantic: The Question of American Exceptionalism in Perspective* (New York: Cambridge University Press, 2002); Charles Lockhart, *The Roots of American Exceptionalism: Institutions, Culture and Policies* (New York: Palgrave Macmillan, 2003); Daniel T. Rodgers, "Exceptionalism," in *Imagined Histories: American Historians Interpret the Past*, ed. Anthony Molho and Gordon S. Wood (Princeton: Princeton University Press, 1998), 21–40; Michael Kammen, "The Problem of American Exceptionalism: A Reconsideration," *American Quarterly* 45 (1993): 1–43; Ian Tyrell, "American Exceptionalism in an Age of International History," *American Historical Review* 96 (Oct. 1991): 1031–1072; Anderson, *Eyes off the Prize*, 4.

16. Koh, "American Exceptionalism," 1479, 1486-1487; Michael Ignatieff, "American Exceptionalism and Human Rights," Keynote Address, Conference on the United States and Global Human Rights, Rothermere American Institute, Oxford University (November 11-13, 2004); Ignatieff and Ruggie refer to this practice of double standards as "exemptionalism" in their essays in the forthcoming *American Exceptionalism and Human Rights.*

17. Koh, "American Exceptionalism," 1497, 1487; see also Rogers Smith, *Stories of Peoplehood: The Politics and Morals of Political Membership* (New York: Cambridge University Press, 2003).

18. *Judgment at Nuremberg,* produced and directed by Stanley Kramer, written by Abby Mann (United Artists, Dec. 1961). This so-called "docudrama" was based on *US* v. *Alstoetter, et al.* (the Justices' Case, 1947); Ingo Müller notes that "the American and West German authorities themselves soon began undoing the results of the [jurists'] trial." Müller, *Hitler's Justice,* 24–42, 273. German archivist Gerhard Jochem explains that "it was the Cold War that diminished the pressure upon us Germans to persecute the murderers among us." He also notes that the Berlin Wall went up in Aug. 1961, after the filming of *Judgment* but before the release of the film. Jochem, "Why Judgment at Nuremberg Was No Success at Nuremberg's Box Offices," RIJONUE website (Germany) (home.t-online.de/home/RIJONUE/judgment.htm, consulted June 23, 2004). See also Douglas, *Memory of Judgment.*

19. Atlantic Charter, point 6; Mandela, *Long Walk to Freedom,* 96.

20. Jonathan D. Greenberg, "Arendt and Weber on Law, Violence, and the State," paper presented at the annual conference of the Law & Society Association, June 4, 2005, Las Vegas; see also Jonathan Schell, *The Unconquerable World: Power, Nonviolence, and the Will of the People* (New York: Metropolitan, 2003); Jonathan D. Greenberg, "Does Power Trump Law?" *Stanford Law Review* 55 (May 2003): 1789–1820; Hannah Arendt, *On Violence* (New York: Harcourt, Brace and World, 1970). I thank Jonathan Greenberg for calling my attention to these sources; see also Brian Z. Tamanaha, *On the Rule of Law: History, Politics, Theory* (New York: Cambridge University Press, 2004); Erik K. Jensen and Thomas C. Heller, *Beyond Common Knowledge: Empirical Approaches to the Rule of Law* (New York: Cambridge University Press, 2004).

21. Hugo Grotius, "Prolegomena," *De Jure Belli ac Pacis Libri Tres* (1625; Carnegie Endowment for International Peace, 1925), rpt. *AJIL* 35 (1941): 206, 208, 205, 213.

22. Harold D. Lasswell, "The Garrison State," *American Journal of Sociology* 46 (Jan. 1941): 455–468; Arendt, *Origins of Totalitarianism,* 568, 375.

23. David Riesman, "Civil Liberties in a Period of Transition," in Carl J. Friedrich and Edward S. Mason, eds., *Public Policy* 3 (Cambridge: Harvard University Press, 1942): 96. I am grateful to Ira Katznelson of Columbia University for guiding me to the Lasswell and Riesman sources. See also Katznelson, *Desolation and Enlightenment,* 75, 25.

24. Susan Sontag, "The Photographs *Are* Us," *Sunday New York Times Magazine,* May 23, 2004, 25–29, 42; Judith Butler, "Indefinite Detention," in *Precarious Life: The Powers of Mourning and Violence* (London: Verso, 2004), 50; Rosemary Foot, "Changing the Script of Modern Statehood: US Human Rights Policy in Asia Post 9/11," paper presented at the Rothermere American Institute, Conference on the United States and Global Human Rights, (November 11-13, 2004) (Foot discusses how Indonesian officials have set up a facility deliberately modeled on the extraterritorial features of the US detention complex at Guantanamo, for example, for the indefinite detention without recourse to legal process of separatist fighters from Aceh province.)

25. "Permission slip" phrase from George W. Bush, 2004 State of the Union Address, Jan. 20, 2004, available at www.whitehouse.gov/news/releases/2004/01; Walter Cronkite in the *Seattle Post-Intelligencer,* May 20, 2004, as quoted in Lisa Hajjar, "Our Heart of

Darkness," Amnesty International, *Amnesty Now,* Summer 2004; Lexington, "The Fear Myth," *Economist,* Nov. 18, 2004; Willkie, *One World,* 134, 137. See also Anthony Lewis, "Making Torture Legal," *New York Review of Books,* July 15, 2004, 4–8; Mark Danner, *Torture and Truth: America, Abu Ghraib, and the War on Terror* (New York: A New York Review Book, 2004); Karen J. Greenberg and Joshua L. Dratel, eds., *The Torture Papers: The Road to Abu Ghraib* (New York: Cambridge University Press, 2004); Sanford Levinson, ed., *Torture: A Collection* (New York: Oxford University Press, 2004).

26. On Grotius's relationship to Machiavelli, see Lauterpacht, "Grotian Tradition," 30–35. Lauterpacht sees a large part of the mission of Grotius's treatise as "curbing the spirit of [Machiavelli's] *The Prince.*" Ibid. Thomas Friedman interview, June 3, 2004, "Fresh Air," National Public Radio, http://www.npr.org.

27. Kagan, *Of Paradise and Power,* 156; Gaddis, *Surprise, Security,* ch. 2; Kathleen Sullivan, Tanner Lectures delivered at Harvard University, 2001, published as *The Tanner Lectures on Human Values* (Salt Lake City: University of Utah Press, 2002); ACLU advertisement quoting former US Navy Admiral and Dean of the Franklin Pierce Law Center John Hutson in the *Economist,* July 3–9, 2004, 5. For a more hopeful vision also premised on a crisis of legitimacy, see Garton Ash, *Free World.*

28. Michael Ignatieff, *The Lesser Evil: Political Ethics in an Age of Terror.* Ignatieff tries to "chart a middle course between a pure civil libertarian position which maintains that no violations of rights can ever be justified and a purely pragmatic position that judges antiterrorist measures solely by their effectiveness." He further asserts, however, that "actions which violate foundational commitments to justice and dignity—torture, illegal detention, unlawful assassination—should be beyond the pale." For Ignatieff, the key corrective measure is transparency and openness, especially "the process of adversarial review that decides these matters. When democrats disagree on substance, they need to agree on process, to keep democracy safe both from our enemies and from our own zeal." Ibid., viii.

29. Joseph S. Nye, Jr., *Soft Power: The Means to Success in World Politics* (New York: Public Affairs, 2004), x; Zbigniew Brzezinski, *The Choice: Global Domination or Global Leadership* (New York: Basic Books, 2004).

30. Jody Williams received the 1997 Nobel Peace prize together with the NGO she coordinates, the International Campaign to Ban Landmines. The Norwegian Nobel Committee chair lauded Williams and her group for "open[ing] up the possibility that this wave of opinion can be channeled into political action." Salam Pax is the pseudonym of an Iraqi weblogger and columnist for the British paper *The Guardian;* his columns are compiled in *The Clandestine Diary of an Ordinary Iraqi* (New York: Grove, 2003). See also "The Nobel Prize for 1997: Speech given by the Chairman of the Norwegian Nobel Committee, Francis Sejerstad (Dec. 10, 1997)," http://www.nobel.no/eng_lect_97a.html (accessed May 1, 2005); Jody Williams and Shawn Roberts, *After the Guns Fall Silent: The Enduring Legacy of Landmines* (Washington, DC: Vietnam Veterans of America Foundation, 1995).

31. For a list of the NGOs consulting to the US mission at the United Nations San Francisco Conference in 1945, see "Charter of the United Nations: Report to the President on the Results of the San Francisco Conference by the Chairman of the United States Delegation, the Secretary of State," June 26, 1945, PSF Trips-1945, Truman Papers HSTPL, Appendix D, 262–266. Hedley Bull, *The Anarchical Society: A Study of Order in World Politics;* Iriye, *Global Community.* The most apposite image for twenty-first-century transborder activity might not be so much mechanical as biological; see, for example, Philip Allot, *The Health of Nations: Society and Law Beyond the State* (Cambridge: Cambridge University Press, 2002), with its cover image of interacting neurons.

32. Rogers Smith, comments on a paper by Elizabeth Borgwardt, "Human Rights Out in the Cold: The 'Four Freedoms' in the Aftermath of World War II," presented at the University of Pennsylvania Law School, conference on "Law and the 'Disappearance' of

Class in 20th century America," Nov. 2002. On the power of ideas, see also Max Weber, "Social Psychology of the World's Religions," in *From Max Weber,* ed. Gerth and Mills, 280; Philpott, *Revolutions in Sovereignty*; Goldstein and Keohane, eds., *Ideas and Foreign Policy.*

33. Terence Ball and J. G. A. Pocock, eds., *Conceptual Change and the Constitution* (Lawrence: University of Kansas Press, 1988), 1; see also Peter Ives, *Gramsci's Politics of Language: Engaging the Bakhtin Circle and the Frankfurt School* (Toronto: University of Toronto Press, 2004), 23, 34–35.

34. Eleanor Roosevelt, *The Moral Basis of Democracy,* 62–63; Grotius, "Law of War and Peace: Prolegomena," 205.

35. Jean Anouilh, *Antigone,* based on the play by Sophocles, original text with Introduction and notes by David I. Grossvogel (Cambridge, Mass: Integral Editions, 1946), 62. First presented in the Théâtre de l'Atelier, Paris, February 1944. Note that in Paris in 1944, audiences would have universally understood the virtuous and doomed figure of Antigone as a symbol of defeated France; they would similarly have understood Antigone's cruel and tyrannical uncle as standing in for the occupying Germans.

Abbreviations

AAAPSS	*Annals of the American Academy of Political and Social Science*
AILC	B. D. Reams, Jr., ed. *American International Law Cases (1783–1968)*. New York: Oceana, 1971.
AJIL	*American Journal of International Law*
Ann. Dig.	J. Fischer Williams and H. Lauterpacht, eds. *Annual Digest of International Law Cases*. London: Longmans, Green, 1932–1953.
ASIL	American Society of International Law
BYIL	*British Yearbook of International Law*
Chapultepec	Inter-American Meeting. Mexico City, Mar. 1945.
CHAR	Chartwell Papers. Churchill College Archives Centre.
CHUR	Churchill Papers. Churchill College Archives Centre.
COHRO	Columbia Oral History Research Office, Butler Library, Columbia University.
EPIL	R. Bernhardt, ed. *Encyclopedia of Public International Law*. 4 vols. North Holland, 2000.
FAO	Food and Agriculture Organization
FDRPL	Franklin D. Roosevelt Presidential Library
Friedman	L. Friedman, ed. *The Law of War: A Documentary History*. 2 vols. New York: Random House, 1972.
FRUS	*Foreign Relations of the United States*. Washington, DC: US GPO. Individual volumes titled topically and/or chronologically.
GA	General Assembly of the United Nations
GAOR	General Assembly of the United Nations, Official Records
Hackworth	G. H. Hackworth. *Digest of International Law*. Washington, DC: US GPO, 1942.
HRLJ	*Human Rights Law Journal*
HSTPL	Harry S. Truman Presidential Library and Archive, Independence, Missouri
IBRD	International Bank for Reconstruction and Development, or World Bank; part of the 1944 Bretton Woods Charters

ICC	International Criminal Court
ICJ	International Court of Justice
ICJ Reports	Reports of the International Court of Justice
ILC	United Nations International Law Commission
ILM	International Legal Materials
IMF	International Monetary Fund, part of the 1944 Bretton Woods Charters
IMT	International Military Tribunal. *Trial of the Major War Criminals, Official Text.* 42 vols. (Nuremberg trial.) Nuremberg: Secretariat of the International Military Tribunal under the Jurisdiction of the Allied Control Authority for Germany, 1947.
IMTFE	International Military Tribunal for the Far East, or Tokyo trial
LC	Library of Congress
NA-Kew	National Archives, Kew, UK (formerly Public Record Office)
NARA	National Archives and Records Administration, Suitland, MD
NGO	Non-governmental organization
NORC	National Opinion Research Center
OMGUS	Office of Military Government in Germany–United States Division (US Military Occupation authority)
OWI	Office of War Information
POQ	*Public Opinion Quarterly*
PPA	*The Public Papers and Addresses of Franklin D. Roosevelt.* (1940–1945). Compiled by Samuel I. Rosenman. New York: Harper, 1941–1948.
PPF	President's Personal Files
PSF	President's Secretary's Files
RdC	Recueil des Cours de l'Académie de la Haye
UNCIO	United Nations Conference on International Organization, Apr.–June 1945
UNRRA	United Nations Relief and Rehabilitation Agency, founded by a conference in June 1943. US Assistant Secretary of State Dean Acheson admitted that nobody really knew what "rehabilitation" meant in the organization's title.
UNWCC	United Nations War Crimes Commission
USDSB	*US Department of State Bulletin*
US GPO	United States Government Printing Office
WSC-FDR	*Churchill and Roosevelt: The Complete Correspondence.* Edited and with commentary by Warren F. Kimball. 3 vols. Princeton: Princeton University Press, 1984.

A Note on the History of Ideas

This book is fundamentally a story of ideas: how ideas about international organization from an earlier era were mediated by individual personalities in the crush of a global conflict, reshaped in contentious negotiations with often-wary allies, and ultimately translated into new institutional realities. Accordingly, the most salient sources have been the texts that historical actors themselves were writing, reading, and debating in the interwar era and in the first half of the 1940s.

Primary sources for such a history of multilateralist debates include influential books and articles by policymakers and commentators such as Sumner Welles, Walter Lippmann, and Wendell Willkie; policy papers and diplomatic correspondence such as those reprinted in the Foreign Relations of the United States documents series; as well as newspapers, political cartoons, speeches, public opinion polls, and the working papers produced by the "think tanks" and activists of the era. These texts were consumed and discussed by elected officials, activist groups, and by the reading public generally, both in the United States and internationally. These "consumers" themselves would then generate additional reactions, often in the form of pamphlets, letters to the editor, or additional speeches. Capturing this iterative dynamic, where ideas often transcended the intent of their framers and were transformed by debate in fluid and contentious times, is the essence of the history of ideas.

Sometimes, research has revealed an illuminating or surprising "backstory" in personal correspondence, internal memoranda, and early drafts of speeches or public statements that show deletions and alterations. Scholarly articles from the time, often drafted by academics who were activists or government officials themselves, are another neglected source for capturing the analysis of contemporary historical actors. Less probative, because more self-serving and further removed in time from the heat of events, are sources such as oral histories and published memoirs. Even these kinds of texts, however, are able to shed light and offer color when read "against the grain" for what they might inadvertently reveal about an author's motives, perceptions, and priorities. For example, the papers of Hamilton Fish Armstrong, the editor of *Foreign Affairs*, convenor of numerous policy study groups, and unofficial advisor to the Department of State, reveal a great deal about how marginal his advising efforts were to shaping official policy, even as Armstrong himself did his best to inflate their importance.

The traditional division between "primary" and "secondary" sources is less sharply delineated here, where many of the key primary sources of the era were often published as part of contemporary political debates. Accordingly, this bibliography highlights several categories of primary sources: unpublished materials (archived collections, diaries, other personal papers, privately-circulated papers of academic or policy study groups, oral histories); published records (including government records, document collections, and bibliographies); works by participants and contemporaries (ordinarily sources published before 1950); in addition to listing a sampling of some of the other relevant secondary sources such as books, articles, dissertations, and websites.

These sources create a sense of how a web of political ideas—about sovereignty, security, legitimacy, and the national interest—was picked apart and rewoven in unsettled and contentious times, and more importantly, how debates about these ideas helped to shape and transform that very context. With the analytical perspective offered by a certain chronological distance, these sources work together to tell the story of a key shift in America's vision of its role in the world.

Unpublished Document Collections; Personal Papers; Oral Histories

American Heritage Center, University of Wyoming: Murray C. Bernays Papers (copies sent by archivist John R. Waggener)

Butler Library, Columbia University: Carnegie Endowment for International Peace Archives; Wellington Koo Papers; Oral History Research Office, transcripts of interviews (Felix Frankfurter; W. Averell Harriman; Robert H. Jackson; Samuel I. Rosenman; James T. Shotwell; Herbert Weschler)

Churchill Archives Centre, Churchill College, Cambridge University: Chartwell Papers; Churchill Papers

Edith Simon Coliver (Nuremberg interpreter), unpublished papers in private collection, San Francisco, CA: diary, "My Trip to the Nuremberg Trials"; diary supplements, "Long Voyage Home" and "Reunion"; interviews with the author in 1997, 1999

Cornell University Law Library: William Donovan Papers, Nuremberg Collection

Arthur W. Diamond Law Library, Columbia University: Telford Taylor Papers (papers and advance copy of finding guide sent by archivist Christopher Laico)

Green Library, Stanford University: Henry L. Stimson Diary (microfilm)

Hoover Institution on War, Revolution and Peace, Stanford, CA: America First Committee Files; Americans United for World Organization File; Commission to Study the Organization of Peace File; Federal Union File; Freedom House File; Robert Murphy File; Harley Notter File; Republican Postwar Policy Association File; San Francisco International Center File; United Nations Association File; Woodrow Wilson Foundation File; Women's Action Committee for Victory and Lasting Peace File

Houghton Manuscript Library, Harvard University, Cambridge: William Castle, Jr., Papers; Joseph Grew Correspondence; Imperial War Museum, London; War Cabinet Rooms

King's College Archives Centre, King's College, Cambridge, UK: Keynes Papers

Langdell Law Library and Reginald F. Lewis International Law Center, Harvard Law

School, Cambridge: International Legal Studies Collection; Legal Periodicals; Nuremberg documents

Library of Congress, Washington, DC: Joseph Alsop Papers; Charles E. Bohlen Papers; Raymond Clapper Papers; Benjamin V. Cohen Papers; Thomas G. Corcoran Papers; Norman H. Davis Papers; Henry P. Fletcher Papers; Green H. Hackworth Papers; Cordell Hull Papers; Harold L. Ickes Papers; Robert H. Jackson Papers; Breckinridge Long Papers; Archibald MacLeish Papers; J. Pierrepont Moffat Papers; Leo Pasvolsky Papers; Robert A. Taft Papers; Henry A. Wallace Papers

London School of Economics and Political Science Archive: William Beveridge Papers; Hugh Dalton Diaries; Charles Kingsley Webster Papers

MacArthur Archive, Norfolk, VA: Bonner Feller Papers

Seeley G. Mudd Library, Princeton University, NJ: Hamilton Fish Armstrong Papers; Bernard Baruch Papers; Council on Books in Wartime, 1942–47; Council on Foreign Relations Collection; Allen Foster Dulles Papers; John Foster Dulles Papers; James Forrestal Papers; Henry Morgenthau, Jr., Papers; Harry Dexter White Papers

National Archives and Records Administration, College Park, MD: General Records of the Department of State (Alger Hiss File; Harley Notter File; Leo Pasvolsky Office Files); Records of the State-War-Navy Central Committee (SWNCC); Senate Foreign Relations Committee Papers

Public Record Office/National Archives, Kew, Surrey, UK: Cabinet Office Records (CAB); Central Office of Information Records; Foreign Office Records (FO); Prime Minister's Office Records (PREM); Treasury Office Records (T)

Franklin Delano Roosevelt Presidential Library, Hyde Park, NY: Adolf A. Berle, Jr., Papers; Oscar Cox Papers; Stephen T. Early Papers; Harry Hopkins Papers; Henry Morgenthau, Jr., Papers; Eleanor Roosevelt Papers; Franklin D. Roosevelt Papers (Atlantic Charter Meeting Files; Official Files; President's Personal Files; President's Secretary Files); Samuel I. Rosenman Papers; Henry A. Wallace Papers; Sumner Welles Papers; Stephen Wise Papers

Rutgers University Oral History Archive of World War II: Mark Addison, John F. Ambos, Lyman Avery, Thomas Bach, Edward J. Barry, Jr., Elliot Bartner, William H. Bauer, Walter H. Berger, Robert Billian, Lowell Blankfort, Lewis M. Bloom, Samuel E. Blum, George Boggs III, Warren Bowers, Roy W. Brown, Walter Bruyere III, M. Leon Canick, George Claflen, Crandon F. Clark, John F. Crane, Edward F. Culwick, Thomas R. Daggett, Frank Dauster, Walter Denise, Carleton C. Dilatush, John Dowling, Jr., James Essig, Robert Feller, Raymond Finley, Jr., Robert Fishkin, Samuel Frankel, Harry A. Galinsky, Marvin Gershenfeld, Richard Gies, William Gillam, William J. Godfrey, Sidney Goff, Livy Goodman, Vincent J. Gorman, Clark J. Gutman, C. Harrison Hill, Stokes Homan, E. Robert Hoppe, Russ Janoff, Kenneth Joel, W. Wallace Kaenzig, Lloyd Kalugin, Joseph W. Katz, Robert Kennedy, James T. Kenny, Tom A. Kindre, Robert C. King, Richard Kleiner, Barton Klion, Vincent Kramer, Harry Kranz, Frederick J. Kroesen, Thomas LaCosta, Robert H. Leaming, Joseph Lerner, Robert D. MacDougall, Joseph B. McCartney, Robert H. McCloughan, Charles W. McDougall, John A. Melrose, Robert F. Moss, Alfred Nisonoff, Aaron Polinsky, John C. Ragone, Walter Reichman, Paul W. Rork, Benjamin B. Roth, Theodore Sattur, Ralph Schmidt, Seymour Silberberg, Robert Strauss, Raymond B. Taub, Justin L. Weiss interviews

Albert and Shirley Small Special Collections Library, University of Virginia: Edward R. Stettinius, Jr., Papers

Kurt Steiner, Tokyo War Crimes Trial prosecutor, unpublished papers in private collection, Stanford, CA: scrapbook; interviews with the author in 1999, 2000

Harry S. Truman Presidential Library, Independence, MO: Dean Acheson Papers; Eleanor Bontecou Papers; George M. Elsey Oral History; Charles P. Kindelberger Oral History;

Charles P. Kindelberger Papers; Katharine Fite Lincoln Letters; Frank McNaughton Papers; Anthony J. Panuch Papers; President's Confidential File; President's Official File; Alvin J. Rockwell Papers; Samuel I. Rosenman Oral History; Samuel I. Rosenman Papers; Durward Sandifer Oral History; United Nations Pamphlet Collection

Government Records and Document Collections

Appadorai, A., and Maurice L. Gwyer. *Speeches and Documents on the Indian Constitution, 1921–1947.* Vol. 2. London: Oxford University Press, 1957.

Buhite, Russell D., and David W. Levy, eds. *FDR's Fireside Chats.* Norman, OK: University of Oklahoma Press, 1992.

Congressional Record.

Dickinson, Asa D. *The Best Books of the Decade 1936–1945.* New York: H. W. Wilson, 1948.

Doenecke, Justus D. *The Literature of Isolationism: A Guide to Non-Interventionist Scholarship.* Colorado Springs: Ralph Myles, 1972.

Drakidis, Philippe. *La Charte de l'Atlantique, 14 août 1941: Source Permanente de Droit des Nations-Unies.* Documents. Bensançon: Centre de Recherche et d'Information Politique et Sociale, 1989.

Ferencz, Benjamin B. *Defining International Aggression, the Search for World Peace: A Documentary History and Analysis.* Vol. 1. Dobbs Ferry, NY: Oceana, 1975.

Green, L. C. *The Contemporary Law of Armed Conflict.* Manchester: Manchester University Press, 1993.

International Military Tribunal. *Trial of the Major War Criminals.* 42 vols. Official text. Nuremberg: Secretariat of the International Military Tribunal under the Jurisdiction of the Allied Control Authority for Germany, 1947.

Ishay, Micheline R., ed. *The Human Rights Reader: Major Political Essays, Speeches, and Documents from the Bible to the Present.* London: Routledge, 1997.

Kyvig, David E., and Mary-Ann Blasio, eds. *New Day/New Deal: A Bibliography of the Great American Depression, 1929–1941.* NY: Greenwood, 1988.

League of Nations. *Chronicle.*

League of Nations. *Treaty Series.*

Mason, Elizabeth B., and Louis M. Starr, eds. *The Oral History Collection of Columbia University.* New York: Oral History Research Office, 1979.

McMahon, Arthur W. *Memorandum on the Postwar International Information Program of the United States.* Department of State Publication 2438. Washington, DC: US GPO, 1945.

Ministry of Foreign Affairs of the USSR. *Correspondence between the Chairman of the Council of Ministers of the USSR and the Presidents of the USA and the Prime Ministers of Great Britain during the Great Patriotic War of 1941–1945.* Vol. 1, *Correspondence with Winston S. Churchill and Clement R. Atlee (July 1941–Nov. 1945)*; Vol. 2, *Correspondence with Franklin D. Roosevelt and Harry S. Truman (Aug. 1941–Dec. 1945).* Moscow: Foreign Languages Publishing, 1957.

Notter, Harley A. *Postwar Foreign Policy Preparation, 1939–1945.* Department of State Publication 3580. General Foreign Policy Series, no. 15. Washington, DC: US GPO, 1949.

Nuremberg Military Tribunals. *Trials of War Criminals.* 15 vols. Washington, DC: US GPO, 1953.

Office of War Information. *Textes de la Liberté: Declarations Officielles Faites au Cours de l'Histoire des États-Unis.* OWI Library Services Division, US Office of Education, 1944.

Pan American Union. *Inter-American Conference on Problems of War and Peace, Mexico City, February 21–March 8, 1945.* Report submitted to the Governing Board of the Pan American Union by the director general. Congress and Conference Series, no. 47. Washington, DC: Pan American Union, 1945.

Polmar, Norman, and Thomas B. Allen. *World War II: The Encyclopedia of the War Years, 1941–1945.* New York: Random House, 1996.

Reisman, W. Michael, and Chris T. Antoniou. *The Laws of War: A Comprehensive Collection of Primary Documents on International Laws Governing Armed Conflict.* New York: Vintage, 1994.

Roberts, Adam, and Richard Guelff, eds. *Documents on the Laws of War.* Oxford: Clarendon, 1982.

Roosevelt, Franklin D. *Complete Presidential Press Conferences of Franklin D. Roosevelt.* New York: DaCapo, 1972.

———. *The Public Papers and Addresses of Franklin D. Roosevelt.* Vols. 10–13 (1940–1945). Compiled by Samuel I. Rosenman. New York: Harper, 1941–1948.

Schindler, Dietrich, and Jiri Toman, eds. *Droits des Conflits Armés: Recueil des Conventions, Resolutions et Autres Documents.* 4th ed. Dordrecht: Martinus Nijhoff; Geneva: Henry Dunant Institute, 1996.

———. *The Laws of Armed Conflicts.* 3rd rev. ed. Dordrecht: Nijhoff, 1988.

Supreme Commander for the Allied Powers. *Political Reconstruction of Japan: September 1945 to September 1948.* Report of the Government Section, Supreme Commander of the Allied Powers. Washington, DC: US GPO, 1949.

Tutorow, Norman E. *War Crimes, War Criminals, and War Crimes Trials: An Annotated Bibliography and Source Book.* Westport, CT: Greenwood, 1986.

United Nations. *Universal Declaration of Human Rights.* G.A. Res. 217, UN GAOR, 3rd Session, 1948. UN Doc. A/10.

United Nations Information Office. *The Atlantic Charter: Some Notes on Background and on United Nations Agreements and Resolutions Including Reference to the Statement: Also Extracts from Relevant Speeches by United Nations Leaders.* New York, c. 1945.

US Congress. *Congressional Record.* 78th Cong., 1st and 2nd sess., 1943–44; 79th Cong., 1st and 2nd sess., 1944–45.

US Department of Commerce. *Historical Statistics of the United States, Colonial Times to 1970s.* Bureau of the Census. Washington, DC, 1975.

US Department of State. *The Axis in Defeat: A Collection of Documents on American Policy toward Germany and Japan.* Department of State Publication 2423. Superintendent of Documents, 1945.

———. *Charter of the United Nations: Report to the President on the Results of the United Nations Conference on International Organization.* Washington, DC: US GPO, 1945.

———. *Report of the Delegation of the United States of America to the Inter-American Conference on Problems of War and Peace, Mexico City, Mexico, February 21–March 8, 1945.* Department of State Publication 2497. Washington, DC: US GPO, 1945.

———. *Peace and War: United States Foreign Policy, 1931–1941.* Washington, DC: US GPO, 1944.

———. *Cooperative War Effort: Declaration by United Nations, Washington, DC, January 1, 1942, and Declaration Known as the Atlantic Charter, August 14, 1941.* Executive Agreement Series, no. 236. Department of State Publication 1732. Washington, DC: US GPO, 1942.

———. *Foreign Relations of the United States: Diplomatic Papers, 1919–1921; 1928; 1941–1946.*

──────. *Bulletin*. Vols. 5–14.

US Department of the Treasury. *Proceedings and Documents of the United Nations Monetary and Financial Conference, Bretton Woods, New Hampshire, July 1–22, 1944*. 2 vols. Washington, DC: US GPO, 1948.

──────. *The Bretton Woods Proposals*. Washington, DC: US GPO, 1945.

US Emergency Management Office. *Four Freedoms and the Arsenal of Democracy*. 1941.

US House of Representatives. Committee on Banking and Currency. *Bretton Woods Agreements Act, Hearings on H.R. 211*. 2 vols. 79th Cong., 1st sess., Mar. 7–May 11, 1945.

──────. *Participation of United States in the International Monetary Fund and the International Bank for Reconstruction and Development*. 79th Cong., 1st sess., 1945. Rept. 629.

──────. Special Committee on Post-War Economic Policy and Planning. *The Post-War Foreign Economic Policy of the United States*. Washington, DC: US GPO, 1945.

──────. Committee on Foreign Affairs. *House Joint Resolution 192*. Hearings, 78th Cong., 2nd sess., 1944.

US Senate. Committee on Banking and Currency. *Bretton Woods Agreements Act, Hearing on H.R. 3314*. 79th Cong., 1st sess., June 12–28, 1945.

──────. Committee on Foreign Relations. *The Charter of the United Nations*. Hearings, 79th Cong., 1st sess., 1945.

──────. Joint Committee on the Investigation of Pearl Harbor. *Report of the Joint Committee Investigating the Pearl Harbor Attack*. 79th Cong., 2nd sess., 1945. S. Doc. 244.

──────. *Participation of the United States in the International Monetary Fund and the International Bank for Reconstruction and Development*. 79th Cong., 1st sess., 1945. Rept. 452.

──────. Committee on Foreign Relations. *Nominations—Department of State*. Hearings, 78th Cong., 2nd sess., 1944.

──────. Subcommittee of the Committee on Armed Services. *Investigation of Action of Army with Respect to Trial of Persons Responsible for the Massacre of American Soldiers, Battle of Bulge, near Malmédy, Belgium, December 1944*. Hearings, 81st Cong., 1st sess., 1949, pursuant to S. Res. 42.

──────. *Senate Report No. 478*. 78th Cong., 1st sess., 1943.

US War Information Office. *The United Nations Fight for the Four Freedoms: The Rights of All Men, Everywhere*. c1942.

Works by Contemporaries

Acton, John E. E. D. [Lord Acton]. *The History of Freedom and Other Essays*. London: Macmillan, 1922.

Adamic, Louis. *Dinner at the White House*. New York: Harper and Bros., 1948.

Adler, Mortimer J. *How to Think about War and Peace*. New York: Simon, 1944.

Alexander, Frederick. *From Paris to Locarno and After: The League of Nations and the Search for Security, 1919–1928*. London: J. M. Dent and Sons, 1928.

Alsop, Joseph, and Robert Kintner. *American White Paper: The Story of American Diplomacy and the Second World War*. New York: Simon and Schuster, 1940.

Alsop, Stewart. "Wanted: A Faith to Fight For." *Atlantic Monthly*, May 1941, pp. 594–597.

American Association for the United Nations. "Washington Letter on the 'United Nations.'" No. 23 (July 7, 1945) and no. 26 (July 31, 1945).

American Bar Association. *Report of Special Committee on Peace and Law through United Nations*. Sept. 1, 1949.

American Society for the Judicial Settlement of International Disputes. *Proceedings of the International Conference under the Auspice of the ASJSID*. Washington, DC, 1910.

Americans United for World Organization. *Congress and Foreign Policy: House and Senate Votes on Major International Issues*. New York: Americans United for World Organization, 1945.

Anderson, C. A. "The Utility of the Proposed Trial and Punishment of Enemy Leaders." *American Political Science Review*, 1943.

Angell, Norman, et al. *America and the New World*. Merrick Lectures. New York: Abingdon-Cokesbury, 1945.

———. *America's Dilemma: Alone or Allied?* New York: Harper and Bros., 1940.

April, Nathan. "An Inquiry into the Juridicial Basis for the Nuernberg War Crimes Trial." *Minnesota Law Review*, 1946, p. 313.

Arendt, Hannah. *The Origins of Totalitarianism*. With an introduction by Samantha Power. 1948; New York: Schocken, 2004.

Arnold, Henry H. *Global Mission*. New York: Harper and Bros., 1949.

Austin, John. *The Province of Jurisprudence Determined: Being the First Part of a Series of Lectures on Jurisprudence; or, The Philosophy of Positive Law*. 2nd ed. Edited by Sarah Austin. London: J. Murray, 1861–1863. (Microfiche. 19th-century legal treatises, no. 13934–13949. Woodbridge, CT: Research Publications, c1986.)

Baer, M. de. "The Treatment of War Crimes Incidental to the War." *The Bulletin of International News*, Feb.–Mar. 1945.

Bailey, Thomas A. *The Man in the Street: The Impact of American Public Opinion on Foreign Policy*. New York: Macmillan, 1948.

———. *Wilson and the Peacemakers*. New York: Macmillan, 1947.

———. *A Diplomatic History of the American People*. 2nd ed. New York: F. S. Crofts, 1942.

Baker, Ray Stannard. *Woodrow Wilson and World Settlement*. 3 vols. Garden City, NY: Doubleday, 1922.

Baldwin, Simeon E. "The International Congresses and Conferences of the Last Century as Forces Working Toward the Solidarity of the World." *American Journal of International Law* 1 (1907): 565.

Barcikowski, W. "Les Nations Unies et l'organisation de la Repression des Crimes de Guerre." *Revue Internationale de Droit Pénale*, 1946, p. 289.

Bartlett, Robert M. *They Work for Tomorrow*. New York: Association Press, 1943.

Bartlett, Ruhl J. *The League to Enforce Peace*. Chapel Hill: University of North Carolina Press, 1944.

Basu. "Tokio Trials." *Indian Review*, 1949, p. 25.

Belloni, G. A. "Criminalità di Guerra." *Giustizia Penale*, 1946, p. 1.

Bemis, Samuel Flagg. *The Latin American Policy of the United States*. New York: Harcourt Brace, 1943.

Bendiner, Robert. *The Riddle of the State Department*. New York: Farrar and Rinehart, 1942.

Ben-Gurion, D. "The Eichmann Case as Seen by Ben-Gurion." *New York Times Magazine*, Dec. 18, 1960, p. 7.

Bennet. "Notes on the German Legal and Penal System." *Journal of Criminal Law and Criminology*, Jan.–Feb. 1947, p. 368.

Berger, J. "The Legal Nature of War Crimes and the Problem of Superior Command." *American Political Science Review*, 1944, p. 1203.

Berle, Beatrice B., and Travis B. Jacobs, eds. *Navigating the Rapids 1918–1971: From the Papers of Adolf A. Berle*. New York: Harcourt Brace Jovanovich, 1973.

Berlin, Isaiah. *The Proper Study of Mankind: An Anthology of Essays*. Edited by Henry
    Hardy and Roger Hausheer. 1949; New York: Farrar, Straus and Giroux, 2000.
———. *Washington Despatches, 1941–1945: Weekly Political Reports from the British
    Embassy*. Edited by Herbert G. Nicholas. Chicago: University of Chicago Press,
    1981.
———. *Mr. Churchill in 1940*. Boston: Houghton Mifflin, 1964.
Bernays, Murray C. "The Legal Basis of the Nuremberg Trials." *Survey Graphic*, 1946,
    pp. 5, 289.
Bernstein, Victor H. *Final Judgment: The Story of Nuremberg*. New York: Boni and Gaer,
    1947.
Bial, L. C. "The Nuremberg Judgment and International Law." *Brooklyn Law Review*,
    1947, p. 34.
Biddle, Francis. *In Brief Authority*. New York: Doubleday, 1962.
———. "The Nuremberg Trial." *Virginia Law Review*, 1947, p. 679. French translation in
    Revue Internationale de Droit Pénale, 1948, p. 1.
Birkett, Justice. "International Legal Theories Evolved at Nuremberg." *International Af-
    fairs*, 1947, p. 317.
Blakeney, B. B. "International Military Tribunal." *American Bar Association Journal*,
    1946, pp. 75, 523.
Blum, John Morton, ed. *The Price of Vision: The Diary of Henry A. Wallace, 1942–1946*.
    Boston: Houghton Mifflin, 1973.
———. *From the Morgenthau Diaries*. Vol. 3, *Years of War, 1941–1945*. Boston:
    Houghton Mifflin, 1967.
Bogoslovsky. "The Nuremberg Trials." *New Jersey State Bar Association Yearbook*, 1946,
    p. 72.
Bohlen, Charles, and Robert H. Phelps. *Witness to History*. New York: Norton, 1973.
Boissarie, A. "La Définition du Crime contre l'Humanité." *Revue Internationale de Droit
    Pénale*, no. 3/4, 1947.
———. "La Repression des Crimes Nazis contre l'Humanité et la Protection des Libertés
    Democratiques." *Revue Internationale de Droit Pénale*, 1947, p. 111.
Borchard, E. "Effects of War on Law." *American Journal of International Law*, 1946.
Bourquin, Maurice. "Grotius est-il le pere du droit des gens?" In *Grandes figures et
    grandes oeuvres juridiques*. Geneva: Librarie de l'Université Georg, 1948.
Brand, G. "The War Crimes Trials and the Laws of War." *British Yearbook of Interna-
    tional Law*, 1949, p. 414.
Brand, J. T. "Crimes against Humanity and the Nuremberg Trials." *Oregon Law Review*,
    1949, p. 93.
Brickner, Richard. "Is Germany Incurable?" *Atlantic Monthly* 171 (1943): 84–93.
Brierly, J. L. "The Covenant and the Charter." *British Yearbook of International Law*,
    1946, p. 83.
———. *The Outlook for International Law*. Oxford: Clarendon, 1944.
Brown, Constance H., comp. "Postwar Planning: A Reading List." *Booklist* 38 (May 1,
    1942): 317–321.
Buell, Raymond L. *Isolated America*. New York: Knopf, 1940.
Bullitt, Orville H., ed. *For the President: Personal and Secret: Correspondence between
    Franklin D. Roosevelt and William C. Bullitt*. With an introduction by George F.
    Kennan. Boston: Houghton Mifflin, 1972.
Bullitt, William C. *The Great Globe Itself: A Preface to World Affairs*. New York: Charles
    Scribner's Sons, 1946.
Butler, Nicholas Murray. *The Family of Nations: Its Need and Its Problems: Essays and
    Addresses*. New York: Charles Scribner's Sons, 1938.
Byrnes, James F. *All in One Lifetime*. New York: Harper, 1958.

Caloyanni, M. "Le Procès de Nuremberg et l'Avenir de la Justice Pénale Internationale." *Revue Internationale de Droit Penal*, 1946, p. 6.

Canadian Institute of International Affairs. *Post-War Reconstruction Studies*. Dec. 22, 1941.

Cantril, Hadley, and Mildred Strunk, eds. *Public Opinion, 1935–1946*. Princeton: Princeton University Press, 1951.

Carnegie Endowment for International Peace. *Consultation between the United Nations and Non-Governmental Organizations: A Working Paper Transmitted by the Interim Committee to Consultative Non-Governmental Organizations*. United Nations Studies, no. 3. New York, Dec. 1949.

———. *Year Book 1945*. Washington, DC, 1945.

———. *Year Book 1944*. Washington, DC, 1944.

———. *Year Book 1943*. Washington, DC, 1943.

———. *Year Book 1942*. Washington, DC, 1942.

———. *Year Book 1920*. Washington, DC, 1920.

———. *Year Book 1913–1914*. Washington, DC, 1914.

———. *Report on the Teaching of International Law in the Educational Institutions of the United States*. Washington, DC, 1913.

Carr, E. H. *The Twenty Years' Crisis: 1919–1939*. 2nd ed. London: Macmillan, 1945.

Carter, E. F. "The Nuremberg Trials: A Turning Point in the Enforcement of International Law." *Nebraska Law Review*, 1949, p. 370.

Chafee, Zechariah, Jr. *How Human Rights Got into the Constitution*. Boston: Boston University Press, 1952.

———. *Documents on Fundamental Rights*. Cambridge: Harvard University Press, 1951.

"Chapultepec." *Life* 18 (Mar. 19, 1945): 30.

Cherne, Leo M. *Bretton Woods: A Cornerstone of Lasting Peace*. New York: Americans United for World Organization, c1945.

Childs, Marquis W. *I Write from Washington*. New York: Harper and Bros., 1942.

———. *They Hate Roosevelt!* Pamphlet circulated by the Democratic National Committee, Hotel Biltmore, New York. New York: Harper and Bros., 1936.

Churchill, Winston S. *Winston and Clementine: The Personal Letters of the Churchills, edited by their daughter Mary Soames*. Boston: Houghton Mifflin, 1999.

———. *My Early Life 1874–1904*. With an introduction by William Manchester. 1930; New York: Simon and Schuster, 1996.

———. *Great Contemporaries*. 1938; Rev. ed., London: Cooper, 1990.

———. *Winston S. Churchill: His Complete Speeches, 1897–1963*. Edited by Robert Rhodes James. 8 vols. New York: Chelsea House Publishers, 1974.

———. *Winston Churchill on America and Britain: A Selection of His Thoughts on Anglo-American Relations*. Foreword by Lady Churchill. Preface by W. Averell Harriman. Collected and edited with an introduction by Kay Halle. New York: Walker, 1970.

———. *The New World*. Vol. 2, *History of the English-Speaking Peoples*. London: Cassell, 1956.

———. *The Second World War*. 6 vols. Vol. 1, *The Gathering Storm*; Vol. 2, *Their Finest Hour*; Vol. 3, *The Grand Alliance*; Vol. 4, *The Hinge of Fate*; Vol. 5, *Closing the Ring*; Vol. 6, *Triumph and Tragedy*. Boston: Houghton Mifflin, 1948–1953.

———. *Secret Session Speeches*. Compiled by Charles Eade. London: Cassell, 1946.

———. *The Unrelenting Struggle: War Speeches by the Right Hon. Winston S. Churchill*. Compiled by Charles Eade. Boston: Little, Brown, 1942.

———. *Address of the Rt. Hon. Winston Churchill, Prime Minister of Great Britain, Delivered before the Senate of the United States and Distinguished Guests, December 26, 1941, Together with the Proceedings Incident Thereto*. Washington, DC: US GPO, 1941.

———. *Freedom's Cause: An Address by the Prime Minister, Mr. Winston Churchill to the*

Meeting of Representatives of Great Britain and Allied Governments, St. James's Palace, June 12, 1941, Together with the Text of the Allied Resolution. New York: British Library of Information, 1941.

Claremont Library. *War Aims and Peace Aims: List of Recent Purchases by Claremont Colleges Library.* Claremont Library Lists, no. 1. Claremont, CA, Apr. 1942.

Clay, Lucius D. *Decision in Germany.* Garden City, NY: Doubleday, 1950.

Colville, John. *The Fringes of Power: Downing Street Diaries, 1939–1945.* London: Hodder and Stoughton, 1985.

Commission on a Just and Durable Peace. *A Message from the National Study Conference on the Churches and a Just and Durable Peace.* New York, 1945.

———. *A Guidebook for Action.* New York, 1944.

———. *A Just and Durable Peace: Statement of Political Propositions.* New York, 1943.

———. *A Message from the National Study Conference on the Churches and a Just and Durable Peace.* New York, 1942.

Commission on the Responsibility of the Authors of the War and on Enforcement of Penalties. "Report." *American Journal of International Law,* 1920, p. 95.

Commission to Study the Organization of Peace. *Ten Year Record, 1939–1949.* New York, 1949.

———. *Bulletin.* 1942–1946.

———. *A Design for a Charter of the General International Organization.* New York, 1944.

———. *Eleven Fundamentals for the Organization of Peace.* New York, 1944.

———. *The Peace We Want.* New York, 1944.

———. *The United States and Postwar International Organization.* New York, 1944.

———. *Fourth Report.* New York, 1943.

———. *Third Report.* New York, 1943.

———. *Second Report: The Transitional Period.* New York, 1942.

———. *Study Course on Immediate Post-War Problems.* New York, 1942.

———. *Toward Greater Freedom.* New York, 1942.

———. *The Atlantic Charter, the Eight-Point Declaration of President Roosevelt and Prime Minister Churchill, August 14, 1941.* New York, 1941.

———. *Comment on the Eight Point Declaration.* New York, 1941.

———. *In Time of War Prepare for Peace.* New York, 1940.

———. *Preliminary Report, November, 1940.* New York, 1940.

———. *A Study of the Organization of Peace.* New York, 1940.

Connally, Tom. *My Name Is Tom Connally.* New York: Crowell, 1954.

Corbett, Percy E. *The Dumbarton Oaks Plan.* Yale Institute of International Studies. Memorandum no. 13. New Haven, CT, Nov. 25, 1944.

———. *Moscow, Teheran, and International Organization.* Yale Institute of International Studies. Memorandum no. 8. New Haven, CT, Mar. 1, 1944.

———. "War Aims and Post-War Plans." American Committee for International Studies, Conference on North Atlantic Relations, Prout's Neck, ME, Sept. 4–9, 1941.

Corbett, Percy E., and Grayson L. Kirk. *The Outlook for a Security Organization.* Yale Institute for International Studies. Memorandum no. 10. New Haven, CT, June 15, 1944.

Corwin, Edward S. *The "Higher Law" Background of American Constitutional Law.* Ithaca: Cornell University Press, 1957.

———. *Total War and the Constitution.* Five lectures delivered for the William W. Cook Foundation, University of Michigan, Mar. 1946. New York: Knopf, 1947.

———. *The Constitution and World Organization.* Princeton: Princeton University Press, 1944.

Cresson, William Penn. *The Holy Alliance: The European Background to the Monroe Doctrine.* New York: Oxford University Press, 1922.

Curti, Merle. *The American Peace Crusade*. Durham, NC: Duke University Press, 1929.

Das, Taraknath. *The Atlantic Charter and India*. New York: India League of America, 1942.

Dean, Vera Micheles. *The Four Cornerstones of Peace*. New York: Whittlesey House / McGraw-Hill, 1946.

Dilks, David, ed. *The Diaries of Sir Alexander Cadogan, O.M., 1938–1945*. London: Cassell, 1971.

Dulles, John Foster. *War or Peace*. New York: Macmillan, 1950.

———. *Long-Range Peace Objectives, Including an Analysis of the Roosevelt-Churchill Eight-Point Declaration*. Statement submitted to the Commission to Study the Bases of a Just and Durable Peace, by its chairman, Mr. John Foster Dulles; together with comments on the paper and suggestions for its use by study groups. New York, Sept. 1941.

Dunant, Henry. *Un Souvenir de Solferino*. Geneva: Joel Cherbuliez, 1862.

Eade, Charles C. *Churchill by Contemporaries*. London: Collins, 1952.

Eagleton, Clyde. *The Forces That Shape Our Future*. New York: New York University Press; London: Oxford University Press, 1945.

Eichelberger, Clark M. *Organizing for Peace: A Personal History of the Founding of the United Nations*. New York: Harper and Row, 1977.

———. *The United Nations Charter: What Was Done at San Francisco*. New York: Harper and Bros., 1945.

———. *Proposals for the United Nations Charter*. New York: Harper and Bros., 1944.

———. *The Time Has Come for Action*. New York: Harper and Bros., 1944.

———. "The League of Nations Association." In *Educating for Peace*, edited by Ida T. Jacobs and John J. DeBoer. New York: Harper and Bros., 1940.

Estorick, Eric. *Stafford Cripps: Master Statesman*. New York: John Day, 1949.

Feis, Herbert. *Churchill, Roosevelt, and Stalin: The War They Waged and the Peace They Sought*. Princeton: Princeton University Press, 1957.

Finney, Nat S. "Joseph H. Ball: A Liberal Dose of Candor." In *Public Men in and out of Office*, edited by J. T. Salter. Chapel Hill: University of North Carolina Press, 1946.

Flynn, John T. *The Roosevelt Myth*. New York: Garden City, 1948.

Ford, Thomas K. "The Genesis of the First Hague Peace Conference." *Political Science Quarterly* 51 (1936): 362–381.

Frank, Jerome. *Law and the Modern Mind*. New York: Brentano's, 1930.

Galloway, George B. *Postwar Planning in the United States*. New York: Twentieth Century Fund, 1942.

Gerhart, Eugene C. *American Liberty and "Natural Law."* With an introduction by Roscoe Pound. 1953; New York: Fred B. Rothman, 1986.

Gilbert, Gustave M. "Hermann Goering, Amiable Psychopath." *Journal of Abnormal and Social Psychology* 46 (Apr. 1948): 211.

———. *Nuremberg Diary*. 1947; New York: Da Capo, 1995.

Gildersleeve, Virginia C. *Many a Good Crusade*. New York: Macmillan, 1954.

Glueck, Sheldon. *War Criminals: Their Prosecution and Punishment*. New York: Knopf, 1944.

———. "Trial and Punishment of Axis War Criminals." *Free World* 4 (Nov. 1942): 143–146.

Gordon, Beate Sirota. *The Only Woman in the Room: A Memoir*. Tokyo: Kondasha International, 1997.

Grafton, Samuel. *All Out! How Democracy Will Defend America, Based on the French Failure, the English Stand, and the American Program*. New York: Simon and Schuster, 1940.

Gross, Leo. "The Peace of Westphalia, 1648–1948." *American Journal of International Law* 42 (Jan. 1948): 20.

Gundlach, Ralph H. "Changing Policies of Peace and Patriotic Societies." *Journal of Social Psychology* 15 (Feb. 1942): 192–195.

Hambro, Carl J. *How to Win the Peace*. Philadelphia: Lippincott, 1942.

Harriman, W. Averell, and Elie Abel. *Special Envoy to Churchill and Stalin, 1941–1946*. New York: Random House, 1975.

Hart, Albert B. "American Ideals of International Relations." *American Journal of International Law* 1 (1907): 624.

Haskins, Charles H. *Some Problems of the Peace Conference*. Cambridge: Harvard University Press, 1920.

Hersey, John. *Into the Valley: A Skirmish of the Marines*. New York: Knopf, 1943.

Hill, David Jayne. "The Net Result at the Hague." *The American Review of Reviews* 36 (Dec. 1907): 727.

Holborn, Louise W. *War and Peace Aims of the United Nations, September 1, 1939–December 31, 1942*. New York: World Peace Foundation, 1943.

Holland, Thomas E. *The Laws of War on Land*. Oxford: Clarendon, 1908.

Holmes, Olive. "The Mexico City Conference and Regional Security." *Foreign Policy Reports* 21 (May 1, 1945): 42.

Hoover, Herbert. *The Ordeal of Woodrow Wilson*. New York: McGraw-Hill, 1958.

Hoover, Herbert, and Hugh Gibson. *The Problems of Lasting Peace*. New York: Harper and Bros., 1942.

Hopkins, Harry. "The Inside Story of My Meeting with Stalin." *American Magazine* 35 (Dec. 1, 1941): 14–15.

House, Edward M., and Charles Seymour, eds. *What Really Happened at Paris: The Story of the Peace Conference, 1918–1919*. New York: C. Scribner's Sons, 1921.

Hull, Cordell. *The Memoirs of Cordell Hull*. 2 vols. New York: Macmillan, 1948.

Humphrey, John P. *Human Rights and the United Nations: A Great Adventure*. Dobbs Ferry, NY: Transnational Publishers, 1984.

Humphrey, R. A. "The Atlantic Charter: Symbol of United Democracy." Public Affairs Bulletin No. 9, Library of Congress Legislative Reference Service. Washington, DC: US GPO, Feb. 1942.

Hunt, Jay B. "The Act of Chapultepec and the United Nations." Masters thesis, Department of History, University of Utah, 1948.

Hyde, Charles Cheney. *International Law, Chiefly as Interpreted and Applied by the United States*. 2nd rev. ed. Boston: Little, Brown, 1945.

Ickes, Harold L. *The Secret Diary of Harold L. Ickes*. 3 vols. New York: Simon and Schuster, 1953–1954.

——. *Autobiography of a Curmudgeon*. New York: Reynal and Hitchcock, 1943.

Idelson, Vladimir R. "The Law of Nations and the Individual." *Transactions of the Grotius Society* 30 (1944): 50–82.

India's Right to Freedom. Pamphlet. Nov. 1944.

Inter-Allied Information Center. Section for Information on Studies in Postwar Reconciliation. *Research and Postwar Planning*. Part 4. New York: The Center, July–Aug. 1942.

Jackson, Robert H. *That Man: An Insider's Portrait of Franklin D. Roosevelt*. Edited by John Q. Barrett. New York: Oxford University Press, 2003.

——. *Report of Robert H. Jackson, United States Representative to the International Conference on Military Trials*. Washington: US GPO, 1949.

——. *The Nürnberg Case: Together with Other Documents*. New York: Knopf, 1947.

——. "Address of Robert H. Jackson, Attorney General of the United States, Inter-American Bar Association, Havana, Cuba, March 27, 1941." Read by the American ambassador, George S. Messersmith. *American Journal of International Law* 35 (1941): 348–359.

———. *The Struggle for Judicial Supremacy: A Study of a Crisis in American Power Politics.* New York: Knopf, 1941.

Janeway, Eliot. "The Four Freedoms vs. the 'New Order.'" In *Smash Hitler's International: The Strategy of Political Offensive against the Axis,* by Edmond Taylor, Edgar Snow, and Eliot Janeway. New York: Greyston, c1941.

Jones, J. Mervyn. *Full Powers and Ratification: A Study in the Development of Treaty-Making Procedure.* Cambridge Studies in International and Comparative Law, no. 2. Cambridge: Cambridge University Press, 1946.

Kelsen, Hans. "The Old and the New League: The Covenant and the Dumbarton Oaks Proposals." *American Journal of International Law* 39 (1945): 45–83.

———. *Law and Peace in International Relations.* Cambridge: Harvard University Press, 1942.

Kennan, George F. *Memoirs, 1925–1950.* New York: Pantheon, 1983.

Kennedy, Sir John. *The Business of War: The War Narrative of Major-General Sir John Kennedy.* London: Hutchinson, 1957.

Kettner, Frederick. *The Four Freedoms: A Basis for a Better World.* Chicago: The Four Freedoms Center, c1943.

Keynes, John Maynard. *The Collected Writings of John Maynard Keynes.* 30 vols. Edited by Donald Moggridge. London: Macmillan for the Royal Economic Society, 1971–1989.

———. *The Economic Consequences of the Peace.* London: Macmillan, 1919.

Kopelmanas, Lazare. "L'Organisation des Nations Unies." Vol. 1, *Les Sources Constitutionelles de l'ONU.* 1947.

———. "Custom as a Means of the Creation of International Law." *The British Yearbook of International Law* 18 (1937): 127–151.

———. "The Problem of Aggression and the Prevention of War." *American Journal of International Law,* 1937.

Labrousse, Roger. "Il Problèma della Originalità di Grozio." *Revista Internazionale di Filosofia del Diritto* 28 (1951): 1.

LaGuardia, Fiorello H. "Interpreting the Atlantic Charter: Its True Intent and Meaning." Delivered at the Opening Ceremonies of Free World House, New York, NY, June 2, 1944. Reprinted in *Vital Speeches of the Day, 555–556.* New York: City News, 1944.

Lake Mohonk Conference on International Arbitration. *Report of the Eleventh Annual Meeting of the Lake Mohonk Conference on International Arbitration.* Lake Mohonk, NY, 1905.

———. *Report of the Seventh Annual Meeting of the Lake Mohonk Conference on International Arbitration.* Lake Mohonk, NY, 1901.

Lape, Esther Everett. *Ways to Peace: Twenty Plans Selected from the Most Representative of Those Submitted to the American Peace Award for the Best Practicable Plan by Which the United States May Co-Operate with Other Nations to Achieve and Preserve the Peace of the World.* New York: Charles Scribner's Sons, 1924.

Lasswell, Harold D. "Public Opinion and British-American Unity." American Committee for International Studies, Conference on North Atlantic Relations, Prout's Neck, ME, Sept. 4–9, 1941.

———. "The Garrison State." *American Journal of Sociology* 46 (Jan. 1941): 455–468.

Laugier, Henry. "A Weak Point in the Atlantic Charter." *Free World* 1 (Jan. 1942): 368–370.

Lauterpacht, Hersch. *International Law and Human Rights.* New York: Praeger, 1950.

———. "The International Protection of Human Rights." *Académie de Droit International, Recueil des Cours* 70 (1947): 3–108.

———. "The Grotian Tradition in International Law." *British Yearbook of International Law* 23 (1946): 1–53.

————. *An International Bill of the Rights of Man*. New York: Columbia University Press, 1945.

Lavine, Harold. "Why the Army Gripes." *The Nation*, Aug. 30, 1941, p. 179–180.

Lerner, Max. *Actions and Passions: Notes on the Multiple Revolutions of Our Times*. New York: Simon and Schuster, 1949.

Lewis, William Draper, and John R. Ellingston, eds. *Essential Human Rights: A Symposium*. Annals of the American Academy of Political and Social Science, Philadelphia, Jan. 1946.

Lincoln, William H. "Remarks." In *Official Report of the Thirteenth Universal Peace Conference*, p. 102. Boston: Boston Peace Conference, 1904.

Lippmann, Walter. *US War Aims*. Boston: Little, Brown, 1944.

————. *US Foreign Policy: Shield of the Republic*. Boston: Little, Brown, 1943.

Lleras, Alberto. "The Inter-American Conference for the Maintenance of Continental Peace and Security." *Bulletin of the Pan-American Union* 81 (Oct. 1947): 527.

Lodge, Henry Cabot. *War Addresses, 1915–1917*. Boston: Houghton Mifflin, 1917.

Luce, Henry L. "New World Colossus." *Time* 45 (Mar. 12, 1945): 25.

————. "The American Century." Pamphlet. New York: Time, Inc., 1941.

Lumsdaine, Arthur A. *The American Soldier: Combat and Its Aftermath*. 2 vols. Princeton: Princeton University Press, 1949.

Lydgate, William A. *What America Thinks*. New York: Thomas Y. Crowell, 1944.

MacVane, John. *Embassy Extraordinary: The US Mission to the United Nations*. Public Affairs pamphlet no. 311. Public Affairs Committee, 1961.

Mandela, Nelson. *Long Walk to Freedom*. Boston: Little, Brown, 1994.

Martin, Sir John. *Downing Street: The War Years*. London: Bloomsbury, 1991.

Masland, John W. "Pressure Groups and American Foreign Policy." *Public Opinion Quarterly* 6 (Mar. 1942): 115–122.

Mayorga, Margaret, ed. "The Four Freedoms." In *Plays of Democracy*. New York: Dodd, Mead, 1944.

Menck, Clara. "The Problem of Reorientation." In *The Struggle for Democracy in Germany*, edited by Gabriel A. Almond. Chapel Hill: University of North Carolina Press, 1949.

Merriam, Charles E. "The National Resources Planning Board: A Chapter in the American Planning Experience." *American Political Science Review* 38 (1944): 1075.

————. *On the Agenda of Democracy*. Cambridge: Harvard University Press, 1941.

Miller, David Hunter. *The Drafting of the Covenant*. New York: G. P. Putnam's Sons, 1928.

————. *My Diary at the Conference of Paris*. New York: Appeal Printing, 1924.

Montague, A. J. "The Supreme Court as a Prototype of an International Court." *American Society for the Judicial Settlement of International Disputes Proceedings*, 1910, p. 210.

Moore, John Bassett. "A Hundred Years of American Diplomacy." *Harvard Law Review* 14 (Nov. 1900): 182.

Morgenthau, Hans. *Politics among Nations: The Struggle for Power and Peace*. New York: Knopf, 1948.

Morgenthau, Henry, Jr. *Germany Is Our Problem*. New York: Harper, 1945.

Morton, Henry V. *Atlantic Meeting: An Account of Mr. Churchill's Voyage in H.M.S. Prince of Wales in August 1941, and the Conference with President Roosevelt which Resulted in the Atlantic Charter*. London: Methuen, 1943.

Mowat, Robert B. *The Concert of Europe*. New York: Macmillan, 1931.

Munro, Dana G. "The Mexico City Conference and the Inter-American System." *USDSB* 12 (Apr. 1, 1945): 525.

Murphy, Robert. *Diplomat among Warriors*. Garden City, NY: Doubleday, 1964.

Murray, Gilbert. *From League to U.N.* London: Oxford University Press, 1948.

National League of Women Voters. "Memorandum: The United Nations: The Road Ahead." Jan. 1946.

National Opinion Research Center. *Report Number 19: The Public Looks at International Organization*. Denver: NORC, 1944.

Neave, Airey. *Nuremberg: A Personal Record of the Trial of the Major Nazi War Criminals in 1945–6*. London: Hodder and Stoughton, 1978.

Neumann, William L. *Making the Peace, 1941–1945*. Washington, DC: Foundation for Foreign Affairs, 1950.

Nicolson, Harold G. *The Congress of Vienna: A Study in Allied Unity, 1812–1822*. New York: Harcourt Brace, 1946.

Nizer, Louis. *What To Do with Germany?* Chicago: Ziff Davis, 1944.

Opie, Redvers. *The Search for Peace Settlements*. Washington, DC: Brookings Institution, 1951.

Oppenheim, Lassa. *International Law, A Treatise*. 3rd ed. Edited by Ronald F. Roxburgh. Vol. 1, *Peace*. New York: Longmans, Green, 1920.

———. "The Science of International Law: Its Task and Method." *American Journal of International Law* 2 (1908): 13.

Osborne, John Ball. "The Influence of Commerce in the Promotion of International Peace." *International Conciliation* 22 (1909): 4.

Pal, Radhabinod. *International Military Tribunal for the Far East: Dissentient Judgment*. Calcutta: Sanyal, 1953.

Pasvolsky, Leo. "The Necessity for a Stable International Monetary Standard." Memorandum prepared for the Seventh General Congress of the International Chamber of Commerce, Vienna, May 29–June 3, 1933. Paris: International Chamber of Commerce, 1933.

Perkins, Frances. *The Roosevelt I Knew*. New York: Viking Press, 1946.

Phillipson, Coleman. *The International Law and Custom of Ancient Greece and Rome*. London: Macmillan, 1911.

Poland and the Four Freedoms. London: St. Clements, 1946.

Pollock, Frederick. "The Sources of International Law." *Columbia Law Review* 2 (1902): 511.

Populus [pseud.]. *My Dear Churchill, and Other Open Letters to Persons in Authority, by Populus*. London: Gollancz, 1941.

Porter, John B. *International Law, Having Particular Reference to the Laws of War on Land. A Course of Twelve Lectures Delivered to the Staff Class of the Army Service Schools by Lieutenant Colonel J. B. Porter*. 2nd rev. ed. Fort Leavenworth, KS: Press of the Army Service Schools, 1914.

Prefaces to Peace: A Symposium Consisting of the Following: One World, by Wendell L. Willkie (complete), The Problems of Lasting Peace, by Herbert Hoover and Hugh Gibson (complete), The Price of Free World Victory, by Henry A. Wallace (from the new book "The Century of the Common Man"), Blue-print for Peace, by Sumner Welles, (from the new book "The World of the Four Freedoms"). New York: Simon and Schuster / Doubleday / Doran / Reynal and Hitchcock / Columbia University Press, 1943.

Reeves, Jesse S. "The Influence of the Law of Nature upon International Law in the United States." *American Journal of International Law* 3 (1909): 547.

Reilly, Michael. *Reilly of the White House*. New York: Simon and Schuster, 1947.

Robinson, Jacob. *Human Rights and Fundamental Freedoms in the Charter of the United Nations*. New York: Institute of Jewish Affairs, 1946.

Rockwell, Norman. *Norman Rockwell: My Adventures as an Illustrator.* With Thomas Rockwell. New York: Harry N. Abrams, 1998.

Romulo, Carlos P., with Beth Day Romulo. *Forty Years: A Third World Soldier at the UN.* Westport, CT: Greenwood Press, 1986.

Roosevelt, Eleanor. *This I Remember.* New York: Harper and Bros., 1949.

———. *The Moral Basis of Democracy.* New York: Howell, Soskin, 1940.

Roosevelt, Elliott. *As He Saw It.* New York: Duell, Sloan, and Pearce, 1946.

Roosevelt, Franklin D. *FDR: His Personal Letters, 1905–1928.* Edited by Elliott Roosevelt. New York: Duell, Sloan and Pearce, 1950.

———. "Our Foreign Policy: A Democratic View." *Foreign Affairs* 6 (July 1928): 585.

Roosevelt, Franklin D., Felix Frankfurter, and Max Freedman. *Roosevelt and Frankfurter: Their Correspondence, 1928–1945.* Boston: Little, Brown, 1968.

Root, Elihu. *Miscellaneous Addresses.* Edited by Robert Bacon and James Brown Scott. Cambridge: Harvard University Press, 1917.

———. *Addresses on International Subjects.* Edited by Robert Bacon and James Brown Scott. Cambridge: Harvard University Press, 1916.

———. "The Need of Popular Understanding of International Law." *American Journal of International Law* 1 (Jan. 1907): 1.

———. "The Sanction of International Law." *American Journal of International Law* 2 (1907): 451.

Rosenman, Samuel I. *Working with Roosevelt.* New York: Harper and Bros., 1952.

Rostow, Eugene V. "The Japanese American Cases—A Disaster." *Yale Law Journal* 54 (1945): 489.

Rowe, Leo S. "Report on the Inter-American Conference on Problems of War and Peace." *Bulletin of the Pan-American Union* 79 (May 1945): 249.

Rusk, Dean. *As I Saw It.* As told to Richard Rusk; edited by Daniel S. Papp. New York: Norton, 1990.

Salomon, Andre. *Le préambule de la Charte bas idéologique de l'O.N.U.* Geneva-Paris: Éditions Trois Collines, 1946.

Sandifer, Durwood. "Rereading Grotius in the Year 1940." *American Journal of International Law* 34 (1940): 459.

Scott, James Brown, ed. *The Hague Conventions and Declarations of 1899 and 1907.* 3rd ed. New York: Oxford University Press, 1918.

———. "Lawyer-Secretaries of Foreign Relations of the United States." *American Journal of International Law* 3 (1909): 942–946.

———. "The Whewell Professorship of International Law." *American Journal of International Law* 2 (1908): 862–865.

Seth, Hira Lal. *Churchill on India: Let His Past Record Speak.* 2nd ed. Lahore: Hero, 1944.

Settel, Arthur, ed. *This is Germany.* New York: William Sloane, 1950.

Sherwood, Robert E. *Roosevelt and Hopkins: An Intimate History.* New York: Harper and Bros., 1948.

Shotwell, James T. *The Great Decision.* New York: Macmillan, 1944.

———. *War as an Instrument of National Policy and Its Renunciation in the Pact of Paris.* New York: Harcourt Brace, 1929.

Shyrock, Harry S., and Hope I. Eldridge. "Internal Migration in Peace and War." *American Sociological Review* 12 (Feb. 1947): 27.

Skillin, Edward S., ed. "The Hemisphere Pact." *Commonweal* 46 (Sept. 12, 1947): 515.

Smith, Dorothy E. *Reading List on the Four Freedoms and the Atlantic Charter.* Chicago: National Council of Teachers, c1943.

Smith, Edwin W. *Events in African History; or, The Atlantic Charter and Africa from an African Standpoint.* New York: Committee on Africa, the War, and Peace Aims, 1942.

Snow, Alpheus H. "International Law and Political Science." *American Journal of International Law* 7 (1913): 315.

Spykman, Nicholas John. *America's Strategy in the World: The United States and the Balance of Power.* New York: Harcourt Brace, 1942.

Starke, J. G. "Monism and Dualism in the Theory of International Law." *British Yearbook of International Law* 17 (1936): 66.

Stettinius, Edward R., Jr. *Roosevelt and the Russians: The Yalta Conference*, ed. Walter Johnson. Garden City, NY: Doubleday, 1949.

Stone, Julius. *The Atlantic Charter: New Worlds for Old.* Sydney: Angus and Robertson, 1943.

Straus, Oscar S. "The Peace of Nations and Peace within Nations." National Arbitration Congress, 1907.

Stronski, Stanislaw. *The Atlantic Charter: No Territorial Guarantees to Aggressors, No Dictatorships.* London: Hutchinson, 1944.

Sulkowski, Joseph. "The Atlantic Charter and the Principle of Self-Determination." *New Europe*, Aug. 1942.

Summers, Robert E., ed. *Dumbarton Oaks.* New York: H. W. Wilson, 1945.

Thompson, Walter H. *Assignment: Churchill.* New York: Farrar, Straus and Young, 1955.

Tully, Grace. *FDR My Boss.* With a foreword by William O. Douglas. New York: Charles Scribner's Sons, 1949.

UNESCO, ed. *Human Rights: Comments and Interpretations.* With an introduction by Jacques Maritain. New York: Columbia University Press, 1949.

Utley, Clifton M., ed. *Modern Men of Destiny: Today's Makers of Tomorrow's World.* Chicago: Pick Hotels, 1945.

Van Alstyne, Richard. *American Diplomacy in Action.* 2nd ed. Stanford: Stanford University Press, 1947.

Vandenberg, Arthur H., Jr., ed. *The Private Papers of Senator Vandenberg.* With the collaboration of Joe Alex Morris. Boston: Houghton Mifflin, 1952.

Visson, Andre. *The Coming Struggle for Peace.* New York: Viking, 1944.

Vreeland, Hamilton. *Hugo Grotius: The Father of the Modern Science of International Law.* New York: Oxford University Press, 1917.

Walters, Francis P. *A History of the League of Nations.* Published under the auspices of the Royal Institute of International Affairs. London: Oxford University Press, 1952.

Webster, Charles K. *The Foreign Policy of Castlereagh, 1812–1815: Britain and the Reconstruction of Europe.* London: G. Bell, 1931.

———. *The Congress of Vienna, 1814–1815.* Published for the Historical Section of the Foreign Office. London: H. Milford / Oxford University Press, 1919.

Welles, Sumner. *Seven Decisions That Shaped History.* New York: Harper and Bros., 1951.

———. *Where Are We Heading?* New York: Harper and Bros., 1946.

———. *An Intelligent American's Guide to the Peace.* New York: Dryden, 1945.

———. *The World We Can Make.* Address delivered under the auspices of the Alumni War Memorial Foundation at Milton Academy, Massachusetts, May 9, 1945.

———. *The Time for Decision.* New York: Harper and Bros., 1944.

———. *The World of the Four Freedoms.* With a foreword by Nicholas Murray Butler. New York: Harper and Bros., 1944.

———. *Address by the Honorable Sumner Welles at the Twenty-Fifth Anniversary Luncheon of the Foreign Policy Association, October 16, 1943.* New York: Woodrow Wilson Foundation, 1943.

Wells, H. G. *The Rights of Man; or, What Are We Fighting For?* Harmondsworth: Penguin, 1940.

West, Rebecca. *A Train of Powder.* London: Macmillan, 1955.

Wheaton, Henry. *Elements of International Law.* Classics of International Law edition. Edited by G. Wilson. Washington, DC: Carnegie Endowment for International Peace, 1939.

White, E. B. *The Wild Flag: Editorials from* The New Yorker *on Federal World Government and Other Matters.* Boston: Houghton Mifflin, 1946.

White, William Allen. *Woodrow Wilson: The Man, His Times, and His Task.* Boston: Houghton Mifflin, 1924.

Whitton, John B., ed. *The Second Chance: America and the Peace.* Princeton: Princeton University Press, 1944.

Willkie, Wendell L. *One World.* New York: Simon and Schuster, 1943.

Wilson, George G. "Grotius: Law of War and Peace: Prolegomena." *American Journal of International Law* 35 (1941): 205–226.

Wilson, Robert W. "International Law in the Treaties of the United States." *American Journal of International Law* 31 (1937): 271–289.

Wright, Quincy. "The United States and International Agreements." *International Conciliation* 411 (May 1945): 379–398.

———. "Human Rights and the World Order." *International Conciliation*, Carnegie Endowment for International Peace, no. 389 (Apr. 1943): 238–262.

———. "International Law and the Balance of Power." *American Journal of International Law* 37 (1943): 97.

Zimmern, Alfred. *The League of Nations and the Rule of Law, 1918–1935.* London: Macmillan, 1936.

Selected Secondary Sources

Abraham, Henry J. *Freedom and the Court: Civil Rights and Liberties in the United States.* 5th ed. Oxford: Oxford University Press, 1988.

Acheson, Dean G. *Present at the Creation: My Years in the State Department.* New York: Norton, 1969.

Ackerman, Bruce A. *We the People.* Vol. 2, *Transformations.* Cambridge: Harvard University Press, Belknap Press, 1998.

———. *We the People.* Vol. 1, *Foundations.* Cambridge: Harvard University Press, Belknap Press, 1991.

Adams, Henry H. *Harry Hopkins: A Biography.* New York: Putnam, 1977.

Adams, Irwin. "The Emergence of the International Law Societies." *Review of Politics* 19 (July 1957): 364.

Adamson, Michael R. "Inventing US Foreign Aid: From Private to Public Funding of Economic Development, 1919–1941." PhD diss., Department of History, University of California, Santa Barbara, Aug. 2000.

Adler, Les K., and Thomas G. Patterson. "Red Fascism: The Merger of Nazi Germany and Soviet Russia in the American Image of Totalitarianism, 1930's-1950's." *American Historical Review* 75 (Apr. 1970): 1046.

"Adolf Eichmann." *The Illustrated London News* 28 (1960): 941.

Albany Law School Board of Trustees. "Robert Hoghwout Jackson 1892–1954." *Albany Law Review* 19 (1955): 1.

Allen, Francis A. *The Decline of the Rehabilitative Ideal: Penal Policy and Social Purpose.* New Haven: Yale University Press, 1981.

Almond, Gabriel A. *The American People and Foreign Policy.* 2nd ed. New York: Harcourt Brace, 1960.

Anderson, Benedict. *Imagined Communities: Reflections on the Origins and Spread of Nationalism.* Rev. ed. London: Verso, 1991.

Anderson, Carol. *Eyes off the Prize: The United Nations and the African-American Struggle for Human Rights, 1944–1955.* Cambridge: Cambridge University Press, 2003.

Andrus, Burton C. *The Infamous of Nuremberg.* London: Leslie Frewin, 1969.

An-Na'im, Abdullah, ed. *Human Rights in Cross-Cultural Perspectives: A Quest for Consensus.* Philadelphia: University of Pennsylvania Press, 1992.

Arendt, Hannah. *Between Past and Future: Eight Exercises in Political Thought.* 1961; New York: Viking, 1968.

Aron, Raymond. *Peace and War.* Garden City, NY: Doubleday, 1966.

Ash, Timothy Garton. *Free World: America, Europe, and the Surprising Future of the West.* New York: Random House, 2004.

Asian Cultural Forum on Development. *Our Voice: NGO Declaration on Human Rights.* Bangkok, 1993.

Aust, Anthony. *Modern Treaty Law and Practice.* Cambridge: Cambridge University Press, 2000.

Backer, John H. *Winds of History: The German Years of Lucius DuBignon Clay.* New York: Van Norstrand Reinhold, 1983.

———. *The Decision to Divide Germany: American Foreign Policy in Transition.* Durham, NC: Duke University Press, 1978.

Bailyn, Bernard. *The Ideological Origins of the American Revolution.* 2nd ed. Cambridge: Harvard University Press, Belknap Press, 1992.

Baldwin, David A., ed. *Neorealism and Neoliberalism: The Contemporary Debate.* New York: Columbia University Press, 1993.

Ball, Howard. *Prosecuting War Crimes and Genocide: The Twentieth-Century Experience.* Lawrence: University Press of Kansas, 1999.

Barber, William J. *Designs within Disorder: Franklin D. Roosevelt, the Economists, and the Shaping of American Economic Policy, 1933–1945.* Cambridge: Cambridge University Press, 1996.

Barnes, Joseph. *Willkie: The Events He Was Part of, the Ideas He Fought For.* New York: Simon and Schuster, 1952.

Bass, Gary J. *Stay the Hand of Vengeance: The Politics of War Crimes Tribunals.* Princeton: Princeton University Press, 2000.

Bazyler, Michael J. "The Holocaust Restitution Movement in Comparative Perspective." In "Fifty Years in the Making: World War II Reparations and Restitutions Claims." Stefan A. Riesenfeld Symposium 2001 special issue, *Berkeley Journal of International Law* 20 (2002).

Bender, Thomas, ed. *Rethinking American History in a Global Age.* Berkeley: University of California Press, 2002.

Benton, Wilbourn E., ed. *Nuremberg: German Views of the War Trials.* Dallas: Southern Methodist University Press, 1955.

Berger, Jason. *A New Deal for the World: Eleanor Roosevelt and American Foreign Policy.* New York: Social Science Monographs, 1981. Distributed by Columbia University Press.

Bernstein, Barton. "The Conservative Achievements of Liberal Reform." In *Towards a New Past,* edited by Barton Bernstein. New York: Pantheon, 1968.

Bernstein, Richard B. *Thomas Jefferson.* New York: Oxford University Press, 2003.

Beschloss, Michael. *The Conquerors: Roosevelt, Truman and the Destruction of Hitler's Germany, 1941–1945.* New York: Simon and Schuster, 2002.

Best, Geoffrey. *Humanity in Warfare: The Modern History of the International Law of Armed Conflicts.* London: Methuen, 1983.

Beyleveld, Deryck, and Roger Brownsword. "The Practical Difference between Natural-Law Theory and Legal Positivism." *Oxford Journal of Legal Studies* 5 (1985): 9.

Birkenhead, Frederick Winston, 2nd Earl. *The Professor and the Prime Minister: The*

Official Life of Professor F. A. Lindemann, Viscount Cherwell. Boston: Houghton Mifflin, 1962.

Black, Conrad. *Franklin Delano Roosevelt: Champion of Freedom.* New York: Public Affairs, 2003.

Bloch, Ernst. *Natural Law and Human Dignity.* Translated by Dennis J. Schmidt. Studies in Contemporary German Social Thought. Cambridge: MIT Press, 1986.

Bloxham, Donald. *Genocide on Trial: War Crimes Trials and the Formation of Holocaust History and Memory.* New York: Oxford University Press, 2001.

Blum, John Morton. *'V' Was for Victory: Politics and American Culture during World War II.* New York: Harcourt Brace Jovanovich, 1976.

———. *Roosevelt and Morgenthau.* Boston: Houghton Mifflin, 1970.

Blumenson, Eric. "Who Counts Morally?" *Journal of Law and Religion* 14 (1999–2000): 1–40.

Boemke, Manfred F., Gerald D. Feldman, and Elizabeth Glaser-Schmidt, eds. *The Treaty of Versailles: A Reassessment after 75 Years.* Cambridge: Cambridge University Press, 1998.

Borgwardt, Elizabeth. "An Intellectual History of the Atlantic Charter: Ideas, Institutions, and Human Rights in American Diplomacy, 1941–1946." PhD diss., Department of History, Stanford University, 2002.

Borstelmann, Thomas. *The Cold War and the Color Line: American Race Relations in the Global Arena.* Cambridge: Harvard University Press, 2001.

———. *Apartheid's Reluctant Uncle: The United States and Southern Africa in the Early Cold War.* New York: Oxford University Press, 1993.

Bosch, William J. *Judgment on Nuremberg: American Attitudes toward the Major German War Crime Trials.* Chapel Hill: University of North Carolina Press, 1970.

Boyle, Francis A. *Foundations of World Order: The Legalist Approach to International Relations, 1898–1922.* Durham, NC: Duke University Press, 1999.

———. "Realism, Positivism, Functionalism and International Law." PhD diss., Political Science, Harvard University, June 1983.

———. "The Law of Power Politics." *Law Forum*, 1981, pp. 901–969.

———. "The Irrelevance of International Law: The Schism between International Law and International Politics." *California Western International Law Journal* 10 (1980): 193–219.

Bradley, Mark, and Patrice Petro, eds. *Truth Claims: Representation and Human Rights.* New Brunswick, NJ: Rutgers University Press, 2002.

Brady, Henry. "Causal Explanation in Social Science." Working paper presented at the Stanford Center for International Security and Cooperation, Stanford University, May 2002.

Breitman, Richard. *The Architect of Genocide: Himmler and the Final Solution.* New York: Knopf, 1991.

Breitman, Richard, and Alan M. Kraut. *American Refugee Policy and European Jewry, 1933–1945.* Bloomington: Indiana University Press, 1987.

Brinkley, Alan. *Culture and Politics in the Great Depression.* Waco, TX: Markham Press Fund, 1999.

———. *Liberalism and Its Discontents.* Cambridge: Harvard University Press, 1998.

———. *The End of Reform: New Deal Liberalism in Recession and War.* New York: Knopf, 1995.

———. *Voices of Protest: Huey Long, Father Coughlin and the Great Depression.* New York: Vintage, 1983.

Brinkley, Douglas, and David R. Facey-Crowther, eds. *The Atlantic Charter.* Franklin and Eleanor Roosevelt Institute Series on Diplomatic and Economic History. New York: St. Martin's, 1994.

Brock, Peter. *Pacifism in the United States: From the Colonial Era to the First World War.* Princeton: Princeton University Press, 1968.

Brogan, Denis W. *The French Nation, 1814–1940: From Napoleon to Pétain.* New York: Harper, 1957.

Brokaw, Tom. *The Greatest Generation.* New York: Random House, 1998.

Brooke, Stephen. "Atlantic Crossing? American Views of Capitalism and British Socialist Thought, 1932–1962." *Twentieth Century British History* 2 (1991): 107–136.

Brooks, Roy L. *When Sorry Isn't Enough: The Controversy over Apologies and Reparations for Human Injustice.* New York: New York University Press, 1999.

Bryant, Arthur. *The Turn of the Tide, 1939–1943.* London: Grafton, 1986.

Buchanan, James M. *The Limits of Liberty.* Chicago: University of Chicago Press, 1975.

Buergenthal, Thomas. *International Human Rights in a Nutshell.* 2nd ed. St. Paul, MN: West Publishing, 1995.

Buergenthal, Thomas, and Dinah Shelton. *Protecting Human Rights in the Americas.* 4th ed. Kehl am Rhein: N. P. Engel, 1995.

Bull, Hedley. *The Anarchical Society: A Study of Order in World Politics.* 1977; 2nd ed., New York: Columbia University Press, 1995.

Bull, Hedley, Benedict Kingsbury, and Adam Roberts, eds. *Hugo Grotius and International Relations.* Oxford: Clarendon, 1990.

Burgers, Jan H. "The Road to San Francisco: The Revival of the Human Rights Idea in the Twentieth Century." *Human Rights Quarterly* 14 (1992): 447–477.

Burns, James MacGregor. *Roosevelt: The Soldier of Freedom.* New York: Harcourt Brace Jovanovich, 1970.

Burns, James MacGregor, and Susan Dunn. *The Three Roosevelts: Patrician Leaders Who Transformed America.* New York: Grove, 2001.

Buscher, Frank M. *The US War Crimes Trial Program in Germany, 1946–1955.* Contributions in Military Studies no. 86. New York: Greenwood, 1989.

Butler, Judith. *Precarious Life: The Powers of Mourning and Violence.* London: Verso, 2004.

Campbell, Thomas M., and George C. Herring. *The Diaries of Edward R. Stettinius, Jr., 1943–1946.* New York: New Viewpoints, 1975.

Caron, David D. "War and International Adjudication: Reflections on the 1899 Peace Conference." *American Journal of International Law* 94 (Jan. 2000): 4–30.

——. "The Legitimacy of the Collective Authority of the Security Council." *American Journal of International Law* 87 (Oct. 1993): 552–586.

Casey, Steven. *Cautious Crusade: Franklin D. Roosevelt, American Public Opinion, and the War against Nazi Germany.* New York: Oxford University Press, 2001.

Cass, Ronald A. *The Rule of Law in America.* Baltimore: Johns Hopkins University Press, 2001.

Cassese, Antonio. *International Law.* New York: Oxford University Press, 2001.

Chace, James. "The Winning Hand." Review of *Franklin Delano Roosevelt: Champion of Freedom,* by Conrad Black, and *Franklin and Winston: An Intimate Portrait of an Epic Friendship,* by Jon Meacham. *New York Review of Books,* Mar. 11, 2004, pp. 17–20.

——. *Acheson: The Secretary of State Who Created the American World.* New York: Simon and Schuster, 1998.

Chambers, John W., II, ed. *The Eagle and the Dove: The American Peace Movement and United States Foreign Policy, 1900–1922.* New York: Garland, 1976.

Chatfield, Charles. *The American Peace Movement: Ideals and Activism.* New York: Twayne, 1992.

Chay, Jongsuk, ed. *Culture and International Relations.* New York: Praeger, 1990.

Chayes, Abram, and Antonia Handler Chayes. *The New Sovereignty: Compliance with International Regulatory Agreements.* Cambridge: Harvard University Press, 1995.

Chodorow, Nancy. *The Power of Feelings*. New Haven: Yale University Press, 1999.

Chua, Amy. *World on Fire: How Exporting Free Market Democracy Breeds Ethnic Hatred and Global Instability*. New York: Doubleday, 2003.

Clark, Ann Marie. *Diplomacy of Conscience: Amnesty International and Changing Human Rights Norms*. Princeton: Princeton University Press, 2001.

Claude, Inis L., Jr. "American Values and Multinational Institutions." In *Institutions for Projecting American Values Abroad*, edited by Kenneth W. Thompson. Lanham, MD: University Press of America, 1983.

Claude, Richard Pierre, and B. H. Weston, eds. *Human Rights in the World Community*. 2nd ed. Philadelphia: University of Pennsylvania Press, 1992.

Cleary, Edward. *The Struggle for Human Rights in Latin America*. Westport, CT: Praeger, 1997.

Cmiel, Kenneth. "Review Essay: The Recent History of Human Rights." *American Historical Review* 109 (Feb. 2004): 117–135.

———. "Freedom of Information, Human Rights, and the Origins of Third-World Solidarity." In *Truth Claims: Representation and Human Rights*, edited by Mark Bradley and Patrice Petro. New Brunswick, NJ: Rutgers University Press, 2002.

———. "The Emergence of Human Rights Politics in the United States. *Journal of American History* 86 (Dec. 1999): 1231–1250.

Cohen, Gary. "The Keystone Kommandos." *Atlantic Monthly* 289 (Feb. 2002): 46–59.

Cohen, Lizabeth. *A Consumers' Republic: The Politics of Mass Consumption in Postwar America*. New York: Knopf, 2003.

———. *Making a New Deal: Industrial Workers in Chicago, 1919–1939*. Cambridge: Cambridge University Press, 1990.

Cohen, Warren I. *America in the Age of Soviet Power, 1945–1991*. Vol. 4 of *Cambridge History of American Foreign Relations*. Cambridge: Cambridge University Press, 1993.

Coicaud, Jean-Marc, and Veijo Heiskanen, eds. *The Legitimacy of International Organizations*. Tokyo: United Nations University Press, 2001.

Commager, Henry Steele. *The American Mind: An Interpretation of American Thought and Character since the 1800s*. New Haven: Yale University Press, 1950.

Conot, Robert E. *Justice at Nuremberg*. New York: Harper and Row, 1983.

Converse, Jean. *Survey Research in the United States*. Berkeley: University of California Press, 1987.

Cooper, John Milton, Jr. *Breaking the Heart of the World: Woodrow Wilson and the Fight for the League of Nations*. Cambridge: Cambridge University Press, 2001.

Cooper, Laura E., and Cooper B. Lee. "The Pendulum of Cultural Imperialism: Popular Music Interchanges between the United States and Britain, 1943–1967." *Journal of Popular Culture* 27 (Winter 1993): 61–78.

Cox, Robert W. *Approaches to World Order*. With Timothy J. Sinclair. Cambridge: Cambridge University Press, 1996.

Crowell, Laura. "The Building of the 'Four Freedoms' Speech." *Speech Monographs* 22 (1955): 268.

Culver, John C., and John Hyde. *American Dreamer: A Life of Henry A. Wallace*. New York: Norton, 2000.

Dadrian, Vahakn. *The History of the Armenian Genocide: Ethnic Conflict from the Balkans to Anatolia to the Caucasus*. Oxford: Berghahn, 2005.

Dahl, Robert. *A Preface to Democratic Theory*. New Haven: Yale University Press, 1956.

Dallek, Robert. *Franklin D. Roosevelt and American Foreign Policy, 1932–1945*. Rev. ed. Oxford: Oxford University Press, 1995.

———. *The American Style of Foreign Policy: Cultural Politics and Foreign Affairs*. New York: Knopf, 1983.

————, ed. *The Roosevelt Diplomacy and World War II*. New York: Holt, Rinehart and Winston, 1970.

Damrosch, Lori F., Louis Henkin, Richard Crawford Pugh, Oscar Schachter, and Hans Smit. *International Law: Cases and Materials*. 4th. ed. St. Paul: West Group, 2001.

Danaher, Kevin. *Ten Reasons to Abolish the IMF and World Bank*. Open Media Pamphlet Series. New York: Seven Stories Press, 2001.

Danner, Mark. *Torture and Truth: America, Abu Ghraib, and the War on Terror*. New York Review of Books, 2004.

Davidson, Eugene. *The Trial of the Germans: An Account of the Twenty-Two Defendants before the International Military Tribunal at Nuremberg*. New York: Macmillan, 1966.

Deak, Istvan, Jan T. Gross, Tony Judt, eds. *The Politics of Retribution in Europe: World War II and Its Aftermath*. Princeton: Princeton University Press, 2000.

Dennet, Raymond, and Joseph E. Johnson, eds. *Negotiating with the Russians*. Boston: World Peace Foundation, 1951.

Desmond, Charles S., Paul A. Freund, Justice Potter Stewart, and Lord Hartley Shawcross. *Mr. Justice Jackson: Four Lectures in His Honor*. New York: Columbia University Press, 1969.

Dimbleby, David, and David Reynolds. *An Ocean Apart: The Relationship between Britain and America in the Twentieth Century*. New York: Random House, 1988.

Divine, Robert A. *Perpetual War for Perpetual Peace*. College Station: Texas A&M University Press, 2000.

————. *The Reluctant Belligerent: American Entry into World War II*. New York: Wiley, c1979.

————. *Foreign Policy and the US Presidential Elections, 1940–1948*. New York: New Viewpoints, 1974.

————. *Roosevelt and World War II*. New York: Penguin, 1970.

————. *Second Chance: The Triumph of Internationalism in America during World War II*. New York: Atheneum, 1967.

Dobson, Alan P. *The Politics of the Anglo-American Economic Special Relationship*. New York: St. Martin's, 1988.

Doenecke, Justus D. *The Battle against Intervention, 1939–1941*. Malabar, FL: Krieger, 1997.

————. *Not to the Swift: The Old Isolationists in the Cold War Era*. Lewisburg, PA: Bucknell University Press, 1979.

————. "Protest Over Malmédy: A Case of Clemency." *Peace and Change* 4 (1977): 28–33.

Donington, Robert. *Opera and Its Symbols: The Unity of Words, Music, and Staging*. New Haven: Yale University Press, 1990.

Donnelly, Jack. *Universal Human Rights in Theory and Practice*. Ithaca: Cornell University Press, 1989.

Donovan, Frank. *Mr. Roosevelt's Four Freedoms: The Story behind the United Nations Charter*. New York: Dodd, Mead, 1966.

Douglas, Lawrence. *The Memory of Judgment: Making Law and History in the Trials of the Holocaust*. New Haven: Yale University Press, 2001.

Doyle, Michael. *Empires*. Ithaca: Cornell University Press, 1986.

————. "Kant, Liberal Legacies, and Foreign Affairs." *Philosophy and Public Affairs* 12 (1983): 205.

Doyle, Michael, and G. John Ikenberry, eds. *New Thinking in International Relations Theory*. Boulder: Westview, 1997.

Draper, G. I. A. D. "Grotius' Place in the Development of Legal Ideas about War." In *Hugo Grotius and International Relations*, edited by Hedley Bull, Benedict Kingsbury, and Adam Roberts. Oxford: Clarendon; New York, Oxford University Press, 1990.

Driscoll, David D., ed. *The International Monetary Fund: Its Evolution, Organization, and Activities*. 1981; 4th ed., Washington, DC: International Monetary Fund, 1984.

Dubin, Martin D. "The Development of the Concept of Collective Security in the American Peace Movement, 1899–1917." PhD diss., Indiana University, 1960.

Dudziak, Mary L. *Cold War Civil Rights: Race and the Image of American Democracy*. Princeton: Princeton University Press, 2000.

Duignan, Peter. *The Rebirth of the West: The Americanization of the Democratic World*. Lanham, MD: Rowman and Littlefield, 1996.

Dutta, Krishna, and Andrew Robinson. *Rabindranath Tagore: The Myriad-Minded Man*. London: Bloomsbury, 1995.

Dworkin, Ronald. "Rawls and the Law." Symposium on Rawls and the Law. *Fordham Law Review* 71 (Apr. 2004): 1387–1405.

———. *Sovereign Virtue: The Theory and Practice of Equality*. Cambridge: Harvard University Press, 2000.

———. *Freedom's Law: The Moral Reading of the American Constitution*. Cambridge: Harvard University Press, 1996.

———. *Taking Rights Seriously*. Cambridge: Harvard University Press, 1977.

Eckes, Alfred E. *A Search for Solvency: Bretton Woods and the International Monetary System, 1941–1971*. Austin: University of Texas Press, 1975.

Edgerton, Robert B. *Death or Glory: The Legacy of the Crimean War*. Boulder: Westview, 1999.

Eichengreen, Barry. *Elusive Stability: Essays in the History of International Finance, 1919–1939*. Cambridge: Cambridge University Press, 1990.

Eide, Asbjørn, and Jan Helgesen, eds. *The Future of Human Rights Protection in a Changing World: Fifty Years since the Four Freedoms Address: Essays in Honour of Torkel Opsahl*. With the collaboration of Teresa Swinehart. Oslo: Norwegian University Press, 1991.

Eide, Asbjørn, et al., eds. *The Universal Declaration of Human Rights: A Commentary*. With the collaboration of Teresa Swinehart. Oxford: Oxford University Press, 1992.

Ekirch, Arthur A., Jr. *Ideologies and Utopias: The Impact of the New Deal on American Thought*. Chicago: Quadrangle Books, 1969.

Elsey, George M. "Some White House Recollections, 1942–53." *Diplomatic History* 12 (Summer 1988): 359.

Etzioni, Amitai. *From Empire to Community: A New Approach to International Relations*. New York: Palgrave Macmillan, 2004.

Falk, Richard A. Introduction to *Hugo Grotius: The Miracle of Holland*. By Charles S. Edwards. Chicago: Nelson-Hall, 1981.

Falk, Richard A., Friedrich Kratochwil, and Saul H. Mendlovitz, eds. *International Law: A Contemporary Perspective*. Boulder: Westview, 1985.

Falk, Richard A., Gabriel Kolko, and Robert Jay Lifton, eds. *Crimes of War: A Legal, Political-Documentary, and Psychological Inquiry into the Responsibility of Leaders, Citizens, and Soldiers for Criminal Acts in Wars*. New York: Random House, 1971.

Farber, Daniel A. "Robert Hoghwout Jackson." In *The Supreme Court Justices: A Biographical Dictionary*, edited by Melvin Urofsky. New York: Garland, 1994.

Feingold, Henry L. *The Politics of Rescue: The Roosevelt Administration and the Holocaust, 1938–1945*. New Brunswick, NJ: Rutgers University Press, 1970.

Feis, Herbert. *Churchill, Roosevelt, Stalin: The War They Waged and the Peace They Sought*. Princeton: Princeton University Press, 1957.

Feldman, Gerald D., and Thomas G. Barnes, eds. *A Documentary History of Modern Europe*. Vol. 4, *Breakdown and Rebirth*. Lanham, MD: University Press of America, 1982.

Feldman, Gerald D., and Wolfgang Seibel, eds. *Networks of Nazi Persecution: Bureaucracy, Business, and the Organization of the Holocaust*. Oxford: Berghahn, 2004.

Ferguson, Niall. "Economic Power and Military Power in the Twentieth Century." Paper presented to the International History Seminar, Stanford University, May 26, 2000.
———. *The Pity of War: Explaining World War I*. New York: Basic Books, 1999.
Finch, George A. "The American Society of International Law 1906–1956." *American Journal of International Law* 50 (1956): 293.
Fink, Carole. *Defending the Rights of Others: The Great Powers, the Jews, and International Minority Protection, 1878–1938*. Cambridge: Cambridge University Press, 2004.
Finnis, John. *Natural Law and Natural Rights*. Oxford: Oxford University Press, 1980.
Foner, Eric. *The Story of American Freedom*. New York: Norton, 1998.
Foot, Rosemary, John Lewis Gaddis, and Andrew Hurrell, eds. *Order and Justice in International Relations*. New York: Oxford University Press, 2003.
Foot, Rosemary, S. Neil MacFarlane, and Michael Mastanduno, eds. *U.S. Hegemony and International Organizations: The United States and Multilateral Institutions*. New York: Oxford University Press, 2003.
Forbath, William E. "The New Deal Constitution in Exile." *Duke Law Journal* 51 (2001): 165.
———. "Caste, Class, and Equal Citizenship." *Michigan Law Review* 98 (Oct. 1999): 1.
———. "Habermas's Constitution: A History, Guide and Critique." *Law and Social Inquiry* 23 (Fall 1998): 969.
Ford, Emmet B. "Diplomacy and the Transmission of Values." In *Institutions for Projecting American Values Abroad*, edited by Kenneth W. Thompson. Lanham, MD: University Press of America, 1983.
Fox, Richard Wightman, and James T. Kloppenberg, eds. *A Companion to American Thought*. Malden, MA: Blackwell, 1995.
Fox, Richard Wightman, and T. J. Jackson Lears, eds. *The Power of Culture: Critical Essays in American History*. Chicago: University of Chicago Press, 1993.
Franck, Thomas M. *The Power of Legitimacy among Nations*. New York: Oxford University Press, 1990.
———. *Human Rights in Third World Perspective*. 3 vols. London: Oceana, 1982.
Frankfurter, Felix. "Foreword." *Columbia Law Review* 55 (Apr. 1955): 435.
Freedman, Max, ed. *Roosevelt and Frankfurter: Their Correspondence, 1928–1945*. Boston: Little, Brown, 1967.
Freund, Paul. "The Humanities and the Constitution." *Humanities* 3 (Aug. 1982): 3.
Fry, Michael, ed. *History, the White House, and the Kremlin: Statesmen as Historians*. New York: Columbia University Press, 1991.
Gaddis, John Lewis. *Surprise, Security, and the American Experience*. Cambridge: Harvard University Press, 2004.
———. *The Landscape of History: How Historians Map the Past*. New York: Oxford University Press, 2002.
———. *We Now Know: Rethinking Cold War History*. New York: Oxford University Press, 1998.
———. *The Long Peace: Inquiries into the History of the Cold War*. New York: Oxford University Press, 1987.
———. *The United States and the Origins of the Cold War, 1941–1947*. New York: Columbia University Press, 1972.
Gardner, Richard N. *Sterling-Dollar Diplomacy: The Origins and Prospects of Our International Economic Order*. 1956; 1969; New York: McGraw-Hill, 1980.
Geertz, Clifford. "Found in Translation: On the Social History of the Moral Imagination." In *Local Knowledge: Further Essays in Interpretive Anthropology*, pp. 36–54. New York: Basic Books, 1983.
———. *The Interpretation of Cultures: Selected Essays*. New York: Basic Books, 1973.

Gelfand, Lawrence E. *The Inquiry: American Preparations for Peace, 1917–1919*. New Haven: Yale University Press, 1963.

Gellman, Irwin F. *Secret Affairs: Franklin Roosevelt, Cordell Hull, and Sumner Welles*. Baltimore: Johns Hopkins University Press, 1995.

George, Alexander L. *Bridging the Gap: Theory and Practice in Foreign Policy*. Washington, DC: United States Institute of Peace, 1993.

Gerhart, Eugene C. *America's Advocate: Robert H. Jackson*. Indianapolis: Bobbs-Merrill, 1958.

Gerstle, Gary. *American Crucible: Race and Nation in the Twentieth Century*. Princeton: Princeton University Press, 2001.

Gerth, H. H., and C. Wright Mills, eds. *From Max Weber: Essays in Sociology*. New York: Oxford University Press, 1958.

Gewirth, Alan. *The Community of Rights*. Chicago: University of Chicago Press, 1996.

Gienow-Hecht, Jessica C. E. *Transmission Impossible: American Journalism as Cultural Diplomacy in Postwar Germany, 1945–1955*. Baton Rouge: Louisiana State University Press, 1999.

———. "Trial by Fire: Newspaper Coverage of the Nuremberg Trial, 1945–46." In *Studies in Periodical and Newspaper History 1995 Annual*, edited by Michael Harris and Tom O'Malley. Westport, CT: Greenwood, 1997.

Gilbert, Felix. *To the Farewell Address: Ideas of Early American Foreign Policy*. Princeton: Princeton University Press, 1961.

Gilbert, Martin, ed. *Winston Churchill and Emery Reeves: Correspondence 1937–1964*. Austin: University of Texas Press, 1997.

———. *The Day the War Ended: May 8, 1945—Victory in Europe*. New York: Henry Holt, 1995.

———. *The First World War: A Complete History*. New York: Henry Holt, 1994.

———. *In Search of Churchill: A Historian's Journey*. London: HarperCollins, 1994.

———. *The Second World War*. London: Weidenfield and Nicholson, 1989.

———. *Winston S. Churchill: Finest Hour, 1939–1941*. London: Heinemann, 1983.

———. *Auschwitz and the Allies*. New York: Holt, Rinehart, and Winston, 1981.

Gilpin, Robert. *War and Change in World Politics*. New York: Cambridge University Press, 1981.

Gimbel, John. *The American Occupation of Germany: Politics and the Military, 1945–1949*. Stanford: Stanford University Press, 1968.

Glaser, Charles L. "Realists as Optimists: Cooperation as Self-Help." *International Security* 19 (Winter 1994–1995): 50.

Glendon, Mary Ann. *A World Made New: Eleanor Roosevelt and the Universal Declaration of Human Rights*. New York: Random House, 2001.

Goldstein, Judith, and Robert O. Keohane, eds. *Ideas and Foreign Policy: Beliefs, Institutions, and Political Change*. Ithaca: Cornell University Press, 1993.

Goldstein, Judith, Anne-Marie Slaughter, and Robert O. Keohane, eds. *Legalization and World Politics*. Cambridge: MIT Press, 2001.

Goldstone, Richard. "Prosecuting War Criminals." Occasional paper no. 10, David Davies Memorial Institute of International Studies, London, Aug. 1996.

Grazia, Victoria de. "Mass Culture and Sovereignty: The American Challenge to European Cinemas, 1920–1960." *Journal of Modern History* 61 (Mar. 1989): 53–87.

Haakonssen, Knud. *Natural Law and Moral Philosophy: From Grotius to the Scottish Enlightenment*. Cambridge: Cambridge University Press, 1996.

Haas, Peter J. *Morality after Auschwitz: The Radical Challenge of the Nazi Ethic*. Philadelphia: Fortress, 1988.

Haber, Stephen, David M. Kennedy, and Stephen D. Krasner. "Brothers under the Skin:

Diplomatic History and International Relations." *International Security* 22 (Summer 1997): 34.

Habermas, Jürgen. *Philosophy in a Time of Terror: Dialogues with Jürgen Habermas and Jacques Derrida*. Interviewed by Giovanna Borradori. Chicago: University of Chicago Press, 2003.

———. *Truth and Justification*. Edited and translated by Barbara Fultner. Cambridge: MIT Press, c2003.

———. *The Liberating Power of Symbols: Philosophical Essays*. Translated by Peter Dews. Cambridge: Polity, 2001.

———. *The Inclusion of the Other: Studies in Political Theory*. Edited by Ciaran Cronin and Pablo DeGreif. Cambridge: MIT Press, 1998.

———. *The Philosophical Discourse of Modernity: Twelve Lectures*. Cambridge: MIT Press, 1997.

———. *Between Facts and Norms: Contributions to a Discourse Theory of Law and Democracy*. Translated by William Rehg. Cambridge: MIT Press, 1996.

Haggard, Steph, and Beth Simmons. "Theories of International Regimes." *International Organization* 41 (Summer 1987): 491.

Hall, John A. *International Order*. Cambridge: Polity, 1996.

Hamby, Alonzo L. *Man of the People: A Life of Harry S. Truman*. New York: Oxford University Press, 1995.

Hansenclever, Andreas, Peter Mayer, and Volker Rittberger. *Theories of International Regimes*. Cambridge: Cambridge University Press, 1997.

Harrod, Roy F. *The Life of John Maynard Keynes*. London: Macmillan, 1951.

Heald, Morrell, and Lawrence S. Kaplan. *Culture and Diplomacy: The American Experience*. Westport, CT: Greenwood, 1977.

Held, David. *Global Covenant: The Social Democratic Alternative to the Washington Consensus*. Cambridge: Polity, 2004.

Henkin, Louis, ed. *The International Bill of Rights: The Covenant on Civil and Political Rights*. New York: Columbia University Press, 1991.

Herman, Sondra R. *Eleven against War: Studies in American Internationalist Thought, 1898–1921*. Stanford: Stanford University Press, 1969.

Hersh, Seymour M. *Chain of Command: The Road from 9/11 to Abu Ghraib*. New York: Harper Collins, 2004.

Hesse, Carla, and Robert Post, eds. *Human Rights in Political Transitions: Gettysburg to Bosnia*. New York: Zone Books, 1999.

Hilberg, Raoul. *The Destruction of the European Jews*. 3 vols. New York: Holmes and Meier, 1985.

Hilderbrand, Robert C. *Dumbarton Oaks: The Origins of the United Nations and the Search for Postwar Security*. Chapel Hill: University of North Carolina Press, 1990.

Hill, Kim Q. *Democracies in Crisis: Public Policy Responses to the Great Depression*. Boulder: Westview, 1988.

Hinsley, F. H. *Power and the Pursuit of Peace: Theory and Practice in the History of Relations between States*. Cambridge: Cambridge University Press, 1963.

Hirschman, Albert. *Exit, Voice, and Loyalty*. Cambridge: Harvard University Press, 1970.

Hitchens, Christopher. "Churchill Takes a Fall." *Atlantic Monthly,* Apr. 2002, pp. 118–137.

Hockett, Jeffrey. *New Deal Justice: The Constitutional Jurisprudence of Hugo L. Black, Felix Frankfurter, and Robert H. Jackson*. Lanham, MD: Rowman and Littlefield, 1996.

Hodgson, Godfrey. *The Colonel: The Life and Wars of Henry Stimson, 1867–1950*. New York: Knopf, 1990.

Hogan, Michael J. *The Marshall Plan: America, Britain, and the Reconstruction of West-*

ern Europe, 1947–1952. Studies in Economic History and Policy, The United States in the Twentieth Century. Cambridge: Cambridge University Press, 1987.

Hoganson, Kristin L. *Fighting for American Manhood: How Gender Politics Provoked the Spanish-American and Philippine-American Wars*. New Haven: Yale University Press, 1998.

Hollinger, David A. "Cultural Relativism." In *The Modern Social Sciences*, edited by Theodore M. Porter and Dorothy Ross. Vol. 7 of *Cambridge History of Science*, edited by David C. Lindberg and Ronald L. Numbers. Cambridge: Cambridge University Press, 2003.

————. "Not Universalists, Not Pluralists: The New Cosmopolitans Find Their Own Way." *Constellations* 8 (2001): 236–248.

Hollinger, David A., and Charles Capper, eds. *The American Intellectual Tradition*. Vol. 2, *1865 to the Present*. 4th ed. New York: Oxford University Press, 2001.

Holman, Frank E. *The Life and Career of a Western Lawyer, 1886–1961*. Baltimore: Port City Press, 1963.

————. *Story of the "Bricker" Amendment*. New York: Committee for Constitutional Government, Inc., 1954.

Holsti, Kalevi J. *Peace and War: Armed Conflicts and International Order, 1648–1989*. New York: Cambridge University Press, 1991.

Hoopes, Townsend, and Douglas Brinkley. *FDR and the Creation of the UN*. New Haven: Yale University Press, 1997.

Horsefield, J. Keith, ed. *The International Monetary Fund, 1945–1965: Twenty Years of International Monetary Cooperation*. 3 vols. Washington, DC: International Monetary Fund, 1969.

Horwitz, Morton J. *The Transformation of American Law, 1870–1960: The Crisis of Legal Orthodoxy*. New York: Oxford University Press, 1992.

Hoschild, Adam. *Bury the Chains: Prophets and Rebels in the Fight to Free an Empire's Slaves*. Boston: Houghton Mifflin, 2005.

Hufton, Olwen, ed. *Historical Change and Human Rights: The Oxford Amnesty Lectures, 1994*. New York: Basic Books, 1995.

Humphrey, John. *No Distant Millennium: The International Law of Human Rights*. Paris: UNESCO, 1989.

Hunt, Michael H. *Ideology and US Foreign Policy*. New Haven: Yale University Press, 1987.

Hutton, Will. *A Declaration of Interdependence: Why America Should Join the World*. New York: Norton, 2003.

Ignatieff, Michael. *The Lesser Evil: Political Ethics in an Age of Terror*. Princeton: Princeton University Press, 2004.

————. *Human Rights as Politics and Idolatry*. Edited by Amy Gutmann. Princeton: Princeton University Press, 2001.

————. *The Rights Revolution*. Toronto: House of Anansi, 2000.

————. "Human Rights: The Midlife Crisis." *New York Review of Books*, May 20, 1999, p. 58.

————. *Isaiah Berlin: A Life*. New York: Metropolitan Books, 1998.

Igo, Sarah. "Constructing American Community: Social Science and the Popular Imagination, 1920–1950." PhD diss., Department of History, Princeton University, 2002. Forthcoming as *America Surveyed: The Making of a Modern Public*.

Ikenberry, G. John. *After Victory: Institutions, Strategic Restraint and the Rebuilding of Order after Major Wars*. Princeton: Princeton University Press, 2001.

————. "Constitutional Politics in International Relations." *European Journal of International Relations* 4 (June 1998): 147–177.

———. "Creating Yesterday's New World Order: Keynesian 'New Thinking' and the Anglo-American Postwar Settlement." In *Ideas and Foreign Policy: Beliefs, Institutions, and Political Change*, edited by Judith Goldstein and Robert O. Keohane, p. 59. Ithaca: Cornell University Press, 1993.

Ikenberry, G. John, David A. Lake, and Michael Mastanduno, eds. *The State and American Foreign Economic Policy*. Ithaca: Cornell University Press, 1988.

"In Search of Global Justice." (Contemporary war crimes trials.) Produced by Public Radio International, aired on National Public Radio, June 28, 2000.

Iriye, Akira. *Global Community: The Role of International Organizations in the Making of the Contemporary World*. Berkeley: University of California Press, 2002.

———. "A Century of NGOs." *Diplomatic History* 23 (Summer 1999): 421.

———. *Cultural Internationalism and World Order*. Baltimore: Johns Hopkins University Press, 1997.

———. *The Globalizing of America, 1913–1945*. Vol. 3 of *The Cambridge History of Foreign Relations*. Cambridge: Cambridge University Press, 1993.

Irons, Peter H. *The New Deal Lawyers*. Princeton: Princeton University Press, 1992.

Jackson, Robert H. "The Weight of Ideas in Decolonization: Normative Change in International Relations." In *Ideas and Foreign Policy: Beliefs, Institutions, and Political Change*, edited by Judith Goldstein and Robert O. Keohane, p. 111. Ithaca: Cornell University Press, 1993.

———. *Quasi-States: Sovereignty, International Relations, and the Third World*. New York: Cambridge University Press, 1990.

Janeway, Michael. *The Fall of the House of Roosevelt: Brokers of Ideas and Power from FDR to LBJ*. New York: Columbia University Press, 2004.

Jervis, Robert. "Realism, Neoliberalism, and Cooperation: Understanding the Debate." *International Security* 24 (Summer 1999): 42.

———. *Systems Effects: Complexity in Political and Social Life*. Princeton: Princeton University Press, 1997.

———. "A Political Science Perspective on the Balance of Power and the Concert." *American Historical Review* 97 (June 1992): 723.

Jonas, Manfred. *Isolationism in America, 1935–1941*. Ithaca: Cornell University Press, 1966.

Jones, Dorothy V. *Toward a Just World: The Critical Years in the Search for International Justice*. Chicago: University of Chicago Press, 2002.

Joseph, Franz M., and Raymond Aron, eds. *As Others See Us: The United States through Foreign Eyes*. Princeton: Princeton University Press, 1959.

Joshi, Vijay, and Robert Skidelsky. "One World?" *New York Review of Books*, Mar. 25, 2004, pp. 19–21.

Joyce, James A. *The New Politics of Human Rights*. London: Macmillan, 1978.

Judt, Tony. *Past Imperfect: French Intellectuals, 1944–1956*. Berkeley: University of California Press, 1992.

Junker, Detlev. "Hitler's Perception of Franklin D. Roosevelt and the United States of America." In *FDR and His Contemporaries: Foreign Perceptions of an American President*, edited by Cornelius A. van Minnen and John F. Sears. New York: St. Martin's, 1992.

Kagan, Robert. *Of Paradise and Power: America and Europe in the New World Order*. New York: Random House, 2003.

Kahn, Paul W. *The Cultural Study of Law: Reconstructing Legal Scholarship*. Chicago: University of Chicago Press, 1999.

Kalman, Laura. *The Strange Career of Legal Liberalism*. New Haven: Yale University Press, 1996.

———. *Legal Realism at Yale, 1927–1960*. Chapel Hill: University of North Carolina Press, 1986.

Kammen, Michael. *American Culture, American Tastes: Social Change and the 20th Century*. New York: Knopf, 1999.

———. *Sovereignty and Liberty: Constitutional Discourse in American Culture*. Madison: University of Wisconsin Press, 1998.

———. *A Machine That Would Go of Itself: The Constitution in American Culture*. 1986; New York: St. Martin's, 1994.

Kaplan, Robert D. "Kissinger, Metternich, and Realism." *Atlantic Monthly*, June 1999, p. 73.

Katz, Barry. *Foreign Intelligence: Research and Analysis in the Office of Strategic Service, 1942–1945*. Cambridge: Harvard University Press, 1989.

Katz, Stanley N. "Constitutionalism and Civil Society." Jefferson Memorial Lecture, University of California at Berkeley, Apr. 25, 2000.

———. *Constitutionalism in East Central Europe: Some Negative Lessons from the American Experience*. German Historical Institute Annual Lecture Series no. 7. Providence: Berghahn, 1994.

Katzenstein, Peter J., Robert O. Keohane, and Stephen Krasner, eds. *Exploration and Contestation in the Study of World Politics*. Cambridge: MIT Press, 1999.

Katznelson, Ira. *Desolation and Enlightenment: Political Knowledge after Total War, Totalitarianism, and the Holocaust*. New York: Columbia University Press, 2003.

Katznelson, Ira, and Martin Shefter, eds. *Shaped by War and Trade: International Influences on American Political Development*. Princeton: Princeton University Press, 2002.

Keck, Margaret, and Kathryn Sikkink. *Activists beyond Borders: Advocacy Networks in International Politics*. Ithaca: Cornell University Press, 1998.

Kei, Ushimura. *Beyond the "Judgment of Civilization": The Intellectual Legacy of the Japanese War Crimes Trials, 1946–1949*. Translated by Steven J. Ericson. Tokyo: International House of Japan 2003.

Kelsen, Hans. *Principles of International Law*. New York: Rinehart, 1952.

Kennedy, David M. *Freedom from Fear: The American People in Depression and War, 1929–1945*. New York: Oxford University Press, 1999.

———. *Over Here: The First World War and American Society*. Oxford: Oxford University Press, 1980.

Kennedy, David W. *The Dark Side of Virtue: Reassessing International Humanitarianism*. Princeton: Princeton University Press, 2004.

———. *International Legal Structures*. Baden-Baden: Nomos, 1987.

———. "Primitive Legal Scholarship." *Harvard International Law Journal* 27 (Winter 1986): 1.

Kennedy, Paul, and William I. Hitchcock, eds. *From War to Peace: Altered Strategic Landscapes in the Twentieth Century*. New Haven: Yale University Press, 2000.

Kennett, Lee B. *G.I.: The American Soldier in World War II*. Norman: University of Oklahoma Press, 1997.

Keohane, Robert O, ed. *Neorealism and Its Critics*. New York: Columbia University Press, 1986.

———. *After Hegemony: Cooperation and Discord in the World Political Economy*. Princeton: Princeton University Press, 1984.

Keohane, Robert O., and Stanley Hoffmann, eds. *The New European Community*. Boulder: Westview, 1991.

Khagram, Sanjeev, James V. Riker, and Kathryn Sikkink, eds. *Restructuring World Politics: Transnational Social Movements, Networks, and Norms*. Minneapolis: University of Minnesota Press, 2002.

Kimball, Warren F. *Swords or Ploughshares? The Morgenthau Plan for Defeated Nazi Germany, 1943–1946*. New York: Lippincott, 1976.

——. *The Most Unsordid Act: Lend-Lease, 1939–1941*. Baltimore: Johns Hopkins University Press, 1969.

Kindleberger, Charles. *The World in Depression, 1929–1939*. Berkeley: University of California Press, 1973.

Kingsbury, Benedict, and Adam Roberts. "Introduction: Grotian Thought in International Relations." In *Hugo Grotius and International Relations*, edited by Hedley Bull, Benedict Kingsbury, and Adam Roberts. Oxford: Clarendon, 1990.

Kirgis, Frederick L. "The Formative Years of the American Society of International Law." *American Journal of International Law* 90 (1996): 559.

Kissinger, Henry A. *Diplomacy*. New York: Simon and Schuster, 1994.

——. *A World Restored: Metternich, Castlereagh and the Problems of Peace, 1812–22*. Boston: Houghton Mifflin, 1957.

Klein, Jennifer. *For All These Rights: Business, Labor, and the Shaping of America's Public-Private Welfare State*. Princeton: Princeton University Press, 2003.

Kloppenberg, James T. *Uncertain Victory: Social Democracy and Progressivism in European and American Thought, 1870–1920*. New York: Oxford University Press, 1986.

Knorr, Klaus, ed. *Historical Dimensions of National Security Problems*. Lawrence: University Press of Kansas, 1975.

Kochavi, Arieh J. *Prelude to Nuremberg: Allied War Crimes Policy and the Question of Punishment*. Chapel Hill: University of North Carolina Press, 1998.

Koessler, Maximilian. "American War Crimes Trials in Europe." *Georgetown Law Journal* 9 (1950): 18.

Kolko, Gabriel. *The Politics of War: The World and United States Foreign Policy, 1943–1945*. New York: Random House, 1968.

Kopelman, Elizabeth. "The Modern Machiavelli: Legitimacy, Conflict, and Power in the International Legal Order." *UCLA Law Review* 43 (Oct. 1995): 139–158.

——. "Ideology and International Law: The Dissent of the Indian Justice at the Tokyo War Crimes Trial." *NYU Journal of International Law and Politics* 23 (Winter 1991): 373–444.

Korey, William. *NGOs and the Universal Declaration of Human Rights: A Curious Grapevine*. New York: St. Martin's, 1998.

——. *The Promises We Keep: Human Rights, the Helsinki Process, and American Foreign Policy*. New York: St. Martin's, 1993.

Koskenniemi, Martti. *The Gentle Civilizer of Nations: The Rise and Fall of International Law, 1870–1960*. Cambridge: Cambridge University Press, 2002.

Kostuch, Gerhart, and Franz Kröger. *Germany Seen through British and American Eyes*. Frankfurt: Moritz Diesterweg, 1969.

Kraske, Gary E. *Missionaries of the Book: The American Library Profession and the Origins of Cultural Diplomacy*. London: Greenwood, 1985.

Krasner, Stephen. *Sovereignty: Organized Hypocrisy*. Princeton: Princeton University Press, 1999.

——, ed. *International Regimes*. Ithaca: Cornell University Press, 1993.

——. "Westphalia and All That." In *Ideas and Foreign Policy: Beliefs, Institutions, and Political Change*, edited by Judith Goldstein and Robert D. Keohane, p. 235. Ithaca: Cornell University Press, 1993.

Kritz, Neil, ed. *Transitional Justice: How Emerging Democracies Reckon with Former Regimes*. 3 vols. Washington, DC: United States Institute of Peace Press, 1995.

Krog, Antjie. *Country of My Skull: Guilt, Sorrow, and the Limits of Forgiveness in the New South Africa*. New York: Times Books, 1999.

Kuklick, Bruce. *American Policy and the Division of Germany: The Clash with Russia over Reparation*. Ithaca: Cornell University Press, 1972.

Kunz, Diane B. *Butter and Guns: America's Cold War Economic Diplomacy*. New York: Free Press, 1997.

LaFeber, Walter. *America, Russia, and the Cold War, 1945–2000*. 9th ed. Boston: McGraw-Hill, 2002.

Laing, Edward A. "The Relevance of the Atlantic Charter for a New World Order." *Indian Journal of International Law* 29 (July–Dec. 1989): 298–325.

Langer, William L., and S. Everett Gleason. *The Undeclared War, 1940–41*. Council on Foreign Relations. New York: Harper and Bros., 1953.

Lauren, Paul Gordon. *The Evolution of International Human Rights: Visions Seen*. Philadelphia: University of Pennsylvania Press, 1998.

———, ed. *Diplomacy: New Approaches in History, Theory, and Policy*. New York: Free Press, 1979.

Layton, Azza Salama. *International Politics and Civil Rights Policies in the United States, 1941–1960*. Cambridge: Cambridge University Press, 2000.

Lears, T. J. Jackson. *No Place of Grace: Antimodernism and the Transformation of American Culture, 1880–1920*. Chicago: University of Chicago Press, 1981.

Lelyveld, Joseph. "The Defendant: Slobodan Milosevic's Trial, and the Debate Surrounding International Courts." *New Yorker,* May 27, 2002, pp. 82–95.

Lerner, Daniel, ed. *Propaganda in War and Crisis: Materials for American Policy*. New York: George W. Stewart, 1951.

Leuchtenburg, William E. *The Supreme Court Reborn: The Constitutional Revolution in the Age of Roosevelt*. New York: Oxford University Press, 1995.

———. *Franklin D. Roosevelt and the New Deal, 1932–1940*. New York: Harper and Row, 1963.

———. "Progressivism and Imperialism: The Progressive Movement and American Foreign Policy, 1898–1916." *Mississippi Valley Historical Review* 39 (1952): 483.

Levi, Primo. *If This Is a Man; The Truce*. London: Vintage, 1996.

Levin, Lawrence W. *Highbrow/Lowbrow: The Emergence of Cultural Hierarchy in America*. Cambridge: Harvard University Press, 1988.

Lewis, David Levering. *W. E. B. DuBois: The Fight for Equality and the American Century, 1919–1963*. New York: Henry Holt, 2000.

Lichtenstein, Nelson. "Human Rights and Global Capitalism: The Rights Revolution." *New Labor Forum* 12 (Spring 2003): 61–73.

———. *Labor's War at Home: The CIO in World War II*. 1982; 2nd ed., Philadelphia: Temple University Press, 2003.

———. *State of the Union: A Century of American Labor*. Princeton: Princeton University Press, 2002.

Lie, John. *Modern Peoplehood*. Cambridge: Harvard University Press, 2004.

Lipset, Seymour Martin. *American Exceptionalism: A Double-Edged Sword*. Cambridge: Harvard University Press, 1965.

Lipstadt, Deborah E. *Beyond Belief: The American Press and the Coming of the Holocaust, 1933–1945*. New York: Free Press, 1986.

"Lookmark: Glimpsing the Forgotten." Depression-era painting and photography. *Doubletake,* Summer 2000, pp. 52–59.

Lowe, Vaughan, and Maglosia Fitzmaurice, eds. *Fifty Years of the International Court of Justice: Essays in Honour of Sir Robert Jennings*. Cambridge: Cambridge University Press, 1996.

Luard, Evan. *A History of the United Nations: The Years of Western Domination, 1945–1955*. New York: St. Martin's Press, 1982.

Luckert, Steven. *The Art and Politics of Arthur Szyk*. Washington, DC: United States Holocaust Memorial Museum, 2002.

Lundestad, Geir. *The American "Empire" and Other Studies of US Foreign Policy in a Comparative Perspective*. Oxford: Oxford University Press, 1990.

Lynch, Aaron. *Thought Contagion: How Belief Spreads through Society*. New York: Basic Books, 1996.

MacMillan, Margaret. *Paris 1919: Six Months that Changed the World*. New York: Random House, 2002.

Maier, Charles S. *In Search of Stability: Explorations in Historical Political Economy*. New York: Cambridge University Press, 1987.

Maier, Pauline. *American Scripture: Making the Declaration of Independence*. New York: Knopf, 1997.

Malloy, Sean. "The Reluctant Warrior: Henry L. Stimson and the Crisis of 'Industrial Civilization.'" PhD diss., Department of History, Stanford University, Aug. 2002.

Manchester, William. *The Last Lion: Winston Spencer Churchill*. 2 vols. Boston: Little, Brown, 1983.

Mangoldt, Hans von, and Volker Rittberger, eds. *The United Nations System and Its Predecessors*. Vol. 2. Oxford: Oxford University Press, 1997.

Mann, Bruce H. *Republic of Debtors: Bankruptcy in the Age of American Independence*. Cambridge: Harvard University Press, 2002.

Marchand, C. Roland. *The American Peace Movement and Social Reform 1898–1918*. Princeton: Princeton University Press, 1972.

Markowitz, Norman D. *The Rise and Fall of the People's Century: Henry A. Wallace and American Liberalism, 1941–1948*. New York: Free Press, 1973.

Martin, Lisa A. "An Institutionalist View: International Institutions and State Strategies." In *International Order and the Future of World Politics*, edited by T. V. Paul and John A. Hall. New York: Cambridge University Press, 1999.

Maurer, Lynn M. "Activist Note: Democracy, Harmony, and Human Rights in the Twenty-First Century." *Peace and Change* 25 (July 2000): 407.

May, Ernest R., and Angeliki E. Laiou, eds. *The Dumbarton Oaks Conversations and the United Nations, 1944–1994*. Cambridge: Harvard University Press, 1998.

McDonald, Forrest. *Novus Ordo Seclorum: The Intellectual Origins of the Constitution*. Lawrence: University Press of Kansas, 1985.

McDougal, Myres H. L., Harold D. Lasswell, and Lung-chu Chen. *Human Rights and World Public Order: The Basic Policies of an International Law of Human Dignity*. New Haven: Yale University Press, 1980.

McElvaine, Robert, ed. *Down and Out in the Great Depression: Letters from the "Forgotten Man."* Chapel Hill: University of North Carolina Press, 1983.

McPherson, James M. *Battle Cry of Freedom: The Civil War Era*. New York: Oxford University Press, 1988.

Meacham, Jon. *Franklin and Winston: An Intimate Portrait of an Epic Friendship*. New York: Random House, 2003.

Mearsheimer, John. "The False Promise of International Institutions." *International Security* 19 (Winter 1994–1995): 9.

Menand, Louis. *The Metaphysical Club: A Story of Ideas in America*. New York: Farrar, Straus and Giroux, 2001.

Mendelsohn, John. *Trial by Document: The Uses of Seized Records in the United States Proceedings at Nuremberg*. New York: Garland, 1988.

Meron, Theodor. "The Humanization of Humanitarian Law." *American Journal of International Law* 94 (Apr. 2000): 243.

Merritt, Anna J., and Richard L. Merritt, eds. *Public Opinion in Semi-Sovereign Germany: The HICOG Surveys, 1949–1955*. Urbana: University of Illinois Press, 1980.

————. *Public Opinion in Occupied Germany: The OMGUS Surveys, 1945–1949*. Urbana: University of Illinois Press, 1970.

Merritt, Richard L. *Democracy Imposed: US Occupation Policy and the German Public, 1945–1949*. New Haven: Yale University Press, 1995.

Middlebrook, Martin, and Patrick Mahoney. *Battleship: The Loss of the* Prince of Wales *and the* Repulse. London: Allen Lane, 1977.

Minear, Richard H., ed. *Dr. Suess Goes to War: The World War II Editorial Cartoons of Theodor Seuss Geisel*. New York: New Press, 1999.

Minnen, Cornelius A. van, and John F. Sears. *FDR and His Contemporaries: Foreign Perceptions of an American President*. New York: St. Martin's, 1992.

Minow, Martha. *Between Vengeance and Forgiveness: Facing History after Genocide and Mass Violence*. Boston: Beacon, 1998.

Miscamble, Wilson. "The Evolution of an Internationalist: Harry S. Truman and American Foreign Policy." *Australian Journal of Politics and History* 23 (Aug. 1977): 268–283.

Moran, Charles McMoran Wilson (Lord). *Churchill at War, 1940–1945*. London: Constable and Robinson, 2002. First published as *Churchill: The Struggle for Survival, 1940–1965*, London: Constable, 1966.

Morsink, Johannes. *The Universal Declaration of Human Rights: Origins, Drafting, and Intent*. Philadelphia: University of Pennsylvania Press, 1999.

Moskowitz, Moses. *International Concern with Human Rights*. Dobbs Ferry, NY: Oceana, 1974.

Müller, Ingo. *Hitler's Justice: The Courts of the Third Reich*. Cambridge: Harvard University Press, 1991.

Murphy, Bruce A. *The Brandeis/Frankfurter Connection: The Secret Political Activities of Two Supreme Court Justices*. New York: Oxford University Press, 1982.

Murray, Stuart, and James McCabe. *Norman Rockwell's Four Freedoms*. New York: Gramercy, 1993.

Nash, Gerald D. *The Great Depression and World War II: Organizing America 1933–1945*. New York: St. Martin's, 1979.

Neustadt, Richard, and Ernest May. *Thinking in Time: The Uses of History for Decision-Makers*. New York: Free Press, 1988.

Niblo, Stephen R. *War, Diplomacy, and Development: The United States and Mexico 1938–1954*. Wilmington, DE: Scholarly Resources, 1995.

Ninkovich, Frank. *The Diplomacy of Ideas: US Foreign Policy and Cultural Relations, 1938–1950*. Cambridge: Cambridge University Press, 1981.

Nobleman, Eli E. *American Military Courts in Germany: With a Special Reference to Historic Practice and Their Role in the Democratization of the German People*. Fort Gordon, GA: US Army Civil Affairs School, 1961.

Norman, Albert. *Our German Policy: Propaganda and Culture*. New York: Vantage, 1951.

Novick, Peter. *The Holocaust in American Life*. Boston: Houghton Mifflin, 1999.

Nye, Joseph S., Jr. *Soft Power: The Means to Success in World Politics*. New York: Public Affairs, 2004.

————. *Bound to Lead: The Changing Nature of American Power*. New York: Basic Books, 1992.

Offner, Arnold A. *Another Such Victory: President Truman and the Cold War, 1945–1953*. Stanford: Stanford University Press, 2002.

Onuf, Peter. "State Politics and Ideological Transformation: Gordon S. Wood's Republican Revolution." *William and Mary Quarterly* 44 (July 1987): 612.

Osiander, Andreas. *The States System of Europe, 1640–1990: Peacemaking and the Conditions of International Stability*. New York: Oxford University Press, 1994.

Osofsky, Hari M. "Domesticating International Criminal Law: Bringing Human Rights Violators to Justice." *Yale Law Journal* 107 (1997): 191.

Parrish, Michael E. *Felix Frankfurter and His Times: The Reform Years.* New York: Free Press, 1982.

Patterson, David S. "The United States and the Origins of the World Court." *Political Science Quarterly* 91 (1976): 279.

Patterson, Dennis, ed. *A Companion to Philosophy of Law and Legal Theory.* Oxford: Blackwell, 1996.

Patterson, James T. *Mr. Republican: A Biography of Robert A. Taft.* Boston: Houghton Mifflin, 1972.

Paul, T. V., and John A. Hall, eds. *International Order and the Future of World Politics.* New York: Cambridge University Press, 1999.

Penrose, E. F. *Economic Planning for the Peace.* Princeton: Princeton University Press, 1953.

Persico, Joseph E. *Nuremberg: Infamy on Trial.* New York: Viking, 1994.

Peterson, Edward. *The Many Faces of Defeat: The German People's Experience in 1945.* New York: Peter Lang, 1990.

Philpott, Daniel. *Revolutions in Sovereignty: How Ideas Shaped Modern International Relations.* Princeton: Princeton University Press, 2001.

Plummer, Brenda Gayle. *Rising Wind: Black Americans and US Foreign Affairs, 1935–1960.* Chapel Hill: University of North Carolina Press, 1996.

Pogue, Forrest. *George C. Marshall: Global Commander.* Colorado Springs: US Air Force Academy, 1968.

Power, Samantha. *"A Problem from Hell": America and the Age of Genocide.* New York: Zone Books, 2001.

Power, Samantha, and Graham Allison, eds. *Realizing Human Rights: Moving from Inspiration to Impact.* New York: St. Martin's, 2000.

Primus, Richard A. *The American Language of Rights.* Cambridge: Cambridge University Press, 1999.

Purcell, Edward A., Jr. *The Crisis of Democratic Theory: Scientific Naturalism and the Problem of Value.* Lexington: University Press of Kentucky, 1973.

Ragazzi, Maurizio. *The Concept of International Obligations Erga Omnes.* Oxford: Clarendon; New York: Oxford University Press, 1997.

Rakove, Jack N. *Declaring Rights: A Brief History with Documents.* Bedford Series in History and Culture. Boston: Bedford, 1998.

———. "Fidelity through History." In "Fidelity in Constitutional Theory." Special issue, *Fordham Law Review* 65 (Mar. 1997): 1587.

———. *Original Meanings: Politics and Ideas in the Making of the Constitution.* New York: Knopf, 1996.

———. "Parchment Barriers and the Politics of Rights." In *A Culture of Rights: The Bill of Rights in Philosophy, Politics, and Law, 1791 and 1991,* edited by Michael J. Lacey and Knud Haakonssen. Washington, DC: Woodrow Wilson International Center for Scholars; Cambridge: Cambridge University Press, 1991.

———. "Gordon S. Wood, the Republican Synthesis, and the Road Not Taken." *William and Mary Quarterly* 44 (July 1987): 617.

Randle, Robert. *The Origins of Peace: A Study of Peacemaking and the Structure of Peace Settlements.* New York: Free Press, 1973.

Rawls, John. *Justice as Fairness: A Restatement.* Edited by Erin Kelly. Cambridge: Harvard University Press, Belknap Press, 2001.

———. *Collected Papers.* Edited by Samuel Freeman. Cambridge: Harvard University Press, 1999.

——. *The Law of Peoples: With, "The Idea of Public Reason Revisited."* Cambridge: Harvard University Press, 1999.

——. *A Theory of Justice.* Rev. ed. Cambridge: Harvard University Press, Belknap Press, 1999.

——. *Political Liberalism.* Rev. ed. John Dewey Essays in Philosophy. New York: Columbia University Press, 1996.

——. *Liberty, Equality and Law: Selected Tanner Lectures in Moral Philosophy.* Edited by Sterling M. McMurrin. Salt Lake City: University of Utah Press, 1987.

Raymond, John M., and Barbara J. Frischoltz. "Lawyers Who Established International Law in the United States, 1776–1914." *American Journal of International Law* 76 (1982): 802.

Rees, David. *Harry Dexter White: A Study in Paradox.* New York: Coward, McCann, and Geoghegan, 1973.

Reston, James. *Deadline.* New York: Random House, 1990.

Reus-Smit, Christian. "The Constitutional Structure of International Society and the Nature of Fundamental Institutions." *International Organization* 51 (Autumn 1997): 555.

Reynolds, David. "The Origins of the Two 'World Wars': Historical Discourse and International Politics." *Journal of Contemporary History* 38 (2003): 29–44.

——. *From Munich to Pearl Harbor: Roosevelt's America and the Origins of the Second World War.* Chicago: Ivan R. Dee, 2001.

——. *The Creation of the Anglo-American Alliance, 1937–41: A Study in Competitive Cooperation.* Chapel Hill: University of North Carolina Press, 1982.

Reynolds, P. A., and E. J. Hughes. *The Historian as Diplomat: Charles Kingsley Webster and the United Nations, 1939–1946.* London: Martin Robinson, 1976.

Rieff, David. "The Precarious Triumph of Human Rights." *New York Times Magazine,* Aug. 8, 1999, p. 37.

Risse, Thomas, Stephen C. Ropp, and Kathryn Sikkink. *The Power of Human Rights: International Norms and Domestic Change.* New York: Cambridge University Press, 1999.

Rittberger, Volker, ed. *Regime Theory and International Relations.* Oxford: Oxford University Press, 1995.

Rivers, William L. *The Opinionmakers.* Boston: Beacon, 1965.

Robertson, Arthur H., and J. G. Merrills. *Human Rights in the World: An Introduction to the International Protection of Human Rights.* New York: St. Martin's, 1996.

Robertson, Geoffrey. *Crimes against Humanity: The Struggle for Global Justice.* New York: New Press, 2000.

Robinson, Greg. *By Order of the President: FDR and the Internment of Japanese Americans.* Cambridge: Harvard University Press, 2001.

Rodgers, Daniel T. *Atlantic Crossings: Social Politics in a Progressive Age.* Cambridge: Harvard University Press, Belknap Press, 1998.

——. *Contested Truths: Keywords in American Politics since Independence.* Cambridge: Harvard University Press, 1987.

Rogers, Jay Logan. "The Bricker Wall: The Fate of Human Rights Treaties in the United States Senate." Seminar Paper. University of Utah Department of History, May 2005

Rosenberg, Emily S. *Spreading the American Dream: American Economic and Cultural Expansion, 1890–1945.* New York: Hill and Wang, 1982.

Rosenberg, Jonathan. "'How Far Is the Promised Land?' World Affairs and the American Civil Rights Movement from the First World War to Vietnam." PhD diss., Harvard University, 1997. Princeton: Princeton University Press, forthcoming.

Rubenfeld, Jed, Anne-Marie Slaughter, Michael J. Glennon, Oona A. Hathaway, and Stacy D. VanDeveer. "What Good is International Law?" *Wilson Quarterly,* Autumn 2003, pp. 21–59.

Ruggie, John G. *Constructing the World Polity: Essays on International Institutionaliza-tion*. London: Routledge, 1998.

———, ed. *Multilateralism Matters: The Theory and Praxis of an Institutional Form*. New York: Cambridge University Press, 1993.

———. "Territoriality and Beyond: Problematizing Modernity in International Rela-tions." *International Organization* 46 (Autumn 1993): 139.

Russell, Ruth B. *A History of the United Nations Charter: The Role of the United States, 1940–1945*. Washington, DC: Brookings Institution, 1958.

Rutherford, Jonathan. *Forever England: Reflections on Race, Masculinity, and Empire*. London: Lawrence and Wishart, 1997.

Ryerson, James. "Richard Rorty's Pragmatic Pilgrimage." *Lingua Franca*, Dec. 2000–Jan. 2001, pp. 42–52.

Said, Edward W. *Humanism and Democratic Criticism*. New York: Columbia University Press, 2004.

Sandel, Michael. *Democracy's Discontent: America in Search of a Public Philosophy*. Cambridge: Harvard University Press, Belknap Press, 1996.

———. *Liberalism and the Limits of Justice*. Cambridge: Cambridge University Press, 1982.

Sands, Philippe, ed. *From Nuremberg to the Hague: The Future of International Criminal Justice*. Cambridge: Cambridge University Press, 2003.

Saul, John Ralston. "The Collapse of Globalism and the Rebirth of Nationalism." *Harper's Magazine,* Mar. 2004, pp. 33–43.

Schachter, Oscar. "The Twilight Existence of Non-Binding International Agreements." *American Journal of International Law* 81 (1977): 296.

Schatz, Arthur W. "The Anglo-American Trade Agreement and Cordell Hull's Search for Peace, 1936–1938." *Journal of American History* 57 (June 1970): 85.

Scheiber, Harry N. "Taking Responsibility: Moral and Historical Perspectives on the Japa-nese War Reparations Issues." In "Fifty Years in the Making: World War II Reparation and Restitution Claims." Stefan A. Riesenfeld Symposium 2001 special issue, *Berkeley Journal of International Law* 20 (2002): 233–249.

Schild, Georg. *Bretton Woods and Dumbarton Oaks: American Economic and Postwar Planning in the Summer of 1944*. London: Macmillan, 1995.

Schlesinger, Arthur M., Jr. *A Life in the Twentieth Century: Innocent Beginnings, 1917–1950*. Boston: Houghton Mifflin, 2000.

———. *The Age of Roosevelt*. 3 vols. Boston: Houghton Mifflin, 1956.

Schlesinger, Stephen C. *Act of Creation: The Founding of the United Nations: A Story of Superpowers, Secret Agents, Wartime Allies and Enemies, and Their Quest for a Peace-ful World*. Boulder: Westview, 2003.

Schmidt, Patrick. "'The Dilemma to a Free People': Justice Robert Jackson, Walter Bagehot, and the Creation of a Conservative Jurisprudence." *Law and History Review* 20 (Fall 2002): 1–21.

Schubert, Glendon. *Dispassionate Justice: A Synthesis of the Judicial Opinions of Robert H. Jackson*. Indianapolis: Bobbs-Merrill, 1969.

Searle, John R. *The Construction of Social Reality*. New York: Free Press, 1995.

Sellars, Kirsten. *The Rise and Rise of Human Rights*. Stroud, Gloucestershire: Sutton Pub-lishing, 2002.

Sen, Amartya. *Development as Freedom*. New York; Oxford University Press, 1999.

———. *Inequality Reexamined*. Cambridge: Harvard University Press, 1992.

———. *Poverty and Famines: An Essay on Entitlement and Deprivation*. Oxford: Claren-don, 1981.

Sheehan, Michael. *The Balance of Power: History and Theory*. London: Routledge, 1996.

Shklar, Judith N. *Legalism: Law, Morals, and Political Trials.* 2nd ed. Cambridge: Harvard University Press, 1986.

Sikkink, Kathryn. "The Power of Principled Ideas: Human Rights Policies in the United States and Western Europe." In *Ideas and Foreign Policy: Beliefs, Institutions, and Political Change,* edited by Judith Goldstein and Robert O. Keohane. Ithaca: Cornell University Press, 1993.

Simmons, Beth A. *Who Adjusts? Domestic Sources of Foreign Economic Policy during the Interwar Years.* Princeton: Princeton University Press, 1994.

Simpson, A. W. Brian. *Human Rights and the End of Empire.* New York: Oxford University Press, 2001.

Simpson, Gerry, ed. *War Crimes Law.* London: Ashgate, 2004.

Singer, Peter. *One World: The Ethics of Globalization.* New Haven: Yale University Press, 2002.

Skidelsky, Robert. "Keynes's Road to Bretton Woods: An Essay in Interpretation." In *International Financial History in the Twentieth Century: System and Anarchy,* edited by Marc Flandreau, Carl-Ludwig Holtfrerich, and Harold James. Publications of the German Historical Institute. Cambridge: Cambridge University Press, 2003.

———. *John Maynard Keynes: A Biography.* Vol. 3, *Fighting for Freedom, 1937–1946.* New York: Viking, 2000.

Skinner, Quentin, Partha Dasgupta, Raymond Guess, Melissa Lane, Peter Laslett, Onora O'Neill, W. G. Runciman, and Andrew Kuper. "Political Philosophy: The View from Cambridge." *Journal of Political Philosophy* 10 (2001): 1–19.

Slaughter, Anne-Marie. *A New World Order.* Princeton: Princeton University Press, 2004.

Smelser, Ronald. *Robert Ley: Hitler's Labor Front Leader.* New York: Berg, 1988.

Smelser, Ronald, and Rainer Zitelmann, eds. *The Nazi Elite.* New York: New York University Press, 1993.

Smith, Bradley F. *The American Road to Nuremberg: The Documentary Record, 1944–1945.* Stanford: Hoover Institution Press, Stanford University, 1982.

Smith, Gaddis. *American Diplomacy during the Second World War, 1941–1945.* New York: John Wiley and Sons, 1965.

Smith, Michael Joseph. *Realist Thought from Weber to Kissinger.* Baton Rouge: Louisiana State University Press, 1986.

Snidal, Duncan. "The Limits of Hegemonic Stability Theory." *International Organization* 35 (Autumn 1985): 579.

Snyder, Frank, and Surakariat Sathirathai, eds. *Third World Attitudes toward International Law: An Introduction.* Dordrecht: Kluwer, 1987.

Sohn, Louis B. *The Human Rights Movement: From Roosevelt's Four Freedoms to the Interdependence of Peace, Development and Human Rights.* Pamphlet. Human Rights Program, Harvard Law School, 1995.

Sontag, Susan. "The Photographs Are Us." *Sunday New York Times Magazine,* May 23, 2004, pp. 25–29, 42.

Sorensen, Thomas C. *The Word War: The Story of American Propaganda.* New York: Harper and Row, 1968.

"Special Report: War Crimes." National Public Radio, July 16, 2000.

Stacks, John F. *Scotty: James B. Reston and the Rise and Fall of American Journalism.* Boston: Little, Brown, 2002.

Starr, June, and Jane F. Collier, eds. *History and Power in the Study of Law: New Directions in Legal Anthropology.* Ithaca: Cornell University Press, 1989.

Stein, Eric. "Lawyers, Judges, and the Making of a Transnational Constitution." *American Journal of International Law* 75 (Jan. 1981): 1.

Steiner, Henry J., and Philip Alston. *International Human Rights in Context: Law, Politics, Morals.* Oxford: Oxford University Press, 1996.

Steinmo, Sven. *Structuring Politics: Historical Institutionalism in Comparative Analysis*. New York: Cambridge University Press, 1992.

Sternsher, Bernard, ed. *Hope Restored: How the New Deal Worked in Town and Country*. Chicago: Ivan R. Dee, 1999.

Stiglitz, Joseph E. *Globalization and Its Discontents*. New York: Norton, 2002.

Stone, Alec. "What Is a Supranational Constitution? An Essay in International Relations Theory." *Review of Politics* 56 (Summer 1994): 441.

Stone, Geoffrey R. "Reflections on the First Amendment: The Evolution of the American Jurisprudence of Free Expression." *Proceedings of the American Philosophical Society* 131 (Sept. 1987).

Storey, Robert G. *The Final Judgment: Pearl Harbor to Nuremberg*. San Antonio: Naylor, 1968.

Sunstein, Cass R. *The Second Bill of Rights: FDR's Unfinished Revolution and Why We Need It More Than Ever.* New York: Basic Books, 2004.

Suu Kyi, Aung San. *Freedom from Fear and Other Writings*. New York: Viking, 1991.

Takaki, Ronald. *Double Victory: A Multicultural History of America in World War II*. Boston: Little, Brown, 2000.

Tananbaum, Duane. *The Bricker Amendment Controversy: A Test of Eisenhower's Political Leadership*. Ithaca: Cornell University Press, 1988.

Taylor, Telford. *The Anatomy of the Nuremberg Trials: A Personal Memoir*. New York: Knopf, 1992.

Teitel, Ruti. *Transitional Justice*. New York: Oxford University Press, 2000.

———. "Transitional Jurisprudence: The Role of Law in Political Transformation." *Yale Law Journal* 106 (1997): 2009.

Terkel, Studs. *"The Good War": An Oral History of World War Two.* New York: Pantheon, 1984.

Thelen, Kathleen. "Historical Institutionalism in Comparative Politics." *Annual Review of Political Science* (Palo Alto: Annual Reviews) 2 (June 1999): 369–404.

Thomas, Daniel. *The Helsinki Effect: International Norms, Human Rights, and the Demise of Communism*. Princeton: Princeton University Press, 2001.

Thompson, Dorothy, and Rose Wilder Lane. *Dorothy Thompson and Rose Wilder Lane: Forty Years of Friendship: Letters, 1921–1960*. Edited by William Holtz. Columbia: University of Missouri Press, 1991.

Thompson, Kenneth W. *Institutions for Projecting American Values Abroad*. Lanham, MD: University Press of America, 1983.

Tierney, Brian. *The Idea of Natural Rights: Studies on Natural Rights, Natural Law and Church Law 1150–1625*. Emory University Studies in Law and Religion. Atlanta: Scholars Press, 1997.

Vagts, Alfred, and Detlev F. Vagts. "The Balance of Power in International Law: The History of an Idea." *American Journal of International Law* 73 (1979): 555.

Vagts, Detlev F. "Taking Treaties Less Seriously." *American Journal of International Law* 92 (1998): 458.

Van Dormael, Armand. *Bretton Woods: Birth of a Monetary System*. New York: Holmes & Meier, 1978.

Van Kley, Dale, ed. *The French Idea of Freedom: The Old Regime and the Declaration of Rights of 1789*. Stanford: Stanford University Press, 1994.

Von Eschen, Penny M. *Race against Empire: Black Americans and Anticolonialism, 1937–1957*. Ithaca: Cornell University Press, 1997.

Walker, Samuel. *In Defense of American Liberties: A History of the ACLU*. 2nd. ed. Carbondale: Southern Illinois University Press, 1999.

Walz, Kenneth. *Theory of International Politics*. New York: McGraw-Hill, 1979.

Walzer, Michael. *Arguing about War.* New Haven: Yale University Press, 2004.

———. *Just and Unjust Wars: A Moral Argument with Historical Illustrations.* New York: Basic Books, 1997.

Wasserstrom, Jeffrey N., Lynn Hunt, and Marilyn B. Young, eds. *Human Rights and Revolutions.* Lanham, MD: Rowman and Littlefield, 2000.

Weiler, Joseph H. H. *The Constitution of Europe: "Do the New Clothes Have an Emperor?" and Other Essays on European Integration.* London: Cambridge University Press, 1999.

Weingartner, James F. *Crossroads of Death: The Story of the Malmédy Massacre.* Berkeley: University of California Press, 1979.

Weintraub, Stanley. *Silent Night: The Story of the World War I Christmas Truce.* New York: Free Press, 2001.

Welles, Benjamin. *Sumner Welles: FDR's Global Strategist.* New York: St. Martin's, 1997.

Westbrook, Robert B. "Fighting for the American Family: Private Interests and Political Obligation in World War II." In *Power of Culture,* ed. Fox and Lears.

White, G. Edward. "Personal versus Impersonal Judging: The Dilemmas of Robert Jackson." In *The American Judicial Tradition: Profiles of Leading American Judges.* 2nd ed. New York: Oxford University Press, 1988.

———. *Alger Hiss's Looking-Glass Wars: The Covert Life of a Soviet Spy.* New York: Oxford University Press, 2004.

White, Stephen K. *The Recent Work of Jürgen Habermas: Reason, Justice, and Modernity.* Cambridge: Cambridge University Press, 1988.

Wiebe, Robert. *The Search for Order, 1877–1920.* New York: Hill and Wang, 1967.

Wight, Martin. "The Balance of Power." In *Diplomatic Investigations,* edited by Herbert Butterfield and Martin Wight. Cambridge: Harvard University Press, 1966.

Willetts, Peter, ed. *The Conscience of the World: The Influence of Non-Governmental Organisations in the UN System.* London: Hurst, 1996.

Williams, Jeffrey. "What about Us? The Conference of Chapultepec: An Example of How World War II Transformed Mexican Foreign Policy." Masters thesis, Department of History, University of Utah, 2004.

Williams, William Appleman. *The Tragedy of American Diplomacy.* 1959; 2nd ed., New York: Dell, 1972.

Willis, James F. *Prologue to Nuremberg: The Politics and Diplomacy of Punishing War Criminals of the First World War.* Westport, CT: Greenwood, 1982.

Wills, Garry. *Lincoln at Gettysburg: Words That Remade American History.* New York: Simon and Schuster, 1992.

Wilson, Theodore A. *The First Summit: Roosevelt and Churchill at Placentia Bay, 1941.* Rev. ed. Lawrence: University Press of Kansas, 1991.

Woetzel, Robert K. *The Nuremberg Trials in International Law. With a Postlude on the Eichmann Case.* New York: Praeger, 1962.

Wolfe, Robert, ed. *Americans as Proconsuls: United States Military Government in Germany and Japan, 1944–1952.* Carbondale: Southern Illinois University Press, 1984.

Woodbridge, George. *UNRRA: The History of the United Nations Relief and Rehabilitation Administration.* 3 vols. New York: Columbia University Press, 1950.

Wooton, Barbara. *Crime and Penal Policy: Reflections on Fifty Years' Experience.* London: George Allen and Unwin, 1978.

The World of Hugo Grotius. Proceedings of the International Colloquium organized by the Grotius Committee of the Royal Netherlands Academy of Arts and Sciences, Rotterdam, Apr. 6–9, 1983. Amsterdam: APA Holland University Press, 1984.

Wyman, David. *The Abandonment of the Jews: America and the Holocaust, 1941–1945.* New York: Pantheon, 1984.

Zakaria, Fareed. *From Wealth to Power: The Unusual Origins of America's World Role.* Princeton: Princeton University Press, 1998.

Zasloff, Jonathan. "Law and the Shaping of American Foreign Policy: The Twenty Years' Crisis." *Southern California Law Review* 77 (2004): 583–682.

———. "Law and the Shaping of American Foreign Policy: From the Gilded Age to the New Era." *New York University Law Review* 78 (2002): 239–373.

Zeiler, Thomas W. *Free Trade: The Advent of GATT.* Chapel Hill: University of North Carolina Press, 1999.

Zimmermann, Warren. *The First Great Triumph: How Five Americans Made Their Country a World Power.* New York: Farrar, Straus, Giroux, 2002.

Internet Sites

American Association for the Advancement of Science. Human Rights Resources on the Internet: http://shr.aaas.org/dhr.htm

American Society for International Law: http://www.asil.org

Amnesty International: http://www.amnesty.org

Columbia University. Guide to UN materials, edited by Silke Sahl: http://library.law.columbia.edu/un

Encyclopedia Britannica Online, Burns Weston, "Human Rights": http://search.eb.com/eb/article?/=109242

Human Rights Watch: http://www.hrw.org

International Bank for Reconstruction and Development (World Bank): http://www.worldbank.org

International Committee of the Red Cross: http://www.icrc.org

International Labor Organization: http://www.ilo.org

International Monetary Fund (IMF): http://www.imf.org

Lawyers' Committee for Human Rights: http://www.lchr.org

Robert H. Jackson Center: http://www.roberthjackson.org

Swarthmore College Peace Collection: http://www.swarthmore.edu.Library/peace

United Nations: http://www.unorg/law; http://untreaty.un.org

United Nations, International Criminal Tribunal for the Former Yugoslavia and Rwanda: http://www.un.org/icty; http://www.un.org/ictr

United Nations, Office of the High Commissioner for Human Rights: http://www.hchr.ch

University of Minnesota Human Rights Library: http://www1.umn.edu/humanrts/

VENONA: http://www.nsa.gov:8080/docs/venona

Yale University. Avalon Project at Yale Law School: Documents in Law, History, and Diplomacy: http://www.yale.edu/lawweb/avalon.htm; Project Diana, An Online Human Rights Archive: http://www.yale.edu/lawweb/avalon/diana

ACKNOWLEDGMENTS

I owe principal thanks to David M. Kennedy of Stanford University, whose enthusiasm for this project has never wavered since he first brought a young international lawyer with an interest in history into Stanford's doctoral program; I am so appreciative of his encouragement, patience, and guidance. I also express my deep gratitude to Barton J. Bernstein who was in effect a co-advisor and whose helpful consultations, insightful bibliographical suggestions, and unparalleled knowledge of the cast of characters contributed to my understanding of the intensity of personal and policy conflicts in United States foreign relations. Jack N. Rakove also offered generous assistance each step along the way, contributing superb editorial suggestions, careful line edits, and useful advice.

At Harvard University Press, Kathleen McDermott improved this project in innumerable ways, and working with her was always a pleasure. She provided detailed line edits, helped clarify key concepts, and creatively supplemented the illustrations in ways that beautifully complement the text. Prospective readers should also share my gratitude to Susan Wallace Boehmer for a superb line edit of the lengthy original draft, along with thought-provoking questions and suggestions. I also thank Kathi Drummy and Mary Kate Maco for the extra time and care they took with this manuscript. Kenneth Cmiel's review of the project for the Press was a model of insightful commentary, for which I am grateful.

My agent, Sarah Chalfant of the Wylie Agency, had an exuberant vision for this book that inspired me from our very first meeting at Harvard Law School. Thanks also to Andrew Woods and Edward Orloff at Wylie for their interest and attention. The gifted intellectual property specialist Zick Rubin encouraged and advised me at critical moments during the manuscript's gestation. Sean Malloy's superb flair for research in visual media was critical to developing the book's art program. Sean also answered a variety of questions based on his own teaching and research in twentieth-century U.S. history and tracked down hard-to-find citations. Christina Koningisor, my energetic and entrepreneurial research assistant, garnered many text and illustration permissions for the book, reviewed and coded the data set of Rutgers Oral Histories, and wrote an excellent summary that supplemented my own analysis.

At the University of Utah, Jeffrey Williams found useful materials on the 1945 Conference of Chapultepec; Christian Clement contributed subtle and excellent German translations; Kate Holvoet spontaneously forwarded useful items on the founding of the United Nations; and Erin Larsen found hundreds of documents as I finalized the text. Peter Kraus responded quickly to my incessant inquiries, hand-delivered materials to me, found me two excellent research assistants, and offered unfailingly entertaining advice. I am grateful to Leslie R. Berlin, who made helpful comments on the penultimate draft; John McGarrahan, who generously allowed me to use his personal collection of Office of War Information posters in presentations; and Ira Katznelson of Columbia University, who provided a thoughtful critique of an early draft of the introduction, as well as encouragement to broaden my conception of the New Deal. I also thank Lewis Bateman, Susan Ferber, Thomas LaBien, and Brigitta von Rheinberg for advice when the manuscript was still in its formative stages.

I wish particularly to thank the director of the Golieb Fellows Program at New York University, William Nelson, as well as participants in the Legal History Colloquium at NYU, for constructive feedback: Felice Batlan, Richard B. Bernstein, Williamjames Hoffer, Deborah Malamud, Mark McGarvie, Tomiko Nagin, Todd Stevens, Howard Venable, and Dennis Vestry. At the Center for the Study of Law and Society at the University of California at Berkeley, I thank Ben Brown, David Caron, Laurel Fletcher, Sanford Kadish, Robert Kagan, David Lieberman, Annette Neirobisz, Harry Scheiber, Jonathan Simon, Steven Sugarman, Dvora Yanow, and especially Rosann Greenspan. In the History Department at Berkeley, I thank Mark Brilliant, David Hollinger, and James Vernon for their interest and advice. Norman Naimark offered a detailed critique of my doctoral prospectus, for which I am in his debt, and allowed me to enroll in his innovative course on Genocide in the Twentieth Century long after I had fulfilled my graduate course requirements.

I thank Mark Bradley, the late Abram Chayes, Paul Chen, Richard Pierre Claude, Mary Dudziak, Richard Falk, William Forbath, Jonathan D. Greenberg, Melanie Greenberg, Richard Goldstone, Risa Goluboff, Robert Gordon, Brad Gregory, the late Gerald Gunther, Edward Harris, Hendrik Hartog, Tsuyoshi Hasegawa, Tom Heller, Godfrey Hodgson, Peter Hoffer, Michael Ignatieff, Robert Johansen, Tony Judt, Laura Kalman, Michael Kammen, Stanley N. Katz, Lorelei Kelly, David W. Kennedy, James Kloppenberg, Walter LaFeber, Melissa Lane, Benjamin Lawrance, Nelson Lichtenstein, George Lopez, Carolyn Lougee-Chappell, David A. Martin, Robert Mnookin, Jack Pole, Richard Polenberg, Samantha Power, David Reynolds, Richard Roberts, Daniel Rodgers, Jonathan Schoenwald, John Setear, Doug Stone, Eric Stover, David Strauss, Jeremi

Suri, Kiyoteru Tsutsui, Detlev Vagts, and Marilyn Young. You have taught me a great deal about the kind of scholar I hope to become.

I thank the Stanford Department of History for a generous fellowship award and several travel grants, the American Historical Association for a Littleton-Griswold Research Award in American Legal History, and the Society for Historians of American Foreign Relations for a Stuart L. Bernath Research Award. For research and institutional support, I am also grateful to the Stanford Center on Conflict and Negotiation, the Stanford Center for International Security and Cooperation, the Golieb Fellowship Program in Legal History at New York University, the MacArthur Foundation, and the Center for the Study of Law & Society at the University of California at Berkeley.

I extend my deep appreciation to L. Ray Gunn and Eric Hinderaker, successive chairs of the Department of History at the University of Utah, for allowing me to accept a postdoctoral fellowship so I could finish a first draft and for granting an extra semester of research leave so I could complete revisions. In the History Department, I am especially appreciative of guidance, advice, and support from Robert A. Goldberg and James R. Lehning. Thanks also to Utah colleagues Lindsay Adams, Megan Armstrong, Beth Clement, Ben Cohen, Alan Coombs, Bruce Dain, Ed Davies, Nadja Durbach, Becky Horn, Colleen McDannell, Glenn Olsen, John Reed, Ron Smelser, and especially James Clayton for their interest in my work and inspirational examples.

I conducted most of the research for this study at the Reginald F. Lewis International Law Center at Harvard Law School, at Harvard's Widener Library, at the Library of Congress, and at the National Archives (formerly the Public Record Office) at Kew, United Kingdom, and of course at the Franklin D. Roosevelt Presidential Library and the Hoover Institution of War, Revolution, and Peace. But for this study, the smaller collections were the key. Thank you to Ben Primer, Dan Linke, and the staff of the Seeley G. Mudd Research Library at Princeton University for going beyond the call of duty, and to Elizabeth Safly, Randy Sowell, and David Clark at the Harry S. Truman Presidential Library in Independence Missouri, who were models of professionalism and responsiveness. The staff of the Churchill College Archives Centre, the MacArthur Library, and the Columbia Oral History Project also went out of their way to help. I am especially grateful to Marci Hoffmann and Wiltrud Harms, international law librarians at Boalt Hall School of Law at the University of California at Berkeley. I also wish to acknowledge the extraordinary responsiveness of archivists who helped me from remote, particularly Christopher Laico of Columbia Law School's Arthur Diamond Law Library and John R. Waggener of the University of Wyoming's American Heritage Center.

For early encouragement of my scholarly aspirations, I thank Richard H. Baker, Martin Brett, Philip Towle, John Lonsdale, Vincent P. O'Brien, the late Hon. Cecil F. Poole, Joachim Whaley, and especially John Paine and Roger Fisher. Roger's generosity, graciousness, and inclusiveness with junior colleagues is legendary and, in my experience, unequaled.

I am grateful for the support of a wonderful set of patient and interested friends, including Elizabeth Brauer, Stan Brenner, Jeff Brown, Bill Cane, Sarah Cane, Philippa Francis-West, Debbi Friedman, John Hiss, William C. Jackson, Susan Johnson, Jeannie Kahwajy, Nancy Katz, Hugh Morgan, Martha Ophir, Alison Tucher, and especially my cousin Brian Ganson.

My mother, Ellen Kaplan Sulkin, was an essential mainstay of practical and emotional support for this project. The rest of my family, David Kopelman, Susan Heifetz Kopelman, Joyce Borgwardt, Jack Borgwardt, Mike Grossman, Casey Sulkin, Alec Sulkin, Gail Kopelman Serruya, Misha Serruya, Andrew Kopelman, Marybeth Borgwardt, Karl Borgwardt, Kim Monke and the late Eric Monke, Sally Kaplan and the late Peter Kaplan, Jill Kargman, Coco and Arie Kopelman, Tina Kopelman and the late Bob Kopelman, supported this project with love and pride. Eva Bella Borgwardt and Jacob Frederic Borgwardt were welcome distractions, even as the advent of a new generation reminded me why I was writing this. For childcare and other indispensable assistance, I thank Jennifer Beeson, Judy Slater, Julie Takagi, Josephine Mannhalter Vick, and especially Catherine Alley and Saina Salakhova.

My husband, Kurt Chandler Borgwardt, made numerous useful suggestions, kept clippings that he thought would be of interest to me, stoically solved an endless stream of computer problems, baked cookies to sustain me through inevitable all-nighters, and formatted the entire manuscript at the dissertation stage. He also took care of our children while I was away at conferences or on research trips and supported me in other innumerable ways while I wrote up my research. I cannot imagine having completed this project without his sustaining love.

This book is dedicated to my grandparents: Ethel Bratt Kaplan, George Irving Kaplan, Ruth Kopelman, Frank Kopelman, Beatrice Eisenman Heifetz, Ralph Heifetz, Mike Barr, and Helene Cahners Kaplan. Ruth Kopelman, in particular, has consistently supported my seemingly endless quest for additional education and my academic career with love and pride. Thank you, Grandma Ruth—I even forgive you for not remembering the Atlantic Charter.

INDEX

Abu Ghraib prison, 296–297

Acheson, Dean: and Bretton Woods Conference, 88–89, 96, 114, 121; and United States Senate, 88–89; and Lend-Lease program, 102, 103, 104; and Food and Agriculture Organization, 115–116, 117; and United Nations Relief and Rehabilitation Agency, 119, 120, 121; and International Monetary Fund, 125; and World Bank, 126; and United Nations Charter, 162

Acton, Lord, 44–45

African Americans, 230; lynching of, 50, 138, 230, 243, 291; and Roosevelt, 50; and Atlantic Charter, 56, 60; and GI Bill of Rights, 139; and United Nations Conference on International Organization, 181, and Dumbarton Oaks Conference, 189; and internationalism, 190; and domestic jurisdiction of United States, 191, 192

Alderman, Sidney B., 239

Alfaro, Ricardo, 262

Allende regime, 269

Alsop, Joseph, 19

Alvarez, José, 265, 269

America First Committee, 24

American Bankers Association, 113, 129

American Institute of Public Opinion, 81

American Jewish Committee, 190

American Peace Society, 64

Anderson, Carol, 60

Anderson, Sir John, 122

Andrus, Burton, 196, 198, 199–200, 201, 203

Annan, Kofi, 277; *In Larger Freedom*, 270–271

Applebaum, Anne, 177

Aquinas, Saint Thomas, 149, 213

Arcadia Conference, 54–55

Arendt, Hannah, 53–54, 242, 295

Argentina, 172, 182

Armenians, 226

Arms control, 4, 25, 26–27, 66. *See also* Security

Ash, Timothy Garton, 35

Atlantic Charter: and Churchill, 4, 5, 23, 28–29, 30, 33, 34, 37, 38, 40, 42, 45, 53, 140; and colonialism, 4, 8–9, 34, 36, 56, 57, 60, 83; and economy, 4, 6, 23, 25, 27, 34, 50, 52, 98; and human rights, 4, 5–6, 29, 34, 58, 60, 85, 142; and individuals, 4, 28, 29, 30, 34, 50, 53, 54, 278, 285; and New Deal, 4, 6, 34, 53, 278; rhetoric of, 4, 8–9, 29, 35, 54, 56, 60, 85, 129, 185, 212, 237, 267, 280–281, 285, 292, 296; and security, 4, 5, 23, 25, 26–27, 50, 163; and trade, 4, 23, 24–26, 28, 34, 52; and multilateralism, 5, 26, 50, 71, 292; and Nuremberg Charter, 5, 42, 44, 204, 236, 237, 241, 277–278; and Roosevelt, 5, 23–24, 26, 33, 35–39, 40, 42, 43–44, 48, 53, 98; and United Nations Charter, 5, 44, 142, 185, 186, 204; and Four Freedoms, 6, 23, 25, 28, 34, 35, 42, 48, 52, 60–61, 285; principles of, 7–8, 22–31, 32, 33, 34–45, 296; and Great Britain, 8–9, 17, 23, 25, 28, 30, 34, 35, 60; and post-World War I mistakes, 14; and internationalism, 23, 24, 25, 26–27, 29, 31, 34, 52, 160, 286; and territory, 23, 25, 52; and United Nations, 30, 40, 190, 193; public reaction to, 32; and equality, 34; and Rockwell, 46; and Beveridge Report, 49; and Ward, 50; and Declaration by United Nations, 55; as entangling alliance, 61; and Food and Agriculture Organization, 118; and banking interests, 129; and Bretton Woods Act, 131; and Bretton Woods institutions, 133; and Bretton Woods Conference, 134–135; and Latin America, 173; and Dumbarton Oaks Conference, 173–174; and Yalta Conference, 178, 179; and postwar treatment of Germany, 208, 299; and war crimes, 212; Jackson on, 224; and Cold War, 250–251; and Bretton Woods Charter, 252; and globalization, 282

421